Tests of hypotheses

Hypotheses	Rejection Region of H_0
$H_0: \mu = \mu_0$ $H_1: \mu > \mu_0$	$\dfrac{\bar{x} - \mu_0}{\sigma/\sqrt{n}} \geq z(\alpha)$
$H_0: \mu = \mu_0$ $H_1: \mu > \mu_0$	$\dfrac{\bar{x} - \mu_0}{s/\sqrt{n}} \geq t(\alpha; n - 1)$
$H_0: \mu_1 = \mu_2$ $H_1: \mu_1 > \mu_2$	$\dfrac{\bar{x} - \bar{y}}{\sqrt{\sigma_1^2/n_1 + \sigma_2^2/n_2}} \geq z(\alpha)$
$H_0: \mu_1 = \mu_2$ $H_1: \mu_1 > \mu_2$	$\dfrac{\bar{x} - \bar{y}}{\sqrt{\dfrac{(n_1 - 1)s_x^2 + (n_2 - 1)s_y^2}{n_1 + n_2 - 2}\left(\dfrac{1}{n_1} + \dfrac{1}{n_2}\right)}} \geq t(\alpha; n_1 + n_2 - 2)$
$H_0: p = p_0$ $H_1: p > p_0$	$\dfrac{y/n - p_0}{\sqrt{\dfrac{p_0(1 - p_0)}{n}}} \geq z(\alpha)$
$H_0: p_1 = p_2$ $H_1: p_1 > p_2$	$\dfrac{y_1/n_1 - y_2/n_2}{\sqrt{\left(\dfrac{y_1 + y_2}{n_1 + n_2}\right)\left(1 - \dfrac{y_1 + y_2}{n_1 + n_2}\right)\left(\dfrac{1}{n_1} + \dfrac{1}{n_2}\right)}} \geq z(\alpha)$
$H_0: \beta_1 = \beta_{10}$ $H_1: \beta_1 > \beta_{10}$	$\dfrac{\hat{\beta}_1 - \beta_{10}}{\sqrt{\dfrac{\sum (y_i - \hat{y}_i)^2/(n - 2)}{\sum (x_i - \bar{x})^2}}} \geq t(\alpha; n - 2)$

Tolerance regions

With normal assumptions, $\bar{x} \pm ks$ covers at least $(100)p$ percent of the population with probability $1 - \alpha$.

$$\frac{\sum z_i x_i - (\sum z_i)(\sum x_i)/n}{\sum z_i^2 - (\sum z_i)^2/n}$$

Applied Statistics for
Engineers and
Physical Scientists

EDITION

2

Applied Statistics for Engineers and Physical Scientists

Robert V. Hogg

Johannes Ledolter

Department of Statistics and Actuarial Science
UNIVERSITY OF IOWA

Macmillan Publishing Company
New York

Maxwell Macmillan Publishers
Toronto

Maxwell Macmillan International
New York   Oxford   Singapore   Sydney

Editor: Robert W. Pirtle
Production Supervisor: Elaine W. Wetterau
Production Manager: Sandra Moore
Text and Cover Designer: Natasha Sylvester
Illustrations: Precision Graphics
This book was set in Times Roman by Santype International Ltd.,
printed and bound by Halliday Printing Co.
The cover was printed by Halliday Printing Co.

Macmillan Publishing Company
866 Third Avenue, New York, New York 10022

Macmillan Publishing Company is part of the
Maxwell Communication Group of Companies.

Maxwell Macmillan Canada
1200 Eglinton Avenue, E.
Suite 200
Don Mills, Ontario M3C 3N1

Library of Congress Cataloging in Publication Data
Hogg, Robert V.
    Applied statistics for engineers and physical scientists/Robert
V. Hogg, Johannes Ledolter.—2nd ed.
        p.   cm.
    Rev. ed. of: Engineering statistics. c1987.
    Includes index.
    ISBN 0-02-355830-X
    1. Engineering—Statistical methods.   I. Ledolter, Johannes.
II. Hogg, Robert V. Engineering statistics.   III. Title.
TA340.H64   1992
620'.0072—dc20   91-12540
                                                                              CIP

Printing: 1 2 3 4 5 6 7 8   Year: 2 3 4 5 6 7 8 9 0 1

Foreword
TO FIRST EDITION

Bob Hogg and Hannes Ledolter have made an important step forward that will hopefully lead to a revolution in how statistics is taught in American universities. They have responded to the need of the customers—engineers who want to use statistical methods to help them do their jobs better—and produced a textbook that discusses those statistical tools most useful to engineers.

In the 1980s we have seen American industry suddenly awaken to the realization that it must improve the quality of its products and services if it is to survive and compete effectively in worldwide markets. The associated debate has identified statistics as a broadly useful tool for improving quality. The need for statistics flows naturally from the recognition that data collection and analysis is necessary to the solution of quality problems. Good decisions are based on facts, not opinions and emotions. We must adopt the view of "In God we trust; others must have data."

Along with this change in the focus of American industry has come the recognition that we must change how we teach statistics. This need has been a concern of many members of the statistical profession. Bob Hogg shared this concern and did something about it. Under Bob's leadership, a workshop on statistical education of engineers was held at The University of Iowa in July 1984. This group of 42 statisticians and engineers, representing both academia and industry, identified among other things five areas that are most important for engineers to have knowledge of:

- Omnipresence of variability.
- High value of graphical analysis.
- Importance and essentials of statistically designed experiments.
- Statistical inference.
- Philosophies of Shewhart, Deming, and others concerning the delivery of quality products and services.

Hogg and Ledolter used the results of the Iowa Workshop as a basis for the contents of this book.

Their book has one key feature that sets it apart from other books on statistics for engineers. The focus of the book is on proper data collection and analysis with emphasis on the use of graphical techniques. The discussion of probability is limited to only that needed to develop an appreciation for statistical methods discussed. The authors have made a concerted effort to strike a balance between the traditional approach to teaching statistics and the need to emphasize problem solving by data collection and analysis. The resulting 40/60 blend, in favor of data collection and analysis, will help us evolve to the approach recommended by the Iowa Workshop. I am confident that, as we use the authors' book, we will also identify ways to improve how we teach the traditional material on probability, tests of significance, confidence intervals, and so on.

Hogg and Ledolter have also made extensive use of data from real problems to give students an understanding of how statistics is used in engineering studies. This has been accomplished through illustrative examples, exercises at the end of the chapters, and the inclusion of case histories. Statistics is most meaningful when you have personal experience with its use. I encourage those who use this book in the classroom to include their own case histories as appropriate; and better yet, assign one or more projects in which the students design a study and collect, analyze, and interpret the results. I believe that teachers and students alike will find the resulting experience both educational and enjoyable.

We are becoming increasingly aware that a company improves its products most rapidly when it moves its focus from product inspection to process control, and then to quality improvement, and finally to quality of product and process design. Statistics provides tools to deal with each of these needs: acceptance sampling plans for inspection, control chart techniques for process control, and design of experiments and regression analysis for quality improvement and the development of product and process design. Each of these important techniques is discussed by Hogg and Ledolter. In the process they are careful to explain both the *how* and the *why*—how techniques are used and the theory underlying the methods. Experience in using the book will tell us if an appropriate balance has been struck and what changes are needed.

The authors are quick to point out that while they consider this book a major step forward in a textbook for the statistical education of engineers, they do not consider their book to be the ultimate answer. One of the fundamentals of quality is the need for constant improvement. Accordingly, I am hopeful that Hogg and Ledolter and other authors will accept the challenge of continually assessing the statistical education needs of engineers and developing textbooks to meet those needs. In the process we will improve our teaching of statistics and help engineers make effective use of statistical methods in the development and improvement of products and services that satisfy customer needs and expectations.

The many changes taking place in our industries, educational system, and other aspects of our society provide the opportunity to make advances that will serve us well for many years to come. I am pleased that Hogg and Ledolter have accepted the challenge of improving the content of our statistical courses for engineers. I share their excitement about the opportunities and encourage you to evaluate their approach in the classroom and report on how the process can be improved.

Ronald D. Snee
E. I. du Pont de Nemours & Co., Inc.

Preface

We are pleased with the reception that was given the first edition of our textbook. The many comments and suggestions that we received from our students and colleagues prompted us to revise and expand the text and to write this second edition.

As with the first edition, this introductory statistics book is written for students with a calculus background. Our revision includes all the topics that are discussed in the first edition, with the exception of some of the discussion on multivariate distributions that many students found difficult. We have added several new topics and many more examples, exercises involving realistic data, and challenging projects. In particular, we have added more discussion on the importance of understanding variability, an introductory section on reliability, material on time-sequence plots (including digidots), and a discussion of distributions that are commonly used in engineering and the physical sciences, such as the Weibull distribution. In addition, the sample correlation coefficient has been introduced in the first chapter along with the method of least squares. Material on statistical quality control has been gathered together and strengthened, and has been placed in an early chapter (Chapter 5).

The entire book, including many of the projects, can be used for a strong two-semester sequence in applied statistics. At the end of this sequence students are familiar with summarizing data, basic probability distributions, sampling distributions, and introductory statistical inference. In addition, they know how to design and analyze experiments and to carry out regression analyses (including basic response surface analyses). However, the book can also be used for several different one-semester (3-semester-hour) courses, depending on the interests of the instructor and the students.

1. Chapters 1–6 provide the basis for a solid introductory statistics course. Such a course includes statistical quality control, but not design of experiments and regression, except for the short introduction to these topics in Chapter 1. We recommend that the instructor assign a few of the projects as they provide valuable hands-on experience with statistics.

2. A course based on Sections 1.1–1.5, Chapters 2–4, and Sections 5.1, 6.1, 6.2, 7.1–7.3, 8.1, 8.3, 8.4, 9.1, and 9.2 includes an introduction to Shewhart control charts, design of experiments, and some regression. We teach a course like this at the University of Iowa. It covers a great deal of material, and unfortunately we find little time to assign and discuss projects. We believe that two-level factorial and fractional factorial designs are very important in practice, and we include Sections 8.3 and 8.4 in our course. Other instructors, however, may want to modify our suggestions and delete some of the design topics.

3. For a first statistics course that emphasizes regression more, but that does not include quality control, consider a variation that covers Chapters 1–3, Sections 4.1–4.5, 6.1, 6.2, 7.1, 7.2, 8.1, and 9.1–9.4.

In the table of contents we have starred a section if it is not needed in subsequent sections. This does not mean that we view these starred sections as unimportant. For example, we believe that Section 4.6 on reliability, Section 5.1 on control charts, and Section 7.3 on blocking are very important; yet we have starred them because they are not essential to understanding the material in subsequent sections. The information on starred sections may help instructors who want to construct an applied statistics course that is tailored to the needs of their students in engineering and the physical sciences.

This book is useful not only to engineers, but also to others who want a solid introduction to applied statistics. For that reason we have changed the title of the book from *Engineering Statistics* to *Applied Statistics for Engineers and Physical Scientists*.

We are indebted to many students and colleagues who have made numerous valuable suggestions and who shared with us data and excercises. We are also very grateful to the participants at two conferences on statistical education held in Iowa City in 1984 and 1990. Especially the first conference in 1984 provided the catalyst for this project. We gratefully acknowledge the help of three very special friends in industry who made unusual contributions to the entire process: Ron Snee (du Pont), who helped in organizing the 1984 conference, made a number of suggestions about the manuscript, and also wrote the foreword; Gerry Hahn (General Electric), who influenced the text, along with very special encouragement; and Bert Gunter (statistical consultant), who contributed the two excellent case studies found in Appendix A.

We are indebted to the Asian Productivity Organization for permission to include Figures 3.5 and 3.7 of their *Guide to Quality Control*, Second Revised Edition, by K. Ishikawa, 1982. We wish to thank the Biometrika Trustees for permission to abridge and adapt Tables 1, 8, 12, 18, and 29 of their *Biometrika Tables for Statisticians*, Vol. 1, Third Edition (1966) and material from an article by W. D. Ewan and K. W. Kemp, in *Biometrika, Vol. 47* (1960). Also we appreciate the permission to use material reprinted from pages 1–2 of *A Million Random Digits with 100,000 Normal Deviates* by the Rand Corporation, New York: The Free Press, 1955 and 1983. We thank the American

Statistical Association for permission to reprint material from F. J. Anscombe's article "Graphs in Statistical Analysis," *The American Statistician, Vol. 27* (1973). We are indebted to McGraw-Hill Book Company for allowing us to use adapted portions of Tables B and C from *Statistical Quality Control* by E. L. Grant and portions of Table 2.1 from *Selected Techniques of Statistical Analysis* by the Columbia University Statistical Research Group.

In the preface to the first edition we wrote: "Although we believe that this book is a big step forward in a textbook for the statistical education of engineers, we do not pretend to have written the ultimate textbook for such a course. As statisticians know, one must be willing to change and experiment when searching for the optimum." Although there is still lots of room for improvement, we believe that with this revision we have taken a further step in the right direction and have come closer to our original goals.

R. V. H.
J. L.

Contents

Introduction   xix

Contents

APPENDIXES

Introduction

The Role of Statistics in Quality Improvement

Improvement of quality is a foremost concern of American industry, and several companies have developed extremely successful programs in that area. Many American companies are starting to realize that poor quality affects their productivity, their competitive position, and thus their profitability. Quality improvements, on the other hand, reduce waste and rework, eliminate the need for frequent costly inspections, decrease warranty costs, increase customer satisfaction, and enhance the reputation of a company.

Unfortunately, not all companies in America have had a long-term respect for quality. This was particularly true for almost three decades, roughly from 1950 to 1980. Management in American industry had simply not created an atmosphere conducive to the manufacturing of high-quality products. It seemed as if being "within specifications" was good enough for many enterprises. This was most apparent when the resulting products were compared to more reliable items manufactured in Japan and other foreign countries. There were, of course, many factors that contributed to the Japanese success. An important one, however, was the utilization of modern *statistical methods* for quality control and process improvement. Japanese industry paid close attention to the advice of several statisticians. One of those was W. Edwards Deming, an internationally renowned expert on quality improvement.

Deming's philosophy is summarized in his 14 points for management that are a guide to improvement in quality and productivity. His insistence upon their use in the Japanese industry has had a significant impact and has revolutionized their thinking about quality and productivity. These principles are also spreading rapidly among American companies. A brief description of these 14 points and a discussion of how they relate to statistics and statistical education for engineers follows. For a more detailed discussion, the reader should refer to Deming's books *Quality, Productivity, and Competitive Position*

(Cambridge, Mass.: MIT Center for Advanced Engineering Study, 1982) and *Out of the Crisis* (Cambridge, Mass.: MIT Center for Advanced Engineering Study, 1986).

1. Create a constancy of purpose toward the improvement of product and service. Consistently aim to improve the design of your products. Innovation, money spent on research and education, and maintenance of equipment will pay off in the long run.

2. Adopt a new philosophy of rejecting defective products, poor workmanship, and inattentive service. Defective items are a terrible drain on a company; the total cost to produce and dispose of a defective item exceeds the cost to produce a good one and defectives do not generate revenues.

3. Do not depend on mass inspection because it is usually too late, too costly and ineffective. Realize that quality does not come from inspection, but from improvements on the process.

4. Do not award business on price tag alone, but also consider quality. Price is only a meaningful criterion if it is set in relation to a measure of quality. A strategy of awarding work to the lowest bidder has the tendency to drive good vendors and good service out of business. Preference should be given to reliable suppliers that use *modern methods of statistical quality control* to assess the quality of their production.

5. Constantly improve the system of production and service. Involve workers in this process, but also use *statistical experts* who can separate special causes of poor quality from common ones.

6. Institute modern training methods. Instructions to employees should be clear and precise. Workers should be well trained.

7. Institute modern methods of supervision. Supervision should not be viewed as passive "surveilance," but as an active participation aimed at helping the employee make a better product.

8. Drive out fear. Great economic loss is usually associated with fear when workers are afraid to ask a question or to take a position. A secure worker will report equipment out of order, will ask for clarifying instructions, and will point to conditions that impair quality and production.

9. Break down the barriers between functional areas. Teamwork among the different departments is needed.

10. Eliminate numerical goals for your work force. Eliminate targets and slogans. Setting goals for other people without providing a plan on how to reach these goals is often counterproductive. It is far better to explain what management is doing to improve the system.

11. Eliminate work standards and numerical quotas. Work standards are usually without reference to produced quality. Work standards, piece work, and quotas are manifestations of the inability to understand and provide supervision. *Quality must be built in.*

12. Remove barriers that discourage the hourly worker from doing his or her job. Management should listen to hourly workers and try to understand their complaints, comments, and suggestions. Management should treat their workers as important participants in the production process and not as opponents across a bargaining table.

13. Institute a vigorous program of training and education. *Education* in simple, but powerful, *statistical techniques* should be required of all employees. *Statistical quality control charts* should be made routinely and they should be displayed in a place where everyone can see them. Such charts document the quality of a process over time. Employees who are aware of the current level of quality are more likely to investigate the reasons for poor quality and find ways of improving the process. Ultimately, such investigations result in better products.

14. Create a structure in top management that will vigorously advocate these 13 points.

Except for the fact that statistical experts, statistical techniques, and the importance of statistical training are mentioned, these 14 points seem to have little to do with statistics. Certainly, we do not want to overemphasize the importance of statistics in engineering and the use of statistical methods in the improvement of quality, but we do believe that statistics plays an important role. In this book we hope to demonstrate that an adequate input of modern statistical ideas can truly make a difference and can result in worthwhile improvements in quality.

As we reread Deming's 14 points, we note the emphasis on *change*: Change the attitude of management, change the methods of supervision, improve programs of training, remove barriers between management and workers and between departments, change ways of awarding business contracts, improve the design of the product, and so on. The improvement of quality means that changes must be made. But how do we decide which changes should be made, for example, if we want to decrease the number of defects or if we want to increase the yield of a certain manufacturing process? Usually, process factors will be involved. Now, to decide which factors to change and by how much, we must first collect information on how the response variable reacts to changes in those factors. The data must be collected in a systematic and planned manner, and they have to be summarized and analyzed by appropriate methods. In this book we show how statistics can contribute to these tasks.

We will also learn how to construct statistically accurate quality control charts. These charts follow the production process over time. They document its quality and alert workers and management to any changes. Control charts are very valuable instruments for monitoring a process. However, listening and monitoring alone cannot produce higher quality. Improvements in quality must come from modifications in the process. That is, we must make changes. We must decide which variables in the system to change and by how much.

We must design studies that reveal how the output, such as quality or yield, responds to these modifications. Knowledge on how to design experiments efficiently can contribute immensely to these answers.

Deming's admonition to drive out fears and to eliminate slogans is excellent. Management and workers must believe that they are members of the same team. It does little good to demand "zero defects" without having some road map—or plan—to achieve that goal. Statistics can help develop that plan. Of course, statistics cannot do it all alone—it is only one of many tools.

Another important message from Deming's 14 points and some of his other writings is that strong support from management is absolutely necessary. *We* are convinced that the use of statistics is important. But statistics also needs that "high-level" backing because, whereas the need for a certain type of engineer in a company may be quite evident, persons do not always see the need for statistics and a statistician. Yet a statistician, or an engineer trained in statistics, can often help identify the problem, determine what data would contribute to its solution, collect such data, and then draw inferences from these data. Furthermore, the statistician could teach management to understand and appreciate the statistical concepts that are used in the solution of the particular problem at hand. Also, once the solution is implemented in the system, the statistician could show the workers in the plant how to use the statistical tools that can help them monitor the process.

As an exercise, we now go through the various stages of a manufacturing process and list several places where statistics can be used. The following list is our particular version and is by no means meant to be exhaustive.

1. In research and product design and development, statistical procedures can be used to compare one procedure, or treatment, or ingredient to others.

2. Statistical acceptance plans can be used to assess the quality of the items that are purchased from suppliers. A statistician can also review the supplier's quality control program to help the supplier to better understand the reliability of incoming parts.

3. Once the production process is operating, statistical measures on the process capabilities are made. Statistical quality control charts are used to make certain that a satisfactory process stays in control.

4. Possible improvements in the process are continually investigated. Factors are changed according to carefully designed experiments and the resulting effects are analyzed by statistical methods.

5. The finished products are tested by accelerated life tests that are analyzed by statistical methods. If the product is unsatisfactory, the process must be improved.

6. Statistical surveys of consumer preferences help in the marketing of the finished product.

Certainly, in a short discussion such as this, we cannot explain in any detail the role that statistics plays in engineering and in quality improvement. We do, however, wish to emphasize that quality affects the competitive position of industries and businesses. Deming's 14 points can be the basis of a solid program in quality. Within such a program of quality improvement, statistics plays an important role. The purpose of this book is to expose the reader to a number of statistical procedures that are useful to an industry that is committed to high quality.

1

Collection and Analysis of Information

1.1 Variability

Statistics deals with the *collection* and the *analysis of data* to solve *real-world problems*. Statistics teaches us how to obtain and analyze data. Of course, all engineers and scientists engage in such activities; so all engineers and scientists deal with statistics. What makes the *discipline* of statistics useful and unique is that it is concerned with the *process* of getting data and understanding problems in the presence of *variability*. Statistical methods are designed to deal with variability. They help us make inferences about underlying processes on the basis of often imperfect and incomplete data.

Variability (or dispersion) in measurements and processes is a fact of life. Virtually all processes vary. Take, for example, a few items from a production line and measure a certain characteristic of these items. If your measurement has sufficient resolution, you will find that these measurements vary. Or count the number of flaws on different bolts of fabric, and you will notice variability among these counts from bolt to bolt. Or measure the thickness of certain thin wafers, the diameter of certain knobs, the yields of chemical batch processes, or the percentage of defective items in successive lots of 10,000. In all these cases, measurements will vary.

There are several reasons for this variability. The variability can come from the slightly different conditions under which each item is made. The variability may reflect differences in raw materials, differences among machines or operators, differences among operating conditions caused by changes in such things as furnace temperature, humidity, production-floor temperature, and so on. Since this variability comes from the process, we refer to it as the *process variability*.

Part of the variability among the recorded values is also *measurement variability*. For example, when you record the weight of an object, the measurement depends on the exact location of the item on the scale, whether the scale is on a level surface, how the scales are calibrated, and so on. When you measure the size of a very small particle, the measurement depends on the accuracy of the measurement instrument, but also on the way you have set up the measurement and how you place the small object into the measurement apparatus. For example, in determining chemical substances, such as aldrin or deldrin, in identical water samples, the results of a gaschromotography do not always give the same concentrations. Similarly, the measured moisture content of a certain pigment paste will not always be the same. Indeed, measurement itself can be thought of as a process and is subject to inputs and outputs, environmental change, and so on; hence it is subject to variability. We refer to this variability as the *measurement variability*, or *analytical test variability*, or the *variability due to the measurement process*, or simply as the *noise* that obscures the true signal of the process.

The simple example given below illustrates these concepts and helps us to distinguish between process and measurement variability. Take a carton of 10 eggs from your refrigerator and measure the length of each egg. Even if you can determine the length of an egg exactly, you find variability among the 10 measurements. Differences among these 10 eggs arise because of the process variability. It arises because the process of producing eggs is not totally uniform; different hens are involved, the feed is not always the same, and so on.

In addition to process variability, measurement variability is usually present. Assume that you measure the length of an egg by putting it "lengthwise" into a hand-held gage. Since this is a rather crude way of measuring length, you find that repeated measurements on the same egg are not identical. Each recorded number contains a measurement error, as measurements depend on how the egg gets placed in the gage, how numbers are rounded, and so on. If you now look at the length measurements on your 10 eggs, you realize that the variation reflects a combination of the process and the measurement variability.

1.1-1   Distributions

There is another important concept that we want to introduce early on in this book; namely that of a *distribution*. Later, in the first chapter, we consider the compressive strengths of certain concrete blocks. We find that compressive strength varies from about 2800 to 6800 pounds per square inch for this one type of block. The majority of the blocks, however, have strengths somewhere between 4000 and 5200. We find fewer blocks with compressive strength between 2800 and 4000, and 5200 and 6800 pounds. So, we find a certain "bunching up" toward the middle of the range from 2800 to 6800. Statisticians search for curves like that in Figure 1.1-1 to describe the variability (or, in other words, the distribution) of their measurements. Figure 1.1-1 depicts a possible distribution of the compressive strength of concrete blocks. On the horizontal axis we record compressive strength, x. On the vertical axis, we record the values of a nonnegative function, $f(x)$. By selecting this curve carefully, the percentage of the total area under the curve between two marks (representing numbers) on the x-axis reflects the percentage of blocks that have strengths between these two numbers. For illustration, roughly 50 percent are between 4000 and 5000, only about 20 percent are between 3000 and 4000, and only a few percent are larger than 6000 or smaller than 3000 pounds. Here these percentages have been estimated "by eye"; but if the equation of the curve is known, the percentages can, of course, be determined by integration. Furthermore, the total area under such a curve must always be 100 percent, as all observations must be between 2800 and 6800.

Such a curve tells us a great deal about the variation in the compressive strength of these concrete blocks. About which value do the observations vary? Here we might answer 4600, which is the value at which the curve assumes its highest point. We call 4600 the *mode* of the distribution of strengths. How much variation is there? Of course, we see that these strengths run between 2800 and 6800. However, more important, the curve describes what percentage of the blocks are between any two points. For example, about 60 percent are between 4000 and 5200 pounds. Or, to say this differently, 60 percent of the observations are within 600 pounds of the mode 4600.

Let us discuss another example to familiarize ourselves with the concept of variability. It happens quite often that whenever a rookie has had a particularly good first year, his or her performance often slips during the second; we can call this phenomenon the "sophomore jinx."

Once we recognize that athletes have performances that are variable, we can find a simple explanation for this phenomenon. We know that the "rookie

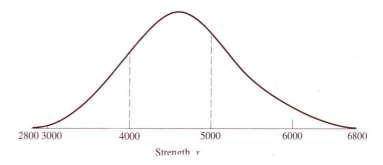

2800 3000   4000   5000   6000   6800

Strength x

FIGURE 1.1-1 Distribution of compressive strength of concrete blocks.

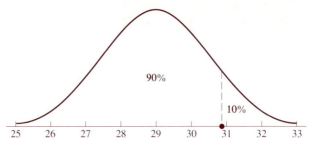

FIGURE 1.1-2   Theoretical distribution of yearly batting percentage of a rookie baseball player under consideration.

of the year" in major league baseball does not often win that title with an average or below-average year. His batting percentage that year is probably about where the *dot* is on the graph in Figure 1.1-2, which depicts the variability in his performance throughout his career. This implies that in the next year, he only has a 10 percent chance to improve on the first performance. Thus, his performance in the second year is likely to be poorer than that in the first. This explains the sophomore jinx. Of course, we should mention at this point that our analysis ignores a learning effect.

Another illustration of the sophomore jinx can be found in the movie industry. Let us ask the movie fans how often they find sequels of hit movies worse than the originals. Although sequel movies often use the same casts and the same directors, frequently the answer to this question is around 90 to 95 percent. The performance in the original "hit" is usually far above the average of that combination of people, and as a consequence, it is extremely difficult to improve upon it. Thus the sequel is frequently worse.

1.1-2   Importance of Variability (or Lack Thereof) for Quality and Productivity Improvement

Managers and engineers must have a basic understanding of variability, as this will help them improve their businesses and industries. But what do distributions and the sophomore jinx have to do with improving quality in business or industry? Actually, a lot! Baseball players are not the only people who have their "ups and downs." Workers and managers do too. Once it is recognized that the performance of a worker will vary, managers should be reluctant to penalize an isolated poor performance or reward an isolated good one. Moreover, it is often the system, or in other words, the process, that is responsible for the variability. Employees are often trapped in a system that gives them little opportunity to affect the results. For example, excessive defects on a production line may be due to poor raw materials and inferior production processes, and the number of defects is often insensitive to the performance of individual workers. In such a situation, it would be inappropriate to punish or reward workers for bad or good production.

With variability in the system, it may be counterproductive to reward iso-lated good performances. Rewards, such as "the worker of the week," often discourage teamwork because it appears as if the "lucky" workers are the favorites of the boss. In the future, others might not be willing to help those "winners." On the other hand, if a worker has had several good performances in succession or maybe even one that appears exceptional when judged against the usual pattern of variability, he or she should be considered carefully for a raise and/or promotion.

A manager, who is a true leader, also recognizes that only he or she can make major improvements in the system. The worker might be able to make some minor changes to improve things, but the manager must be the one to initiate changes that result in substantial improvements.

Suppose that the variability of a process is not about the target value, as in Figure 1.1-3(a). Assume that in this example we are concerned about the bore size in a certain gear blank. Suppose that the target value is 10 centimeters, with lower and upper specification limits of 9.9 and 10.1 centimeters, respec-tively. Production outside the specification limits cannot be shipped out and must be scrapped. Our production process in (a) is not very successful in meeting these requirements. The bore sizes of a relatively large proportion (about 15 percent) of our production are below the lower specification limit. We also notice that our production is off the target. Changes in the process

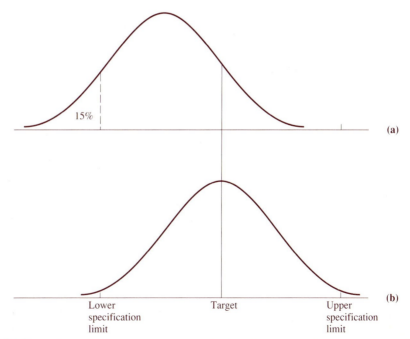

FIGURE 1.1-3 Two distributions compared with the target and lower/upper specifi-cation limits.

must be made to shift the distribution to the right. We notice that the production in Figure 1.1-3(b) is right on target and that most of the produced gear blanks satisfy the required specification limits.

The example in Figure 1.1-3 illustrates how the shift of a distribution can bring a process close to a desired target. Such shifts require level adjustments which are often easy to carry out. However, they leave the extent of the variability unchanged. So, making level adjustments and shifting the distribution to the right or left does not always solve the problem.

Let us now consider a second example and let us study the distribution in Figure 1.1-4(a). The percentage of items outside the specification limits is much too large. Adjustments to reduce the variability must be made to bring most, if not all, items within specifications. Figure 1.1-4(b) shows the results of such changes. The variability is reduced and the items are within the specification limits. Changes that decrease the variability of a process are often more expensive than those needed to change the level of the process.

We also want to point out that producing zero defects is often not good enough. Consider the two distributions in Figure 1.1-5. In either case, all items are within the specification limits, and yet a larger percentage of items is closer to the target T in case (b). Japanese manufacturers have learned that it is often not sufficient just to produce within specifications and they know that each deviation from the target decreases quality. Many of their efforts are directed toward continuous reduction of the variability, to come closer and closer to the target. The parts of the final product will simply fit better if each component is closer to its target value.

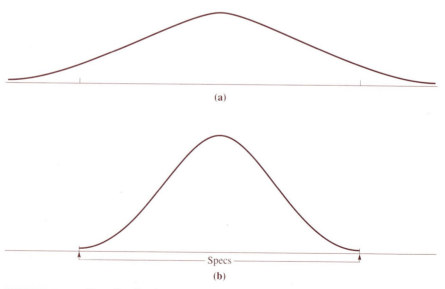

(a)

Specs

(b)

FIGURE 1.1-4   Two distributions compared to their specification limits.

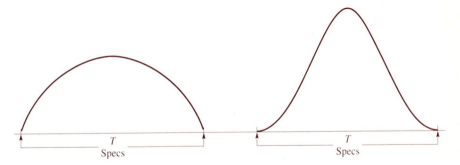

FIGURE 1.1-5   Two distributions resulting in zero defects.

Let us emphasize that the reduction of variation is a key element in improving quality and productivity. The 14 points by W. Edwards Deming are relevant here, as they encourage this reduction. Let us consider them again in a somewhat reworded form.

1. Constancy of purpose certainly reduces variation.
2. The new philosophy of continual improvement eliminates the high cost of defectives.
3. Quality does not come from inspection, but from improvements in the design and the process.
4. Select a few reliable suppliers. This will reduce the variability that comes from too many suppliers.
5. Statistical experts (with the help of the worker) can often distinguish between the inherent variation in the system and that created by special causes. The latter should be eliminated, if possible. Then, if the process is still not satisfactory, attempts must be made to reduce the inherent variation.
6. Training helps improve the uniformity of the product.
7. Good leaders understand that they must reduce variation and move the distribution to a better level by helping the worker and by improving the design and the process.
8. Drive out fear so that workers are not afraid to make suggestions and ask questions, thus improving the product.
9. Teamwork, throughout the company, reduces variation.
10. Managers who understand variability can then take steps to deal with it.
11. Quotas, like 100 per day, may affect quality. For example, consider the foreman who has 90 good items and 10 questionable ones. He ships all 100 to make his quota of 100, but clearly he has not helped the reputation of the company.

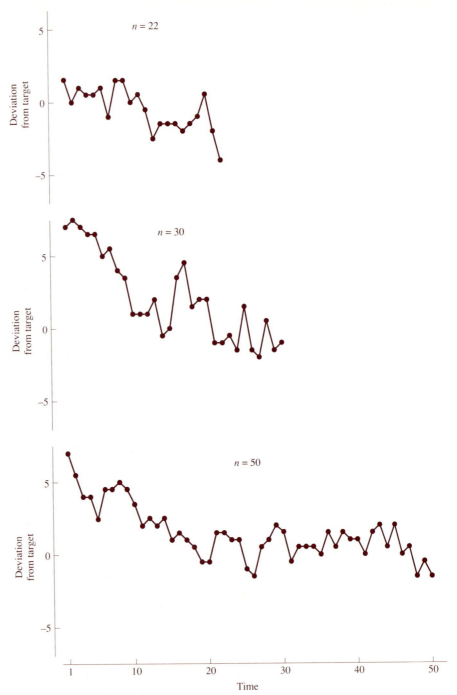

FIGURE 1.1-7   Time-sequence plots for metal cutting example. Deviations from target are expressed as inches $\times 10^4$.

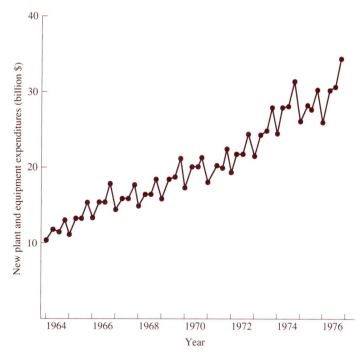

FIGURE 1.1-8   Quarterly new plant and equipment expenditures in U.S. industries (in billions of dollars), first quarter 1964 to fourth quarter 1976.

are shipped to consumers, the producer will receive many complaints from dissatisfied customers and, if a warranty exists, an excessive number of warranty claims. Ultimately, customers will lose confidence in the product and will select a different and more reliable supplier.

Also, a rigorous inspection program cannot inspect quality into a product. Assume, for example, that products are 100 percent inspected and that most products that are outside specification limits are in fact identified. Since unacceptable products have to be either scrapped, reworked, or sold as seconds, the company faces additional costs. If the producer wants to maintain profits, these costs have to be passed on to the consumer; thus prices have to be raised. As a consequence, consumers will look for suppliers who keep their processes within tight specification limits and who succeed in reducing the variability of their products, because such suppliers can offer their products at a lower price. This simple illustration shows that the competitive position of a company depends to a large extent on its success in controlling the variability in the production process. This illustrates that it is very important to keep a close watch on the stability of a process and to find ways of reducing process variability. There exist very simple statistical techniques that can be used to monitor the variability of a process; they require taking periodic measurements on the process and displaying the results in a prominent place. This effectively communicates the most current state of the process. Much more will be said about process variability in later sections of this book, and in Chapter 5 we give an introduction to *control charts*. We think that it is important to introduce control charts in an introductory book on statistics, as they represent an important and very successful application of statistical methods.

Let us illustrate the basic ideas behind control charts with two simple illustrations. Let us first assume that our plant produces ball-point pens in lots of 10,000. Now an easy check of whether or not the quality of our production has changed is to take representative samples of size 100 from each lot, determine the fraction of defectives, and enter the fractions from successive lots on a chart. A plot of the fraction of defectives from successive lots will give a very useful description of the overall quality of the production process. Such a time-sequence chart, displayed in a prominent place, will alert workers and management to changes in the process (either slippage or improvement). Usually, control limits will be added to these charts; points above the upper control limit indicate that the process has deteriorated and that certain modifications should be made. The construction of control limits will be explained later; all that we want to say at this point is that they are based on the natural variability in the fraction of defectives that can be expected from repeated representative samples.

In the preceding example we measured the quality of a component on a pass–fail basis. We analyzed what are called *attribute data*, that is, data that describe the presence or absence of a certain characteristic. However, the classification of an item as defective or as being outside specification limits requires measurements of certain engineering variables: for example, the diameter of a knob that is supposed to be within certain specifications, or the thickness of a wafer for integrated circuits that has to be within certain limits, or the pull strength of a weld that has to exceed a certain value. By classifying the items according to two outcomes only, we actually throw away information; the pass–fail data do not tell us by how much we exceed or are within given specification limits. Thus it can be argued that it is better to analyze the variability in the original measurements instead of the variability in the implied attribute data. Just as we can monitor the variability in the fraction of defectives from successive lots, we can monitor the diameter of knobs. We can sample a small number of knobs each hour or from each production shift, determine the diameters of the sampled knobs, and display the sample average and the range (which is the difference between the largest and the smallest measurement in the sample) on control charts. Details are given in Chapter 5.

We pointed out that we cannot inspect quality into an item; improvements in quality can only come from changes in the process. Control charts, however, are very helpful in suggesting what changes should be made. Points outside the limits, as well as patterns in these charts, will lead to discussions and investigations toward finding the reason why certain lots have more defectives than others. We can search for patterns in these charts and relate them to changes that have taken place in the production process. For example, why is it that there were many more defectives during the last several lots? Is it due to a bad batch of ink? If the records show that these batches were produced with ink purchased from a new supplier, we might hypothesize that it is the switch to a new supplier that is responsible for the sudden increase. Or why is it that the number of defectives is drifting upward? Is it because the machines have not been serviced for a while? Checks of the service records and whether previous overhauling of machines has eliminated such drifts could provide some justification for this hypothesis. Also, if we find that one of the machines has not been serviced for a long time, it may pay to observe this machine and check whether it could be the cause of the decrease in quality. Suppose that every tenth lot contains more defectives than the others. If we produce 10 lots a day and the problem lot is always the first one produced, the problem could be related to the startup of the production line. If the number of defectives from the weekend's production is always higher than the number of defectives produced on weekdays, we could hypothesize that the inexperienced weekend staff needs more training. This discussion shows that the information from control charts is very helpful because it will lead to discussions and investigations that try to determine the causes of such deviations. Usually, this discussion leads to the formation of certain hypotheses about the factors that could have affected the response.

1.2 Representation of Data

1.2-1 Summary and Display of Measurement Data

Let us now discuss how to summarize and display data that are obtained by measuring objects. For example, we may have measured several items by determining their weight, width, length, strength, diameter, deflection, and so on. Often, measurements are made on a sample of n items taken from a much larger data set, which in statistics is called the *population*. For example, we may have made measurements on a sample of 100 pens that were taken from a lot of size 10,000. Or we may have obtained measurements on a sample of 10 garden tractors from a day's production totaling 200. Or we may determine the concentrations of various pollutants from water samples that are obtained from 20 different sites on a large lake. Or we may have obtained yearly incomes of a sample of 100 civil engineers. Usually, we want to generalize the results obtained from the sample to the population from which the sample was selected. The inference from the sample to the population is discussed in later chapters; this inference is possible only if the sample is a representative part of the population.

Data sets are often large, so that data must be organized, summarized, and displayed before any interpretation can be attempted. Graphical displays, such as plots and diagrams, are especially useful to uncover unknown features in the data. Pictures stimulate insight and force us to notice what we frequently never expected to see.

Let us start with an example. Table 1.2-1 lists measurements of compressive strength (in units of 100 pounds per square inch) that were made on 90 concrete blocks. These measurements were taken to investigate the variability among blocks purchased from the traditional supplier. Table 1.2-1, without summary and display, is not very informative.

To get more insight, we could construct a *dot diagram* of the observations. In a dot diagram we mark the observations on the horizontal axis; for illustration we have used the first 10 observations of Table 1.2-1. The dot diagram in Figure 1.2-1(a) gives a visual display of the variability among these 10 observations.

For 90 observations such a diagram would not be too informative because we would have many points bunched together. For large data sets it is better to construct a frequency distribution, as in Table 1.2-2, and to display the results in form of a *histogram*, as in Figure 1.2-1(b).

To determine the frequency distribution, we first rank the n observations, say $x_1, x_2, \ldots, x_n$, from the smallest value, x_{min}, to the largest, x_{max}. The range of the data $R = x_{max} - x_{min}$ tells us about the extent of their variability. In our example, $x_{min} = 28.7$, $x_{max} = 67.2$, and $R = 38.5$. Then we group the data into nonoverlapping intervals (cells or classes) that are usually of equal length (width). There are no universally applicable rules for determining the number of cells. Experience and experimentation with different lengths of the class intervals usually provide the best guide. However, it is generally desirable to have somewhere between 7 and 15 cells. Of course, this will depend on the number of observations; if there are more observations, we can use more classes with shorter class widths (lengths). Let us assume, in our example, that we have 10 classes, each of width 4.0. The first class starts with 28.0 and goes up to (but not including) 32.0, the second from 32.0 to 36.0, ..., the last from

TABLE 1.2-1   Compressive Strength of Concrete Blocks (100 Pounds per Square Inch)

49.2	53.9	50.0	44.5	42.2	42.3	32.3	31.3	60.9	47.5
43.5	37.9	41.1	57.6	40.2	45.3	51.7	52.3	45.7	53.4
51.0	45.7	45.9	50.0	32.5	67.2	55.1	59.6	48.6	50.3
45.1	46.8	47.4	38.3	41.5	44.0	62.2	62.9	56.3	35.8
38.3	33.5	48.5	47.4	49.6	41.3	55.2	52.1	34.3	31.6
38.2	46.0	47.0	41.2	39.8	48.4	49.2	32.8	47.9	43.3
49.3	54.5	54.1	44.5	46.2	44.4	45.1	41.5	43.4	39.1
39.1	41.6	43.1	43.7	48.8	37.2	33.6	28.7	33.8	37.4
43.5	44.2	53.0	45.1	51.9	50.6	48.5	39.0	47.3	48.8

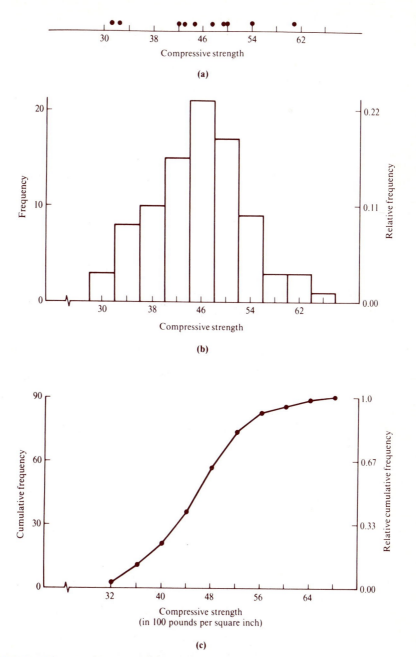

FIGURE 1.2-1   Graphical display of the compressive strength measurements in Table 1.2-1: (a) dot diagram of the first 10 observations; (b) histogram; (c) cumulative frequencies and a plot of the ogive.

TABLE 1.2-2   Frequency Distribution

Interval	Midpoint	Tally	Frequency f_i	Relative Frequency f_i/n	Cumulative Frequency $fcum_i$	Relative Cumulative Frequency $fcum_i/n$
28.0–32.0	30.0	‖‖	3	0.033	3	0.033
32.0–36.0	34.0	‖‖‖ ‖‖	8	0.089	11	0.122
36.0–40.0	38.0	‖‖‖ ‖‖‖	10	0.111	21	0.233
40.0–44.0	42.0	‖‖‖ ‖‖‖ ‖‖‖	15	0.167	36	0.400
44.0–48.0	46.0	‖‖‖ ‖‖‖ ‖‖‖ ‖‖‖ ‖	21	0.233	57	0.633
48.0–52.0	50.0	‖‖‖ ‖‖‖ ‖‖‖ ‖‖	17	0.189	74	0.822
52.0–56.0	54.0	‖‖‖ ‖‖‖‖	9	0.100	83	0.922
56.0–60.0	58.0	‖‖‖	3	0.033	86	0.955
60.0–64.0	62.0	‖‖‖	3	0.033	89	0.988
64.0–68.0	66.0	‖	1	0.012	90	1.000
			90	1.000		

64.0 to 68.0. The end points of each class are called the *cell boundaries*; the middle is called the *midpoint*. Next, we count the number of values that belong to each class and we make a frequency distribution table. We use the convention that an observation that falls exactly on a boundary is allocated to the class that has this boundary as the lower limit. Thus each observation in Table 1.2-2 falls in one and only one class. Apart from the (*absolute*) *frequencies* f_i ($i = 1, 2, \ldots, k$, where k is the number of classes), we also list the *relative frequencies* f_i/n, the *cumulative frequencies*

$$fcum_i = \sum_{j=1}^{i} f_j = f_1 + \cdots + f_i \qquad (i = 1, 2, \ldots, k),$$

and the *relative cumulative frequencies*

$$\frac{fcum_i}{n} = \frac{1}{n} \sum_{j=1}^{i} f_j.$$

Note that the absolute frequencies of the classes add to n, and the relative frequencies add to 1.

The frequency table can be better visualized if it is displayed graphically. The histogram in Figure 1.2-1(b) is a bar graph that associates the frequencies (either the absolute or the relative frequencies) with the data intervals. The histogram shows how the values of our variable of interest are distributed. It condenses a set of data for easy visual comprehension of its general characteristics, such as typical values, spread, and shape. It also helps to detect unusual observations in a data set.

The histogram in Figure 1.2-1(b) is approximately *symmetric*, with a single peak, or hump, in the middle. The peak represents the most frequent class; in our example, it is the class from 44 to 48. The midpoint of this class, 46, is also called the *mode*; it stands for the most frequent value in the data set if we assume that the values in each cell equal its midpoint.

Symmetric distributions with a single peak in the middle are very common with measurement data. In fact, they are so common that many of them are called "normal distributions." In Chapter 4 we discuss the theory that explains why this particular type of histogram is so common.

However, as the histograms in Figure 1.2-2 show, symmetric distributions with a single hump in the middle are not the only possible histograms. The first is a histogram of the CO emissions of 794 cars (see Exercise 1.2-9 for the data). The second is a histogram of the lengths of life of more than 1 million human beings (see Exercise 1.2-10 for the data). The third is a histogram of the thickness of the ears of 150 paint cans (*ears* are tabs used to secure the lid of large paint cans). The data are listed in Exercise 1.2-8.

The histogram in Figure 1.2-2(a) has a single hump but is *not* symmetric. We call such a nonsymmetric distribution *skewed*. The histogram in Figure 1.2-2(a) is said to be *skewed to the right* because it has a long right tail of relatively large numbers. The histogram in Figure 1.2-2(b) is also skewed. Since it has a long left tail of relatively small numbers, we call it *skewed to the left*. Note that the frequency of failure (death) is relatively high in the first age interval, from 0 to 5 years. This is due to the fact that the infant mortality rate is somewhat higher than the mortality rate during the teen years. Histograms of the failure time of items for which there is an increasing failure rate (i.e., the older it gets, the more likely it is to fail) are skewed to the left. However, some items may also fail early in life, and the increasing failure rate may apply only to items that survived past a certain point. In such cases we would observe a pattern such as that in Figure 1.2-2(b).

Figure 1.2-2(c) shows a histogram with two peaks (or two modes). We call such a histogram *bimodal*, as compared to the *unimodal* histograms in Figures 1.2-1(b) and 1.2-2(a). The bimodal nature can be explained by the fact that the hopper, from which the paint cans were selected, collected cans from two different machines that produced ears of different thickness (see Exercise 1.2-8).

So far we have considered the absolute and relative frequencies. The cumulative frequencies in the last columns of Table 1.2-2 show that 36 of 90 measurements, or 40 percent, are smaller than 44; similarly, 89 of 90 measurements, or 98.8 percent, are smaller than 64. In Figure 1.2-1(c) we plot the (relative) cumulative frequencies against the upper limits of the intervals. An *ogive* is a line graph that connects these points. The definition of cumulative frequencies implies that this ogive is nondecreasing and always between zero and 1.

A histogram condenses a set of data for easy *visual* comprehension of its general characteristics. Frequently, however, we also want to summarize the information *numerically* and obtain a few statistics that characterize the data set. In particular, we want measures of the location and of the dispersion.

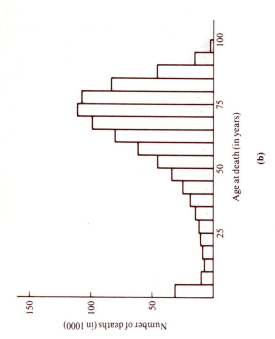

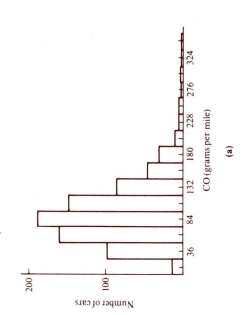

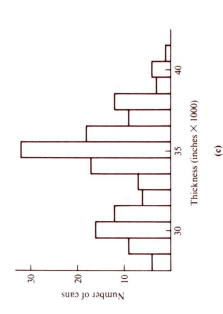

FIGURE 1.2-2 Three histograms: (a) CO emissions of 794 cars; (b) ages at death for a cohort of people; (c) thickness of the ears of 150 paint cans.

1.2-2   Measures of Location

For a given data set $x_1, x_2, \ldots, x_n$, the most familiar measure of location is the arithmetic average of the n observations. Since the data set usually corresponds to a sample from a larger population (in our example the population could be the set of all concrete blocks that are in our inventory), we refer to this average as the *sample mean* and denote it by

$$\bar{x} = \frac{1}{n}(x_1 + x_2 + \cdots + x_n) = \frac{1}{n}\sum_{i=1}^{n} x_i.$$

Note that the deviations of the observations from the sample mean, $x_i - \bar{x}$, $i = 1, 2, \ldots, n$, always add to zero; that is,

$$\sum_{i=1}^{n}(x_i - \bar{x}) = \sum_{i=1}^{n} x_i - n\bar{x} = \sum_{i=1}^{n} x_i - \sum_{i=1}^{n} x_i = 0.$$

One can think of the sample mean as the fulcrum point that keeps a weightless ruler, on which each observation is represented by the same weight, in perfect balance.

If we consider only the first 10 observations in Table 1.2-1, we find that

$$\bar{x} = \frac{454.1}{10} = 45.41.$$

For the complete set of 90 observations, the average is 45.51.

One problem with the mean as the center of a data set is that it is affected by the presence of a single observation that lies very far to one side of the other values. We call such an observation an *outlier*. For example, assume that the third observation in the first row of Table 1.2-1 gets recorded incorrectly as 5.0 instead of 50.0. This is clearly an outlying observation, as a simple dot diagram of the 10 observations would show (see Figure 1.2-3). The sample mean becomes $\bar{x} = 40.91$, a considerable change from 45.41.

The *median* of a sample is a measure of location that is much less sensitive to a single observation. The median is the middle observation when the observations are arranged in increasing order of magnitude if n is an odd number. If n is even, there is no unique middle and the median is usually taken to be the average of the middle pair of numbers. The median has the property that one-half of the observations lie below and one-half lie above this value (if n is odd, we can think of splitting that middle value). Take the first 10 observations in Table 1.2-1 and arrange them in increasing order:

31.3   32.3   42.2   42.3   44.5   47.5   49.2   50.0   53.9   60.9

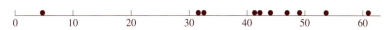

FIGURE 1.2-3   A simple dot diagram.

Since n is even, we take the average of the 5th and 6th largest observations. We find that the median is Md $= (44.5 + 47.5)/2 = 46.0$. Note that the one outlier (5.0 instead of 50.0) in the sample of the first 10 observations affects the median just slightly; Md $= (42.3 + 44.5)/2 = 43.4$. In general, the changes in the median are usually much smaller than the ones for the mean when outliers are introduced. The median for all 90 observations is the average of the 45th and 46th largest; it is 45.5.

We could have used the ogive in Figure 1.2-1(c) to determine the median, at least approximately. Since, by definition, half of the observations are below the median, we look for the intersection of the ogive and the relative cumulative frequency of 0.5. The x coordinate of this point of intersection is our median. Of course, this method is only approximate (but still very good) because we are using only the grouped data in Table 1.2-2, not the individual observations.

For symmetric distributions such as the one in Figure 1.2-1(b), the mean, the median, and the mode (which is the most frequent value, or in the case of grouped data the midpoint of the most frequent class) will be about the same. For this particular data set of $n = 90$ observations we have found that $\bar{x} = 45.51$, Md $= 45.5$, and Mode $= 46.0$. For skewed distributions they are no longer equal. Take, for example, the CO data in Exercise 1.2-9, which were used to construct the skewed histogram in Figure 1.2-2(a). There the mode is 84, and as you will see by working Exercise 1.2-9, the median and mean are given by Md $= 87.9$ and $\bar{x} = 94.2$. For frequency distributions that are skewed to the right, it is usually true that mode $<$ median $<$ mean. Similarly, for distributions that are skewed to the left, we usually find that mode $>$ median $>$ mean. You can use the data in Exercise 1.2-10 and Figure 1.2-2(b) to illustrate this fact.

The median divides the data set into two parts. A finer partition can be obtained by dividing the data set into more than two parts. For example, we can order the n observations $x_1, x_2, \ldots, x_n$ from the smallest one $x_{(1)}$, the second smallest one $x_{(2)}, \ldots,$ to the largest one $x_{(n)}$. The ordered observations are called the *order statistics* $x_{(1)} \leq x_{(2)} \leq \cdots \leq x_{(n)}$; the numbers in parentheses are the *ranks* of the observations. The smallest observation $x_{(1)}$ represents the first $100/n$ percent of the distribution of the sample. If we take the midpercentage, $100/2n = 100[(1 - 0.5)/n]$, as the representative value, we say that the smallest observation $x_{(1)}$ is the $100[(1 - 0.5)/n]$th *percentile* of the sample. The second smallest observation $x_{(2)}$ represents the second $100/n$ percent of the distribution of the sample. The midpoint of this second $100/n$ percent region, $100[(2 - 0.5)/n]$, is the representative percentage; thus we say that $x_{(2)}$ is the $100[(2 - 0.5)/n]$th percentile of the sample. In general, the ith order statistic $x_{(i)}$ is the $100[(i - 0.5)/n]$th percentile of the sample. We also call it the *quantile of order* $(i - 0.5)/n$. For example, take $n = 10$. Here each order statistic represents $100/10 = 10$ percent of the distribution. The order statistics $x_{(1)}, x_{(2)}, \ldots, x_{(10)}$ are the respective 5th, 15th, $\ldots,$ 95th percentiles of the sample.

Frequently, we want to calculate a certain percentile from the data. Since the ith order statistic is the $100P = 100[(i - 0.5)/n]$th percentile, it follows that the $(100P)$th percentile of the sample is the observation with rank $nP + 0.5$. If this is not an integer, we take the average of the two order statistics whose ranks are closest to this number. Take the 50th percentile, or the median, as an example; it is the observation with rank $(n/2) + 0.5 = (n + 1)/2$. If n is an odd number, we take the middle observation with rank $(n + 1)/2$. If n is even, we take the average of the two middle observations with ranks $(n/2)$ and $(n/2) + 1$. To find the 25th percentile, which is also called the *lower (first) quartile* Q_1, we take the observation with rank $(n/4) + 0.5$. Again, if this is not an integer but a fraction, we average the two order statistics whose ranks are closest to this number. Similarly, the 75th percentile, or the *upper (third) quartile* Q_3, is the observation with rank $n(3/4) + 0.5$. For example, if $n = 10$, the first quartile Q_1 is the observation with rank $(10/4) + 0.5 = 3$. The 75th percentile, or upper quartile Q_3, is the $10(3/4) + 0.5 = 8$th largest observation. The 50th percentile, or median, or second quartile Q_2, is the average of $x_{(5)}$ and $x_{(6)}$. For the 10 data items in the first row of Table 1.2-1, we find $Q_1 = 42.2$, $Q_2 = 46.0$, and $Q_3 = 50.0$. With $n = 90$, Q_1 is the observation with rank 23, Q_3 the one with rank 68, and the median Q_2 is the average of $x_{(45)}$ and $x_{(46)}$.

Remarks   Some authors and some computer programs use a slightly different definition for percentiles. One popular scheme is the following. Since the order statistics divide the data set into $n + 1$ segments, they define the ith order statistic as the $100[i/(n + 1)]$th percentile. Accordingly, the $(100P)$th percentile is the observation with rank $(n + 1)P = nP + P$. If n is not too small and P is between 0.1 and 0.9, there is very little difference between the two definitions. ∎

Example 1.2-1   A manufacturer claims that his fabric consists of 80 percent cotton. To check his claim we take a small swatch from each bolt of fabric and determine its cotton content. The results of 25 such samples are given below.

$$77 \quad 81 \quad 76 \quad 86 \quad 79 \quad 79 \quad 80 \quad 77 \quad 89 \quad 77 \quad 78 \quad 85 \quad 80$$

$$75 \quad 79 \quad 88 \quad 81 \quad 78 \quad 82 \quad 80 \quad 76 \quad 83 \quad 81 \quad 85 \quad 79.$$

The 25 order statistics are

$$75 \leq 76 \leq 76 \leq 77 \leq 77 \leq 77 \leq 78 \leq 78 \leq 79 \leq 79 \leq 79 \leq 79 \leq 80 \leq$$

$$80 \leq 80 \leq 81 \leq 81 \leq 81 \leq 82 \leq 83 \leq 85 \leq 85 \leq 86 \leq 88 \leq 89.$$

The fourth order statistic $x_{(4)} = 77$ is the $100[(4 - 0.5)/25)] = 14$th percentile and $x_{(19)} = 82$ is the $100[(19 - 0.5)/25] = 74$th percentile. The median is the order statistic with rank $25/2 + 0.5 = 13$; that is, $x_{(13)} = 80$. The first and third quartiles have ranks $25/4 + 0.5 = 6.75$ and $(25)3/4 + 0.5 = 19.25$, respectively. Thus those respective quartiles are $[x_{(6)} + x_{(7)}]/2 = (77 + 78)/2 = 77.5$ and $[x_{(19)} + x_{(20)}]/2 = (82 + 83)/2 = 82.5$. Alternatively, one could interpolate by taking the weighted averages $(0.25)x_{(6)} + (0.75)x_{(7)} = 77.75$ and $(0.75)x_{(19)} + (0.25)x_{(20)} = 82.25$. The differences, however, will usually be quite small. ∎

There is yet one other measure of location, the *trimmed mean*. In calculating the 100α percent trimmed mean, $\bar{x}_\alpha$, we ignore (or trim) the $n\alpha$ smallest and the $n\alpha$ largest observations and calculate the arithmetic average of the remaining $n(1 - 2\alpha)$ observations. For example, a 10 percent trimmed mean, calculated from a sample of size $n = 10$, trims $(10)(0.1) = 1$ observation from each end of the ordered data set. Ignoring the smallest and largest observations of the first 10 observations in Table 1.2-1 (i.e., 31.3 and 60.9) leads to the 10 percent trimmed mean, $\bar{x}_{0.1} = 45.24$.

1.2-3   Measures of Variation

We have discussed the fact that variability or dispersion is an integral and natural part of all measurements. The sample mean, median, mode, and trimmed mean do not capture the dispersion as they are estimates of location.

The simplest measure of dispersion is the *range*. It is defined as the difference between the largest and the smallest observations. For example, the minimum of the first 10 observations in Table 1.2-1 is 31.3, the maximum is 60.9, and therefore the range of those $n = 10$ observations is $R = 60.9 - 31.3 = 29.6$.

A drawback of this measure is that it is very sensitive to outliers. Just one large (or small) observation can influence its value a great deal. A more reliable measure of dispersion is the *interquartile range*, which is the difference between the third and first quartiles. For our 10 observations the interquartile range is $50.0 - 42.2 = 7.8$.

The units for the range and the interquartile range are the same as the units of the observations x. In our example strength is measured in units of 100 pounds per square inch. Thus the interquartile range is 780 pounds per square inch.

The most common measures of variability, however, are the *sample variance* and its square root, the *sample standard deviation*. The square $(x_i - \bar{x})^2$ of the distance $|x_i - \bar{x}|$ of an observation x_i from the overall average $\bar{x}$ provides some information about the variability, $i = 1, 2, \ldots, n$. The *sample variance* is a special average of these n squared distances and is defined as

$$s^2 = \frac{1}{n-1}[(x_1 - \bar{x})^2 + (x_2 - \bar{x})^2 + \cdots + (x_n - \bar{x})^2] = \frac{1}{n-1}\sum_{i=1}^{n}(x_i - \bar{x})^2.$$

We just said that it is the average of n such components, but we have divided the sum by $n - 1$ instead of n. Why? A formal reason for this change will be given in a later chapter. For the time being, however, consider the following intuitive explanation. We noted before that the n deviations $x_i - \bar{x}$, $i = 1, \ldots, n$, add up to zero. Thus we really need only $(n - 1)$ of these deviations to calculate s^2. We can always obtain the last deviation from

$$(x_n - \bar{x}) = -\sum_{i=1}^{n-1}(x_i - \bar{x}).$$

Thus it seems justified to divide by $n - 1$ instead of n. At any rate, using the divisor $(n - 1)$ instead of n makes almost no numerical difference provided that the number of observations is reasonably large.

There is also a convenient shortcut method for calculating the sample variance that avoids working out the deviations from the mean. It is given by

$$s^2 = \frac{1}{n-1}\left[\sum_{i=1}^{n} x_i^2 - \frac{(\sum_{i=1}^{n} x_i)^2}{n}\right].$$

See Exercise 1.2-4. For the first 10 observations in Table 1.2-1 we find that $\sum x_i = 454.1$ and $\sum x_i^2 = 21{,}364.27$; thus $s^2 = (1/9)[21{,}364.27 - (454.1)^2/10] = 82.62$. Similarly, we can calculate the sample variance of the 90 observations in Table 1.2-1; we find that $s^2 = (1/89)[191{,}605.04 - (4095.6)^2/90] = 58.74$.

The variance $s^2 \geq 0$ measures the scatter of the observations around their mean. If $s^2 = 0$, there is no variation at all because all n observations must be the same. However, there is a drawback to the variance as a measure of variation as its unit is not the same as the unit of our observations. Since s^2 is an average of squares, its unit is the square of the unit of the measurements x; if the x's are measured in pounds, the unit of s^2 is (pounds)^2.

To return to the original units of measurement, we take the square root of the sample variance. This gives a measure known as the *sample standard deviation*,

$$s = \sqrt{s^2} = \sqrt{\frac{1}{n-1}\sum_{i=1}^{n}(x_i - \bar{x})^2}.$$

For our 10 observations, the standard deviation is $s = \sqrt{82.62} = 9.1$. Its unit is the same as that of the observations, 100 pounds per square inch. The standard deviation is 910 pounds per square inch.

So far we have learned how to calculate sample variances and sample standard deviations. Calculation is important, but in today's computer age, where these summary statistics are calculated by machines, it is even more important to understand their meaning. Here we give an intuitive interpretation of the sample standard deviation. Looking at the preceding equation for s, we see that the distances from the observations to the sample mean vary about one standard deviation. Or, to say this differently, observations, on the average, are *approximately* one standard deviation from the mean. Here we wish to emphasize the word *approximately* because the average actually involves the square, after which the square root is taken. In our example of $n = 10$ observations, we find that 7 of the 10 observations lie within one standard deviation, $s = 9.1$, on either side of the mean $\bar{x} = 45.4$. The other three, 31.3, 32.3, and 60.9, lie beyond these limits, so that all 10 distances from the mean average to be *about* one standard deviation. In general, we find that usually over half of the observations will be within plus or minus one standard deviation from the mean. More than three-fourths of the observations, and often even much more than that, will lie within plus or minus two standard deviations of the mean;

and almost all the observations will be within three standard deviations. In a subsequent chapter we discuss this in more detail.

A note on computation is now in order. Measures such as mean and variance are easy to calculate for small samples. However, in many realistic applications we may be facing very large data sets. Sophisticated electronic recording devices may give you measurements every second and it may be necessary to summarize 10,000 or more observations. Certainly, we would use a computer program in such circumstances. However, in writing such programs statisticians have to worry about the efficient calculation of these statistics. Take, for example, the sample variance that we get by averaging the squares of 10,000 deviations. Since, typically, $\bar{x}$ is rounded off, we introduce this rounding error into 10,000 squares $(x_i - \bar{x})^2$; and the result will probably not be very satisfactory. Also, the shortcut method is not very good if the observations are large in magnitude but vary only little. Here we do not go into these issues. If you want to learn more about this, consult books on statistical computing.

We often express the standard deviation as a percentage of the mean. The measure

$$CV = \frac{100s}{\bar{x}}$$

is called the *coefficient of variation*. Since s and $\bar{x}$ are expressed in the same units, we find that this measure does not depend on the unit of measurement. This measure says that the observations lie, on the average, within approximately CV percent of the mean. In our example with 10 observations we found that $\bar{x} = 45.41$ and $s = 9.1$. Thus the observations lie, on average, within $(100)(9.1)/45.41 = 20$ percent of the mean.

Exercises 1.2

1.2-1 The tensile strengths (in pounds per square inch) of eight synthetic fiber samples are given by

$$12 \quad 15 \quad 18 \quad 16 \quad 15 \quad 14 \quad 16 \quad 17$$

(a) Construct a dot diagram.
(b) Calculate the sample mean, variance, and standard deviation.
(c) Calculate the quartiles and the interquartile range.

1.2-2 A manufacturer of metal alloys is concerned about customer complaints concerning the lack of uniformity in the melting points of one of the firm's alloy filaments. Fifty filaments are selected and their melting points are determined. The following results are obtained:

320	326	325	318	322	320	329	317	316
331	320	320	317	329	316	308	321	319
322	335	318	313	327	314	329	323	327
323	324	314	308	305	328	330	322	310
324	314	312	318	313	320	324	311	317
325	328	319	310	324				

(a) Construct a frequency distribution and display the histogram.

(b) Calculate the mean, median, quartiles, sample variance, and standard deviation. How many observations lie within one standard deviation from the mean? Within two standard deviations?

Hint The use of a computer would be helpful in these calculations.

1.2-3 The following 64 observations are a sample of daily weekday afternoon (3 to 7 P.M.) lead concentrations [in micrograms per cubic meter ($\mu g/m^3$)]. The data were recorded at an air monitoring station near the San Diego Freeway in Los Angeles during the fall of 1976.

```
6.7   5.4   5.2   6.0   8.7   6.0   6.4   8.3   5.3   5.9
7.6   5.0   6.9   6.8   4.9   6.3   5.0   6.0   7.2   8.0
8.1   7.2  10.9   9.2   8.6   6.2   6.1   6.5   7.8   6.2
8.5   6.4   8.1   2.1   6.1   6.5   7.9   5.1   9.5  10.6
8.4   8.3   5.9   6.0   6.4   3.9   9.9   7.6   6.8   8.6
8.5  11.2   7.0   7.1   6.0   9.0  10.1   8.0   6.8   7.3
9.7   9.3   3.2   6.4
```

(a) Construct a frequency distribution and display the results in form of a histogram. Is this distribution symmetric?

(b) Calculate the mean, median, quartiles, interquartile range, sample variance, and sample standard deviation.

1.2-4 Show that the sample variance can be calculated from

$$s^2 = \frac{1}{n-1}\left[\sum_{i=1}^{n} x_i^2 - \frac{\left(\sum_{i=1}^{n} x_i\right)^2}{n}\right].$$

Hint Write

$$\sum_{i=1}^{n} (x_i - \bar{x})^2 = \sum_{i=1}^{n} (x_i^2 - 2\bar{x}x_i + \bar{x}^2)$$

and recall that

$$\sum_{i=1}^{n} 2\bar{x}x_i = 2\bar{x}\sum_{i=1}^{n} x_i, \qquad \sum_{i=1}^{n} \bar{x}^2 = n\bar{x}^2.$$

1.2-5 Obtain the last 50 annual precipitation totals for the city in which you live. Construct a histogram.

Calculate the mean, the quartiles, and the standard deviation. Interpret your findings.

Can you think of other informative data displays? What about plotting the annual totals over time? What can you learn from such a plot?

1.2-6 Take 10 eggs from your refrigerator and measure their *lengths*. Describe your measurement procedure and discuss the factors that may have caused the variability in these 10 observations. Construct a dot diagram of these measurements, and calculate their mean, sample variance, and sample standard deviation.

Of course, one source of the variability are actual size differences, despite the fact that all these eggs probably come from a carton of large (or medium, or extra-large) eggs. Another source of the variability could come from your measurement procedure; for example, you may not always line up the egg in exactly the same way when you measure its length. To learn more about this measurement variability, obtain another round of measurements with the *same* 10 eggs. This will give you two measurements for each egg. Note, however, that these two *replicated* measurements are *not* obtained by lining up each egg once and then taking two measurements. If that were done, we would only obtain information on the variability that is due to the measurement *instrument*, not on the variability that is due to the measurement *procedure*.

Display the variability in the resulting 20 observations. You could make a histogram of these 20 measurements, but if you do that, you are not separating the sources of the variability, that is, the variability due to actual size differences and the measurement variability. Think about other ways of displaying your data which reflect the fact that you have obtained two measurements on each egg and display the variability that is due to the measurement procedure.

1.2-7 Discuss how you would measure the breaking strength of ordinary household plastic wrap. Obtain 10 measurements, display their variability, discuss the factors that affect your measurements, and comment on how we could learn more about their contributions to this variability.

1.2-8 Snee has measured the thickness of paint can ears. At periodic intervals, samples of five paint cans are taken from a hopper that collects the production from two machines and the thickness of each ear is measured. The results (in inches × 1000) of 30 such samples follow.

Sample	Measurements
1	29　36　39　34　34
2	29　29　28　32　31
3	34　34　39　38　37
4	35　37　33　38　41
5	30　29　31　38　29
6	34　31　37　39　36
7	30　35　33　40　36
8	28　28　31　34　30
9	32　36　38　38　35
10	35　30　37　35　31
11	35　30　35　38　35
12	38　34　35　35　31
13	34　35　33　30　34
14	40　35　34　33　35
15	34　35　38　35　30
16	35　30　35　29　37
17	40　31　38　35　31
18	35　36　30　33　32
19	35　34　35　30　36
20	35　35　31　38　36
21	32　36　36　32　36
22	36　37　32　34　34
23	29　34　33　37　35
24	36　36　35　37　37
25	36　30　35　33　31
26	35　30　29　38　35
27	35　36　30　34　36
28	35　30　36　29　35
29	38　36　35　31　31
30	30　34　40　28　30

Construct a histogram. Since there are many observations, it makes sense to use about 15 intervals of equal length. Interpret the shape of the histogram. You will notice that this histogram has two "humps" or modes. We call such a histogram *bimodal*, as compared to the unimodal histograms that we have seen in Figure 1.2-2, for example. What could be the reason for this bimodal nature?

Experiment with a different number, k, of classes. For example, try $k = 10$ and $k = 6$. You will notice

that the two humps will eventually collapse into one This shows that the choice of k can change the appearance of the histogram. Be aware that searching for a shape that serves the experimenter's purpose in the best possible way and ignoring all others could be a misuse of histograms.

Can you think of any other useful displays of this information?

Hint What could you learn from a plot of the 30 sample averages over time?

[R. D. Snee, "Graphical Analysis of Process Variation Studies," *Journal of Quality Technology*, 15: 76–88 (April 1983).]

1.2-9 The following data on the carbon monoxide emissions of 794 cars, grouped into intervals of 24 grams per mile, were taken from an article by Snee and Pfeifer.

Interval	Interval Midpoint	Frequency
0–24	12	13
24–48	36	98
48–72	60	161
72–96	84	189
96–120	108	148
120–144	132	85
144–168	156	45
168–192	180	30
192–216	204	10
216–240	228	5
240–264	252	5
264–288	276	1
288–312	300	2
312–336	324	1
336–360	348	1

(a) Calculate the relative frequencies, the cumulative frequencies, and the relative cumulative frequencies. Construct a histogram and plot the ogive. Determine the median and the interquartile range.

(b) Calculate the sample mean, the sample variance, and the sample standard deviation.

[R. D. Snee and C. G. Pfeifer, "Graphical Representation of Data," in *Encyclopedia of Statistical Sciences*, S. Kotz and N. L. Johnson, eds., Vol. 3 (New York: Wiley, 1983), pp. 488–511.]

Hint   Here we have listed the grouped data; the individual observations are not available. In the calculation of the mean and variance from such grouped data we usually assume that within each class the observations are distributed fairly evenly and that it is reasonable to represent each observation in a given class by the midpoint M_i, $i = 1, 2, \ldots, k$. Then we approximate the mean as

$$\bar{x} = \frac{\sum_{i=1}^{k} f_i M_i}{\sum_{i=1}^{k} f_i}$$

and the variance as

$$s^2 = \frac{\sum_{i=1}^{k} f_i (M_i - \bar{x})^2}{\left(\sum_{i=1}^{k} f_i\right) - 1}.$$

To calculate the $(100P)$th percentile, or the quantile of order P, we must locate the observation with rank $r = Pn + 0.5$. Obtain the cumulative frequencies and determine the class that includes the percentile; it is the class whose cumulative frequency is the first to exceed r. Denote the lower and upper limits of this class by L and U, the frequency of this class by f, and the number of observations that are smaller than L by m; of course, $m < r$. Then the $(100P)$th percentile is given by

$$L + \frac{r - m}{f}(U - L).$$

As an illustration, let us calculate the 20th percentile. Since $n = 794$, we have to locate the observation with rank $r = (0.20)(794) + 0.5 = 159.3 \cong 159$. This percentage is in the third class from 48–72, which has frequency $f = 161$. Since the cumulative frequency of the class with upper limit $L = 48$ is $m = 13 + 98 = 111$, we find that the 20th percentile is given by

$$48 + \frac{159\text{–}111}{161}(72 - 48) = 55.2.$$

Of course, we could also obtain this value from the ogive, at least approximately. It is the point where the ogive crosses the horizontal line that is drawn at relative cumulative frequency of $P = 0.20$.

1.2-10   An analysis of human mortality data has led to the following frequency distribution of the length of life.

Age Group	Number of Deaths (1000s)	Age Group	Number of Deaths (1000s)
0–5	39.3	55–60	76.4
5–10	12.0	60–65	99.9
10–15	9.5	65–70	123.3
15–20	10.8	70–75	138.6
20–25	12.3	75–80	134.2
25–30	14.6	80–85	103.6
30–35	18.1	85–90	56.6
35–40	23.2	90–95	18.6
40–45	30.8	95–100	3.0
45–50	41.7		
50–55	56.7		

Construct a histogram. Determine the mean, mode, and median. Use the hint in Exercise 1.2-9.

1.2-11 (Project)   Machine tools in the metal-cutting industry have to machine parts within close tolerances, sometimes in the range of ± 0.0005 inch. The tools involved in the cutting process wear with time. These changes cause drift in the dimensional properties between the cutting tool and the workpiece. This drift pattern needs to be monitored and controlled.

In this exercise we study several tool offset systems for a Cincinnati Milacron Cinturn lathe. The study focuses on the bore size of various sizes of gear blanks for large tractors. Several different correction algorithms are developed and tested in the manufacturing environment. The algorithms estimate the drift in the measurement of the bore and recommend suitable tool offsets.

For boring operations the drift may be in the positive direction, which means that the bore of the part has become oversized, or in the negative direction implying that the bore of the part has become too small. In either case, it becomes necessary to offset the tool in the opposite direction of the observed change and of such a magnitude that the dimensions of the parts are restored to acceptable limits.

Measurements of the finished bore size are taken by the operator. Based on the bore size measurement, the required tool offset for the next piece is calculated. The feedback control algorithm is implemented by a computer program. Note that in this context adjustments are highly desirable, as the observations come from a changing system. This is different from the "tampering" in a stable system.

The data sets given below represent the outcome of several experiments on a Cincinnati Milacron lathe (machine 1282). The first three experiments are conducted to obtain *process capability data*. This means that the tool is kept at its nominal position and is not changed over time. These data tell us about the capability of the process when it is not adjusted. The measurements (deviations from target, in inches $\times 10^5$) are given below (read across):

Experiment 1 (*n* = 22)

```
 15    0   10    5    5   10  -10   15   15 0
  5   -5  -25  -15  -15  -15  -20  -15  -10 5
-20  -40
```

Experiment 2 (*n* = 30)

```
 70   75   70   65 65   50   55 40   35   10
 10   10   20   -5  0   35   45 15   20   20
-10  -10   -5  -15 15  -15  -20  5  -15  -10
```

Experiment 3 (*n* = 50)

```
 70   55   40   40   25   45   45   50   45   35
 20   25   20   25   10   15   10    5   -5   -5
 15   15   10   10  -10  -15    5   10   20   15
 -5    5    5    5    0   15    5   15   10   10
  0   15   20    5   20    0    5  -15   -5  -15
```

The results for experiments 4 and 5 summarize the target deviations that are obtained after implementing the feedback controller. The tool offset depends on the readings that are collected on previously machined parts. If the target deviations are within certain control limits (called the deadband), the readings are treated as good as nominal and no offsets are made. If readings are outside these limits, the algorithm, in its simplest version, calculates the offset as a percentage of the (negative) target deviation of the bore measurement. Two experiments with slightly different versions of this feedback controller are carried out and the results are listed below.

Experiment 4 (*n* = 70)

```
  7.5    0    -2.5  -10    17.5    7.5  17.5    7.5    7.5  -2.5
 -2.5  12.5  -10.0   2.5   -7.5    5.0  -7.5    2.5   -5.0  -7.5
-10    -5     7.5    7.5    7.5    7.5   7.5    5     17.5 -17.5
  7.5   5     7.5    0      7.5    0     7.5   -2.5    7.5   7.5
  7.5   5     7.5    7.5   -2.5    7.5   7.5    5      7.5   5
  7.5  20     0     -2.5    0      0     0      2.5    5     0
 20     0     2.5   -5     -7.5  -12.5   0     10     -2.5  -7.5
```

Experiment 5 (*n* = 134)

```
 10   10    5    0  -15    5   15  -5    0    0
  0  -10  -10   10    5   10   10   5   -5   10
  5    0    0    0   -5  -10  -10  20    5    5
  0    5   10   10    0    5    5   5    5   -5
  0   -5   -5    5    0  -10  -15  10   10   10
  5   10    0    0   10    5    5  20   -5    0
 -5   -5  -15   10    0   10   -5   5    5   10
 -5    5    5   10    0    0   -5   0   10    5
 10   15   10    5   15   10   10  10    5    0
  5    0    5   10  -15   20   10  -5    5    0
-10  -10   15  -10    5    0   -5  10    5    0
 -5    5    5  -10   10    5   10  10   10    5
  0    5   10   10    5    0   10  10    5    0
  5   10   10    5
```

Discuss the information that is contained in these data sets. Your analysis should contain time-sequence plots as in Figure 1.1-7. Discuss whether or not trend components are present in the data. If there are, describe their nature and discuss possible reasons for their occurrence. You may notice that the initial deviations in experiments 1 to 3 are always positive and quite large. Can you explain why?

Has feedback control made a difference? Define and calculate for each experiment a summary measure for "closeness to the target." Interpret your findings. In addition, use the graphical techniques discussed in Section 1.2 to compare the five distributions.

1.2-12 (Project) In the following table we report the monthly number of motor vehicle fatalities on Iowa roads (1950/1 through 1979/12). Data were provided by the Iowa Department of Public Safety.

```
1950: 31 40 32 39 41 56 59   60 59   57 60 53
1951: 45 39 46 39 42 56 48   57 60   68 46 63
1952: 29 23 39 32 46 45 53   71 58   47 50 38
1953: 29 29 37 38 48 45 76   70 54   54 48 73
1954: 51 35 40 46 52 40 62   60 71   49 59 47
1955: 48 35 35 48 56 40 56   60 63   59 56 53
1956: 63 50 41 45 53 57 79   71 55   63 62 61
1957: 35 54 41 59 68 62 57   72 62   56 54 70
1958: 55 48 38 44 39 34 46   63 40   72 61 58
1959: 57 40 52 60 58 40 49   54 65   87 48 69
1960: 43 26 35 49 38 59 53   54 58   85 56 63
1961: 40 37 46 54 57 55 57   72 54   69 43 52
1962: 30 26 38 38 37 73 58   78 50   69 49 72
```

1963: 30 35 47 46 53 58 86   56 77   58 70 79
1964: 49 60 61 49 63 63 85   89 75   83 75 82
1965: 53 44 43 54 63 72 53   92 83   76 86 77
1966: 45 57 57 68 70 66 91   91 98   92 89 80
1967: 53 37 65 44 63 73 98   80 75   89 81 60
1968: 56 39 70 64 85 77 77 100 81   69 77 75
1969: 40 42 54 63 79 66 61   82 81   88 74 51
1970: 64 61 57 60 84 63 84   92 90 107 70 80
1971: 48 49 53 65 57 70 72   87 86 112 63 66
1972: 44 44 62 43 71 72 85   97 82   91 91 92
1973: 50 48 60 67 79 83 67 104 63   77 67 48
1974: 41 46 41 49 46 56 74   73 71   60 67 68
1975: 38 28 56 48 67 76 83   57 56   52 61 52
1976: 49 50 46 45 75 88 93   91 72   71 50 55
1977: 49 39 47 48 52 50 73   57 55   65 43 62
1978: 29 29 33 45 72 77 61   73 60   55 75 41
1979: 36 42 37 45 53 66 54   61 60   69 56 53

In addition, we report annual (1950–1979) and monthly (1978 and 1979) data on vehicle miles of travel in Iowa. These data were provided by the Iowa Department of Transportation.

Annual traffic volume (millions of miles traveled):

1950: 9,434	1960: 11,255	1970: 16,053
1951: 9,350	1961: 11,471	1971: 16,581
1952: 9,721	1962: 11,687	1972: 17,127
1953: 9,970	1963: 12,036	1973: 17,690
1954: 9,811	1964: 12,384	1974: 17,250
1955: 10,244	1965: 12,733	1975: 17,853
1956: 10,382	1966: 13,439	1976: 18,440
1957: 10,227	1967: 14,145	1977: 19,028
1958: 10,609	1968: 15,047	1978: 19,466
1959: 10,971	1969: 15,542	1979: 18,959

Monthly traffic volume (millions of miles traveled):

1978:	1319	1295	1520	1598	1774	1778
	1854	1863	1694	1707	1553	1511
1979:	1249	1299	1470	1607	1731	1712
	1757	1792	1648	1653	1510	1531

Analyze this information. You should address the following issues:

(a) Discuss the time trend and the seasonal pattern in the traffic fatality sequence. Speculate on the factors (variables) that may be responsible for the trend and the seasonality. Discuss whether the change in the traffic speed limit from 70 mph to 55 mph beginning January 1974 has made a difference.

Hints   Construct time-sequence plots of monthly fatalities, as well as yearly totals. Compare the number of fatalities before and after the speed limit change. Calculate monthly averages (where for each month the average is taken over the 30 years) and plot them against month.

(b) Discuss the time trend and the seasonal pattern in the data on traffic volume.

(c) Has it become safer to drive? Support your answer with appropriate plot(s). Your analysis should take traffic volume into account. Would it make sense to consider the number of fatalities per million miles traveled?

1.2-13 (Project)   A producer of gasoline additives is interested to learn whether or not a new diesel additive increases fuel economy. The company hires an independent research institute to conduct a fuel consumption test utilizing class 8 diesel trucks. The purpose of the testing is to evaluate the benefits in improving fuel economy that are derived from using this new product.

The procedure chosen for this evaluation is the joint TMC/SAE Fuel Consumption Test Procedure Type II, developed by the Engineering Society for Advancing Mobility Land Sea Air and Space (SAE J1321). This recommended practice provides a standardized test procedure for comparing the in-service fuel consumption of a vehicle operated under two conditions. An unchanging control vehicle is run in tandem with a test vehicle to provide reference fuel consumption data.

A test with two different trucks as test vehicles is conducted. The two trucks used in the test program are two identical 1987 International tractor/trailer combinations with the same type of engine, transmission, drive axle, tires, trailer, and identical 80,000-pound load of concrete blocks. The two trucks, with mileage of 250,000 and 275,000 miles, are leased from a brick manufacturer. Both trucks are first checked on a chassis dynamometer to ensure that the engines are performing properly.

The test route chosen represents a typical long-haul interstate highway operation. A low-density 20-mile-long traffic portion of I-80 between Iowa City and Amana is used in the experiment.

The test procedure is divided into two segments, the baseline and the test segment. During the baseline the test truck uses ordinary diesel (Gulf No. 2); during the test segment the additive is mixed at a ratio of 1 part additive and 500 parts fuel. Ordinary Gulf No. 2 diesel without additive is used in the control truck, for both the baseline and the test segments.

The two trucks enter I-80 in Iowa City with the second truck following the lead truck at a distance of approximately 1/2 mile. Fuel consumption is measured over a distance of exactly 40 miles, 20 miles westbound and 20 miles eastbound on I-80, at a steady speed of 60 mph. After accelerating to 60 mph westbound the driver starts the fuel meter upon reaching mile marker 262. At mile marker 242 the meter is stopped and the quantity of fuel used is recorded. The same procedure is used for the eastbound leg of the trip between markers 242 and 262. The same two drivers operate their assigned truck throughout the test program. The drivers take 10 test laps as practice to establish familiarity with the trucks and the route. The fuel consumption (in pounds) for laps during the baseline testing program (baseline laps 11–27) are given in the following table.

Baseline Laps			Test Laps		
Lap No.	Control	Test	Lap No.	Control	Test
11	50.1488	51.8912	1	50.0354	49.4885
12	49.2472	50.6840	2	50.3589	48.7868
13	50.7082	51.9655	3	49.8449	48.3581
14	49.6399	50.5968	4	50.8973	49.3284
15	50.4372	51.8736	5	51.2444	50.2403
16	50.2273	51.6166	6	55.9998	54.1003
17	50.0609	50.8950	7	55.0668	53.7085
18	50.2046	50.9899	8	52.0332	50.0265
19	50.4621	51.6013	9	51.3607	50.7168
20	50.1678	51.3997	10	51.0776	50.1817
21	49.6908	50.9830	11	50.8610	49.3742
22	49.6244	50.5118	12	50.5268	49.1016
23	47.5206	49.7935	13	49.1427	48.6476
24	49.7272	50.1476			
25	46.9486	48.8342			
26	47.9234	48.9613			
27	48.7489	49.1496			

After completing the baseline experiment, the fuel tank of the test truck is drained and filled with fuel containing the diesel additive. The test truck is then driven 5000 miles using the treated fuel. This is done to condition the engine to the new fuel supply and to

maximize the additive's potential. After this conditioning period, 13 laps are run during the testing stage (test laps 1 to 13). The results of these test laps are also given in the table.

(a) Consider the fuel consumption of the control truck during the baseline laps. Describe the variability by constructing a dot diagram or a histogram of the 17 observations. Calculate the mean, median, standard deviation, and interquartile range.

(b) Repeat part (a) for the test truck during the baseline laps. To facilitate easy comparisons among the two trucks, display the dot diagrams on the same scale.

(c) What conclusions can you draw from the analysis in parts (a) and (b)? Speculate on the factors that cause the variability in fuel consumption. Would there be a better way to compare the fuel efficiencies of the two trucks? Consider the differences or the ratios in the fuel consumption of the test and the control trucks, and repeat the exercise in part (a). What conclusion can you draw from this analysis? Discuss why this is a better way to compare the two trucks than a comparison of the dot diagrams in parts (a) and (b).

(d) The main interest in this experiment is to compare the effectiveness of the diesel additive. It is recommended that one consider the ratio (diesel use of test truck)/(diesel use of control truck). Construct a dot diagram of the 13 test lap ratios and compare it to the dot diagram of the 17 baseline lap ratios. Again, to facilitate the comparison, you should make these plots on the same scale.

1.2-14 (Group Project) W. E. Deming (*Out of the Crisis*, 1986, p. 327) asserts: "If anyone adjusts a stable process to try to compensate for a result that is undesirable, or for a result that is extra good, the output that follows will be worse than if he had left the process alone." Variation is a fact of life, even in stable processes. If one changes a stable process on the basis of a defective item or a complaint of a single customer, one makes things worse and increases the variability of the output. Improvements of a stable process (i.e., a reduction of its variability) can only come through fundamental changes in the system, not through tampering with the process. The following experiment (the "funnel experiment," taken from Deming) demonstrates the loss that is due to overadjustment.

(a) Consider the following experiment with a stable

process: Designate a point on a table as the target. Assume that the coordinates of the target are (0, 0). Take a funnel and construct a holder for the funnel which suspends it about 3 feet off the table. Take a rubber or Styrofoam ball, drop it through the funnel, and mark the spot on the table where it comes to rest. Repeat the experiment 50 times. Leave the funnel fixed, aimed at the target. Note that this experiment describes a stable system. There will be variation among the locations of impact, even if the funnel is located directly above the target. Comment briefly on the sources of variability. Analyze the results of your experiment. Note that each point is characterized by two coordinates. Define and use an appropriate distance measure in your analysis. Discuss.

(b) Repeat the same experiment, but adjust the position of the funnel after each drop. If the ball at drop k ($k = 1, 2, \ldots$) comes to rest at point z_k, move the funnel the distance $-z_k$ from its last position. More specifically, denote the position of the funnel at trial k by $po_x(k)$ and $po_y(k)$, and the position of the ball at trial k, relative to the target (0, 0), by $x(k)$ and $y(k)$. Then the position of the funnel at trial $k + 1$ is given by $po_x(k + 1) = po_x(k) - x(k)$ and $po_y(k + 1) = po_y(k) - y(k)$. Analyze the resulting data. Obtain a measure for the variability from the target and interpret the results. Does the experiment confirm Dr. Deming's claim?

(c) Consider an adjustment procedure that sets the funnel at time $k + 1$ over the point $-z_k$, measured from the target. That is, set $po_x(k + 1) = -x(k)$ and $po_y(k + 1) = -y(k)$. Generate 50 observations, analyze the data, and interpret the findings. Compare the results to the ones in part (b).

1.3   Exploratory Data Analysis

Histograms are very valuable tools for displaying the variability of observations and they help the analyst develop an understanding of a data set. However, a disadvantage of histograms is that individual data points cannot be identified because all data falling in an interval are indistinguishable. In recent years, statisticians have looked for other, more informative graphical descriptions of the data, and have developed new graphical procedures for data analysis. John Tukey, in particular, has created several imaginative and very useful data displays. Since they are usually performed at the initial exploratory stage of the analysis, these displays are known as *exploratory data analysis* (EDA). Here we introduce a few of the simpler ideas; for additional discussion consult the books by J. W. Tukey, *Exploratory Data Analysis* (Reading, Mass.: Addison-Wesley, 1977) or P. Velleman and D. Hoaglin, *Applications, Basics, and Computing of Exploratory Data Analysis* (Boston: Duxbury Press, 1981).

1.3-1   Stem-and-Leaf Displays

The easiest way to begin is with an illustration. Suppose that we have $n = 58$ test scores.

76	93	42	66	60	56	60	75	78	81
61	70	58	64	67	73	49	52	74	91
76	82	86	59	69	73	74	64	94	65
48	59	72	68	66	64	88	80	51	82
77	60	66	86	85	51	90	91	53	63
69	73	67	61	86	80	72	65		

We note that 42 and 94 are the smallest and largest scores, respectively. Of course, we could construct a histogram, together with the usual tabulation. But we can do much the same thing with a *stem-and-leaf display* and not lose the original values as we do with tally marks. In this data set, take the first number 76 and record it as follows: The 7 in the "tens" place is treated as the *stem* and the 6 in the "units" place is the corresponding *leaf*. Note that the leaf 6 comes after the stem 7 in Table 1.3-1. The second number, 93, is represented by the leaf 3 after the stem 9; the third number, 42, by the leaf 2 after the stem 4; the fourth number, 66, by the leaf 6 after the stem 6; the fifth number, 60, by the leaf 0 after the stem 6 (note that this is the second leaf on the stem 6); and so on. The reader is urged to complete such a table, carefully lining up the leaves vertically to give the same effect as a histogram. Of course, here the original numbers are not lost as they are with tally marks.

Sometimes, to help us find percentiles and other characteristics of the data, we order the leaves according to magnitude, giving an *ordered stem-and-leaf display* as in Table 1.3-2. For illustration, since $n = 58$ is even, the median is the average of observations with rank 29 and 30; that is, Md $= (69 + 69)/2 = 69$. The first quartile is the observation with rank $(58)(0.25) + 0.5 = 15$; $Q_1 = 61$. The third quartile is the observation with rank $(58)(0.75) + 0.5 = 44$; $Q_3 = 80$. The 20th percentile, or the second *decile* as it is often called, is the observation with rank $(58)(0.2) + 0.5 = 12.1 \cong 12$, which is 60. Note here that we violated our earlier rule and did not average the 12th and 13th order statistics to obtain the 20th percentile. Since there really is no unique rule among statisticians, we prefer this particular approximation, as 12.1 is about equal to 12. The 85th percentile is the $(58)(0.85) + 0.5 = 49.8 \cong$ 50th largest observation, 86 (again noting that 49.8 is about equal to 50).

The stem-and-leaf tables as given here are equivalent to a histogram with

TABLE 1.3-1   Stem-and-Leaf Display

Stem	Leaf																			Frequency
4	2	9	8																	3
5	6	8	2	9	9	1	1	3												8
6	6	0	0	1	4	7	9	4	5	8	6	4	0	6	3	9	7	1	5	19
7	6	5	8	0	3	4	6	3	4	2	7	3	2							13
8	1	2	6	8	0	2	6	5	6	0										10
9	3	1	4	0	1															5

TABLE 1.3-2   Ordered Stem-and-Leaf Display

Stem	Leaf	Frequency
4	2 8 9	3
5	1 1 2 3 6 8 9 9	8
6	0 0 0 1 1 3 4 4 4 5 5 6 6 6 7 7 8 9 9	19
7	0 2 2 3 3 3 4 4 5 6 6 7 8	13
8	0 0 1 2 2 5 6 6 6 8	10
9	0 1 1 3 4	5

six classes. Suppose that we desire more classes. It is easy to increase the number of classes with the modification given in Table 1.3-3. Here a stem with * has the leaves 0, 1, 2, 3, 4 and a stem with · has the leaves 5, 6, 7, 8, 9.

As a second illustration, consider $n = 44$ scores on a test that was based upon 40 points. The scores, ranging from 12 to 37, are as follows:

$$
\begin{array}{cccccccccc}
17 & 22 & 36 & 28 & 30 & 33 & 19 & 21 & 20 & 29 \\
34 & 26 & 27 & 23 & 20 & 12 & 18 & 24 & 14 & 37 \\
25 & 30 & 24 & 27 & 18 & 15 & 35 & 33 & 29 & 24 \\
26 & 20 & 15 & 24 & 16 & 22 & 31 & 23 & 32 & 25 \\
29 & 26 & 32 & 19 & & & & & &
\end{array}
$$

A stem-and-leaf display after ordering the data is given in Table 1.3-4. Here the leaves are recorded in the following manner: 0, 1 after a stem with *; 2, 3 after a stem with t (t for twos and threes); 4, 5 after a stem with f (f for fours and fives); 6, 7 after a stem with s (s for sixes and sevens); 8, 9 after a stem with ·. The median is the observation with rank 22.5, that is, the average of the 22nd and 23rd largest scores, that is, $(24 + 25)/2 = 24.5$.

TABLE 1.3-3   Ordered Stem-and-Leaf Display

Stem	Leaf	Frequency
4*	2	1
4·	8 9	2
5*	1 1 2 3	4
5·	6 8 9 9	4
6*	0 0 0 1 1 3 4 4 4	9
6·	5 5 6 6 6 7 7 8 9 9	10
7*	0 2 2 3 3 3 4 4	8
7·	5 6 6 7 8	5
8*	0 0 1 2 2	5
8·	5 6 6 6 8	5
9*	0 1 1 3 4	5

TABLE 1.3-4   Ordered Stem-and-Leaf Display

Stem	Leaf						Frequency
1t	2						1
1f	4	5	5				3
1s	6	7					2
1·	8	8	9	9			4
2∗	0	0	0	1			4
2t	2	2	3	3			4
2f	4	4	4	4	5	5	6
2s	6	6	6	7	7		5
2·	8	9	9	9			4
3∗	0	0	1				3
3t	2	2	3	3			4
3f	4	5					2
3s	6	7					2

Imagination must be used to create stem-and-leaf displays. In some instances modifications must be made, which may lead to a small loss of information. As an illustration, consider the compressive strengths of $n = 90$ concrete blocks given in Table 1.2-1. First, we could round off our numbers a little, writing 49.2 as 49, 53.9 as 54, 43.5 as 44, 53.4 as 53, and so on. Then we could start the stem-and-leaf display with the 2· having possible leaves of 5, 6, 7, 8, 9; 3∗ with leaves of 0, 1, 2, 3, 4; and ending with the stem 6· having possible leaves of 5, 6, 7, 8, 9. Such a scheme would provide nine classes.

If the person describing the data, however, does not want to lose information by rounding (although this is usually not serious), we could create stems with double leaves: 49.2 would be recorded as the leaf 92 after the stem 4·, 53.9 as the leaf 39 after the stem 5t, and so on. Thus, in the concrete block illustration, stems would run from 2· to 6s, for a total of 20 classes. For illustration, with the stem 4s, we have

4s   75   68   74   74   60   70   79   62   73

representing the numbers 47.5, 46.8, 47.4, 47.4, 46.0, 47.0, 47.9, 46.2, and 47.3. Thus the frequency of the class with stem 4s is 9. The reader is asked to complete this stem-and-leaf display in Exercise 1.3-1.

1.3-2   Box-and-Whisker Displays

In box-and-whisker displays (also called *box plots*) we depict the three quartiles, together with the two extremes of the data. The box in these displays, aligned either horizontally or vertically, encloses the interquartile range

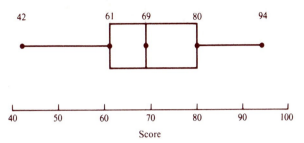

FIGURE 1.3-1   Box-and-whisker display for the 58 test scores.

with the left (or lower) line identifying the 25th percentile (lower quartile) and the right (or upper) line the 75th percentile (upper quartile). A line sectioning the box displays the 50th percentile (median) and its relative position within the interquartile range. The whiskers at either end extend to the extreme values. In large data sets, where the sample size is at least 50 or 100, the whiskers may extend only to the 10th and 90th percentiles or the 5th and 95th percentiles instead of the extreme values. Then extreme values may also be displayed as unconnected dots. Figure 1.3-1 illustrates the box-and-whisker display for the data given in Table 1.3-2, recalling that those five numbers (minimum, first quartile, median, third quartile, maximum), in that order, are 42, 61, 69, 80, and 94. The stem-and-leaf display in Table 1.3-2 shows that the distribution of these scores is fairly symmetric around the center value. We can also see this from the box-and-whisker display in Figure 1.3-1; the left and right whiskers are about equal in length and the lengths of the left and right boxes around the median are about the same.

For the data in Table 1.3-4, the minimum, first quartile, median, third quartile, and maximum are 12, 20, 24.5, 29.5, and 37, respectively. The box-and-whisker display is depicted in Figure 1.3-2. Again, the distribution of these observations looks quite symmetric.

On the other hand, many data sets are not symmetric. For example, consider the CO concentrations in Figure 1.2-2(a), incomes of engineers, or losses from automobile accidents; these distributions are skewed to the right. Consider the $n = 794$ CO concentrations in Exercise 1.2-9. There the 5th, 25th,

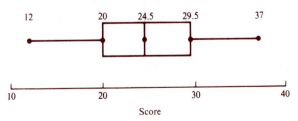

FIGURE 1.3-2   Box-and-whisker display of the data in Table 1.3-4.

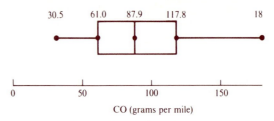

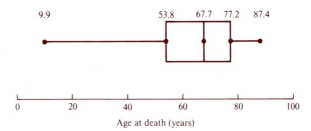

FIGURE 1.3-3   Box-and-whisker display of the CO emissions in Exercise 1.2-9.

FIGURE 1.3-4   Box-and-whisker display of ages at death in Exercise 1.2-10.

50th, 75th, and 95th percentiles are given by 30.5, 61.0, 87.9, 117.8, and 180.2 grams/mile, respectively. The box-and-whisker display in Figure 1.3-3 shows that the right whisker is longer than the left one, and the right box is larger than the left; we say that the distribution is skewed to the right.

The histogram of the number of deaths in various age groups in Figure 1.2-2(b) illustrates a distribution that is skewed to the left. From the data in Exercise 1.2-10 we calculate the 5th, 25th, 50th, 75th, and 95th percentiles as 9.9, 53.8, 67.7, 77.2, and 87.4 years. The box-and-whisker display in Figure 1.3-4 shows that the left whisker and the left box are larger than the right whisker and the right box. Thus these data are skewed to the left.

1.3-3   Digidot Plots

John Tukey's stem-and-leaf display is a simple but useful idea for replacing a collection of numbers and the corresponding histogram with a single graphical display that preserves the original numbers. However, stem-and-leaf displays, as well as histograms, ignore the time order in which the measurements were produced. We emphasized before that a time-sequence plot of the observations should always be made if measurements are taken sequentially and if one has reason to believe that "time" is an important variable. More recently, J. Stuart Hunter [*American Statistician*, 42: 54 (1988)] has enhanced the stem-and-leaf display by combining it with a time-sequence plot. Since time-series observations are shown as connected dots and because the stem-and-leaf is displayed in the left-hand margin, Hunter proposed the name *digidot plot*.

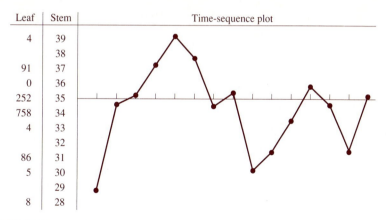

Leaf	Stem	Time-sequence plot
4	39	
	38	
91	37	
0	36	
252	35	
758	34	
4	33	
	32	
86	31	
5	30	
	29	
8	28	

FIGURE 1.3-5   A digidot plot.

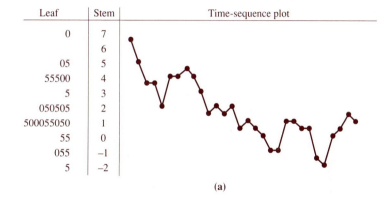

Leaf	Stem	Time-sequence plot
0	7	
	6	
05	5	
55500	4	
5	3	
050505	2	
500055050	1	
55	0	
055	−1	
5	−2	

(a)

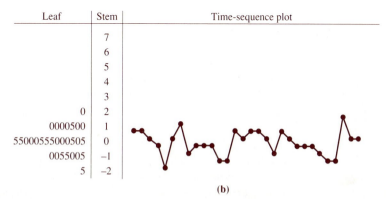

Leaf	Stem	Time-sequence plot
	7	
	6	
	5	
	4	
	3	
0	2	
0000500	1	
55000555000505	0	
0055005	−1	
5	−2	

(b)

FIGURE 1.3-6   Digidot plots for metal-cutting example. Plots for experiments 3 and 4 are made on the same scale.

His illustration involved 15 observations recorded in the following sequence (read across):

28.8	34.8	35.2	37.1	39.4	37.9	34.5	35.5
30.5	31.6	33.4	36.0	34.7	31.8	35.2.	

As each observation becomes available, it is placed as a dot on the time-sequence plot in Figure 1.3-5, and simultaneously, the last digit is recorded on the stem-and-leaf display at the left. Of course, here the stems are 28, 29, 30, ..., 39. Thus the time history is saved in a digidot plot, which often gives it an advantage over the usual stem-and-leaf display.

As another example, let us consider the data in Exercise 1.2-11, which describe a metal-cutting process on a lathe. In Figure 1.3-6(a) and (b), we display digidot plots for the first 30 deviations from the target for experiments 3 and 4. Recall that experiment 3 corresponds to the uncontrolled situation where the cutting tool is not adjusted. The digidot plot in (a), as well as our previous discussion in Section 1.1, shows that the measurements drift over time. The variability, displayed in the stem-and-leaf display on the left margin, is rather large and mostly due to "time" or tool wear. Note that a stem-and-leaf display or a histogram alone will not reveal the importance of time. The data in experiment 4 are obtained under feedback control which adjusts the position of the cutting tool according to the previous deviations from the target. The digidot plot shows that the drift has disappeared, and the stem-and-leaf display on the left margin indicates that the variability in the deviations is considerably smaller if a feedback controller is applied.

Exercises 1.3

1.3-1 Use the data on compressive strength of concrete blocks given in Table 1.2-1. Complete a stem-and-leaf display using double leaves with stems 2·, 3∗, 3t, 3f, 3s, 3·, 4∗, and so on.

1.3-2 Consider the data in Exercises 1.2-2, 1.2-3, and 1.2-8.

(a) Construct ordered stem-and-leaf displays.

(b) Construct box-and-whisker displays.

1.3-3 The following data represent $n = 38$ hurricane losses (in million dollars). Since these hurricanes occurred over a period of 30 years, these figures are adjusted for inflation. The observations are already ordered from the smallest to the largest.

2.73	3.08	4.47	6.77	7.12	10.56
14.47	15.35	16.98	18.38	19.03	25.30
29.11	30.15	33.73	40.60	41.41	47.91
49.40	52.60	59.92	63.12	77.81	102.94
103.22	123.68	140.14	192.01	198.45	227.34
329.51	361.20	421.68	513.59	545.78	750.39
863.88	1638.00				

(a) Calculate the sample mean and standard deviation.

(b) The losses range from about zero to 1650. If we construct a histogram with 10 equal-sized intervals, we find that 27 of the 38 observations are in the first class from 0 to 165 and that some cells are completely empty. In some instances, involving skewed data, statisticians often use transformations such as $\sqrt{x}$ or $\log x$ to make the distribution more symmetric. For each of these transformations, construct a stem-and-leaf display for the transformed hurricane data.

1.3-4   Consider the following yields of 30 consecutive batches (read across):

72.4	75.3	72.7	74.2	75.6
75.0	73.3	73.1	74.4	77.5
75.8	74.0	73.2	74.8	76.2
72.7	68.2	79.1	73.8	75.5
74.7	75.7	72.9	72.1	77.7
76.6	73.2	75.1	75.5	71.7

Construct a digidot plot and a box-and-whisker display for these $n = 30$ observations. If you had a detailed account of the special circumstances that accompanied each batch (e.g., if you knew that certain batches were produced by the day shift while others were produced by the night shift; or if you knew that some batches used raw material from supplier A while others used material of supplier B; or if you knew that a machine malfunctioned during batch 17), how could you use this information to assign some of the variability to these causes?

1.3-5   Consider the data in Exercise 1.2-11.

(a) Construct digidot plots for the data from experiments 1, 2, and 4. Interpret your findings.

(b) Use the data from experiment 5 and construct a box-and-whisker display.

1.3-6   Use the data in Exercise 1.2-13. Construct a digidot plot for the fuel consumption of the control truck during the baseline laps.

1.4   Comparisons of Samples

Probably the most important problem faced in data analysis is the comparison of two or more distributions or, rather, two or more samples that are taken from different populations. Comparisons are often made to determine the best way of performing certain tasks. The populations can be created by different medical treatments, different brands of paints, different types of automobiles, different educational systems, and so on.

Let us begin our discussion with an illustration taken from a case study by J. H. Sheesley which is reported in R. D. Snee, L. B. Hare, and J. R. Trout, *Experiments in Industry* (Milwaukee, Wis.: American Society for Quality Control, 1985). He was comparing the performance of two different types of lead wires that were needed in the production of ordinary household light bulbs. The company had noticed that during assembly a certain percentage of lead wires did not feed properly into machines that produced components of these light bulbs. Since this resulted in lost production, the company changed the way it produced the lead wires. It was interested in evaluating whether the lead wires produced by the new process perform better than those from the old one. In Sheesley's report there were several other important variables besides the two types of wires, such as different machines, shifts, plants, and so on. Here we ignore these and suppose that each type of wire, new and old, was "being treated fairly"; that is, there were no biases created by using one type of wire under better conditions than the other (such as with a better shift or

TABLE 1.4-1   Average Hourly Number of Misfeeding Leads

Old:	17.6	18.3	10.8	19.2	18.0	39.4	21.4	19.9	23.7	22.7	23.2	19.6
New:	12.4	28.1	11.5	7.8	16.7	16.8	25.6	23.7	26.9	11.2	21.5	18.9

running one on Wednesday and the other on Monday). An experiment was conducted, and for each production run, the average number of leads per hour that missed was recorded. The results of 24 production runs, 12 with the old and 12 with the new type of lead wire, are given in Table 1.4-1.

It is always instructive to compare the histograms (or the dot diagrams, if the number of observations in each group is small). To facilitate the graphical comparison one should draw these histograms (or dot diagrams) on the same scale (see Figure 1.4-1).

Another useful graphical tool is a comparison of box-and-whisker displays. The two sets of order statistics are

Old:	10.8	17.6	18.0	18.3	19.2	19.6	19.9	21.4	22.7	23.2	23.7	39.4
New:	7.8	11.2	11.5	12.4	16.7	16.8	18.9	21.5	23.7	25.6	26.9	28.1

The smallest value, first quartile, median, third quartile, and the largest value (after appropriate averaging and rounding) for each group separately are given in the box-and-whisker display in Figure 1.4-2. From these data it looks as if the new process has lowered somewhat the number of misfeeding leads. But the evidence from these few observations is certainly not very strong. In later sections we study formal statistical procedures that provide a quantitative assessment as to whether differences between two or more samples are really significant.

In addition to the comparative histograms (dot diagrams) and box-and-whisker displays, there is another interesting graphical method for comparing two samples or distributions; it is called a *q–q plot*. The reason for its name is that the $(100P)$th percentile is often called the *quantile of order P*, and in a *q–q* plot, quantiles of one sample (distribution) are plotted against the corresponding quantiles of the other. By plotting 5 to 15 pairs of corresponding quantiles, we can get a good visual comparison of the two samples. For illustration, consider the wire data. Since both samples are of equal size, $n = 12$, it is con-

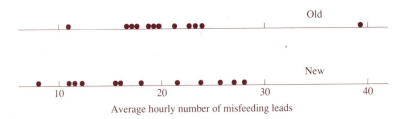

Average hourly number of misfeeding leads

FIGURE 1.4-1   Dot diagrams for Sheesley's data in Table 1.4-1.

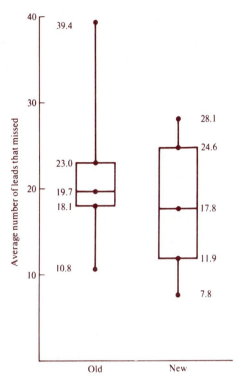

FIGURE 1.4-2   Box-and-whisker displays for Sheesley's data in Table 1.4-1.

venient to use the quantiles of order $(i - 0.5)/12$, $i = 1, 2, \ldots, 12$. That is, we simply use the two sets of order statistics, and in Figure 1.4-3 we plot the order statistics of the new method against the order statistics of the old one.

A line with slope 1 is drawn through the origin to help with the comparison. If all points are on this 45-degree line, there is absolutely no difference between the two samples; in particular, their centers and their spreads are exactly the same since all their corresponding quantiles are equal. If all points are below this line, however, the quantiles in the old sample are larger than the corresponding ones in the new sample. On the other hand, if all the points are above this line, this indicates that the quantiles of the new sample are larger than the ones in the old. In Figure 1.4-3 it appears that there are more points below the 45° line. Thus there is some evidence that the new wires produce fewer misfeeds than the old ones. This is essentially the same conclusion that we have drawn from the box-and-whisker displays.

From the q–q plot we can also get information on the spreads of the two distributions. If the plotted points increase with a slope greater than 1, this means that the sample plotted on the horizontal (in our case the old wires) is not as spread out as that plotted on the vertical axis. On the other hand, a slope of less than 1 means that the sample plotted on the horizontal axis is spread out more than that on the vertical axis. In Figure 1.4-3 we notice that

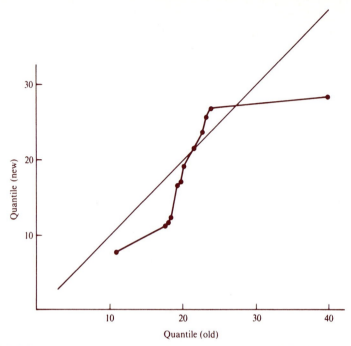

FIGURE 1.4-3   Quantile–quantile (q–q) plot for Sheesley's data in Table 1.4-1.

except for the extreme quantiles, the sample of the old wires is closer together than that of the new. This feature could also be seen in the dot diagrams and the box-and-whisker displays; the interquartile range for the old wire is less than that of the new wire. Practical experience with q–q plots, as well as related plots that are studied later, will help the practicing engineer understand the relationships between two samples (or distributions).

This discussion has illustrated the comparison of two groups. The following examples show how we can assess, graphically, the differences among three or more samples.

Example 1.4-1   A civil engineer wishes to compare the strength properties of three different types of beams, one (A) made of steel and two (B and C) made of different and more expensive alloys. The engineer determines the strength of a beam by setting it in a horizontal position, supported only on each end, applying a force of 3000 pounds at the center and measuring the deflection (in

TABLE 1.4-2   **Ordered Deflections**

A:	79	82	83	84	85	86	86	87
B:	74	75	76	77	78	82		
C:	77	78	79	79	79	82		

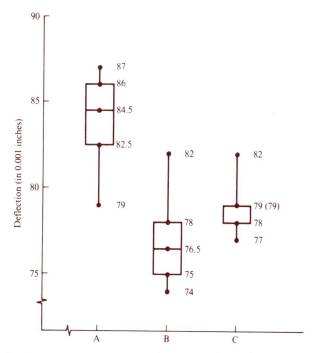

FIGURE 1.4-4   Comparative box-and-whisker displays for the data in Table 1.4-2.

units of 0.001 inch). The ordered observations for three samples of sizes $n_1 = 8$, $n_2 = 6$, and $n_3 = 6$ are given in Table 1.4-2. The corresponding box-and-whisker displays are depicted in Figure 1.4-4. A similar picture emerges if one compares the three dot diagrams. The deflection seems to be greatest in A, while B and C are more or less the same. But, of course, with only eight and six observations in the groups, it is difficult to tell for certain.   ∎

Example 1.4-2   A company divides its production of 4-foot by 8-foot wood-grained panels into three different quality groups. Ten samples of 100 panels each were taken from each group and the number of imperfections per 100 panels was counted. The results are listed in Table 1.4-3. The corresponding box-and-whisker displays are given in Figure 1.4-5.

TABLE 1.4-3   **Number of Imperfections per 100 Panels**

Quality Group	Observations									
I	0	2	1	1	0	1	0	2	3	0
II	4	1	7	1	4	0	2	5	6	9
III	6	7	18	4	14	10	10	15	11	9

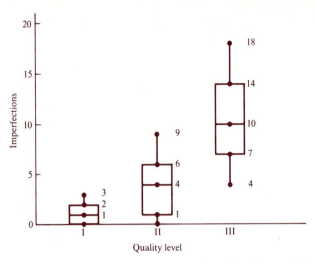

FIGURE 1.4-5 Comparative box-and-whisker displays for the number of flaws in Table 1.4-3.

It is quite obvious from this figure that there is a difference in the number of imperfections among the three quality levels. Moreover, the variability (i.e., the spread of the distribution) becomes larger with poorer quality. It is interesting to note that the spreads, as measured by the respective interquartile

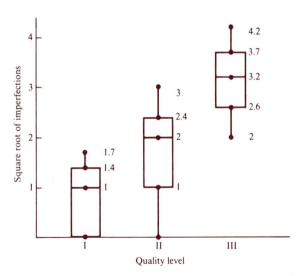

FIGURE 1.4-6 Comparative box-and-whisker displays for the transformed data in Table 1.4-3.

ranges of 2, 5, and 7, are roughly proportional to the square root of the middle values, as measured by the medians 1, 4, and 10. From statistical theory, statisticians know that under such conditions, a square-root transformation of these data should make the spreads about the same. In Figure 1.4-6 we show the box-and-whisker displays of $\sqrt{x}$, where x is the number of imperfections that are given in Table 1.4-3. The new respective interquartile ranges are 1.4, 1.4, and 1.1, which are now much more equal than the old ones. Reexpressing the data by taking a square-root transformation simplifies the comparison, as the three groups differ only with respect to their levels, and not with respect to their variability. ■

Exercises 1.4

1.4-1 (Continuation of Exercise 1.2-3). During the fall of 1977, the weekday afternoon lead concentrations (in $\mu g/m^3$) at the measurement station near the San Diego Freeway in Los Angeles were as follows:

```
9.5 10.7  8.3  9.8  9.1  9.4  9.6 11.9  9.5 12.6
10.5  8.9 11.4 12.0 12.4  9.9 10.9 12.3 11.0  9.2
9.3  9.3 10.5  9.4  9.4  8.2 10.4  9.3  8.7  9.8
9.1  2.9  9.8  5.7  8.2  8.1  8.8  9.7  8.1  8.8
10.3  8.6 10.2  9.4 14.8  9.9  9.3  8.2  9.9 11.6
8.7  5.0  9.9  6.3  6.5 10.2  8.8  8.0  8.7  8.9
6.8  6.6  7.3 16.7
```

(a) Construct a histogram and a box-and-whisker display and compare them with the ones you have made for the 1976 data in Exercise 1.2-3 and 1.3-2. Make sure that you draw the 1976 and 1977 displays on the same scale. Interpret the displays.
(b) Compare the 1976 and 1977 samples using a q–q plot. Here the sample sizes for the two groups are the same and you can plot the order statistics of one sample against the order statistics of the other (you need not plot all pairs of corresponding order statistics). How would you have proceeded if the sample sizes had not been the same?
[J. Ledolter and G. C. Tiao, "Statistical Methods for Ambient Air Pollutants with Special Reference to the

Los Angeles Catalyst Study (LACS) Data," *Environmental Science and Technology*, 13: 1233–1240 (1979).]

Remark In the spring of 1977 a new traffic lane was added to the freeway. This reduced traffic congestion, increased the traffic speed, and thus increased the lead concentrations. ■

1.4-2 The precipitation of platinum sulfide by three different methods led to the following results (already ordered in magnitude):

Method	Platinum Recovered from 10.12 milligrams Pt
1	10.28 10.29 10.31 10.33 10.33 10.33 10.34
2	10.22 10.23 10.23 10.24 10.27 10.28 10.29
3	10.22 10.25 10.30 10.33 10.36 10.38 10.38

Compare the quality of the three methods. Make the best graphical presentation and comparison you can. Use dot diagrams, box-and-whisker displays, q–q plots, and so on.
[J. W. Tukey, *Exploratory Data Analysis* (Reading, Mass.: Addison-Wesley, 1977).]

1.4-3 Jaffe, Parker, and Wilson have investigated

the concentrations of several hydrophobic organic substances (such as hexachlorobenzene, chlordane, heptachlor, aldrin, dieldrin, endrin) in the Wolf River in Tennessee. Measurements were taken downstream of an abandoned dump site that had previously been used by the pesticide industry to dispose of its waste products.

It was expected that these hydrophobic substances might have a nonhomogeneous vertical distribution in the river because of differences in density between these compounds and water and because of the adsorption of these compounds on sediments, which could lead to higher concentrations on the bottom. It is important to check this hypothesis because the standard procedure of sampling at six-tenths of the depth could miss the bulk of these pollutants if the distribution were not uniform.

Grab samples were taken with a La Motte–Vandorn water sampler of 1 liter capacity at various depths of the river. This sampler consists of a horizontal plexiglass tube of 7 centimeters diameter and a plunger on each side which shuts the sampler when the sampler is at the desired depth. Ten surface, 10 middepth, and 10 bottom samples were collected, all within a relatively short period. Until they were analyzed the samples were stored in 1-quart mason jars at low temperatures.

In the analysis of the samples, a 250-milliliter water sample was taken from each mason jar and was extracted with 1 milliliter of either hexanes or petroleum ether. A sample of the extract was then injected into a gas chromatograph and the output was compared against standards of known concentrations. The test procedure was repeated two more times, injecting different samples of the extract in the gas chromatograph. The average aldrin and hexachlorobenzene (HCB) concentrations (in nanograms per liter) in these 30 samples was as follows:

Surface		Middepth		Bottom	
Aldrin	HCB	Aldrin	HCB	Aldrin	HCB
3.08	3.74	5.17	6.03	4.81	5.44
3.58	4.61	6.17	6.55	5.71	6.88
3.81	4.00	6.26	3.55	4.90	5.37
4.31	4.67	4.26	4.59	5.35	5.44
4.35	4.87	3.17	3.77	5.26	5.03
4.40	5.12	3.76	4.81	6.26	6.48
3.67	4.52	4.76	5.85	3.76	3.89
5.17	5.29	4.90	5.74	8.07	5.85
5.17	5.74	6.57	6.77	8.79	6.85
4.35	5.48	5.17	5.64	7.30	7.16

(a) Consider aldrin. Compare the box-and-whisker displays for the surface, middepth, and bottom samples. Do you think that a transformation should be considered? If so, which transformation? Make appropriate plots to support your claim. Consider the logarithmic transformation and repeat your analysis. Do you think that the vertical distribution of this substance is homogeneous?

(b) Repeat the analysis with hexachlorobenzene. [P. R. Jaffe, F. L. Parker, and D. J. Wilson, "Distribution of Toxic Substances in Rivers," *Journal of the Environmental Engineering Division*, 108: 639–649 (1982).]

1.4-4 Consider the data from experiments 4 and 5 in Exercise 1.2-11. Note that these target deviations are obtained from experiments that use slightly different versions of a feedback controller. Compare the histograms and box-and-whisker displays. Construct a q–q plot. Can you conclude that one controller leads to smaller target deviations than the other?

1.4-5 Consider the data in Exercise 1.2-13. Analyze the ratio in part (d) (diesel use of test truck)/(diesel use of control truck). Compare the ratios for baseline and test conditions. What conclusions do you reach?

1.5   Graphical Techniques, Correlation, and Least Squares

There are many statistical techniques that can help engineers and scientists make wise decisions, but one simple and always effective method is to display the relevant data in appropriate graphical form. We have illustrated the effectiveness of graphics in our previous discussion on time-sequence plots, dot diagrams, histograms, digidot plots, and box-and-whisker displays.

1.5-1   The *Challenger* Disaster

We now give a further illustration, using data from the *Challenger* explosion on January 28, 1986. You may recall that the *Challenger* space shuttle was launched from Cape Kennedy in Florida on a very cold January morning. Meteorologists had predicted temperatures at launch to be around 30 degrees. The night before the launch there was much debate among engineers and NASA officials whether a launch under such low-temperature conditions would be advisable. Several engineers advised against a launch because they thought that O-ring failures were related to temperature. Data on O-ring failures experienced in previous launches were available and were studied the night before the launch. There were seven previous incidents of known distressed O-rings. Figure 1.5-1 displays this information; it is a simple scatter plot of the number of distressed rings per launch against temperature at launch.

From this plot alone there does not seem to be a strong relationship between the number of O-ring failures and temperature. Based on this information, along with many other technical and political considerations, it was decided to launch the *Challenger* space shuttle. As you all know, the launch resulted in disaster: the loss of seven lives and billions of dollars, and a serious setback to the space program.

One may argue that engineers looked at the scatter plot of the number of failures against temperature but could not see a relationship. However, this argument misses the fact that engineers did not display *all the data that were relevant to this question.* They looked only at instances where there were fail-

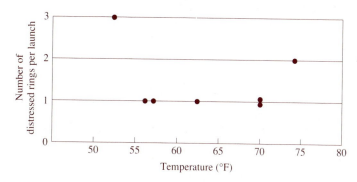

FIGURE 1.5-1   Scatter plot of number of distressed rings per launch against temperature.

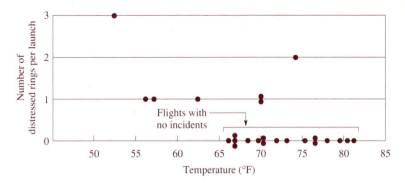

FIGURE 1.5-2 Scatter plot of number of distressed rings per launch against temperature (all data).

ures; they ignored the cases where there were no failures. In fact, there were 17 prior launches in which no failures occurred. A scatter plot of the number of distressed rings per launch against temperature using data from all previous shuttle launches is given in Figure 1.5-2.

It is difficult to look at these data and not see a relationship between failures and temperature. Moreover, one recognizes that an extrapolation is required and that an inference about the number of failures outside the observed range of temperature is needed. The temperature at *Challenger*'s launch was only 31° F, while the lowest temperature recorded at a previous launch was 53° F. It is always very dangerous to extrapolate inferences to a region for which one does not have data. If NASA officials had looked at this plot, certainly the launch would have been delayed.

The Rogers Commission, which investigated the *Challenger* disaster, saw the data in Figure 1.5-2 and reported that "a careful analysis of the flight history of O-ring performance would have revealed the correlation of O-ring damage in low temperature." This example shows why it is so important to have statistically minded engineers involved in important decisions. Applied statisticians like R. Snee have told us time and time again: "In God We Trust; Others Must Have Data."

This example raises two important points. It illustrates the importance of scatter plots where we plot one variable against another. Earlier versions of such scatter plots are the time-sequence plots, where we plot the variable of interest against time. The other point that is made so well in the *Challenger* example is the importance of plotting *relevant data*. Yes, it is true that some data were used in making the decision. But not all the relevant data were utilized. It takes knowledge of statistics to make good decisions, as well as subject knowledge, common sense, and an ability to question the relevance of information.

1.5-2   The Sample Correlation Coefficient As a Measure of Association in a Scatter Plot

Scatter plots are useful graphical tools, as they show the nature and the strength of relationships between two variables. We give another example of a scatter plot and introduce a simple measure of association. Figure 1.5-3 gives a scatter plot of fuel consumption y (in gallons of fuel per hundred miles traveled) against weight x (in 1000 pounds) of $n = 10$ automobiles. The data are given in Table 1.5-1. This plot reveals several features.

1. It shows a *positive* association between these two variables since, as expected, heavier cars require more fuel than lighter ones.

2. It also shows a relationship that is roughly *linear*; over the studied range of weights from 1900 to 4100 pounds, each added unit of weight increases fuel consumption by roughly the same amount. In Figure 1.5-3 we have drawn in such a "best-fitting" straight line; there is much more on that in Section 1.5-3 and in Chapter 9.

3. The plot also shows that the relationship between these two variables is fairly *strong*; the scatter around this best-fitting line is quite tight.

Scatter plots tell us graphically what these relationships are like. Sometimes, however, it is useful to attach to these plots a numeric value that assesses the association in terms of a single number. This is especially useful if one compares different data sets (e.g., scatter plots of fuel consumption against

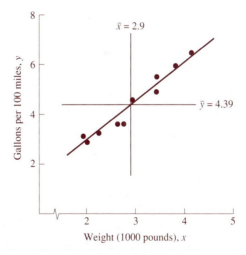

FIGURE 1.5-3   Scatter plot of fuel consumption (gallons per 100 miles traveled) against weight.

TABLE 1.5-1   **Weight x (1000 Pounds) and Fuel Consumption y (Gallons per 100 Miles)**

Car	x	y	$(x - \bar{x})(y - \bar{y})$	$(x - \bar{x})^2$	$(y - \bar{y})^2$
AMC Concord	3.4	5.5	0.555	0.25	1.2321
Chevy Caprice	3.8	5.9	1.359	0.81	2.2801
Ford Country Squire Wagon	4.1	6.5	2.532	1.44	4.4521
Chevette	2.2	3.3	0.763	0.49	1.1881
Toyota Corona	2.6	3.6	0.237	0.09	0.6241
Ford Mustang Ghia	2.9	4.6	0.000	0.00	0.0441
Mazda GLC	2.0	2.9	1.341	0.81	2.2201
AMC Sprint	2.7	3.6	0.158	0.04	0.6241
VW Rabbit	1.9	3.1	1.290	1.00	1.6641
Buick Century	3.4	4.9	0.255	0.25	0.2601

Source: Data from H. V. Henderson and P. F. Velleman, "Building Multiple Regression Models Interactively," *Biometrics*, 37: 391–411 (1981).

weight for domestic and imported cars, or scatter plots for different model years). The *sample correlation coefficient* is one such measure. It quantifies the degree of *linear* association among two variables. It is important to emphasize that it only picks up the linear association; it may miss more complicated associations where the variables are related in a nonlinear fashion. There is always a danger when one characterizes a scatter plot with just a single summary statistic, as this one number may miss certain aspects of the data that are discernible to the eye; the sample correlation coefficient is no exception.

In Figure 1.5-3 we have also drawn in a vertical line at the average $\bar{x}$, and a horizontal line at the average $\bar{y}$. These lines divide the scatter into four quadrants. The deviations $x_i - \bar{x}$ and $y_i - \bar{y}$ are important components in developing this measure of association. Standardized deviations, $(x_i - \bar{x})/s_x$ and $(y_i - \bar{y})/s_y$, are in fact preferable, as we are looking for a measure of association that does not depend on the unit of measurement. Here s_x and s_y are the standard deviations of the x and y measurements. Since $(x_i - \bar{x})$ and s_x are expressed in terms of the same unit, their ratio is dimensionless and is not affected by changes in the measurement unit. For example, it does not matter whether we measure weight in pounds, 1000 pounds, kilograms, or tons, or fuel consumption in gallons, quarts, or liters.

The sample correlation coefficient depends on the products

$$[(x_i - \bar{x})/s_x][(y_i - \bar{y})/s_y].$$

In case of a positive association, these products are mostly positive, as larger (smaller)-than-average y-values usually occur together with larger (smaller)-than-average x-values. Negative products are not as common in positive association as it is rarer to observe larger (smaller)-than-average y-values with smaller (...

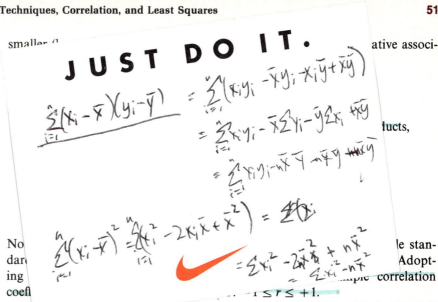

...ative associ-

...ucts,

No...
dar...
ing...
coef... $-1 \leq r \leq +1.$

T... ...on coefficient measures the direction and the strength of a linear association. The *sign* of the coefficient tells us about the direction of the association; positive values imply a positive or direct association, and negative values imply a negative or indirect one. The *absolute value* of this coefficient tells us about the strength of the linear association. A coefficient of $+1$ or -1 implies that there is a perfect linear association; the scatter plot in such a situation shows that all points lie on a straight line, exactly. A coefficient of zero, on the other hand, implies that there is no linear association.

As an illustration we use the fuel consumption and weight of the 10 automobiles in Table 1.5-1 to calculate the sample correlation coefficient. We find that, rounded to three decimal digits, the sample means and sample standard deviations are given by $\bar{x} = 2.9$, $s_x = 0.759$ and $\bar{y} = 4.39$, $s_y = 1.273$. The last three columns in Table 1.5-1 list the products $(x_i - \bar{x})(y_i - \bar{y})$ and the squares $(x_i - \bar{x})^2$ and $(y_i - \bar{y})^2$. Substituting sums of these columns into the expression for the sample correlation coefficient, we obtain

$$r = \frac{8.49}{\sqrt{(5.18)(14.589)}} = 0.977.$$

It implies a positive association that is very strong. It confirms the conclusions that we have drawn from the scatter plot in Figure 1.5-3.

Remark There is yet another equivalent expression for the correlation coefficient,

$$r = \frac{\sum x_i y_i - (\sum x_i)(\sum y_i)/n}{\sqrt{[\sum x_i^2 - (\sum x_i)^2/n][\sum y_i^2 - (\sum y_i)^2/n]}}.$$

This is computationally useful, as it avoids some of the rounding errors that are made with the earlier formula. For the data in Table 1.5-3 we find that

$\sum x_i = 29.0$, $\sum y_i = 43.9$, $\sum x_i^2 = 89.28$, $\sum y_i^2 = 207.31$ and $\sum x_i y_i = 135.8$.
Accordingly,

$$r = \frac{135.80 - (29.0)(43.9)/10}{\sqrt{[89.28 - (29.0)^2/10][207.31 - (43.9)^2/10]}} = 0.977.$$ ∎

1.5-3   Introduction to Least Squares

In Sections 1.5-1 and 1.5-2, we have introduced scatter plots. Moreover, the
fuel consumption data in Table 1.5-1 are plotted in Figure 1.5-3 along with the
"best-fitting" straight line. We now discuss in what sense this line is best-
fitting among all possible straight lines that could be drawn through these
points.

More generally, suppose that we wish to fit a curve, $y = h(x; \alpha, \beta)$, that
depends on two parameters, α and β, to n pairs of points: (x_1, y_1), (x_2, y_2), ...,
(x_n, y_n). The height of the curve at x_i is $h(x_i; \alpha, \beta)$ and the height of the
observed point is y_i. The distance between these heights is $|y_i - h(x_i; \alpha, \beta)|$,
and the square of this distance measures, in some sense, how badly the curve
misses the point. In the method of least squares, we select the parameters α
and β so as to minimize the sum of the squares of these n distances, hence the
name "least squares." That is, we find α and β to minimize

$$S(\alpha, \beta) = \sum_{i=1}^{n} [y_i - h(x_i; \alpha, \beta)]^2.$$

In the special case when $h(x; \alpha, \beta) = \alpha + \beta x$ is a linear function of x, this is
a rather easy mathematical problem. Here

$$S(\alpha, \beta) = \sum_{i=1}^{n} (y_i - \alpha - \beta x_i)^2.$$

Thus, if we set the two first partial derivatives equal to zero, we obtain

$$\frac{\partial S(\alpha, \beta)}{\partial \alpha} = \sum_{i=1}^{n} 2(y_i - \alpha - \beta x_i)(-1) = 0,$$

$$\frac{\partial S(\alpha, \beta)}{\partial \beta} = \sum_{i=1}^{n} 2(y_i - \alpha - \beta x_i)(-x_i) = 0.$$

These two linear equations in α and β are equivalent to

$$\sum_{i=1}^{n} y_i = n\alpha + \left(\sum_{i=1}^{n} x_i\right)\beta,$$

$$\sum_{i=1}^{n} x_i y_i = \left(\sum_{i=1}^{n} x_i\right)\alpha + \left(\sum_{i=1}^{n} x_i^2\right)\beta.$$

If we multiply the first equation by $\sum x_i$ and the second by n and then subtract

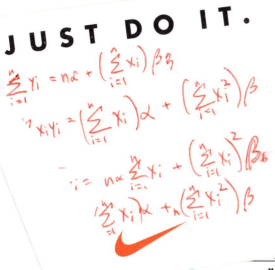

JUST DO IT.

$\sum_{i=1}^{n} y_i = n\hat{\alpha} + \left(\sum_{i=1}^{n} x_i\right)\hat{\beta}$

$\sum_{i=1}^{n} x_i y_i = \left(\sum_{i=1}^{n} x_i\right)\alpha + \left(\sum_{i=1}^{n} x_i^2\right)\beta$

$\cdots_i = n\alpha \sum_{i=1}^{n} x_i + \left(\sum_{i=1}^{n} x_i\right)^2 \hat{\beta}$

$\sum_{i=1}^{n} x_i \hat{\alpha} + n\left(\sum_{i=1}^{n} x_i^2\right)\beta$

ninates the α term), we obtain the solution,

$$\frac{\sum y_i - (\sum x_i)(\sum y_i)/n}{\sum x_i^2 - (\sum x_i)^2/n} = \frac{\sum (x_i - \bar{x})(y_i - \bar{y})}{\sum (x_i - \bar{x})^2}.$$

y related to the sample correlation $1)s_x s_y$, discussed in Section 1.5-2. Since $\sum (x_i - \bar{x})^2 = (n-1)s_x^2$, we find that

$$\frac{r s_x s_y}{)s_x^2} = r \frac{s_y}{s_x}.$$

he first equation, namely

$+ (\sum x_i)\beta,$

$$\frac{\cdots}{n} = \bar{y} - \hat{\beta}\bar{x} = \bar{y} - \left(r\frac{s_y}{s_x}\right)\bar{x}.$$

Thus the best-fitting line in the sense of least squares is

$$\hat{y} = \left(\bar{y} - r\frac{s_y}{s_x}\bar{x}\right) + \left(r\frac{s_y}{s_x}\right)x$$

$$= \bar{y} + \left(r\frac{s_y}{s_x}\right)(x - \bar{x}),$$

where $\bar{x}, \bar{y}, s_x, s_y,$ and r are the computed characteristics of the data.

For the data in Table 1.5-1, these minimizing values are

$$\hat{\beta} = 1.639, \qquad \hat{\alpha} = -0.363.$$

The slope 1.639 implies that for each additional 1000 pounds of weight, driving 100 miles requires an additional 1.639 gallons of fuel. Since our data set includes only cars with weights between 1900 and 4100 pounds, it does not make sense to extrapolate the least-squares line to $x = 0$, and thus the intercept -0.363 by itself has no real meaning.

For more complicated functions h, the least-squares fit is not as easy to obtain. Suppose that we wish to fit the exponential function, $y = \alpha e^{\beta x}$. The minimization of

$$S(\alpha, \beta) = \sum_{i=1}^{n} (y_i - \alpha e^{\beta x_i})^2$$

is quite difficult since the partial derivatives of $S(\alpha, \beta)$ are no longer linear functions of α and β. However, there are many computer programs, known as nonlinear least-squares procedures, that can be used to determine the coefficients.

This problem does suggest one other technique that is frequently used in fitting data, and that is transformations. In this specific case a logarithmic

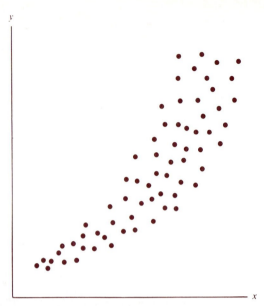

FIGURE 1.5-4   Scatter plot of y against x, indicating a nonlinear functional relationship.

transformation of y proves beneficial. Then we would use the data points $(x_i, y_i^* = \ln y_i)$ to fit the function $\ln y = \ln \alpha + \beta x$ or, equivalently, $y^* = \alpha^* + \beta x$, where $\alpha^* = \ln \alpha$. That is, we fit a straight line to (x_i, y_i^*), $i = 1, 2, \ldots, n$. This would be particularly desirable if the spread of the y values increases with larger y values. As a matter of fact, it is an ideal transformation if the spread of the y values is proportional to the level of the corresponding y.

The best advice is first to plot the raw data (x_i, y_i), $i = 1, 2, \ldots, n$. Then look for a transformation that produces a linear relationship. For illustration, if the points plot as in Figure 1.5-4, consider $y^* = \sqrt{y}$ or $y^* = \ln y$ or, more generally, $y^* = y^p$, $p < 1$. These transformations would tend to straighten out that upward curve and also decrease the spread in the points with large y values. The use of transformations on y and x in curve fitting requires much practice and a little "mathematical common sense."

Exercises 1.5

1.5-1   Consider the aldrin and hexachlorobenzene (HBC) concentrations of the 30 water samples in Exercise 1.4-3. Explore the relationship between these two variables. Make a scatter plot of aldrin against HCB. Do you think that there may be a problem with some of the observations? Which are the most likely candidates?

Calculate the sample correlation coefficient. Calculate r, with and without the suspicious observation(s).

1.5-2 By the method of least squares, fit $y = \beta x$ to the following $n = 6$ points.

x	3	1	5	6	3	4
y	4	2	4	8	6	5

Note that here we are forcing the line through the origin. Draw the fitted line on the scatter plot.

1.5-3 By the method of least squares, fit $y = \alpha + \beta x^2$ to the $n = 8$ points

x	−2	3	−1	0	−3	1	5	−3
y	7	15	3	1	11	6	30	16

1.5-4 Fisher presents the following data, which give the logarithm (base 10) of the volume occupied by algal cells on successive days, taken over a period over which the relative growth rate was approximately constant.

Day (x)	log Volume (log y)
1	3.592
2	3.823
3	4.174
4	4.534
5	4.956
6	5.163
7	5.495
8	5.602
9	6.087

Plot log y against x. Do you think that the logarithmic transformation is appropriate? If so, why?

Calculate and interpret the sample correlation coefficient. By the method of least squares, fit log $y = \alpha + \beta x$ to the $n = 9$ data points.
[R. A. Fisher, *Statistical Methods for Research Workers* (Edinburgh: Oliver & Boyd, 1925).]

1.5-5 Tukey discusses the relationship between the vapor pressure of B-trimethylborazole (y, in millimeters of mercury) and temperature (x, in °C).

x	y	x	y
13.0	2.9	56.1	51.4
19.5	5.1	64.4	74.5
22.5	8.5	71.4	100.2
27.2	10.3	80.5	143.7
31.8	14.6	85.7	176.9
38.4	21.3	91.5	216.9
45.7	30.5		

Plot y against x. How can we straighten this plot? Try various transformations on y and/or x: for example, square root and logarithmic transformations.
[J. W. Tukey, *Exploratory Data Analysis* (Reading, Mass.: Addison-Wesley, 1977).]

1.5-6 In a statistical analysis of air pollution data, Ledolter and Tiao analyzed hourly carbon monoxide (CO) averages that were recorded on summer weekdays at a measurement station in Los Angeles. This particular station was established by the Environmental Protection Agency as part of a larger study to assess the effectiveness of the catalytic converter. The measurement station was located about 25 feet from the San Diego Freeway, which in this particular area is located at 145° north. The measurement station was located such that winds from 145 to 325° (which in the summer are the prevalent wind directions during the daylight hours) transport the CO emissions from the highway toward the measurement station. For each hour 1 to 24, we have listed the average summer weekday CO concentration (in parts per million), the average weekday traffic density TD = traffic count/traffic speed, and the average perpendicular wind-speed component:

$$WS_p = \text{wind speed} \times \cos(\text{wind direction} - 235°).$$

Hour	CO	TD	WS_p	Hour	CO	TD	WS_p
1	2.4	50	−0.2	13	5.8	179	4.6
2	1.7	26	0.0	14	5.5	178	5.4
3	1.4	16	0.0	15	5.9	203	5.9
4	1.2	10	0.0	16	6.8	264	5.9
5	1.2	12	0.1	17	7.0	289	5.6
6	2.0	41	−0.1	18	7.4	308	4.9
7	3.4	157	−0.1	19	6.4	267	3.8
8	5.8	276	−0.2	20	5.0	190	2.5
9	6.8	282	0.2	21	3.8	125	1.4
10	6.6	242	1.0	22	3.5	120	0.6
11	6.6	200	2.3	23	3.3	116	0.4
12	6.3	186	3.8	24	3.1	87	0.1

(a) Make a map of the area and discuss why WS_p is a meaningful measure.

(b) Construct diurnal plots of CO, traffic density TD, and perpendicular wind-speed component. (Diurnal plots are plots against hour of the day.)

(c) Interpret your graphs. For example, does it appear that CO is proportional to TD, and that WS_p plays the role of transport as well as diffusion?

(d) Ignore traffic density for the moment and assume that there is information on wind speed and direction. How can you change the diurnal CO plot such that it also shows wind speed and direction?

Hint Represent wind direction by the vane direction on 360° with north on top, and wind speed by the length of the vane.

[J. Ledolter and G. C. Tiao, "Statistical Methods for Ambient Air Pollutants with Special Reference to the Los Angeles Catalyst Study (LACS) Data," *Environmental Science and Technology*, 13: 1233–1240 (1979).]

1.5-7 Consider the times it took Ledolter to ride his bicycle from his office in the Engineering School to the Princeton train station when he was a visitor there during the academic year 1985–86. He usually left his office shortly after 5 P.M. as he had to catch a train at 5:20.

Date	Time (seconds)	Date	Time (seconds)
Sept. 3, 1985 (Tuesday)	290	Sept. 19	305
4	305	20	360
5	310	23	340
6	365	24	275
9	280	25	320
10	300	26	305
11	410	27	385
12	305	30	280
13	345	Oct. 1	315
16	260	2	320
17	295	3	290
18	290	4	330

Many factors affected his time. The most important were traffic conditions: He had to cross two major busy roads and at times had to wait, especially on Fridays, when the traffic was particularly heavy. Other factors were the weather conditions, his energy level, the condition of the bicycle, and whether he stopped along the way to chat with someone (e.g., this was the case on September 11).

Analyze the data. Display the variability. Check whether the day of week had an influence on the times. Check whether times got faster (or slower) with experience.

Conduct a similar experiment and record the time it takes you to get to a certain class. Obtain measurements for the next 20 days. Keep a log of the special circumstances that affect your times, and analyze the 20 observations in any way you think is appropriate.

1.5-8 The following $n = 15$ pairs of observations are the ACT Math and ACT Verbal test scores of 15 students.

(16, 19) (18, 17) (22, 18) (20, 23) (17, 20)
(25, 21) (21, 24) (23, 18) (24, 18) (31, 25)
(27, 29) (28, 24) (30, 24) (27, 23) (28, 24)

Construct a scatter plot of Math against Verbal test scores and calculate the sample correlation coefficient. Find the best-fitting straight line by the method of least squares.

1.5-9 (Possible Class Project) Ask each of your students to supply the following information (of course, without giving their names): gender (male/female), height (inches), weight (pounds), age (years), current grade-point average, current smoking status (no/yes), current drinking status (no/moderate/heavy), television exposure (hours/day). Enter the data into a computer file and make the data accessible to all students. Data on categorical variables should be coded: 0 (male) and 1 (female) for gender; 0 (no) and 1 (yes) for smoking; and 0 (no), 1 (moderate), and 2 (heavy) for drinking status.

Ask the students to analyze the information using simple graphical procedures and summary statistics, such as sample means, standard deviations, and correlation coefficients. For example, discuss the relationship between weight and height (here you should carry out the analysis for males and females combined, as well as for males and females separately). Explore differences in grade-point averages and smoking/drinking patterns among females and males. Is there a relationship between grade-point average and drinking? Is grade-point average related to television exposure? Can you answer whether extensive television exposure drives you to drink, or whether drinking makes you watch TV?

*1.6   The Importance of Experimentation

The information that one obtains by listening to ongoing processes gives a picture of what these processes are like. Such data provide the bases of *descriptive* (or, as Deming calls it, *enumerative*) studies. However, one must keep in mind that the analysis of such data represents a passive use of statistics, because these data occur without any active participation of the investigator. Although much can be learned by "listening" to a process, much more can be learned by active questioning, testing, and experimenting, much as a doctor does with a patient. It is through these *comparative* (*analytic*) studies that we learn how to improve our products and services.

Observing a patient's responses on several stress tests will provide more information than can be obtained from measurements taken during normal resting periods. The same is true for industrial processes. Much can be learned about a process by changing the factors that are thought to have an influence according to a specified plan. Measurements on how a process responds to such changes provide the investigator with valuable information on the effects of these factors. Such investigations involve the collection and analysis of data from carefully planned experiments. *Design of experiments*, a very important area of statistics, teaches engineers and physical scientists how to perform experiments that ensure the validity of experimental results and that lead, in relatively few experimental runs, to precise estimates of the effects of these factors on the response.

1.6-1   Design of Experiments

A poorly designed experiment may not shed light on a particular question that we would like to have answered. Thus it is important to have an experimental plan *before* information is collected; trying to rescue the experiment at the data analysis stage *after* it has been run usually fails. Consulting a statistician after an experiment is finished often amounts simply to asking for a postmortem examination; the statistician cannot save the investigation at this point and can only suggest from which oversight it has failed. Thus it is important to design the experiment such that the validity of the experimental results is assured.

In good experimental designs relatively few runs are needed to get precise estimates of the effects on the response of the factors studied. R. A. Fisher, an eminent statistician and scientist who developed this subject, said that a complete overhaul of an experimental design may often increase the precision of the results 10- or 12-fold for the same cost in time and labor.

Example 1.6-1   This example illustrates the importance of carefully planned experiments. Assume that it is thought that one possible reason for the increased fraction of defectives is a change in the supplier of one of the raw materials needed in production: say, the ink in our ball-point-pen example of Section 1.1-4. To follow up on this hypothesis, the plant engineer produces a total of 40 lots of pens: 20 are produced from the old raw material A and 20 are produced from the new one, B. Since the plant can manufacture only 10 lots a day, it takes all day Thursday and Friday to produce the 20 lots from the old material and all day Saturday and Sunday to produce the 20 lots from the new material. Subsequent sample inspection shows that the old material includes 1.5 percent defectives, whereas the new one includes 5.8 percent. The engineer takes this as conclusive evidence that the new material is indeed worse than the old one. A worker on the assembly line, however, raises the point that on Thursday and Friday the line is staffed by experienced workers, whereas on Saturday and Sunday the company uses inexperienced part-time help. He documents his observation by pointing out that in the past the rejection rates for weekend production were usually higher than those on weekdays. Thus, he says, the difference in the percentage of defectives could just as well be due to the different experience levels of the workers.   ■

Of course, the worker is correct. In this experiment we observed only experienced workers, who use the old raw material, and inexperienced workers, who use the new one. We say that the two factors are *confounded*. From this experiment alone it is not possible to separate the effects of these two factors. The observed difference in the percentage of defectives could be due to differences of raw materials, worker experience, or perhaps both.

This is an example of a poorly designed experiment. How could we have done better? If we believe that experience matters, each group of workers should have produced pens from both raw materials. Thus the weekday group, as well as the weekend group, should have processed 10 lots from A and 10 lots from B. If we fear that the process varies somewhat from day to day, we should, each day, produce five lots with A and five lots with B. Such a design could "block out" a possible day effect because comparisons can now be made *within* each day. The day represents a block, and the principle of allocating both raw materials (i.e., the different treatments) to each block is called *blocking* an experiment.

The original experiment has failed here because we have chosen a design in which our variable of interest is completely confounded with another variable that is believed to have an influence on the response. Usually, we can think of many variables besides the variable of interest that could influence the response. In our example it was "day," but it could be batch, furnace run, location, plant, and so on. We refer to factors that can affect the response but which are not of main interest as the *blocking variables*. A good design makes sure that the levels of the variable of interest are not confounded with the levels of these other variables.

If we know how these other factors change over the course of the experiment, we can always choose a design that avoids confounding. But what should we do if these factors and the way they change over the course of the experiment are unknown? How can we protect the validity of our results and guard against the effects of all these unspecified and unknown factors? The answer to this is *randomization*, which is another important principle in the design of experiments. In the context of our example we would randomize the order of the experiments within each day. For example, the particular order of the 10 runs on Thursday (the five from *A* and five from *B*) would be randomized. We can get such a random arrangement by putting in a bowl five paper slips designated *A* and five slips designated *B*, mixing the slips, and drawing one after the other. For example, the sequence *ABAABABBAB* would specify the order in which the experiments should be carried out. We start with a lot that uses material *A*, the next uses *B*, the next two use *A*, and so on. We would repeat such a drawing three more times; the resulting sequences would give us the order for the experiments on Friday, Saturday, and Sunday. This randomization spreads the risk of unspecified factors evenly over the levels of our factor of interest. A random arrangement would be much safer than a deterministic pattern in which on each day the five *A*'s are run first and the five *B*'s second; the deterministic arrangement would be particularly bad if there are trends in the quality of the production process.

In summary, the principles of *blocking* and *randomization* ensure the validity of the experimental results. If we know of certain factors that may affect the comparison, we should block the experiment with respect to these factors and make sure that the experiment is designed so that comparisons can be made within each block. To guard against all other unspecified factors, we should randomize the treatments within each block. The risk that this random order is confounded with some other important factor is quite small. Thus we can say that randomization guarantees the validity of the inference in the face of unspecified disturbances. A simple rule of thumb is to *block what you can and randomize what you cannot block.*

Example 1.6-2   Let us consider another experiment. Assume that you are an engineer for a major car manufacturer. Your job is to design a new disk for front disk brakes that is more durable than the one currently in use. After experimentation you come up with a new alloy component that you think is more durable than the old one. You have already made several test runs in the laboratory and have found that the new material is indeed better than the old one. However, before the company makes a decision to install these disks in their new cars, they want you to run an experiment that shows this advantage under general driving conditions.

For your study you select a sample of 12 brand-new cars that are all of the same type. In 6 of those 12 cars you install the new experimental disks in the front brakes. You have just learned the importance of randomization. Even though you were told that the 12 cars are identical, you divide these 12 cars at random into two groups. You carry out the randomization by assigning a number to each car and drawing these numbers at random. The first six numbers drawn identify the cars on which the new brake disks should be installed. Next, you have to assign these 12 cars to 12 test drivers who drive the cars for 5000 miles. You know that there will be differences among drivers; there are always a few of us who drive faster and use their brakes more often than others. Thus you allocate the drivers to the cars at random. You can do this by preparing a list of these 12 drivers, putting 12 slips of paper that identify the cars into a bowl, and selecting one slip after the other. The first car selected would be driven by the first driver on your list, the second car by the next driver on your list, and so on. After you have made these assignments, the test drivers are instructed to use the cars for their normal day-to-day driving. After 5000 miles the cars are brought back to the factory and the loss of material on the disks is measured.

When the experiment is finished, you obtain 12 measurements: six on each material. Probably the first thing that you would do with this information is to plot the material loss on a simple line graph and construct a dot diagram. As in Figure 1.6-1, you may want to use two different symbols to distinguish between the new material *A* (use ×, for example), and the old material *B* (say o). You could also calculate the averages of these two groups of six; the averages are indicated by the arrows. Note that, based on tests of 12 cars, the average material loss for brake pads made of material *A* is slightly smaller than the one for pads made of material *B*. However, does this really mean that material *A* is better than material *B*? Probably not, as there is large variability among the individual measurements. Referring to Figure 1.6-1, we see that the "×'s" and the "o's" are pretty well mixed up. One also notices that cars equipped with type *A* disks lead to the smallest as well as the largest material loss. Judging from this diagram, we cannot say that this small difference in the averages is sufficient evidence that *A* is better than *B*. Based on the information from this experiment, we cannot say that there is a difference among these two materials. Of course, our engineer is very disappointed, since this evidence conflicts with his findings in the lab. What went wrong?

Again, this is a poorly designed experiment. Yes, it is true that we have randomized the driver and car assignment to make sure that not all fast drivers drive cars equipped with *A* and all slow ones drive those with *B*.

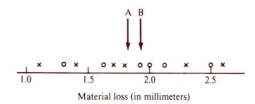

Material loss (in millimeters)

FIGURE 1.6-1 Loss of brake disk lining for 12 cars. Material *A* was used for the disks on six of the cars; their resulting material losses are marked by ×. Material *B* was used on the remaining six cars, and their results are denoted by o. The arrows indicate the averages for *A* and *B*.

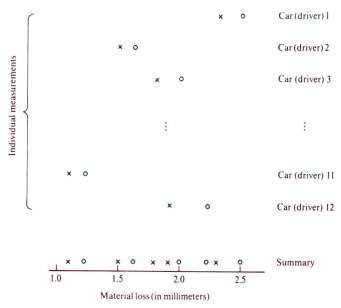

FIGURE 1.6-2   Loss of brake disk lining from an experiment with 12 cars. Both materials were mounted on each car (× corresponds to type *A*, and ○ corresponds to type *B*). To simplify the graphical comparison, we have shown only the results of five cars.

Although we have spread the possible driver effect evenly among the two treatments, the price that we paid is in terms of a rather large variability among our measurements. We could have done much better. Blocking with respect to driver and car would have eliminated a major source of variability. It is easy to block here because in each car we can install both types of disks. We can put one type on the left front wheel, and the other type on the right. Actually, we could flip a coin to decide whether type *A* goes on the right wheel or on the left. This random assignment would guard against right–left biases. At the conclusion of this experiment we obtain two measurements on each of the 12 cars (drivers): one on *A* and one on *B*. The analysis of the difference eliminates the variability that is due to the drivers. Since variability among drivers is a major component, it makes the comparison between *A* and *B* much more precise. This is what R. A. Fisher meant when he said that a complete overhaul of the experimental design may often increase the precision of the results 10- or 12-fold for the same cost in time and effort. Figure 1.6-2 shows this very clearly. The measurements from every car show that the material loss for *A* is less than that for *B*. This provides strong evidence that material *A* is indeed better. However, if this experiment had not been blocked with respect to drivers, the conclusion would have been quite different. The summary diagram at the bottom of the figure shows little difference between *A* and *B*. ■

Example 1.6-3 Assume that we want to compare the fuel efficiency of two specific trucks, *A* and *B*. A possible but very bad experimental design is to obtain fuel consumption measurements on *n* consecutive test runs of fixed length with truck *A*, followed by *n* consecutive runs with truck *B*. Since the runs are not carried out under the same weather, road, and traffic conditions, it is impossible to make a fair comparison. A design that runs the trucks in tandem, described in Exercise 1.2-13, is preferable as the fuel consumption of both trucks is obtained under the same conditions. An analysis of the ratios (or the differences) in fuel consumption for the *n* runs will tell us which of the two trucks is the more efficient one.

A comparison of truck fuel efficiency may not be the real goal of the investigation. In Exercise 1.2-13 it is the question whether a certain fuel additive improves fuel efficiency, and the question which of the two trucks is more fuel efficient is of minor interest. Nevertheless, we can use the "tandem-type" design to evaluate this question. We can compare the ratio in fuel consumption that we obtained when both trucks use the same fuel to the ratio that is obtained when one of the trucks uses the additive. A difference in these ratios tells us whether the fuel additive has an effect. ■

1.6-2   Design of Experiments with Several Factors and the Determination of Optimum Conditions

There is usually a rather long list of factors (variables) that are thought to have an effect on the response variable. For example, the yield of a chemical process may depend on the reaction time, on the pressure and the temperature under which the reaction is completed, on the concentration of a certain additive, on the type of catalyst that is used in the reaction, and so on. The roughness of the finish of certain metal strips in a metallurgical process may depend on the solution temperature, the solution concentration, the roll size, the roll tension, and so on. The impurity of a certain chemical product may depend on the type of polymer that is used, the polymer concentration, and the amount of a certain additive. How should we conduct experiments that allow us to estimate the effects of these factors, and how should we locate regions that lead to the largest (or smallest) possible response? In the case of yield as the response, we would look for a maximum; in case of impurity or roughness, we would look for a minimum.

If there is only one factor, this problem is relatively straightforward. We would ask the operator in charge of the process, or a chemist, or an expert in metallurgy about the range over which the factor should be varied and would inquire which factor level is currently being used. Then we would conduct several experiments at various levels of this factor, measure the response, plot the responses on graph paper, and locate the direction in which we should move in order to increase (or decrease) the response.

But how should we proceed if there are $k = 5$ or $k = 10$ factors, particularly if there are constraints on the numbers of runs that we can perform? Economy in the number of experimental runs is usually of great importance. For instance, if the experiments are performed on-line (i.e., during the normal production schedule), the operator is going to be very reluctant to make too many changes. Frequently, each change requires lengthy preparations and setup costs. Also, there is always the concern that with some of the changes recommended, the output may in fact be poor and substantial losses may result. Experiments in the laboratory, away from the production process, are also often very time consuming and expensive. Of course, the cost of an experiment depends on the particular setting. Usually, however, the information from a well-designed experiment will outweigh the cost of experimentation.

Before you read further, think how you would design an experiment if you wanted to study the effects of $k = 5$ factors on the yield of a certain process. Assume that you know the feasible range of these five factors and the settings at which the process is currently run. In particular, think about how to specify the values of these five factors, called the design variables, and how you would analyze the results. By now you are probably convinced that you need a plan or a design for choosing the levels of the design variables and a method for analyzing the results.

One way, but, in fact, in many cases a very bad one, is to change the factors one at a time. To make our discussion simpler, assume that there are only $k = 2$ factors, say temperature and pressure, that affect the yield of a certain chemical reaction. In the "one factor at a time" approach the experimenter fixes one of the factors at a certain level, say temperature at 220°C, which may have been the value that was suggested by the chemist. Then, with temperature fixed at 220°C, the experimenter changes pressure and conducts runs at various pressure levels; say, at 80, 90, 100, 110, and 120 pounds per square inch (psi). She analyzes the yields at these levels, plots the responses on graph paper (yield against pressure), and locates the pressure that leads to the highest yield. Assume that the maximum is obtained when pressure is at 100 psi (this is the maximum for the fixed temperature of 220°C). She then fixes pressure at this value and changes temperature; suppose that she conducts experiments with temperature at 180, 200, 220, 240, and 260°C. Again she analyzes the results, plots the yields against temperature, and finds the maximum; assume that it is somewhere between 220 and 240°C, say at 230°C. From these experiments the engineer claims that the optimum of the process is at temperature 230°C and pressure 100 psi.

Figure 1.6-3(a) shows that this conclusion is *wrong*, and it illustrates the problems with the "change one factor at a time" approach. In this graph we have connected the settings of temperature (x_1) and pressure (x_2) that lead to the same response (y); these connecting curves are called the *contours* and the plot is called a *contour plot*. We can obtain these contours by plotting the response y for given values of x_1 and x_2 in the three-dimensional (x_1, x_2, y) space and then slicing through this surface at various heights y; here the y are chosen as 70, 65, and 60. This contour plot shows that the point

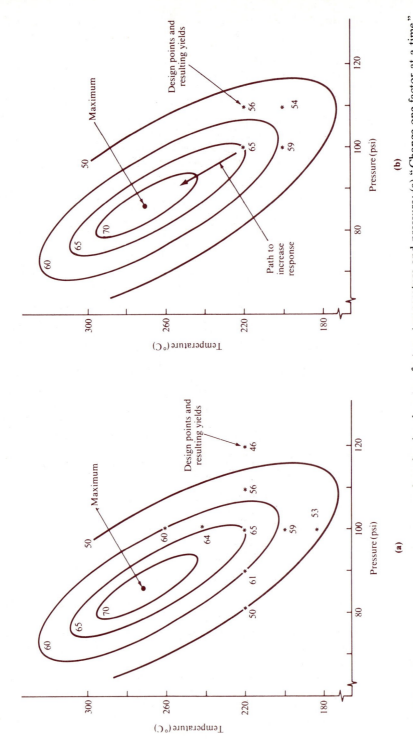

FIGURE 1.6-3 Contour plot of a response surface that involves two factors, temperature and pressure: (a) "Change one factor at a time" approach (the *incorrect* approach); (b) changing the factors together (the *correct* approach).

(temperature = 230°C, pressure = 100 psi) which we have obtained by changing the factors one at a time is *not* the maximum. The maximum is achieved when temperature is at 270°C and pressure at about 85 psi.

The "change one factor at a time" approach has failed here because it assumes that the effects of changes in one factor are independent of the value of the other factor; it assumes that the maximum with respect to one factor is independent of the settings of the other. This is not true in the illustration given in Figure 1.6-3, and thus this approach fails.

To locate the optimal region, we have to change the factors *together*. For example, it is much better to start the experiment at the points (temperature = 200°C, pressure = 100 psi), (220°C, 100 psi), (200°C, 110 psi), and (220°C, 110 psi); see Figure 1.6-3(b). Observations at these four points would tell us to move in the northwest direction (i.e., increase temperature and lower pressure). Additional experiments could be performed on this path, and usually, with very few runs, we would locate the maximum.

This simple example shows quite clearly that we should change the factors *together*, not one at a time. In this book we discuss very simple but extremely useful arrangements that allow us to determine the effects of several factors on a response and to determine whether the effects of one factor depend on the levels of the other. [Note that the four runs given in Figure 1.6-3(b) show that the effect of a 20°C temperature increase, from 200°C to 220°C, is three times larger at a pressure of 100 psi than at 110 psi.] In these designs we select a low and a high level for each factor and conduct experiments at every possible factor-level combination. The design in Figure 1.6-3(b) is one such example with $k = 2$ factors; there we start with $2^2 = 4$ runs. If there are $k = 3$ factors, we have to conduct experiments at $2^3 = 8$ different factor-level combinations. The results of these experiments, properly analyzed, give us information on the effects of these factors and tell us how to change these factors to increase the yield.

Exercises 1.6

1.6-1 Purchase a bag of rubber bands containing bands of different lengths, widths, and colors. You are interested in the breaking strength of rubber bands. In particular, you would like to know whether length, width, or color affects the strength. Think about appropriate ways of measuring strength and discuss how you would carry out the experiment.

Carry out a small experiment and analyze your data in the form of graphs and simple summary statistics.

1.6-2 There are many other experiments with rubber bands of different sizes and colors that you could carry out.

(a) For example, you could shoot rubber bands at a target some distance away and measure the accuracy (i.e., the deviation from the specified target). Study how distance to the target and diameter of the rubber band affect your shooting accuracy. What about the effects of color? Does it make a difference if several individuals shoot at the target?

(b) Study the percent elongation of cut rubber bands that you obtain by adding a certain weight to one end of the band. How does this elongation depend on the length, width, and color of the rubber band? How does it depend on the weight?

(c) Study the travel distance that you obtain when shooting rubber bands from a ruler. In particular, stretch the rubber bands to 8, 9, and 10 inches on your ruler, and let go. Do the width, the length, and the color of the rubber band make a difference? Discuss.

1.6-3 You would like to learn how the distance from the basket and the angle to the basket affects your shooting percentage in basketball. Design an experiment that allows you to study these two factors. Make sure that your results are not confounded by other factors, such as possible "fatigue" or "time of the day" effects.

Carry out the experiment and present your results.

2 Probability Models

2.1 Probability

In applied mathematics we are usually concerned with either *deterministic* or *probabilistic* models, although in many instances these are intertwined. As an illustration, say that we are interested in the half-life of a certain substance, say plutonium-241, ^{241}Pu. In many situations involving decay, we can assume that the rate of decay of an amount, x, is proportional to that amount. That is, we have the simple differential equation

$$\frac{dx}{dt} = bx,$$

where b is the constant of proportionality. The solution of this equation is easily shown to be

$$x = ce^{bt},$$

where c is another constant. If we are given x at two different times, one of which is usually $t = 0$, the constants b and c can be found. To determine the half-life, we find that t for which the amount equals one-half of the original; it is $t = (-\ln 2)/b > 0$, since $b < 0$. We have thus found a solution of a problem described by what is commonly called a *deterministic model* because everything is known once the differential equation and the two boundary conditions are specified.

It is interesting to observe, however, that such a deterministic problem can easily involve a *probabilistic* or *stochastic* element. For instance, suppose that the observation on x at a time point $t \neq 0$ is the true value plus some random noise, which could be a measurement error or which could be due to changes in the experimental conditions. That is, if we repeated the experiment on several occasions, we would get slightly different values of x at a given time t. More generally, if we take n pairs of observations, say (t_1, x_1), (t_2, x_2), ..., (t_n, x_n), where some of the time points $t_1, t_2, ..., t_n$ differ, we usually find that they do not lie exactly on one curve of the form $x = ce^{bt}$. Then the problem is to determine the constants b and c so that the curve $x = ce^{bt}$ seems to "fit" the n observed points (t_1, x_1), (t_2, x_2), ..., (t_n, x_n) in some reasonable manner. To describe in more detail a situation that involves noise components, we need a probabilistic model involving random elements.

Remarks   Many engineers, scientists, and applied statisticians believe that in an introductory course in statistics there should be very little on basic probabilistic concepts. We have tried to keep these to a minimum and yet have enough so that we can develop the basic probability models. In addition, there is often criticism of use of coins, cards, chips, and dice in illustrating some of these concepts because those in practice believe that real examples should be used. There is a great deal of truth in this, but we find that it requires much longer discussions to explain these real situations, and that defeats the attempt to minimize the material on probability. Hence, in this and the next sections, we do use coins, cards, chips, and dice; but in most cases we find that students enjoy computing a few probabilities involving them. As a matter of fact, a probability course can be very entertaining and educational; for example, many students like to be able to compute the probability of the caster winning in "craps" and the chances of winning Lotto America.   ■

Random experiments have *outcomes* that cannot be determined with certainty before the experiments are performed. To understand such experiments we have to learn something about the basic concepts of probability. Let us begin with a very simple random experiment that we understand from everyday life—a flip of an unbiased coin. Clearly, the outcome is either heads (H) or tails (T), but it cannot be predicted with certainty. The collection of all possible outcomes, namely $S = \{H, T\}$, is called the *sample space*. Suppose that we are interested in a subset A of our sample space; for example, in our case, let $A = \{H\}$ represent heads. Repeat this random experiment a number of times, say n, and count the number of times, say f, that the experiment ended in A. Here f is called the *frequency* of the *event* A and the ratio f/n is called the *relative frequency* of the event A in these n trials of the experiment.

We actually flipped a coin a large number of times and recorded in Table 2.1-1 the frequencies and relative frequencies for a number of different values of n. We note that the relative frequency, f/n, is unstable for small values of n but tends to stabilize as n increases. We associate the number about which f/n stabilizes with the event A. Clearly, to arrive at a single number we would need to repeat the experiment a very large number of times. Since this is often

TABLE 2.1-1   Results of Coin Flips

n	f	f/n
10	3	0.300
20	11	0.550
50	23	0.460
100	52	0.520
200	96	0.480
500	241	0.482
1000	489	0.489

not feasible in practice, we usually take an approximate value of that number. For example, in the coin-tossing experiment, we might associate 1/2 with $A = \{H\}$ because we believe that the relative frequency of heads in a sequence of flips of an unbiased coin would stabilize around 1/2. We denote this association by $P(A) = 1/2$ and call $P(A)$ the *probability of the event A*.

In practice, $P(A) = 1/2$ is probably only an approximation of the probability of "heads" in a coin-tossing experiment because of some bias in the coin or of some bias in the way the experiment is performed. Clearly, we know of experiments (with dice or cards) in which biases do exist (loaded dice or crooked dealers).

The preceding interpretation of probability is referred to as the *relative frequency approach*, and it obviously depends on the fact that an experiment can be repeated under essentially identical conditions. Many persons, however, extend probability to other situations, treating it as a rational measure of belief. For example, if B is the event of rain tomorrow, they might say that $P(B) = 2/5$ is their *personal* or *subjective* probability of that event. Hence, if they are not opposed to gambling, this could mean a willingness on their part to bet on the outcome B so that the two possible payoffs are in the ratio $P(B)/[1 - P(B)] = (2/5)/(3/5) = 2/3$. Often, with this probability, they say that the *odds* for rain are 2 to 3. If they truly believe that $P(B) = 2/5$ is correct, they would be willing to accept either side of the bet: (1) win 3 units if B occurs and lose 2 units if it does not occur, or (2) win 2 units if B does not occur and lose 3 units if it does.

With either of these interpretations of probability, however, the basic laws of probability are the same. Although we could develop these mathematically from certain given axioms, we find that most of them appeal to the reader's intuition about probability, whether using the relative frequency or the subjective approach. Therefore, we simply list these laws using the well-known terminology from the algebra of sets. In addition, since most readers are familiar with an ordinary deck of 52 playing cards, we give very simple illustrations involving a draw of a card at random from that deck. To check our intuition about probability at this point, consider the following probability assignments:

$$P(B_1) = \frac{13}{52}, \text{ where } B_1 \text{ represents the event that our random draw results}$$

in a spade.

$$P(B_2) = \frac{4}{52}, \text{ where } B_2 \text{ represents the event that we have drawn a king,}$$

$$P(B_1 \cap B_2) = \frac{1}{52}, \text{ as the intersection } B_1 \cap B_2 \text{ represents a draw of the king of}$$

spades.

2.1-1   The Laws of Probability

We now discuss the laws of probability. Since the frequency f of the event A in $n \geq 1$ trials of the experiment is such that $0 \leq f \leq n$, we have that $0 \leq f/n \leq 1$. Hence $P(A)$ equals a number between zero and 1, possibly including those end points:

Law 2.1-1 $0 \leq P(A) \leq 1.$

Since the frequency of the null set, say ϕ, is zero and the frequency of the sample space (universal set), say S, is n, the respective relative frequencies of $0/n = 0$ and $n/n = 1$ suggest the second law:

Law 2.1-2 $P(\phi) = 0$ and $P(S) = 1.$

If A_1 and A_2 are disjoint sets, (i.e., their intersection has no elements, so $A_1 \cap A_2 = \phi$), we say that events A_1 and A_2 are *mutually exclusive*. The probability that A_1 or A_2 occurs is clearly the sum of the individual probabilities; that is,

$$P(A_1 \cup A_2) = P(A_1) + P(A_2),$$

where $A_1 \cup A_2$ is the union of the two disjoint sets. For illustration, in a notation that is rather obvious, we have

$$P(\text{draw results in a spade or a heart}) = \frac{13}{52} + \frac{13}{52} = \frac{26}{52}.$$

This can be extended to several mutually disjoint sets, say $A_1, A_2, \ldots, A_k$ where $A_i \cap A_j = \phi$, $i \neq j$, to give the third law:

Law 2.1-3   If $A_1, A_2, \ldots, A_k$ are mutually exclusive events, then

$$P(A_1 \cup A_2 \cup \cdots \cup A_k) = P(A_1) + P(A_2) + \cdots + P(A_k).$$

The probability of not getting the event A is denoted by $P(A')$, where A' is the complement of A. It is obvious that

$$P(\text{draw does not result in a spade}) = \frac{39}{52} = 1 - \frac{13}{52}$$

$$= 1 - P(\text{draw results in a spade}),$$

which suggests the next law:

Law 2.1-4 $P(A') = 1 - P(A).$

From Law 2.1-4 we note that in the definition of odds the ratio $P(B)/[1 - P(B)]$ can be written as $P(B)/P(B')$. That is, the odds for event B equal the ratio of the probability that B occurs and the probability that B does not occur. Of course, the odds *against* B equal the ratio $P(B')/P(B)$. For illustration, the odds against a spade in a random draw of a card from an ordinary deck of 52 cards are $(39/52)/(13/52)$, that is, 3 to 1.

Suppose now that we consider two events, A_1 and A_2, that are not mutually exclusive. Then the probability of the union $A_1 \cup A_2$ is less than $P(A_1) + P(A_2)$ because the probability of the intersection $A_1 \cap A_2$ is counted twice, once in $P(A_1)$ and once in $P(A_2)$. This leads to the following law:

Law 2.1-5 $P(A_1 \cup A_2) = P(A_1) + P(A_2) - P(A_1 \cap A_2).$

Actually, Law 2.1-5 can be extended to the probability of the union of several events: adding the probabilities of the "singles," subtracting the probabilities of the "doubles," adding the probabilities of the "triples," and so on. In particular,

$$P(A_1 \cup A_2 \cup A_3) = P(A_1) + P(A_2) + P(A_3) - P(A_1 \cap A_2)$$

$$- P(A_1 \cap A_3) - P(A_2 \cap A_3) + P(A_1 \cap A_2 \cap A_3).$$

The reader can see this by considering the *Venn diagram* in Figure 2.1-1, noting that the double intersections are counted twice, except for the common triple intersection, which is counted three times. Thus subtracting the probabilities of the three doubles means that $A_1 \cap A_2 \cap A_3$ is not counted at all. Thus we must add the term $P(A_1 \cap A_2 \cap A_3)$.

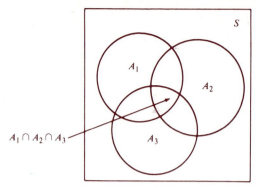

FIGURE 2.1-1   Venn diagram.

Example 2.1-1   For illustration, assume that a large inventory of coated lenses includes 5 percent scratched lenses, 2 percent poorly coated lenses, and 1 percent that are both scratched as well as poorly coated. If you pick one lens at random from this inventory, the probability of selecting a defective lens (one that is *either* scratched *or* poorly coated) is

$$P(A_1 \cup A_2) = P(A_1) + P(A_2) - P(A_1 \cap A_2)$$

$$= \frac{5}{100} + \frac{2}{100} - \frac{1}{100} = \frac{6}{100},$$

or 6 percent.   ■

We now consider a rule that allows us to assign probabilities to certain events under an "equally likely" assumption. Let $A_1, A_2, \ldots, A_k$ be mutually exclusive and *exhaustive* events. That is, not only do we have $A_i \cap A_j = \phi$, $i \neq j$, but the union of the sets exhausts the sample space,

$$A_1 \cup A_2 \cup \cdots \cup A_k = S.$$

Thus we have, from Laws 2.1-2 and 2.1-3, that

$$P(A_1) + P(A_2) + \cdots + P(A_k) = P(S) = 1.$$

Suppose, further, that we can assume that each of the events $A_1, A_2, \ldots, A_k$ has the same probability; that is,

$$P(A_1) = P(A_2) = \cdots = P(A_k).$$

Then we have

$$kP(A_i) = 1 \quad \text{and} \quad P(A_i) = \frac{1}{k}, \qquad i = 1, 2, \ldots, k.$$

If another event, B, is the union of r of these k mutually exclusive events, say

$$B = A_1 \cup A_2 \cup \cdots \cup A_r, \qquad r \leq k,$$

then

$$P(B) = P(A_1) + P(A_2) + \cdots + P(A_r) = \frac{r}{k}.$$

Sometimes, for this particular partition of S, the integer k is said to be the *total number* of ways in which the random experiment can end, and the integer r is said to be the number of ways that are *favorable* to the event B. Thus when we can assume these "equally likely" partitions, the probability of B is equal to the number of favorable ways divided by the total ways of ending an experiment. Please note that the *assumption* of equal probability of $1/k$ must be checked before we can assign probabilities in this manner.

Example 2.1-2   It is really this rule about the assignment of probability that gave us the probabilities in the draw of a card. Let a card be drawn at random from an ordinary deck of 52 playing cards. Let us assume that each of the 52 outcomes in S has the same probability of $1/52$. Let B_1 be the set of outcomes that are spades, so that $r_1 = 13$, and B_2 be the set of outcomes that are kings, so that $r_2 = 4$. Then

$$P(B_1) = \frac{13}{52} = \frac{1}{4} \quad \text{and} \quad P(B_2) = \frac{4}{52} = \frac{1}{13}.$$

Moreover, since $B_1 \cap B_2$ equals the king of spades with $r = 1$, we have that

$$P(B_1 \cap B_2) = \frac{1}{52}$$

and

$$P(B_1 \cup B_2) = P(\text{draw resulting in either a spade or a king})$$

$$= \frac{13}{52} + \frac{4}{52} - \frac{1}{52} = \frac{16}{52} = \frac{4}{13}.$$ ■

In Example 2.1-2, the probabilities were easy to compute because there was no difficulty in the determination of the appropriate values of r and k. However, instead of drawing only one card, suppose that five cards are taken, at random and without replacement, from the deck. We can think of each five-card hand as being an outcome in a sample space. It is reasonable to assume that each of these outcomes has the same probability. It is shown in many elementary mathematics books that the number of possible five-card hands is

$$k = \binom{52}{5} = \frac{52!}{5!\,47!} = 2{,}598{,}960,$$

where $n! = n(n-1) \cdots (3)(2)(1)$ and $0! = 1$. We refer to $n!$ as "n factorial."

In general, if n is a positive integer and y is a nonnegative integer with $y \leq n$, the binomial coefficient

$$\binom{n}{y} = \frac{n!}{y!\,(n-y)!}$$

is equal to the number of combinations of n distinct items taken y at a time. In our illustration involving five cards, suppose that we want to determine the probability of the event B_1 that all five cards are spades. Since there are

$$r_1 = \binom{13}{5} = \frac{13!}{5!\,8!} = 1287$$

different ways of selecting five spades out of 13, we find that

$$P(B_1) = \frac{r_1}{k} = \frac{\binom{13}{5}}{\binom{52}{5}} = 0.0005.$$

Next, let B_2 be the event that at least one of the five cards is a spade. Then B_2' is the event that no card is a spade and all five cards are drawn from the remaining 39. Thus

$$P(B_2') = \frac{\binom{39}{5}}{\binom{52}{5}} = 0.2215.$$

Of course, $P(B_2) = 1 - P(B_2') = 0.7785$.

Now suppose that B_3 is the event in which exactly three cards are kings and exactly two cards are queens. We can select the three kings in $\binom{4}{3}$ ways and the two queens in $\binom{4}{2}$ ways. By the multiplication rule in the study of counting, the number of ways favorable to B_3 is $r_3 = \binom{4}{3}\binom{4}{2} = (4)(6) = 24$. Multiplication is appropriate here, as we can combine each selection of three kings (there are four of them) with each possible choice of two queens (there are six of those). Thus

$$P(B_3) = \frac{\binom{4}{3}\binom{4}{2}}{\binom{52}{5}} = 0.0000092.$$

Finally, in this illustration, let B_4 be the event in which there are exactly two kings, two queens, and one jack. Then

$$P(B_4) = \frac{\binom{4}{2}\binom{4}{2}\binom{4}{1}}{\binom{52}{5}} = 0.0000554,$$

because the numerator of this fraction is the number of ways favorable to B_4.

Example 2.1-3   A lot, consisting of 100 fuses, is inspected by the following procedure. Five of the fuses are selected at random and tested. If all five "blow" at the correct amperage, the lot is accepted. If, in fact, there are 20 defective fuses in the lot (and thus 80 good fuses), the probability of accepting the lot is

$$\frac{\binom{80}{5}}{\binom{100}{5}} = 0.32,$$

approximately. Note that this is a fairly high probability of acceptance for such a poor lot of fuses.   ∎

Example 2.1-4   In Lotto America, the player selects six of the first 54 positive integers. Later six numbers are drawn at random and without replacement. The player wins the "big" prize if all six of the drawn numbers match the player's number (say, event B_1). There are other prizes to be won also; for example, if exactly five of the numbers drawn match the player's numbers (say, event B_2). If we suppose that the player's numbers (displayed on certain balls in a big urn) are red in color, the probability of drawing all six red balls is

$$P(B_1) = \frac{\binom{6}{6}\binom{48}{0}}{\binom{54}{6}} = \frac{(6)(5)(4)(3)(2)(1)}{(54)(53)(52)(50)(49)(48)} = (4.114)(10^{-8}),$$

since $\binom{6}{6} = \binom{48}{0} = 1$. Similarly,

$$P(B_2) = \frac{\binom{6}{5}\binom{48}{1}}{\binom{54}{6}} = (1.185)(10^{-5}).$$

∎

Exercises 2.1

2.1-1   To test the quality of a shipment of crystal glasses, we selected 50 glasses at random. We found that one was scratched and chipped, three had only scratches, and two were only chipped. Consider the following events: A is a chipped glass, and B is a scratched glass. Determine the relative frequencies of A, B, $A \cup B$, and $A \cap B$.

2.1-2   To 125 students that took last semester's engineering statistics course, the instructor gave 30 A's, 40 B's, 35 C's, 15 D's and 5 F's. Calculate the relative frequencies of these five events. Calculate the relative frequency of getting a grade that is better than C.

2.1-3   Consider rolling a single die (one of a pair of dice). Assume that each upside is equally likely. What is the probability that the experiment ends in rolling a "4"? What is the probability that it ends in an even number?

2.1-4 A person has purchased 5 of 1000 tickets sold in a certain raffle. To determine the 10 prize winners, 10 tickets are drawn at random and without replacement.

(a) Compute the probability that this person wins exactly one prize.

(b) Compute the probability that he wins at least one prize.

Hint First compute the probability that he does not win a prize.

2.1-5 A bowl contains 20 chips, of which nine are red, eight are white, and three are blue. Six chips are taken at random and without replacement. Find the probability that **(a)** each of the six chips is red; **(b)** there are three red, two white, and one blue among these six chips; **(c)** none of the six chips are blue; and **(d)** there is at least one white and one blue among the six.

Hint Consider the complement of at least one white and one blue.

2.1-6 A lot of 100 fuses is accepted if each of 10 fuses taken at random "blows" at the correct amperage. If there are exactly 20 defectives among the 100 fuses, what is the probability of accepting the lot?

2.1-7 Compute the probability of being dealt at random and without replacement a 13-card bridge hand consisting of **(a)** four spades, four hearts, three diamonds, and two clubs; and **(b)** 13 cards of the same suit.

2.2   Conditional Probability and Independence

2.2-1   Conditional Probability

Let us begin with a simple problem. Suppose that a bowl contains 10 chips of equal size: five red, three white, and two blue. We draw one at random and define the events

$$A \text{ as the draw of a red or a blue chip}$$

and

$$B \text{ as the draw of a red or a white chip.}$$

Of course, $A \cap B$ is the draw of a red chip. Assuming each chip to be equally likely, we would assign $P(A) = 7/10$, $P(B) = 8/10$, and $P(A \cap B) = 5/10$. Suppose, however, we are told that the draw resulted in either a red or a white chip but not in a blue chip. This means that B has occurred. Intuitively, the probability of A, given the information that a blue chip has been ruled out, would be 5/8, as there are five red chips among the eight chips that are red or white. That is, the conditional probability, $P(A \mid B)$, of event A given that the event B has occurred is

$$P(A \mid B) = \frac{5}{8} = \frac{5/10}{8/10} = \frac{P(A \cap B)}{P(B)}.$$

This illustration suggests the following definition.

Definition 2.2-1   *The conditional probability of an event A given that event B has occurred is defined by*

$$P(A \mid B) = \frac{P(A \cap B)}{P(B)}$$

provided that $P(B) > 0$.

In this definition we can think of B as a *reduced sample space*. It is called "reduced" because we consider only those outcomes that result in B. So $P(A \mid B)$ is the probability that event A occurs given that we are considering this new sample space B.

Example 2.2-1   Let us toss a nickel and a dime at random and record the result as an ordered pair: (result on nickel, result on dime). Thus the sample space consists of the four pairs (T, T), (T, H), (H, T), and (H, H), where T represents "tails" and H represents "heads." Assuming that these four pairs are equally likely, we assign a probability of 1/4 to each. If the event A represents (H, H) and if the event B is the event of having at least one head, then

$$P(A \mid B) = \frac{P(A \cap B)}{P(B)} = \frac{P(A)}{P(B)} = \frac{1/4}{3/4} = \frac{1}{3}.$$

Here A is a subset of B, thus $A \cap B = A = \{(H, H)\}$, and B is the reduced sample space $\{(T, H), (H, T), (H, H)\}$. Further, if C is the event in which heads appears on the nickel, then

$$C \cap B = \{(H, T), (H, H)\}$$

and

$$P(C \mid B) = \frac{P(C \cap B)}{P(B)} = \frac{2/4}{3/4} = \frac{2}{3}.$$

But if D is the event in which tails appears on the nickel, then

$$D \cap B = \{(T, H)\}$$

and

$$P(D \mid B) = \frac{P(D \cap B)}{P(B)} = \frac{1/4}{3/4} = \frac{1}{3}. \qquad \blacksquare$$

Example 2.2-2   The following probabilities apply to the waiting time in front of a bank teller: $P(A_1$: no waiting time$) = 1/2$; $P(A_2$: minor waiting time$) = 1/3$; $P(A_3$: considerable waiting time$) = 1/6$. Assume that you are told that there is some waiting time. Then the conditional probability of considerable waiting time is

$$P(A_3 \mid A_2 \cup A_3) = \frac{P(A_3)}{P(A_2 \cup A_3)} = \frac{1/6}{1/3 + 1/6} = \frac{1}{3}.$$

Here we have used the fact that $A_3 \cap (A_2 \cup A_3) = A_3$. ■

Example 2.2-3   Let us draw five cards at random and without replacement from an ordinary deck of 52 cards. Let us obtain the conditional probability of an all-spade hand (event A) given that there are at least four spades in the hand (event B). Since $A \cap B = A$, we find that

$$P(A \mid B) = \frac{P(A \cap B)}{P(B)} = \frac{P(A)}{P(B)} = \frac{\binom{13}{5} \Big/ \binom{52}{5}}{\left[\binom{13}{4}\binom{39}{1} + \binom{13}{5}\right] \Big/ \binom{52}{5}} = 0.0441.$$ ■

The equation in Definition 2.2-1 of conditional probability is sometimes written as

$$P(A \cap B) = P(B)P(A \mid B),$$

or as

$$P(A \cap B) = P(A)P(B \mid A),$$

since the roles of A and B can be interchanged. Written in either one of these forms, it is called the *multiplication rule*. Many times it is easier to assign the probabilities $P(B)$ and $P(A \mid B)$ and obtain $P(A \cap B)$ than it is to assign $P(A \cap B)$ and $P(B)$ to find $P(A \mid B)$.

Example 2.2-4   A bowl contains six white and four blue chips of the same size. Two chips are drawn at random in succession and without replacement. The probability that the first chip is white (event A) and the second chip is white (event B) is

$$P(A \cap B) = P(A)P(B \mid A) = \frac{6}{10} \cdot \frac{5}{9} = \frac{1}{3}.$$

Here it is reasonable to assign $P(A) = 6/10$, because there are six white chips among the 10 and $P(B \mid A) = 5/9$, since after it is given that the first draw is white, there are only five white and four blue chips. ■

The multiplication rule can be extended to three or more events. We have

$$P(A_1 \cap A_2 \cap A_3) = P(A_1 \cap A_2)P(A_3 | A_1 \cap A_2)$$
$$= P(A_1)P(A_2 | A_1)P(A_3 | A_1 \cap A_2),$$
$$P(A_1 \cap A_2 \cap A_3 \cap A_4) = P(A_1 \cap A_2 \cap A_3)P(A_4 | A_1 \cap A_2 \cap A_3)$$
$$= P(A_1)P(A_2 | A_1)P(A_3 | A_1 \cap A_2)$$
$$\times P(A_4 | A_1 \cap A_2 \cap A_3),$$

and so on.

Example 2.2-5   Three cards are dealt at random in succession and without replacement. The probability of three spades (i.e., spade on first, A_1, spade on second, A_2, and spade on third, A_3) is

$$\left(\frac{13}{52}\right)\left(\frac{12}{51}\right)\left(\frac{11}{50}\right) = 0.0129.$$

The first factor occurs because there are 13 spades among 52 equally likely cards. If a spade occurs on the first, there are 12 spades left in the 51 remaining cards; this gives us the factor 12/51. Finally, if spades occur on the first two draws, there are 11 spades left in the remaining 50 cards, hence the factor 11/50. [Note that this probability can also be calculated from $\binom{13}{3}/\binom{52}{3}$.]   ■

2.2-2   Independence

In practice it often happens that $P(A | B) = P(A)$ and $P(B | A) = P(B)$. That is, the fact that B has occurred does not change the probability of A, and the fact that A has occurred does not change the probability of B. In this case the multiplication rule becomes

$$P(A \cap B) = P(A)P(B)$$

and we say that A and B are independent events.

Definition 2.2-2   *Events A and B are independent if and only if*

$$P(A \cap B) = P(A)P(B).$$

Otherwise, A and B are dependent events.

Example 2.2-6   When we toss the nickel and the dime at random, it is reasonable to assume that the two resulting events are independent. Thus

$$P(\text{H on nickel and H on dime}) = \left(\frac{1}{2}\right)\left(\frac{1}{2}\right) = \frac{1}{4}.$$

In an obvious notation we also have

$$P(T, T) = P(T, H) = P(H, T) = \left(\frac{1}{2}\right)\left(\frac{1}{2}\right) = \frac{1}{4},$$

which was our assumption in Example 2.2-1.   ■

Example 2.2-7   The event, A_1, that a certain part of a spaceship works during a flight is determined to be 0.99. Since the engineers are reluctant to risk the probability 0.01 of failure, they insert another part in parallel. This means that failure occurs if and only if both parts fail. Let the event A_2 stand for the success of the second part. Assume that it has been determined that $P(A_2) = 0.99$ and that A_1 and A_2 are independent events; thus

$$P(A_1 \cap A_2) = P(A_1)P(A_2) = 0.9801.$$

Then the probability of failure (which means that both parts fail) is

$$P[(A_1 \cup A_2)'] = 1 - P(A_1 \cup A_2)$$
$$= 1 - [P(A_1) + P(A_2) - P(A_1 \cap A_2)]$$
$$= 1 - (0.99 + 0.99 - 0.9801) = 0.0001.$$

Alternatively, we could calculate the probability that both parts fail from

$$P(A_1' \cap A_2') = P(A_1')P(A_2') = (0.01)(0.01) = 0.0001.$$ ■

Remark   In our alternative calculation in Example 2.2-7, we used the fact (but had not proved it) that if A_1 and A_2 are independent, so are A_1' and A_2'. Furthermore, it is also true that A_1 and A_2' are independent, as are A_1' and A_2. We prove the latter and the other two are shown in a similar manner. Namely, we show that for independent events A_1 and A_2,

$$P(A_1' \cap A_2) = P(A_1')P(A_2).$$

Since $A_1 \cup A_1' = S$,

$$P(A_2) = P[(A_1 \cup A_1') \cap A_2] = P[(A_1 \cap A_2) \cup (A_1' \cap A_2)]$$
$$= P(A_1 \cap A_2) + P(A_1' \cap A_2),$$

because $A_1 \cap A_2$ and $A_1' \cap A_2$ are mutually exclusive. Thus, by the independence of A_1 and A_2,

$$P(A_2) = P(A_1)P(A_2) + P(A_1' \cap A_2)$$

and

$$P(A_1' \cap A_2) = P(A_2) - P(A_1)P(A_2) = [1 - P(A_1)]P(A_2) = P(A_1')P(A_2).$$ ■

The concept of independence can be extended to more than two events. Events $A_1, A_2, \ldots, A_k$ are *mutually independent* if and only if

$$P(A_{r_1} \cap A_{r_2} \cap \cdots \cap A_{r_i}) = P(A_{r_1})P(A_{r_2}) \cdots P(A_{r_i}),$$

where $r_1, r_2, \ldots, r_i$ are any i distinct integers from $\{1, 2, \ldots, k\}$ with $i = 2, 3,$ $\ldots, k$. In particular, with $i = 2$, note that the events must be *pairwise independent*, that is,

$$P(A_{r_1} \cap A_{r_2}) = P(A_{r_1})P(A_{r_2}), \qquad r_1 \neq r_2.$$

More important, with $i = k$, we must have that

$$P(A_1 \cap A_2 \cap \cdots \cap A_k) = P(A_1)P(A_2) \cdots P(A_k).$$

Example 2.2-8 The probability that a certain type of component works successfully is 0.99. However, this part is so critical that three such components are placed in parallel; with this system at least one must work to ensure the success of the operation. If we can assume that the outcomes associated with the three components are independent, the probability that all fail is

$$(0.01)(0.01)(0.01) = 0.000001.$$

Thus the probability of the complement of the event that all fail (i.e., that at least one works successfully) is

$$1 - 0.000001 = 0.999999.$$

That is, by placing three such components in parallel we increase the probability of success to 0.999999. ∎

*2.2-3 Bayes' Theorem

Let us start our discussion with a simple example. Assume that we produce components for a very complicated piece of machinery and assume that 5 percent of the components are defective. Furthermore, suppose that prior to a lengthy and expensive assembly process it is impossible to determine for sure whether a component is defective. However, suppose that we have developed a quick, but not totally reliable method for screening out defective items. We know that this test rejects good parts as defective in 1 percent of the cases; moreover, the test accepts defective parts as good ones in 10 percent of the cases.

We apply this new method to a newly produced item and the test indicates that it is a good one. What is the probability that this item is in fact a defective one?

Let us introduce some notation. Let D denote the event that the item is defective; $P(D) = 0.05$, $P(D') = 0.95$. Furthermore, let TD be the event that the test indicates a defect; according to our assumptions, $P(TD \mid D') = 0.01$ and $P(TD' \mid D) = 0.10$, where TD' is the event that the test indicates a good item.

This implies that the probabilities of the complements are $P(TD'|D') = 1 - P(TD|D') = 0.99$ and $P(TD|D) = 1 - P(TD'|D) = 0.90$. The objective is to find

$$P(D\,|\,TD') = \frac{P(D\cap TD')}{P(TD')} = \frac{P(TD'|D)P(D)}{P(TD')},$$

using Definition 2.2-1. Good, as well as bad items, can pass our test; thus $TD' = (TD'\cap D)\cup(TD'\cap D')$. Since the events in this union are disjoint (an item cannot be good and defective at the same time), we can use Law 2.1-3 and the multiplication rule to write

$$P(TD') = P(TD'\cap D) + P(TD'\cap D')$$

$$= P(TD'|D)P(D) + P(TD'|D')P(D').$$

Therefore, our desired probability is

$$P(D\,|\,TD') = \frac{P(TD'|D)P(D)}{P(TD'|D)P(D) + P(TD'|D')P(D')}$$

$$= \frac{(0.10)(0.05)}{(0.10)(0.05) + (0.99)(0.95)} = 0.0053.$$

If we ship without any screening, we ship 5 percent defectives. The probability $P(D) = 0.05$ that a randomly selected item is defective is called the *prior probability* of being defective. If we apply our imperfect screening test and ship only items that pass the test, we reduce the probability of shipping defective items to 0.53 percent. The probability $P(D\,|\,TD') = 0.0053$ is called the *posterior probability* of being defective, as it is calculated after obtaining the additional information that the item has passed the test.

In general, we can state

Bayes Theorem   Assume that a random experiment can result in k mutually exclusive and exhaustive outcomes $A_1, A_2, \ldots, A_k$, with *prior probabilities* $P(A_1)$, $P(A_2)$, $\ldots$, $P(A_k)$. Suppose that there is another event B for which the conditional probabilities $P(B|A_1)$, $P(B|A_2)$, $\ldots$, $P(B|A_k)$ can be given. Then the *posterior probability* of A_i given B is

$$P(A_i\,|\,B) = \frac{P(A_i\cap B)}{P(B)} = \frac{P(B|A_i)P(A_i)}{\sum_{j=1}^{k} P(B|A_j)P(A_j)}.$$

The proof is straightforward because first

$$P(A_i\cap B) = P(A_i)P(B\,|\,A_i).$$

Furthermore, since $B = (A_1\cap B)\cup(A_2\cap B)\cup\cdots\cup(A_k\cap B)$ partitions B into k mutually exclusive events, we have

$$P(B) = P(A_1)P(B\,|\,A_1) + P(A_2)P(B\,|\,A_2) + \cdots + P(A_k)P(B\,|\,A_k).$$

Example 2.2-9 Items in your inventory are produced at three different plants: 50 percent come from plant A_1, 30 percent from plant A_2, and 20 percent from plant A_3. You are aware that your plants produce at different levels of quality: A_1 produces 5 percent defectives, A_2 produces 7 percent defectives, and A_3 yields 8 percent defectives. You select an item from your inventory and it turns out to be defective. Then the probability that this item is from plant A_1 is

$$P(A_1 \mid D) = \frac{(0.05)(0.50)}{(0.05)(0.50) + (0.07)(0.30) + (0.08)(0.20)} = 0.403.$$

Note that the prior probability $P(A_1) = 0.50$ is larger than the posterior probability $P(A_1 \mid D) = 0.403$ because A_1 tends to produce fewer defectives than do A_2 and A_3. Similarly, we can calculate the probability that the defective part comes from plant 2, $P(A_2 \mid D) = 0.339$, and the probability that it comes from plant 3, $P(A_3 \mid D) = 0.258$. These two posterior probabilities are larger than their corresponding prior probabilities.   ∎

Exercises 2.2

2.2-1 A bowl contains ten chips: six red and four blue. Three chips are drawn at random and without replacement. Compute the conditional probability that **(a)** two are red and one blue, given that at least one red is among the three chips; and **(b)** all three are red, given that at least two red chips are in the sample of three chips.

2.2-2 A hand of 13 cards is dealt at random and without replacement from an ordinary deck of 52 playing cards. Find the conditional probability that there are at least three aces in the hand given that there are at least two aces.

2.2-3 Five cards are to be drawn successively at random and without replacement from an ordinary deck of cards. Compute the probability that the sequence "spade, club, club, heart, and spade" is observed in that particular order.

2.2-4 Consider flipping at random two coins, one a nickel and the other a dime, and recording either H or T for each. What is the sample space of this random experiment? Assume that the flips are independent. What is the probability of getting two heads? What is the probability of getting exactly one head? What is the probability of getting at least one head?

2.2-5 Consider flipping one unbiased coin at random seven times, recording the sequence of H's and T's. How many different outcomes are in the sample space? That is, how many different sequences are possible? If the flips are independent, what is the probability of getting seven heads? What is the probability of getting exactly six heads?

Hint How many outcomes in the sample space have exactly six heads, and what is the probability of each?

2.2-6 You are rolling two unbiased dice, one red and one blue, recording the ordered pair (spots up on red die, spots up on blue die). Determine the possible outcomes of this experiment. If the results on the dice are independent, determine the probabilities of the following events: **(a)** a "1" on the red die; **(b)** a "1" on each die; **(c)** a "1" on at least one of the two dice; **(d)** the sum of the two values equals 7; **(e)** the sum of the two values is an even number; **(f)** the number on the blue die is at least as large as the number on the red die; **(g)** getting equal numbers on the two dice.

2.2-7 At each of five defense stations the probability of downing an attacking airplane is 0.10. If a plane has to pass all five defense stations before arriving at its target, what is the probability that it gets shot down before it reaches the target?

Hint Assume independence and compute the probability that it will successfully pass all defense stations.

2.2-8 Suppose that the numbers 0 through 9 comprise the possible outcomes of a random experiment, and assume that each number is equally likely. Define the following events: A_1, the number is even; A_2, the number is between 4 and 7, inclusive.

(a) Are A_1 and A_2 mutually exclusive events?

(b) Calculate $P(A_1)$, $P(A_2)$, $P(A_1 \cap A_2)$, and $P(A_1 \cup A_2)$.

(c) Are A_1 and A_2 independent events?

2.2-9 A device for checking welds in pipes is designed to signal if the weld is defective. The probability assignment for the status of the weld and the response of the device is as follows:

	Device response	
Status	Signal	No signal
Defective	0.05	0.01
Not defective	0.02	0.92

This means, for example, $P(\text{defective} \cap \text{signal}) = 0.05$. Choose a pipe at random.

(a) What is the probability that it is defective?

(b) What is the probability that it is not defective?

(c) If the device signals a defect, what is the conditional probability that the pipe is actually not defective?

(d) If the device does not signal a defect, what is the conditional probability that the device is, in fact, defective?

2.2-10 A company's management made a certain proposal to its sales representatives in different sales regions. Questionnaires were sent to each representative, and the results were as follows:

	Region			
Opinion	East	Midwest	West	Total
Opposed	50	80	50	180
Not opposed	100	120	200	420
Total	150	200	250	600

(a) What is the probability that a questionnaire selected at random is that of a western sales representative in favor of the proposal?

(b) What is the probability that it is that of a midwestern sales representative?

(c) If a questionnaire is selected at random from the group that responded unfavorably to the proposal, what is the conditional probability that the respondent comes from the East?

(d) Are regional district and opinion on the proposal independent? If yes, prove your assertion. If no, with the same marginal totals, specify what the numbers in the cells of the table would have been had the two factors been independent.

Hint If the regions are denoted by A_1, A_2, A_3 and opinions are called B_1, B_2, respectively, is it true that $P(A_i \cap B_j) = P(A_i)P(B_j)$, for all $i = 1, 2, 3$ and $j = 1, 2$? If so, regions and opinions would be independent.

2.2-11 A survey organization asked respondents' views on the probable future direction of the economy and on how they voted for president in the last election. The following table shows the fractions of respondents in nine classifications.

	View on Economy		
	Optimistic	Pessimistic	Neutral
Voted for the president	0.20	0.08	0.12
Voted against the president	0.08	0.15	0.12
Did not vote	0.07	0.08	0.10

(a) What is the probability that a randomly chosen respondent voted for the president?

(b) What is the probability that a randomly chosen respondent is pessimistic about the economy?

(c) What is the conditional probability that a respondent who voted for the president will be pessimistic about the economy?

(d) What is the conditional probability that a respondent who is pessimistic about the economy voted for the president?

(e) Are views on the economy independent of how respondents voted?

Hint See Exercise 2.2-10.

2.2-12 Two inspectors review the quality of a manufactured component and classify the items as "good," "repairable," and "scrap." Each inspector looks at every item, but they do not always classify the items in the same way. Describe the sample space, and assign probabilities to the nine possible outcomes. Make certain that they are nonnegative and add to 1; the probability of the sample space has to equal 1. For your chosen assignment, calculate the marginal probabilities for each inspector. Do the inspectors act independently?

2.2-13 A popular gambling game called craps is played as follows. A player (called the "caster") rolls two dice and the sum of the two numbers that appear is observed. If that sum is 7 or 11, the caster wins the game immediately. If the sum equals 2, 3, or 12, the player loses immediately and that collection of numbers is usually referred to as "craps." If, however, the sum on the first roll is 4, 5, 6, 8, 9, 10, the game continues and that value is called the caster's "point." The caster can then win by rolling again and again until that sum (the caster's point) occurs a second time before the sum of 7 appears once. If the 7 is obtained before caster's point is observed a second time, the caster loses.

(a) Refer to Exercise 2.2-6 and establish the following probabilities for the sum resulting from a single roll of a pair of unbiased dice (clearly the fact that they were colored in that exercise does not influence these probabilities):

Sum	2	3	4	5	6	7	8	9	10	11	12
Probability	1/36	2/36	3/36	4/36	5/36	6/36	5/36	4/36	3/36	2/36	1/36

(b) The probability of winning with the sum of 7 or 11 on the first roll is 8/36. Why?

(c) The probability of winning with the sum of 4 on the first roll is computed by

P(4 on 1st)P(4 the 2nd time before 7|4 on 1st).

The first factor is, of course, 3/36. The second is the conditional probability of 4 given that the sequence of rolls ends in either 4 or 7, which have the respective probabilities of 3/36 and 6/36. Thus the answer is

$$\left(\frac{3}{36}\right)\left(\frac{3/36}{3/36 + 6/36}\right) = \frac{1}{36}$$

Using similar arguments, show that the probability of winning with a 5, 6, 8, 9, 10 on the first roll are 2/45, 25/396, 25/396, 2/45, 1/36, respectively.

(d) Thus the probability that the caster wins at craps is

$$\frac{8}{36} + 2\left(\frac{1}{36} + \frac{2}{45} + \frac{25}{396}\right) \approx 0.493.$$

2.2-14 Bowl A_1 contains three red and two white chips and bowl A_2 contains two red and five white chips. A fair die is cast. If the outcome is "five or six," a chip is taken from A_1, otherwise a chip is taken from A_2.

(a) Compute the probability that a white chip (say B) is taken.

Hint Note that $B = (B \cap A_1) \cup (B \cap A_2)$ and $(B \cap A_1) \cap (B \cap A_2) = \phi$.

(b) Given that a white chip is observed, compute the conditional (posterior) probability that it came from A_1.

(c) Compare $P(A_1|B)$ determined in part (b) with the prior probability $P(A_1)$. Does the result agree with your intuition?

2.2-15 Suppose that we wish to determine whether a rare but very costly flaw is present (event F). Let us assume that this flaw is indeed rare and that $P(F) = 0.01$ and thus $P(F') = 0.99$. A fairly simple test procedure is proposed to test for this flaw. However, the test is preliminary as the probabilities of reaching the wrong conclusion are large. About 5 percent of the time the test indicates a flaw (TF) when no flaw is present, and about 3 percent of the time it indicates the absence of a flaw when a flaw is present. That is, $P(TF|F') = 0.05$, but $P(TF'|F) = 0.03$.

(a) Show that the probability that the test indicates a flaw is $P(TF) = 0.0592$.

(b) Show that the posterior probability that there is no flaw, given that the test has indicated a flaw, is $P(F'|TF) = 0.8361$.

Remark Armed with these probabilities, a statistician would argue very strongly for better test procedures. The error rates of the present test, in particular, $P(TF|F') = 0.05$, are much too large relative to the proportion of flaws in the population [$P(F) = 0.01$]. More reliable test procedures must be found. ■

2.3 Random Variables and Expectations

2.3-1 Random Variables and Their Distributions

Engineers and scientists are often interested in quantities that cannot be predicted with certainty; for example, consider (1) the number of defects in lots of fuses, (2) the thickness of a lens, (3) the compression strength of a concrete block, (4) the tear strength of paper, and (5) the number of flaws in 1000 feet of wire. Note that these measurements can be thought to depend on the outcomes of experiments that cannot be predicted with certainty. For example, suppose that we are interested in the compressive strength of certain concrete blocks. Let us select a concrete block from a lot of concrete blocks and measure its compressive strength. This gives us a certain number. However, we could repeat the entire experiment, select a different block, and obtain a different value. Not all blocks are identical; process variability is usually present and not all items that leave the production line are the same. The measurement equipment and procedures may also influence the outcome; it is often the case that repeated measurements on the same item lead to different results. In summary, measurements can be thought of as functions of the outcomes of random experiments. Such functions are called *random variables*, since their values cannot be predicted with certainty before the random experiment is performed. That is, random variables are functions of the outcomes of random experiments. Thus engineers want to know something about the characteristics of random variables to be able to deal with the processes that produce them. It is the purpose of this section to introduce some useful terminology. We begin with an example.

Example 2.3-1 Let an unbiased coin be tossed at random three independent times. Let the random variable X be the number of heads observed in these three tosses. Here the random variable is a function of the outcomes of these three trials and it can take on one of the values 0, 1, 2, or 3. We say that the *space* of all possible values of X is $R = \{0, 1, 2, 3\}$. A random variable that can take on distinct values only is called a *discrete* random variable, so here X is a discrete random variable. Later we consider *continuous* random variables that can take any value in a continuum. It is easy to show that in this particular example the probabilities associated with the events $X = x$, $x = 0, 1, 2, 3$, are given by

$$P(X = x) = \binom{3}{x}\left(\frac{1}{2}\right)^3, \qquad x = 0, 1, 2, 3.$$

Recall that the number of combinations of n distinct objects taken r at a time is

$$\binom{n}{r} = \frac{n!}{r!\,(n-r)!}, \qquad r = 0, 1, 2, \ldots, n,$$

where $0! = 1$ and $k! = (k)(k-1)(k-2)\cdots(3)(2)(1)$. In our case we have

$$\binom{3}{0} = \frac{3!}{0!\,3!} = 1, \qquad \binom{3}{1} = \frac{3!}{1!\,2!} = 3, \qquad \binom{3}{2} = 3, \qquad \binom{3}{3} = 1.$$

To illustrate the calculation of these probabilities, consider $P(X = 2)$. We can get exactly two heads in three trials in three different ways: (T, H, H), (H, T, H), and (H, H, T). Thus

$$P(X = 2) = P(\text{T, H, H}) + P(\text{H, T, H}) + P(\text{H, H, T}).$$

Due to the independence of the tosses, we have

$$P(X = 2) = \left(\frac{1}{2}\right)\left(\frac{1}{2}\right)\left(\frac{1}{2}\right) + \left(\frac{1}{2}\right)\left(\frac{1}{2}\right)\left(\frac{1}{2}\right) + \left(\frac{1}{2}\right)\left(\frac{1}{2}\right)\left(\frac{1}{2}\right) = 3\left(\frac{1}{2}\right)^3 = \frac{3}{8}.$$

In similar fashion we find that

$$P(X = 0) = \frac{1}{8}, \qquad P(X = 1) = \frac{3}{8}, \qquad P(X = 3) = \frac{1}{8}.$$

∎

Often, the probability $P(X = x)$ is denoted by $f(x)$ and is called the *probability function*, the *frequency function*, the *probability mass function*, or the *probability density function* of a random variable of the *discrete type*. We use the latter expression and frequently abbreviate probability density function by *p.d.f.*, or simply *density*.

Since $f(x) = P(X = x)$ is a probability density function defined on the space R, it enjoys the following properties:

1. $f(x) \geq 0$, $x \in R$, because probability is nonnegative.
2. $\sum_{x \in R} f(x) = 1$, because the sum of the probabilities must equal 1.
3. $P(X \in A) = \sum_{x \in A} f(x)$, where A is a subset of R.

Example 2.3-2   Toss an unbiased coin a number of independent times until a head appears. Let X be the number of trials needed to obtain that first head. Here X is a random variable of the discrete type and the space of X is $R = \{1, 2, 3, 4, \ldots\}$. To achieve $X = x$, there must be tails on the first $x - 1$ trials and then a head on the xth trial, the probability of which is

$$P(\overbrace{\text{T, T, \ldots, T}}^{x-1}, \text{H}) = \overbrace{\left(\frac{1}{2}\right)\left(\frac{1}{2}\right) \cdots \left(\frac{1}{2}\right)}^{x-1}\left(\frac{1}{2}\right) = \left(\frac{1}{2}\right)^x.$$

That is,

$$f(x) = \left(\frac{1}{2}\right)^x, \qquad x \in R = \{1, 2, 3, 4, \ldots\}.$$

Of course, $(1/2)^x \geq 0$, provided that $x = 1, 2, 3, \ldots$. Furthermore,

$$\sum_{x=1}^{\infty} f(x) = \sum_{x=1}^{\infty} \left(\frac{1}{2}\right)^x = \frac{1/2}{1 - 1/2} = 1$$

because this is the sum of an infinite geometric series whose first term is $a = 1/2$ and whose common ratio is $r = 1/2$. Also, for example, the probability that we need between 3 and 5 tosses of the coin to get that first head is

$$P(X = 3, 4, 5) = \sum_{x=3}^{5} \left(\frac{1}{2}\right)^x = \left(\frac{1}{2}\right)^3 + \left(\frac{1}{2}\right)^4 + \left(\frac{1}{2}\right)^5 = \frac{7}{32}.$$ ■

Sometimes we let the function $F(x)$ represent the cumulative sum of all the probabilities less than or equal to x. That is,

$$F(x) = P(X \leq x) = \sum_{t \in A} f(t),$$

where $A = \{t; t \in R \text{ and } t \leq x\}$. Since $F(x)$ cumulates all the probability less than or equal to x, it is called the *cumulative distribution function* (c.d.f.) of X or, more simply, the *distribution function* of X. The c.d.f. for the random variable in Example 2.3-2 is, for $x = 1, 2, 3, \ldots$,

$$F(x) = \sum_{t=1}^{x} \left(\frac{1}{2}\right)^t = \frac{(1/2) - (1/2)(1/2)^x}{1 - 1/2} = 1 - \left(\frac{1}{2}\right)^x.$$

To find $F(x)$ here, we used the result for the sum of x terms of a geometric series with $a = r = 1/2$. Note that the c.d.f. is defined for any x value, not just for the ones in the space R. For x values that are different from the integers $1, 2, 3, \ldots$, the c.d.f. is $F(x) = 1 - (1/2)^{[x]}$, where $[x]$ is the largest nonnegative integer that is smaller than x. More specifically, $F(x) = 0$ for $x < 1$, $F(x) = 1 - 1/2$ for $1 \leq x < 2$, $F(x) = 1 - (1/2)^2$ for $2 \leq x < 3$, and so on.

Using $F(x)$ of our illustration, we note that

$$P(X = 3, 4, 5) = P(X \leq 5) - P(X \leq 2) = F(5) - F(2)$$

$$= \left[1 - \left(\frac{1}{2}\right)^5\right] - \left[1 - \left(\frac{1}{2}\right)^2\right] = \frac{1}{4} - \frac{1}{32} = \frac{7}{32}.$$

More generally, if X is a random variable of the discrete type with an outcome space R consisting of integers, then

$$P(a \leq X \leq b) = F(b) - F(a - 1),$$

where $a \in R$ and $b \in R$. Most tables of well-known discrete probability distributions are given in terms of their c.d.f. $F(x)$.

2.3-2   Expectations of Random Variables

Suppose that we once again refer to Example 2.3-1, where X is the number of heads in three independent tosses of an unbiased coin and

$$f(x) = \binom{3}{x}\left(\frac{1}{2}\right)^3, \qquad x = 0, 1, 2, 3.$$

Let us play a game and award X^2 dollars to the person flipping the coin. Before we consider a charge for playing such a game, we observe that the player receives 0, 1, 4, or 9 dollars for the respective x values of 0, 1, 2, 3. The probabilities of 1/8, 3/8, 3/8, and 1/8 are associated with the respective amounts 0, 1, 4, and 9. That is, if the game is played a large number of times, about 1/8 of the trials lead to a payment of zero dollars, about 3/8 of them to a payment of one dollar, about 3/8 of them to a payment of four dollars, and about 1/8 of them to a payment of nine dollars. Thus the average payment is

$$(0)\left(\frac{1}{8}\right) + (1)\left(\frac{3}{8}\right) + (4)\left(\frac{3}{8}\right) + (9)\left(\frac{1}{8}\right) = 3.$$

This is a weighted average of the possible outcomes of the random variable X^2, namely 0, 1, 4, 9, with respective weights 1/8, 3/8, 3/8, and 1/8. Note that this average of 3 does not equal any of the possible amounts of 0, 1, 4, and 9. If we let $u(X) = X^2$, we denote this weighted average by

$$E[u(X)] = \sum_{x \in R} u(x)f(x)$$

and call it the *mathematical expectation* or the *expected value* of $u(X)$. Incidentally, since in this illustration $E(X^2) = 3$, it is likely that the person would be charged something like \$3.25 for a game to provide the organizer of the game a profit of 25 cents per play *on the average*.

Remark   It should be pointed out that $u(X)$ itself is a random variable, say Y, taking on values in some space R_1. Suppose that we find the p.d.f. of Y to be $g(y)$. Then $E(Y)$ is given by

$$\sum_{y \in R_1} yg(y).$$

But does this equal

$$\sum_{x \in R} u(x)f(x)?$$

It seems that it should, as these two different summations are seemingly computing the average of $Y = u(X)$. In fact, these two summations are equal, and this is illustrated in Exercise 2.3-8.

It is easy to show (Exercise 2.3-7) that the mathematical expectation E is a *linear* or *distributive operation* enjoying the following properties:

1. $E(c) = c$, where c is a constant.

2. $E\left[\sum_{i=1}^{k} c_i u_i(X)\right] = \sum_{i=1}^{k} c_i E[u_i(X)],$

where $c_1, c_2, \ldots, c_k$ are constants. In particular,

$$E[c_1 u_1(X) + c_2 u_2(X)] = c_1 E[u_1(X)] + c_2 E[u_2(X)].$$

Example 2.3-3   Using the setup of Example 2.3-1, we let $u_1(X) = X$ and $u_2(X) = X^2$. We already know that $E[u_2(X)] = 3$. Thus, if we had a payment equal to $3X + 2X^2$, then

$$E[3u_1(X) + 2u_2(X)] = (3)\left(\frac{3}{2}\right) + (2)(3) = \frac{21}{2}$$

because

$$E[u_1(X)] = \sum_{x=0}^{3} xf(x) = (0)\left(\frac{1}{8}\right) + (1)\left(\frac{3}{8}\right) + (2)\left(\frac{3}{8}\right) + (3)\left(\frac{1}{8}\right) = \frac{3}{2}. \quad \blacksquare$$

In Chapter 1, we defined the (sample) mean of a set of numbers by their average, where each number is given the same weight. Here we define the mean of a random variable X as the expected value of $u(X) = X$. It is a weighted average of all possible outcomes; each outcome $x \in R$ is weighted by its probability $f(x)$. We denote this expectation by the Greek letter mu:

$$\mu = E(X) = \sum_{x \in R} xf(x).$$

We call $\mu = E(X)$ the *mean* of X or the mean of the distribution of X. In Example 2.3-3 we note that the mean of the X of Example 2.3-1 is $\mu = E(X) = 3/2$.

Example 2.3-4   Using the number of trials needed to obtain the first head as the random variable X with p.d.f. $f(x) = (1/2)^x$, $x = 1, 2, 3, \ldots$, we have

$$\mu = E(X) = \sum_{x=1}^{\infty} x\left(\frac{1}{2}\right)^x = (1)\left(\frac{1}{2}\right) + (2)\left(\frac{1}{2}\right)^2 + 3\left(\frac{1}{2}\right)^3 + \cdots = 2.$$

To see that this infinite series sums to 2, consider

$$\left(\frac{1}{2}\right)\mu = (1)\left(\frac{1}{2}\right)^2 + (2)\left(\frac{1}{2}\right)^3 + (3)\left(\frac{1}{2}\right)^4 + \cdots.$$

The difference of the expressions for μ and $(1/2)\mu$ equals

$$\frac{\mu}{2} = (1)\left(\frac{1}{2}\right) + (1)\left(\frac{1}{2}\right)^2 + (1)\left(\frac{1}{2}\right)^3 + \cdots = \frac{1/2}{1 - 1/2} = 1.$$

Thus $\mu = 2$. Incidentally, it is interesting to observe that $\mu = 2$ is the weighted average of the infinite set of numbers 1, 2, 3, 4, ... Clearly, the weight associated with a large value of x, such as 1000, must be small; it is, as $f(1000) = (1/2)^{1000}$.   ■

A (sample) variance of a set of numbers with equal weights was also defined in Chapter 1. Here we define the *variance of X* (or the variance of the distribution of X) as the weighted average of $(X - \mu)^2$, that is,

$$\sigma^2 = E[(X - \mu)^2] = \sum_{x \in R} (x - \mu)^2 f(x),$$

where σ is the Greek lowercase letter sigma. Sometimes we use the expression $\text{var}(X) = \sigma^2$. Since $f(x) \geq 0$, the variance is nonnegative. The positive square root of the variance is called the *standard deviation* of X:

$$\sigma = \sqrt{\text{var}(X)} = \sqrt{E[(X - \mu)^2]}.$$

The standard deviation σ is expressed in the same units as the random variable X. Since $(X - \mu)^2$ equals σ^2 *on the average*, we can think of the standard deviation σ as the *approximate* average distance from several outcomes of the random variable X to the mean μ.

There is another way of computing the variance. We have

$$\sigma^2 = E[(X - \mu)^2] = E[X^2 - 2\mu X + \mu^2].$$

However, since the expectation is a linear operation and $E(\mu^2) = \mu^2$, we obtain

$$\sigma^2 = E(X^2) - 2\mu E(X) + \mu^2 = E(X^2) - 2\mu^2 + \mu^2 = E(X^2) - \mu^2.$$

Thus $\sigma^2 = E(X^2) - \mu^2$ and the standard deviation equals

$$\sigma = \sqrt{E(X^2) - \mu^2}.$$

Example 2.3-5   Let X have a p.d.f. given by

x	1	2	3	4
$f(x)$	0.4	0.2	0.3	0.1

Hence

$$\mu = E(X) = (1)(0.4) + (2)(0.2) + (3)(0.3) + (4)(0.1) = 2.1,$$

$$E(X^2) = 1^2(0.4) + 2^2(0.2) + 3^2(0.3) + 4^2(0.1) = 5.5,$$

$$\sigma^2 = E(X^2) - \mu^2 = 5.5 - 4.41 = 1.09,$$

and

$$\sigma = \sqrt{1.09} = 1.044.$$ ■

We determine the mean μ and the standard deviation σ for each of two important discrete distributions in the next two sections. Those who have studied mechanics recognize the mean μ as the centroid of a system of weights given by $f(x)$, while σ is the radius of gyration. It is also helpful here to note for later consideration that if $Y = cX$, where c is a constant, then

$$\mu_Y = E(Y) = E(cX) = cE(X) = c\mu_X,$$

$$\sigma_Y^2 = E[(Y - \mu_Y)^2] = E[(cX - c\mu_X)^2] = c^2 E[(X - \mu_X)^2] = c^2 \sigma_X^2,$$

and

$$\sigma_Y = |c|\sigma_X.$$

For example, if Y is in inches and X is the same measurement in feet, so that $Y = 12X$, then $\mu_Y = 12\mu_X$, $\sigma_Y^2 = 144\sigma_X^2$, and $\sigma_Y = 12\sigma_X$.

Exercises 2.3

2.3-1 Let the p.d.f. of X be defined by $f(x) = x/10$, $x = 1$, 2, 3, 4. Determine **(a)** $P(X \le 2)$, **(b)** $P(2 \le X \le 4)$, **(c)** $\mu = E(X)$, and **(d)** $\sigma^2 = E[(X - \mu)^2]$.

2.3-2 For each of the following, determine the constant c so that $f(x)$ enjoys the properties of a p.d.f.
(a) $f(x) = cx$, $x = 1, 2, \ldots, 25$.
(b) $f(x) = c(x + 1)^3$, $x = 0, 1, 2$.
(c) $f(x) = c(1/3)^x$, $x = 1, 2, 3, \ldots$.

2.3-3 Let X have the p.d.f. $f(x) = (1/6)(5/6)^{x-1}$, $x = 1, 2, 3, \ldots$.
(a) Show that $f(x)$ is a valid p.d.f.
(b) Determine $F(x) = P(X \le x)$, $x = 1, 2, 3, \ldots$.
(c) Compute $P(4 \le X \le 7)$.
(d) Evaluate $\mu = E(X)$.

2.3-4 Suppose that the probability density function $f(x)$ of the length X of an international telephone call, to the nearest minute, is given by

x	1	2	3	4
$f(x)$	0.2	0.5	0.2	0.1

(a) Calculate $P(X \le 2)$, $P(X < 2)$, and $P(X \ge 1)$.
(b) Calculate and plot the cumulative distribution function $F(x)$ against x. Note that this is a step function; at each $x = 1, 2, 3, 4$ the function will jump to a new level. The height of the step at x is $f(x)$.
(c) Calculate the mean $\mu = E(X)$.
(d) Calculate $E(X^2)$ and use this to determine the variance, $\sigma^2 = E(X^2) - [E(X)]^2$.

(e) Calculate the variance using the formula $\sigma^2 = E[(X - \mu)^2]$, and show that it is the same as that found in part (d).

2.3-5 The yearly number X of large contracts that are awarded to a company is a random variable with p.d.f.

x	0	1	2	3
$f(x)$	0.2	0.4	0.3	0.1

Calculate the mean, variance, and standard deviation of this distribution.

2.3-6 Let X have the p.d.f. $f(x) = x^2/30$, $x = 1, 2, 3, 4$. Suppose that a game has payoff $u(X) = (4 - X)^3$. Compute the expected value of the payoff, $E[(4 - X)^3]$.

2.3-7 Using the definition of the mathematical expectation, show that

$$E\left[\sum_{i=1}^{k} c_i u_i(X)\right] = \sum_{i=1}^{k} c_i E[u_i(X)],$$

where $c_1, c_2, \ldots, c_k$ are constants.
Hint   Write

$$E\left[\sum_{i=1}^{k} c_i u_i(X)\right] = \sum_{x \in R}\left[\sum_{i=1}^{k} c_i u_i(x)\right] f(x)$$

$$= \sum_{i=1}^{k} \sum_{x \in R} c_i u_i(x) f(x)$$

after interchanging the order of summation.

2.3-8 With the random variable X of Example 2.3-1, argue that the random variable $Y = X^2$ has the p.d.f. $g(y)$ given by

y	0	1	4	9
$g(y)$	1/8	3/8	3/8	1/8

(a) Evaluate $E(Y) = \sum_{y \in R_1} yg(y)$, where $R_1 = \{0, 1, 4, 9\}$.

(b) Evaluate $E(X^2) = \sum_{x \in R} x^2 f(x)$, where $f(x)$ and R are described in Example 2.3-1.

(c) Note from parts (a) and (b) that

$$\sum_{y \in R_1} yg(y) = \sum_{x \in R} x^2 f(x).$$

More generally, if $Y = u(X)$, then

$$E(Y) = \sum_{x \in R} u(x)f(x) = \sum_{y \in R_1} yg(y),$$

where $g(y)$ is the p.d.f. of $Y = u(X)$ with space R_1.

2.3-9 Let X have the p.d.f. $f(x) = x^3/36$, $x = 1, 2, 3$.

(a) Show that $Y = X^3$ has p.d.f. $g(y) = y/36$, $y = 1, 8, 27$.

(b) Evaluate the two summations

$$\sum_{x=1}^{3} x^3 f(x) \quad \text{and} \quad \sum_{y \in R_1} yg(y),$$

where

$$R_1 = \{1, 8, 27\}.$$

2.4   The Binomial and Related Distributions

2.4-1   Bernoulli Trials

Consider a random experiment, the outcome of which can be classified in one of two mutually exclusive and exhaustive ways. We frequently call these two ways *success* and *failure*, but these words could stand for *heads* and *tails*, *female* and *male*, *death* and *life*, *defective* and *nondefective*, and so on. If this random experiment is repeated a number of times so that:

1. The outcomes of these trials are mutually independent, and
2. The probability p of success is the same in each trial,

this sequence of trials is called a sequence of *Bernoulli trials*.

Let X be a random variable associated with one Bernoulli trial in such a way that $X = 1$ represents success and $X = 0$ represents failure. Since

$$P(X = 1) = p \quad \text{and} \quad P(X = 0) = 1 - p = q,$$

we can write the p.d.f. of X as

$$f(x) = P(X = x) = p^x(1 - p)^{1-x} = p^x q^{1-x}, \quad x = 0, 1.$$

The mean and the variance of X are, respectively,

$$\mu = (0)(1 - p) + (1)(p) = p$$

and

$$\sigma^2 = E(X^2) - p^2 = [(0)^2(1 - p) + (1)^2(p)] - p^2 = p(1 - p) = pq.$$

Let X_i be the random variable associated with the ith Bernoulli trial, $i = 1, 2, \ldots, n$. Thus each X_i has the same p.d.f., mean, and variance, namely,

$$f(x) = p^x q^{1-x}, \qquad x = 0, 1; \quad \mu = p; \quad \sigma^2 = pq.$$

The fact that the outcomes of the n trials are mutually independent means that all events like

$$X_1 = 1, \quad X_2 = 0, \quad X_3 = 0, \quad \ldots, \quad X_{n-1} = 1, \quad X_n = 0$$

are mutually independent (see Section 2.2), and thus we call $X_1, X_2, \ldots, X_n$ *mutually independent random variables.* In general, a collection of n mutually independent random variables, each having the same distribution, is called a *random sample.*

The probability of getting a particular sequence of successes and failures is easily calculated because of the independence. If $n = 5$, the probability of the sequence (success, success, failure, success, failure) is

$$P(X_1 = 1, X_2 = 1, X_3 = 0, X_4 = 1, X_5 = 0) = ppqpq = p^3 q^2.$$

More generally, if x_i equals zero or 1, $i = 1, 2, \ldots, n$, then from the independence we have

$$P(X_1 = x_1, X_2 = x_2, \ldots, X_n = x_n)$$
$$= f(x_1)f(x_2) \cdots f(x_n)$$
$$= p^{x_1}(1-p)^{1-x_1} p^{x_2}(1-p)^{1-x_2} \cdots p^{x_n}(1-p)^{1-x_n}$$
$$= p^{\Sigma x_i}(1-p)^{n-\Sigma x_i} = p^y(1-p)^{n-y} = p^y q^{n-y}$$

where $y = \sum_{i=1}^{n} x_i$ is the number of 1's (successes) among $x_1, x_2, \ldots, x_n$. This agrees with our result when $n = 5$ and the number of successes is $y = 3$.

In practice the common probability, p, associated with the Bernoulli trials is usually unknown. For example, we often do not know the exact probability p of producing a defective part in a certain manufacturing process. How, then, can we estimate p once the random sample is observed to be $x_1, x_2, \ldots, x_n$, where each x_i is equal to zero or 1? The intuitive answer to this question is to take the relative frequency of defectives $\hat{p} = \sum_{i=1}^{n} x_i/n$. The numerator $\sum_{i=1}^{n} x_i$ is the number of defectives; the "hat" above p indicates that we have an estimate of p.

2.4-2   The Binomial Distribution

Since $Y = \sum_{i=1}^{n} X_i$, the number of successes in n Bernoulli trials, is an important statistic in estimating p, we should learn more about its distribution. Clearly, the space of Y is $R = \{0, 1, 2, \ldots, n\}$. If exactly y successes occur, where $y = 0, 1, 2, \ldots, n$, there must be $n - y$ failures. Since the trials are independent, the probability of one such sequence is $p^y(1 - p)^{n-y}$. There are, however,

$$\binom{n}{y} = \frac{n!}{y!(n-y)!}$$

ways in which exactly y *ones* can be assigned to y of the variables $X_1, X_2, \ldots, X_n$. Thus $g(y) = P(Y = y)$ is the sum of the probabilities of these $\binom{n}{y}$ mutually exclusive events, each with probability $p^y(1 - p)^{n-y}$. That is,

$$g(y) = \binom{n}{y} p^y (1 - p)^{n-y}, \qquad y = 0, 1, 2, \ldots, n.$$

This is the p.d.f. of the *binomial distribution* with *parameters n* and *p*. This p.d.f. is often abbreviated as $b(n, p)$. It is called a binomial distribution because these $n + 1$ probabilities given by $g(y)$, $y = 0, 1, 2, \ldots, n$, are equal to the respective $n + 1$ terms in the expansion of a certain binomial raised to the nth power, namely,

$$1 = [(1 - p) + p]^n = \sum_{y=0}^{n} \binom{n}{y} p^y (1 - p)^{n-y}.$$

Incidentally, this equation shows that the binomial probabilities, $g(y)$, $y = 0, 1, 2, \ldots, n$, sum to 1.

We find the mean of Y by considering

$$\mu = E(Y) = \sum_{y=0}^{n} y \frac{n!}{y!(n-y)!} p^y (1 - p)^{n-y}$$

$$= \sum_{y=1}^{n} \frac{n!}{(y-1)!(n-y)!} p^y (1 - p)^{n-y}$$

because $y/y! = 1/(y - 1)!$ when $y = 1, 2, \ldots, n$. We rewrite this as follows:

$$\mu = (np) \sum_{y=1}^{n} \frac{(n-1)!}{(y-1)!(n-y)!} p^{y-1} (1 - p)^{n-y}$$

$$= (np)[(1 - p)^{n-1} + (n - 1)p(1 - p)^{n-2} + \cdots + p^{n-1}]$$

$$= (np)[(1 - p) + p]^{n-1} = np.$$

That is, $\mu = E(Y) = np$ is the mean of the number of successes in n Bernoulli trials, each with probability p of success. For illustration, if $n = 100$ and $p = 1/4$, the mean is $np = (100)(1/4) = 25$. We expect 25 successes, a result that agrees with our intuition.

The variance of Y is found by noting that

$$E(Y^2) = E[Y(Y - 1)] + E(Y).$$

It can be shown (Exercise 2.4-5) that $E[Y(Y - 1)] = n(n - 1)p^2$; thus

$$\sigma^2 = \text{var}(Y) = E(Y^2) - (np)^2$$

$$= n(n - 1)p^2 + np - (np)^2 = np(1 - p).$$

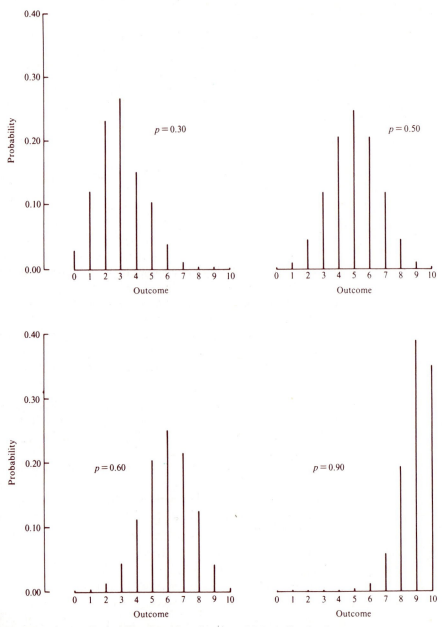

FIGURE 2.4-1   Probability densities of various $b(10, p)$ distributions.

Thus we have demonstrated that if Y is $b(n, p)$, then

$$E(Y) = np \quad \text{and} \quad \text{var}(Y) = E[(Y - np)^2] = np(1 - p).$$

With these expectations it is easy to find the mean and the variance of the estimator, $\hat{p} = Y/n$, of p. The mean of $\hat{p}$ is

$$E(\hat{p}) = E\left(\frac{Y}{n}\right) = \left(\frac{1}{n}\right)E(Y) = \frac{1}{n}(np) = p,$$

and $\text{var}(\hat{p})$ equals

$$E[(\hat{p} - p)^2] = E\left[\left(\frac{Y}{n} - p\right)^2\right] = \frac{1}{n^2} E[(Y - np)^2]$$

$$= \frac{1}{n^2} [np(1 - p)] = \frac{p(1 - p)}{n}.$$

Remark Here we call $\hat{p} = Y/n$ an *estimator* of the parameter p. Say that we actually performed the experiment n independent times and observed y successes; that is, here y is a known number. For illustration, suppose that $n = 50$ and $y = 17$. Then we call $y/n = 17/50 = 0.34$ an *estimate* of p. That is, the random variable, Y/n, is an estimator of p *before* performing the experiment; but *after* the experiment results in a given number of successes, say y, the known value, y/n is called an estimate of p. In general, an estimator is a random variable and an estimate is an observation of that random variable. ∎

The fact that the c.d.f. $F(y) = P(Y \le y)$ of the binomial distribution is tabled for $p = 0.05, 0.10, \ldots, 0.50$ when $n \le 20$ (Table C.2) helps in the computation of binomial probabilities. Incidentally, if $p = 0.55, 0.60, \ldots, 0.95$, we simply redefine success as failure and failure as success to obtain a value of p of less than 0.50. That is, if $W = n - Y$ is the number of failures, then W is $b(n, 1 - p)$. For illustration, if Y is binomial with $n = 10$ and $p = 0.6$, then $P(Y = 1, 2, 3) = P(W = 7, 8, 9)$, where W is $b(10, 0.4)$. This binomial p.d.f., together with those associated with $n = 10$ and $p = 0.3, 0.5$, and 0.9, is given in Figure 2.4-1.

Example 2.4-1 Let Y be $b(n = 14, p = 0.15)$. Then

$$P(Y = 3, 4, 5) = \sum_{y=3}^{5} \binom{14}{y}(0.15)^y(0.85)^{14-y}$$

$$= P(Y \le 5) - P(Y \le 2) = F(5) - F(2)$$

$$= 0.9885 - 0.6479 = 0.3406.$$ ∎

Example 2.4-2   Let Y be $b(n = 8, p = 0.75)$ so that $E(Y) = (8)(0.75) = 6$ and var$(Y) = 8(0.75)(0.25) = 1.5$. To find $P(Y = 6, 7)$, let $W = 8 - Y$ equal the number of failures in the eight Bernoulli trials so that W is $b(8, 0.25)$. That is,

$$P(Y = 6, 7) = P(W = 1, 2) = F(2) - F(0) = 0.6785 - 0.1001 = 0.5784. \quad \blacksquare$$

Example 2.4-3   The probability that a certain type of transformer fails in the first 10 years of operation is $p = 0.05$. If we observe $n = 20$ such transformers and if we can assume independence, we know that the number, Y, of transformers failing in the first 10 years is $b(n = 20, p = 0.05)$. Therefore, $E(Y) = (20)(0.05) = 1$ is the expected number that fail in those 10 years. The probability that between one and four transformers (inclusive) fail is

$$P(Y = 1, 2, 3, 4) = \sum_{y=1}^{4} \binom{20}{y}(0.05)^y(0.95)^{20-y}$$

and can be found from Table C.2. It is equal to

$$P(Y \leq 4) - P(Y \leq 0) = 0.9974 - 0.3585 = 0.6389. \quad \blacksquare$$

Remarks   Independence is important here. Independence, intuitively, means that the status of one transformer does not depend on the status of another. Independence, for example, would probably not be present if the transformers are taken sequentially from the production line and if we believe that there is some carryover in the production of consecutive items.

The application of the binomial distribution also requires that the probability of failure is the same for all transformers. Suppose that you take the 20 transformers from two groups: say, a certain fraction from lots that come from machine A and the rest from lots that were produced by machine B. If there is reason to believe that these two machines produce transformers of different quality, it would be inappropriate to combine them into one group. This would certainly violate the assumption that the probabilities of failure are the same. In most cases, however, violation of the independence assumption causes a greater change in the distribution of Y than do slight changes of p from trial to trial. $\quad \blacksquare$

*2.4-3   The Negative Binomial Distribution

Let us consider the problem of observing a sequence of Bernoulli trials until exactly r successes occur, where r is a fixed positive integer. Let the random variable Z denote the number of trials needed to observe the rth success. Of course, the space of Z is $R = \{r, r + 1, r + 2, \ldots\}$, the collection of an infinite, but countable, number of values. If z is an element of R, the event $Z = z$ occurs when there are exactly $r - 1$ successes in the first $z - 1$ trials followed by a success on the zth trial. Since the latter two events are independent, we obtain $P(Z = z)$ by multiplying their probabilities. That is, the p.d.f. of Z is

$$h(z) = P(Z = z) = \left[\binom{z-1}{r-1} p^{r-1}(1-p)^{z-r}\right](p)$$

$$= \binom{z-1}{r-1} p^r (1-p)^{z-r} \qquad \text{for } z = r, r+1, r+2, \dots .$$

We say that Z has a *negative binomial distribution* with parameters r and p.

Example 2.4-4   A process is continued until the first defective is produced. Assume that the trials are independent (which may not always be a good assumption in practice). If the process produces $p = 0.05$ defectives, the probability that the first defective appears on the fifth trial is

$$P(Z = 5) = \binom{4}{0}(0.05)(0.95)^4 = 0.0407.$$

The probability that the first defective occurs on or before the fifth trial is

$$P(Z \le 5) = \sum_{z=1}^{5} \binom{z-1}{0}(0.05)(0.95)^{z-1} = 0.2262. \qquad \blacksquare$$

*2.4-4   The Hypergeometric Distribution

Consider a collection of $N = N_1 + N_2$ objects, N_1 of them belonging to one of two distinct classes (say, defective items) and N_2 of them to the other (say, good items). Take n of these objects at random and *without replacement* from these N objects. We wish to find the probability that exactly w of these n sampled objects belong to the first class (i.e., are defective). Here w is a non-negative integer satisfying the inequalities $w \le n$, $w \le N_1$, and $n - w \le N_2$. Of course, if $n \le N_1$ and $n \le N_2$, then the space of W, the number of items in the first class, is $R = \{0, 1, 2, \dots, n\}$. The p.d.f. of W is

$$k(w) = P(W = w) = \frac{\dbinom{N_1}{w}\dbinom{N_2}{n-w}}{\dbinom{N_1 + N_2}{n}}, \qquad w = 0, 1, \dots, n,$$

and it is said to be the p.d.f. of a *hypergeometric distribution*.

The hypergeometric and the binomial distribution are closely related. Their difference lies in the adopted sampling scheme. The binomial distribution assumes independent trials and constant success probabilities. It assumes a sampling scheme *with replacement* so that trials are independent and the probability of success is constant across trials. In the hypergeometric distribution, on the other hand, the trials are no longer independent. Because sampling is *without replacement*, the probability of success at the ith trial depends on the outcomes of the previous ones.

However, if N_1 and N_2 are large compared to n, the hypergeometric distribution can be approximated by the binomial. This is intuitive, as in this case the probability of a success does not change much from one trial to the next and is close to $p = N_1/(N_1 + N_2)$.

This approximation can also be shown formally. To see this, write $k(w)$ as

$$k(w) = \frac{\dfrac{N_1!}{w!\,(N_1 - w)!}\,\dfrac{N_2!}{(n - w)!\,(N_2 - n + w)!}}{\dfrac{(N_1 + N_2)!}{n!\,(N_1 + N_2 - n)!}}$$

$$= \frac{n!}{w!\,(n - w)!}$$

$$\times \frac{[N_1(N_1 - 1)\cdots(N_1 - w + 1)][N_2(N_2 - 1)\cdots(N_2 - n + w + 1)]}{(N_1 + N_2)(N_1 + N_2 - 1)\cdots(N_1 + N_2 - n + 1)}$$

$$\approx \binom{n}{w}p^w q^{n-w} = \binom{n}{w}p^w(1 - p)^{n-w},$$

where $p = N_1/(N_1 + N_2)$ and $q = 1 - p = N_2/(N_1 + N_2)$. This approximation is valid, as the expression above for $k(w)$ includes w factors of the form $(N_1 - r_1)/(N_1 + N_2 - r_2) \approx p$ and $n - w$ factors of the form $(N_2 - r_3)/(N_1 + N_2 - r_4) \approx q$, where the integers r_1, r_2, r_3, and r_4 are small relative to N_1 and N_2.

Example 2.4-5   A lot of 1000 items consists of $N_1 = 100$ defective and $N_2 = 900$ good items. A sample of $n = 20$ items is taken at random and without replacement from this lot. The probability that the sample contains two or less defective items is

$$P(W \leq 2) = \sum_{w=0}^{2} k(w) = \sum_{w=0}^{2} \frac{\dbinom{100}{w}\dbinom{900}{20 - w}}{\dbinom{1000}{20}} = 0.6772.$$

This can be closely approximated using a binomial distribution $b(n = 20,$ $p = 100/1000 = 0.1)$; that is,

$$P(W \le 2) \approx \sum_{w=0}^{2} \binom{20}{w}(0.1)^w(0.9)^{20-w} = 0.6769.$$ ■

Exercises 2.4

2.4-1 The probability of producing a defective item is 0.02.
(a) What is the probability that out of 10 items that are selected independently none is defective?
(b) How many defective items do you expect in a sample of 100 items?

2.4-2 The university football team has 11 games on its schedule. Assume that the probability of winning each game is 0.40 and that there are no ties. Assuming independence (which may not be a good assumption here because there are streaks of wins and losses), calculate the probability that this year's team will have a winning season (i.e., wins at least six games).

2.4-3 The probability of producing a high-quality color print is 0.10. How many prints do we have to produce such that the probability of producing at least one quality print is larger than 0.90?

2.4-4 A roofing contractor offers an inexpensive method to fix leaky roofs. However, this is no fool-proof method, as he estimates that after the job is done, 10 percent of the roofs will still leak.
(a) The resident manager of an apartment complex hires this contractor to fix the roofs on six buildings. What is the probability that after the work has been done, at least two of these roofs will still leak?
(b) The contractor offers a guarantee that pays $100 if a roof still leaks after he has worked on it. If he works on 81 roofs, find the mean and standard deviation of the amount of money that he will have to pay as a result of this guarantee.

2.4-5 If Y follows a $b(n, p)$ distribution, show that $E[Y(Y - 1)] = n(n - 1)p^2$.

Hint   Write

$$E[Y(Y - 1)] = \sum_{y=0}^{n} y(y - 1) \frac{n!}{y!(n - y)!} p^y(1 - p)^{n-y}$$

$$= \sum_{y=2}^{n} y(y - 1) \frac{n!}{y!(n - y)!} p^y(1 - p)^{n-y}$$

because the $y = 0$ and $y = 1$ terms equal zero. Use $y(y - 1)/y! = 1/(y - 2)!$ when $y \ge 2$. Factor out $n(n - 1)p^2$ and note that the remaining summation equals $[(1 - p) + p]^{n-2} = 1$.

2.4-6 If a student answers questions on a true-false test randomly (i.e., assume that $p = 0.5$) and independently, determine the probability that
(a) the first correct answer is that of question 4,
(b) at most four questions must be answered to get the first correct answer.

2.4-7 The probability that a machine produces a defective item is $p = 0.05$. Each item is checked as it is produced. Assuming independence among items, compute the probability that the third defective item is found **(a)** on the 20th trial, and **(b)** on or before the 20th trial.

2.4-8 Of 10 fish in a pond, four of them are tagged. If $n = 3$ fish are caught at random and not replaced, what is the probability that **(a)** two of the three are tagged, and **(b)** two or less are tagged?

2.4-9 Suppose that there are 100 defectives in a lot of 2000 items. If a sample of size $n = 10$ is taken at random and without replacement,
(a) Determine the probability that there are two or less defectives in the sample.

(b) Approximate the probability in part (a) using the binomial distribution.

2.4-10 Assume that the probability of a male birth is 0.5, and that the binomial distribution is applicable. What is the probability that a couple with (a) three, [(b) five] children has at least two boys? (c) What are the corresponding probabilities if the probability of a male birth is 0.53?

2.4-11 Electric switches are shipped in packages of eight items. The probability that an item is defective is 0.1. What is the probability that a package contains (a) at least one defective switch, and (b) less than two defective switches? Apply the binomial dis-

tribution. (c) Calculate the expected number of defectives in a package.

2.4-12 A customer is supplied with four randomly selected packages (see Exercise 2.4-11). What is the probability that (a) each package contains at least one defective, and (b) at least one package contains less than two defectives?

2.4-13 Assume that the probability for a switch to be defective (see Exercise 2.4-11) has been reduced to 0.05. What are now the probabilities for parts (a) and (b) in Exercise 2.4-12? What are the probabilities of having (c) at least 3 [(d) less than 5] defectives in a single package of 40 items?

2.5 Poisson Distribution and Poisson Process

2.5-1   The Poisson Distribution

A binomial probability can be approximated by another important probability when the number of trials, n, is large and the probability of success, p, is small. To find this approximating probability distribution, we investigate the limit of a binomial probability when $n \to \infty$ and $p \to 0$ such that $np = \lambda$, where the Greek lowercase letter lambda represents a positive constant. Replacing p by λ/n and keeping y fixed, we have

$$\lim_{n \to \infty} P(Y = y) = \lim_{n \to \infty} \left[\frac{n!}{y!\,(n-y)!} \left(\frac{\lambda}{n}\right)^y \left(1 - \frac{\lambda}{n}\right)^{n-y} \right]$$

$$= \lim_{n \to \infty} \left[\frac{n(n-1)\cdots(n-y+1)}{n^y} \left(\frac{\lambda^y}{y!}\right) \frac{(1-\lambda/n)^n}{(1-\lambda/n)^y} \right]$$

$$= \lim_{n \to \infty} \left[(1)\left(1 - \frac{1}{n}\right)\cdots\left(1 - \frac{y-1}{n}\right) \right] \left(\frac{\lambda^y}{y!}\right)\left[\frac{\lim_{n \to \infty}(1-\lambda/n)^n}{\lim_{n \to \infty}(1-\lambda/n)^y} \right]$$

$$= \frac{\lambda^y e^{-\lambda}}{y!},$$

since we know from calculus that

$$\lim_{n \to \infty} \left(1 - \frac{\lambda}{n}\right)^n = e^{-\lambda}$$

and since the limits of the other factors, other than $\lambda^y/y!$ (which does not depend upon n), equal 1. The space of y, which is $\{0, 1, 2, \ldots, n\}$ in the binomial distribution, now includes all nonnegative integers, $\{0, 1, 2, 3, \ldots\}$, in this limiting process.

We show that

$$h(y) = \frac{\lambda^y e^{-\lambda}}{y!}, \qquad y = 0, 1, 2, \ldots,$$

satisfies the properties of a p.d.f. Since $\lambda > 0$, it is clear that $h(y) \geq 0$. In addition,

$$\sum_{y=0}^{\infty} h(y) = \sum_{y=0}^{\infty} \frac{\lambda^y e^{-\lambda}}{y!}$$

$$= e^{-\lambda}\left(1 + \frac{\lambda}{1!} + \frac{\lambda^2}{2!} + \frac{\lambda^3}{3!} + \cdots\right).$$

However, the infinite sum in this last expression is the MacLaurin's expansion (special case of Taylor's expansion) of e^{λ}. Thus

$$\sum_{y=0}^{\infty} h(y) = e^{-\lambda}e^{\lambda} = 1.$$

So $h(y)$ satisfies the properties of a p.d.f. of a random variable of the discrete type. It is called a *Poisson p.d.f.* with parameter λ.

Since np is the mean of the binomial distribution, we suspect that the parameter λ is the mean of the Poisson distribution. We investigate this conjecture by evaluating

$$\mu = E(Y) = \sum_{y=0}^{\infty} y \frac{\lambda^y e^{-\lambda}}{y!}$$

$$= (0)e^{-\lambda} + (1)\frac{\lambda e^{-\lambda}}{1!} + (2)\frac{\lambda^2 e^{-\lambda}}{2!} + (3)\frac{\lambda^3 e^{-\lambda}}{3!} + \cdots$$

$$= e^{-\lambda}\left(\lambda + \frac{\lambda^2}{1!} + \frac{\lambda^3}{2!} + \cdots\right)$$

$$= (e^{-\lambda})(\lambda)\left(1 + \frac{\lambda}{1!} + \frac{\lambda^2}{2!} + \cdots\right) = (e^{-\lambda})(\lambda)(e^{\lambda}) = \lambda.$$

Thus the mean of the Poisson distribution is indeed λ, as we suspected.

The variance of the binomial distribution is $np(1 - p) = \lambda(1 - \lambda/n)$, which equals λ in the limit as $n \to \infty$. Could it be that λ is also the variance of the Poisson distribution? This is indeed the case, as shown below. Note that

$$E(Y^2) = E[Y(Y - 1)] + E(Y).$$

Since $E[Y(Y - 1)] = \lambda^2$ as demonstrated in Exercise 2.5-7, we have that

$$\sigma^2 = E(Y^2) - \lambda^2 = \lambda^2 + \lambda - \lambda^2 = \lambda.$$

Thus we observe that the Poisson distribution is one in which the mean and the variance are equal to a common value λ. This is a very important characteristic of the Poisson distribution.

The c.d.f. $F(y) = P(Y \le y)$ of the Poisson distribution is given in Table C.3 for various values of λ. This is useful in the calculation of certain probabilities.

Example 2.5-1   Let Y be the number of the $n = 20$ transformers of Example 2.4-3 that fail in the first 10 years. That is, Y is $b(n = 20, \ p = 0.05)$. Here $n = 20$ is not too large, but it is still interesting to see how various values of the binomial c.d.f., with $n = 20$, $p = 0.05$, compare with the Poisson c.d.f. with $\lambda = 20(0.05) = 1$ (see Table 2.5-1).

TABLE 2.5-1   Two Cumulative Distribution Functions $F(y) = P(Y \le y)$

y	Binomial c.d.f.	Poisson c.d.f.
0	0.3585	0.3679
1	0.7358	0.7358
2	0.9245	0.9197
3	0.9841	0.9810
4	0.9974	0.9963

Even with a small value of n such as 20, the approximation is quite good; it is extremely good with much larger values of n.

Example 2.5-2   Let Y be $b(n = 50, \ p = 0.96)$. Obviously, p is not small, but the Poisson approximation can still be used if the roles of *success* and *failure* are interchanged. That is, the number of failures $W = 50 - Y$ is $b(50, \ p = 0.04)$. Thus

$$P(Y = 46, 47, 48, 49, 50) = P(W = 0, 1, 2, 3, 4)$$

$$\approx F(4) = 0.947,$$

where $F(4)$ comes from Table C.3 with $\lambda = (50)(0.04) = 2$.

2.5-2   The Poisson Process

We have discovered that the Poisson distribution is a good approximation to the binomial distribution when n is large and p is small. However, the Poisson distribution is also an appropriate model for many other random phenomena. For illustrations, the number of flaws on a casting or the number of breakdowns of a certain machine in a given period of time may very well be random variables that have (at least approximate) Poisson distributions. To see this intuitively, consider the casting and divide its surface into n equal parts. Let n be large so that each part is small and not likely to have more than one flaw. If λ is the average number of flaws per casting and we have divided a casting into n equal parts, it is reasonable to assign to each part a probability of λ/n that there is one flaw. Moreover, since each part is so small, suppose that the probability of two or more flaws in it is zero. Since the probability of a flaw in a given part is λ/n, the probability of the part not having a flaw is $1 - \lambda/n$. If we can assume that the outcomes (either flaw or nonflaw in each part) are mutually independent with common probability λ/n of a flaw, we have, in essence, n Bernoulli trials. The probability of y defects in these n trials is

$$\frac{n!}{y!(n-y)!} \left(\frac{\lambda}{n}\right)^y \left(1 - \frac{\lambda}{n}\right)^{n-y}$$

However, we have proved that this expression approaches $h(y) = \lambda^y e^{-\lambda}/y!$ as $n \to \infty$.

Let us describe this more formally and let us consider the assumptions of a *Poisson process*. This process generates a number of "changes" (occurrences, accidents, flaws, claims, etc.) in a fixed "interval" (time, space, length, etc.). Suppose that the number of changes, Y, in a fixed interval satisfy the following assumptions:

1. The probability of exactly one change in a very short interval of length h is approximately proportional to h, that is, it equals λh, where λ is the constant of proportionality.

2. The probability of two or more changes in this short interval of length h is approximately equal to zero.

3. The numbers of changes in nonoverlapping intervals are mutually independent.

If we then count the number of changes, Y, in a fixed interval of length w, it can be shown that Y has a Poisson distribution with mean λw. In particular, if $w = 1$, the mean is λ. Note that in our example with $w = 1$ casting we assumed independence from part to part and assumed that the probability of exactly *one* flaw in one such part is proportional to λ, and the probability of more than one is zero. Before any model is used in practice, the assumptions must be checked to see if they are appropriate. *Certainly*, before using the Poisson model, one should assess whether the independence from part to part appears reasonable. Namely, is it a reasonable assumption that the quality of the casting is more or less uniform, or are there regions where the flaws occur in groups?

Example 2.5-3   Let the number, Y, of traffic deaths per week in a certain state have an approximate Poisson distribution with mean $\lambda = 7$. It is reasonable to assume a Poisson distribution in this case, as one can use either one of the following two justifications. There are many drivers (n large), and the probability of someone being involved in a fatal traffic accident is quite small (p small). Alternatively, we can use the results of the Poisson process to argue that the distribution of weekly traffic deaths is Poisson. The week can be divided into short periods, say hours. The probability of observing exactly one accident during such a short period should be proportional to the length of the period, and the probability of observing more than one should be negligible. Assuming, furthermore, that the accidents occur more or less independently would also lead us to the Poisson distribution.

For illustration, the probability of more than nine accidents is

$$P(Y \geq 10) = 1 - P(Y \leq 9)$$

$$= 1 - 0.830 = 0.170,$$

where $F(9) = 0.830$ from Table C.3 with $\lambda = 7$. The probability of exactly five weekly traffic deaths is

$$P(Y = 5) = P(Y \leq 5) - P(Y \leq 4) = F(5) - F(4)$$

$$= 0.301 - 0.173 = 0.128.$$ ■

Example 2.5-4   For 10,000 feet of a particular type of power-line wire, the number, Y, of failures per year has a Poisson distribution with $\lambda = 0.2$. The probability that there is more than one failure during the year is given by

$$P(Y > 1) = 1 - P(Y \leq 1) = 1 - 0.982 = 0.018,$$

from Table C.3.   ■

As with the parameter p of the binomial distribution, the parameter λ of a Poisson distribution is often unknown. Since λ is the mean of this distribution, it is reasonable to estimate it by observing several values of Y, say $Y_1, Y_2, \ldots, Y_n$, and determining the mean of these observations, say $\bar{Y}$. That is, $\hat{\lambda} = \bar{Y}$ is an estimator of the unknown quantity λ. Here, as with the estimator of the parameter p of a binomial, we use the "hat" above λ to denote an estimator.

As an example, assume that your company manufactures wood panels and that there are good reasons to believe that the number of flaws follow a Poisson distribution. But you do not know λ. To estimate it, you are planning to take a sample of, say, $n = 20$ panels. Before you actually look at the sampled items, the number of flaws, Y_i, is a random variable, $i = 1, 2, \ldots, 20$; it could be zero with probability $e^{-\lambda}$, 1 with probability $\lambda e^{-\lambda}$, and so on. Thus the estimator $\hat{\lambda} = \bar{Y} = \sum Y_i/20$ is a random variable and has a distribution with a certain mean and a certain variance (we will study such distributions in a later section). But once you have inspected the 20 panels and have determined the number of flaws, say,

2 4 1 0 0 3 2 1 5 3 0 1 1 0 4 3 2 2 1 0

you can calculate the average $\bar{y} = 35/20 = 1.75$ and take this number as an estimate of the unknown parameter λ in the Poisson distribution. For this to be a good estimate, we have to take a representative sample. Ideally, we would like a *random sample* from the population in which we are interested. If our interest is in today's production, we should give each item produced an equal chance of being in our sample; we should not simply go to machine 1, or worker *B*, or pile *H* and take all items from these groups. However, it may turn out that the average number of flaws, and thus the parameter λ in the Poisson distribution, are large. The next logical step would be to ask why. For example, is it because of machine 1, or worker *B*, or because of variability in the raw material? To learn more about that, one could take samples from each machine and compare their numbers of flaws. This brings us back to the techniques of Section 1.4, where we compared different samples.

Exercises 2.5

2.5-1   If the probability is 0.04 that a single item is defective, what are the probabilities that a sample of 100 will contain **(a)** exactly zero defectives, **(b)** exactly four defectives, and **(c)** more than five defectives? Use the Poisson approximation.

2.5-2   On the average, 2.5 telephone calls per minute are received at a corporation's switchboard. Making appropriate assumptions about the distribution (provide justification), find the probability that in any given minute there will be more than two calls.

2.5-3   A telephone switchboard receives on average 300 calls an hour but can make only 10 connections during any given minute. Determine the probability that the switchboard cannot handle all incoming calls in a given minute.

Hint   Assume that the number of incoming calls per minute follows a Poisson distribution with parameter $\lambda = 300/60 = 5$.

2.5-4   The daily number of plant shutdowns follows a Poisson distribution with mean 2.0. What is the probability that there are **(a)** more than three shutdowns in a day, and **(b)** at least one in a day? **(c)** Assume that the company loses $1000 on each shutdown. Calculate the expected daily loss.

2.5-5   Suppose that in one year the number of industrial accidents *X* follows a Poisson distribution with mean 3.0. If each accident leads to an insurance claim of $5000, how much money would an insurance company need to keep in reserve to be 95 percent certain that the claims are covered?

2.5-6   Bortkiewicz (1898; Das Gesetz der kleinen Zahlen) collected data on the number of horsemen, *Y*, that were killed by kicks from horses in each of 10 Prussian cavalry regiments. Data for 20 years (thus in total 200 observations) are as follows:

Number of Fatalities	Observed Frequency
0	109
1	65
2	22
3	3
4	1
5	0

Assume that the data come from a Poisson distribution. Note that this makes sense, since those fatalities are very rare events. Calculate an estimate of the parameter λ. Using this estimate, calculate the probabilities and expected frequencies of $Y = 0, 1, 2, 3, 4$ and ≥ 5, and compare them with the observed frequencies. Comment on the "fit."

2.5-7   Show that for the Poisson distribution,

$$E[Y(Y-1)] = \lambda^2.$$

Hint   Note that

$$E[Y(Y-1)] = \sum_{y=0}^{\infty} y(y-1) \frac{\lambda^y e^{-\lambda}}{y!} = \sum_{y=2}^{\infty} \frac{\lambda^y e^{-\lambda}}{(y-2)!}$$

and factor λ^2 out of the last summation.

2.5-8   A furniture factory found that the number of reclamations concerning wood delivered by a certain supplier was on average six per year. What is the probability of having no reclamation in **(a)** all of next year, and **(b)** the next quarter?

3 Continuous Probability Models

In Chapter 2 we have considered only random variables of the discrete type; for example, the binomial random variable can take only one of the values 0, 1, 2, ..., n, and the Poisson random variable must equal a non-negative integer. We recognize, however, that many random variables, such as weight of an item, tear strength of a paper, and length of life of a motor, can assume any value in certain intervals. These random variables are said to be of the *continuous type* because their realizations fall in a given continuum, which is usually an interval.

3.1-1 Empirical Distributions

Let us suppose that we have a random sample from a distribution of either the discrete or continuous type. Before the sample is drawn, the future observations, $X_1, X_2, ..., X_n$, are treated as mutually independent random variables, each coming from the same underlying distribution. Once the sample is observed, the resulting observations are denoted by the lowercase letters x_1, $x_2, ..., x_n$, respectively. If we now assign a weight of $1/n$ to each of these n observations, we have in effect created a distribution of the discrete type because the weights are nonnegative and sum to 1. This distribution is called the *empirical distribution*.

We can find the mean and the variance of this empirical distribution according to the same procedure that we use with any other discrete distribution. Since each value x_i has the "probability" (weight) $1/n$, we find that the mean and the variance are, respectively,

$$\sum_{i=1}^{n} x_i \left(\frac{1}{n}\right) = \frac{1}{n} \sum_{i=1}^{n} x_i = \bar{x}$$

and

$$\sum_{i=1}^{n} (x_i - \bar{x})^2 \left(\frac{1}{n}\right) = \frac{1}{n} \sum_{i=1}^{n} (x_i - \bar{x})^2 = \frac{1}{n} \sum_{i=1}^{n} x_i^2 - \bar{x}^2 = v.$$

We note that the mean of the empirical distribution and the sample mean are the same, $\bar{x}$. Moreover, the variance, v, of the empirical distribution and the sample variance, s^2, are related by the expression $v = (n-1)s^2/n$; thus they are almost equal for large, or moderately large, n.

The empirical distribution can help us model the underlying distribution from which the sample is taken. To illustrate this, let us refer to the compressive strengths of $n = 90$ concrete blocks given in Section 1.2. There we described the variability of these measurements with a histogram. In the histogram in Figure 1.2-1(b), the height above each class is either the frequency of the class, say f_i, or the relative frequency f_i/n. Now let us go one step further and let us choose the height of the bar such that the *area* associated with that class is equal to the relative frequency, f_i/n. Since the length of each class interval in that example is 4 units, the heights become $f_i/4n$. Let us call the resulting histogram a *normalized relative frequency histogram* $h(x)$. It is called normalized because the area under this histogram is 1. It is clear that we can obtain the relative frequency of a number of classes simply by integrating $h(x)$ over those classes. For example, the relative frequency of the three classes from 48.0 to 60.0 is equal to

$$\int_{48}^{60} h(x)\, dx = 4 \cdot \frac{17}{(90)(4)} + 4 \cdot \frac{9}{(90)(4)} + 4 \cdot \frac{3}{(90)(4)} = \frac{29}{90}.$$

One might think that this procedure is quite complicated when it is much easier to sum the frequencies 17, 9, and 3 and divide by $n = 90$, obtaining 29/90. This more difficult scheme, however, leads to a generalization that proves very valuable when we have histograms with unequal class widths.

Say that the *class boundaries* for the k classes are

$$[c_0, c_1), [c_1, c_2), \ldots, [c_{k-1}, c_k).$$

We use this notation because we remember that the class intervals are closed on the left; that is, a value on a boundary point is assigned to the class that has this value as its lower boundary. The (normalized) *relative frequency histogram* is defined by

$$h(x) = \frac{f_i/n}{c_i - c_{i-1}} \qquad \text{for } c_{i-1} \leq x < c_i, \quad i = 1, 2, \ldots, k,$$

where n is the number of observations and f_i is the frequency of the class $[c_{i-1}, c_i)$. In this definition it is *not* necessary for the classes to be of equal length, and in some cases we can describe the distribution of the data better by making the class lengths unequal. Also note that the relative frequency of an interval $[a, b)$, where $c_0 \leq a < b \leq c_k$, can always be approximated by the integral

$$\int_a^b h(x)\, dx.$$

If $a < b$ are boundary points associated with the classes, this integral gives the exact relative frequency of the interval $[a, b)$. If either a or b is not a boundary point, the integral provides an approximation to the relative frequency of the interval $[a, b)$. Since relative frequency is an approximation to probability, this integral can be thought of as an approximation to the probability $P(a \leq X < b)$, where X is the random variable under consideration.

Example 3.1-1   In W. Nelson, *Applied Life Data Analysis* (New York: Wiley, 1982), we find $n = 19$ times to breakdown of an insulating fluid between electrodes recorded at the voltage of 34 kilovolts. These times (in minutes), already ordered from smallest to largest, are

0.19   0.78   0.96   1.31   2.78   3.16   4.15   4.67   4.85   6.50

7.35   8.01   8.29   12.06   31.75   32.52   33.91   36.71   72.89

Since with $n = 19$, $(5 - 0.5)/19 = 0.24$, $(10 - 0.5)/19 = 0.50$, and $(15 - 0.5)/19 = 0.76$, we have that $x_{(5)} = 2.78$, $x_{(10)} = 6.50$, and $x_{(15)} = 31.75$ equal the 24th, 50th, and 76th percentiles, respectively. Thus an approximate box-and-whisker diagram is as given in Figure 3.1-1. It clearly shows that these data are highly skewed to the right. A histogram with equal class intervals is inappropriate in this situation as many classes would be empty. There is clearly no unique way to construct a relative frequency histogram, and an engineer must use his or her judgment in the selection of the number k and the lengths of the class intervals. For example, with these data, we question whether we want to show a second smaller mode that seemingly appears around 33. We think not

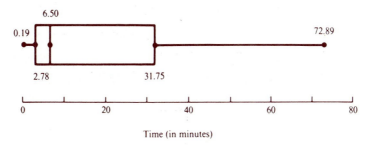

FIGURE 3.1-1   Box-and-whisker plot of breakdown times.

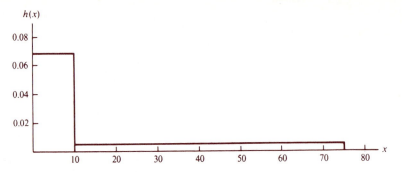

FIGURE 3.1-2   Relative frequency histogram of breakdown times.

because there is no apparent reason in this experiment for that second mode to appear, and thus we would rather smooth it out. As a matter of fact, we believe that these data can be described fairly well with only $k = 2$ classes, $[0, 10)$ and $[10, 75)$. However, other persons might disagree with our selection of

$$h(x) = \begin{cases} \dfrac{13/19}{10} = 0.0684, & 0 \le x < 10, \\[2ex] \dfrac{6/19}{65} = 0.0049, & 10 \le x < 75. \end{cases}$$

We feel, however, that $h(x)$, as depicted in Figure 3.1-2, is a relatively smooth, yet accurate description of the situation. Better than other relative frequency histograms, it suggests an underlying model, described by some $f(x)$. We could be wrong, however, and we ask (Exercise 3.1-1) readers to find other relative frequency histograms that, in their opinion, achieve a better balance between smoothness and providing an accurate description of these data. In any case, make certain that the total area under $h(x)$ is equal to 1; in our case, it is

$$\int_0^{75} h(x)\, dx = (10)\left(\frac{13/19}{10}\right) + (65)\left(\frac{6/19}{65}\right) = \frac{13}{19} + \frac{6}{19} = 1. \qquad \blacksquare$$

3.1-2   Distribution of Continuous Random Variables

In order to describe the variability of a continuous random variable X, we must find a *probability density function* $f(x)$ that gives us the probabilities $P(a \le X < b)$ through the integral

$$P(a \le X < b) = \int_a^b f(x)\, dx.$$

That is, the probability $P(a \le X < b)$ is the area between the graph of $f(x)$, the x axis, and the vertical lines $x = a$ and $x = b$, as depicted in Figure 3.1-3. In

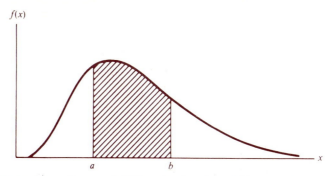

FIGURE 3.1-3 Plot of a probability density $f(x)$. The shaded area represents $P(a \leq X < b)$.

some sense, $f(x)$ is the limit of the normalized relative frequency histogram $h(x)$ as n increases and the lengths of the class intervals go to zero.

Since areas, such as $P(a \leq X < b)$ for all $a < b$, represent probabilities, we require that the total area between the graph of $f(x)$ and the x axis be equal to 1. That is,

$$\int_R f(x)\, dx = 1,$$

where the integral is taken over R, the outcome space of the random variable X. Moreover, since probabilities are nonnegative, we also need that

$$f(x) \geq 0, \qquad x \in R.$$

Then, if A is a subset of R, the probability of the event $\{X \in A\}$ is given by

$$P(X \in A) = \int_A f(x)\, dx.$$

It is interesting to observe that if A consists of a single point, say $x = b$, then

$$P(X = b) = \int_b^b f(x)\, dx = 0,$$

because the integral over a single point is equal to zero. This agrees with our intuition because if the space R is really an interval with an uncountable infinity of points, the probability of one particular point is certainly zero. Of course, in practice, we usually record an observation only to so many decimal points (for illustration, three, and thus the number $\sqrt{2}$ is recorded as 1.414). This "rounding" really forces us back into a discrete situation where we have a finite, but very large, number of possible outcomes. Nevertheless, it is often more convenient to approximate their probabilities by an appropriate continuous probability model. So in a practical situation, we look for a p.d.f. $f(x)$ from which we can compute the probabilities, at least approximately. Let us consider a simple example.

As in the discrete case, it is frequently beneficial to use the (*cumulative*) *distribution function* (c.d.f.)

$$F(x) = P(X \le x) = P(X < x) = \int_{-\infty}^{x} f(w) \, dw,$$

which is the area between the graph of the p.d.f. and the x axis up to the vertical line through the general point x. Of course, from the fundamental theorem of calculus, we know that

$$F'(x) = f(x)$$

for x values where the derivative $F'(x)$ exists. Note that since $F(x)$ cumulates the probability up to and including x, it is a nondecreasing function such that

$$\lim_{x \to -\infty} F(x) = 0 \qquad \text{and} \qquad \lim_{x \to \infty} F(x) = 1.$$

The point, x_p, $0 < p < 1$, for which

$$F(x_p) = P(X \le x_p) = \int_{-\infty}^{x_p} f(x) \, dx = p$$

is called the (*100p*)*th percentile* of the distribution. It is also called the *quantile of order p*. The 50th percentile is the median; the 25th and 75th percentiles are the first and third quartiles of the distribution. These three values are also called quantiles of orders 0.5, 0.25, and 0.75, respectively.

Example 3.1-4   Let us hit the spinner, of Example 3.1-2, $n = 3$ independent times, obtaining three independent observations, X_1, X_2, X_3. Let Y equal the maximum value of these three observations. Since $Y \le y$, $0 \le y < 1$, if and only if each observation is less than or equal to y, namely $X_1 \le y$, $X_2 \le y$, and $X_3 \le y$, we have that the distribution function of Y is

$$G(y) = P(Y \le y) = P(X_1 \le y, X_2 \le y, X_3 \le y)$$
$$= P(X_1 \le y)P(X_2 \le y)P(X_3 \le y).$$

This last step follows from the independence of the events

$$(X_1 \le y), \quad (X_2 \le y), \quad \text{and} \quad (X_3 \le y).$$

Furthermore,

$$P(X_i \le y) = \int_0^y 1 \cdot dx = y, \qquad i = 1, 2, 3,$$

implies that

$$G(y) = y^3, \qquad 0 \le y < 1.$$

Accordingly, the p.d.f. of Y is

$$g(y) = G'(y) = 3y^2, \qquad 0 \le y < 1.$$

For illustration, the probability that the maximum spin exceeds 0.8 is

$$P(Y > 0.8) = \int_{0.8}^{1} 3y^2 \, dy = 1 - (0.8)^3 = 0.488.$$

It is also easy to calculate the percentiles of the distribution of $Y = \max(X_1, X_2, X_3)$. They are given by $G(y_p) = y_p^3 = p$ or $y_p = p^{1/3}$. For example, the median is 0.794, and the first and third quartiles are 0.630 and 0.909, respectively.   ■

For random variables of the continuous type, the definition and the rules associated with *mathematical expectation* are the same as in the discrete case except that integrals replace summations. That is,

$$E[u(X)] = \int_R u(x)f(x) \, dx = \int_{-\infty}^{\infty} u(x)f(x) \, dx$$

is the expected value of $u(X)$. The *mean* and *variance* of X are

$$\mu = E(X) = \int_{-\infty}^{\infty} xf(x) \, dx$$

and

$$\sigma^2 = E[(X - \mu)^2] = \int_{-\infty}^{\infty} (x - \mu)^2 f(x) \, dx$$

$$= \int_{-\infty}^{\infty} x^2 f(x) \, dx - \mu^2 = E(X^2) - \mu^2.$$

Example 3.1-5   Let X have the p.d.f. of Example 3.1-2,

$$f(x) = 1, \qquad 0 \le x < 1.$$

Then

$$\mu = E(X) = \int_0^1 x \cdot 1 \cdot dx = \left[\frac{x^2}{2} \right]_0^1 = \frac{1}{2}$$

and

$$\sigma^2 = E(X^2) - \left(\frac{1}{2} \right)^2 = \int_0^1 x^2 \cdot 1 \cdot dx - \frac{1}{4} = \frac{1}{3} - \frac{1}{4} = \frac{1}{12}.$$ ■

Example 3.1-6   For $Y = \max(X_1, X_2, X_3)$ of Example 3.1-4,

$$\mu = E(Y) = \int_0^1 y(3y^2) \, dy = \frac{3}{4}$$

and

$$\sigma^2 = \text{var}(Y) = \int_0^1 y^2(3y^2)\, dy - \left(\frac{3}{4}\right)^2 = \frac{3}{5} - \frac{9}{16} = \frac{3}{80}.$$

Thus the standard deviation of Y is

$$\sigma = \sqrt{\text{var}(Y)} = \sqrt{\frac{3}{80}} = 0.19.$$

■

Exercises 3.1

3.1-1 For the data in Example 3.1-1, construct other relative frequency histograms by trying other values of k and different boundary values.

Hint As a start, take $k = 4$ with classes of $[0, 10)$, $[10, 30)$, $[30, 40)$, and $[40, 80)$. Compare your plots to that in Figure 3.1-2.

3.1-2 Nelson has recorded the operating hours on $n = 22$ transformers until failure, where the data are already ordered from smallest to largest.

10	314	730	740	990	1046	1570	1870
2020	2040	2096	2110	2177	2306	2690	3200
3360	3444	3508	3770	4042	4186		

(a) Draw a box-and-whisker diagram.
(b) Construct a normalized relative frequency histogram.
[W. Nelson, *Applied Life Data Analysis* (New York: Wiley, 1982), p. 137.]

3.1-3 Hogg and Tanis have reported on 40 losses due to wind-related catastrophes in 1977. These data include only those losses of $2,000,000 or more, and are recorded to the nearest $1,000,000 (in units of $1,000,000).

2	2	2	2	2	2	2	2	2	2
2	2	3	3	3	3	4	4	4	5
5	5	5	6	6	6	6	8	8	9
15	17	22	23	24	24	25	27	32	43

(a) Draw a box-and-whisker diagram.
(b) Construct a normalized relative frequency histogram.
[R. V. Hogg and E. A. Tanis, *Probability and Statistical Inference*, 3rd ed. (New York: Macmillan, 1988), pp. 38–40.]

Hint The authors used $k = 4$ with classes $[1.5, 2.5)$, $[2.5, 6.5)$, $[6.5, 29.5)$, and $[29.5, 49.5)$. However, try others, such as $k = 5$ and $[1.5, 2.5)$, $[2.5, 9.5)$, $[9.5, 20.5)$, $[20.5, 28.5)$, and $[28.5, 45.5)$. Compare the results.

3.1-4 Let X have the p.d.f. $f(x) = 3(1 - x)^2$, $0 \le x < 1$. Compute
(a) $P(0.1 < X < 0.5)$.
(b) $P(X > 0.4)$.
(c) $P(0.3 < X < 2)$.
Hint In part (c), recognize that the outcome space of X is $0 \le x < 1$.

3.1-5 Find the mean and the variance of each of the distributions given by the following densities.
(a) $f(x) = 2x$, $0 \le x < 1$.
(b) $f(x) = 6x(1 - x)$, $0 \le x < 1$.

3.1-6 Find the 50th percentile (*median*), the 25th percentile (*first quartile*), the 75th percentile (*third quartile*), and the 90th percentile (also called the *ninth decile*) for the following densities.
(a) $f(x) = 4x^3$, $0 \le x < 1$.
(b) $f(x) = e^{-x}$, $0 \le x < \infty$.

3.1-7 Consider the uniform (rectangular) distribution on the space $[a, b]$, where $a < b$, with p.d.f.

$$f(x) = \frac{1}{b - a}, \qquad a \le x < b.$$

(a) Obtain the cumulative distribution function $F(x)$. Plot $f(x)$ and $F(x)$. Determine the median and the first and third quartiles.
(b) Calculate the mean and the variance.

3.1-8 Suppose that the p.d.f. of the life (in weeks) of a certain part is $f(x) = 3x^2/(400)^3$, $0 \le x < 400$.

(a) Show that the probability of a part failing in the first 200 weeks is 1/8.

(b) To decrease this probability, four independent parts are placed in *parallel* so that all must fail if the system is to fail. Show that the p.d.f. of the life Y of this parallel system is $g(y) = 12y^{11}/(400)^{12}$, $0 \leq y < 400$.

Hint

$$P(Y \leq y) = P(X_1 \leq y)P(X_2 \leq y)P(X_3 \leq y)P(X_4 \leq y),$$

where X_1, X_2, X_3, X_4 are the lives of the respective parts.

(c) Determine $P(Y \leq 200)$ and compare it to the answer in part (a).

3.2 The Normal Distribution

The normal distribution is the most important distribution in the study of statistics. This is true not only because many data sets are almost normally distributed, but also because many estimators, such as $\hat{p}$ from the binomial model and $\hat{\lambda}$ from the Poisson model, have approximate normal distributions. We comment much more on this fact in Section 4.2.

If X has a *normal distribution* with mean μ and variance σ^2, its p.d.f. is

$$f(x) = \frac{1}{\sqrt{2\pi}\,\sigma}\exp\left[-\frac{(x-\mu)^2}{2\sigma^2}\right], \qquad -\infty < x < \infty.$$

We abbreviate this by saying that X is $N(\mu, \sigma^2)$. The graph of $f(x)$ is the well-known bell-shaped curve displayed in Figure 3.2-1. The graph of the $N(\mu, \sigma^2)$ p.d.f. is symmetric about $x = \mu$ and reaches its highest value at that point. The more mathematical reader may want to verify that

$$\int_{-\infty}^{\infty} f(x)\,dx = 1, \qquad E(X) = \int_{-\infty}^{\infty} xf(x)\,dx = \mu,$$

$$\mathrm{var}(X) = \int_{-\infty}^{\infty} (x-\mu)^2 f(x)\,dx = \sigma^2$$

and that the points of inflection of $f(x)$ are at $\mu - \sigma$ and $\mu + \sigma$; see Exercise 3.2-9, in which helpful hints are given.

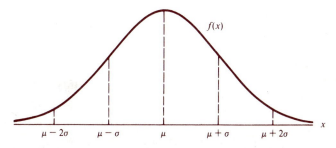

FIGURE 3.2-1   Probability density function of the $N(\mu, \sigma^2)$ distribution.

Let us accept the fact that $f(x)$ is a p.d.f. with mean μ and variance σ^2. Then, if the random variable Z has a normal distribution with mean zero and variance 1, that is, Z is $N(0, 1)$, its p.d.f. is

$$f(z) = \frac{1}{\sqrt{2\pi}} e^{-z^2/2}, \qquad -\infty < z < \infty$$

and Z is said to have a *standard normal distribution*. For such a Z, let us try to compute some probabilities, such as

$$P(-1 < Z < 1.5) = \int_{-1}^{1.5} \frac{1}{\sqrt{2\pi}} e^{-z^2/2}\, dz.$$

We notice quickly that we cannot find an antiderivative of $f(z)$; that is, we cannot find a simple function $F(z)$ such that $F'(z) = f(z)$. Thus we are not able to use the fundamental theorem of calculus to evaluate this integral, and we are forced to use numerical methods. Fortunately, statisticians have faced these integrals for years and tabled the (cumulative) distribution function (c.d.f.) of the $N(0, 1)$ distribution, namely,

$$\Phi(z) = P(Z \le z) = \int_{-\infty}^{z} \frac{1}{\sqrt{2\pi}} e^{-w^2/2}\, dw.$$

We give one such tabulation in Table C.4 in Appendix C. For example, the probability $\Phi(1.5) = 0.9332$ in this table corresponds to the shaded area in Figure 3.2-2(a). A plot of $\Phi(z)$, the c.d.f. of the $N(0, 1)$ distribution, is given in Figure 3.2-2(b). It has a very characteristic "S-shaped" pattern. Note that the shaded area in Figure 3.2-2(a) is the ordinate of the c.d.f. at z in Figure 3.2-2(b). Although the c.d.f. and p.d.f. can supply the same information, we find the p.d.f. more descriptive of the distribution.

With this notation, we can write our required probability as

$$P(-1 < Z < 1.5) = \Phi(1.5) - \Phi(-1);$$

that is, we determine the area under the p.d.f. up to 1.5 and subtract the area under the curve up to -1. However, we do not find $\Phi(-1)$ in Table C.4 since the function $\Phi(z)$ is given only for positive arguments. But due to the symmetry of $f(z)$ about $z = 0$, it follows that $\Phi(-1) = 1 - \Phi(1)$ or, more generally,

$$\Phi(-z) = 1 - \Phi(z).$$

Thus we find

$$P(-1 < Z < 1.5) = \Phi(1.5) - [1 - \Phi(1)]$$

$$= 0.9332 - (1 - 0.8413) = 0.7745.$$

The entries in Table C.4 can be used to find the percentiles of the $N(0, 1)$ distribution. The $(100p)$th percentile (or the quantile of order p) is the value z_p for which $\Phi(z_p) = P(Z \le z_p) = p$. For example, we find that the 95th percentile

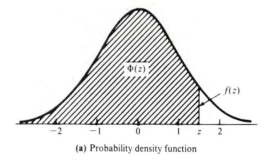

(a) Probability density function

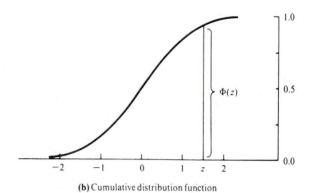

(b) Cumulative distribution function

FIGURE 3.2-2   Plot of the p.d.f. $f(z)$ and the c.d.f. $\Phi(z) = P(Z \le z)$ of the $N(0, 1)$ distribution.

is $z_{0.95} = 1.645$. The symmetry of the p.d.f. around zero implies that $z_{1-p} = -z_p$; thus the 5th percentile is $z_{0.05} = -1.645$. Similarly, you can check that the first, 25th, 50th, 75th, and 99th percentiles are given by -2.326, -0.675, 0.0, 0.675, and 2.326, respectively.

So far we have learned how to find probabilities associated with the standard $N(0, 1)$ distribution. Suppose, however, that X is $N(\mu = 75, \sigma^2 = 100)$ and we want a probability such as $P(70 < X < 90)$. In general, say that X is $N(\mu, \sigma^2)$ and we wish to determine

$$P(a < X < b) = \int_a^b \frac{1}{\sqrt{2\pi}\,\sigma} \exp\left[-\frac{(y - \mu)^2}{2\sigma^2} \right] dy.$$

If we change the variable of integration by letting $w = (y - \mu)/\sigma$ so that $y = \mu + \sigma w$ and $dy/dw = \sigma$, we find that

$$P(a < X < b) = \int_{(a-\mu)/\sigma}^{(b-\mu)/\sigma} \frac{1}{\sqrt{2\pi}} e^{-w^2/2}\, dw.$$

Since the integrand in this integral is the p.d.f. of the $N(0, 1)$ distribution, we can use the entries in Table C.4 to evaluate these probabilities. Thus we have that

$$P(a < X < b) = \Phi\left(\frac{b - \mu}{\sigma}\right) - \Phi\left(\frac{a - \mu}{\sigma}\right).$$

That is, to compute this probability we use the c.d.f. of the $N(0, 1)$ distribution after standardizing the bounds of the interval, namely a and b. The standardization is carried out by subtracting the mean μ and dividing by the standard deviation σ.

Note that the values of X that satisfy $(a < X < b)$ are the same as the ones that satisfy

$$\left(\frac{a - \mu}{\sigma} < \frac{X - \mu}{\sigma} < \frac{b - \mu}{\sigma}\right).$$

Thus

$$P(a < X < b) = P\left(\frac{a - \mu}{\sigma} < \frac{X - \mu}{\sigma} < \frac{b - \mu}{\sigma}\right) = \Phi\left(\frac{b - \mu}{\sigma}\right) - \Phi\left(\frac{a - \mu}{\sigma}\right).$$

Thus we have actually proved that if X is $N(\mu, \sigma^2)$, the random variable

$$Z = \frac{X - \mu}{\sigma} \quad \text{is} \quad N(0, 1).$$

The percentiles of the $N(\mu, \sigma^2)$ distribution are linearly related to the percentiles of the $N(0, 1)$ distribution. Using the transformation from the $N(\mu, \sigma^2)$ to the $N(0, 1)$ distribution, we find that

$$p = P(X \le x_p) = P\left(\frac{X - \mu}{\sigma} \le \frac{x_p - \mu}{\sigma}\right) = P\left(Z \le \frac{x_p - \mu}{\sigma}\right).$$

Therefore,

$$\frac{x_p - \mu}{\sigma} = z_p \quad \text{and} \quad x_p = \mu + \sigma z_p,$$

where z_p is the percentile of the $N(0, 1)$ distribution.

Example 3.2-1   If X is $N(75, 100)$, then

$$P(70 < X < 90) = \Phi\left(\frac{90 - 75}{10}\right) - \Phi\left(\frac{70 - 75}{10}\right)$$

$$= \Phi(1.5) - \Phi(-0.5)$$

$$= 0.9332 - (1 - 0.6915) = 0.6247,$$

$$P(80 < X < 95) = \Phi\left(\frac{95 - 75}{10}\right) - \Phi\left(\frac{80 - 75}{10}\right)$$

$$= \Phi(2.0) - \Phi(0.5)$$

$$= 0.9772 - 0.6915 = 0.2857,$$

and

$$P(55 < X < 65) = \Phi\left(\frac{65 - 75}{10}\right) - \Phi\left(\frac{55 - 75}{10}\right)$$

$$= \Phi(-1) - \Phi(-2) = [1 - \Phi(1)] - [1 - \Phi(2)]$$

$$= \Phi(2) - \Phi(1) = 0.9772 - 0.8413 = 0.1359.$$

The 95th percentile of this distribution is given by $75 + (10)(1.645) = 91.45$. Similarly, the three quartiles are given by 69.02, 75.0, and 80.98, respectively.

∎

Example 3.2-2 Say that the time, X, to assemble an item is a normally distributed random variable with mean $\mu = 15.8$ minutes and standard deviation $\sigma = 2.4$ minutes. The probability that the next item will take more than 17 minutes to assemble is

$$P(X > 17) = P\left(\frac{X - 15.8}{2.4} > \frac{17 - 15.8}{2.4}\right)$$

$$= 1 - \Phi(0.5) = 1 - 0.6915 = 0.3085.$$ ∎

To gain a greater appreciation of the normal distribution and the relationship of its probabilities to the parameters μ and σ, consider the following discussion. If X is $N(\mu, \sigma^2)$, then, with $k > 0$, we have

$$P(\mu - k\sigma < X < \mu + k\sigma) = \Phi\left(\frac{\mu + k\sigma - \mu}{\sigma}\right) - \Phi\left(\frac{\mu - k\sigma - \mu}{\sigma}\right)$$

$$= \Phi(k) - \Phi(-k) = 2\Phi(k) - 1.$$

For selected values of k, we obtain the following probabilities:

k	1	1.282	1.645	1.96	2	2.576	3
$P(\mu - k\sigma < X < \mu + k\sigma)$	0.6826	0.80	0.90	0.95	0.9544	0.99	0.9974

These results imply that about 68 percent of normally distributed observations are between $\mu - \sigma$ and $\mu + \sigma$; about 95 percent are in the interval given by $\mu \pm 2\sigma$, and almost all (99.74%) are within three standard deviations of the mean μ. We call the bounds of the interval, $\mu - k\sigma$ to $\mu + k\sigma$, the $100[2\Phi(k) - 1]$ percent *tolerance limits* of a normal distribution.

What do these results imply in a real situation? Say that we find that the inside diameter of a washer that our company produces has the following characteristics: mean $= 0.503$ and standard deviation $= 0.005$. If we can assume that these diameters are normally distributed, then 99 percent of them are between $0.503 \pm 2.576(0.005)$, that is, roughly between 0.490 and 0.516. If the specifications for these diameters were 0.500 ± 0.005 (i.e., the diameter of a useful washer should be between 0.495 and 0.505), this finding causes some concern because we would probably want at least 99 percent of our washers to be within specifications. Questions should be asked: Are the specifications realistic and necessary; and if so, what changes should be made in our process to get a larger number of washers within these specifications? In our particular example it would be desirable to shift the mean to 0.500 and reduce the standard deviation as much as possible. The shifting of the mean may not be too difficult to achieve, but the reduction of the variance could require very expensive modifications of our production process.

Exercises 3.2

3.2-1 Let Z be $N(0, 1)$. Determine the probabilities.
(a) $P(-0.7 < Z < 1.3)$.
(b) $P(0.2 < Z < 1.1)$.
(c) $P(-1.9 < Z < -0.6)$.
3.2-2 Let X be $N(25, 16)$. Determine the probabilities.
(a) $P(22 < X < 26)$.
(b) $P(19 < X < 24)$.
(c) $P(X > 23)$.
(d) $P(|X - 25| < 5)$.
3.2-3 If X is $N(5, 4)$, find each c so that
(a) $P(X < c) = 0.8749$.
(b) $P(c < X) = 0.6406$.
(c) $P(X < c) = 0.95$.
(d) $P(|X - 5| < c) = 0.95$.
3.2-4 The weight of the cereal in a box is a random variable with mean 12.15 ounces and standard deviation 0.2 ounce. What percentage of the boxes have contents that weigh under 12 ounces? If the manufacturer claims there are 12 ounces in a box, does this percentage cause concern? If so, what two things could be done to correct the situation? Which would probably be cheaper immediately but might cost more in the long run?
3.2-5 Suppose that the specifications on the diameter of a rotor shaft are 0.25 ± 0.002. If these diameters are distributed normally with $\mu = 0.251$ and $\sigma = 0.001$, what percentage of them are within specifications?
3.2-6 The thickness of manufactured metal plates is the variable of interest. Due to many factors, such as

slight variations in the metal, different operators, and different machines, the thickness varies and can be considered a normal random variable with mean $\mu = 20$ mm and standard deviation $\sigma = 0.04$ mm. How much scrap can be expected if the thickness of the metal plates
(a) Has to be at least 19.95 mm?
(b) Can be at most 20.10 mm?
(c) Can differ at most 0.05 mm from the target 20 mm?
(d) How would one have to set the tolerance limits $20 - c$ and $20 + c$ such that one produces at most 5 percent scrap?
(e) Assume that the mean has shifted to $\mu = 20.10$. Calculate the percentage of metal plates that exceed the tolerance limits in part (d).
3.2-7 A machine fills 100-pound bags of dry concrete mix. The actual weight of the mix that is put in each bag is a random variable with standard deviation $\sigma = 0.5$ pound. The mean of the distribution can be set by the operator. At what mean weight should the machine be set such that only 5 percent of the bags are underweight?
3.2-8 The average weight of a certain brand of refrigerator is 31 pounds. Due to variability in raw materials and production conditions, weight is a random variable; assume that the distribution is normal with a standard deviation of $\sigma = 0.5$ pound.
(a) What is the probability that a randomly selected refrigerator is heavier than 32.0 pounds?
(b) What is the probability that the weight of a ran-

domly selected refrigerator is between 30.0 and 30.5 pounds?

3.2-9 Let $f(x)$ be a p.d.f. associated with $N(\mu, \sigma^2)$.

(a) Show that

$$I = \int_{-\infty}^{\infty} f(x)\, dx = 1.$$

Hint Change the variables by letting $y = (x - \mu)/\sigma$, obtaining

$$I = \int_{-\infty}^{\infty} \frac{1}{\sqrt{2\pi}}\, e^{-y^2/2}\, dy.$$

Write

$$I^2 = \int_{-\infty}^{\infty} \int_{-\infty}^{\infty} \frac{1}{2\pi}\, e^{-(y^2 + z^2)/2}\, dy\, dz$$

and use polar coordinates $y = r\cos\theta$, $z = r\sin\theta$ to evaluate I^2.

(b) Show that

$$\int_{-\infty}^{\infty} xf(x)\, dx = \mu$$

Hint Prove that

$$\int_{-\infty}^{\infty} \left(\frac{x - \mu}{\sigma}\right) f(x)\, dx = 0$$

by finding an antiderivative of the integrand; then use the result of part (a).

(c) Show that

$$\int_{-\infty}^{\infty} (x - \mu)^2 f(x)\, dx = \sigma^2$$

by integrating by parts.

(d) Prove that the points of inflection of $f(x)$ are at $\mu - \sigma$ and $\mu + \sigma$.

Hint Set $f''(x) = 0$.

3.3 Other Useful Distributions

Let X be a continuous random variable that represents the length of life of a component (such as light bulbs, windings, parts, human beings, etc.). Say the p.d.f. and c.d.f. of X are $f(x)$ and $F(x)$, respectively, with outcome space $0 \le x < \infty$. We are often interested in the probability that a component fails in the interval $(x, x + \Delta x)$, given that it has lasted at least x units. Since the event $(x < X < x + \Delta x)$ is a subset of $(X > x)$, this conditional probability equals

$$P(x < X < x + \Delta x \mid X > x) = \frac{P(x < X < x + \Delta x)}{P(X > x)} \approx \frac{f(x)\,\Delta x}{1 - F(x)}.$$

The right side of the equation above is an approximation because, for a small Δx, the probability of failing in the interval $(x, x + \Delta x)$ is approximately equal to $f(x)\,\Delta x$. If Δx denotes one unit, the conditional probability approximately equals

$$\lambda(x) = \frac{f(x)}{1 - F(x)};$$

and $\lambda(x)$ is called the *failure rate function*. That is, the failure rate at x is the height of the p.d.f. at x divided by the probability of exceeding x. It is the approximate conditional probability of failing in the next unit given that the component has already lasted x units of time. Frequently, since parts (and people) "wear out," this tends to be an increasing function of x, but there are illustrations in which $\lambda(x)$ is a constant or decreasing function of x ("old is as good or better than new").

Of course, with $\lambda(t) = f(t)/[1 - F(t)]$, and $F'(t) = f(t)$, we have

$$\int_0^x \lambda(t)\,dt = \int_0^x \frac{f(t)}{1 - F(t)}\,dt$$

$$= \{-\ln[1 - F(t)]\}_0^x$$

$$= -\ln[1 - F(x)] + \ln[1 - F(0)].$$

However, X is the length of life and thus $P(X \le 0) = F(0) = 0$, so

$$\int_0^x \lambda(t)\,dt = -\ln[1 - F(x)]$$

and

$$F(x) = 1 - \exp\left[-\int_0^x \lambda(t)\,dt\right], \qquad 0 \le x < \infty.$$

Accordingly,

$$f(x) = F'(x) = \lambda(x) \exp\left[-\int_0^x \lambda(t)\,dt\right], \qquad 0 \le x < \infty.$$

By considering various failure rate functions, we can generate a number of continuous-type distribution functions and their corresponding density functions.

3.3-1   Weibull Distribution

Let the failure rate be proportional to a power of x, say $\lambda(x) = \alpha x^{\alpha-1}/\beta^\alpha$, $0 \le x < \infty$, where the parameters α and β are positive. Then

$$f(x) = \frac{\alpha x^{\alpha-1}}{\beta^\alpha} \exp\left[-\left(\frac{x}{\beta}\right)^\alpha\right], \qquad 0 \le x < \infty.$$

This was the p.d.f. used in Example 3.1-3 with $\beta = 8$ and $\alpha = 1.8$. The p.d.f. $f(x)$ is said to be that of a *Weibull distribution* with parameters α and β and is very useful in many engineering applications. In particular, if $\alpha = 1$, we obtain the p.d.f. of an *exponential distribution*:

$$f(x) = \frac{1}{\beta} e^{-x/\beta}, \qquad 0 \le x < \infty.$$

Several examples of Weibull densities with $\beta = 10$ are given in Figure 3.3-1.

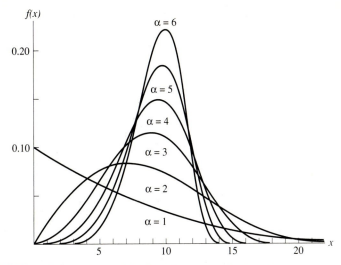

FIGURE 3.3-1   Graphs of several Weibull densities with $\beta = 10$.

*3.3-2   Gompertz Distribution

Human mortality (failure rate) increases about exponentially once a person reaches his or her middle twenties. As a matter of fact, this increase equals roughly 10 percent each year; hence

$$\lambda(x) \approx c(1.1)^x = ce^{bx},$$

where $b = \ln(1.1)$. The corresponding p.d.f., with parameters $b > 0$ and $c > 0$, is

$$f(x) = ce^{bx} \exp\left(-\frac{c}{b} e^{bx} + \frac{c}{b} \right), \qquad 0 \le x < \infty.$$

The function $f(x)$ is known as the p.d.f. of the *Gompertz distribution*. It is widely used in actuarial science because it provides an excellent description of the distribution of the length of human life.

In Figure 3.3-2, we display the failure rates and density functions of an exponential, a Weibull, and a Gompertz distribution.

Engineers study the same p.d.f. $f(x)$ as that of Gompertz, but they usually replace the coefficient b by $1/\delta$ and c/b by $e^{-\lambda/\delta}$. With this change, which only amounts to a relabeling or reparameterization of the coefficients, the p.d.f. becomes

$$f(x) = \frac{1}{\delta} \exp\left(\frac{x - \lambda}{\delta} \right) \exp\left[-\exp\left(\frac{x - \lambda}{\delta} \right) + \exp\left(\frac{-\lambda}{\delta} \right) \right],$$

for $0 \le x < \infty$. The new parameters are $\delta > 0$ and $-\infty < \lambda < \infty$.

express the gamma function as $\Gamma(\alpha) = (\alpha - 1)(\alpha - 2) \cdots (\alpha - r)\Gamma(\alpha - r)$, where $\alpha - r$ is a number between 0 and 1. The gamma function for arguments between 0 and 1 can be obtained from standard mathematical tables; for example, $\Gamma(1) = 1$ and $\Gamma(0.5) = \sqrt{\pi}$.

The gamma distribution arises as the distribution of waiting times. In Section 2.5 we have learned that for a Poisson process the number of occurrences in an interval of length w follows a Poisson distribution with

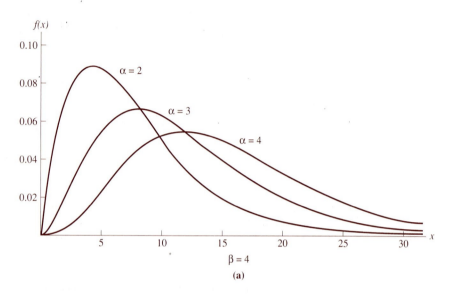

(a)

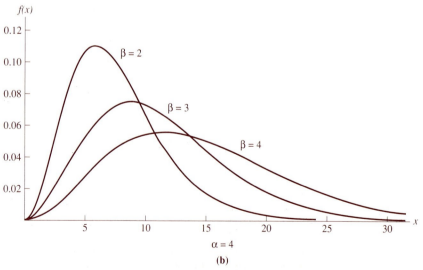

(b)

FIGURE 3.3-3   Graphs of several gamma densities.

parameter λw, where λ is the mean occurrence in an interval of length 1. Similarly, one can show that the time it takes to obtain exactly k occurrences has a gamma distribution with parameters $\alpha = k$ and $\beta = 1/\lambda$.

As a special case of the gamma distribution with $k = \alpha = 1$, we obtain the exponential distribution with parameter $\beta = 1/\lambda$. It is the distribution of the waiting time to the first occurrence. To see the effect of the parameters on the shape of the gamma p.d.f., several combinations of α and β have been used for the graphs displayed in Figure 3.3-3.

3.3-5   Chi-Square Distribution

Another special case of the gamma distribution that statisticians frequently use is that in which $\alpha = r/2$, where r is a positive integer and $\beta = 2$. A random variable Y that has the p.d.f.

$$f(y) = \frac{1}{\Gamma(r/2)2^{r/2}} \, y^{(r/2)-1} e^{-y/2}, \qquad 0 \leq y < \infty,$$

is said to have a *chi-square distribution* with parameter r. For no obvious reason at this time, we call the parameter r the *number of degrees of freedom* of this chi-square distribution, which is written, for brevity, $\chi^2(r)$.

*3.3-6   Lognormal Distribution

Let the random variable X be $N(\mu, \sigma^2)$ and consider the random variable $Y = e^X$ or, equivalently, $X = \ln(Y)$. The distribution function of Y is

$$G(y) = P(Y \leq y) = P(X \leq \ln y), \qquad 0 \leq y < \infty.$$

That is,

$$G(y) = \int_{-\infty}^{\ln y} \frac{1}{\sqrt{2\pi}\,\sigma} \exp\left[-\frac{(x - \mu)^2}{2\sigma^2} \right] dx.$$

The p.d.f. of Y is

$$g(y) = G'(y) = \frac{1}{\sqrt{2\pi}\,\sigma y} \exp\left[-\frac{(\ln y - \mu)^2}{2\sigma^2} \right], \qquad 0 \leq y < \infty.$$

Because this distribution results from the transformation $X = \ln Y$, the random variable Y is said to have a *lognormal distribution* with parameters μ and σ. See Figure 3.3-4 for the graphs of several lognormal densities. Incidentally, we now see why a log transformation of a positive random variable that is skewed to the right frequently creates a distribution that is more normal-like.

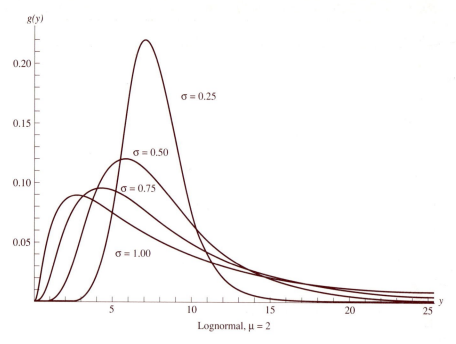

Lognormal, $\mu = 2$

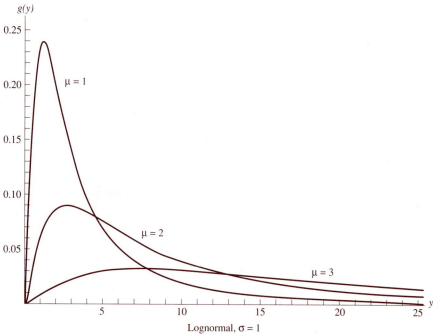

Lognormal, $\sigma = 1$

FIGURE 3.3-4   Graphs of several lognormal densities.

TABLE 3.3-1   Important Continuous Distributions

Distribution	p.d.f.	Mean	Variance
Normal	$\dfrac{1}{\sqrt{2\pi}\,\sigma}\exp\left[-\dfrac{(x-\mu)^2}{2\sigma^2}\right],$ $-\infty < x < \infty$	μ	σ^2
Gamma	$\dfrac{1}{\Gamma(\alpha)\beta^\alpha}\,x^{\alpha-1}e^{-x/\beta},$ $0 \le x < \infty$	$\alpha\beta$	$\alpha\beta^2$
Exponential $(\alpha = 1)$	$\dfrac{1}{\beta}\,e^{-x/\beta}$	β	β^2
Chi-square $(\alpha = r/2;\ \beta = 2)$	$\dfrac{1}{2^{r/2}\Gamma(r/2)}\,x^{(r/2)-1}e^{-x/2}$	r	$2r$
Weibull	$\dfrac{\alpha x^{\alpha-1}}{\beta^\alpha}\exp\left[-\left(\dfrac{x}{\beta}\right)^\alpha\right]$ $0 \le x < \infty$	$\beta\Gamma\left(\dfrac{1}{\alpha}+1\right)$	$\beta^2\left\{\Gamma\left(\dfrac{2}{\alpha}+1\right)-\left[\Gamma\left(\dfrac{1}{\alpha}+1\right)\right]^2\right\}$
Lognormal	$\dfrac{1}{\sqrt{2\pi}\,\sigma y}\exp\left[-\dfrac{(\ln y-\mu)^2}{2\sigma^2}\right]$ $0 \le y < \infty$	$e^{\mu+\sigma^2/2}$	$e^{2\mu+\sigma^2}(e^{\sigma^2}-1)$

In Table 3.3-1 we summarize the most important continuous distributions by recording their densities and the corresponding means and variances. In Exercises 3.2-9, 3.3-12, and 3.3-13, hints are given on how to compute the means and variances of the normal, gamma, and Weibull distributions.

Exercises 3.3

3.3-1 Let X have the Weibull p.d.f. with $\alpha = 4$ and $\beta = 60$. Compute probabilities such as $P(60 < X < 80)$ and $P(20 < X < 40)$. Discuss whether this model could serve as a p.d.f. for the length of a human life.

3.3-2 Let X have an exponential p.d.f. with $\beta = 500$; that is, $f(x) = (1/500)\exp(-x/500)$, $0 \le x < \infty$.
(a) Compute $P(X > 500)$.

(b) Compute the conditional probability

$$P(X > 1000 \mid X > 500) = P(X > 1000)/P(X > 500).$$

(c) Note the answers in parts (a) and (b) are the same. Show, in general, that

$$P(X > x + c \mid X > x) = P(X > c).$$

Since the exponential distribution has a constant

failure rate we could have expected this result. That is, for this model, "old is as good as new."

3.3-3 Let X_1, X_2, and X_3 be $n = 3$ independent observations from a Weibull distribution with parameters α and β. Define Y as the minimum value of these three observations. If $0 \leq y < \infty$, note that $Y > y$ is equivalent to $X_1 > y$, $X_2 > y$, and $X_3 > y$, so that

$$G(y) = 1 - P(Y > y)$$

$$= 1 - P(X_1 > y, X_2 > y, X_3 > y).$$

Show that $g(y) = G'(y)$ is a Weibull p.d.f. with parameters α and $\beta/3^{1/\alpha}$.

3.3-4 Telephone calls enter a college switchboard according to a Poisson process on the average of three every 4 minutes (i.e., at a rate of $\lambda = 0.75$ per minute). Let W denote the waiting time in minutes until the second call.

(a) What is the p.d.f. of W?

(b) Compute $P(W > 1.5$ minutes).

3.3-5 Let X equal the number of alpha particle emissions of carbon-14 that are counted by a Geiger counter per second. Assume that X has a Poisson distribution with mean 8. Let W be the time in seconds before the second count is made. Determine $P(W \leq 0.5)$ and $P(W > 0.75)$.

3.3-6 Let Y have a lognormal distribution with parameters $\mu = 5$ and $\sigma = 1$. Obtain its mean, variance, and standard deviation. Sketch its p.d.f. Compute $P(Y < 91)$.

Hint $P(Y < 91) = P(\ln Y < \ln 91)$.

3.3-7 Nelson reports that the life, in thousands of miles, of a certain type of electronic control for locomotives has an approximate lognormal distribution with parameters $\mu = 2.236$ and $\sigma = 0.320$, where he has taken common (base 10) logarithms. Show that the fraction of these that would fail on an 80,000-mile warranty is 0.15. Nelson notes that this fraction was so high that the control had to be redesigned.

Hint $P(X < 80) = P(\log_{10} X < \log_{10} 80)$; use the fact that $\log_{10} X$ has a normal distribution with mean 2.236 and standard deviation 0.320.

3.3-8 Start with a uniform random variable U on the interval $[0, 1]$. Let $X = -b \ln(1 - U)$. Show that X has an exponential distribution.

Hint   Find the cumulative distribution function of X and use the fact that $X \leq x$ if and only if $U \leq 1 - \exp(-x/b)$.

3.3-9 Consider the p.d.f. of the extreme value distribution

$$g(y) = \frac{1}{\delta} \exp\left(\frac{y - \lambda}{\delta}\right) \exp\left[-\exp\left(\frac{y - \lambda}{\delta}\right)\right],$$

$$-\infty < y < \infty.$$

(a) Show that it is a valid p.d.f., and that it reaches its maximum at λ; that is, λ is the *mode*. This explains why we refer to λ as the location parameter.

(b) Show that the percentiles are given by $y_p = \lambda + \delta \ln[-\ln(1 - p)]$. This explains why we refer to δ as the scale parameter. An increase in δ will stretch the distribution, and thus change the scale.

3.3-10 Let three parts be placed in *series* so that the failure of any one of them results in the failure of the system. Assume that the lengths X_1, X_2, and X_3 of lives of the parts have independent distributions with failure rates $\lambda_1(x)$, $\lambda_2(x)$, and $\lambda_3(x)$, respectively.

(a) Show that $Y = \min(X_1, X_2, X_3)$, the length of life of the system, has distribution function

$$G(y) = 1 - \exp\left\{-\int_0^y [\lambda_1(x) + \lambda_2(x) + \lambda_3(x)]\, dx\right\}$$

so that the failure rate of Y is $\lambda_1(y) + \lambda_2(y) + \lambda_3(y)$.

Hint $P(Y \leq y) = 1 - P(Y > y)$
$$= 1 - P(X_1 > y)P(X_2 > y)P(X_3 > y).$$

(b) If $\lambda_i(x) = x^2/9$, $i = 1, 2, 3$, find the p.d.f. of Y. What type of distribution is this?

3.3-11 Show that $\Gamma(\alpha) = (\alpha - 1)\Gamma(\alpha - 1)$, provided that $\alpha > 1$.

Hint   Integrate

$$\Gamma(\alpha) = \int_0^\infty w^{\alpha - 1} e^{-w}\, dw$$

by parts one time.

3.3-12 Let Y have a gamma distribution with parameters α and β. Show that the mean and the variance are $\alpha\beta$ and $\alpha\beta^2$, respectively.

Hint   In the integrals representing $E(Y)$ and $E(Y^2)$, change variables by writing $w = y/\beta$ and use the result of Exercise 3.3-11 to obtain $E(Y) = \beta\Gamma(\alpha + 1)/\Gamma(\alpha) = \alpha\beta$ and $E(Y^2) = \beta^2\Gamma(\alpha + 2)/\Gamma(\alpha) = (\alpha + 1)\alpha\beta^2$.

3.3-13 Let Y have a Weibull distribution with parameters α and β. Show that the mean and the variance are $\beta\Gamma(1/\alpha + 1)$ and $\beta^2\{\Gamma(2/\alpha + 1) - [\Gamma(1/\alpha + 1)]^2\}$, respectively.

Hint   In the integrals representing $E(Y)$ and $E(Y^2)$, let $w = (y/\beta)^\alpha$.

3.4   Fitting and Testing Models

3.4-1   Checking for Normality

Until now we have viewed the normal distribution as a theoretical model that describes the variability in a variable X, and we have assumed that the parameters μ and σ^2 are known. Now suppose that they are unknown and that we want to estimate them from a sample of n observations $x_1, x_2, \ldots, x_n$. Since the two parameters in the normal distribution correspond to the mean and the variance, the natural estimates are the sample mean

$$\bar{x} = \frac{1}{n} \sum_{i=1}^{n} x_i$$

and the sample variance

$$s^2 = \frac{1}{n-1} \sum_{i=1}^{n} (x_i - \bar{x})^2.$$

Given that $\bar{x}$ and s are the estimates of the unknown parameters μ and σ, we still may not know whether the normal distribution provides an appropriate model for the variability of the observations under consideration. How can we check whether a sample of n observations, $x_1, x_2, \ldots, x_n$, seemingly comes from a normal distribution? For example, take the $n = 90$ observations in Table 1.2-1, which represent compressive strength measurements on 90 concrete blocks. Could these observations be from a normal distribution? In this section we discuss several graphical methods.

Probably the simplest way to check whether observations come from a normal distribution is to plot the histogram of the observations. Since the relative frequency histogram is an estimate of the probability density, we have to check whether it resembles the bell-shaped curve of the normal distribution in Figure 3.2-1. The histogram of the 90 measurements in Figure 1.2-1(b) looks more-or-less bell-shaped. We could say that the distribution is roughly normal. However, it is quite difficult to assess normality from a histogram if there are only a few observations. For example, it is difficult to say whether the 10 observations in the dot diagram in Figure 1.2-1(a) come from a normal distribution.

In addition to the histogram, which when scaled correctly is an estimate of the p.d.f., we can calculate an estimate of the c.d.f. and assess whether this estimate looks like the c.d.f. of a normal distribution. The *empirical* distribution was defined in Section 3.1; associated with it is the *empirical c.d.f.*, which is given by

$$F_n(x) = \frac{\#(\{x_i : x_i \le x\})}{n},$$

where $\#(\{x_i: x_i \le x\})$ is the number of observations that are less than or equal to x. $F_n(x)$ is the relative frequency of measurements that are smaller than or equal to x. As an illustration we have used the first 10 observations in Table 1.2-1 to construct the empirical c.d.f. in Figure 3.4-1. The 10 observations, ordered from smallest to largest, are

$$31.3 \quad 32.3 \quad 42.2 \quad 42.3 \quad 44.5 \quad 47.5 \quad 49.2 \quad 50.0 \quad 53.9 \quad 60.9$$

The ordered observations are written as $x_{(i)}$, $i = 1, 2, \ldots, n$ and are called the *order statistics* of the sample (see Section 1.2). For example, $x_{(1)}$ is the smallest observation and $x_{(n)}$ is the largest; the number in parentheses denotes the rank of the observation.

The empirical c.d.f. is defined for any real-valued x; it is a nondecreasing step function of x, with jumps of magnitude $1/n$ at each of the n observations. Now, to determine whether the observations are normally distributed, we can check whether the empirical c.d.f. resembles the "S-shaped" curve in Figure 3.2-2(b) that we expect from a normal distribution.

It is usually difficult for us to recognize nonlinear patterns. The human eye is much better at recognizing linear tendencies. Thus it would be more convenient if we could stretch the y axis and create a special graph paper such that, under normality, the points $(x_{(i)}, P_i = (i - 0.5)/n)$ would plot on a straight line. Recall that $x_{(i)}$ is the $100(i - 0.5)/n$ sample percentile. Such special graph paper

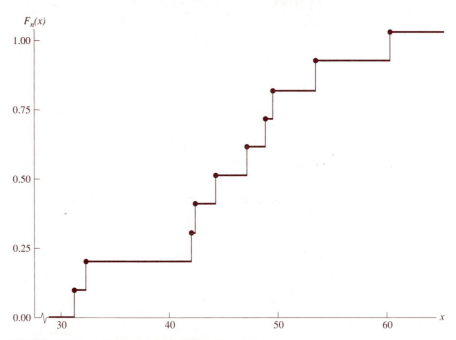

FIGURE 3.4-1   Empirical c.d.f. (step function) $F_n(x)$.

is, in fact, available and is known as *normal probability paper*. It looks like ordinary graph paper, except that the distances on the y axis, where we plot the values $P_i = (i - 0.5)/n$, $i = 1, 2, \ldots, n$, become larger as one moves away from the centerline at $P = 0.5$. For example, the distance between $P = 0.3$ and 0.4 (which, due to the symmetry of the normal distribution, is the same as the one from 0.6 to 0.7) is larger than the distance between $P = 0.4$ and 0.5.

There is another, and equivalent, way to think about this transformation of the y axis. The ith largest observation in our sample, $x_{(i)}$, is the sample quantile of order $P_i = (i - 0.5)/n$. One can also calculate the quantile of order P_i of the $N(\mu, \sigma^2)$ distribution. This distributional quantile is given by $q_i = \mu + \sigma z_i$, where z_i is the corresponding quantile of the $N(0, 1)$ distribution. The quantiles $z_1, z_2, \ldots, z_n$, which satisfy $P_i = P(Z \leq z_i) = \Phi(z_i)$ for $i = 1, \ldots, n$, are called the *standardized normal scores* (quantiles) associated with the n ordered observations $x_{(1)}, x_{(2)}, \ldots, x_{(n)}$. Now if the data do in fact come from the $N(\mu, \sigma^2)$ distribution, then $q_i \cong x_{(i)}$ and the points on the scatter plot of q_i against $x_{(i)}$ should about fall on a 45-degree line through the origin. Such a plot is called a *q–q plot*, as we plot the quantile of one distribution (theoretical) against the corresponding quantile of another (empirical). That is, we plot two quantiles against each other: an observed quantile and one that is implied by a certain theoretical distribution.

The normal quantiles, q_i, depend on the parameters μ and σ^2. In practice, we can replace those parameters by their estimates $\bar{x}$ and s^2. Alternatively, we can simply plot the standardized normal scores z_i directly against the observed quantiles $x_{(i)}$. Since $q_i = \bar{x} + s z_i$ and since, under normality, $x_{(i)} \cong q_i$, we find that the points on the scatter plot of z_i against $x_{(i)}$ should lie approximately on a straight line with slope $1/s$ that goes through the point $(\bar{x}, 0)$. Such a graph is called a *normal probability plot*. Deviations from a linear pattern provide evidence that the underlying distribution is not normal. It is also easy to estimate from this plot, at least approximately, the parameters μ and σ of the normal distribution. The reciprocal of the slope gives us an estimate of the standard deviation; the intersection of a horizontal line at $z_i = 0$ with the approximate straight line gives us the estimate of μ.

We illustrate this plot with the first 10 observations from Table 1.2-1. We determine the ranks of the observations (if there were ties, we would assign the average rank), and calculate $P_i = (i - 0.5)/n$. The standardized normal scores satisfy $P_i = P(Z \leq z_i) = \Phi(z_i)$, $i = 1, 2, \ldots, n$, and are determined from Table C.4. For example, z_1 satisfies $P_1 = (1 - 0.5)/10 = 0.05 = P(Z \leq z_1)$ and is given by $z_1 = -1.645$. The second one, z_2, satisfies $P_2 = (2 - 0.5)/10 = 0.15 = P(Z \leq z_2)$ and is $z_2 = -1.04$; and so on. They are listed in the last column of Table 3.4-1. A plot of the normal scores against the observations is given in Figure 3.4-2. Since this plot exhibits a fairly good linear relationship, we have reason to believe that these data come from a normal distribution. We can also get a quick estimate of the standard deviation. Note that the slope in Figure 3.4-2 is about $(2)(1.6)/30 = 0.11$, and its reciprocal is 9.4. This is very close to the sample standard deviation $s = 9.1$.

TABLE 3.4-1   First 10 Observations from Table 1.2-1 and Their Normal Scores

Observation	Rank i	$P_i = \dfrac{i - 0.5}{n}$	Normal Score
49.2	7	0.65	0.39
53.9	9	0.85	1.04
50.0	8	0.75	0.67
44.5	5	0.45	−0.13
42.2	3	0.25	−0.67
42.3	4	0.35	−0.39
32.3	2	0.15	−1.04
31.3	1	0.05	−1.64
60.9	10	0.95	1.64
47.5	6	0.55	0.13

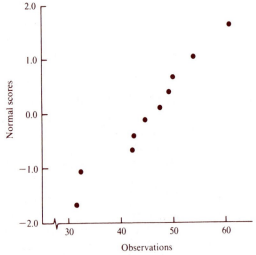

FIGURE 3.4-2   Normal probability plot. Scatter plot of the normal scores against the observations.

Remark   Here we have taken the ith order statistic $x_{(i)}$ as the quantile of order $P_i = (i - 0.5)/n$. In the statistics literature there are some slight differences in the definition of sample quantiles; this fact was mentioned in Section 1.2. Some authors define $x_{(i)}$ as the quantile of order $i/(n + 1)$, and some (e.g., the authors of the computer software MINITAB) define it as the quantile of order $[i - (3/8)]/[n + (1/4)]$. Thus the standardized normal scores (quantiles) could differ somewhat depending on the particular definition one has adopted. Interestingly, each of the three different definitions can be justified on different theoretical grounds. For our purposes, however, it will suffice to say that for reasonably large samples these three definitions will give very similar results. ∎

*3.4-2 Checking Other Models

At the beginning of Section 3.4-1, we fit an assumed normal model by equating the sample moments, $\bar{x}$ and s^2, to those of the model, namely μ and σ^2. Such a procedure of obtaining estimates of the unknown parameters is called *estimation by the method of moments*. Of course, it can also be used with other distributional models.

Remark Strictly speaking, estimation by the method of moments requires that the moments of the theoretical distribution be equated to the moments of the empirical distribution, as defined in Section 3.1-1. Thus, for the normal model, the estimates by the method of moments are

$$\hat{\mu} = \bar{x} \quad \text{and} \quad \hat{\sigma}^2 = v = \frac{1}{n} \sum_{i=1}^{n} (x_i - \bar{x})^2.$$

However, there is little difference and there is some advantage (to be explained later) using s^2 rather than v in the latter equation. ■

For illustration, suppose that by studying the histogram of a skewed set of data, we believe that a gamma distribution will provide a fairly good fit. If we equate the first two theoretical moments (i.e., $\mu = \alpha\beta$ and $\sigma^2 = \alpha\beta^2$; see Table 3.3-1), to the corresponding sample moments, we obtain

$$\alpha\beta = \bar{x} \quad \text{and} \quad \alpha\beta^2 = s^2.$$

The solutions of these equations provide the estimates

$$\hat{\alpha} = \frac{\bar{x}^2}{s^2} \quad \text{and} \quad \hat{\beta} = \frac{s^2}{\bar{x}}.$$

Example 3.4-1 Referring to Exercise 3.1-3, in which 40 losses due to wind-related catastrophes are given, we find that $\bar{x} = 9.225$ and $s_x = 10.237$. Since only losses above 1.5 (in millions) are considered, we subtract 1.5 from each observation, say $y = x - 1.5$, to obtain $\bar{y} = 7.725$ and $s_y = 10.237$. (Note that the standard deviation is not affected if one subtracts a constant from each observation.) If we believe that a gamma distribution provides a reasonable model for the distribution of y values, we estimate the parameters by

$$\hat{\alpha} = \left(\frac{7.725}{10.237}\right)^2 = 0.569 \quad \text{and} \quad \hat{\beta} = \frac{(10.237)^2}{7.725} = 13.566.$$

It is interesting to compare the fitted gamma p.d.f.,

$$g(y) = \frac{y^{0.569-1} e^{-y/13.566}}{\Gamma(0.569)(13.566)^{0.569}}, \quad 0 \le y < \infty,$$

to the relative frequency histogram using the $k = 4$ classes $[0, 1)$, $[1, 5)$, $[5, 28)$, and $[28, 48)$ (see Figure 3.4-3). ■

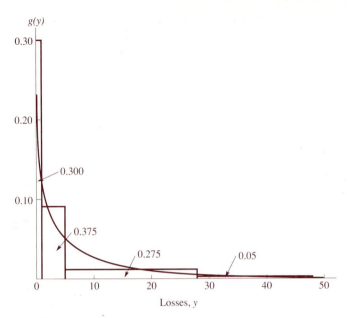

FIGURE 3.4-3 Relative frequency histogram of losses due to wind-related catastrophes and the p.d.f. of the corresponding fitted gamma distribution.

We can also use quantile–quantile plots, similar to the normal probability plot discussed earlier, to check whether a set of observations comes from a specified theoretical distribution function, $F(x) = P(X \leq x)$. Let $x_{(1)} \leq x_{(2)} \leq \cdots \leq x_{(n)}$ be the order statistics. For several values of i (possibly all if n is small), determine q_i, where

$$\frac{i - 0.5}{n} = F(q_i).$$

Of course, here we assume that the c.d.f. $F(x)$ is of a form that allows easy calculation of the theoretical quantiles. We then plot the implied theoretical quantiles q_i against the observed quantiles (order statistics) $x_{(i)}$; this gives us a q–q graph. If these points lie fairly close to a straight 45-degree line through the origin, we say that $F(x)$ provides a reasonable model for the underlying distribution.

Example 3.4-2 Suppose that someone thought the data of Exercise 3.1-3 could be fit with an exponential distribution once 1.5 had been subtracted from the $n = 40$ observations. From Example 3.4-1 we know that the mean of the 40 values

0.5	0.5	0.5	0.5	0.5	0.5	0.5	0.5	0.5	0.5
0.5	0.5	1.5	1.5	1.5	1.5	2.5	2.5	2.5	3.5
3.5	3.5	3.5	4.5	4.5	4.5	4.5	6.5	6.5	7.5
13.5	15.5	20.5	21.5	22.5	22.5	23.5	25.5	30.5	41.5

is given by $\bar{y} = 7.725$. Equating this to the mean, β, of the exponential distribution (see Table 3.3-1), we find that the fitted exponential density is

$$g(y) = \frac{1}{7.725} e^{-y/7.725}, \qquad 0 \le y < \infty.$$

The corresponding distribution function is

$$G(y) = \int_0^y g(w) \; dw = 1 - e^{-y/7.725}, \qquad 0 \le y < \infty.$$

The quantile, q_p, of order p is found by solving

$$p = 1 - e^{-q_p/7.725}.$$

It is

$$q_p = -7.725 \ln(1 - p).$$

Let us consider every third order statistic. For example, the 3rd order statistic, 0.5, is the $100(3 - 0.5)/40 = 6.25$ percentile; the 6th order statistic, 0.5, is the $100(6 - 0.5)/40 = 13.75$ percentile; and so on until the 39th order statistic, 30.5, which is the $100(39 - 0.5)/40 = 96.25$ percentile of the data. These observed quantiles, together with the implied theoretical quantiles $q_p = -7.725 \ln(1 - p)$, are listed in Table 3.4-2. Figure 3.4-4 gives the scatter plot of these 13 quantiles.

TABLE 3.4-2   Observed and Theoretical Quantiles

	Quantile	
p	Observed	Theoretical
0.0625	0.5	0.50
0.1375	0.5	1.14
0.2125	0.5	1.85
0.2875	0.5	2.62
0.3625	1.5	3.48
0.4375	2.5	4.44
0.5125	3.5	5.55
0.5875	4.5	6.84
0.6625	4.5	8.39
0.7375	7.5	10.33
0.8125	20.5	12.93
0.8875	22.5	16.88
0.9625	30.5	25.36

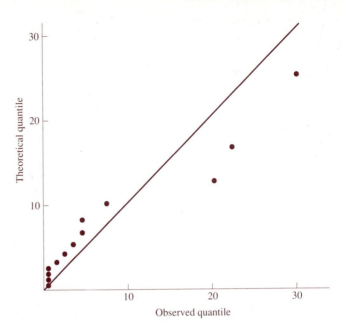

FIGURE 3.4-4 q–q plot for Example 3.4-2. Theoretical quantiles are calculated from the exponential distribution with $\beta = 7.725$.

The q–q plot in Figure 3.4-4 does not exhibit a straight-line pattern with slope 45 degrees through the origin. Although it is not an impossible fit, a better one would have been achieved if the smaller quantiles of the theoretical distribution were smaller and the larger quantiles bigger. That is exactly what was achieved in Example 3.4-1 by fitting the gamma p.d.f. ■

We mentioned earlier that we can purchase special normal probability graph paper. If the n observations are from a normal distribution, a plot of the points $[x_{(i)}, P_i = (i - 0.5)/n]$ on that special paper should exhibit, at least approximately, a linear relationship. Special graph paper is also available for many other distributions. As a matter of fact, the Weibull distribution is so important in engineering that there is a Weibull graph paper. A plot of $[x_{(i)}, P_i = (i - 0.5)/n]$ on this special graph paper allows the user to check whether the observations could have come from a Weibull distribution; if the points fit a straight line, the Weibull distribution provides an appropriate model. Furthermore, the user can obtain estimates of α and β from this plot. This is much the same idea as finding the estimate of σ from the reciprocal of the slope in the normal probability paper.

Exercises 3.4

3.4-1 Consider the following 25 observations.

10.1   37.5   8.4   99.0   12.8
66.0   31.0   85.3   63.6   73.8
98.5   11.8   83.5   88.7   99.6
65.5   80.1   74.4   69.9   9.9
91.5   80.3   44.1   12.6   63.6

(a) Construct a relative frequency histogram and sketch the empirical c.d.f.

(b) Determine the normal scores (implied theoretical quantiles) of the observations, and plot the normal scores against the observations. From this normal probability plot, and from the graphs in part (a), comment whether or not these observations are from a normal distribution. If you find that they are not from a normal distribution, what other models (distributions) are suggested by the data?

3.4-2 In this chapter we suggested a quantile plot to check for normality. Similar quantile plots can be made to check whether the observations come from certain other distributions. Consider the exponential distribution with the density $g(y) = (1/\beta)\exp(-y/\beta)$, $0 < y < \infty$.

(a) Show that $y_p = -\beta \ln(1 - p)$ is the quantile of order p.

(b) A plot of $-\ln(1 - P_i)$ against the order statistics $y_{(i)}$, where i is the rank of the observation and $P_i = (i - 0.5)/n$, is suggested as a check whether the data are from an exponential distribution. Explain why this is appropriate and discuss how one could estimate the parameter β from such a plot.

(c) It is hypothesized that the times to failure of certain welds that are exposed to continuous vibrations of specified frequency and amplitude follow an exponential distribution. The times to failure (in units of 1000 cycles) of 10 welded pieces follow.

580   300   990   240   1900
480   1040   1500   50   280

Check whether this hypothesis is valid.

3.4-3 Consider the $n = 90$ data in Table 1.2-1. Check whether these observations come from a normal distribution. Estimate μ and σ from the normal probability plot.

3.4-4 Check whether the melting points in Exercise 1.2-2 could possibly come from a normal distribution. Obtain rough estimates of μ and σ from the normal probability plot.

3.4-5 Consider the carbon monoxide emissions in Exercise 1.2-9. Construct and interpret a normal probability plot. Since the data are already grouped you may want to use the upper class limits as the observed order statistics in your q–q plot.

3.4-6 Assume that Y follows a lognormal distribution with parameters μ and σ (see Section 3.3-6).

(a) Show that the quantile of order p, y_p, is given by $y_p = e^{\mu + \sigma z_p}$, where z_p is the quantile of the $N(0, 1)$ distribution.

(b) Consider a scatter plot of the logarithms of the order statistics, $\ln y_{(i)}$, against z_i, where z_i is the normal score satisfying $P_i = (i - 0.5)/n = \Phi(z_i)$. Why is this a useful plot for checking whether the observations are from a lognormal distribution?

(c) Apply this plot to the carbon monoxide emissions that were studied in Exercise 3.4-5. Which of the two models, normal or lognormal, is more plausible?

The fact that the outcomes $X_1 = x_1$, $X_2 = x_2$, ..., $X_n = x_n$ occur with probability $g(x_1, x_2, ..., x_n)$ implies a distribution for the random variable $Y = u(X_1, X_2, ..., X_n)$. Quite often this distribution can be determined explicitly. A good example is the binomial distribution. There we looked at the number of successes $Y = \sum_{i=1}^{n} X_i$ among n independent Bernoulli trials [i.e., $P(X_i = 1) = p$ and $P(X_i = 0) = 1 - p$ for $i = 1, 2, ..., n$]. We found that Y can take on integer values $y = 0, 1, ..., n$, with probability

$$P(Y = y) = \binom{n}{y} p^y (1 - p)^{n - y}.$$

Important characteristics of the sampling distribution are its mean and variance. Since the outcomes $X_1 = x_1$, $X_2 = x_2$, ..., $X_n = x_n$ occur with probability $g(x_1, x_2, ..., x_n)$, it is natural to define the expected value of the estimator $Y = u(X_1, X_2, ..., X_n)$ as

$$\mu_Y = E(Y) = E[u(X_1, X_2, ..., X_n)]$$
$$= \sum_{x_1} \sum_{x_2} \cdots \sum_{x_n} u(x_1, x_2, ..., x_n) g(x_1, x_2, ..., x_n).$$

Each possible outcome $u(x_1, x_2, ..., x_n)$ is weighted by its corresponding probability of occurrence.

How can we calculate the variance of the estimator $Y = u(X_1, X_2, ..., X_n)$? Using the definition of variance, we can write

$$\sigma_Y^2 = \text{var}(Y) = \text{var}[u(X_1, X_2, ..., X_n)]$$
$$= \sum_{x_1} \sum_{x_2} \cdots \sum_{x_n} [u(x_1, x_2, ..., x_n) - \mu_Y]^2 g(x_1, x_2, ..., x_n).$$

Alternatively, we can calculate it from

$$\sigma_Y^2 = E(Y^2) - \mu_Y^2,$$

where

$$E(Y^2) = \sum_{x_1} \sum_{x_2} \cdots \sum_{x_n} [u(x_1, x_2, ..., x_n)]^2 g(x_1, x_2, ..., x_n).$$

Integration replaces summation in the case of continuous random variables. For example,

$$E[u(X_1, X_2, ..., X_n)]$$
$$= \int_{x_1} \int_{x_2} \cdots \int_{x_n} u(x_1, x_2, ..., x_n) g(x_1, x_2, ..., x_n) \, dx_1 \, dx_2 \cdots dx_n.$$

The equations above are valid for general joint probability density functions. Simplifications in these expressions occur for random samples. There the random variables X_1, X_2, ..., X_n are mutually independent and come from the same distribution with p.d.f. $f(x)$. In this case

$$g(x_1, x_2, ..., x_n) = f(x_1) f(x_2) \cdots f(x_n).$$

4.1-1   Linear Functions of Independent Random Variables

We begin the study of sampling distribution theory by considering linear functions of mutually independent random variables because many estimators can be written as linear functions of $X_1, X_2, \ldots, X_n$. After considering the general linear function $\sum_{i=1}^{n} a_i X_i$, we study $\bar{X} = \sum_{i=1}^{n} X_i/n$ as a special case.

Let us start our discussion with two independent random variables X_1 and X_2 with possibly different densities $f_1(x)$ and $f_2(x)$ and joint p.d.f. $g(x_1, x_2) = f_1(x_1)f_2(x_2)$. Let us calculate the expectation of the linear combination $Y = a_1 X_1 + a_2 X_2$, where a_1 and a_2 are constants. According to our previous definition, we find that

$$
\begin{aligned}
\mu_Y = E(Y) &= E(a_1 X_1 + a_2 X_2) \\
&= \sum_{x_1} \sum_{x_2} (a_1 x_1 + a_2 x_2) f_1(x_1) f_2(x_2) \\
&= a_1 \left[\sum_{x_2} f_2(x_2) \right]\left[\sum_{x_1} x_1 f_1(x_1) \right] + a_2 \left[\sum_{x_1} f_1(x_1) \right]\left[\sum_{x_2} x_2 f_2(x_2) \right] \\
&= a_1 E(X_1) + a_2 E(X_2) = a_1 \mu_1 + a_2 \mu_2,
\end{aligned}
$$

where $\mu_1 = E(X_1)$ and $\mu_2 = E(X_2)$ are the expectations of X_1 and X_2. The expectation of a linear combination of random variables is the linear combination of the respective expectations. We say that the expectation is a *linear operation*.

This linearity property is also used in the calculation of the variance of $Y = a_1 X_1 + a_2 X_2$. We find that

$$
\begin{aligned}
\sigma_Y^2 = \text{var}(Y) &= E[(Y - \mu_Y)^2] = E[(a_1 X_1 + a_2 X_2 - a_1 \mu_1 - a_2 \mu_2)^2] \\
&= E\{[a_1(X_1 - \mu_1) + a_2(X_2 - \mu_2)]^2\} \\
&= E[a_1^2(X_1 - \mu_1)^2 + a_2^2(X_2 - \mu_2)^2 + 2a_1 a_2(X_1 - \mu_1)(X_2 - \mu_2)] \\
&= a_1^2 E[(X_1 - \mu_1)^2] + a_2^2 E[(X_2 - \mu_2)^2] \\
&\quad + 2a_1 a_2 E[(X_1 - \mu_1)(X_2 - \mu_2)] \\
&= a_1^2 \sigma_1^2 + a_2^2 \sigma_2^2,
\end{aligned}
$$

since for independent random variables

$$
\begin{aligned}
E[(X_1 - \mu_1)(X_2 - \mu_2)] &= \sum_{x_1} \sum_{x_2} (x_1 - \mu_1)(x_2 - \mu_2) f_1(x_1) f_2(x_2) \\
&= \left[\sum_{x_1} (x_1 - \mu_1) f_1(x_1) \right]\left[\sum_{x_2} (x_2 - \mu_2) f_2(x_2) \right] \\
&= [E(X_1) - \mu_1][E(X_2) - \mu_2] = 0.
\end{aligned}
$$

This shows that the variance of a linear combination $Y = a_1 X_1 + a_2 X_2$ of independent random variables is

$$\sigma_Y^2 = a_1^2 \sigma_1^2 + a_2^2 \sigma_2^2$$

where σ_1^2 and σ_2^2 are the variances of the random variables X_1 and X_2.

It is an easy exercise to generalize these results for a linear function of n mutually independent random variables, $Y = \sum_{i=1}^{n} a_i X_i$. Say that $\mu_i = E(X_i)$ and $\sigma_i^2 = \text{var}(X_i)$ are the mean and the variance of the random variable X_i, $i = 1, \ldots, n$. One can show that the mean and the variance of Y are

$$\mu_Y = \sum_{i=1}^{n} a_i \mu_i \qquad \text{and} \qquad \sigma_Y^2 = \sum_{i=1}^{n} a_i^2 \sigma_i^2.$$

Note that the variance σ_Y^2 is a weighted sum of the individual variances. For the special case when all $a_i = 1$, we find that the variance of a sum of independent random variables is the sum of the individual variances. Furthermore, this equation shows that the variance of the difference of independent random variables is the sum of the individual variances.

Example 4.1-1 Let the independent random variables X_1 and X_2 have respective means $\mu_1 = 6$, $\mu_2 = 4$ and variances $\sigma_1^2 = 16$, $\sigma_2^2 = 9$. Then $Y = 3X_1 + 2X_2$ has mean $\mu_Y = (3)(6) + (2)(4) = 26$ and variance $\sigma_Y^2 = (3^2)16 + (2^2)9 = 180$. On the other hand, $W = 3X_1 - 2X_2$ has mean $\mu_W = (3)(6) - (2)(4) = 10$ and variance $\sigma_W^2 = (3)^2 16 + (-2)^2 9 = 180$. ∎

Example 4.1-2 In constructing certain products (e.g., a house), operations must be done in sequence. Assume that the three times, T_1, T_2, T_3, needed to complete a certain product, are mutually independent random variables with respective means $\mu_1 = 16$, $\mu_2 = 7$, $\mu_3 = 21$ and variances $\sigma_1^2 = 13$, $\sigma_2^2 = 9$, $\sigma_3^2 = 17$. Then the respective mean and variance of the total time $Y = T_1 + T_2 + T_3$ needed to complete the product are, respectively.

$$\mu_Y = 16 + 7 + 21 = 44, \qquad \sigma_Y^2 = 13 + 9 + 17 = 39.$$ ∎

4.1-2 Distribution of the Sample Mean $\bar{X}$

Let $X_1, X_2, \ldots, X_n$ be a *random sample* of size n from a distribution with mean μ and variance σ^2. Recall that the term "random sample" implies that (1) $X_1, X_2, \ldots, X_n$ are drawn from the *same* distribution, and (2) the drawings are *mutually independent*.

Let us consider the sample mean

$$\bar{X} = \frac{1}{n} \sum_{i=1}^{n} X_i = \left(\frac{1}{n}\right) X_1 + \left(\frac{1}{n}\right) X_2 + \cdots + \left(\frac{1}{n}\right) X_n,$$

and let us study its sampling distribution. Let us first determine the mean and the variance of the sampling distribution of $\bar{X}$. The sample mean is a linear combination of $X_1, X_2, \ldots, X_n$, with weights $a_i = 1/n$. Also, $X_1, X_2, \ldots, X_n$ are mutually independent and from the same distribution; thus $E(X_i) = \mu_i = \mu$, $\text{var}(X_i) = \sigma_i^2 = \sigma^2$. From our earlier result about the mean and variance of a linear combination of independent random variables, it follows that

$$E(\bar{X}) = \sum_{i=1}^{n} \left(\frac{1}{n}\right)\mu = \mu \qquad \text{and} \qquad \text{var}(\bar{X}) = \sum_{i=1}^{n} \left(\frac{1}{n}\right)^2 \sigma^2 = \frac{\sigma^2}{n}.$$

That is, the mean of $\bar{X}$ is the same as that of the underlying distribution; the variance, however, is that of the underlying distribution divided by the sample size n.

The sample mean $\bar{X}$ is the usual estimator of the population mean μ. Now, almost certainly the mean of one particular sample will not equal μ unless the investigator is extremely lucky. Moreover, the sample means will vary with repeated samples. However, the result $E(\bar{X}) = \mu$ shows that the mean of this sampling distribution is the same as the mean of the underlying distribution that we want to estimate. We call such an estimator an *unbiased estimator*.

The second result, $\text{var}(\bar{X}) = \sigma^2/n$, shows that the variability of the estimator $\bar{X}$ around the population mean μ goes to zero as the number of observations in the sample increases. In the limit, as n becomes larger and larger, we essentially look at all elements in the population, and we can estimate μ precisely.

The sample mean is an unbiased estimator of μ. But one can think of many other unbiased estimators of the population mean. For example, the average of the first three observations in the sample, $(X_1 + X_2 + X_3)/3$, or the sixth observation that gets recorded, X_6, are also unbiased estimators. However, since $\bar{X}$ uses more information than the other two estimators, our intuition tells us to prefer $\bar{X}$. This intuition is quite correct since, for $n > 3$, $\text{var}(\bar{X}) = \sigma^2/n$ is smaller than

$$\text{var}\left(\frac{X_1 + X_2 + X_3}{3}\right) = \frac{\sigma^2}{3} \qquad \text{and} \qquad \text{var}(X_6) = \sigma^2.$$

The sample mean $\bar{X}$, calculated from all n observations, is less variable than the other two estimators. We certainly prefer an estimator that varies around the population parameter as little as possible. This is the reason we say that $\bar{X}$ is *more efficient or more reliable* than the other two estimators.

We have already determined the mean and the variance of the sampling distribution of $\bar{X}$, and found that $E(\bar{X}) = \mu$ and $\text{var}(\bar{X}) = \sigma^2/n$. We also know that, for any random variable W, the mean of the linear function $bW + c$ is

$$E(bW + c) = bE(W) + c = b\mu_W + c$$

and its variance is

$$\text{var}(bW + c) = b^2 \text{var}(W) = b^2\sigma_W^2.$$

Adding a nonrandom constant c to a random variable shifts its mean but does not affect its variance. Thus

$$Z = \frac{\bar{X} - \mu}{\sigma/\sqrt{n}} = \left(\frac{\sqrt{n}}{\sigma}\right)\bar{X} - \frac{\sqrt{n}\,\mu}{\sigma}$$

has mean

$$\mu_Z = \frac{\sqrt{n}}{\sigma}\mu - \frac{\sqrt{n}\,\mu}{\sigma} = 0$$

and variance

$$\sigma_Z^2 = \left(\frac{\sqrt{n}}{\sigma}\right)^2 \text{var}(\bar{X}) = \left(\frac{n}{\sigma^2}\right)\left(\frac{\sigma^2}{n}\right) = 1.$$

We say that $Z = (\bar{X} - \mu)/(\sigma/\sqrt{n})$ is a standardized random variable having mean zero and variance 1.

What more can we say about the distribution of $\bar{X}$, or, if we prefer, the distribution of Z? There is a theorem in mathematical statistics that says that a linear combination of normal random variables (which, in general, need not be independent) is again normally distributed. This theorem implies the following result:

> If we sample from a normal distribution with mean μ and variance σ^2, then the distribution of $\bar{X}$ is $N(\mu, \sigma^2/n)$ and the distribution of Z is $N(0, 1)$.

Example 4.1-3 Let $\bar{X}$ be the mean of a random sample of size $n = 25$ taken from the normal population $N(75, 100)$. Thus the distribution of $\bar{X}$ is normal with mean 75 and standard deviation $10/\sqrt{25} = 2$. We can calculate probabilities, such as

$$P(71 < \bar{X} < 79) = P\left(\frac{71 - 75}{2} < \frac{\bar{X} - 75}{2} < \frac{79 - 75}{2}\right)$$

$$= \Phi(2) - \Phi(-2) = 0.9544.$$

This result implies that the *mean of 25 observations* has a 0.9544 chance of falling between 71 and 79. Compare this with the probability that an *individual observation X* falls within these limits, that is,

$$P(71 < X < 79) = P\left(\frac{71 - 75}{10} < \frac{X - 75}{10} < \frac{79 - 75}{10}\right)$$

$$= \Phi(0.4) - \Phi(-0.4)$$

$$= 0.6554 - (1 - 0.6554)$$

$$= 0.3108.$$

Of course, the probability of an individual observation falling between 71 and 79 is much smaller than that of a sample average $\bar{X}$ that is based on $n = 25$ observations. ∎

Exercises 4.1

4.1-1 Let the independent random variables X_1 and X_2 have respective means $\mu_1 = 4$, $\mu_2 = 9$ and variances $\sigma_1^2 = 6$, $\sigma_2^2 = 8$. Consider $Y = 3X_1 - 2X_2$, and find the mean and variance of Y.

4.1-2 Let T_1, T_2, T_3, T_4 represent four independent sequential times needed to complete some operation. Find the mean and variance of the total time $Y = \sum T_i$ if the four means are $\mu_1 = 3$, $\mu_2 = 11$, $\mu_3 = 9$, $\mu_4 = 6$ and the four variances are $\sigma_1^2 = 4$, $\sigma_2^2 = 9$, $\sigma_3^2 = 7$, $\sigma_4^2 = 5$, respectively.

4.1-3 Let $\bar{X}$ be the mean of a random sample of size $n = 10$ from a distribution with p.d.f. $f(x) = 6x(1 - x)$, $0 < x < 1$. Find the mean and variance of $\bar{X}$.

4.1-4 Let X_1, X_2 be a random sample of size $n = 2$ from a discrete uniform distribution with p.d.f. $f(x) = 1/3$, $x = 1, 2, 3$. Let $Y = X_1 + X_2$.
(a) Compute the mean μ_X and variance σ_X^2 of the underlying distribution and use them to determine μ_Y and σ_Y^2.
(b) Find the p.d.f. $g(y) = P(Y = y)$, $y = 2, 3, 4, 5, 6$, and use it to compute μ_Y and σ_Y^2.

4.1-5 A cereal manufacturer packages cereal in boxes that have 12-ounce label weight. Suppose that the actual distribution of weights is $N(12.2, 0.04)$.
(a) What percentage of the boxes have cereal weighing under 12 ounces?
(b) If $\bar{X}$ is the mean weight of the cereals in $n = 4$ boxes selected at random, compute $P(\bar{X} < 12)$.

4.1-6 Show that the mean and the variance of a linear function of mutually independent random variables X_1, X_2, ..., X_n, namely $Y = \sum_{i=1}^{n} a_i X_i$, are

$$\mu_Y = \sum_{i=1}^{n} a_i \mu_i \quad \text{and} \quad \sigma_Y^2 = \sum_{i=1}^{n} a_i^2 \sigma_i^2.$$

4.1-7 Let W have the triangular p.d.f. $f(w) = 2w$, $0 < w < 1$.
(a) Show that the mean and the variance of W are 2/3 and 1/18, respectively.
(b) What are the mean and variance of $U = \sqrt{18(W - 2/3)}$?
(c) Find the distribution function $G(u) = P(U \le u)$ and the p.d.f. $g(u) = G'(u)$.
(d) What type of distribution does U have?

4.1-8 Let X_1 and X_2 be two independent observations of the spinner in Example 3.1-2. Let $Y = X_1 + X_2$. Draw the space of (X_1, X_2) and, using a geometric argument, determine the probability

$$G(y) = P(Y \le y) = P(X_1 + X_2 \le y).$$

Distinguish between the two cases, $0 < y \le 1$ and $1 < y < 2$. Show that

$$g(y) = G'(y) = \begin{cases} y, & 0 < y \le 1, \\ 2 - y, & 1 < y < 2. \end{cases}$$

4.2 Central Limit Theorem

The result that $\bar{X}$ is $N(\mu, \sigma^2/n)$ applies if each X arises from the normal distribution $N(\mu, \sigma^2)$. But what can we say if the underlying distribution is not normal? For example, if we sample from a uniform, or an exponential, or some other distribution? The central limit theorem provides the answer to this question.

Central Limit Theorem	If $\bar{X}$ is the mean of a random sample $X_1, X_2, \ldots, X_n$ from a distribution with mean μ and finite variance $\sigma^2 > 0$, then the distribution of $$Z = \frac{\bar{X} - \mu}{\sigma/\sqrt{n}} = \frac{\sum X_i - n\mu}{\sigma\sqrt{n}}$$ approaches a distribution that is $N(0, 1)$ as n becomes large.

This theorem says that for a sufficiently large sample size n the distribution of $\bar{X}$ can be approximated by a distribution that is $N(\mu, \sigma^2/n)$. Similarly, the distribution of the sum $\sum_{i=1}^{n} X_i$ can be approximated by the $N(n\mu, n\sigma^2)$ distribution.

Example 4.2-1　Since we have not given a formal proof of this theorem (this would require more mathematics), we include a simulation experiment that should convince you that this theorem is, in fact, correct.

Consider the list of random numbers that are given in Table C.10. Each number from zero to nine occurs with equal probability and, furthermore, the occurrences are independent. Independence means that there are no long "runs" of 4's, or runs of 9's, or that certain sequences of numbers occur more often than others. These numbers can be thought of as the outcomes of independent drawings from a discrete uniform distribution that assigns equal probability of 1/10 to each integer from zero through nine. One could generate such a table by putting 10 slips of paper with labels zero to nine in a hat and drawing with replacement, making sure that the slips are well mixed after each draw. Although this mechanism for generating such random numbers is instructive, it is not one that is used in practice. In today's computer age, the standard software packages contain programs that will generate numbers with the characteristics of random numbers. Computer-produced random numbers are frequently called *pseudorandom numbers.* The prefix "pseudo" is used because the programs take a certain starting number (the "seed" number) and determine all subsequent numbers by certain arithmetic operations. Yet despite their deterministic origin, these computer-produced numbers do behave as if they were truly randomly generated.

Before we describe the experiment that illustrates the central limit theorem, let us discuss how we might check whether the numbers in Table C.10 are indeed random drawings from a discrete uniform distribution on the integers zero through nine. One could simply take these 2000 numbers and obtain the relative frequencies of the numbers zero through nine; these frequencies should be about 0.10. But this alone would not be sufficient; one should also check the independence among the numbers. For that, one could determine the frequencies of the 100 different pairs of adjacent numbers (0, 0), (0, 1), ..., (9, 8), (9, 9); again, these frequencies should be about the same. The same type of analysis should be made for adjacent triples, quadruples, and so on.

Now let us return to our original objective, which was to illustrate the central limit theorem. Let us sample from the uniform distribution on 0 to 1 having p.d.f. $f(x) = 1$ for $0 \le x < 1$. In Example 3.1-5 it is shown that $E(X) = 0.5$ and $\text{var}(X) = 1/12$. Let us generate random numbers from this distribution. This can be achieved approximately by taking nonoverlapping sets of five consecutive numbers from Table C.10, and dividing the resulting numbers by 100,000. This creates numbers that are distributed uniformly between 0.00000 and 0.99999; actually, these numbers follow a distribution with discrete outcomes but can be approximated by a continuous uniform distribution. The fact that we take nonoverlapping sets of numbers guarantees their independence. Now let us consider random samples of size n (where $n = 1, 2, 5, 10,$ and 30), calculate the sample means $\bar{x}$ and the standardized means $z = (\bar{x} - 0.5)/\sqrt{1/(12n)}$, and repeat this for each sample size, say, 500 times. As an example, take the case $n = 2$. Using the numbers in the fifth column of Table C.10, we find that the first sample average is

$$\bar{x} = \frac{1}{2}(0.44999 + 0.89435) = 0.67217,$$

the second sample average is

$$\bar{x} = \frac{1}{2}(0.20151 + 0.69861) = 0.45006,$$

and so on, until we have generated the 500 averages. Fortunately, most statistical computer packages include programs that generate random samples from various distributions, including the uniform.

In Figure 4.2-1 we summarize the results of the 500 samples and we plot, for each n separately, the histogram of $(\bar{x} - 0.5)/\sqrt{1/12n}$. The smooth curve on these figures corresponds to the p.d.f. of the $N(0, 1)$. These histograms are centered at zero, and their variance is about 1. For $n = 1$, the distribution is uniform since the "averages" correspond to individual observations from a uniform distribution. The distribution of the means from samples of size $n = 5$ already starts to look normal, despite the fact that we sample from a uniform distribution. As we expect from the central limit theorem, the approximation to the $N(0, 1)$ distribution becomes better and better as we increase the sample size n. For $n = 30$, this approximation is already extremely good. This experiment shows that for sufficiently large sample size, the distribution of the sample mean is approximately normal, even if we sample from a distribution that is quite different from a normal. ∎

Example 4.2-2   One can also use a theoretical example to illustrate the approximation. Consider $Y = X_1 + X_2$, the sum of two independent observations from the uniform distribution $f(x) = 1$, $0 \le x < 1$. Since $\mu = 1/2$ and $\sigma^2 = 1/12$, the mean and the variance of Y are $E(Y) = 1$ and $\text{var}(Y) = 1/6$.

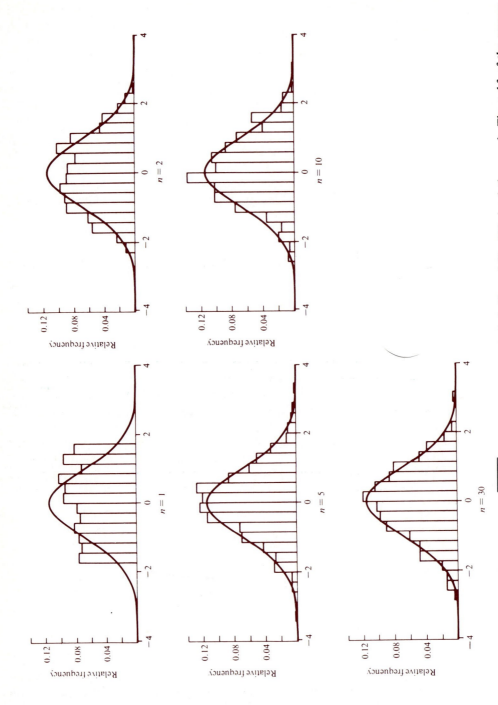

FIGURE 4.2-1 Histograms of $(\bar{x} - 0.5)/\sqrt{1/(12n)}$ for sample sizes $n = 1, 2, 5, 10$, and 30; 500 simulations each. The p.d.f. of the approximating $N(0, 1)$ distribution is given for comparison.

Even though $n = 2$ is extremely small, let us use the normal approximation to find

$$P(0.5 < Y < 1.5) = P\left(\frac{-0.5}{1/\sqrt{6}} < \frac{Y-1}{1/\sqrt{6}} < \frac{0.5}{1/\sqrt{6}}\right)$$

$$\approx \Phi(0.5\sqrt{6}) - \Phi(-0.5\sqrt{6})$$

$$= 2\Phi(1.22) - 1 = 0.7776.$$

The exact p.d.f. of Y was determined in Exercise 4.1-8. Using this result, we find that the exact probability is

$$P(0.5 < Y < 1.5) = \int_{0.5}^{1.5} g(y)\, dy$$

$$= 1 - 2\int_{0}^{0.5} y\, dy = 1 - 0.25 = 0.75.$$

Even for such a small n the normal approximation is not too bad; it will improve for larger n. ■

4.2-1   Normal Approximation of the Binomial Distribution

The central limit theorem implies that the binomial distribution with parameters n and p can be approximated by the $N[np, np(1 - p)]$ distribution. The reason for this is that a binomial random variable Y can be thought of as the sum $\sum_{i=1}^{n} X_i$, where $X_1, X_2, \ldots, X_n$ is a random sample from a Bernoulli distribution with mean p and variance $p(1 - p)$. However, note that Y can only take on integer values, $0, 1, 2, \ldots, n$, and thus we approximate a discrete probability distribution by a continuous p.d.f. $f(y)$, which is $N[np, np(1 - p)]$. Thus it is natural to approximate the true probability $P(Y = k)$, where k is one of those integers, by the area under the normal p.d.f. between $k - 0.5$ and $k + 0.5$. That is,

$$P(Y = k) \approx \int_{k-0.5}^{k+0.5} f(y)\, dy.$$

Since $f(y)$ is the p.d.f. of a $N[np, np(1 - p)]$, this probability is

$$P(Y = k) \approx \Phi\left(\frac{k + 0.5 - np}{\sqrt{np(1 - p)}}\right) - \Phi\left(\frac{k - 0.5 - np}{\sqrt{np(1 - p)}}\right).$$

The following example illustrates this approximation.

Example 4.2-3 Let Y be binomial with $n = 16$, $p = 1/2$. Although n is not very large here, we have selected a symmetric binomial distribution; this improves the approximation. If p is different from $1/2$, we would need a larger

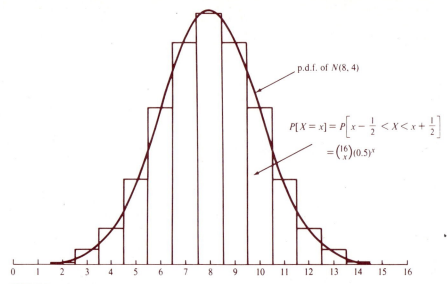

FIGURE 4.2-2 The p.d.f. of the $b(n = 16, p = 0.5)$ distribution and of the approximating $N(8, 4)$ distribution.

value of n to attain the same quality of approximation. With $n = 16$ we can use the table of binomial probabilities (Table C.2) to compare the approximations with the exact probabilities. In Figure 4.2-2 we have drawn a probability histogram, $b(n = 16, p = 0.5)$, together with the normal p.d.f. of $N[np = 8, np(1 - p) = 4]$. The normal p.d.f. approximates the shape of the probability histogram quite well. For example, the approximation of $P(Y = 7)$ is

$$P(6.5 < Y < 7.5) \approx \Phi\left(\frac{7.5 - 8}{2}\right) - \Phi\left(\frac{6.5 - 8}{2}\right)$$

$$= \Phi(-0.25) - \Phi(-0.75) = 0.7734 - 0.5987 = 0.1747.$$

From the binomial tables with $n = 16$ and $p = 0.5$, the true probability is

$$P(Y = 7) = P(Y \le 7) - P(Y \le 6) = 0.4018 - 0.2272 = 0.1746;$$

thus the approximation and the exact probability are in excellent agreement. As another illustration with this same distribution, consider the probability

$$P(Y = 6, 7, 8, 9, 10) = P(5.5 < Y < 10.5)$$

$$\approx \Phi\left(\frac{10.5 - 8}{2}\right) - \Phi\left(\frac{5.5 - 8}{2}\right) = 2(0.8944) - 1 = 0.7888.$$

This agrees well with the exact probability

$$P(Y \le 10) - P(Y \le 5) = 0.8949 - 0.1051 = 0.7898.$$

Exercises 4.2

4.2-1 Let $\bar{X}$ be the mean of a random sample of size $n = 48$ from the uniform distribution on the interval (0, 2); that is, $f(x) = 1/2, 0 < x < 2$. Approximate the probability $P(0.9 < \bar{X} < 1.1)$.

4.2-2 Let $\bar{X}$ be the mean of a random sample of size $n = 15$ from a distribution with p.d.f. $f(x) = (3/2)x^2, -1 < x < 1$. Approximate $P(-0.02 < \bar{X} < 0.1)$.

4.2-3 Let $\bar{X}$ be the mean of a random sample of size $n = 36$ from an exponential distribution with mean 4. Approximate $P(3.1 < \bar{X} < 4.6)$.

4.2-4 Let $\bar{X}$ be the mean of a random sample of size $n = 12$ from a chi-square distribution with six degrees of freedom. Approximate $P(5.1 < \bar{X} < 7.2)$.

4.2-5 Let Y be $b(n = 16, p = 0.2)$. This particular binomial distribution is quite skewed.
(a) From the binomial tables, find $P(Y = 1, 2, 3, 4)$.
(b) Use the normal distribution to approximate the probability in part (a).
Hint Write it as $P(0.5 < Y < 4.5)$.
(c) Is the approximation as good in this skewed case as in the symmetric case with $n = 16$?

4.2-6 Let Y have a Poisson distribution with mean $\lambda = 9$.
(a) Find $P(7 \leq Y \leq 11)$ from the Poisson table.
(b) Approximate the probability in part (a) using the normal p.d.f. $N(9, 9)$.
Hint Since Y has a discrete distribution, first write that probability as $P(6.5 < Y < 11.5)$. It is true that Y has an approximate normal distribution, as it can be thought of as the sum of $n = \lambda = 9$ independent Poisson variables, each with mean and variance equal to 1.

4.2-7 In Example 4.2-1 we discussed how to generate independent realizations from a uniform distribution on zero to 1. Here we illustrate how we can use these random numbers to generate independent realizations from a continuous random variable with c.d.f. $F(x)$. It is easy to see that $U = F(X)$ follows a uniform distribution because the c.d.f. of U is

$$P[F(X) \leq u] = P[X \leq F^{-1}(u)] = F(F^{-1}(u)) = u,$$

which is the c.d.f. of the uniform distribution on space zero to 1. Moreover, the converse of this result is true: If U has the uniform distribution on zero to one, then the X defined by $U = F(X)$ has a distribution with c.d.f. $F(x)$. Therefore, we can first generate a uniform random number, say u, and then determine the corresponding quantile x_u such that $u = F(x_u)$. The number x_u is a realization from the distribution with c.d.f. $F(x)$. Furthermore, since the u's are random numbers that enjoy the property of independence, it follows that the corresponding x_u's represent independent realizations from the distribution with c.d.f. $F(x)$.
(a) Using the numbers from Table C.10, generate 20 realizations from a uniform distribution on zero to 1.
(b) Use those numbers to generate 20 realizations of the following two distributions: (1) the exponential distribution with p.d.f. $f(x) = (1/3)\exp(-x/3)$, and (2) the $N(2, 9)$ distribution.
Hint In (1) we can find the c.d.f. $F(x)$ in closed form. Do it and solve $u = F(x_u)$ for x_u. In (2) we must use the normal tables, as we cannot determine $F(x)$ explicitly.

4.3 Confidence Intervals for Means

If a random sample $X_1, X_2, \ldots, X_n$ arises from a distribution with unknown mean μ and variance $\sigma^2 > 0$, then the sample mean $\bar{X}$ is an unbiased estimator of μ; that is, $E(\bar{X}) = \mu$. We now study the reliability of $\bar{X}$ as an estimator and develop an interval that covers the unknown mean μ with high probability. We use the distribution of $\bar{X}$, which, according to the central limit theorem, is approximately $N(\mu, \sigma^2/n)$, provided that n is large. Of course, $\bar{X}$ is exactly $N(\mu, \sigma^2/n)$ if the underlying distribution is $N(\mu, \sigma^2)$. Thus the following probability statements should be read as approximate or exact, depending on whether $\bar{X}$ has an approximate or exact normal distribution. In either case, the distribution of $\bar{X}$ is said to be a sampling distribution, here $N(\mu, \sigma^2/n)$, because it describes how $\bar{X}$ varies from sample to sample.

For a given probability $1 - \alpha$ (usually, α is small, i.e., 0.01, 0.05, 0.10), we can find a value, say $z(\alpha/2)$, from the normal table such that

$$P\left[-z(\alpha/2) \leq \frac{\bar{X} - \mu}{\sigma/\sqrt{n}} \leq z(\alpha/2)\right] = 1 - \alpha.$$

Make a graph of the normal p.d.f. and convince yourself that $z(\alpha/2)$ is the $100(1 - \alpha/2)$ percentile of the $N(0, 1)$ distribution; that is, $P[Z \leq z(\alpha/2)] = 1 - \alpha/2$. Since $P[Z \geq z(\alpha/2)] = \alpha/2$, $z(\alpha/2)$ is also called the *upper $100(\alpha/2)$ percentage point* of the $N(0, 1)$ distribution. Since the $N(0, 1)$ distribution is symmetric around zero,

$$P[Z \leq -z(\alpha/2)] = P[Z \geq z(\alpha/2)] = \alpha/2.$$

For example, if $1 - \alpha = 0.95$, then $z(\alpha/2) = z(0.025) = 1.96$, and if $1 - \alpha = 0.90$, then $z(\alpha/2) = z(0.05) = 1.645$.

The inequalities

$$-z(\alpha/2) \leq \frac{\bar{X} - \mu}{\sigma/\sqrt{n}} \leq z(\alpha/2)$$

are equivalent to the following statements:

$$-z(\alpha/2) \frac{\sigma}{\sqrt{n}} \leq \bar{X} - \mu \leq z(\alpha/2) \frac{\sigma}{\sqrt{n}},$$

$$-\bar{X} - z(\alpha/2) \frac{\sigma}{\sqrt{n}} \leq -\mu \leq -\bar{X} + z(\alpha/2) \frac{\sigma}{\sqrt{n}},$$

and

$$\bar{X} - z(\alpha/2) \frac{\sigma}{\sqrt{n}} \leq \mu \leq \bar{X} + z(\alpha/2) \frac{\sigma}{\sqrt{n}}.$$

Thus the probabilities of each set of inequalities is exactly the same, $1 - \alpha$. In particular,

$$P\left[\bar{X} - z(\alpha/2) \frac{\sigma}{\sqrt{n}} \leq \mu \leq \bar{X} + z(\alpha/2) \frac{\sigma}{\sqrt{n}}\right] = 1 - \alpha.$$

Note that the random variable $\bar{X}$ is in the extremes of these inequalities and the constant, but unknown, parameter μ is in the middle. Thus the probability that the *random interval*

$$\left[\bar{X} - z(\alpha/2) \frac{\sigma}{\sqrt{n}}, \bar{X} + z(\alpha/2) \frac{\sigma}{\sqrt{n}} \right]$$

includes the unknown mean μ is $1 - \alpha$. For simplicity, we sometimes write the random interval as $\bar{X} \pm z(\alpha/2)\sigma/\sqrt{n}$.

Suppose that an experiment is carried out and we observe the sample x_1, $x_2, \ldots, x_n$ and compute the sample mean $\bar{x}$. Assuming that σ is known, we can then compute the interval

$$\left[\bar{x} - z(\alpha/2) \frac{\sigma}{\sqrt{n}}, \bar{x} + z(\alpha/2) \frac{\sigma}{\sqrt{n}} \right]$$

or, more simply, $\bar{x} \pm z(\alpha/2)\sigma/\sqrt{n}$. Now this computed interval either includes μ or it does not. However, since prior to sampling the random interval includes μ with probability $1 - \alpha$, we continue to associate that number $1 - \alpha$ with the computed interval. We say that we are $100(1 - \alpha)$ percent *confident* that the computed interval $\bar{x} \pm z(\alpha/2)\sigma/\sqrt{n}$ includes μ. More formally, $\bar{x} \pm z(\alpha/2)\sigma/\sqrt{n}$ is referred to as a $100(1 - \alpha)$ percent *confidence interval* for μ and $1 - \alpha$ is called the *confidence coefficient*.

Example 4.3-1   A random sample of size $n = 25$ from the distribution $N(\mu, \sigma^2 = 4)$ results in the sample mean $\bar{x} = 13.2$. Then $\bar{x} \pm 2(\sigma/\sqrt{n})$ provides a 95.44 percent confidence interval for μ. That is, $13.2 \pm 2(2/5)$ or, equivalently, the interval from 12.4 to 14.0 is a 95.44 percent confidence interval for μ. Note that it is easy to remember how to form a 95.44 percent confidence interval for μ: Take $\bar{x}$ and add and subtract two standard deviations of the sample mean.

Example 4.3-2   The mean breaking strength of a sample of $n = 32$ steel beams equals $\bar{x} = 42,196$ pounds per square inch (psi). From past experience we know that the standard deviation of an individual measurement is about $\sigma = 500$ psi. Thus $\bar{x} \pm 1.645\sigma/\sqrt{32}$, which equals $42,196 \pm 1.645(500/\sqrt{32})$, or $(42,051; 42,341)$, provides an approximate 90 percent confidence interval for the population mean μ. This means that we are 90 percent confident that the unknown mean μ is within this interval.

We would like to remark in the context of this example that it is always important to identify clearly from which population we have sampled. For example, taking only beams from the scrap pile and testing their breaking strengths may tell us nothing about the overall breaking strength of our production. We would only learn about the breaking strength of the rejected beams, which most likely would be different from the rest of the production. If we want to get information on today's production, we have to sample from today's production and make certain that we give each beam the same chance of being selected.

Of course, if the population mean μ is unknown, then in many situations the population standard deviation σ is also unknown and we cannot compute the interval $\bar{x} \pm z(\alpha/2)(\sigma/\sqrt{n})$. If the sample size is quite large (at least 30), most statisticians simply approximate σ by the sample standard deviation s, and use $\bar{x} \pm z(\alpha/2)(s/\sqrt{n})$ as an approximate $100(1 - \alpha)$ percent confidence interval for μ. This is usually quite satisfactory, particularly if we recognize that this involves an additional approximation so that a quoted 95 percent confidence interval might really be one of 93 percent, 96.5 percent, or some other percentage number reasonably close to 95.

Example 4.3-3   In Example 4.3-2 we assumed that the standard deviation of individual measurements is known. Let us now take a more realistic position and suppose that σ is estimated by the sample standard deviation s. From the $n = 32$ observations, we not only compute $\bar{x} = 42,196$, but also the sample standard deviation $s = 614$. If these 32 observations suggest that the underlying distribution is fairly symmetric, an approximate 95 percent confidence interval for μ is given by $\bar{x} \pm (1.96)s/\sqrt{n}$. Since this is an approximation anyway, we may as well replace $z(0.025) = 1.96$ by 2 and use $\bar{x} \pm 2s/\sqrt{n}$ as an approximate 95 percent confidence interval. This equation is easy to remember. In our example the approximate 95 percent confidence interval for μ is given by $42,196 \pm 2(614)/\sqrt{32}$, or $(41,979; 42,413)$. ∎

4.3-1   Determination of the Sample Size

We are now planning an experiment and want to be $100(1 - \alpha)$ percent confident that our estimate is within h units of the unknown parameter μ. For example, we may want to be 95 percent confident that our estimate is within $h = 2$ units of μ. How large must we choose our sample size n in order to estimate μ with such accuracy?

Since we know that

$$P\left[\bar{X} - z(\alpha/2)\frac{\sigma}{\sqrt{n}} \le \mu \le \bar{X} + z(\alpha/2)\frac{\sigma}{\sqrt{n}}\right] = 1 - \alpha,$$

we must choose n such that $h = z(\alpha/2)(\sigma/\sqrt{n})$ or, equivalently,

$$n = \frac{\sigma^2[z(\alpha/2)]^2}{h^2}.$$

This requires knowledge of σ^2. In many situations, the experimenter may have a reasonable approximation for σ^2. That is, results from pilot studies or from experiments with other related variables can suggest an appropriate planning value for σ^2.

The expression for n above shows that the required sample size increases with increasing confidence coefficient $1 - \alpha$ and decreases with increasing half-width h. Sometimes we may require too much accuracy, and as a result we find that n is very large. If we cannot afford to collect that many observations, we may want to reduce the confidence coefficient or, alternatively, increase the half-width h.

Example 4.3-4 An existing process used to manufacture paint yields, on the average, 70 tons of paint each day. Daily yields, however, vary from day to day due to changes in raw materials and plant conditions.

Suppose, however, it is fairly well established that the daily yields are normally distributed, that the variability from one day to the other is more or less independent, and that the standard deviation is $\sigma = 3$ tons.

Because of increasing demand for this type of paint, certain modifications are suggested and we are interested in estimating the mean yield of this modified process. How many sample observations do we have to obtain if we want to be 95 percent certain that our estimate is within 1 ton of the true but unknown mean yield μ? Here $\sigma = 3$ and $z(0.025) = 1.96$. Thus $n = (9)(1.96)^2/1 = 34.6$; that is, we must sample at least 35 days. ■

4.3-2   Confidence Intervals for $\mu_1 - \mu_2$

Let $X_1, X_2, \ldots, X_{n_1}$ and $Y_1, Y_2, \ldots, Y_{n_2}$ be random samples of sizes n_1 and n_2 from two *independent* distributions with respective parameters μ_1, σ_1^2 and μ_2, σ_2^2. For example, the two populations may correspond to the breaking strengths of two different fabrics: fabric A, an "all-synthetic" material, and fabric B, a material with 15 percent cotton content. From fabric A, the investigator selects at random n_1 small pieces of cloth and determines their breaking strengths, $X_1, X_2, \ldots, X_{n_1}$. Similarly, $Y_1, Y_2, \ldots, Y_{n_2}$ are the breaking strengths of n_2 fabric specimens that are taken at random from the production of fabric B.

The sample means $\bar{X}$ and $\bar{Y}$ are estimators of μ_1 and μ_2. If the samples are taken from normal distributions, the respective distributions of $\bar{X}$ and $\bar{Y}$ are exactly $N(\mu_1, \sigma_1^2/n_1)$ and $N(\mu_2, \sigma_2^2/n_2)$. However, even if the samples arise from nonnormal distributions, the distributions of $\bar{X}$ and $\bar{Y}$ are *approximately* normal according to the central limit theorem, provided that the sample sizes n_1 and n_2 are large enough.

The appropriate estimator for $\mu_1 - \mu_2$ is the difference of the sample means $\bar{X} - \bar{Y}$. Since we assumed that the two random samples are selected independently, it follows that $\bar{X}$ and $\bar{Y}$ are independent also. Hence (see Section 4.1),

$$\text{var}(\bar{X} - \bar{Y}) = \text{var}(\bar{X}) + \text{var}(\bar{Y}) = \frac{\sigma_1^2}{n_1} + \frac{\sigma_2^2}{n_2}.$$

Thus the sampling distribution of $\bar{X} - \bar{Y}$ is

$$N\left(\mu_1 - \mu_2, \frac{\sigma_1^2}{n_1} + \frac{\sigma_2^2}{n_2}\right).$$

Accordingly,

$$P\left[-z(\alpha/2) \le \frac{\bar{X} - \bar{Y} - (\mu_1 - \mu_2)}{\sqrt{\sigma_1^2/n_1 + \sigma_2^2/n_2}} \le z(\alpha/2)\right] = 1 - \alpha.$$

Rewriting these inequalities so that $\mu_1 - \mu_2$ is in the middle expression, we find that the probability that the random interval

$$\left[\bar{X} - \bar{Y} - z(\alpha/2)\sqrt{\frac{\sigma_1^2}{n_1} + \frac{\sigma_2^2}{n_2}}, \ \bar{X} - \bar{Y} + z(\alpha/2)\sqrt{\frac{\sigma_1^2}{n_1} + \frac{\sigma_2^2}{n_2}}\right],$$

includes $\mu_1 - \mu_2$ is $1 - \alpha$. Once the samples are observed so that we can compute $\bar{x}$ and $\bar{y}$, we obtain the interval

$$\left[\bar{x} - \bar{y} - z(\alpha/2)\sqrt{\frac{\sigma_1^2}{n_1} + \frac{\sigma_2^2}{n_2}}, \ \bar{x} - \bar{y} + z(\alpha/2)\sqrt{\frac{\sigma_1^2}{n_1} + \frac{\sigma_2^2}{n_2}}\right].$$

This is a $100(1 - \alpha)$ percent confidence interval for $\mu_1 - \mu_2$.

Here we have assumed that σ_1^2 and σ_2^2 are known. If they are unknown but the sample sizes are large, we can replace σ_1^2 by the sample variance s_x^2 and σ_2^2 by s_y^2 and use

$$\bar{x} - \bar{y} \pm z(\alpha/2)\sqrt{\frac{s_x^2}{n_1} + \frac{s_y^2}{n_2}}$$

as an approximate $100(1 - \alpha)$ percent confidence interval for $\mu_1 - \mu_2$.

Example 4.3-5 The analysis of the breaking strength (in pounds per square inch) of $n_1 = 35$ selected specimens from the all-synthetic fabric A led to the mean $\bar{x} = 25.2$ and standard deviation $s_x = 5.2$. The $n_2 = 30$ specimens from fiber B resulted in the mean $\bar{y} = 28.5$ and standard deviation $s_y = 5.9$. Since the sample sizes are quite large, we can use the sample variances in place of the unknown population variances. Using 2 in place of 1.96, we find that an approximate 95 percent confidence interval for the unknown difference of the population means is given by

$$25.2 - 28.5 \pm 2\sqrt{\frac{(5.2)^2}{35} + \frac{(5.9)^2}{30}},$$

or, equivalently, $(-6.0, -0.6)$. We are approximately 95 percent confident that this interval covers the unknown difference $\mu_1 - \mu_2$. Since this interval does not include zero, the data provide some evidence that $\mu_1 - \mu_2$ is negative, and that the mean breaking strength of the all-synthetic fabric is less than that of the one that includes some cotton. ∎

Remark The derivation of this confidence interval for $\mu_1 - \mu_2$ depends heavily on the independence of the two random samples, as the variance of $\bar{X} - \bar{Y}$ is calculated under the independence assumption. How does one know whether it is safe to make this assumption? It depends on the way the experiment is conducted! An experiment that assigns two treatments (say, paints A and B) *randomly* to *different* experimental units (say, wooden boards in a durability comparison) guarantees, in general, independence among the two samples. However, the situation is different if two treatments are assigned to the same experimental unit. Assume, for example, that both paints are applied to the same board and that n such boards are used in the comparison. Observations made on the same board are most likely similar (if one paint scores higher than average, so will the other). In this case the independence assumption is no longer valid and confidence intervals, as calculated in this section, are no longer appropriate. ∎

Exercises 4.3

4.3-1 A random sample of size $n = 36$ from $N(\mu, 25)$ has mean $\bar{x} = 49.2$. Find a 90 percent confidence interval for μ.

4.3-2 The mean and standard deviation of $n = 42$ mathematics SAT test scores (selected at random from the entering freshman class of a large private university) are $\bar{x} = 680$ and $s = 35$. Find an approximate 99 percent confidence interval for the population mean μ.

4.3-3 Let a population have mean μ and standard deviation $\sigma = 5$. Find the sample size n such that we are 95 percent confident that the estimate $\bar{x}$ is within ± 1.5 units of the true mean μ.

4.3-4 The average biological oxygen demand (BOD) at a particular station has to be estimated. From measurements at other similar stations we know that the variance of BOD samples is about 8.0 $(mg/liter)^2$. How many observations should we sample if we want to be 90 percent confident that the true mean is within 1 mg/liter of our sample average?

4.3-5 In comparing the times until failure (in hours) of two different types of light bulbs, we obtain the

sample characteristics $n_1 = 45$, $\bar{x} = 984$, $s_x^2 = 8742$ and $n_2 = 52$, $\bar{y} = 1121$, $s_y^2 = 9411$. Find an approximate 90 percent confidence interval for the difference of the two population means. Interpret the result and explain why we can use the normal table here despite the fact that the distribution of individual failure times is probably exponential or Weibull.

4.3-6 We are interested in comparing the biological oxygen demand (BOD) at a river station before and after a certain chemical plant has made "improvements" in treating its waste. We are planning to take n observations before and n observations after these improvements are made. From past experience we know that the variance of individual BOD measurements, both before and after, is about 8.0 $(mg/liter)^2$. How large must we choose n such that we are 95 percent confident that the estimated before/after difference in BOD is within 2 mg/liter of the true change?

4.3-7 Consider the melting points of the $n = 50$ alloy filaments in Exercise 1.2-2. Calculate a 95 percent confidence interval for the mean melting point μ.

4.4   Inferences with Small Samples and Unknown Variances

In Section 4.3 we considered confidence intervals for means and differences of means when either the populations had known variances or the sample sizes were large enough so that the sample variances could be used to approximate those of the populations. However, what should we do if the sample size is small, such as $n = 13$? Then we do not have as much reliance on s as an approximation to σ. Accordingly, we must replace the value $z(\alpha/2)$ by a larger value and thus lengthen the interval to take this additional uncertainty into account. The amount of the increase from $z(\alpha/2)$ raises another interesting sampling distribution problem that we now consider.

Let us assume that the random sample $X_1, X_2, \ldots, X_n$ arises from the normal distribution $N(\mu, \sigma^2)$. Normality is important here as the following discussion depends on this assumption. The estimators $\bar{X}$ and $S^2 = [1/(n-1)] \sum (X_i - \bar{X})^2$ of μ and σ^2 are random variables, and in our usual notation they are denoted by capital letters. We already know that the distribution of the sample mean $\bar{X}$ is $N(\mu, \sigma^2/n)$. Although we cannot prove it at this level, it can be shown that $\bar{X}$ and the sample variance S^2 are independent random variables. Moreover, $W = (n-1)(S^2/\sigma^2) = \sum_{i=1}^{n} (X_i - \bar{X})^2/\sigma^2$ has that very special distribution, which is called *chi-square with $n - 1$ degrees of freedom* and which was first considered in Section 3.3. Recall, for brevity, we say that W is $\chi^2(r = n - 1)$. Chi-square densities for three different values of the parameter r are given in Figure 4.4-1. Upper percentage points $\chi^2(\alpha; r)$ for

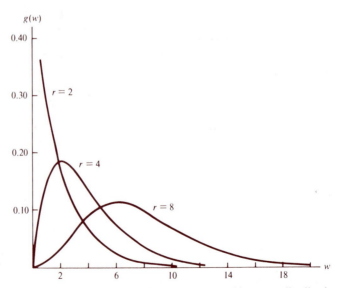

FIGURE 4.4-1   Probability densities of three different chi-square distributions.

selected tail probabilities α such that $P[W > \chi^2(\alpha; r)] = \alpha$ are given in Table C.5, Appendix C.

Example 4.4-1   Let W be $\chi^2(8)$. Then the value d for which $P(W > d) = 0.05$ is $d = \chi^2(0.05; 8) = 15.507$. This is the upper fifth percentage point or, equivalently, the 95th percentile of the distribution of W. We also find that $P(W > 2.180) = 0.975$ and $P(W > 20.090) = 0.01$. ■

Several other properties of chi-square random variables should be noted here:

1. The mean of a $\chi^2(r)$ random variable is r while the variance is $2r$.
2. Z^2, the square of a $N(0, 1)$ random variable, follows a $\chi^2(1)$ distribution; see Exercise 4.4-5 for a proof.
3. The sum of m independent chi-square random variables with $r_1, r_2, \ldots, r_m$ degrees of freedom, respectively, has a chi-square distribution with $r = r_1 + r_2 + \cdots + r_m$ degrees of freedom.

The first property and the fact that $(n - 1)(S^2/\sigma^2)$ follows a chi-square distribution with $n - 1$ degrees of freedom imply that

$$E\left[(n - 1)\frac{S^2}{\sigma^2}\right] = n - 1$$

and hence $E(S^2) = \sigma^2$. This shows that the sample variance is an unbiased estimator of the variance σ^2. This explains why the division of $\sum_{i=1}^{n}(X_i - \bar{X})^2$ by $(n - 1)$ instead of n is preferable in defining the sample variance. Since $E[\sum(X_i - \bar{X})^2/n] = (n - 1)\sigma^2/n \neq \sigma^2$, we find that $\sum(X_i - \bar{X})^2/n$ is a slightly *biased* estimator of σ^2.

This brings us to the study of the ratio we want to consider,

$$\frac{\bar{X} - \mu}{S/\sqrt{n}}$$

where σ in $(\bar{X} - \mu)/(\sigma/\sqrt{n})$ has been replaced by S. But this ratio can be written as

$$T = \frac{\bar{X} - \mu}{S/\sqrt{n}} = \frac{(\bar{X} - \mu)/(\sigma/\sqrt{n})}{\sqrt{\dfrac{(n - 1)S^2}{\sigma^2}\bigg/(n - 1)}} = \frac{Z}{\sqrt{W/r}},$$

where $r = n - 1$ and where the random variables $Z = (\bar{X} - \mu)/(\sigma/\sqrt{n})$ and $W = (n - 1)(S^2/\sigma^2)$ are independent $N(0, 1)$ and $\chi^2(r)$ variables, respectively.

It was exactly this ratio that W. S. Gosset considered in the earlier part of the twentieth century. He found that it had a very special distribution. However, his employer (an Irish brewery) did not want the other breweries to

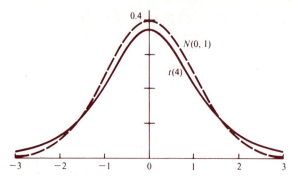

FIGURE 4.4-2   Probability densities of the $N(0, 1)$ and $t(4)$ distributions.

know that they were using statistical methods, so he was asked to publish his result under a pseudonym. Gosset selected "A Student" and since that day this very special distribution has been called *Student's t-distribution with $r = n - 1$ degrees of freedom.*

The p.d.f. of Student's t-distribution with r degrees of freedom is

$$h(t) = \frac{c}{(1 + t^2/r)^{(r+1)/2}}, \qquad -\infty < t < \infty,$$

where c is selected so that the area under $h(t)$ is 1. For convenience, we say T is $t(r)$. It can be shown that $E(T) = 0$ and $var(T) = r/(r - 2)$, $r > 2$. As we might suspect, this density looks very much like that of the $N(0, 1)$, particularly when r is large. It is symmetric about zero, but has thicker tails than the standard normal distribution (see Figure 4.4-2). Upper percentage points for selected tail probabilities α, such that $P[T > t(\alpha; r)] = \alpha$, are recorded in Table C.6. Since the distribution of T is symmetric about zero, we have that

$$P[T < -t(\alpha; r)] = P[T > t(\alpha; r)].$$

Example 4.4-2   If $r = 8$, then

$$P(T > 2.306) = 0.025.$$

As r increases, say $r = 25$, then

$$P(T > 2.060) = 0.025;$$

and we note that with larger r values, $t(0.025; r)$ approaches the value $z(0.025) = 1.96$ associated with the $N(0, 1)$ distribution.   ■

Once we accept the fact that $T = (\bar{X} - \mu)/(S/\sqrt{n})$ is $t(n - 1)$, we can write

$$P\left[-t(\alpha/2; n - 1) \le \frac{\bar{X} - \mu}{S/\sqrt{n}} \le t(\alpha/2; n - 1) \right] = 1 - \alpha.$$

However, as before, this can be rewritten as

$$P\left[\bar{X} - t(\alpha/2; n-1)\,\frac{S}{\sqrt{n}} \leq \mu \leq \bar{X} + t(\alpha/2; n-1)\,\frac{S}{\sqrt{n}}\right] = 1 - \alpha.$$

Once the sample is observed and the characteristics $\bar{x}$ and s are computed,

$$\left[\bar{x} - t(\alpha/2; n-1)\,\frac{s}{\sqrt{n}},\ \bar{x} + t(\alpha/2; n-1)\,\frac{s}{\sqrt{n}}\right]$$

provides a $100(1 - \alpha)$ percent confidence interval for μ. Again, for ease of presentation, we frequently write this as $\bar{x} \pm t(\alpha/2; n-1)s/\sqrt{n}$.

Let us recall that this result about the sampling distribution of $T = (\bar{X} - \mu)/(S/\sqrt{n})$ required that the random sample be taken from $N(\mu, \sigma^2)$. What if the underlying distribution is not normal? We still tend to use $\bar{x} \pm t(\alpha/2; n-1)s/\sqrt{n}$ for the confidence interval for μ unless we believe that the sample has come from an underlying distribution with very long and thick tails or one that is highly skewed. One or two extreme observations, or outliers, in the sample are usually an indication of the latter situations. If this is the case, *robust methods* must be used to form confidence intervals for μ. These procedures are discussed in more advanced courses.

Example 4.4-3   The mean μ of the times it takes a lab technician to perform a certain task is of interest. The lab technician was observed at $n = 16$ different occasions and the mean and standard deviation of these 16 times were $\bar{x} = 4.3$ minutes and $s = 0.6$ minute. Thus $r = n - 1 = 15$, and with $\alpha = 0.05$ so that $\alpha/2 = 0.025$ and $t(0.025; 15) = 2.131$, a 95 percent confidence interval for μ is $4.3 \pm (2.131)(0.6/4)$. Our best estimate for the mean time is 4.3 minutes. Furthermore, we are 95 percent confident that the interval (3.98 minutes, 4.62 minutes) covers the unknown mean time μ. ■

*4.4-1   Tolerance Limits

Confidence intervals assess the reliability of point estimates of unknown population parameters. The fact that prior to sampling a certain interval covers the population parameter μ in $100(1 - \alpha)$ percent of the cases allows us to judge the quality of the estimate that we calculate from our sample. Although a confidence interval for an unknown mean μ of a distribution is extremely important, the production supervisor frequently wants a different interval. He wants an interval that contains most of the individual measurements. It is hoped that the latter interval is within the specifications of the process because otherwise some measurements will fall outside the specification limits. That is, defectives will be produced. For illustration, suppose that the inside diameter of a washer is normally distributed with $\mu = 0.503$ and $\sigma = 0.005$. Then we know, for example, that 99 percent of them are between $0.503 \pm 2.576(0.005)$ or, equivalently, between 0.490 and 0.516. If the specifications for these diameters are given by 0.500 ± 0.005 (i.e., the diameter of a useful washer should be between 0.495 and 0.505), this observation causes some concern because the interval (0.490, 0.516) is not within specifications and some washers will be outside the specification limits. Possibly, the specifications are unrealistic, and they could be taken wider without harming the usefulness of the washers. However, if the specifications are correct, we must make certain changes to the process in order to bring the washers within specifications. Certainly, in this illustration, the mean μ should be shifted to 0.500 and the standard deviation should be reduced.

Unfortunately, we do not always know μ and σ, and hence they must be estimated by $\bar{x}$ and s. Once this is done, however, the interval $\bar{x} \pm (2.576)s$ does not necessarily contain 99 percent of the measurements, as μ and σ have only been approximated by $\bar{x}$ and s. If we restrict ourselves to intervals such as $\bar{x} \pm ks$, what value of k is needed so that the probability that the random interval $\bar{X} \pm kS$ covers at least $100p$ percent of the population is large, say $1 - \alpha$? For illustration, p and α might be 0.99 and 0.05, respectively. The theoretical problem to be solved is this: Find the k so that

$$P[F(\bar{X} + kS) - F(\bar{X} - kS) \geq p] = 1 - \alpha,$$

where F is the cumulative distribution function of a distribution that is $N(\mu, \sigma^2)$. The solution is beyond the scope of this course, but statisticians have prepared tables of k values for various p and α, and one adaptation is Table C.9. Once we select k and determine the observed interval $\bar{x} \pm ks$, we say that $(\bar{x} - ks, \bar{x} + ks)$ is a $100(1 - \alpha)$ percent *tolerance interval* for at least $100p$ percent of the population (distribution). Since we wish to cover at least $100p$ percent of the population rather than simply the mean μ, $\bar{x} \pm ks$ must be much wider than the confidence interval for μ, $\bar{x} \pm t(\alpha/2; n - 1)s/\sqrt{n}$.

In Example 4.4-3, the interval 3.98 to 4.62 is a 95 percent confidence interval for the mean μ. If, however, we want a 95 percent tolerance interval for at least $100p = 90$ percent of the population of the lab technician's times, we find from Table C.9 that for $n = 16$, $k = 2.437$. Thus

$$4.3 \pm (2.437)(0.6)$$

is the desired tolerance interval, since $\bar{x} = 4.3$ and $s = 0.6$. That is, we are 95 percent confident that the interval 2.84 to 5.76 minutes covers at least 90 percent of the individual times. The latter interval is much wider than the 95 percent confidence interval for μ, as it should be. Also note that for large n the constant k approaches 1.645. This is nothing else than the upper fifth percentage point of the $N(0, 1)$ distribution. For large n the estimates $\bar{x}$ and s approximate the population parameters and we can use the normal table to construct the tolerance interval.

Example 4.4-4 In a personal communication, George S. Kalemkarian of Deere & Company reported that an engineer in that company's Corporate

Engineering Standards group was interested in the hardness of certain castings. The engineer mentioned casually that he wanted to construct "a reasonably accurate interval that would describe the hardness of most castings." After some discussion, it became apparent that he was not interested in an interval for the *mean* hardness of a casting, but that he wanted an interval for the *individual hardness* values. That is, he wanted a tolerance interval rather than a confidence interval for the mean. These two types of intervals are quite different, but, nevertheless, they are often confused in practice. While the length of the confidence interval for the mean becomes very small with large sample sizes, the bounds in the tolerance interval approach, with large *n*, the corresponding percentiles of the population.

Table 4.4-1 lists the Brinell hardness numbers (BHN) of 105 tested castings in form of an ordered stem-and-leaf display. This display serves as a histogram for these data and describes the variability that we can expect among the different castings.

The product specifications for the hardness of such castings call for a target value of 214 BHN, with a lower specification of 173 BHN and an upper specification of 255 BHN. Table 4.4-1 shows that all 105 castings are within the specification limits. An interesting feature of this data set is that it consists of only seven different values—197, 207, 212, 217, 223, 229, and 241—even though, in theory, Brinell hardness is measured on a continuous scale. This feature is due to the particular measurement procedure that is used. A discussion with the engineer who was taking these measurements revealed that hardness is determined by impressing a 3000-kilogram load into a surface of the casting and measuring the ball indentation diameter to the nearest 0.1 millimeter (mm). For illustration, a diameter of 4.1 mm converts to 217 BHN. Due to rounding, our data set includes only these seven discrete points. Incidentally, the measurements were taken by the same person; this eliminates person-to-person variation.

If we take this rounding into account, it appears that apart from the one unusual value at 241 the distribution of these data is fairly symmetric. It also seems that the variability in these measurements can be approximated, at least roughly, by a normal distribution. Once we accept the fact that the normal distribution provides an adequate description of the variability, we can use

TABLE 4.4-1   Hardness Values (BHN) of 105 Engine Castings

Stem	Leaf
19	7 7 7 7 7 7 7 7 7 7 7 7 7 7 7 7
20	7 7 7 7 7 7 7 7 7 7 7 7 7 7 7 7 7 7 7
21	2 2 7 7 7 7 7 7 7 7 7 7 7 7 7 7 7 7 7 7 7 7 7 7 7 7 7 7 7 7 7 7 7 7 7 7 7 7 7 7 7 7 7 7 7 7 7 7
22	3 3 3 3 9 9 9 9 9 9 9 9 9 9 9 9 9 9 9 9 9 9 9 9 9 9 9 9
23	
24	1

subsequent sample information to construct tolerance intervals and check whether the manufactured items are within specifications. For example, suppose that the Brinell hardness values of a sample of $n = 10$ recently produced items are

$$217 \quad 217 \quad 197 \quad 207 \quad 217 \quad 223 \quad 229 \quad 229 \quad 217 \quad 217$$

Here $\bar{x} = 217$ and $s = 9.57$. From Table C.9, with $n = 10$, we find that $k = 2.839$ if we want to be 95 percent confident that the resulting tolerance interval $(\bar{x} - ks, \bar{x} + ks)$ includes at least 90 percent of *all* casting hardness values. That is, we have that

$$\text{upper tolerance limit} = 217 + (2.839)(9.57) = 244.2,$$

$$\text{lower tolerance limit} = 217 - (2.839)(9.57) = 189.8.$$

This result implies that we are very confident that at least 90 percent of our castings are within the specification limits of 173 and 255 BHN. Similarly, 95 percent tolerance limits for at least 95 percent of the values are 184.7 and 249.3; again they are within specifications. If we establish 95 percent tolerance limits for at least 99 percent of the values, we note that a very small percentage may be outside the specifications. In summary, it appears that at the moment we produce castings that are within specifications. However, we know that processes vary, and thus we should check at regular intervals whether we continue to produce at a satisfactory level.

Incidentally, it is interesting to observe that the 95 percent confidence interval for the mean μ of the population is

$$\bar{x} \pm t(0.025; 9) \frac{s}{\sqrt{n}} = 217 \pm 2.262 \frac{9.57}{\sqrt{10}},$$

or, equivalently, 210.2 to 223.8. Of course, this interval is much shorter than the tolerance interval. ∎

4.4-2   Confidence Intervals for $\mu_1 - \mu_2$

Let us consider two independent populations in which σ_1^2 and σ_2^2 are unknown but the sample sizes, n_1 and n_2, are small. The confidence intervals for $\mu_1 - \mu_2$ in Section 4.3-2 may be poor approximations, as sample variances calculated from small samples are imprecise estimates of variances. We must make additional assumptions to obtain a confidence interval for $\mu_1 - \mu_2$. The additional assumptions are that the underlying independent populations are normal and the unknown variances are equal (or nearly so); that is, $\sigma_1^2 = \sigma_2^2 = \sigma^2$. With these assumptions, we know that

$$\frac{(n_1 - 1)S_X^2 + (n_2 - 1)S_Y^2}{\sigma^2}$$

is $\chi^2(r)$, where $r = n_1 + n_2 - 2$, since $(n_1 - 1)S_X^2/\sigma^2$ and $(n_2 - 1)S_Y^2/\sigma^2$ are independent $\chi^2(n_1 - 1)$ and $\chi^2(n_2 - 1)$. Here we used the fact that the sum of independent chi-square random variables has a chi-square distribution. Thus the ratio

$$T = \frac{\bar{X} - \bar{Y} - (\mu_1 - \mu_2)}{\sqrt{\sigma^2/n_1 + \sigma^2/n_2}} \Bigg/ \sqrt{\frac{(n_1 - 1)S_X^2 + (n_2 - 1)S_Y^2}{\sigma^2} \Bigg/ (n_1 + n_2 - 2)}$$

has a Student's t-distribution with $r = n_1 + n_2 - 2$ degrees of freedom because the numerator is $N(0,1)$, the denominator is the square root of a chi-square random variable divided by its degrees of freedom, and the numerator and denominator are independent. This can be rewritten as

$$T = \frac{\bar{X} - \bar{Y} - (\mu_1 - \mu_2)}{\sqrt{\dfrac{(n_1 - 1)S_X^2 + (n_2 - 1)S_Y^2}{n_1 + n_2 - 2}\left(\dfrac{1}{n_1} + \dfrac{1}{n_2}\right)}} = \frac{\bar{X} - \bar{Y} - (\mu_1 - \mu_2)}{\sqrt{S_p^2\left(\dfrac{1}{n_1} + \dfrac{1}{n_2}\right)}}.$$

The expression

$$S_p^2 = \frac{(n_1 - 1)S_X^2 + (n_2 - 1)S_Y^2}{n_1 + n_2 - 2}$$

is called the *pooled variance* because it "pools" or combines the variance estimates from the two samples in proportion to their degrees of freedom. Since S_X^2 and S_Y^2 are unbiased estimators of the common variance, it follows that $E(S_p^2) = \sigma^2$. The inequalities, with $r = n_1 + n_2 - 2$, in

$$P[-t(\alpha/2; r) \le T \le t(\alpha/2; r)] = 1 - \alpha$$

can be rewritten as

$$\bar{X} - \bar{Y} - t(\alpha/2; r)S_p\sqrt{\frac{1}{n_1} + \frac{1}{n_2}} \le \mu_1 - \mu_2 \le \bar{X} - \bar{Y} + t(\alpha/2; r)S_p\sqrt{\frac{1}{n_1} + \frac{1}{n_2}}.$$

Once the samples are observed,

$$\bar{x} - \bar{y} \pm t(\alpha/2; r = n_1 + n_2 - 2)s_p\sqrt{\frac{1}{n_1} + \frac{1}{n_2}}$$

provides a $100(1 - \alpha)$ percent confidence interval for $\mu_1 - \mu_2$.

Remark   The use of a pooled estimate of σ^2 is not recommended if there is a suspicion that the variances of the two distributions are not the same. Pooling is especially dangerous in this circumstance if the sample sizes n_1 and n_2 are quite different. In such a case it is safer to use the approach in Section 4.3-2 and calculate a confidence interval that uses $s_x^2/n_1 + s_y^2/n_2$ as the estimate of $\mathrm{var}(\bar{X} - \bar{Y})$.   ■

Example 4.4-5   An accelerated life testing experiment compared the durability of two types of exterior house paint; type A was an oil-based paint, while type

B was a latex paint. A total of $n_1 = 10$ and $n_2 = 12$ wood panels were covered with paint A and B, respectively. These panels were then exposed to a sequence of tests that involved extreme temperature, light, and moisture conditions. At the end of the experiment the quality of the painted surface was rated on several characteristics (such as paint loss, luster of painted surface, cracking, and peeling). Scores between 0 (extremely poor) and 100 (excellent) were assigned to the 22 panels. For paint A it was found that with $n_1 = 10$, $\bar{x} = 52$ and $s_x^2 = 400$; for paint B, with $n_2 = 12$, $\bar{y} = 46$ and $s_y^2 = 340$. Since individual scores are often based on several characteristics through averaging, it is reasonable to assume that they are normally distributed. We could check this assumption by constructing normal probability plots (one for each group); see Section 3.4. A comparison of $s_x^2 = 400$ and $s_y^2 = 340$ shows that the sample variances are quite similar. This provides evidence that the population variances are about equal and justifies the pooling of the individual sample variances. A formal procedure for assessing whether two population variances are the same is given in Section 4.5-1.

Using the preceding theory, we can construct a 90 percent confidence interval for $\mu_1 - \mu_2$. Since $t(\alpha/2 = 0.05; n_1 + n_2 - 2 = 20) = 1.725$, this interval is given by

$$(52 - 46) \pm (1.725)\sqrt{367}\sqrt{\frac{1}{10} + \frac{1}{12}},$$

where the pooled variance is

$$s_p^2 = \frac{(9)(400) + (11)(340)}{10 + 12 - 2} = 367.$$

Since the interval 6 ± 14.1, or $(-8.1, 20.1)$ includes zero, we find no evidence in these data that the mean durability of these two paints is different. ∎

Exercises 4.4

4.4-1 The mean μ of the tear strength of a certain paper is under consideration. The $n = 22$ determinations (taken at random) yielded $\bar{x} = 2.4$ pounds.
(a) If the standard deviation of an individual measurement is known to be $\sigma = 0.2$, find an approximate 95 percent confidence interval for μ.
(b) If the standard deviation σ is unknown but the sample standard deviation is $s = 0.2$, determine a 95 percent confidence interval for μ.

4.4-2 Let W be $\chi^2(12)$.
(a) Determine the mean and variance of W.

(b) Find d_1, d_2, d_3, and d_4 so that $P(W > d_1) = 0.05$, $P(W > d_2) = 0.99$, $P(W > d_3) = 0.005$, and $P(W < d_4) = 0.025$.

4.4-3 Let T be $t(r = 11)$.
(a) Determine the mean and variance of T.
(b) Determine d_1 if $P(T > d_1) = 0.05$.
(c) Find d_2 if $P(-d_2 < T < d_2) = 0.95$.

4.4-4 Let μ be the mean mileage of a certain brand of tire. A sample of $n = 14$ tires was taken at random, resulting in $\bar{x} = 32,132$ and $s = 2596$ miles. Find a 99 percent confidence interval for μ.

4.4-5 Let X be $N(\mu, \sigma^2)$. Then $Z = (X - \mu)/\sigma$ is $N(0, 1)$. Find the distribution function of $W = Z^2$, that is, $G(w) = P(W \le w) = P(-\sqrt{w} \le Z \le \sqrt{w})$, $0 < w$, so

$$G(w) = 2 \int_0^{\sqrt{w}} \frac{1}{\sqrt{2\pi}} \exp\left(\frac{-z^2}{2}\right) dz.$$

Show that the p.d.f. $g(w) = G'(w)$ of W is $\chi^2(1)$.
Hint From calculus we know that

$$\frac{d}{dx}\left[\int_a^{u(x)} g(y)\, dy \right] = g[u(x)]\, \frac{d}{dx}\, u(x).$$

4.4-6 We stated without proof that the quantity $(n - 1)S^2/\sigma^2$ follows a chi-square distribution with $n - 1$ degrees of freedom if our random sample is from $N(\mu, \sigma^2)$. Convince yourself that this is true by performing the following experiment. Take samples of size $n = 4$ from the $N(10, 4)$ distribution. Use a computer program that generates such normal random variables. From the samples of size 4, calculate $\bar{x}$, s^2, and $(n - 1)(s^2/\sigma^2) = 3s^2/4$. Repeat the experiment 500 times and make a normalized relative frequency histogram of $3s^2/4$. Compare the relative frequencies from the simulations with the p.d.f. of the $\chi^2(3)$ distribution, which is $f(w) = cw^{1/2}e^{-w/2}$; here $c = 0.4$.

4.4-7 The effectiveness of two methods of teaching statistics is compared. A class of 24 students is randomly divided into two groups and each group is taught according to a different method. Their test scores at the end of the semester show the following characteristics:

$$n_1 = 13, \quad \bar{x} = 74.5, \quad s_x^2 = 82.6$$

and

$$n_2 = 11, \quad \bar{y} = 71.8, \quad s_y^2 = 112.6$$

Assuming underlying normal distributions with $\sigma_1^2 = \sigma_2^2$, find a 95 percent confidence interval for $\mu_1 - \mu_2$.

4.4-8 Two rubber compounds were tested for tensile strength. Rectangular materials were prepared and pulled in a longitudinal direction. A sample of 14 specimens, seven from compound A and seven from compound B, was prepared, but it was later found that two B specimens were defective, and they had to be removed from the test. The tensile strength (in units of 100 pounds per square inch) are as follows:

A: 32 -30 33 32 29 34 32
B: 33 35 36 37 35

Calculate a 95 percent confidence interval for the difference in the mean tensile strengths of the two rubber compounds. State your assumptions.

4.4-9 Consider the ratio (diesel use of test truck)/ (diesel use of control truck) for the data in Exercise 1.2-13. Compare the baseline and the test runs and construct a 95 percent confidence interval for the mean difference.

4.4-10 Refer to Exercises 4.4-1 and 4.4-4 and, in each case, compute a 95 percent tolerance interval for 95 percent of the individual values in the population.

4.5   Other Confidence Intervals

In Sections 4.3 and 4.4 we discussed confidence intervals for the population means. In this section we extend the discussion to other population parameters: the variance σ^2 and the proportion p.

4.5-1   Confidence Intervals for Variances

A critical assumption in the following development of confidence intervals for σ^2 is that we sample from a normal distribution. Let $S^2 = \sum_{i=1}^{n} (X_i - \bar{X})^2/ (n - 1)$ be the sample variance from a random sample of size n taken from a

$N(\mu, \sigma^2)$ distribution. We know from the preceding section that S^2 is an unbiased estimate of σ^2 and that the sampling distribution of $(n-1)S^2/\sigma^2$ is $\chi^2(n-1)$. Thus

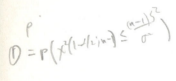

$$P\left[\chi^2(1-\alpha/2; n-1) \le \frac{(n-1)S^2}{\sigma^2} \le \chi^2(\alpha/2; n-1)\right] = 1 - \alpha,$$

where $\chi^2(\alpha/2; n-1)$ is the upper $100(\alpha/2)$ percentage point [or, in other words, the $100(1-\alpha/2)$ percentile] of the $\chi^2(n-1)$ distribution. Rearranging the terms within the probability statement such that σ^2 is in the middle of the interval leads to

$$P\left[\frac{(n-1)S^2}{\chi^2(\alpha/2; n-1)} \le \sigma^2 \le \frac{(n-1)S^2}{\chi^2(1-\alpha/2; n-1)}\right] = 1 - \alpha.$$

This shows that under these particular assumptions (i.e., sampling from a normal distribution) the interval

$$\left[\frac{(n-1)S^2}{\chi^2(\alpha/2; n-1)}, \frac{(n-1)S^2}{\chi^2(1-\alpha/2; n-1)}\right]$$

represents a $100(1-\alpha)$ percent confidence interval for the unknown population variance σ^2. Furthermore, since the probability statement above is unchanged by taking the square root of the three terms, we find that a $100(1-\alpha)$ percent confidence interval for the standard deviation σ is given by

$$\left[\sqrt{\frac{(n-1)S^2}{\chi^2(\alpha/2; n-1)}}, \sqrt{\frac{(n-1)S^2}{\chi^2(1-\alpha/2; n-1)}}\right].$$

Example 4.5-1   In Example 4.4-3 we studied the times it takes a lab technician to complete a certain task. A sample of $n = 16$ times led to the sample mean $\bar{x} = 4.3$ minutes and standard deviation $s = 0.6$ minute. With $r = n - 1 = 15$, $\chi^2(0.025; 15) = 27.488$, and $\chi^2(0.975; 15) = 6.262$ we find that a 95 percent confidence interval for σ^2 is given by $[(15)(0.6)^2/27.488, (15)(0.6)^2/6.262]$ or $(0.20, 0.86)$. Taking the square root of each of these limits, we are 95 percent confident that the interval from 0.44 minute to 0.93 minute will cover the unknown σ. Note that this interval is quite large.   ■

Remark   Confidence intervals for σ^2 and σ are usually quite wide unless the sample size is very large. An estimate of a variance will always be less precise than an estimate of a mean, as an average of squared observations is more variable than an average of observations.   ■

Now suppose that we have two independent normal distributions and we want to compare their variances σ_1^2 and σ_2^2 by finding a confidence interval for their ratio, σ_1^2/σ_2^2. Before we can do this, we have to introduce another distribution, the F-distribution. As we will see later, this is a very important distribution in statistics.

Let U and V be independent chi-square random variables with r_1 and r_2 degrees of freedom, respectively. Then we say that

$$F = \frac{U/r_1}{V/r_2}$$

has an *F-distribution with r_1 and r_2 degrees of freedom*; for brevity, we say that F is $F(r_1, r_2)$. Clearly, the reciprocal of F,

$$\frac{1}{F} = \frac{V/r_2}{U/r_1},$$

must be $F(r_2, r_1)$, because U and V (and the associated degrees of freedom r_1 and r_2) have exchanged roles. The probability density functions of F-distributions look very much like the right skewed densities of chi-square distributions in Figure 4.4-1 except that they are centered around 1 and that the two parameters r_1 and r_2 allow greater flexibility. The upper percentage points $F(\alpha; r_1, r_2)$, such that $P[F > F(\alpha; r_1, r_2)] = \alpha$, for tail probabilities $\alpha = 0.05$ and $\alpha = 0.01$ are given in Table C.7. Since $\alpha = P[F > F(\alpha; r_1, r_2)] = P[1/F < 1/F(\alpha; r_1, r_2)]$ and since $1/F$ has an $F(r_2, r_1)$ distribution, it follows that $F(1 - \alpha; r_2, r_1) = 1/F(\alpha; r_1, r_2)$.

Example 4.5-2   Let F be $F(5, 8)$. Then

$$P(F > 3.69) = 0.05 \quad \text{and} \quad P(F \leq 6.63) = 0.99$$

since $F(0.05; 5, 8) = 3.69$ and $F(0.01; 5, 8) = 6.63$. Also, $P(F < 1/4.82 = 0.21) = 0.05$ because $F(0.05; 8, 5) = 4.82$. ∎

We can use the F-distribution to find confidence intervals for σ_1^2/σ_2^2. With random samples of sizes n_1 and n_2 from the respective independent $N(\mu_1, \sigma_1^2)$ and $N(\mu_2, \sigma_2^2)$ distributions, we know that

$$\frac{(n_1 - 1)S_1^2}{\sigma_1^2} \text{ is } \chi^2(n_1 - 1),$$

$$\frac{(n_2 - 1)S_2^2}{\sigma_2^2} \text{ is } \chi^2(n_2 - 1),$$

and, since we sample from two independent distributions, these two random variables are independent. Hence

$$F = \frac{\dfrac{(n_2 - 1)S_2^2}{\sigma_2^2} \Big/ (n_2 - 1)}{\dfrac{(n_1 - 1)S_1^2}{\sigma_1^2} \Big/ (n_1 - 1)} = \frac{\sigma_1^2 S_2^2}{\sigma_2^2 S_1^2}$$

is $F(r_1 = n_2 - 1, r_2 = n_1 - 1)$ and therefore

$$P\left[F(1 - \alpha/2; r_1, r_2) \le \frac{\sigma_1^2 S_2^2}{\sigma_2^2 S_1^2} \le F(\alpha/2; r_1, r_2)\right] = 1 - \alpha.$$

Since $F(1 - \alpha/2; r_1, r_2) = 1/F(\alpha/2; r_2, r_1)$, the inequality can be written as

$$P\left[\frac{1}{F(\alpha/2; r_2, r_1)} \frac{S_1^2}{S_2^2} \le \frac{\sigma_1^2}{\sigma_2^2} \le F(\alpha/2; r_1, r_2) \frac{S_1^2}{S_2^2}\right] = 1 - \alpha.$$

That is, the probability that the random interval, with $r_1 = n_2 - 1$ and $r_2 = n_1 - 1$,

$$\left[\frac{1}{F(\alpha/2; r_2, r_1)} \frac{S_1^2}{S_2^2}, F(\alpha/2; r_1, r_2) \frac{S_1^2}{S_2^2}\right]$$

includes σ_1^2/σ_2^2 is $1 - \alpha$. Once the samples are observed and s_1^2 and s_2^2 computed, the corresponding computed interval provides a $100(1 - \alpha)$ percent confidence interval for σ_1^2/σ_2^2.

Example 4.5-3 Let us refer to Example 4.4-5 about accelerated life testing of paints. There $n_1 = 10$, $s_1^2 = 400$ and $n_2 = 12$, $s_2^2 = 340$. Thus $F(0.05; 11, 9) = 3.10$ and $F(0.05; 9, 11) = 2.90$, and the interval

$$\left[\left(\frac{1}{2.90}\right)\left(\frac{400}{340}\right), (3.10)\left(\frac{400}{340}\right)\right]$$

or, equivalently, [0.41, 3.65] is a 90 percent confidence interval for σ_1^2/σ_2^2. This interval contains the number 1, and thus we would not doubt the statement that the variances, σ_1^2 and σ_2^2, are equal. Note, however, that this interval is very wide. This is a common, and objectionable, feature of confidence intervals for σ_1^2/σ_2^2. ■

4.5-2 Confidence Intervals for p and $p_1 - p_2$

Let us now discuss confidence intervals for an unknown population *proportion p*. For example, the proportion p of manufactured items that are acceptable (or flawed) or the proportion p of companies that use statistical techniques for process control. Since each sampled item (product, company, etc.) can be classified according to one of two categories, say "success" and "failure," the outcomes in a random sample correspond to realizations of n independent Bernoulli trials with unknown probability of success p. Let Y be the number of successes in our random sample, and let Y/n be the sample proportion (i.e., relative frequency of success). Thus Y follows a binomial distribution with mean np and variance $np(1 - p)$, and the sample proportion

$\hat{p} = Y/n$ is an unbiased estimator of p. Furthermore, the central limit theorem implies that

$$\frac{Y - np}{\sqrt{np(1-p)}} = \frac{(Y/n) - p}{\sqrt{p(1-p)/n}}$$

is approximately $N(0, 1)$. This means that

$$P\left[-z(\alpha/2) \leq \frac{(Y/n) - p}{\sqrt{p(1-p)/n}} \leq z(\alpha/2) \right] \approx 1 - \alpha.$$

The inequalities in the probability statement can be written as

$$\frac{Y}{n} - z(\alpha/2) \sqrt{\frac{p(1-p)}{n}} \leq p \leq \frac{Y}{n} + z(\alpha/2) \sqrt{\frac{p(1-p)}{n}}.$$

However, once Y is observed to be y, these limits cannot be evaluated because they still contain the unknown p. But if p in those limits is approximated by the sample proportion of successes, y/n, we obtain the approximate $100(1 - \alpha)$ percent confidence interval

$$\frac{y}{n} \pm z(\alpha/2) \sqrt{\frac{(y/n)(1 - y/n)}{n}}$$

for p.

Example 4.5-4 We interview $n = 200$ voters, of which $y = 104$ say that they plan to vote for a certain candidate. Then, with $\alpha = 0.10$ and $z(\alpha/2) = 1.645$, we find that

$$\frac{104}{200} \pm 1.645 \sqrt{\frac{(0.52)(0.48)}{200}}$$

or, equivalently, $[0.462, 0.578]$ is an approximate 90 percent confidence interval for p, the fraction of all voters favoring this candidate. ∎

We want to emphasize at this point that it is very important that the subjects be selected *randomly* from the underlying population. If they are not selected at random, the binomial distribution may no longer be appropriate and we cannot attach confidence intervals to our estimates.

Example 4.5-5 Let Y be $b(n, p)$. How large should the sample size n be such that we are $100(1 - \alpha)$ percent confident that our estimate is within h units of the unknown population proportion; for example, 99.74 percent certain that it is within $h = 0.03$, or three percentage points, of p? Since

$$P\left[\left| \frac{Y}{n} - p \right| \leq z(\alpha/2) \sqrt{\frac{p(1-p)}{n}} \right] = 1 - \alpha,$$

we find that

$$h = z(\alpha/2)\sqrt{\frac{p(1-p)}{n}} \quad\text{and}\quad n = p(1-p)\left[\frac{z(\alpha/2)}{h}\right]^2.$$

Now, p is unknown; but $p(1-p)$ reaches a maximum when $p = \frac{1}{2}$. Hence if we let $p = \frac{1}{2}$, then, since here $z(0.0013) = 3.0$,

$$n = \frac{1}{4}\left[\frac{z(\alpha/2)}{h}\right]^2 = \frac{1}{4}\left(\frac{3.0}{0.03}\right)^2 = 2500$$

is a more than adequate sample size to be 99.74 percent confident that the estimate is within three percentage points of p. This is the reason many of the well-known polls interview from 2000 to 3000 persons to obtain a reliable estimate of the percentage of voters favoring a certain candidate.   ■

If there are two different methods of performing a certain task, we may want to compare their probabilities of success, say p_1 and p_2. Let Y_1 and Y_2 be the respective numbers of successes from the two independent random samples of sizes n_1 and n_2. The random variables Y_1 and Y_2 have binomial distributions $b(n_1, p_1)$ and $b(n_2, p_2)$, respectively. From the central limit theorem we know that the distributions of Y_1 and Y_2, or of Y_1/n_1 and Y_2/n_2, can be approximated by normal distributions. Hence their difference $Y_1/n_1 - Y_2/n_2$ has an approximate normal distribution with mean $p_1 - p_2$ and variance $p_1(1-p_1)/n_1 + p_2(1-p_2)/n_2$. The standardized random variable

$$Z = \frac{Y_1/n_1 - Y_2/n_2 - (p_1 - p_2)}{\sqrt{p_1(1-p_1)/n_1 + p_2(1-p_2)/n_2}}$$

has an approximate $N(0, 1)$ distribution. Rewriting the inequalities in

$$P[-z(\alpha/2) \le Z \le z(\alpha/2)] \approx 1 - \alpha,$$

we find that the probability that the random interval

$$\frac{Y_1}{n_1} - \frac{Y_2}{n_2} \pm z(\alpha/2)\sqrt{\frac{p_1(1-p_1)}{n_1} + \frac{p_2(1-p_2)}{n_2}}$$

includes $p_1 - p_2$ is about $1 - \alpha$. Performing the experiments and observing y_1 and y_2, and approximating p_1 and p_2 under the radical sign by y_1/n_1 and y_2/n_2, respectively, we obtain the approximate $100(1-\alpha)$ percent confidence interval for $p_1 - p_2$, that is,

$$\frac{y_1}{n_1} - \frac{y_2}{n_2} \pm z(\alpha/2)\sqrt{\frac{(y_1/n_1)(1-y_1/n_1)}{n_1} + \frac{(y_2/n_2)(1-y_2/n_2)}{n_2}}.$$

Example 4.5-6   A company suspects that its two major plants produce different proportions of "grade A" items. Samples of sizes $n_1 = n_2 = 300$ were selected from a week's production of the two factories, and $y_1 = 213$ and $y_2 = 189$

items were classified as grade A. Thus an approximate 95.44 percent confidence interval for $p_1 - p_2$ is

$$0.71 - 0.63 \pm 2 \sqrt{\frac{(0.71)(0.29)}{300} + \frac{(0.63)(0.37)}{300}},$$

or, equivalently, [0.004, 0.156]. Since the confidence interval does not include zero, we conclude that the first factory produces, on average, a higher percentage of grade A items than the second. ∎

Exercises 4.5

4.5-1   Refer to Exercise 4.3-2. Calculate 95 percent confidence intervals for σ^2 and σ.

4.5-2   Refer to Exercises 4.4-7 and 4.4-8 and, in each case, compute 90 percent confidence intervals for σ_1^2/σ_2^2, the ratio of the population variances.

4.5-3   One tire manufacturer found that after 5000 miles, $y = 32$ of $n = 200$ steel belted tires selected at random were defective. Find an approximate 99 percent confidence interval for p, the proportion of defective tires in the total production.

4.5-4   To test two different training methods, 200 workers were divided at random into two groups of 100 each. At the end of the training program there were $y_1 = 62$ and $y_2 = 74$ successes, respectively. Find an approximate 90 percent confidence interval for $p_1 - p_2$, the difference of the true proportions of success.

4.5-5   A sample of $n = 21$ observations leads to $\bar{x} = 74.2$ and $s^2 = 562.8$. Determine a 90 percent confidence interval for σ^2.

4.5-6   Let Y be $b(n, p)$. When Y is observed to be y, we want $y/n \pm 0.05$ to be an approximate 95 percent confidence interval for p.
(a) If we know p is around 1/4, how should we choose the sample size n?
(b) If we did not have the prior information that p was about 1/4, what size sample should we take?

4.5-7   We want to be 90 percent confident that the difference of two sample proportions is within 0.06 of the difference of the population proportions, $p_1 - p_2$. If we take n observations from each population, how should we select this value of n?

*4.6   Introduction to Reliability

The *reliability* of a product or a system is related to the probability that it will function properly for a certain period of time. In Section 3.3, certain basic concepts associated with reliability are introduced. In particular, the *failure rate function* of a system was defined by

$$\lambda(x) = \frac{f(x)}{1 - F(x)},$$

where $f(x)$ is the p.d.f. and $F(x) = P(X \leq x)$ is the c.d.f. of the random variable X, the time to failure. We learned that $\lambda(x) \Delta x$ is the conditional probability that an item fails in the interval $(x, x + \Delta x)$, given that its lifetime (i.e., the time to failure) X exceeds x.

Frequently, $R(x) = 1 - F(x) = P(X > x)$ is called the *reliability function*, as it expresses the probability that an item will function longer than x. The failure rate function can then be written as $\lambda(x) = f(x)/R(x)$.

We also learned in Section 3.3 how to obtain the p.d.f. $f(x)$ from a given failure rate function $\lambda(x)$,

$$f(x) = \lambda(x)\exp\left[- \int_0^x \lambda(t)\, dt \right], \qquad 0 \leq x < \infty.$$

For the failure rate $\lambda(x) = \alpha x^{\alpha-1}/\beta^\alpha$, with $\alpha > 0$ and $\beta > 0$, we obtained the *Weibull* p.d.f.

$$f(x) = \frac{\alpha x^{\alpha-1}}{\beta^\alpha} \exp\left[-\left(\frac{x}{\beta}\right)^\alpha \right], \qquad 0 \leq x < \infty.$$

This is a commonly used distribution model in reliability. Of course, if $\alpha = 1$, then $f(x)$ is the exponential p.d.f. with mean $\beta = 1/\lambda$, namely

$$f(x) = \frac{1}{\beta} e^{-x/\beta} = \lambda e^{-\lambda x}, \qquad 0 \leq x < \infty.$$

The failure rate function for this distribution is constant, $\lambda(x) = \lambda$. The parameter $\lambda = 1/\beta$ is known as the failure rate of the exponential distribution.

Let us now consider a system of components that is arranged in *series* like that depicted in Figure 4.6-1. For this system to function, all components, C_1, $C_2, \ldots, C_n$, must function properly. Thus, if the random variable X_i represents the lifetime of component C_i, $i = 1, 2, \ldots, n$, then the lifetime, say Y, of the system is the minimum of $X_1, X_2, \ldots, X_n$. That is,

$$Y = \min(X_1, X_2, \ldots, X_n).$$

The lifetimes $X_1, X_2, \ldots, X_n$ of the components are often mutually independent. In which case, the reliability function, $R(y)$, of the series system equals

$$R(y) = P(Y > y) = P(X_1 > y)P(X_2 > y) \cdots P(X_n > y)$$

$$= R_1(y)R_2(y) \cdots R_n(y),$$

where $R_i(y) = P(X_i > y)$, $i = 1, 2, \ldots, n$. That is, the reliability function of this series system is equal to the product of the individual reliability functions. Of

FIGURE 4.6-1 A series system.

course, we have to assume that the lifetimes of the individual components are independent.

If each individual lifetime X_i has an exponential distribution with failure rate $\lambda_i = 1/\beta_i$, $i = 1, 2, \ldots, n$, then

$$R_i(y) = \int_y^\infty \lambda_i e^{-\lambda_i x}\, dx = e^{-\lambda_i y}$$

and

$$R(y) = e^{-\lambda_1 y} e^{-\lambda_2 y} \cdots e^{-\lambda_n y} = e^{-(\Sigma\, \lambda_i)y}.$$

That is, the failure rate of the system is the sum of the individual failure rates, namely $\lambda_y = \sum_{i=1}^n \lambda_i$, and the lifetime Y of the system has an exponential distribution with mean $1/\lambda_y$.

Example 4.6-1 Suppose that an electronic circuit has four transistors arranged in series. Assume that the lifetimes of these transistors are independent and that they have exponential distributions with respective failure rates $\lambda_1 = 0.00006$, $\lambda_2 = 0.00003$, $\lambda_3 = 0.00012$, and $\lambda_4 = 0.000018$. Assume that these failure rates are in terms of failures per minute. A failure rate of $\lambda_1 = 0.00006$, for example, implies that the average time to failure is $1/0.00006 = 16,667$ minutes, or about 278 hours. For our system with these four transistors arranged in series we can expect $\lambda_y = \sum_{i=1}^4 \lambda_i = 0.000228$ failure per minute. Moreover, the lifetime, Y, of the system has an exponential distribution with mean $1/\lambda_y = 1/0.000228 = 4386$ minutes, or about 73 hours. ∎

If the proper functioning of a system is extremely important (e.g., failure could mean loss of life or great economic loss), a system is often constructed by placing components in *parallel*, as depicted in Figure 4.6-2. Here all components are active simultaneously. For this system to function properly, *at least* one of the components must function. Thus the lifetime, say Z, of this

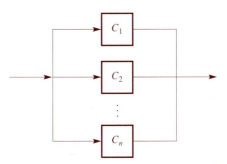

FIGURE 4.6-2   A parallel system.

system is the maximum of the lifetimes, $X_1, X_2, \ldots, X_n$, of the individual components. That is,

$$Z = \max(X_1, X_2, \ldots, X_n).$$

If $X_1, X_2, \ldots, X_n$ are mutually independent, the reliability function, $R(z)$, of the system is

$$
\begin{aligned}
R(z) = P(Z > z) &= 1 - P(Z \le z) \\
&= 1 - P(X_1 \le z)P(X_2 \le z) \cdots P(X_n \le z) \\
&= 1 - [1 - R_1(z)][1 - R_2(z)] \cdots [1 - R_n(z)],
\end{aligned}
$$

where $R_i(z) = P(X_i > z) = 1 - P(X_i \le z)$ is the reliability function of the ith component, $i = 1, 2, \ldots, n$.

Example 4.6-2 Suppose that the four transistors in Example 4.6-1 are arranged in parallel. Then the reliability function of the system is

$$R(z) = 1 - [1 - e^{-(0.00006)z}][1 - e^{-(0.00003)z}]$$
$$\times [1 - e^{-(0.00012)z}][1 - e^{-(0.000018)z}].$$

This expression cannot be simplified much more, and we would need to investigate $R(z)$ further by substituting various values of z. A graph of $R(z) = P(Z > z)$ is given in Figure 4.6-3. It shows that for this particular system there is a 20 percent chance that the lifetime exceeds 100,000 minutes, and about a 5 percent probability that it exceeds 170,000 minutes. The median lifetime is somewhere between 50,000 and 60,000 minutes. ∎

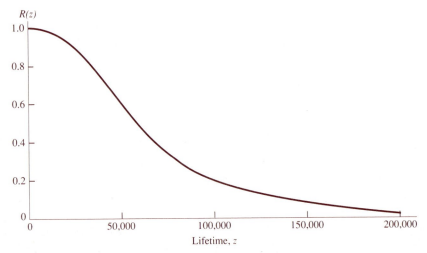

FIGURE 4.6-3 Plot of $R(z) = P(Z > z)$ in Example 4.6-2.

In the formulation of a parallel system all components are active simultaneously, and thus the lifetime of this system equals the maximum lifetime of the individual components. Clearly, it would be better if we could devise a system in which only one component is active at a time and another component starts only when the current component fails. In this *standby* system, the procedure continues until all n components have failed one at a time. Clearly, the lifetime, say W, of the system is equal to the sum of the individual lifetimes. That is, $W = X_1 + X_2 + \cdots + X_n$. If the individual X_i, for $i = 1, 2, \ldots, n$, are mutually independent with means μ_i and variances σ_i^2,

$$\mu_W = E(W) = \sum_{i=1}^{n} \mu_i$$

and

$$\sigma_W^2 = E[(W - \mu_W)^2] = \sum_{i=1}^{n} \sigma_i^2.$$

However, to determine the reliability function of this system, we must find the distribution of W and then evaluate the probability

$$R(w) = P(W > w).$$

For illustration, suppose that X_i, for $i = 1, 2, \ldots, n$, has a gamma distribution with parameters α_i and common β,

$$f(x) = \frac{1}{\Gamma(\alpha_i)\beta^{\alpha_i}} x^{\alpha_i - 1} e^{-x/\beta}, \qquad 0 \le x < \infty;$$

see Section 3.3. Then it is known that also the sum W has a gamma distribution with parameters $\sum_{i=1}^{n} \alpha_i$ and β. In particular, if $\alpha_1 = \alpha_2 = \cdots = \alpha_n = 1$ so that each X_i has the same exponential distribution with $\beta = 1/\lambda$, W has a gamma distribution with parameters n and $\beta = 1/\lambda$. Thus in the latter case we have

$$R(w) = \int_w^{\infty} \frac{1}{(n-1)!\beta^n} y^{n-1} e^{-y/\beta} \, dy,$$

and $\mu_W = n\beta = n/\lambda$ and $\sigma_W^2 = n\beta^2 = n/\lambda^2$.

Exercises 4.6

4.6-1 Let X have the p.d.f. $f(x) = 1/x^2$, $1 \le x < \infty$. Determine and sketch the reliability function $R(x) = P(X > x)$ and the failure rate function $\lambda(x) = f(x)/R(x)$.

4.6-2 Let X have the p.d.f. $f(x) = (xe^{-x/\beta})/\beta^2$, $0 \le x < \infty$. Determine and sketch the reliability function $R(x)$ and the failure rate function $\lambda(x)$.

4.6-3 Three components are arranged in series. Moreover, suppose that their respective lifetimes are mutually independent with exponential distributions having failure rates $\lambda_1 = 0.003$, $\lambda_2 = 0.010$, and $\lambda_3 = 0.008$.

(a) Determine the reliability function, $R(y)$, and the failure rate function of the series system.

(b) What is μ_Y, the mean time to failure of this system?

(c) Evaluate $R(\mu_Y)$.

4.6-4 Repeat Exercise 4.6-3(a), but assume that the components are now placed in parallel.

4.6-5 Three identical components are connected in parallel. Their lifetimes are mutually independent, and each lifetime has an exponential distribution with $\lambda = 0.02$.

(a) If at least one must operate for the system to function properly, evaluate the reliability function at 15.

(b) Suppose the system is designed so that at least two must operate for the system to function properly. Evaluate the reliability function of this system at 15. Compare this answer to that of part (a).

(c) If these three components can be placed in a standby system, evaluate the reliability function of this system at 15. Does this make sense in light of the answers in parts (a) and (b)?

4.6-6 Consider a parallel system with $k > 1$ components. Assume that the lifetime of each of these components follows an exponential distribution with failure rate λ and suppose that the k lifetimes are mutually independent. Obtain an expression for the $(100p)$th percentile of the lifetime distribution for the parallel system.

CHAPTER

5 Statistical Quality Control

All processes have some variation. When we manufacture a product, measurements on the final product will show inevitable variation from unintentional process changes as well as random variation. Many different factors enter into a production process, and a change in each will cause some variation in the final product. This variation may come from differences among machines, lot-to-lot variation, differences in suppliers and incoming raw materials, changes in the plant environment, and so on. Despite the fact that considerable effort is generally directed toward controlling the variability in each of these factors, there will still be variability in the final product. In the end it is this variability that has to be controlled.

Statistical *control charts* or, more generally, statistical process control methods are procedures for monitoring the process variation and for generating information on the stability of the process. It is important to check the stability of processes, since unstable processes will result in lost production, defective products, poor quality, and, in general, loss of consumer confidence. For example, in the production of integrated-circuit boards, which involves several welding procedures, it may be the weld strength that is of importance. Selecting a small sample of such boards at regular intervals and measuring the weld strength by a certain pull test to destruction will provide valuable information on the stability of the welding process. In the production of concrete cylinders, it is the compressive strength that is of importance and that needs to be controlled. Measurements on a small number of concrete cylinders, say twice during each production shift, can give us valuable information on the variability of this process. In the production of thin wafers for integrated-circuit devices by high-temperature furnace oxide growth processes, it is the thickness of these very thin wafers that needs to be controlled. Measurements on the thickness of a few selected wafers from every other furnace run can indicate whether the thickness of the product is stable. Here we have given only three examples. Many others can be found, and we encourage the reader to think of still others.

5.1-1 $\bar{x}$-Charts and *R*-charts

A control chart is a *plot* of a summary statistic from samples that are taken *sequentially in time*. Usually, it is the sample mean and a measure of the sample variability, such as the standard deviation or the range, that are plotted on such control charts. The charts in Figures 5.1-1 and 5.1-2 are two examples. The chart in Figure 5.1-1 shows the average compressive strengths of concrete blocks from samples of size $n = 5$. Twice during each shift, five concrete blocks are taken from the production line, their compressive strengths are determined, and the average is entered on the chart. Since we plot averages, we call this an $\bar{x}$-chart. In Figure 5.1-2 we display the variability within the samples over time and plot the *ranges* of successive samples; we call such a plot an *R-chart*.

Control charts also include bounds, or *control limits*, which help us determine whether a particular average (or range) is "within acceptable limits" of random variation. Through these limits, control charts try to distinguish between the variation that can normally be expected (the variation due to

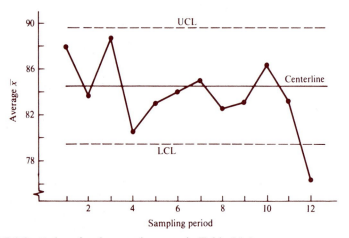

FIGURE 5.1-1 $\bar{x}$-chart for the sample means in Table 5.1-1.

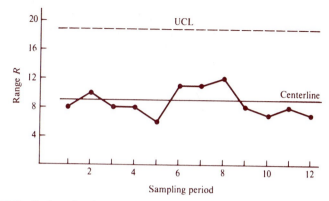

FIGURE 5.1-2 R-chart for the sample ranges in Table 5.1-1.

common causes, as Deming calls it) and the variation that is caused by unexpected changes (i.e., the variation due to *special causes*). One should not tamper with the process if the measurements on these charts fall within the control limits. However, if one notices shifts in the process level on the $\bar{x}$-chart and if the plotted averages are outside the control limits, we conclude that something has happened to the process. Similarly, if the process *variation* as measured on the R-chart changes by more than what could be expected under usual circumstances, we conclude that the process variability is no longer stable. Steps have to be taken in these circumstances to uncover the special causes and to keep them from recurring in the future.

The theoretical explanation of the control limits in the $\bar{x}$-chart is as follows. Let us suppose that our observations are from a stable distribution with mean μ and variance σ^2. Then the mean $\bar{X}$ of a random sample of size n from this distribution has an approximate normal distribution with mean μ and variance σ^2/n. If these averages are plotted on a chart, the probability that a sample average $\bar{X}$ falls between $\mu - 3\sigma/\sqrt{n}$ and $\mu + 3\sigma/\sqrt{n}$ is 0.9974. If μ and σ are known, we call $\mu - 3\sigma/\sqrt{n}$ and $\mu + 3\sigma/\sqrt{n}$ the *lower control limit* (LCL) and the *upper control limit* (UCL), respectively. Thus, with a stable process, the probability of $\bar{X}$ falling between the LCL and UCL is very large. Consequently, it is very rare that a sample average $\bar{X}$ from such a stable process would fall *outside* the control limits.

Unfortunately, we usually do not know whether our process is stable, nor do we know the values of μ and σ. Thus we begin by taking several samples, each of size n. Let us say that there are k such samples. Let $\bar{x}_1, \bar{x}_2, \ldots, \bar{x}_k$ and $s_1, s_2, \ldots, s_k$ be the means and standard deviations of these samples. Then we can estimate σ by the average of the standard deviations, namely $\bar{s} = (s_1 + \cdots + s_k)/k$. Moreover, if we are reasonably satisfied with the overall average of the nk observations in these k samples, we can use $\bar{\bar{x}} = (\bar{x}_1 + \cdots + \bar{x}_k)/k$ as the centerline in our control charts; that is, use $\bar{\bar{x}}$ as an estimate of μ.

With these estimates, the control limits around the centerline $\bar{\bar{x}}$ are given by $\bar{\bar{x}} - A_3 \bar{s}$ and $\bar{\bar{x}} + A_3 \bar{s}$, where the constant A_3 is chosen in such a way that $A_3 \bar{s}$ is a good estimate of $(3/\sqrt{n})\sigma$. The constant A_3 depends on the sample size n and is given in Table C.1. The development behind the selection of the constant A_3 is beyond the scope of this book. Note that A_3 in Table C.1 is always slightly larger than $3/\sqrt{n}$; this is because we use an estimate $\bar{s}$ instead of the unknown standard deviation σ. Also note that for moderately large sample sizes, A_3 and $3/\sqrt{n}$ are quite similar; for $n = 5$, $A_3 = 1.43$ while $3/\sqrt{5} = 1.34$; for $n = 10$, $A_3 = 0.98$ while $3/\sqrt{10} = 0.95$; for larger n, the difference disappears almost completely.

However, the calculation of the standard deviations involves a considerable amount of computation. An alternative, and simpler, procedure for estimating $3\sigma/\sqrt{n}$ proceeds as follows. Let $R_1, R_2, \ldots, R_k$ be the ranges of the k samples. Calculate the average range $\bar{R} = (R_1 + \cdots + R_k)/k$. It can be shown that $A_2 \bar{R}$ is a good estimate of $3\sigma/\sqrt{n}$ when sampling from a normal distribution. The constant A_2 depends on the sample size n, and it is also given in Table C.1. With this modification, the $\bar{x}$-chart consists of a centerline at $\bar{\bar{x}}$, which is an estimate of μ, and control limits $\bar{\bar{x}} - A_2 \bar{R}$ and $\bar{\bar{x}} + A_2 \bar{R}$.

There are several control charts for measures of variability. Either the range R or the standard deviation s of samples of size n can be used to measure variability, and R- and s-charts can be constructed. In this book we concentrate on R-charts, where we plot ranges of successive samples.

We approximate the centerline of the R-chart with the average of the k values of R, namely $\bar{R}$. The lower and upper control limits are taken to be $\text{LCL} = D_3 \bar{R}$ and $\text{UCL} = D_4 \bar{R}$, respectively. The constants D_3 and D_4, and thus the limits, are chosen so that for a stable process the probability of an individual R falling between the LCL and UCL is extremely large. The constants D_3 and D_4 are also given in Table C.1.

In summary, the construction of the control charts is very simple. We take samples of a few observations (usually, the sample size n is 4 or 5) at various times. It is usually recommended that $k = 10$ to 20 such samples be obtained before constructing the control limits. Depending on the application, these samples can be taken every 4 hours (see the weld strength example), twice a shift (compressive strength), from every other furnace run (wafer example), every hour, from every tenth batch, and so on. The frequency of the sampling depends on the stability of the process; the more stable the process, the longer the time between samples. It also depends on the potential loss that is caused when deteriorations of the process are not recognized on time, and of course on the cost of the sampling inspection. From each sample we calculate the average $\bar{x} = \sum_{i=1}^{n} x_i/n$ and the range $R = \max(x_1, \ldots, x_n) - \min(x_1, \ldots, x_n)$, and enter these quantities on the $\bar{x}$-chart and R-chart. From the k sample averages and ranges, we compute the grand average (average of averages),

$$\bar{\bar{x}} = \frac{1}{k} \sum_{j=1}^{k} \bar{x}_j,$$

and the average of the ranges,

$$\bar{R} = \frac{1}{k} \sum_{j=1}^{k} R_j.$$

These quantities form the respective centerlines in the $\bar{x}$-chart and the R-chart. The control limits (the lower control limit, LCL, and the upper control limit, UCL) in the $\bar{x}$-chart are given by

$$LCL = \bar{x} - A_2 \bar{R} \qquad \text{and} \qquad UCL = \bar{x} + A_2 \bar{R}.$$

The control limits in the R-chart are given by

$$LCL = D_3 \bar{R} \qquad \text{and} \qquad UCL = D_4 \bar{R}.$$

The constants A_2, D_3, and D_4 can be found in Table C.1 in Appendix C; they depend on the sample size n. These constants are chosen such that almost all future averages $\bar{x}$ and ranges R will fall within the respective control limits, provided that the process has stayed in control (which means that the level has not shifted and the variability has not changed). If the process is stable, it is very rare that a sample average or sample range fall outside the control limits. On the other hand, if there are shifts and drifts in the process, the averages and/or the ranges will probably exceed the limits and generate an alarm.

We should also point to a limitation of the R-chart. Table C.1 shows that the constants D_3 and thus also the lower control limit $D_3 \bar{R}$ are zero for sample sizes smaller than seven. This implies that for small n the R-chart can warn about increases in variability, but not about reductions. This is unfortunate, as in quality improvement applications one would also like to know whether certain actions have led to a reduction in variability.

Consider the data in Table 5.1-1, in which we list the compressive strength measurements from $k = 10$ samples of size $n = 5$. The process was sampled twice during each production shift, and the observations were taken while the process was under control, or at least thought to be under control. With $n = 5$ observations in each sample, we find from Table C.1 that the constants are $A_2 = 0.577$, $D_3 = 0$, and $D_4 = 2.115$. Thus the control limits for the $\bar{x}$-chart are

$$LCL = \bar{x} - A_2 \bar{R} = 84.52 - (0.577)(8.9) = 79.38$$

and

$$UCL = \bar{x} + A_2 \bar{R} = 84.52 + (0.577)(8.9) = 89.66.$$

The limits on the R-chart are $LCL = D_3 \bar{R} = (0)(8.9) = 0$ and $UCL = D_4 \bar{R} = (2.115)(8.9) = 18.82$. These are the limits that are shown in Figures 5.1-1 and 5.1-2. We see that the averages and ranges of all 10 samples are within these limits. We could have expected this because we were told that the process was in control when these observations were taken. But let us plot the results of the next two samples, also given in Table 5.1-1, on these charts. There we find that the twelfth average $\bar{x} = 76.4$ is smaller than the lower control limit on the $\bar{x}$-chart. This fact should alert the user that this particular sample represents

TABLE 5.1-1   Compressive Strength of Concrete (kg/cm^2)

	Sample	Compressive Strength					$\bar{x}$	R
	1	91	88	88	90	83	88.0	8
	2	84	89	80	79	87	83.8	10
	3	93	90	87	89	85	88.8	8
Samples	4	76	84	82	79	82	80.6	8
used to	5	83	85	81	80	86	83.0	6
determine	6	84	84	90	79	83	84.0	11
the control	7	83	89	80	82	91	85.0	11
limits	8	78	79	90	81	85	82.6	12
	9	82	81	87	86	79	83.0	8
	10	88	90	83	84	87	86.4	7
Mean							$\bar{\bar{x}} = 84.52$	$\bar{R} = 8.9$
	11	79	87	82	85	83	83.2	8
	12	72	79	76	77	78	76.4	7

an unusual event, called a special cause. This finding should lead to an investigation (i.e., discussions with workers on the production line, checking whether there were changes in raw materials, looking for any other unusual condition) that will identify an assignable cause for this event. Finally, these causes should be eliminated.

Control charts are very useful methods that help us assess whether a process is stable. They alert the user to situations in which something has shifted. A point outside the control limits forces us to find an assignable cause for this unusual event and, more important, to make certain changes in the process that prevent such conditions from happening again. Control charts will uncover many external sources that lead to shifts in the mean level and in the variability of the process. Their graphical simplicity makes them a very valuable instrument for process control. The requirement to identify assignable causes and to eliminate them forces management and workers to take an aggressive attitude toward maintaining the quality of their work.

Remark   The use of control charts and a strategy of investigating and eliminating special causes will lead to stable processes. However, we want to make it very clear at this point that control limits and specification limits are *not* the same. A stable process (or, to say it differently, a process that is under control) implies that we have been successful in eliminating special, unusual causes. The variability that is due to the common causes, however, is still present and may lead to products that are outside the specification limits.

The first step in improving processes is to bring them under control. Once we have eliminated special causes and have made the process stable, we can check whether the process also satisfies the required specification limits. This can be done in the following way.

Since $A_2 \bar{R}$ is an estimate of $3\sigma/\sqrt{n}$, where n is the size of each sample, we find that $\sqrt{n}\,A_2\bar{R}$ is an estimate of 3σ. Thus $\bar{\bar{x}} \pm \sqrt{n}\,A_2\bar{R}$ is an estimate of $\mu \pm 3\sigma$. If the underlying distribution is approximately normal (unimodal and fairly symmetric without long tails), almost all items should be between $\bar{\bar{x}} - \sqrt{n}\,A_2\bar{R}$ and $\bar{\bar{x}} + \sqrt{n}\,A_2\bar{R}$. If these two bounds are within specifications (specs), most items must be within specs too. However, if one or both of the bounds, $\bar{\bar{x}} \pm \sqrt{n}\,A_2\bar{R}$, are outside the specification limits, it is very likely that some of the items are outside specification limits. The situation should be reviewed carefully. Questions like "How many items are outside specs?" and "Were the specs determined correctly?" should be addressed.

If a stable process is not capable of producing items within the specification limits, we must think about making changes to our process. In later chapters on design of experiments we will learn how to decide which changes are most favorable. ∎

5.1-2   *p*-Charts and *c*-Charts

Control charts are not only useful for averages and ranges, but also for proportions, such as the proportion of defectives. Also, control charts are useful not just in manufacturing applications, but also in other areas, such as the service industry. In fact, they can be applied to virtually all situations in which data are taken sequentially in time.

Assume, for example, that we simply judge whether or not a manufactured item is satisfactory. That is, although we prefer to take more accurate measurements, here we just check an item on a pass–fail basis, whether it is within or outside specifications. Assume that an inspector on the production line checks a sample of n items at certain stated periods (hour, half-day, day, etc., depending on the numbers of items produced each day) and observes the number of defectives, say d, in these n items. If this is done for k periods, we obtain $d_1, d_2, \ldots, d_k$ defectives, respectively. The average fraction of defectives is

$$\bar{p} = \frac{d_1 + d_2 + \cdots + d_k}{nk}.$$

Statistical theory implies that in a stable process (i.e., a process that produces defectives at a rate of $\bar{p}$) almost all of the future fraction defectives, d/n, will be between the respective lower and upper control limits:

$$\text{LCL} = \bar{p} - 3\sqrt{\frac{\bar{p}(1-\bar{p})}{n}},$$

$$\text{UCL} = \bar{p} + 3\sqrt{\frac{\bar{p}(1-\bar{p})}{n}}.$$

These 3-sigma limits are obtained from the sampling distribution of proportions, which has variance $p(1-p)/n$. These control limits, together with the centerline at $\bar{p}$, are plotted on a chart; since we are plotting fractions of defectives or percentages, we call it a *p-chart*. Fractions outside these limits suggest that the process has gone out of control and that the fraction of defectives has changed. In particular, a point exceeding the upper control limit indicates that the process has deteriorated. In such a situation we should look for possible reasons for the sudden increase in the number of defectives.

Example 5.1-1 Each hour $n = 50$ fuses are tested. For the first $k = 20$ hours we find the following number of defectives:

$$1 \quad 1 \quad 3 \quad 0 \quad 2 \quad 4 \quad 0 \quad 0 \quad 1 \quad 2 \quad 3 \quad 2 \quad 0 \quad 1 \quad 1 \quad 1 \quad 3 \quad 0 \quad 0 \quad 2$$

Thus, since $nk = 1000$,

$$\bar{p} = \frac{27}{1000} = 0.027$$

is the average fraction of defectives. We must first decide if this is an acceptable fraction for our particular process. If it is, then

$$\text{LCL} = 0.027 - 3\sqrt{\frac{(0.027)(0.973)}{50}} = -0.042,$$

$$\text{UCL} = 0.027 + 3\sqrt{\frac{(0.027)(0.973)}{50}} = 0.096.$$

Since LCL < 0, and since the fraction defective d/n can never be less than zero, we usually plot the LCL at zero, or omit it entirely. In Figure 5.1-3 we have plotted these 20 values of the fraction defective together with six more recent

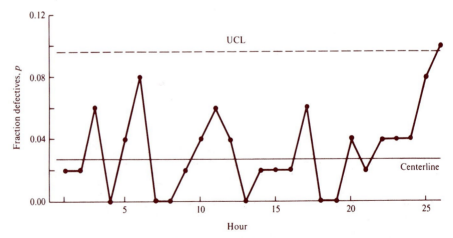

FIGURE 5.1-3   *p*-chart for the data in Example 5.1-1.

ones, those with d values of 1, 2, 2, 2, 4, and 5. Additional values would also be plotted as long as the process is "in control." However, we find that the sixth additional fraction defective is above the UCL. This suggests that the process has become unstable and that corrective action should be taken. In this example we have assumed that 2.7 percent defective is acceptable and that we are willing to produce at this level; this may not be the case for other items. ■

The *c-chart* is very similar to the *p*-chart except that here we count the number of flaws or defectives for a certain unit (bolt of fabric, length of wire, and so on) rather than the number of defectives in n items. Suppose that we determine the number, c, of blemishes in 50 feet of a continuous strip of tin plate. This is done each hour for k hours, resulting in $c_1, c_2, \ldots, c_k$ with an average of

$$\bar{c} = \frac{1}{k} \sum_{i=1}^{k} c_i.$$

The *c*-chart is a time-sequence plot of the number of defectives c_i. Its center-line is given by $\bar{c}$ and the respective lower and upper control limits for the *c*-chart are

$$\text{LCL} = \bar{c} - 3\sqrt{\bar{c}},$$
$$\text{UCL} = \bar{c} + 3\sqrt{\bar{c}}.$$

These are approximations to the 3-sigma limits $\lambda \pm 3\sqrt{\lambda}$ of a Poisson distribution. The Poisson distribution with parameter λ is appropriate in this context, as it approximates the distribution of the number of defectives. The control limits are obtained after replacing the parameter λ (which is the mean as well as the variance of this distribution) by the sample mean.

Example 5.1-2   We observe $k = 15$ 50-foot tin strips and obtain the following numbers of blemishes:

$$2 \quad 1 \quad 1 \quad 0 \quad 5 \quad 2 \quad 3 \quad 1 \quad 1 \quad 2 \quad 0 \quad 0 \quad 4 \quad 3 \quad 1$$

The average is $\bar{c} = 26/15 = 1.73$ and

$$\text{LCL} = 1.73 - 3\sqrt{1.73} = -2.22, \qquad \text{UCL} = 1.73 + 3\sqrt{1.73} = 5.68.$$

These 15 points, together with the 10 additional observations

$$3 \quad 1 \quad 1 \quad 0 \quad 2 \quad 2 \quad 5 \quad 0 \quad 1 \quad 2$$

are plotted on the *c*-chart in Figure 5.1-4. Of course, as long as the process is in control, as with these 10 additional points, future points are plotted on this *c*-chart. Occasionally, new control limits are calculated if the points continue to fall within the control limits; thus the control limits may change slightly. Points outside the control limits, however, indicate that the process has become unstable. Assignable causes for these unusual events should be found and eliminated. ■

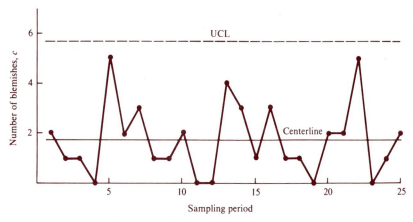

FIGURE 5.1-4 c-chart for the data in Example 5.1-2.

The control charts that we discussed in this section were developed in the late 1920s by Shewhart in the United States and by Dudding and Jennet in Great Britain. In the United States they are usually referred to as Shewhart control charts.

Remark   When viewing time-sequence plots such as Shewhart charts, you should guard against reading too much into short sequences of points. For example, in the desire to improve, a foreman may believe that three successive decreasing points on a p-chart are an indication that the process has improved. Of course, we recognize that the probability of getting three points of decreasing magnitude is fairly large, even if the process has stayed unchanged. It is 1/6 as there are 3! = 6 equally likely ways of arranging three points. Sales managers, especially, are known to misinterpret their graphs. Two consecutive sales periods with increasing sales are often taken as evidence of improvement. Is this enough to claim improvement when, with no actual changes, the probability of such an arrangement is 1/2? Certainly not. Maybe four increasing observations in succession would be more reason for celebration. The probability of such an event is 1/24 as there are 4! = 24 equally likely ways of arranging four observations. Since this probability is rather small, it seems more likely that some significant improvement has taken place.

Exercises 5.1

5.1-1   Grant notes that a particular dimension determines the fit of a molded plastic rheostat knob in its assembly. The dimension was specified by the engineering department as 0.140 ± 0.003 inch. A special gage was designed to permit quick measurement of the actual value of this dimension. Five knobs from each hour's production were selected and measured. The averages and the ranges (in units of 0.001 inch) for the first 20 hours were as follows:

Hour	Average, $\bar{x}$	Range, R	Hour	Average, $\bar{x}$	Range, R
1	137.8	9	11	139.6	12
2	143.0	8	12	141.4	9
3	141.2	15	13	141.2	3
4	139.8	6	14	140.6	8
5	140.0	10	15	141.6	9
6	139.2	8	16	140.4	13
7	141.2	10	17	140.0	6
8	140.0	8	18	141.8	8
9	142.0	7	19	140.4	8
10	139.2	13	20	138.8	6

Construct an $\bar{x}$-chart and an R-chart. Is this process in control? If so, does it satisfy the specification limits?
[E. L. Grant, *Statistical Quality Control*, 2nd ed. (New York: McGraw-Hill, 1952), p. 23.]

5.1-2 Astro Electronics, an RCA division, uses statistical quality control tools to assure proper weld strength of several of their welding procedures. Weld

Date	Time	Average	Range (pounds)
1/3	7:30	5.48	1.4
	11:25	5.42	1.6
	16:20	5.42	1.4
	20:00	5.40	0.5
	23:30	5.52	1.7
1/4	7:20	5.32	0.7
	11:25	5.34	1.6
	16:20	5.58	1.2
	20:20	4.54	0.6
	23:00	5.42	1.6
1/7	7:40	5.58	0.5
	10:20	5.06	1.4
	14:00	4.82	1.9
	20:20	4.86	1.3
	23:00	4.68	0.9
1/8	8:00	5.28	1.6
	11:20	4.68	1.1
	14:00	4.94	0.6
1/9	9:00	4.90	1.0
1/10	7:40	4.96	0.7
	11:00	5.06	1.8
	14:00	5.22	0.8

strength is measured by a pull test to destruction. A sample of a small number of items (in this case, five) is taken periodically throughout the production process, usually at the beginning, the middle, and the end of each shift. The averages and the ranges of 22 such samples, taken from an article by Shecter, are listed in the table for this exercise. Construct $\bar{x}$- and R-charts. Interpret your results and comment on the stability of the process.

Note that the frequency of sampling should depend on the stability of the process. Actually, Shecter reports that initially the samples were taken every hour, but the data showed a relatively stable process; thus, sampling about every 4 hours (or less) was thought appropriate.
[E. Shecter, "Process Control for High Yields," *RCA Engineer*, 30(3): 38–43 (1985).]

5.1-3 A 1-month record of daily 100 percent inspection of a single critical quality characteristic of a part of an electrical device led to an average fraction defective $\bar{p} = 0.0145$. After this month of 100 percent inspection, the company switched to a sampling plan under which a sample of 500 units was selected each day. During the first 10 days the inspector found 8, 10, 7, 20, 13, 15, 8, 12, 45, and 30 defectives. Plot this information on a p-chart using $\bar{p} = 0.0145$ as a centerline, and interpret your findings.

5.1-4 A company that produces certain bolts considers its output quality adequate as long as the proportion of defectives is not larger than 2.5 percent. To monitor the quality, the company takes a random sample of 100 bolts each hour and counts the number of defective bolts. With $p = 0.025$, calculate the lower and upper control limits of the appropriate control chart. Now suppose that the number of defectives in the last six samples were 3, 0, 2, 1, 7, and 8. What conclusions would you draw from this information?

5.1-5 Past experience has shown that the number of defects per yard of material follows a Poisson distribution with $\lambda = 1.2$. This information was used to establish the control limits of the c-chart. If the average number of defects shifts to 2.0, what is the probability that it will be detected by the c-chart on the first observation following the shift? What is the probability that this shift is not recognized for the next 10 (20) observations?

5.1-6 In the production of stainless steel pipes the number of defects per 100 feet should be controlled.

From 15 randomly selected 100-foot-long pipes, we obtained the following data on the number of defects: 6, 10, 8, 1, 7, 9, 7, 4, 5, 10, 3, 4, 9, 8, 5. Construct a control chart. Is this process under control?

5.1-7 The following data give the results of inspection of 100-yard pieces of woolen textile. The number of defects among the last 12 samples are: 3, 6, 3, 0, 5, 2, 4, 0, 1, 0, 3, 4. Calculate the control limits of the c-chart. Is this process under control?

5.1-8 A company that produces electronic components considers its quality adequate as long as the proportion of defectives is not larger than 2 percent. To monitor the quality the company takes a random sample of 80 components each hour and counts the number of defective items.

(a) Calculate the centerline and the lower and upper control limits of the appropriate control chart.

(b) Suppose that the number of defectives in the last six samples were 2, 0, 4, 1, 3, 7. What conclusions would you draw from this information?

5.1-9 We are concerned that the level of a process increases from a specified acceptable level μ_0. Assume that successive observations X_t are independent with standard deviation σ. Suppose that one uses the Shewhart chart for individual observations ($n = 1$) with centerline at μ_0 and upper control limit $h = \mu_0 + k\sigma$.

Define the *run length* T as the time period at which the process exceeds the control limit for the first time. It is a random variable that can take on integer values 1, 2, ... The expectation of this random variable, $E(T)$, is called the *average run length* (ARL).

(a) Show that the average run length ARL for the one-sided Shewhart chart above (i.e., our only concern is whether we exceed the upper control limit) is given by

$$\text{ARL} = \frac{1}{P(X_t > h)}.$$

(b) Assume that the X_t come from a normal distribution. Calculate the average run length for $k = 2.0, 2.5, 3.0$.

(c) Calculate the average run lengths in part (b) for a two-sided chart where one is concerned about increases as well as decreases in the level.

Hint The average run length is given by

$$\text{ARL} = (1)P(T = 1) + (2)P(T = 2) + (3)P(T = 3) + \cdots$$
$$= (1)P(X_1 > h) + (2)P(X_2 > h \text{ and } X_1 < h)$$
$$+ (3)P(X_3 > h \text{ and } X_2 < h \text{ and } X_1 < h) + \cdots.$$

You can show the result using the independence assumption (which implies that the probability of an intersection of events is the product of the individual probabilities) and facts about geometric sums.

---

*5.2 Cusum Charts

Shewhart control charts provide a very useful display of the data and give us a simple rule for making decisions as to whether a process has started to become unstable. Such charts require that measurements on a process be taken on a regular basis and that the results be prominently displayed. They create an atmosphere where the quality of the process is checked on a regular basis. They enhance our awareness of the present state of the process and make us "listen to" the process.

A disadvantage of these charts, however, is their relative insensitivity to small or moderate changes in the mean value. For illustration, consider a chart for *individual observations* ($n = 1$) and assume that the mean has shifted by one standard deviation, from μ to $\mu + \sigma$. Then, as the following calculation shows, we have to plot 44 observations (on the average) on the control chart before one observation exceeds the upper control limit. This is quite easy to see; under the assumption that the observations come from a $N(\mu + \sigma, \sigma^2)$ distribution, the probability

$$P(X > \mu + 3\sigma) = 1 - P(X \le \mu + 3\sigma) = 1 - \Phi\left(\frac{\mu + 3\sigma - (\mu + \sigma)}{\sigma}\right)$$

$$= 1 - \Phi(2) = 0.02275$$

while $P(X < \mu - 3\sigma) \approx 0$. Thus, if the mean increases by one standard deviation, only about 2.275 percent or one observation among 44 will exceed the upper control limit. To say this differently, on the average about 44 points have to be plotted until the upper control limit is exceeded.

The responsiveness to changes in the mean level can be improved by plotting the Shewhart $\bar{x}$-chart with two additional sets of limits, namely at 1- and 2-sigma deviations of the sample mean. That is, if μ and σ are known, we plot additional lines at $\mu \pm \sigma/\sqrt{n}$ and $\mu \pm 2\sigma/\sqrt{n}$. Of course, most of the time, these must be approximated by $\bar{x} \pm A_2 \bar{R}/3$ and $\bar{x} \pm 2A_2 \bar{R}/3$, respectively, since $A_2 \bar{R}$ is an estimate of $3\sigma/\sqrt{n}$. The rules that are often used with these additional lines appear in the *Western Electric Company Handbook* (1956) and, more recently, have been discussed by Andrew C. Palm in the *Journal of Quality Technology*, 22: 289–298 (1990). They are

1. A lack of control is indicated whenever a single point ($\bar{x}$) falls outside the 3-sigma control limits approximated by $\bar{x} \pm A_2 \bar{R}$. (This is the usual rule.)

2. A lack of control is indicated whenever at least two out of three successive points fall on the same side of the center line (approximated by $\bar{x}$) and outside the 2-sigma limits approximated by $\bar{x} \pm 2A_2 \bar{R}/3$.

3. A lack of control is indicated whenever at least four out of five successive points fall on the same side of the centerline and outside the 1-sigma limits approximated by $\bar{x} \pm A_2 \bar{R}/3$.

4. A lack of control is indicated whenever at least eight successive points fall on the same side of the centerline.

The more of these rules are used simultaneously, the more sensitive the chart will be to shifts in the mean. However, the more rules used, the higher the probability that the process will be stopped unnecessarily. For example, if only the usual procedure (rule 1) is used, the probability of claiming lack of control when in fact the process is in control is about 0.003. Using rules 1 and 2 together, this probability is about 0.005. With rules 1, 2, and 3 together it is about 0.008, and with all four rules it is just a little over 0.01. Although none of these probabilities is very large, we gain a great deal of protection if the mean actually shifts. For example, if the mean shifts 1-sigma to $\mu + \sigma/\sqrt{n}$ (or to $\mu + \sigma$ if $n = 1$) and we use all four rules simultaneously, we need only about 9 points on the average to detect this shift. This number is a lot smaller than the 44, which we can expect if we use only rule 1. For gains like this, many persons are quite willing to let the probability of a "false alarm" increase from 0.003 to 0.01.

The Shewhart charts and, to a lesser extent, their modifications are weighted against concluding that a small change in the mean has taken place. The **cumulative sum (cusum) charts**, on the other hand, are much more responsive to small changes in the mean level. In cusum charts, we consider the deviations of the observations (again $n = 1$) from a reference value k, $x_i - k$, and calculate the cumulative sums

$$S_1 = x_1 - k,$$

$$S_2 = (x_2 - k) + (x_1 - k) = (x_2 - k) + S_1,$$

$$S_3 = (x_3 - k) + (x_2 - k) + (x_1 - k) = (x_3 - k) + S_2,$$

$$\vdots$$

$$S_r = \sum_{i=1}^{r} (x_i - k) = (x_r - k) + S_{r-1}.$$

These cumulative sums, or *cusums* as they are often abbreviated, are then plotted against r.

In the following discussion we consider the deviations from an acceptable mean level μ, and choose $k = \mu$. If the mean level stays at μ, the cumulative sum path should be roughly horizontal because there should be about as many observations below μ as above μ. A moderate change in the level, which would go largely undetected on the Shewhart chart, leads to a noticeable change in the slope of the plotted cumulative sums. This is due to the fact that the change in the level gets cumulated with each new observation. As an illustration, we have taken 40 random drawings from a $N(0, 1)$ distribution and then have added one standard deviation to the last 20 observations. [To take random drawings from a $N(0, 1)$ distribution, use standard computer software.] The jump in the level after the first 20 observations goes undetected on the Shewhart chart in Figure 5.2-1(a); the 3σ limits are not exceeded. In Figure 5.2-1(b) we plot the cumulative sums $S_r = \sum_{i=1}^{r} x_i$, because here $k = 0$. There we clearly notice a change in the slope after about the 20th observation.

In cusum charts it is the average slope of the cusum line that is of importance. Horizontal segments on such charts correspond to periods where the mean value of the process and the reference value are the same. The farther the current mean is away from the reference value, the steeper the graph on the cusum chart.

A rising cusum path indicates that the process mean may have increased. One must now develop rules that help us to decide whether such an increase in the cusum path, in fact, comes from a change in the level, or whether it is just due to random fluctuations in the process. One such rule calls for action if the current point on the chart exceeds the lowest point of the cusum path by more than a fixed amount h. Woodward and Goldsmith, in *Cumulative Sum*

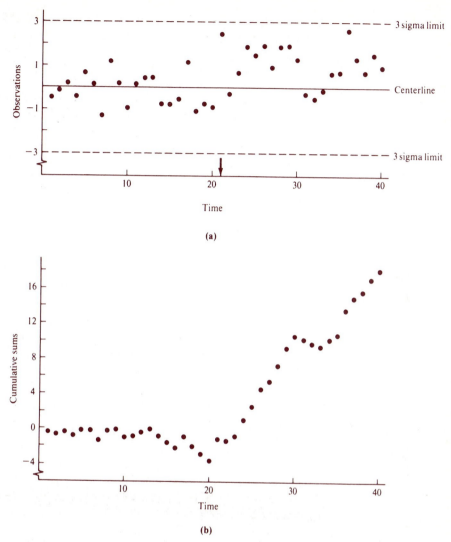

FIGURE 5.2-1   Plot of 40 generated $N(0, 1)$ random variables with a mean increase of one standard deviation after observation 20: (a) Shewhart $\bar{x}$-chart; (b) cusum chart.

Techniques (Edinburgh: Oliver & Boyd, 1964), give an excellent survey of cusum methods and discuss the following procedure, proposed by E. S. Page ["Continuous Inspection Schemes," *Biometrika*, 41: 100–115 (1954)] and later modified by W. D. Ewan and K. W. Kemp ["Sampling Inspection of Continuous Processes with No Autocorrelation Between Successive Results," *Biometrika*, 47: 363–380 (1960).]

Assume that we are concerned about increases in the mean level. Suppose that the *acceptable quality level* (AQL) is μ_0, while the unacceptable level, or the *rejectable quality level* (RQL), is μ_1, where $\mu_0 < \mu_1$. The reference value k is now taken midway between the acceptable and rejectable quality levels; thus $k = (\mu_0 + \mu_1)/2$. Note that with this particular reference value the cumulative sums $S_r = \sum_{i=1}^{r}(x_i - k)$ will slope downward if the process is at the AQL and slope upward if the process is at the RQL. Our rule calls for action if the cumulative sum exceeds the previous lowest point of the cusum path by more than h units; h is referred to as the *length of the decision interval*. That is, we check whether $d_r = S_r - \min_{i=0, 1, \ldots, r} S_i > h$, for $r = 1, 2, 3, \ldots$. An increase in the average quality level is indicated at the first index r where this inequality occurs. The initial cumulative sum is taken as $S_0 = 0$, because we assume that prior to the first observation the process is in control.

Instead of plotting the cusums and measuring distances from the previous lowest point in the cusum path, we can plot these distances directly. It is easy to see that

$$d_r = \max[0, d_{r-1} + (x_r - k)].$$

If x_r is above the reference value k, then $d_r = d_{r-1} + (x_r - k)$. If x_r is below k, then $d_r = \max[0, d_{r-1} + (x_r - k)]$, because d_r cannot be negative. The recursive equation for d_r is initialized with $d_0 = 0$.

On the modified cusum chart we plot the differences d_r against r and check whether these differences exceed the length of the decision interval, h. The advantage of this particular cusum version is that only points that are relevant toward making a decision are plotted. If at a time t the cusum path is at its lowest value, then there is no need to plot the cumulative sum for the subsequent observation if it is smaller than the reference value. However, as soon as an observation exceeds k, the distance of the cusum from its previous minimum is plotted; if the path of these distances crosses h, then we say that the mean level has shifted to an unacceptable level; the process has gone out of control.

The advantage of this particular cusum scheme is that during periods of satisfactory production it is usually not necessary to calculate and plot the cumulative sums at all. Also, this technique can be applied in tabular form, without any recourse to graphs.

The question now becomes how to choose h; one approach makes this determination according to *average run lengths*. The average run length is defined as the mean number of points that have to be plotted on the control chart before an action is signaled. This number should be large if the process is stable and the average quality level is acceptable, but it should be small if the mean level has shifted to the rejectable level μ_1. For normal distributions, Ewan and Kemp have evaluated the average run length when the mean is at the AQL, μ_0, and also the one when the mean is at the RQL, μ_1. Of course, these average run lengths depend on the size of the decision interval h. However, they also depend on the distance of the reference value k from μ_0 and μ_1, and on the standard deviation $\sigma/\sqrt{n}$ if averages $\bar{x}_i$ are used in the cusum. Of course, $n = 1$ if individual measurements are considered.

TABLE 5.2-1   **Average Run Lengths for Several Cusum Schemes**

Average Run Length Under:		$\dfrac{\lvert k - \mu_0 \rvert \sqrt{n}}{\sigma}$	$\dfrac{h\sqrt{n}}{\sigma}$
μ_0	μ_1		
1000	3	1.12	2.40
1000	7	0.65	4.06
500	3	1.04	2.26
500	7	0.60	3.80
250	3	0.94	2.11
250	7	0.54	3.51

Table 5.2-1 lists the average run lengths for a few selected schemes. Assume, for example, that $\mu_0 = 12.0$, $\mu_1 = 12.2$, and the standard deviation of individual observations is $\sigma = 0.3$. Suppose that we want a scheme with an average run length at AQL of 500 and one at RQL of 7. From Table 5.2-1 we find that $(k - \mu_0)\sqrt{n}/\sigma = 0.6$ and $h\sqrt{n}/\sigma = 3.80$. Since $k = (\mu_0 + \mu_1)/2 = 12.1$ and $\sigma = 0.3$ are known, we can solve for n and h. This leads to $(0.1)\sqrt{n} = (0.6)(0.3)$, or $\sqrt{n} = 1.8$ and $n = 3.24$, and $h = (0.3)(3.8)/1.8 = 0.63$. This says that we should consider samples of size 4 and use the successive averages $\bar{x}_r$ to calculate and plot

$$d_r = \max[0, d_{r-1} + (\bar{x}_r - k)]; \qquad d_0 = 0.$$

If d_r exceeds $h = 0.63$, we conclude that the performance of the process has become unacceptable.

How should one set the limit h if n is fixed in advance? We get two equations from Table 5.2-1, but have only one unknown, h. Usually, we cannot choose h such that both equations are satisfied. Thus, by choosing h, it is only possible to satisfy one of the average run lengths, say the one at the AQL; the average run length at RQL is in turn implied by this choice.

Ewan and Kemp have developed charts, called nomograms, that can be used to set h such that a given average run length at AQL is achieved. We have reproduced these charts in Figure 5.2-2. To illustrate these nomograms, consider our 40 generated random variables with variance 1 that are plotted in Figure 5.2-1(a). There we had increased the mean after the first 20 observations by one unit. Let us assume that we are concerned about increases in the level from AQL, $\mu_0 = 0$, to RQL, $\mu_1 = 1$, and that we want a cusum scheme that leads to a false rejection signal in only one among 700 observations. Here $n = 1$ and $\sigma = 1$. Passing a line through $\lvert k - \mu_0 \rvert \sqrt{n}/\sigma = 0.5$ on the left axis and the average run length at AQL of 700 on the right axis in Figure 5.2-2(a), we find that $h\sqrt{n}/\sigma \cong 4.7$, and thus $h = 4.7$. The nomogram in Figure 5.2-2(b) can be used to determine the average run length at RQL that is implied by

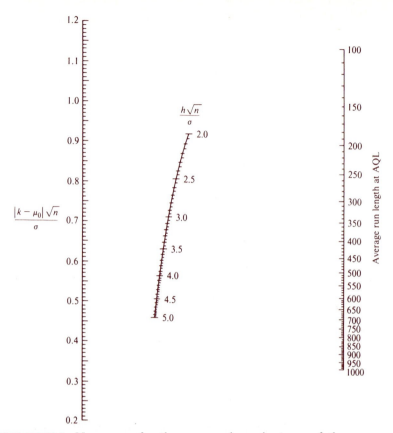

FIGURE 5.2-2(a) Nomogram for the cusum scheme in terms of the average run length at AQL = μ_0. [Reproduced with permission from W. D. Ewan and K. W. Kemp, "Sampling Inspection of Continuous Processes with No Autocorrelation Between Successive Results," *Biometrika*, 47: 363–380 (1960).]

this particular value of h. This is done by passing a straight line through $|\mu_1 - k|\sqrt{n}/\sigma = 0.5$ and $h\sqrt{n}/\sigma = 4.7$. The intersection of this line with the axis on the left side determines the average run length at RQL. For our sample it turns out to be about 10. Thus our cusum scheme with $h = 4.7$ leads to average run lengths of 700 at AQL and 10 at RQL, respectively.

Compare this to the performance of the Shewhart chart. There the probability of exceeding the upper 3σ limit by chance is $P(X > \mu_0 + 3\sigma) = 0.00135$, which also corresponds to an average run length at AQL of about 700. But as shown earlier in this section, it takes an average of 44 points before a 1σ change in the level is detected. This shows that a cusum chart responds much quicker to a change in the level. This can also be seen from the 40 generated observations that we had plotted in Figure 5.2-1(a). The differences $d_r =$

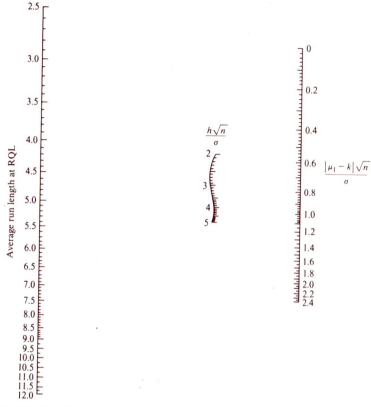

FIGURE 5.2-2(b) Nomogram for the cusum scheme in terms of the average run length at RQL $= \mu_1$. [Reproduced with permission from W. D. Ewan and K. W. Kemp, "Sampling Inspection of Continuous Processes with No Autocorrelation Between Successive Results," *Biometrika*, 47: 363–380 (1960).]

$\max[0, d_{r-1} + (x_r - 0.5)]$, $r = 1, 2, 3, \ldots, 40$, are calculated in Table 5.2-2 and are plotted in Figure 5.2-3. We find that these differences exceed $h = 4.7$ for the first time at observation number 26; this is only six observations after the change in mean has occurred. On the other hand, the Shewhart chart has not detected the change, even after 20 observations.

It is interesting to note that a Shewhart chart with the four rules given in the *Western Electric Company Handbook* would have declared the process out of control at observation number 28, as four out of five observations, namely observations at times 24, 25, 26, and 28, are above the 1-sigma limit. Note that in this particular example, these rules declare the process out of control at roughly the same place as does the cusum. Some people find these four rules easier to use than a cusum, although in general the latter may be slightly better.

TABLE 5.2-2   Calculation of $S_r = \sum_{i=1}^{r} (x_i - 0.5)$ and $d_r = \max[0, d_{r-1} + (x_r - 0.5)]$ from 40 Simulated Values; $d_0 = 0$.

r	x_r	$x_r - 0.5$	S_r	d_r	r	x_r	$x_r - 0.5$	S_r	d_r
1	−0.44	−0.94	−0.94	0	21	2.46	1.96	−11.61	1.96
2	−0.09	−0.59	−1.53	0	22	−0.26	−0.76	−12.37	1.20
3	0.18	−0.32	−1.85	0	23	0.64	0.14	−12.23	1.34
4	−0.44	−0.94	−2.79	0	24	1.88	1.38	−10.85	2.72
5	0.65	0.15	−2.64	0.15	25	1.51	1.01	−9.84	3.73
6	0.07	−0.43	−3.07	0	26	1.94	1.44	−8.40	5.17
7	−1.29	−1.79	−4.86	0	27	0.93	0.43	−7.97	5.60
8	1.18	0.68	−4.18	0.68	28	1.85	1.35	−6.62	6.95
9	0.18	−0.32	−4.50	0.36	29	1.93	1.43	−5.19	8.38
10	−0.96	−1.46	−5.96	0	30	1.29	0.79	−4.40	9.17
11	0.12	−0.38	−6.34	0	31	−0.29	−0.79	−5.19	8.38
12	0.42	−0.08	−6.42	0	32	−0.57	−1.07	−6.26	7.31
13	0.45	−0.05	−6.47	0	33	−0.17	−0.67	−6.93	6.64
14	−0.80	−1.30	−7.77	0	34	0.65	0.15	−6.78	6.79
15	−0.76	−1.26	−9.03	0	35	0.71	0.21	−6.57	7.00
16	−0.53	−1.03	−10.06	0	36	2.68	2.18	−4.39	9.18
17	1.19	0.69	−9.37	0.69	37	1.37	0.87	−3.52	10.05
18	−1.07	−1.57	−10.94	0	38	0.72	0.22	−3.30	10.27
19	−0.78	−1.28	−12.22	0	39	1.49	0.99	−2.31	11.26
20	−0.85	−1.35	−13.57	0	40	0.95	0.45	−1.86	11.71

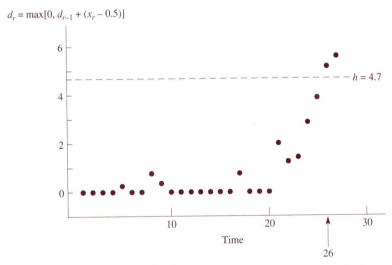

FIGURE 5.2-3   Plot of $d_r = \max[0, d_{r-1} + (x_r - 0.5)]$ for the generated observations in Figure 5.2-1(a).

Remark   Here we have discussed the cusum chart for detecting *increases* in the mean level. Charts for detecting *decreases* in the mean are similar, and they are discussed in Exercise 5.2-4. If closeness to a target is of interest and if one is concerned about increases and decreases alike, one can combine the two one-sided charts. One concludes that a change in the level has taken place if either chart indicates an out-of-control signal. Of course, the ARL for this combined chart will be somewhat smaller than the ones for the one-sided charts. ■

Exercises 5.2

5.2-1 Consider the data given in Exercise 5.1-1. Calculate and plot the cumulative sums of successive subgroup averages. Use the reference value $k = 140.0$. Interpret your findings.

5.2-2 Consider cumulative sums of independent $N(0, \sigma^2)$ random variables; $S_r = \sum_{i=1}^{r} X_i$. Show that var$(S_r) = r\sigma^2$ and convince yourself that consecutive cumulative sums S_r and S_{r+1} are closely related (i.e., if S_r is large, so is S_{r+1}). To learn more about the nature of a cusum path for a process that is under control, take a sample of size 100 from a $N(0,1)$ distribution and plot the corresponding cusums. Use the computer to generate these random variables. Repeat and plot several of these paths. You will notice that a plot of S_r will give the appearance of a slowly changing path that at times can drift upward or downward.

5.2-3 Several times during a shift a company inspector takes five cans of tomatoes from the production line, opens each can, and weighs the solid contents. The cans should have a drained weight of $\mu_0 = 21.5$ ounces (AQL). The averages from samples of size $n = 5$ taken over the last several days are as follows (read across):

22.9	22.0	21.4	22.0	21.5	21.9	20.8	20.0
21.5	21.6	20.2	20.5	20.5	21.7	21.1	21.8
21.6	20.8	21.9	21.2	20.7	21.5	22.6	21.3
21.3	20.1	21.4	20.0	21.2	21.6		

The standard deviation of individual measurements is about 1.25. Due to a loss in revenue, the company is concerned that too much contents is put into each can, and it considers a mean weight $\mu_1 = 22.0$ an unacceptable value. Construct a cusum chart that leads to an average run length at AQL of about 500. Plot the cusums as well as the length of the decision interval. Determine the run length at the RQL. [E. L. Grant, *Statistical Quality Control*, 2nd ed. (New York: McGraw-Hill, 1952).]

5.2-4 In this section we have described a cusum rule for detecting an increase in the average quality level. If we are concerned about a decrease from AQL of μ_0 to RQL of $\mu_1 < \mu_0$, then we consider $d_r^* = S_r - \max_{i=0, 1, \ldots, r} S_i = \min[0, d_{r-1}^* + (\bar{x}_r - k)]$ with $d_0^* = 0$, and conclude that the average quality level has become unacceptable if $d_r^* < -h$. Table 5.2-1 and the nomograms in Figure 5.2-2 can be used to determine h. Consider the data in Exercise 5.2-3, and suppose that the inspector of the U.S. Food and Drug Administration is concerned that too little contents is put in each can; that is, from the consumers' point of view, $\mu_1 = 21.0$ is considered unacceptable. Construct a cusum chart with an average run length at AQL of about 500.

5.2-5 The deflection of a 10-foot steel beam should be around $\mu_0 = 0.01$ inch. The company has started a rigorous control program because an average deflection of $\mu_1 = 0.012$ inch would definitely be unacceptable to its customers. From each production batch, the inspector selects a sample of $n = 4$ beams and determines their deflections. The averages from the last 20 batches (in units of 0.001 inch) are as follows (read across):

11.0	11.6	8.6	11.4	9.0	10.2	9.4
10.5	10.9	11.4	12.8	12.3	11.4	11.6
10.0	12.8	11.0	10.9	13.0	12.1	

The standard deviation of individual measurements

is approximately 3 units. Construct a cusum chart with an average run length at AQL of about 700 observations. Determine the average run length at RQL.

5.2-6   Suppose that the average breaking strength of a certain synthetic material should be about 20 pounds per square inch and assume that an average of 16 pounds per square inch (psi) is unacceptable. The standard deviation of an individual measurement is 5 psi. Set up a cusum chart that leads to average run lengths at AQL and RQL of 1000 and 7, respectively. Use results in Exercise 5.2-4.

*5.3 Acceptance Sampling

Manufactured parts (items) are often shipped from a supplier (the producer) to another company (the consumer) that uses these parts in the construction of some final product. These could be sent in boxes—or even boxcars—and a *standard* grouping of these items is often called a *lot*. Let each lot consist of N parts, where N can range from 10 or so to several thousands, depending on the nature of the part. Unfortunately, some of these parts are probably defective; here we let p represent the fraction defective in the lot. That is, there are Np defective items among the N parts. If p is small, the supplier is providing acceptable quality; but a large p suggests that the quality is unacceptable and that the lot should be rejected and not be shipped. However, we do not know p nor the number Np of defectives in the lot. We must find an estimate of p to help us decide whether to accept or to reject the lot. Of course, we could inspect all parts in the lot. However, *100 percent inspection* is usually extremely expensive (sometimes more costly than the production) and sometimes impossible—for example, in the case of destructive inspection, in which an item (e.g., a fuse) is destroyed in the testing. Thus, in most instances, we resort to sampling to determine whether the lot should be accepted or rejected. By observing just a sample (only a fraction of the items in the lot), we may accept certain lots that we would reject if we looked at every item, and we may reject others that we would accept in 100 percent inspection. To decide whether the acceptance sampling plan is a desirable one, we should consider the probabilities of making these two types of errors.

Example 5.3-1   Let a lot of $N = 1000$ items contain Np defectives, where $0 \leq p \leq 1$. We take $n = 10$ items at random and without replacement and test them; if all are satisfactory, we accept the lot; otherwise, we reject it. If we consider the multiplication rule of probabilities, the probability of obtaining n good items, and thus accepting the lot, is

$$\left(\frac{N - Np}{N}\right)\left(\frac{N - Np - 1}{N - 1}\right)\left(\frac{N - Np - 2}{N - 2}\right) \cdots \left[\frac{N - Np - (n - 1)}{N - (n - 1)}\right]$$

$$= (1 - p)\left(1 - \frac{Np}{N - 1}\right)\left(1 - \frac{Np}{N - 2}\right) \cdots \left[1 - \frac{Np}{N - (n - 1)}\right].$$

With $n = 10$ and $N = 1000$, it is easy to see that

$$\frac{N}{N-1} \approx \frac{N}{N-2} \approx \cdots \approx \frac{N}{N-(n-1)} \approx 1.$$

Thus the probability of accepting the lot is approximately equal to the binomial probability $(1-p)^{10}$. This is the probability that we would have obtained if we had taken the $n = 10$ items at random and with replacement, that is, replacing each selected item before selecting the next. The procedure of sampling with replacement is not too practical, however. Nevertheless, if N is considerably larger than n, this binomial probability provides an excellent approximation to the true probability and we very frequently use it.

The probability of accepting the lot is called the *operating characteristic (or OC) curve*. In this example, it is approximated by

$$OC(p) \approx (1-p)^{10}.$$

The OC curve is a function of p, and its graph is given in Figure 5.3-1. The values $OC(0.05) = 0.60$, $OC(0.10) = 0.35$, $OC(0.15) = 0.20$, $OC(0.20) = 0.11$, $OC(0.25) = 0.06$, $OC(0.30) = 0.03$ can be found in the binomial tables under $P(X \leq 0)$ with $n = 10$. The reader may find this OC curve highly undesirable because there is a probability of 0.35 of accepting the lot, even though there are $1000(0.10) = 100$ defective items among the $N = 1000$ items in the lot. That is, there is a 35 percent chance of accepting a seemingly undesirable lot that has 10 percent defectives. In addition, the probability of accepting a desirable lot, say with $p = 0.02$, is

$$(1 - 0.02)^{10} = (0.98)^{10} = 0.82.$$

This means the probability of rejecting a lot with only 2 percent defectives is 0.18, and this is undesirable too. That is, in this example, the probabilities of the two types of errors, the *producer's risk* of rejecting a satisfactory lot and

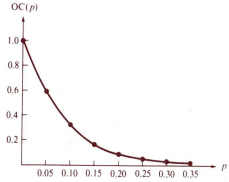

FIGURE 5.3-1 OC curve: Probability of accepting a lot as a function of the proportion of defectives, p.

the *consumer's risk* of accepting an undesirable lot, are too high: 0.18 and 0.35, respectively. The only way that we can correct this is by taking a larger sample size and redesigning the acceptance sampling procedure. ∎

There are two major observations that should be made concerning Example 5.3-1.

1. The true probability of accepting the lot can be written as

$$\prod_{i=1}^{10}\left[\frac{N - Np - (i-1)}{N - (i-1)}\right] = \frac{\binom{Np}{0}\binom{N-Np}{10}}{\binom{N}{10}}.$$

The numerator of the expression on the right side is the number of ways of selecting zero from the Np defectives times the number of ways of selecting 10 from the $N - Np$ good items. Of course, the denominator is the total number of ways of selecting 10 from the N items in the lot. In general, the probability of obtaining y defectives in a sample of size n taken at random and without replacement is given by the *hypergeometric probability*

$$\frac{\binom{Np}{y}\binom{N-Np}{n-y}}{\binom{N}{n}},$$

and this was studied in Section 2.4. The numerator is the number of ways of selecting exactly y from Np defectives and $n - y$ from $N - Np$ nondefectives, while the denominator is the number of ways of selecting n from the N items in the lot. If N is much larger than n, so that the probability of getting a defective does not change much from drawing to drawing, then we can approximate the hypergeometric probability by the binomial probability or the Poisson probability (with reasonably large n and small p), namely,

$$\binom{n}{y}p^y(1-p)^{n-y} \quad \text{or} \quad \frac{(np)^y e^{-np}}{y!}.$$

2. The two values of p that were used in the example, $p_0 = 0.02$ and $p_1 = 0.10$, are frequently called *acceptable quality level* (AQL) and *lot tolerance fraction defective* (LTFD). The probabilities of errors at AQL = 0.02 and LTFD = 0.10, which in our example are $\alpha = 0.18$ and $\beta = 0.35$, have special names. The probability, $\alpha = 0.18$, of rejecting a good lot of AQL = 0.02 is called the *producer's risk* because the producer is hurt if a good lot is rejected. The probability, $\beta = 0.35$, of accepting a bad lot of LTFD = 0.10 is called the *consumer's risk* because the consumer loses if a bad lot is accepted.

Example 5.3-2 Suppose that we wish to design an acceptance sampling plan for lots of $N = 5000$ items. In reference to the particular item that we are manufacturing, let us suppose that $p_0 = \text{AQL} = 0.02$ and $p_1 = \text{LTFD} = 0.06$. Furthermore, we want the probabilities of errors at those two values of p to be *about* $\alpha = 0.05$ and $\beta = 0.10$. That is, we desire an OC curve such as that in Figure 5.3-2. To achieve such an OC curve, it seems as if the sample size must be fairly large; so we begin by using the Poisson approximation. The scheme is to take a sample of size n and accept the lot if the number of defectives is less than or equal to an *acceptance number,* say Ac. Let us begin with an initial guess of $n = 100$ as the sample size. With $\lambda = (100)(0.02) = 2$, we see from the Poisson table that if $\text{Ac} = 4$, then $\text{OC}(0.02) = P(Y \le 4) = 0.947$. Since $1 - 0.947 = 0.053$, this is quite close to the desired α. However, $(100)(0.06) = 6$ and $\text{Ac} = 4$ imply, according to the Poisson table with $\lambda = 6$, that $\text{OC}(0.06) = P(Y \le 4) = 0.285$, which is much larger than the desired β value of 0.10. To lower this probability $\text{OC}(0.06)$, we must increase the sample size. Let us try $n = 150$, which gives the two lambdas $150(0.02) = 3$ and $150(0.06) = 9$. Choosing $\text{Ac} = 6$ so that

$$\text{OC}(0.02) = P(Y \le 6) = 0.966$$

means that $1 - 0.966 = 0.034$ is the probability of rejecting a lot of acceptable quality of $\text{AQL} = 0.02$. This probability of 0.034 is close to the desired $\alpha = 0.05$.

However,

$$\text{OC}(0.06) = P(Y \le 6) = 0.207$$

is still too high and not desirable. Trying various λ values so that the ratio between them is $0.06/0.02 = 3$, we see that $\lambda = 4$ and $\lambda = 12$ with $\text{Ac} = 7$ provide the respective OC values of 0.949 and 0.090, probabilities that are close to the desired $1 - \alpha = 0.95$ and $\beta = 0.10$. Also, $(n)(0.02) = 4$ and $(n)(0.06) = 12$ imply that $n = 200$. That is, a highly desirable sampling plan is

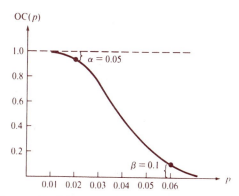

FIGURE 5.3-2 OC curve for Example 5.3-2. Probability of accepting a lot as a function of the proportion of defectives, p.

described by $n = 200$ and Ac $= 7$: Take a sample of $n = 200$ items from each lot. If there are not more than 7 defectives, accept the lot; otherwise, reject it. The approximate operating characteristic curve of this sampling plan is

$$OC(p) \approx \sum_{y=0}^{7} \frac{(np)^y e^{-np}}{y!},$$

where $n = 200$.   ∎

Most of the time engineers do not need to construct acceptance sampling plans because the plans are dictated by the companies or the federal government. Even though plans such as a Military Standard 105D (MIL-STD-105D) plan are required, we believe that it is always advisable to determine their corresponding OC curves.

Example 5.3-3   Suppose that we have a lot of $N = 1000$ items and we desire an AQL $= 0.025$ or 2.5 percent. From a MIL-STD-105D table that is found in most books on quality control, we find that we should use $n = 80$ and Ac $= 5$ and the *rejection number* Re $= 6$, which means that we should reject the lot if six or more defectives are found in the sample of $n = 80$ items. In most instances, engineers simply use the scheme that is designated by MIL-STD-105D. However, we believe that the engineer should also learn more about the implications of such a plan. This can be done by constructing an OC curve. Using the Poisson approximation, we calculate the probability of accepting the lot, namely

$$OC(p) = P(Y \le 5) = \sum_{y=0}^{5} \frac{(80p)^y e^{-80p}}{y!}.$$

From the Poisson table we obtain OC(0.02 or $\lambda = 1.6$) $= 0.994$, OC(0.025 or $\lambda = 2.0$) $= 0.983$, OC(0.03 or $\lambda = 2.4$) $= 0.964$, OC(0.05 or $\lambda = 4.0$) $= 0.785$,

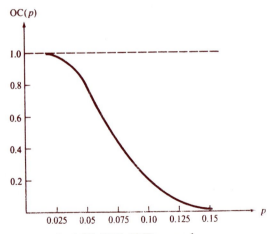

FIGURE 5.3-3   OC curve for MIL-STD-105D example.

OC(0.10 or $\lambda = 8.0$) = 0.191, and OC(0.15 or $\lambda = 12.0$) = 0.020. This OC curve is given in Figure 5.3-3. Although the probability $\alpha = 1 - 0.983 = 0.017$ is desirably small at AQL = 0.025, we may be somewhat concerned about the high probability of accepting the lot, OC(0.10) = 0.191, if the lot is 10 percent defective. Thus we may want to reduce (if possible) the acceptance number to Ac = 4, which provides, when $n = 80$,

$$OC(0.025 \text{ or } \lambda = 2.0) = 0.947$$

and

$$OC(0.10 \text{ or } \lambda = 8.0) = 0.100.$$

This seems, to us, a better plan; but, of course, the federal government may dictate one based on MIL-STD and may not let us use it. ■

There is one final concept associated with an acceptance sampling plan that we consider in this section. If a lot with fraction defective p is accepted, it is allowed to continue on into the production process. If it is rejected, an agreement is usually made with the supplier that it is to be 100 percent inspected and that bad items are replaced with good ones before the lot is sent on into the production process. In the first case, the fraction defective entering the process is p; in the second case it is zero because after replacing the bad items, all items are good. To get an *average outgoing quality* (AOQ), we must average the values p and zero, with weights OC(p) and $1 - $ OC(p), which are their respective probabilities of occurring. That is, the AOQ is the expected value

$$AOQ(p) = (p)[OC(p)] + (0)[1 - OC(p)] = p[OC(p)].$$

The maximum of the AOQ curve is called the *average outgoing quality limit* (AOQL). It tells us about the worst possible average of outgoing quality. It is usually determined by calculus or empirical means. The AOQ curve associated with the MIL-STD-105D plan of Example 5.3-3 is plotted in Figure 5.3-4; the AOQL is about 4 percent.

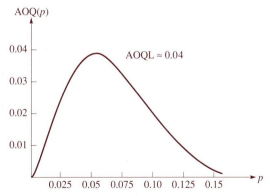

FIGURE 5.3-4 AOQ curve for the MIL-STD-105D example.

Example 5.3-4   In Example 5.3-1, we found that $OC(p) \approx (1 - p)^{10}$, thus

$$AOQ(p) \approx p(1 - p)^{10}.$$

which has the maximizing solution of $p = 1/11$. Thus

$$AOQL = AOQ\left(p = \frac{1}{11}\right) = \left(\frac{1}{11}\right)\left(\frac{10}{11}\right)^{10} = 0.035.$$ ∎

Acceptance sampling plans are important because we want to avoid letting too many defectives into the consumer's production process. However, we must realize that *quality cannot be inspected into products*. Products have to be built properly in the first place! Therefore, if a supplier has a good quality control program, it would be possible to eliminate the acceptance sampling procedures altogether. Reliable suppliers can be trusted and there is no need to inspect their products. But until all suppliers can be classified in this manner, acceptance sampling plans are definitely needed.

Exercises 5.3

5.3-1   A sampling plan uses a sample size of $n = 15$ and an acceptance number Ac = 1.

(a) Using hypergeometric probabilities, calculate the respective probabilities of accepting lots of $N = 50$ items that are 2, 6, 10, and 20 percent defective. Sketch the OC curve.

(b) The sampling plan is used for large lots. Use binomial probabilities to compute an approximation to the probabilities in part (a).

5.3-2   A sampling plan uses $n = 100$ and Ac = 3. The lot size N is large compared to the sample size n.

(a) Sketch the OC curve.

(b) Calculate the producer's risk at AQL = 0.02.

(c) Calculate the consumer's risk at LTFD = 0.10.

(d) Assume that a rejected lot is 100 percent inspected and that defectives are replaced by good items. Plot the AOQ curve and find approximately the average outgoing quality limit AOQL.

5.3-3   A sampling plan for the fraction of defectives consists of sampling $n = 50$ items and rejecting the lot if there are more than two defectives. Suppose that the lot size N is large enough to permit us to use the Poisson approximation. Calculate the pro-

ducer's risk at AQL = 0.05 and the consumer's risk at LTFD = 0.10.

5.3-4   A sampling plan consists of sampling $n = 300$ items from a lot of $N = 5000$ items. The acceptance number is Ac = 1. The plan stipulates that rejected lots are 100 percent inspected and that defective items are replaced by good ones.

(a) Plot the OC curve and observe the producer's risk α at AQL = 0.002 and the consumer's risk β at LTFD = 0.010.

(b) Plot the AOQ curve and determine the approximate value of AOQL.

5.3-5   Design an acceptance sampling plan for large lots with AQL = 0.02 and LTFD = 0.08. Control the probabilities of errors at those two values of p at about $\alpha = 0.05$ and $\beta = 0.10$.

5.3-6   The following sampling plan is used: (1) Select a sample of size 2 from a lot of 20. If both items are good, accept the lot. If both are defective, reject it. If one is good and one defective, take a second sample of one item. (2) If the item in the second sample is good, accept the lot. Otherwise, reject it. If the lot is $p = 0.2$ fraction defective, what is the probability that we accept the lot? Repeat your calculations for several other values of the fraction defective p and plot the OC curve.

Note This sampling scheme is called a *double-sampling plan*, since it allows the possibility of delaying the decision on the lot until a second sample is chosen. The sampling schemes that we have discussed in this section are *single-sampling plans*, since we accept or reject a lot on the basis of a single sample.

5.3-7 Specifications require that the product has certain quality characteristics, which can only be determined by a destructive test. The product is made in batches of $N = 1000$. The current inspection scheme is to select $n = 4$ items from each batch. If all four articles meet the quality specification, we accept the lot. If two or more fail, we reject the lot. If one fails, we take another sample of two. If both pass the inspection, we accept the lot. Otherwise, we reject it. What is the probability that we accept a batch that contains 5 percent defectives? Sketch the OC curve of this double-sampling plan.

*5.4   Problem Solving

The statistical methods that we have discussed so far in this chapter help us monitor processes. They indicate whether something has gone wrong and needs to be fixed. However, it is often quite difficult to determine exactly what has gone wrong and, once the reason is found, how to fix it. Engineers face such problems constantly and university education should prepare them for these situations. However, "problem solving" is a difficult subject to teach, and we ourselves are not sure how best to do it. Experience, common sense, and subject knowledge are needed as much as anything. It helps to gain this experience by observing and working with experienced problem solvers.

When confronted with difficult problems, we do advise that a team of experts familiar with the process be gathered to "brainstorm" the situation. Of course, the workers who know much about processes and machines must be included. Other possible members on the team are foremen, supervisors, managers, and of course, engineers. It is beneficial to include all members who are associated, directly or indirectly, with the project. The size of the team is often determined by the magnitude of the problem: two or three persons can frequently handle a minor problem; more may be needed for a major one.

Of course, reliable data are usually needed to help the team make wise decisions. Information must be collected to reveal facts that help solve the problem at hand. Here we give several examples. To identify the most prevalent defect in a manufacturing process, we collect information on the frequencies of the various defects. To be able to eliminate the most important defects, we have to collect, summarize, and analyze information on their causes. We collect and display information on the percentage of defectives in successive lots to assess whether a production process is stable and to identify possible sources for its instability: for example, variation in the raw materials, weekday–weekend differences, or lack of machine maintenance. We might measure the width, length, weight, or diameter of certain items to check whether they are within specifications. We take measurements on various types of products to determine which type is the best. Processes are run at various settings to determine which factors are important and to learn how we can reach the optimum. Water samples from different locations in a lake are analyzed to discover whether the levels of a particular pollutant depend on location. The amounts of hydrocarbons that are emitted from car engines with and without catalytic converters are obtained to assess the effect of the catalytic converter on these emissions. The fuel efficiency of various types of automobiles is measured to see how they differ. Also, we may want to check whether fuel efficiency is related to the weight of the car, the design of its engine, the wind resistance of its chassis, and so on. Information on the durability of a certain consumer product is collected to help estimate the amount of money that a company will have to spend on warranty repairs.

Reliable *data* provide the information that is needed to make decisions. Data, properly collected and analyzed, can help us understand and solve open problems. Data are routinely used to assess the variability of measurements, decide whether a process is in control, compare the effectiveness of various methods, suggest various ways of improving a process, assess the relationships among variables, find optimum conditions, and much more. Proper ways of obtaining and presenting the information are extremely important.

5.4-1   Pareto Diagram

Let us start our discussion with a simple *Pareto diagram* that displays the frequencies of various defects. Since this diagram identifies the main sources of defects, it has become a valuable tool in industry.

Defects can arise from a number of sources. For example, in a lens-polishing process an item can be defective because the lenses are too thick or thin, scarred, unfinished, or poorly coated. In a rubber molding process, the items may show surface scars, have cracks, be misshaped, or be incomplete. The major contributors to the defects have to be identified because only then can an appropriate strategy be pursued to eliminate the most important defect(s). The various sources can be identified through a Pareto diagram.

As an example, consider a lens-polishing company which has found that the number of defectives has increased recently. The company is looking for the major contributors to these defectives and has classified the total number of defectives from a day's production ($N = 110$) according to several major causes. The data are given in the first column of Table 5.4-1.

A Pareto diagram is a bar graph that shows the frequencies of the various defects. In Figure 5.4-1 we have arranged the bars in decreasing order of the frequencies: the most frequent cause is on the left and the least frequent on the right. Note that with qualitative variables such as type of defect, type of engineer (civil, industrial, electrical, etc.), or type of machine, the ordering of types is really arbitrary. However, in the particular context in which we are looking

TABLE 5.4-1   **Major Causes of Lens-Coating Defects**

	Before	After
Lenses too thick or thin	10	8
Scarred	30	32
Cracked	6	8
Unfinished	15	12
Poorly coated	45	16
Others	4	4
	110	80

for the most common type of defect, it makes sense to order them in decreasing order of occurrence. In our example, the most important defect arises from "poorly coated lenses"; there are 45 defectives or $100(45/110) = 40.9$ percent in this category. The second most important cause is "scarred lenses," contributing another 27.3 percent.

The line graph on the Pareto diagram connects the cumulative percentages of the k ($k = 1, 2, \ldots, 5$) most frequent defects. For example, the two most frequent defects, "poorly coated lenses" and "scarred lenses," represent $(45 + 30)/110 = 0.68$ or 68 percent of all defective lenses. The three most fre-

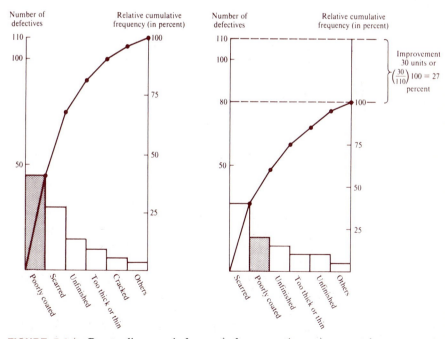

FIGURE 5.4-1   Pareto diagrams before and after corrective action was taken.

quent defects ("poorly coated lenses," "scarred lenses," and "unfinished lenses") represent $(45 + 30 + 15)/110 = 0.82$ or 82 percent, and so on.

Pareto diagrams show that usually only two or three defects will account for over 75 percent of the losses. A Pareto diagram is an important aspect of any quality improvement program because it focuses everyone's attention on the one or two categories that lead to the most defects. It is usually easier to reduce the occurrence of a more frequent defect by half than it is to reduce the one occurrence of a rare defect to zero. Rare defects are more or less inevitable, occurring every now and then.

After viewing this information, the company started an effort to improve their lens-coating operation. It turned out that a switch to a cheaper, yet less reliable supplier of the lens-coating solution had caused an increase in poorly coated lenses. The company decided to return to the original supplier, and in the process it reduced the number of defects due to poorly coated lenses by about two-thirds. A summary of the distribution of defects after corrective action had been taken is given in the second column of Table 5.4-1. A comparison of the two Pareto displays in Figure 5.4-1 also gives a nice summary of the improvements that can be attributed to the corrective action that was taken. Furthermore, these diagrams show that scarring is the next most-important defect. Possible causes for scarring should now be investigated. We could start such an investigation by constructing Ishikawa cause-and-effect diagrams, which are discussed in the next section.

5.4-2 Diagnosis of Causes of Defects

A main objective of many investigations is to *improve* quality, that is, to take actions that lead to better products. Measures must be taken to correct the causes of low quality. Finding the dominant cause of a defect, such as poor coating of lenses or excessive wobble during machine rotation, can be a lengthy project, since we can usually think of many factors that may have contributed to low quality. Kaoru Ishikawa, a Japanese control engineer, has developed certain *cause-and-effect diagrams* which depict the variables that may have affected the response. These diagrams are also called *fishbone diagrams* because they resemble the skeleton of a fish. There are several different methods for constructing cause-and-effect diagrams, depending on how the information is organized and presented. We reproduce two such diagrams in Figure 5.4-2. Figure 5.4-2(a) lists the main factors that affect wobble during machine rotation, as well as the factors that influence those main factors. Machine wobble is thought to be a major cause of production defects. Why does machine wobble occur? One possible factor is the variability among materials. Thus "materials" is written on the diagram as a branch. Why does dispersion in the materials occur? It could be because of the variability in the G axle bearing. Thus "G axle bearing" becomes a twig on the branch. Why does dispersion in the G axle bearing occur? It could be due to variability in

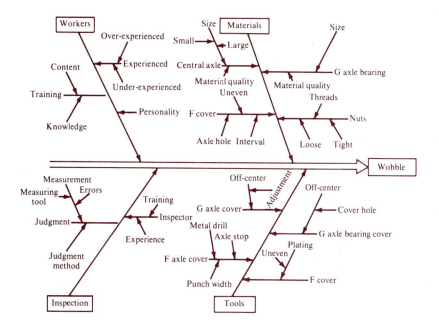

(a) Cause-and-effect diagram for wobbling during machine rotation.

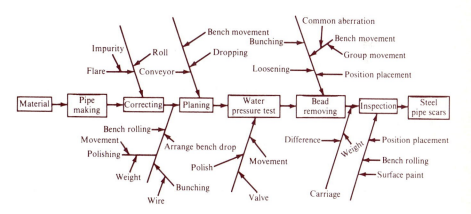

(b) Cause-and-effect diagram for steel pipe scarring.

FIGURE 5.4-2   Two cause-and-effect diagrams. [From Ishikawa, K., *Guide to Quality Control*, Second Revised Edition (Tokyo: Asian Productivity Organization, 1982).]

the size of the G axle bearing. Thus "size" becomes a twig on the twig, and so on. Such a diagram shows why excess wobble may occur and it helps to organize and relate the factors that influence the wobble. The second diagram lists the causes that may affect the scarring of steel pipes. Here the diagram follows the production process and lists the components that may affect the scarring at the various stages of production.

Cause-and-effect diagrams are very useful first steps for recognizing the factors that may be of importance. Successfully composed diagrams usually enhance the communication among those who attempt to improve the process. However, after a set of possible factors has been identified, we have to study and quantify their effects in more detail. Well-designed experiments have to be conducted to quantify the cause-and-effect relationships.

Exercises 5.4

5.4-1 (Possible Projects for Teams)
(a) A large supermarket receives complaints about the quality of its baked goods. Suppose that you are in charge of the bakery. Develop an Ishikawa fishbone diagram that could help you locate the causes of poor quality.
(b) The quality of health care that is provided by a hospital to its patients is the variable of interest. Discuss how one could measure quality of health care, and develop an Ishikawa fishbone diagram that could be a guide to improving quality.
(c) Assume that you are the owner of a painting business that specializes in residential house painting. You are concerned about the quality of your work because customers will not pay you for repairs if the paint peels prematurely. Construct a fishbone diagram to locate some of the factors that may be responsible for early peeling.
(d) You notice that a number of color computer display terminals are returned by customers because of misconvergence errors among the three primary colors, red, green, and blue. How would you *initiate* a process that ultimately leads to the construction of a cause-and-effect diagram?
(e) Universities depend on the "quality" of their

instruction. Discuss ways of measuring the quality of classroom instruction and construct a diagram that lists the factors that affect the quality.
(f) Think of a problem associated with your engineering education. Form groups, which might include several of your instructors and the dean of the College of Engineering, to brainstorm about this problem. Develop an Ishikawa fishbone diagram.
(g) Consider the registration process at your particular university. You are concerned because it always seems to take too long to register for next semester's courses. How would you go about improving the registration process? Identify the main factors that affect registration time and develop appropriate cause-and-effect diagrams.
5.4-2 Students were asked about their views on the engineering statistics course: 55 students thought that the presentation of the material was too theoretical; 35 wished that they had a better handout on the use of computer software for statistical analysis; 15 thought that the tests were too difficult; 10 felt that the instructor was not always prepared; and 5 students had difficulty locating the instructor during office hours. Prepare a Pareto chart and discuss ways of improving the course.

CHAPTER

6 Tests of Statistical Hypotheses

6.1 Tests of Characteristics of a Single Distribution

The collection and analysis of data are important components of the *scientific method* of learning. Data are used to confirm or refute existing theories, as well as to revise them and to formulate new ones. Theories and hypotheses should always be confirmed by data from carefully planned experiments. If the data contradict existing theories, one must search for better theoretical explanations. The data, especially the discrepancies between the observations and the values that are implied by theory, often provide the information for necessary revisions of inadequate theory. In cases where there is no existing theory, an exploratory analysis of the data usually provides a good starting point for formulating theories.

These introductory remarks illustrate the fact that sample data are routinely used to decide between competing hypotheses. *Statistical testing of hypotheses* is an area of statistics that deals with procedures for confirming and refuting hypotheses about distributions of random variables. The hypotheses are usually framed in terms of population parameters. For example, two competing hypotheses may specify that the mean breaking strength of a certain alloy is greater (not greater) than 2000 pounds, that the mean yield of product A is smaller (not smaller) than the one of product B, that the variability in process A is larger (not larger) than the one in process B, that the mean tensile strengths of five different alloys are the same (not the same), and so on. In the following discussion we motivate this decision-theoretic concept with an example.

is not enough evidence to reject H_0, that the mean tar content is 11.5. Equivalently, we could then have based the decision on the p value $= P(Z \leq -1.05) = \Phi(-1.05) = 0.147 > \alpha = 0.10$. ∎

So far we have discussed how to test whether or not a mean has decreased. How do we have to change our procedure if we want to test whether there has been an increase, and test $H_0: \mu = \mu_0$ against $H_1: \mu > \mu_0$? In this case we reject H_0 in favor of H_1 when $\bar{X} \geq c$. If you are uncertain about the orientation of the critical region, go through the same steps that led to Figure 6.1-4, but reverse H_0 and H_1. If we want a test with significance level α, we require that the probability of a false rejection of H_0 is α; that is,

$$P(\bar{X} \geq c; \mu = \mu_0) = P\left(Z = \frac{\bar{X} - \mu_0}{\sigma/\sqrt{n}} \geq \frac{c - \mu_0}{\sigma/\sqrt{n}} \right) = \alpha.$$

Thus we reject H_0 if the standardized test statistic

$$\frac{\bar{X} - \mu_0}{\sigma/\sqrt{n}} \geq z(\alpha) \qquad \text{or} \qquad \bar{X} \geq \mu_0 + z(\alpha)\frac{\sigma}{\sqrt{n}}.$$

Equivalently, we could base our decision on the

$$p \text{ value} = P(\bar{X} \geq \bar{x}; \mu = \mu_0) = 1 - \Phi\left(\frac{\bar{x} - \mu_0}{\sigma/\sqrt{n}} \right).$$

Example 6.1-3 Let p be the average fraction of "grade A" items produced by a certain company. In the past, p has been about 0.62. Of the remaining 38 percent, 3 percent were scrap and 35 percent were "seconds." A new method is proposed that is thought to increase p. Under the new method, $n = 250$ items are produced and $y = 172$ grade A items are found among them. Under the null hypothesis $H_0: p = 0.62$, the distribution of the number of grade A items Y has mean $250(0.62) = 155$, variance $250(0.62)(0.38) = 58.9$, and standard deviation $\sqrt{58.9} = 7.675$. Approximating this distribution by a normal distribution (due to the central limit theorem), we can calculate the approximate

$$\text{probability value} = P(Y \geq 172; p = 0.62) = P\left(\frac{Y - 155}{7.675} \geq \frac{171.5 - 155}{7.675} \right)$$

$$= 1 - \Phi(2.15) = 0.0158.$$

Since this is smaller than 0.05, for example, we reject $H_0: p = 0.62$ and accept $H_1: p > 0.62$ at the $\alpha = 0.05$ significance level. ∎

Tests of $H_0: \mu = \mu_0$ against $H_1: \mu < \mu_0$ or $H_0: \mu = \mu_0$ against $H_1: \mu > \mu_0$ are called *one-sided* tests because the alternative hypotheses are one-sided, not two-sided as in $H_1: \mu \neq \mu_0$. There are occasions when two-sided tests are appropriate. Suppose that in the past mathematics test scores have had a mean of about 75 points. Assume that there has been an intervention (say, a new type of standardized test is being used); and we *really* do not know whether scores will increase, decrease, or stay about the same. Thus we wish to test the null (no change) hypothesis $H_0: \mu = 75$ against the two-sided alternative, $H_1: \mu \neq 75$.

Assume that test scores are normally distributed with mean μ and variance $\sigma^2 = 100$. We reject $H_0: \mu = \mu_0$ if the standardized test statistic $(\bar{X} - \mu_0)/(\sigma/\sqrt{n})$ is large in absolute value. A test with significance level α rejects H_0 in favor of H_1 if

$$\left| \frac{\bar{X} - \mu_0}{\sigma/\sqrt{n}} \right| \geq z(\alpha/2),$$

because the probability of this event is α when $H_0: \mu = \mu_0$ is true. Alternatively, in terms of the (not standardized) test statistic $\bar{X}$ we reject H_0 if either $\bar{X} \leq \mu_0 - z(\alpha/2)\sigma/\sqrt{n}$ or $\bar{X} \geq \mu_0 + z(\alpha/2)\sigma/\sqrt{n}$. Figure 6.1-6 illustrates this graphically.

Assume that we find the average to be $\bar{x} = 72$ with a sample of $n = 25$ tests. Then $(\bar{x} - \mu_0)/(\sigma/\sqrt{n}) = (72 - 75)/(10/5) = -1.5$. Since its absolute value is smaller than $z(\alpha/2) = z(0.025) = 1.96$, we accept H_0 at the $\alpha = 0.05$ significance level. The probability value in this two-sided example is

$$p \text{ value} = 2P\left(Z \geq \left| \frac{\bar{x} - \mu_0}{\sigma/\sqrt{n}} \right| \right) = 2P(Z \geq 1.5) = 0.134.$$

We double the probability here because we can reject H_0 with large or small values of the standardized variable Z.

There is an obvious relationship between confidence intervals and two-sided tests. If a $100(1 - \alpha)$ percent confidence interval $\bar{X} \pm z(\alpha/2)(\sigma/\sqrt{n})$ does not include the value μ_0, then $|(\bar{X} - \mu_0)/(\sigma/\sqrt{n})| > z(\alpha/2)$, and we reject $H_0: \mu = \mu_0$ and accept $H_1: \mu \neq \mu_0$ at significance level α; the converse is also true. For illustration, if a confidence interval does not include zero, we can reject $H_0: \mu = 0$. If zero is included, we accept H_0.

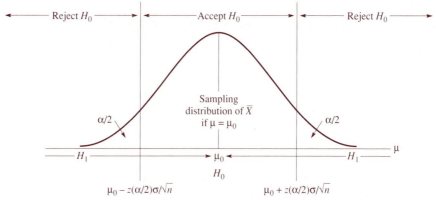

FIGURE 6.1-6   Graphical illustration of the two-sided test $H_0: \mu = \mu_0$ against $H_1: \mu \neq \mu_0$.

So far we have assumed that the variance of the underlying distribution is known. Since the sampling distribution of $(\bar{X} - \mu)/(\sigma/\sqrt{n})$ is $N(0, 1)$ (either exactly if the X values are normally distributed or approximately if X is not normal but the sample size is large enough), we have used the normal tables to determine the critical values. Now, let us assume that the underlying distribution of the X values is normal but that the variance σ^2 is estimated by the sample variance S^2. The sampling distribution of $(\bar{X} - \mu)/(S/\sqrt{n})$ is a t-distribution with $n - 1$ degrees of freedom, and the critical values $z(\alpha)$ must be replaced by $t(\alpha; n - 1)$. Of course, if n is large (at least 30), we can use the normal table.

Example 6.1-4   A company claims that the mean deflection of their 10-foot steel beams is 0.012 inch. A construction contractor who purchases large quantities of steel beams suspects that the manufacturer misleads its customers and that the true deflection is, in fact, larger than the one claimed. To see whether this suspicion is justified, the contractor selects $n = 10$ beams at random from his inventory, determines their deflection, and conducts a test of $H_0: \mu = 0.012$ against $H_1: \mu > 0.012$. From the 10 measurements,

$$0.0132 \quad 0.0138 \quad 0.0108 \quad 0.0126 \quad 0.0136$$
$$0.0112 \quad 0.0124 \quad 0.0116 \quad 0.0127 \quad 0.0131$$

he calculates the mean $\bar{x} = 0.0125$ and the standard deviation $s = 0.0010$. The test statistic is $(0.0125 - 0.012)/(0.001/\sqrt{10}) = 1.56$. Since it is smaller than the critical value $t(0.05; n - 1 = 9) = 1.833$, this sample alone does not provide enough evidence to reject H_0 at significance level $\alpha = 0.05$. Until more measurements are taken, the contractor cannot claim that the company has made a false claim.   ■

Exercises 6.1

6.1-1   In the introductory illustration of this section, let $n = 300$ and using the Poisson approximation show that the critical region of $Y \leq 5$ (acceptance region of $Y \geq 6$) has an OC curve such that $OC(0.03) = 0.884$ and $OC(0.01) = 0.084$.

6.1-2   Let $\bar{X}$ be the mean of a random sample of size $n = 36$ from $N(\mu, 9)$. Our decision rule is to reject $H_0: \mu = 50$ and to accept $H_1: \mu > 50$ if $\bar{X} \geq 50.8$. Determine the $OC(\mu)$ curve and evaluate it at $\mu = 50.0, 50.5, 51.0$, and 51.5. What is the significance level of the test?

6.1-3   Let p be the fraction of engineers who do not understand certain basic statistical concepts. Unfortunately, in the past, this number has been high, about $p = 0.73$. A new program to improve the knowledge of statistical methods has been started and it is expected that under this program p would decrease from 0.73. To test $H_0: p = 0.73$ against $H_1: p < 0.73$, 300 engineers in this new program were tested and 204 (i.e., 68 percent) did not comprehend certain basic statistical concepts. Compute the probability value to determine if this indicates progress. That is, can we reject H_0 in favor of H_1? Use $\alpha = 0.05$.

6.1-4 In a certain industry about 15 percent of the workers showed some signs of ill effects due to radiation. After the management had claimed that improvements had been made, 140 workers were tested and 19 experienced some ill effects due to radiation. Does this support the management's claim? Use $\alpha = 0.05$.

6.1-5 The time to repair breakdowns of a certain copying machine has a mean of 93 minutes. The company claims that breakdowns of its new improved model are easier to fix. To test this claim, $n = 73$ breakdowns of the new model were observed, resulting in a mean repair time of $\bar{x} = 88.8$ minutes and a standard deviation of $s = 26.6$ minutes. Use the significance level $\alpha = 0.025$ to check the company's claim.

6.1-6 In an industrial training program, students have been averaging about 65 points on a standardized test. The lecture system was replaced by teaching machines with a lab instructor. There was some doubt as to whether the scores would decrease, increase, or stay about the same. Hence $H_0: \mu = 65$ was tested against the two-sided alternative $H_1: \mu \neq 65$. A sample of $n = 50$ students using the teaching machines were tested. This resulted in $\bar{x} = 68.2$ and $s = 13.2$. Using significance level $\alpha = 0.05$, what is your conclusion?

6.1-7 Consider a $N(\mu, \sigma^2 = 40)$ distribution. To test $H_0: \mu = 32$ against $H_1: \mu > 32$, we reject H_0 if the sample mean $\bar{X} \geq c$. Find the sample size n and the constant c such that $OC(\mu = 32) = 0.90$ and $OC(\mu = 35) = 0.15$.

6.1-8 Let Y have a binomial distribution with parameters n and p. In a test of $H_0: p = 0.25$ against $H_1: p < 0.25$, we reject H_0 if $Y \leq c$. Find n and c if $OC(p = 0.25) = 0.90$ and $OC(p = 0.20) = 0.05$. State your assumptions.

6.1-9 Let $X_1, X_2, \ldots, X_{10}$ be a random sample from a Poisson distribution with mean λ. In a test of $H_0: \lambda = 1.1$ against $H_1: \lambda < 1.1$, we reject H_0 if the sum of these 10 observations, Y, is less than or equal to 8. Using the Poisson table, find the $OC(\lambda)$ curve at $\lambda = 0.5, 0.7, 0.9$, and 1.1. What is the significance level of the test?

Hint Use the fact that a sum of n independent Poisson random variables with parameter λ is again Poisson with parameter $n\lambda$.

6.1-10 A recent commuter was told that it takes on average 60 minutes to travel by car from Philadelphia to Princeton, New Jersey. Anxious to learn whether this is correct, our commuter takes measurements on $n = 20$ consecutive weekdays and finds that the average time was 68 minutes and the standard deviation was 6 minutes. Is there enough evidence that our commuter was given a time that was too low? State the assumptions that you have made in your analysis.

6.1-11 Let $\bar{X}$ be the mean of a random sample of size $n = 16$ from a normal distribution with mean μ and standard deviation $\sigma = 8$. To test $H_0: \mu = 35$ against $H_1: \mu > 35$, we reject H_0 if $\bar{X} \geq 36.5$.
(a) Determine the OC-curve at $\mu = 35, 36$, and 38.5.
(b) What is the probability of a type I error?
(c) What is the probability of a type II error at $\mu = 36$?

6.1-12 Sixty-four randomly selected fuses were subjected to a 20 percent overload and the time to failure was recorded. It was found that the sample average and standard deviation were $\bar{x} = 8.5$ and $s = 2.4$.
(a) Compute a 99 percent confidence interval for μ, the mean time to failure under such conditions.
(b) Test $H_0: \mu = 8$ against $H_1: \mu > 8$; use significance level $\alpha = 0.05$. What is your conclusion?

6.2   Tests of Characteristics of Two Distributions

One of the most important tests made in statistics is that in which two different "methods" are compared. We may compare the effectiveness of two educational systems, the durability of two different paints, the effectiveness of two medical treatments, the gas mileage of two makes of automobiles, the measurements under the "old" method and a "new" one, and so on. Usually, we are interested in comparing the means of two distributions. That is, we want to show that on average the "scores" under the new method are higher than the ones under the old method. Hence we wish to test the null (no difference) hypothesis H_0: $\mu_1 = \mu_2$, against the alternative hypothesis H_1: $\mu_1 > \mu_2$, where μ_1 and μ_2 are the means of the score distributions under the new and the old methods. In other applications, we may want to test H_0: $\mu_1 = \mu_2$ against H_1: $\mu_1 < \mu_2$ or H_0: $\mu_1 = \mu_2$ against H_1: $\mu_1 \neq \mu_2$.

6.2-1   Comparing Two Independent Samples

Let us consider random samples from each of two *independent* distributions with respective means μ_1, μ_2 and variances σ_1^2, σ_2^2. We denote these random samples of respective sizes, n_1 and n_2, by $X_1, X_2, \ldots, X_{n_1}$ and $Y_1, Y_2, \ldots, Y_{n_2}$. Of course, the sample means, $\bar{X}$ and $\bar{Y}$, are approximately $N(\mu_1, \sigma_1^2/n_1)$ and $N(\mu_2, \sigma_2^2/n_2)$, where the approximation is exact in case the underlying distributions are normal. For the moment, we assume that σ_1^2 and σ_2^2 are known.

Under the null hypothesis, H_0: $\mu_1 = \mu_2$ or $\mu_1 - \mu_2 = 0$, the random variable

$$Z = \frac{\bar{X} - \bar{Y}}{\sqrt{\sigma_1^2/n_1 + \sigma_2^2/n_2}}$$

is $N(0, 1)$. Thus, if a sample realization of Z is much larger than zero, we believe that the alternative hypothesis, H_1: $\mu_1 > \mu_2$, is true. We reject H_0 and accept H_1 when $Z \geq z(\alpha)$; then the significance level of the test is α.

If the variances σ_1^2 and σ_2^2 are unknown, they can be replaced by the sample variances S_X^2 and S_Y^2. Then the critical region $Z \geq z(\alpha)$ provides an approximate α-level test, provided that the sample sizes n_1 and n_2 are reasonably large (not smaller than 20).

Example 6.2-1   In this example we illustrate how to obtain the operating characteristic curve of such a test. Let $\bar{X}$ and $\bar{Y}$ be the means of the respective random samples of sizes $n_1 = 22$ and $n_2 = 34$ from independent normal distributions $N(\mu_1, \sigma_1^2 = 115)$ and $N(\mu_2, \sigma_2^2 = 96)$. Then the variance of $\bar{X} - \bar{Y}$ is $(115/22) + (96/34) = 8.05$. Accordingly, a test of H_0: $\mu_1 = \mu_2$ against H_1: $\mu_1 > \mu_2$ with significance level $\alpha = 0.025$ rejects H_0 when $Z = (\bar{X} - \bar{Y})/\sqrt{8.05} \geq 1.96$, or $(\bar{X} - \bar{Y}) \geq 1.96\sqrt{8.05}$.

What can we say about the probabilities of this event when $\theta = \mu_1 - \mu_2$ is not equal to zero, and how can we determine the OC(θ) curve? Since the operating characteristic curve is the probability of accepting H_0, for different values of $\theta = \mu_1 - \mu_2$, we find that

$$OC(\theta) = P(\bar{X} - \bar{Y} < 1.96\sqrt{8.05}; \theta = \mu_1 - \mu_2)$$

$$= P\left(\frac{\bar{X} - \bar{Y} - \theta}{2.84} < 1.96 - \frac{\theta}{2.84}; \theta\right)$$

$$= \Phi\left(1.96 - \frac{\theta}{2.84}\right),$$

because $(\bar{X} - \bar{Y} - \theta)/2.84$ is $N(0, 1)$. The OC curve evaluated for a few θ values is as follows:

θ	0	2	4	6	8	10
$OC(\theta)$	0.9750	0.8962	0.7088	0.4404	0.1949	0.0594

The probability of a type I error is $\alpha = 1 - 0.975 = 0.025$ and the probability of a type II error at $\theta = \mu_1 - \mu_2 = 8$, for example, is $\beta = 0.1949$. This says that the probability of accepting H_0, if in fact the mean level of group 1 is 8 units larger than the one of group 2, is 0.1949. If the magnitude of this type II error probability is unacceptable, we must increase the sample sizes or increase the probability α of the type I error. ∎

If the sample sizes n_1 and n_2 are fairly small, we must make additional assumptions to carry out the test. We must assume that the underlying distributions are normal and the variances σ_1^2 and σ_2^2 are about equal. If $\sigma_1^2 = \sigma_2^2$, we can obtain an estimate S_p^2 of the common variance by pooling the sample variances S_X^2 and S_Y^2, in proportion to $n_1 - 1$ and $n_2 - 1$, respectively. Under the null hypothesis $H_0: \mu_1 = \mu_2$, the random variable

$$T = \frac{\bar{X} - \bar{Y}}{\sqrt{S_p^2\left(\dfrac{1}{n_1} + \dfrac{1}{n_2}\right)}} = \frac{\bar{X} - \bar{Y}}{\sqrt{\dfrac{(n_1 - 1)S_X^2 + (n_2 - 1)S_Y^2}{n_1 + n_2 - 2}\left(\dfrac{1}{n_1} + \dfrac{1}{n_2}\right)}}$$

has a Student's $t(n_1 + n_2 - 2)$ distribution (see Section 4.4). If we reject H_0 and accept $H_1: \mu_1 > \mu_2$ when $T \geq t(\alpha; n_1 + n_2 - 2)$, we obtain a test with significance level α.

Similarly, in a test of $H_0: \mu_1 = \mu_2$ against $H_1: \mu_1 < \mu_2$, we accept H_1 if $T \leq -t(\alpha; n_1 + n_2 - 2)$. In a test of $H_0: \mu_1 = \mu_2$ against $H_1: \mu_1 \neq \mu_2$, we reject H_0 and accept H_1 if $|T| \geq t(\alpha/2; n_1 + n_2 - 2)$.

Example 6.2-2 An experiment is conducted to compare the crash resistance of two different types of car bumpers. Twenty cars of the same model type are divided into two groups of $n_1 = 11$ and $n_2 = 9$ cars. Type A bumpers are

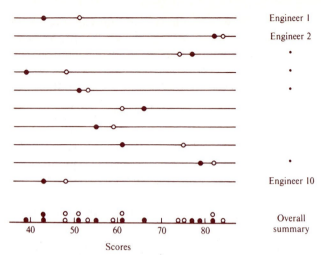

FIGURE 6.2-2   Graphical display of the data in Example 6.2-3. The symbols ● and ○ correspond to measurements before and after the training.

tions. It is true that we would obtain more degrees of freedom for the t-statistic in the independent situation, $n_1 + n_2 - 2 = 18$, instead of the $n - 1 = 9$ in the paired t-test, but the variability among engineers would have "drowned out" the difference $\bar{x} - \bar{y} = 3.9$. That is, the calculated test statistic assuming independent samples is very small (in fact, it is $3.9/6.7 = 0.58$), and we would not have rejected H_0. This can be seen very clearly from the dot diagram in Figure 6.2-2. Although for 8 out of 10 engineers the program has been successful, the overall summary in Figure 6.2-2, where measurements are viewed as realizations from two independent samples, would show little difference.

Thus more precise comparisons can be made by grouping the experimental units into homogeneous blocks, which may be subjects, days, plots of land, temperatures, animals from the same litter, specimens from the same batch, and so on. The precision of the blocked (or paired) comparisons is increased, since this grouping or *blocking* eliminates the differences among the experimental units from the measurements. As in the paired-sample t-test, a blocked comparison leads to a smaller denominator in our test statistic and gives us a better chance of detecting a true difference between the two methods. Much more will be said about blocking in Section 7.3.   ■

6.2-3   Test of $p_1 = p_2$

We consider a test of the equality of means from two independent Bernoulli distributions, namely p_1 and p_2, which are the probabilities of success resulting from two different processes. For illustration, a pump manufacturer claims that a larger percentage of his pumps will be operating without repairs in three years than those of a competitor. That is, he claims that $p_1 > p_2$, where p_1 and p_2 are the respective fractions of pumps that operate without repairs after three years.

To test $H_0: p_1 = p_2$ against $H_1: p_1 > p_2$ we select n_1 and n_2 items at random from the two respective populations. The numbers of successes, Y_1 and Y_2, have independent binomial distributions, $b(n_1, p_1)$ and $b(n_2, p_2)$, which can be approximated by normal distributions. Also, the sample proportions $\hat{p}_i = Y_i/n_i$ are approximately $N[p_i, p_i(1 - p_i)/n_i]$, $i = 1, 2$. Since Y_1 and Y_2 are assumed to be independent, the variance of $\hat{p}_1 - \hat{p}_2 = Y_1/n_1 - Y_2/n_2$ is the sum of the variances, namely

$$\frac{p_1(1 - p_1)}{n_1} + \frac{p_2(1 - p_2)}{n_2}.$$

If the null hypothesis $H_0: p_1 = p_2 = p$, where p is unknown, is true, then

$$Z = \frac{\hat{p}_1 - \hat{p}_2}{\sqrt{\dfrac{p(1 - p)}{n_1} + \dfrac{p(1 - p)}{n_2}}}$$

follows a $N(0, 1)$ distribution, at least approximately. Since p is unknown, we cannot compute Z from our sample results. To avoid this difficulty, we replace the common p by the pooled estimate $\hat{p} = (Y_1 + Y_2)/(n_1 + n_2)$ and calculate the test statistic

$$Z = \frac{\hat{p}_1 - \hat{p}_2}{\sqrt{\hat{p}(1 - \hat{p})(1/n_1 + 1/n_2)}}.$$

We reject $H_0: p_1 = p_2$ in favor of $H_1: p_1 > p_2$ if the calculated test statistic is greater than or equal to $z(\alpha)$. An identical test can be performed by finding the probability value associated with the computed Z and then seeing if this probability value is less than or equal to α.

Example 6.2-4 To test the pump manufacturer's claim, $H_1: p_1 > p_2$, we checked on $n_1 = n_2 = 100$ pumps from each of the companies and found $y_1 = 67$ and $y_2 = 62$ working pumps. Here the pooled estimate of p is $\hat{p} = 129/200 = 0.645$. Since the calculated test statistic

$$z = \frac{0.67 - 0.62}{\sqrt{(0.645)(0.355)(1/100 + 1/100)}} = 0.74$$

is rather small and does not exceed $z(0.05) = 1.645$, we have insufficient evidence to reject $H_0: p_1 = p_2$. That is, until more data are observed, it would be difficult to accept the manufacturer's claim.   ■

*6.2-4   Test of $\sigma_1^2 = \sigma_2^2$

In concluding this section, we look at a test of the equality of the variances, σ_1^2 and σ_2^2, of two independent normal distributions. Let S_X^2 and S_Y^2 be the respective variances of the samples of sizes n_1 and n_2. We know that

$$F = \frac{S_X^2/\sigma_1^2}{S_Y^2/\sigma_2^2}$$

has an F distribution with $n_1 - 1$ and $n_2 - 1$ degrees of freedom. Thus if H_0: $\sigma_1^2 = \sigma_2^2$ is true, $F = S_X^2/S_Y^2$ is $F(n_1 - 1, n_2 - 1)$. Suppose that the alternative hypothesis is H_1: $\sigma_1^2 > \sigma_2^2$. For example, we may want to test whether the variability in the incoming material from a new supplier (σ_2^2) is smaller than the one from the current supplier (σ_1^2). We reject H_0: $\sigma_1^2 = \sigma_2^2$ and accept H_1: $\sigma_1^2 > \sigma_2^2$ if $S_X^2/S_Y^2 \geq F(\alpha; n_1 - 1, n_2 - 1)$. For illustration, say that observations on both suppliers resulted in $n_1 = 12$, $\bar{x} = 26.2$, $s_x^2 = 29.1$ and $n_2 = 10$, $\bar{y} = 25.9$, $s_y^2 = 14.6$. Then $s_x^2/s_y^2 = 29.1/14.6 = 1.99 < F(0.05; 11, 9) = 3.10$ [which is an interpolation between $F(0.05; 10, 9) = 3.14$ and $F(0.05; 12, 9) = 3.07$ found in Table C.7]. We find that there is not enough evidence to reject H_0: $\sigma_1^2 = \sigma_2^2$. Figure 6.2-3 shows this graphically.

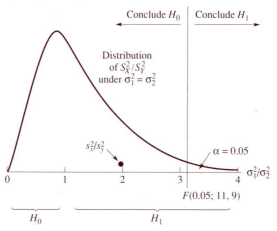

FIGURE 6.2-3   Graphical description of the test H_0: $\sigma_1^2 = \sigma_2^2$ against H_1: $\sigma_1^2 > \sigma_2^2$.

We should note here that even though the ratio of the two sample variances is almost two, we still do not reject the equality of $\sigma_1^2 = \sigma_2^2$. As a matter of fact, that ratio would have to be greater than 3.10 to result in the rejection of H_0: $\sigma_1^2 = \sigma_2^2$. For this reason, most statisticians find this test not to be very useful.

Exercises 6.2

6.2-1 Two producers of light bulbs each claim that they have the longer lasting bulbs. Accordingly, 100 bulbs were selected at random from each producer and tested. This resulted in means of $\bar{x} = 798$ and $\bar{y} = 826$ hours with respective variances of $s_x^2 = 7982$ and $s_y^2 = 9001$. Test $H_0\colon \mu_1 = \mu_2$ against the two-sided alternative $H_1\colon \mu_1 \neq \mu_2$ at the $\alpha = 0.05$ significance level.

6.2-2 Let $\bar{X}$ and $\bar{Y}$ be means of random samples of sizes $n_1 = 14$ and $n_2 = 18$ from the respective normal distributions $N(\mu_1, \sigma_1^2 = 26)$ and $N(\mu_2, \sigma_2^2 = 21)$. Let $\theta = \mu_1 - \mu_2$. Construct a test of $H_0\colon \theta = 0$ against $H_1\colon \theta < 0$ that has significance level $\alpha = 0.025$. Determine the $OC(\theta)$ curve for $\theta = -5, -4, -3, -2, -1, 0$, and graph this function.

6.2-3 In Exercise 6.2-2 take equal sample sizes $n = n_1 = n_2$. Find n so that $\alpha = 0.025$ and $\beta = 0.05$ when $\theta = -3$.

6.2-4 An engineer wishes to compare the strengths of two types of beams, the first made of steel and the second made of an alloy. Several beams of each type are selected at random and the deflections (in units of 0.001 inch) are measured when submitted to a force of 3000 pounds. The respective sample characteristics are $n_1 = 10$, $\bar{x} = 82.6$, $s_x^2 = 6.52$ and $n_2 = 12$, $\bar{y} = 78.1$, $s_y^2 = 7.02$. Compute the appropriate test statistic and test whether the mean deflection of steel beams is larger than the mean deflection of those made of our alloy.

6.2-5 The golf scores of two competitors, A and B, are recorded over a period of 10 days. Golfer A claims that her game is better than that of B. Use the following data to test this claim.

Golfer	Day									
	1	2	3	4	5	6	7	8	9	10
A	87	86	79	82	78	87	84	81	83	81
B	89	85	83	87	76	90	85	78	85	84

Note Since the playing conditions on different days may be quite different, it may be better to pair or block the comparison with respect to day.

6.2-6 A certain washing machine manufacturer claims that the fraction p_1 of his washing machines that need repairs in the first five years of operation is less than the fraction p_2 of another brand. To test this claim, we observe $n_1 = n_2 = 200$ machines of each brand, and find that $y_1 = 21$ and $y_2 = 37$ machines need repairs. Do these data support the manufacturer's claim? Use $\alpha = 0.05$.

6.2-7 Two different fabrics are compared on a Martindale wear tester that can compare two materials in a single run. The weight losses (in milligrams) from seven runs are as follows:

Fabric	Run						
	1	2	3	4	5	6	7
A	36	26	31	38	28	37	22
B	39	27	35	42	31	39	21

Analyze the data and discuss whether one fabric is better than the other.

6.2-8 Use the data in Table 1.4-1 and test whether the new process has led to a significant reduction in the average number of lead wires that misfeed during production. State and check your assumptions carefully.

6.2-9 To measure air pollution in a home, the amount of suspended particle matter is measured during a 24-hour period. We sample from homes in which there are no smokers and from homes in which there is at least one smoker. Say that these respective samples yielded $n_1 = 16$, $\bar{x} = 67.1$, $s_x^2 = 7.82$ and $n_2 = 13$, $\bar{y} = 132.3$, $s_y^2 = 24.12$.

(a) Test $H_0\colon \sigma_1^2 = \sigma_2^2$ against $H_1\colon \sigma_1^2 < \sigma_2^2$ at $\alpha = 0.05$ using $F = s_y^2/s_x^2$.

(b) If $\sigma_1^2 = \sigma_2^2$ is not rejected in part (a), investigate $H_0\colon \mu_1 = \mu_2$ against $H_1\colon \mu_1 < \mu_2$ at $\alpha = 0.05$ using a t-test. If $\sigma_1^2 = \sigma_2^2$ is rejected in part (a), we suggest that you test H_0 against H_1 using $(\bar{x} - \bar{y})/\sqrt{s_x^2/n_1 + s_y^2/n_2}$, even though the sample sizes are not as large as we might like.

6.2-10 The depletion of carbon in steel billets is an important indicator of breaking strength and is monitored by steel producers as well as their customers (automotive industry). The manager of

Northstar Steel suspects that measurements made by the customer show higher depletion of carbon than measurements taken by the in-house metallurgist. He wants to investigate this suspicion by carrying out an experiment. He plans to pick billets at random, remove two small adjacent segments from each billet, give one to the in-house metallurgist, and send the other to the customer's laboratory. From previous experiments he knows something about the variability of measurement differences on the same item; he believes that the standard deviation among measurement differences is about 10 units. How many billets does he have to sample such that the probability of concluding incorrectly that the customer's measurements are higher is at most 0.05, and that a difference of 5 units is detected with probability 0.80?

Hint This is a blocked experiment. Analyze the differences.

6.2-11 We want to determine whether or not a new applied project-oriented way of teaching statistics helps students increase their understanding of probabilistic concepts. The experimenter has developed a set of videotaped instructional materials for both a traditional course and the new applied project-oriented course. He plans to select an equal number of students for each program, have them view the videotapes, and test them on a sequence of new problems. Tests are scored between 0 and 100 and it is known from prior experience that the interquartile range (i.e., the difference between the third and first quartiles) of the test scores is about 15 points. How many students should he select in each of the two groups if (1) the error of concluding incorrectly that the new program leads to higher scores is at most 0.05 when, in fact, the traditional and new programs have the same mean, and (2) an increase of 5 points in the new over the traditional method is detected with probability 0.90?

Hint Assume normality and calculate σ from the interquartile range.

Exercises 6.2-12 to 6.2-14 are longer than most and can be assigned as projects. We thank D. L. Hawkins for suggesting Exercises 6.2-13 and 6.2-14.

6.2-12 (Continuation of Exercise 1.2-13) Three such tests are conducted with trucks A, B, and C. The first test uses truck A as the control truck and truck B as the test truck. Truck A is the control and C is the

test truck in test 2, while truck C is the control and A is the test truck in test 3. The fuel consumption (in pounds) for baseline and test laps are given for each of these three tests.

Test 1

Baseline Laps			Test Laps		
Lap No.	Control	Test	Lap No.	Control	Test
11	50.1488	51.8912	1	50.0354	49.4885
12	49.2472	50.6840	2	50.3589	48.7868
13	50.7082	51.9655	3	49.8449	48.3581
14	49.6399	50.5968	4	50.8973	49.3284
15	50.4372	51.8736	5	51.2444	50.2403
16	50.2273	51.6166	6	55.9998	54.1003
17	50.0609	50.8950	7	55.0668	53.7085
18	50.2046	50.9899	8	52.0332	50.0265
19	50.4621	51.6013	9	51.3607	50.7168
20	50.1678	51.3997	10	51.0776	50.1817
21	49.6908	50.9830	11	50.8610	49.3742
22	49.6244	50.5118	12	50.5268	49.1016
23	47.5206	49.7935	13	49.1427	48.6476
24	49.7272	50.1476			
25	46.9486	48.8342			
26	47.9234	48.9613			
27	48.7489	49.1496			

Test 2

Baseline Laps			Test Laps		
Lap No.	Control	Test	Lap No.	Control	Test
1	55.3113	55.7334	1	49.8147	50.5716
2	53.6337	54.1822	2	48.9365	50.1891
3	51.7796	51.8036	3	48.8112	49.7914
4	50.5123	50.2009	4	55.7907	54.8131
5	50.4743	51.1479	5	53.0183	52.7244
6	50.0646	50.3411	6	52.7069	52.4025
7	53.2571	52.9607	7	50.8575	50.6479
8	51.4892	50.3907	8	50.9064	51.2019
9	50.7879	50.7934	9	52.2317	51.8950
10	52.4796	51.9957	10	53.4323	52.3988
11	50.2225	51.3380	11	54.7146	55.0461
12	51.9174	53.2850	12	49.7150	49.9162
13	51.1354	52.3657	13	49.4545	49.5722
14	51.5383	51.7294	14	49.8251	48.1274
15	50.9109	52.4779	15	50.0902	51.0376
			16	49.4245	49.6365
			17	49.4206	49.1149

Test 3

Baseline Laps			Test Laps		
Lap No.	Control	Test	Lap No.	Control	Test
1	53.1619	53.0108	1	52.3952	51.7054
2	51.7278	51.8493	2	52.7375	51.2310
3	51.7645	51.9223	3	54.1094	53.1208
4	51.3215	50.8417	4	53.9236	52.8810
5	52.8214	51.7060	5	50.3270	49.2826
6	51.2873	49.9220	6	51.0103	48.9047
7	51.7809	50.6570	7	52.0884	51.4040
8	54.7923	54.0798	8	55.7383	55.1146
9	53.6278	53.3307	9	53.2446	52.3117
10	52.9175	52.5211	10	51.7210	51.1680
11	53.5807	52.1636	11	52.2943	51.3923
12	53.4555	54.1245	12	51.5441	51.2498
13	53.9870	53.7951	13	52.3488	52.0088
14	52.6708	51.3502	14	53.3372	52.3147
15	52.4845	53.5616	15	52.7943	52.4803
16	50.4069	50.4483	16	55.2126	54.7778
17	51.7267	50.8487			
18	50.6869	50.8670			
19	51.3805	51.3316			

(a) Analyze the data and discuss whether the company can make the claim that their fuel additive improves fuel economy.

(b) Discuss the strengths and weaknesses of the design.

Hint   For each test consider the ratio (diesel use of test truck)/(diesel use of control truck).

6.2-13   We want to investigate whether the temperature of water has an effect on how much pinto beans grow when soaked. We would like to find out whether or not the temperature of the soaking solution affects the expansion of the bean. Perform the following experiment: Select two levels of water temperature: room-temperature water (treatment A) and refrigerated water (at about $40°F$ as treatment B). From a bag of pinto beans select $2n$ beans as your experimental units and assign them randomly to each treatment. The soaking time is 8 hours for all beans. Let X_i and Y_i be the length differences in the two treatment groups; that is,

X_i = soaked length − dry length,

in treatment group A,

Y_i = soaked length − dry length,

in treatment group B.

(a) Assume that we want to test $H_0: \mu_x = \mu_y$ against $H_1: \mu_x > \mu_y$ at significance level $\alpha = 0.05$ and power (i.e., the probability of rejecting H_0) of 0.95 if $\mu_x - \mu_y = 1$ mm. How large should n be?

In your sample size calculations you may assume that the observations X_i and Y_i come from normal distributions with respective means μ_x and μ_y and that the two standard deviations σ_x and σ_y are the same. You will have to perform a pilot study to estimate the required standard deviation. Give all the data, summary statistics, and your conclusion.

(b) Using n as obtained in part (a), run the experiment with n experimental units per treatment. Carefully describe the method you use in allocating experimental units to the treatment groups.

(c) Test the equality of σ_x and σ_y at the $\alpha = 0.05$ significance level. Report appropriate plots, summary statistics, and conclusions.

(d) Using the appropriate test, test $H_0: \mu_x = \mu_y$ against the one-sided alternative $H_1: \mu_x > \mu_y$. Report your conclusion, as well as summary statistics, p-values, and appropriate plots of the data. Also, check whether a transformation of the data would be useful. Remember that transformations, such as logs, should be used if the variability in the groups increases with their levels.

6.2-14   Repeat the experiment in Exercise 6.2-13 but in a matched-pairs design with $2n$ experimental units. You have to select the matching variable. For example, you may want to block with respect to variables such as weight, thickness, or length of the dry beans. Sorting through your bag of beans you can identify pairs of beans of equal length; one from the pair is selected at random and soaked in room-temperature water while the other is soaked in refrigerated water.

(a) Obtain the required sample size that satisfies the requirements in Exercise 6.2-13(a). Remember that it is the standard deviation of the *difference* $W = X - Y$ that enters the sample size calculation. Your pilot study must be designed to estimate σ_W.

(b) Carefully describe the method you use to allocate the experimental units to the treatment groups.

(c) Test the hypothesis $H_0: \mu_W = 0$ against $H_1: \mu_W > 0$ at significance level $\alpha = 0.05$, where $\mu_W = \mu_X - \mu_Y$. Report your conclusion, as well as test statistics, p-values, and appropriate plots of the data.

for a test having significance level α. The alternative hypothesis, H_1, consists of all alternatives to H_0, namely, all cases where there is at least one inequality $p_i \neq p_{i0}$. Note that with one such inequality, there must be at least one other.

Example 6.3-1   One famous Mendelian theory concerning the crossing of two types of peas states that the respective probabilities are

$$H_0: p_1 = \frac{9}{16}, \quad p_2 = \frac{3}{16}, \quad p_3 = \frac{3}{16}, \quad p_4 = \frac{1}{16}$$

for the four mutually exclusive and exhaustive classifications: (1) round and yellow, (2) wrinkled and yellow, (3) round and green, (4) wrinkled and green. It is interesting to note that these probabilities can be obtained by multiplying $(0.75 + 0.25)$ by itself, which might suggest how Mendel arrived at his theory. To test H_0, suppose that we performed $n = 80$ independent experiments, observing the frequencies $y_1 = 42$, $y_2 = 17$, $y_3 = 13$, and $y_4 = 8$. Since the respective expected values are $(80)(9/16) = 45$, $(80)(3/16) = 15$, $(80)(3/16) = 15$, and $(80)(1/16) = 5$, we find that the observed value of Q_3, which is denoted by a lowercase letter, is

$$q_3 = \frac{(42 - 45)^2}{45} + \frac{(17 - 15)^2}{15} + \frac{(13 - 15)^2}{15} + \frac{(8 - 5)^2}{5} = 2.533.$$

Since Q_3 is approximate $\chi^2(3)$ and $q_3 = 2.533 < \chi^2(0.05; 3) = 7.815$, we do not reject H_0 at the $\alpha = 0.05$ level. Mendel's hypothesis is not rejected by these data.   ∎

In using the chi-square approximation to the distribution of Q_{k-1}, many statisticians suggest that n should be large enough so that $np_{i0} \geq 5$, $i = 1, 2, \ldots, k$. However, in many cases the approximation also works very well for $np_{i0} \geq 1$, provided that the term $(y_i - np_{i0})^2/np_{i0}$ does not contribute too much to q_{k-1} when np_{i0} is small. We do not want a small denominator np_{i0} to inflate $(y_i - np_{i0})^2/np_{i0}$ such that it dominates the other terms in q_{k-1}.

In the basic chi-square test, the probabilities $p_1, p_2, \ldots, p_k$ are completely specified by the null hypothesis. We call such a null hypothesis a *simple* null hypothesis. Sometimes this is not the case, as the probabilities in H_0 may be functions of other parameters that are unknown. We call such a null hypothesis a *composite* null hypothesis.

The following two examples should illustrate the difference between a simple and a composite null hypothesis. Take Example 6.3-1, where we considered probabilities of events that are associated with the crossing of two types of peas. There we tested whether or not $p_1 = 9/16$, $p_2 = p_3 = 3/16$, and $p_4 = 1/16$. We pointed out that these specific values are the terms in the expression $[p + (1 - p)]^2$, where $p = 3/4$. This is an example of a simple null hypothesis. Now, consider the case where we test whether or not the probabilities are given by the terms in the expansion $[p + (1 - p)]^2$, but leave p unspecified. Since $H_0: p_1 = p^2$, $p_2 = p_3 = p(1 - p)$, $p_4 = (1 - p)^2$, includes an unspecified parameter, we call it a composite null hypothesis. As another example, say that we are interested in testing whether the numbers of defectives, X, in samples of size 10 follow a binomial distribution with $p = 0.10$. Under H_0: $p = 0.10$ the probability of the event $(X = i)$ is given by $p_i = \binom{10}{i} p^i (1 - p)^{10-i}$, $i = 0, 1, \ldots, 10$. Since p is specified, we are looking at a simple null hypothesis. On the other hand, if we just want to test whether X follows a binomial distribution $b(10, p)$ and leave p unspecified, we are talking about a composite null hypothesis.

If p_i are not completely specified under H_0, we cannot compute Q_{k-1} once realizations of $Y_1, Y_2, \ldots, Y_k$ are observed because we cannot evaluate their expected values, np_i, $i = 1, 2, \ldots, k$. However, there is a way out of this difficulty. The probabilities $p_1, p_2, \ldots, p_k$ in

$$Q_{k-1} = \sum_{i=1}^{k} \frac{(Y_i - np_i)^2}{np_i}$$

are usually functions of a smaller set of parameters $\theta_1, \theta_2, \ldots, \theta_h$, where $h < k - 1$. This was the case in our illustrations. For example, the 11 probabilities p_i, $i = 0, 1, \ldots, 10$ were functions of just one unknown, the parameter p. Thus, also, Q_{k-1} is a function of $\theta_1, \theta_2, \ldots, \theta_h$. Let us find estimates of these h parameters, so that Q_{k-1} is minimized. We call those estimates the *minimum chi-square estimates* of $\theta_1, \theta_2, \ldots, \theta_h$. These estimates, in turn, provide estimates of $p_1, p_2, \ldots, p_k$, since the latter are functions of $\theta_1, \theta_2, \ldots, \theta_h$. Substituting these estimates for p_i, we obtain the minimum value of Q_{k-1}. The distribution of this minimum value Q_{k-1} can be approximated by a chi-square distribution with $k - 1 - h$ degrees of freedom. The only adjustment that we have to make when going from a simple to a composite null hypothesis is in the degrees of freedom of the chi-square distribution. In the context of composite null hypotheses, we lose one degree of freedom for each estimated parameter. We reject the composite null hypothesis if the calculated minimum value q_{k-1} exceeds the critical value $\chi^2(\alpha; k - 1 - h)$.

Remark   In many situations, the parameters are *not* estimated by minimizing Q_{k-1} because this is sometimes a difficult problem. If other estimates are used, the computed q_{k-1} is not the smallest possible value, and hence there is a greater chance of rejecting H_0 when comparing that computed q_{k-1} to $\chi^2(\alpha; k - 1 - h)$. Accordingly, the significance level will be somewhat higher than α. Nevertheless, this approximation is still not too bad, particularly if the parameters are estimated as a function of the frequencies $Y_1, Y_2, \ldots, Y_k$. ■

6.3-1   Contingency Tables

A major application of this result is in the context of *contingency tables*. Let the result of a random experiment be classified by two attributes. For example, a radio receiver may be classified as having low, average, or high fidelity and as having low, average, or high selectivity; or graduating engineering students may be classified according to their starting salary and their grade-point average. In general, let us label the mutually exclusive and exhaustive levels of the first attribute by $A_1, A_2, \ldots, A_a$, and those of the second by $B_1, B_2, \ldots, B_b$. This leads to the mutually exclusive and exhaustive classification $A_i \cap B_j$, $i = 1, 2, \ldots, a$ and $j = 1, 2, \ldots, b$. Let us repeat the experiment n independent times and let Y_{ij} denote the frequencies of the $k = ab$ groups in the classification $A_i \cap B_j$. For example, we determine the fidelity and selectivity of n radio receivers, or we ask n graduating engineers about their starting salary and grade-point average. For a test of the simple null hypothesis $H_0: P(A_i \cap B_j) = p_{ij}$, where p_{ij} are $k = ab$ specified probabilities that add to 1, we use

$$Q_{ab-1} = \sum_{i=1}^{a} \sum_{j=1}^{b} \frac{(Y_{ij} - np_{ij})^2}{np_{ij}}.$$

Under this null hypothesis the distribution of Q_{ab-1} is approximately $\chi^2(ab - 1)$, provided that n is large enough to make each np_{ij} reasonably large.

Often, we wish to test the independence of the two attributes. For example, is the level of the fidelity of a radio receiver independent of the level of selectivity; or is the level of the starting salary for an engineer independent of the grade-point average of that engineer? Let us denote the individual (or marginal) probabilities $P(A_i)$ by $p_{i\cdot}$ and $P(B_j)$ by $p_{\cdot j}$, so that

$$p_{i\cdot} = P(A_i) = \sum_{j=1}^{b} p_{ij} \quad \text{and} \quad p_{\cdot j} = P(B_j) = \sum_{i=1}^{a} p_{ij}.$$

Then the hypothesis of independence,

$$H_0: P(A_i \cap B_j) = P(A_i)P(B_j) \qquad \text{for all } A_i \text{ and } B_j,$$

can be written as

$$H_0: p_{ij} = p_{i\cdot} p_{\cdot j}, \qquad \begin{array}{l} i = 1, 2, \ldots, a, \\ j = 1, 2, \ldots, b. \end{array}$$

Note that H_0 is a composite null hypothesis with unknown parameters $p_{1\cdot}$, $\ldots, p_{a-1,\cdot}$ and $p_{\cdot 1}, \ldots, p_{\cdot, b-1}$; here we need just these $a - 1$ and $b - 1$ parameters, since

$$p_{a\cdot} = 1 - (p_{1\cdot} + \cdots + p_{a-1,\cdot}) \qquad \text{and} \qquad p_{\cdot b} = 1 - (p_{\cdot 1} + \cdots + p_{\cdot, b-1}).$$

That is, these $a - 1 + b - 1 = a + b - 2 = h$ parameters are our θ values. These unknown parameters can be estimated by

$$\hat{p}_{i\cdot} = \frac{Y_{i\cdot}}{n}, \qquad \text{where } Y_{i\cdot} = \sum_{j=1}^{b} Y_{ij}, \quad i = 1, 2, \ldots, a,$$

and

$$\hat{p}_{\cdot j} = \frac{Y_{\cdot j}}{n}, \qquad \text{where } Y_{\cdot j} = \sum_{i=1}^{a} Y_{ij}, \quad j = 1, 2, \ldots, b.$$

If we replace $p_{ij} = p_{i \cdot} p_{\cdot j}$ in Q_{ab-1} by the product $\hat{p}_{i \cdot} \hat{p}_{\cdot j}$ of these estimates, then, according to the rule above, Q_{ab-1} has an approximate chi-square distribution with

$$ab - 1 - (a + b - 2) = (a - 1)(b - 1)$$

degrees of freedom. If the computed Q_{ab-1} gets too large, namely, exceeds $\chi^2[\alpha; (a-1)(b-1)]$, we reject the hypothesis $H_0: p_{ij} = p_{i \cdot} p_{\cdot j}$ that the two attributes are independent.

Example 6.3-2 Ninety graduating male engineers were classified by two attributes: grade-point average (low, average, high) and initial salary (low, high). The following results were obtained.

Salary	Grade-Point Average			
	Low	Average	High	
Low	15	18	7	40
High	5	22	23	50
	20	40	30	90

Note that here $y_{1 \cdot} = 40$, $y_{2 \cdot} = 50$ and $y_{\cdot 1} = 20$, $y_{\cdot 2} = 40$, $y_{\cdot 3} = 30$, and

$$\hat{p}_{1 \cdot} = \frac{4}{9}, \quad \hat{p}_{2 \cdot} = \frac{5}{9} \quad \text{and} \quad \hat{p}_{\cdot 1} = \frac{2}{9}, \quad \hat{p}_{\cdot 2} = \frac{4}{9}, \quad \hat{p}_{\cdot 3} = \frac{3}{9}.$$

Assuming independence of the attributes (H_0), we estimate the joint probabilities by $\hat{p}_{ij} = \hat{p}_{i \cdot} \hat{p}_{\cdot j}$. Under H_0, the estimated expected values $n \hat{p}_{i \cdot} \hat{p}_{\cdot j}$ are

$$90 \left(\frac{4}{9} \right) \left(\frac{2}{9} \right) = 8.89, \qquad 90 \left(\frac{4}{9} \right) \left(\frac{4}{9} \right) = 17.78, \qquad 90 \left(\frac{4}{9} \right) \left(\frac{3}{9} \right) = 13.33,$$

$$90 \left(\frac{5}{9} \right) \left(\frac{2}{9} \right) = 11.11, \qquad 90 \left(\frac{5}{9} \right) \left(\frac{4}{9} \right) = 22.22, \qquad 90 \left(\frac{5}{9} \right) \left(\frac{3}{9} \right) = 16.67.$$

The computed Q_5 is

$$q_5 = \frac{(15 - 8.89)^2}{8.89} + \frac{(18 - 17.78)^2}{17.78} + \frac{(7 - 13.33)^2}{13.33}$$

$$+ \frac{(5 - 11.11)^2}{11.11} + \frac{(22 - 22.22)^2}{22.22} + \frac{(23 - 16.67)^2}{16.67}$$

$$= 4.20 + 0.00 + 3.01 + 3.36 + 0.00 + 2.40 = 12.97.$$

Since $(a - 1)(b - 1) = (1)(2) = 2$ and $12.97 > \chi^2(0.05; 2) = 5.991$, we reject the hypothesis of independence. That is, based on these data, we conclude that starting salaries and grade-point averages are dependent. ∎

6.3-2 Goodness-of-Fit Tests

Sometimes we conjecture that X has a certain kind of distribution that involves one or more parameters. For example, we may think that the number of flaws, X, on a bolt of material has a Poisson distribution with an unknown parameter λ. Or we may conjecture that the compression strengths of concrete cylinders come from a normal distribution with certain mean and variance. Suppose that we divide the outcome space of the variable X into k mutually exclusive and exhaustive cells. From a sample of size n, we can determine the frequencies of those k cells. Let us denote those frequencies by $Y_1, Y_2, \ldots, Y_k$; of course, $\sum_{i=1}^{k} Y_i = n$. The probabilities $p_1, p_2, \ldots, p_k$, where $\sum_{i=1}^{k} p_i = 1$, and the expected values $E(Y_i) = np_i$ are determined from the distribution of X. If the parameters of the distribution are specified (say, $\lambda = 1$ for the Poisson, and $\mu = 45$ and $\sigma^2 = 90$ for the normal), then we know that

$$Q_{k-1} = \sum_{i=1}^{k} \frac{(Y_i - np_i)^2}{np_i}$$

has an approximate chi-square distribution with $k - 1$ degrees of freedom. However, usually those parameters are unknown and to compute Q_{k-1} we need to estimate a number of parameters of the distribution of X, say h of them. For example, $h = 1$ in the Poisson and $h = 2$ in the normal case. The use of the estimates of these parameters in Q_{k-1} produces a statistic that has an approximate $\chi^2(k - 1 - h)$ distribution. The null hypothesis H_0 that X has that specified underlying distribution is questioned if the computed q_{k-1} is too large; namely, if it exceeds $\chi^2(\alpha; k - 1 - h)$.

Example 6.3-3   We observe $n = 85$ values of a random variable X that is thought to have a Poisson distribution, obtaining

x	0	1	2	3	4	5
Frequency	41	29	9	4	1	1

The sample average is the appropriate estimate of $\lambda = E(X)$. It is given by

$$\hat{\lambda} = \frac{(41)(0) + (29)(1) + (9)(2) + (4)(3) + (1)(4) + (1)(5)}{85} = 0.8.$$

With this estimated λ value the expected frequencies for the first three cells are

$$85(0.449) = 38.2, \qquad 85(0.360) = 30.6, \qquad 85(0.144) = 12.2.$$

We can use Table C.3 to determine these Poisson probabilities. The expected frequency for the cell $\{3, 4, 5, \ldots\}$ is $85(0.047) = 4.0$. Here we have combined several of the original cells to obtain an expected value that is not much smaller than 5. The computed Q_3, with $k = 4$ after that combination, is

$$q_3 = \frac{(41 - 38.2)^2}{38.2} + \frac{(29 - 30.6)^2}{30.6} + \frac{(9 - 12.2)^2}{12.2} + \frac{(6 - 4)^2}{4}$$

$$= 0.21 + 0.08 + 0.84 + 1.00 = 2.13.$$

Comparing this value with $\chi^2(0.05; 4 - 1 - 1 = 2) = 5.991$, we certainly find no reason to reject the Poisson distribution. ∎

Exercises 6.3

6.3-1 We cast a certain die $n = 120$ independent times and find the number of times 1, 2, 3, 4, 5, 6 spots are on the "up side" to be 16, 21, 22, 14, 19, 28, respectively. Does it seem as if this die is biased? That is, can we reject H_0: $p_i = 1/6$, $i = 1, 2, \ldots, 6$, using $\alpha = 0.05$?

6.3-2 A manufacturer of men's underwear claims that 91 percent of the products are of the "best" quality, 8 percent are "seconds," and only 1 percent are defective. To test this claim, 500 garments selected at random are inspected; this results in the respective frequencies of 434, 48, and 18. Can we reject the claim at the $\alpha = 0.05$ level?

6.3-3 The starting salaries of $n = 200$ engineers were classified as in the lower 25 percent (A_1), second 25 percent (A_2), third 25 percent (A_3), and the upper 25 percent (A_4). In addition, these 200 engineers were classified according to the color of their eyes. The results are summarized in the following table.

Eyes	Salary				
	A_1	A_2	A_3	A_4	
Blue	22	17	21	20	80
Brown	14	20	20	16	70
Other	14	13	9	14	50
	50	50	50	50	200

Are the color of eyes and the starting salary independent attributes? Use $\alpha = 0.05$. If not, you may be able to claim discrimination.

6.3-4 A test of the equality of two or more multinomial distributions can be made by using calculations that are associated with a contingency table. For example, $n = 100$ light bulbs were taken at random from each of three brands and were graded as A, B, C, or D.

Brand	Grade				
	A	B	C	D	
1	27	42	21	10	100
2	23	39	25	13	100
3	22	36	23	19	100
	72	117	69	42	300

Clearly, we want to test the equality of three multinomial distributions, each with $k = 4$ cells. Since under H_0 the probability of falling into a particular grade category is independent of brand, we can test this hypothesis by computing Q_{11} and comparing it with $\chi^2(\alpha; (2)(3) = 6)$. Use $\alpha = 0.025$.

6.3-5 The number X of telephone calls received each minute at a certain switchboard in the middle of a working day is thought to have a Poisson distribution. Data were collected, and the results were as follows:

x	0	1	2	3	4	5	6
Frequency	40	66	41	28	9	3	1

Fit a Poisson distribution. Then find the estimated expected value of each cell after combining $\{4, 5, 6, \ldots\}$ to make one cell. Compute Q_4, since $k = 5$, and compare it to $\chi^2(\alpha = 0.05; 3)$. Why do we use three degrees of freedom? Do we accept or reject the Poisson distribution?

6.3-6 Use the compression strength data of Section 1.2. Check to see if a normal curve fits the frequency distribution given in Table 1.2-2. Combine the first two cells and the last three so that $k = 7$. Use $\alpha = 0.05$. Why do we use four degrees of freedom? Note that the goodness-of-fit test provides a formal test for normality. It complements the normal probability plots in Section 3.4.

CHAPTER

7

Experiments with
One Factor

Frequently, experimenters want to compare more than two treatments. For example, plant breeders compare the yields of different corn hybrids, computer scientists investigate the times between failures of various computer systems, and company managers compare the productivities of several plants within their company. Engineers study the effect of different gas additives on pollutant emissions, the effectiveness of several rust inhibitors on corrosion, the effects of various catalysts on process yields, and the durabilities of various types of materials. Experiments have to be designed to investigate possible treatment effects. These experiments have to be designed properly and the resulting data have to be analyzed correctly.

In Section 6.2 we discussed how to compare two treatments. We emphasized the principles of *randomization* and *blocking*. Randomization, which allocates the treatments randomly to the experimental units, guarantees the validity of the inference in the face of unspecified disturbances. It makes certain that the risk of unspecified disturbances is spread fairly evenly among the treatments. Without such randomization it could be that the treatment differences are confounded with other variables that cannot be controlled by the experimenter. The following example reiterates this important concept. Assume that we want to study how two different drying methods affect the compressive strength of concrete cylinders. Suppose that the plant has produced a total of 30 such cylinders. Since these cylinders were made from separate batches of concrete, we can expect some variability among the cylinders. That is, we should expect variability even though the foreman claims that these batches were mixed exactly the same way. However, these differences among the experimental units should not bias our comparison. Thus we use randomization and assign the two treatments (the two drying methods) to the experimental units (concrete blocks) at random. We could carry out this randomization by numbering the blocks from 1 through 30 and then selecting these numbered blocks at random and without replacement until we have filled our first group of 15 blocks. Then we could flip a coin to determine which of the two drying methods should be applied to this group.

Blocking is the other important concept in the design of comparative experiments. In Section 6.2 we discussed how blocking, or running the experiment in pairs if there are only two treatments, can eliminate unwanted sources of variation and can improve the precision of the comparison. Let us assume that in our illustration the batches of concrete were just large enough to produce two concrete cylinders from each batch. Obviously, the two cylinders from the same batch would show less variability than cylinders that come from different batches. Accordingly, we would be better off by assigning the two treatments to the two cylinders in each batch (block) and then analyzing their differences in compressive strength. This would eliminate the variability that is introduced by the differences among batches. Randomization would still play a role in the assignment of treatments to the experimental units within each batch. We would flip a coin to determine whether the first cylinder in each batch should be assigned to drying method A or B.

7.1   Completely Randomized One-Factor Experiments

In this and the following two sections we extend the analysis from two to k levels (treatments) of a single factor. Here and in Section 7.2 we analyze the data from the *completely randomized experiment*. There the k treatments are randomly allocated to the experimental units. In the analysis that corresponds to this design we assume that the samples that we observe from the k treatment groups are independent. In Section 7.3 we analyze the data from the *randomized complete block experiment*. In this design the experimental units are grouped into homogeneous blocks, and the k treatments are randomly assigned to every block.

Let us assume that there are k different treatments (factor levels) under study. For the ith treatment, the response Y is a random variable that varies around an unknown treatment mean μ_i, $i = 1, 2, \ldots, k$. We assume that for each treatment group the distribution of the response Y around its group mean is normal and that the variances are the same for all treatment groups. The latter assumption specifies that the "precision" of the observations is the same in each group. An example with $k = 3$ treatment distributions is shown in Figure 7.1-1.

Now, let us suppose that we observe n_i independent realizations from the distribution that is associated with the ith treatment. Furthermore, we assume

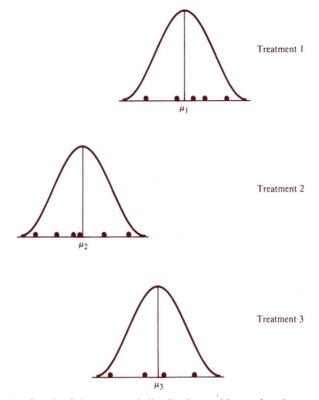

FIGURE 7.1-1 Graph of three normal distributions with equal variances and a set of possible realizations.

that these random samples from the different treatment groups are drawn independently; this is an extremely important assumption in the analysis of data from a completely randomized design. This means that the observations in one treatment group are independent of the ones in the others. As an example, we have plotted hypothetical results of samples of respective sizes $n_1 = 5$, $n_2 = 6$, and $n_3 = 4$ in Figure 7.1-1.

The assumptions above specify that the deviations from the respective group means are independent and normally distributed, with mean zero and constant variance, say σ^2. Thus we can write

$$Y_{ij} = \mu_i + \varepsilon_{ij}, \qquad i = 1, 2, \ldots, k \quad \text{and} \quad j = 1, 2, \ldots, n_i,$$

where Y_{ij} is the value of the response variable in the jth trial for the ith treatment, μ_i is the ith treatment mean, and ε_{ij} are independent $N(0, \sigma^2)$ random variables. This equation describes a *statistical model* that links the observations and the parameters of the underlying populations.

The data analysis that is described in this section depends on these assumptions. Thus we should always check whether the assumptions in this model are

TABLE 7.1-1   One-Factor Experiment

Treatment	Observations	Sample Mean
1	$Y_{11}, Y_{12}, \ldots, Y_{1n_1}$	$\bar{Y}_1 = \dfrac{1}{n_1} \sum\limits_{j=1}^{n_1} Y_{1j}$
$\vdots$		$\vdots$
i	$Y_{i1}, Y_{i2}, \ldots, Y_{in_i}$	$\bar{Y}_i = \dfrac{1}{n_i} \sum\limits_{j=1}^{n_i} Y_{ij}$
$\vdots$		$\vdots$
k	$Y_{k1}, Y_{k2}, \ldots, Y_{kn_k}$	$\bar{Y}_k = \dfrac{1}{n_k} \sum\limits_{j=1}^{n_k} Y_{kj}$

consistent with the nature of the experiment. This model is appropriate, for example, if we study the breaking strength of three different alloys and have obtained several independent measurements on their breaking strength. Moreover, the measurements must be approximately normally distributed with common variance. It is also an appropriate model if in a study of the effectiveness of four different dietary supplements we have obtained the percentage weight gains of N subjects that were randomly divided into the four dietary groups. We must also assume that the gains in each group are at least approximately normally distributed with common variance. However, this model is not appropriate for an experiment in which each subject receives all four treatments, because then the assumption of independence would probably be violated. In the latter case, an analysis that uses the subject as a block would be more appropriate; this is considered in Section 7.3.

The experimenter wants to determine whether or not the means $\mu_1, \mu_2, \ldots, \mu_k$ of the k levels (treatments) of this one factor are equal. If they are equal, we say that there is no difference due to the different levels of this factor; that is, we say that there are no factor effects. If we find that the μ_i are different, we want to determine how they differ. For example, are they different because μ_1 is larger than $\mu_2 = \mu_3$, or is it because all three are different? Those two issues, testing whether or not the means are the same and follow-up tests to determine how they are different, are discussed in this and the next section.

The data from comparative one-factor experiments can be arranged as in Table 7.1-1. The unknown treatment means $\mu_1, \mu_2, \ldots, \mu_k$ are estimated by the sample means

$$\bar{Y}_i = \frac{1}{n_i} \sum_{j=1}^{n_i} Y_{ij}, \qquad i = 1, 2, \ldots, k.$$

Example 7.1-1   A civil engineer wishes to compare the strength properties of three different types of beams. Type A is made of steel, while types B and C are made of two different and more expensive alloys. The engineer measures the

TABLE 7.1-2 Deflections of Three Types of Beams

Type	Observations								$\bar{y}_i$	$\sum_{j=1}^{n_i} (y_{ij} - \bar{y}_i)^2$
A (steel)	82	86	79	83	85	84	86	87	84	48
B	74	82	78	75	76	77			77	40
C	79	79	77	78	82	79			79	14

strength of a beam by setting it in a horizontal position, supported only on each end, and by applying a force of 3000 pounds at the center and then measuring the deflection. The deflection, measured in units of 1/1000 inch, for respective samples of sizes $n_1 = 8$, $n_2 = 6$, and $n_3 = 6$ are given in Table 7.1-2. The engineer was assured that these beams were representative random samples from the ones that were kept in inventory, not just the first six or eight beams that could be reached most easily. The engineer was also concerned that the measurement procedures may influence the comparison. To make sure that the order in which the experiments were carried out did not affect the comparison, the engineer randomized the order. She did this by assigning to each beam a different number from 1 to 20, drawing numbers without replacement, and performing the measurements in that particular (random) order. The sample means $\bar{Y}_i$ and the sums of squared deviations of the observations from their respective sample means, $\sum_{j=1}^{n_i} (Y_{ij} - \bar{Y}_i)^2$, $i = 1, 2, 3$, are also given in Table 7.1-2. Dot diagrams of the observations in each treatment group are given in Figure 7.1-2.

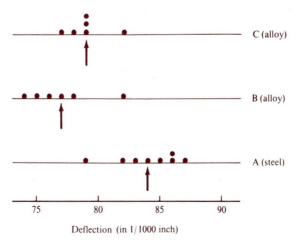

FIGURE 7.1-2 Dot diagrams of the observations in three groups. Group means are indicated by arrows.

It is always useful to display data graphically, either by separate dot diagrams or by box plots if there are many observations in each treatment group. Dot diagrams of the observations by treatment groups show (1) the variability of the observations from their group average (the *within-treatment* variability), and (2) the variability between the group averages (the *between-treatment* variability). If the between-treatment variability is larger than what could be expected from the variation that occurs within the treatments, we would question whether the population means $\mu_1, \mu_2, \ldots, \mu_k$ are the same. Also note that this graphical display of the data gives us a visual method to check whether the variability in the various treatment groups is roughly the same.

In the case of a single random sample, we used the sum of squares $\sum_{j=1}^{n_i} (Y_{ij} - \bar{Y}_i)^2$ and the sample variance

$$S_i^2 = \frac{1}{n_i - 1} \sum_{j=1}^{n_i} (Y_{ij} - \bar{Y}_i)^2$$

to describe the internal variability in the data. For a single random sample from a normal distribution, we know that $\sum_{j=1}^{n_i} (Y_{ij} - \bar{Y}_i)^2/\sigma^2$ has a chi-square distribution with $n_i - 1$ degrees of freedom. Since we have k independent samples, we know from Section 4.4 that the sum of the k independent chi-square random variables

$$\frac{\sum_{i=1}^{k} \sum_{j=1}^{n_i} (Y_{ij} - \bar{Y}_i)^2}{\sigma^2}$$

is chi-square with degrees of freedom equal to $\sum_{i=1}^{k} (n_i - 1) = N - k$, where $N = \sum_{i=1}^{k} n_i$ is the total number of observations. The numerator of this chi-square variable is the pooled sum of squares

$$SS_{Error} = \sum_{i=1}^{k} \sum_{j=1}^{n_i} (Y_{ij} - \bar{Y}_i)^2 ;$$

it is called the *within-treatment sum of squares* or the *error sum of squares*. This quantity, divided by the degrees of freedom $N - k$, is known as the *mean square error* (or *mean square due to error*)

$$MS_{Error} = \frac{SS_{Error}}{N - k} = \frac{\sum_{i=1}^{k} \sum_{j=1}^{n_i} (Y_{ij} - \bar{Y}_i)^2}{N - k}.$$

It is a weighted average of the sample variances S_i^2: $MS_{Error} = \sum_{i=1}^{k} w_i S_i^2$, where $w_i = (n_i - 1)/(N - k)$. It is an unbiased estimator of the common σ^2, which measures the internal variability. Note that it is an unbiased estimate of σ^2 whether or not the treatment means $\mu_1, \mu_2, \ldots, \mu_k$ are the same.

In our example, we find that the within-treatment sum of squares equals

$$SS_{Error} = 48 + 40 + 14 = 102$$

and its degrees of freedom are given by $(8-1)+(6-1)+(6-1)=17$. A pooled estimate of σ^2 is

$$MS_{Error} = \frac{102}{17} = 6.0$$

Now there is another type of variability that can be calculated, namely the variation of the treatment averages around the grand mean. The grand mean

$$\bar{Y} = \frac{1}{N} \sum_{i=1}^{k} \sum_{j=1}^{n_i} Y_{ij}$$

is the sum of all observations divided by the total number of observations. If each mean $\bar{Y}_i$ is given its sample size n_i as its weight in computing a sum of squares, that sum of squares,

$$SS_{Treatment} = n_1(\bar{Y}_1 - \bar{Y})^2 + n_2(\bar{Y}_2 - \bar{Y})^2 + \cdots + n_k(\bar{Y}_k - \bar{Y})^2$$

$$= \sum_{i=1}^{k} n_i(\bar{Y}_i - \bar{Y})^2,$$

is called the *between-treatment sum of squares* or simply the *treatment sum of squares*. It measures the variability among the treatment means; it is zero if the treatment means are equal. There are k components in this sum of squares; however, there is also one restriction, namely

$$\sum_{i=1}^{k} n_i(\bar{Y}_i - \bar{Y}) = \sum_{i=1}^{k} n_i \bar{Y}_i - \bar{Y} \sum_{i=1}^{k} n_i = 0.$$

Thus intuitively, this sum of squares has $k-1$ degrees of freedom, and we call the ratio

$$MS_{Treatment} = \frac{SS_{Treatment}}{k-1}$$

the *mean square due to treatment*.

In our example we find that the treatment sum of squares is given by

$$SS_{Treatment} = 8(84 - 80.4)^2 + 6(77 - 80.4)^2 + 6(79 - 80.4)^2$$

$$= 184.8.$$

Since there are $k-1=3-1=2$ degrees of freedom, the mean square due to treatment is

$$MS_{Treatment} = \frac{184.8}{2} = 92.4.$$

7.1-1   Analysis-of-Variance Table

We have defined two types of variation: the *within* and the *between* treatment sum of squares. We now show that we can write the total sum of squares around the grand mean, SSTO, as the sum of these two sums of squares.

$$\text{SSTO} = \sum_{i=1}^{k} \sum_{j=1}^{n_i} (Y_{ij} - \bar{Y})^2 = \sum_{i=1}^{k} \sum_{j=1}^{n_i} [(Y_{ij} - \bar{Y}_i) + (\bar{Y}_i - \bar{Y})]^2$$

$$= \sum_{i=1}^{k} \sum_{j=1}^{n_i} (\bar{Y}_i - \bar{Y})^2 + \sum_{i=1}^{k} \sum_{j=1}^{n_i} (Y_{ij} - \bar{Y}_i)^2$$

$$+ 2 \sum_{i=1}^{k} \sum_{j=1}^{n_i} (Y_{ij} - \bar{Y}_i)(\bar{Y}_i - \bar{Y})$$

$$= \sum_{i=1}^{k} n_i(\bar{Y}_i - \bar{Y})^2 + \sum_{i=1}^{k} \sum_{j=1}^{n_i} (Y_{ij} - \bar{Y}_i)^2$$

$$= \text{SS}_{\text{Treatment}} \quad + \text{SS}_{\text{Error}},$$

since

$$\sum_{i=1}^{k} \sum_{j=1}^{n_i} (Y_{ij} - \bar{Y}_i)(\bar{Y}_i - \bar{Y}) = \sum_{i=1}^{k} (\bar{Y}_i - \bar{Y}) \sum_{j=1}^{n_i} (Y_{ij} - \bar{Y}_i) = 0$$

because

$$\sum_{j=1}^{n_i} (Y_{ij} - \bar{Y}_i) = 0, \qquad i = 1, 2, \ldots, k.$$

This sum-of-squares decomposition is frequently recorded in a table. Since this table concerns various sums of squares or estimates of variances, it is called the *analysis-of-variance table* or *ANOVA table*. It is given in Table 7.1-3. The first column identifies the sources of variation, the second and third columns the corresponding sums of squares and degrees of freedom; the fourth column gives the mean squares, and the last column contains the F-ratio, $F = \text{MS}_{\text{Treatment}}/\text{MS}_{\text{Error}}$, which will be explained later.

TABLE 7.1-3   ANOVA Table for the Completely Randomized Design

Source	SS	df	MS	F
Treatment	$\sum_{i=1}^{k} n_i(\bar{Y}_i - \bar{Y})^2$	$k-1$	$\text{MS}_{\text{Treatment}} = \dfrac{\text{SS}_{\text{Treatment}}}{k-1}$	$\dfrac{\text{MS}_{\text{Treatment}}}{\text{MS}_{\text{Error}}}$
Error	$\sum_{i=1}^{k} \sum_{j=1}^{n_i} (Y_{ij} - \bar{Y}_i)^2$	$N-k$	$\text{MS}_{\text{Error}} = \dfrac{\text{SS}_{\text{Error}}}{N-k}$	
Total	$\sum_{i=1}^{k} \sum_{j=1}^{n_i} (Y_{ij} - \bar{Y})^2$	$N-1$		

The sum-of-squares contributions are usually calculated by computer programs. If they are calculated by hand, it is more convenient to calculate them from

$$\text{SSTO} = \sum_{i=1}^{k} \sum_{j=1}^{n_i} (Y_{ij} - \bar{Y})^2 = \sum_{i=1}^{k} \sum_{j=1}^{n_i} Y_{ij}^2 - \frac{\left(\sum_{i=1}^{k} \sum_{j=1}^{n_i} Y_{ij} \right)^2}{N},$$

$$\text{SS}_{\text{Treatment}} = \sum_{i=1}^{k} n_i (\bar{Y}_i - \bar{Y})^2 = \sum_{i=1}^{k} \frac{\left(\sum_{j=1}^{n_i} Y_{ij} \right)^2}{n_i} - \frac{\left(\sum_{i=1}^{k} \sum_{j=1}^{n_i} Y_{ij} \right)^2}{N},$$

and

$$\text{SS}_{\text{Error}} = \text{SSTO} - \text{SS}_{\text{Treatment}}.$$

Note that one sum of squares in Table 7.1-3 can always be calculated from the other two.

Example 7.1-2   We use the data on the deflection of steel bars. We find that $k = 3$, $n_1 = 8$, $n_2 = n_3 = 6$, and thus $N = 20$. In addition,

$$\sum_{i=1}^{k} \sum_{j=1}^{n_i} Y_{ij} = 82 + 86 + \cdots + 82 + 79 = 1608,$$

$$\sum_{i=1}^{k} \sum_{j=1}^{n_i} Y_{ij}^2 = 82^2 + 86^2 + \cdots + 82^2 + 79^2 = 129{,}570,$$

$$\sum_{j=1}^{n_1} Y_{1j} = 82 + 86 + \cdots + 87 = 672,$$

$$\sum_{j=1}^{n_2} Y_{2j} = 74 + 82 + \cdots + 77 = 462,$$

$$\sum_{j=1}^{n_3} Y_{3j} = 79 + 79 + \cdots + 79 = 474.$$

Hence

$$\text{SSTO} = 129{,}570 - \frac{(1608)^2}{20} = 286.8,$$

$$\text{SS}_{\text{Treatment}} = \frac{(672)^2}{8} + \frac{(462)^2}{6} + \frac{(474)^2}{6} - \frac{(1608)^2}{20} = 184.8,$$

$$\text{SS}_{\text{Error}} = 286.8 - 184.8 = 102.0.$$

The ANOVA table is given by

Source	SS	df	MS	F
Treatment	184.8	2	92.4	15.4
Error	102.0	17	6.0	
Total	286.8	19		

7.1-2   *F*-Test for Treatment Effects

We want to test the null hypothesis that all treatment means are the same, $H_0: \mu_1 = \mu_2 = \cdots = \mu_k$, against the alternative hypothesis that there is at least one that is different, H_1: not all μ_i are the same. We need to construct a test statistic and obtain its distribution under the null hypothesis. The $F = \mathrm{MS_{Treatment}/MS_{Error}}$ ratio in the last column of the ANOVA table is the appropriate statistic. The numerator, and thus the ratio itself, is "small" if H_0 is true, as in this case the sample treatment means are about the same. On the other hand, the numerator is "large" if H_1 is true, as in this case the sample means are different. A more formal justification is given as follows.

We saw earlier that the within-treatment mean-square $\mathrm{MS_{Error}}$ is an estimate of σ^2. This is true irrespective of whether or not the treatment means μ_1, $\mu_2, \ldots, \mu_k$ are the same; that is, $E(\mathrm{MS_{Error}}) = \sigma^2$. Also, the between-treatment mean-square $\mathrm{MS_{Treatment}}$ provides an estimate of σ^2, but only if the treatment means are the same. If they are different, $\mathrm{MS_{Treatment}}$ tends to be much larger than σ^2. In general, it can be shown (see Exercises 7.1-7 and 7.1-8) that

$$E(\mathrm{MS_{Treatment}}) = \sigma^2 + \frac{\sum_{i=1}^{k} n_i \tau_i^2}{k-1}$$

where $\tau_i = \mu_i - \mu$ are the deviations from the overall (weighted) mean $\mu = (\sum_{i=1}^{k} n_i \mu_i)/N$. These deviations are also called the treatment effects, and it is true that $\sum_{i=1}^{k} n_i \tau_i = 0$.

If $\mu_1 = \mu_2 = \cdots = \mu_k(=\mu)$, then $\tau_i = 0$ for all i, and $E(\mathrm{MS_{Treatment}}) = \sigma^2$. In this case the numerator and the denominator of the F-ratio estimate the same quantity. Moreover, it can be shown that under H_0, $\mathrm{SS_{Treatment}}/\sigma^2$ and $\mathrm{SS_{Error}}/\sigma^2$ are independent chi-square random variables and thus

$$F = \frac{(\mathrm{SS_{Treatment}}/\sigma^2)/(k-1)}{(\mathrm{SS_{Error}}/\sigma^2)/(N-k)} = \frac{\mathrm{MS_{Treatment}}}{\mathrm{MS_{Error}}}$$

has an F distribution with $k-1$ and $N-k$ degrees of freedom. It is easy to remember the degrees of freedom, since they correspond to the MS entries in the ANOVA table. If some of the means $\mu_1, \mu_2, \ldots, \mu_k$ are different, the numerator in the F-ratio and thus the F-ratio itself tend to be larger. This leads to the following test procedure. If $F \geq F(\alpha; k-1, N-k)$, accept H_1. In such a case we say that the F-statistic is significant and that there are statistically significant differences among the group means. On the other hand, if the F-ratio is smaller than the critical value, there is not enough evidence in the data to reject $H_0: \mu_1 = \mu_2 = \cdots = \mu_k$.

An identical test procedure uses the *probability value* (or *p value*), which is calculated by most computer programs. Here it is defined as

$$p \text{ value} = P[F(k-1, N-k) \geq F],$$

where F is the observed F-ratio $\mathrm{MS_{Treatment}/MS_{Error}}$; that is, it is the probability of obtaining a realization from the $F(k-1, N-k)$ distribution which is at least as large as the observed F-ratio. If this p value is less than or equal to α, we accept H_1; otherwise, we accept H_0 until further data are obtained.

Example 7.1-3   In Example 7.1-2, the F-ratio is $92.4/6.0 = 15.4$. The critical value with $\alpha = 0.05$ is $F(0.05; \ 2, \ 17) = 3.59$; for $\alpha = 0.01$, it is $F(0.01; \ 2, 17) = 6.11$. Thus there is very strong evidence that the treatment means are different, as we reject $H_0: \mu_1 = \mu_2 = \mu_3$ at both significance levels $\alpha = 0.05$ and $\alpha = 0.01$. In the next section we indicate how to follow up on this test.   ■

7.1-3   Graphical Comparison of k Samples

The numerical analysis of the ANOVA table should always be supplemented by a graphical display of the data. If there are only a few observations in each group, one can construct k separate dot diagrams and put them side by side, or, as we have done in Figure 7.1-2, put one below the other. If there are many observations in each group, one should construct box plots for each group and arrange them side by side on the same scale. This was shown in Figures 1.4-4, 1.4-5, and 1.4-6. If there is considerable overlap among the boxes of the various groups, the F-statistic from the ANOVA table will tend to be insignificant. The box plots also give us information on the variability of the observations within each group, tell us whether the observations need to be transformed, alert us to outliers, and give us a quick summary of the main features of the data. They should be part of any data analysis.

Exercises 7.1

7.1-1   In a one-factor experiment with four treatments, the following results were obtained:

Treatment	n_i	$\bar{y}_i$	s_i^2
1	20	40.2	900
2	20	38.6	800
3	18	43.5	960
4	18	50.0	720

Construct the ANOVA table and test whether there are differences among the treatment means (use $\alpha = 0.05$).

7.1-2   The female cuckoo lays her eggs into the nest of foster parents. The foster parents are usually deceived, probably because of the similarity of sizes of the eggs. Latter investigated this possible explanation and measured the lengths of cuckoo eggs (in millimeters) that were found in the nests of the following three species.

Hedge sparrow: 22.0 23.9 20.9 23.8 25.0
24.0 21.7 23.8 22.8 23.1
23.1 23.5 23.0 23.0

Robin: 21.8 23.0 23.3 22.4 23.0
23.0 23.0 22.4 23.9 22.3
22.0 22.6 22.0 22.1 21.1
23.0

Wren: 19.8 22.1 21.5 20.9 22.0
21.0 22.3 21.0 20.3 20.9
22.0 20.0 20.8 21.2 21.0

$$s^2 = \frac{1}{n-1} \sum_{i=1}^{n} (x_i - \bar{x})^2$$

Display the information in appropriate graphs. Construct an ANOVA table. Is there a difference in the mean lengths? Investigate.
[O. H. Latter, "The Cuckoo's Egg," *Biometrika*, 1: 164–176 (1901).]

7.1-3 Montgomery discusses a case in which the tensile strength of a synthetic fiber used to make cloth for men's shirts is of interest to a manufacturer. It is suspected that the strength is affected by the percentage of cotton in the fiber. Five levels of cotton percentage are considered, and five observations are taken at each level. The 25 experiments are run in random order.

Percentage of Cotton	Tensile Strength (pounds per square inch)				
15	7	7	15	11	9
20	12	17	12	18	18
25	14	18	18	19	19
30	19	25	22	19	23
35	7	10	11	15	11

(a) Are there differences in the mean breaking strengths due to the percentage of cotton used? Make comparative dot diagrams and construct the ANOVA table.
(b) Plot the treatment averages against percentage of cotton and interpret your findings.
[D. C. Montgomery, *Design and Analysis of Experiments*, 2nd ed. (New York: Wiley, 1984), p. 51.]

7.1-4 An operator of a feed lot wants to compare the effectiveness of three different cattle feed supplements. He selects a random sample of 15 one-year-old heifers from his lot of over 1000 and divides them into three groups at random. Each group gets a different feed supplement. Upon noting that one heifer in group A was lost due to an accident, the gains in weight over a 6-month period were as follows:

Group	Weight Gain (pounds)				
A	500	650	530	680	
B	700	620	780	830	860
C	500	520	400	580	410

(a) Are there differences in the mean weight gains due to the three different feed supplements?

(b) If you could start the experiment over, can you suggest improvements in the design of this experiment that could help to make the conclusions more precise? For example, would a blocking arrangement on initial weight be helpful?

7.1-5 Three workers with different experience manufacture brakewheels for a magnet brake. Worker A has four years' experience, worker B has seven years, and worker C has one year. The company is concerned about product quality, which is measured by the difference between the specified diameter and the actual diameter of the brakewheel. On a given day the supervisor selects at random nine brakewheels from the output of each worker. The following table lists the differences between specified and actual diameter.

Worker	Precision (1/100 inch)								
A	2	3	2.3	3.5	3	2	4	4.5	3
B	1.5	3	4.5	3	3	2	2.5	1	2
C	2.5	3	2	2.5	1.5	2.5	2.5	3	3.5

Are there statistically significant differences in quality among the three different workers?

7.1-6 In an experiment to compare different arithmetic teaching methods, 45 students were randomly divided into five equal-sized groups. Two groups were taught by the current method, while the other three were taught by one of three new methods. At the end each student took a standardized test, with the following results:

Group A:	17	14	24	20	24	23	16	15	14
Group B:	21	23	13	19	13	19	20	21	16
Group C:	28	30	29	24	27	30	28	28	23
Group D:	19	28	26	26	19	24	24	23	22
Group E:	21	14	13	19	15	15	10	18	20

Analyze the data. Note that the first step of any data analysis should be a summary and graphical representation of the information. Calculate the group means, medians, quartiles, interquartile ranges, and standard deviations, and then construct comparative box-and-whisker displays. What can you conclude from these displays?

The students are allocated to the five groups at random. Thus it is appropriate to conduct statistical inferences, such as tests of hypotheses. Go ahead and make your test. Discuss whether the conclusion from the ANOVA table gives you more, or less, or different information than the comparative box-and-whisker display.

Is it always true that a statistically significant difference is also of practical importance? Discuss.
[G. B. Wetherill, *Elementary Statistical Methods*, 3rd ed. (London: Methuen, 1982).]

7.1-7 Show that the model $Y_{ij} = \mu_i + \varepsilon_{ij}$, where $i = 1, 2, \ldots, k$ and $j = 1, 2, \ldots, n_i$, can also be written as $Y_{ij} = \mu + \tau_i + \varepsilon_{ij}$, where $\mu = (\sum_{i=1}^{k} n_i \mu_i)/N$ is a weighted average of the treatment means, $\tau_i = \mu_i - \mu$ are the treatment effects, and $\sum_{i=1}^{k} n_i \tau_i = 0$.

7.1-8 Use the representation in Exercise 7.1-7 and show that

$$E(\mathrm{MS_{Treatment}}) = \sigma^2 + \frac{1}{k-1} \sum_{i=1}^{k} n_i \tau_i^2.$$

The following hints should help the mathematically interested reader to derive this result.

(a) Use the definition of $\mathrm{SS_{Treatment}}$ to show that

$$E(\mathrm{SS_{Treatment}}) = \sum_{i=1}^{k} n_i E[(\bar{Y}_i - \bar{Y})^2].$$

(b) Show that

$$\bar{Y}_i - \bar{Y} = \sum_{j=1}^{n_i} \left(\frac{1}{n_i} - \frac{1}{N} \right) Y_{ij} + \sum_{h \neq i} \sum_{j=1}^{n_h} \left(-\frac{1}{N} \right) Y_{hj}.$$

(c) Show that $E(\bar{Y}_i - \bar{Y}) = \tau_i$ and

$$\mathrm{var}(\bar{Y}_i - \bar{Y}) = \sigma^2 \left[\frac{1}{N^2} (N - n_i) + n_i \left(\frac{1}{n_i} - \frac{1}{N} \right)^2 \right]$$

$$= \frac{(N - n_i)\sigma^2}{Nn}.$$

(d) Use the fact that for any random variable W, with finite variance, $E(W^2) = \mathrm{var}(W) + [E(W)]^2$ to obtain $E[(\bar{Y}_i - \bar{Y})^2]$. Substitute this result into part (a) and obtain

$$E(\mathrm{MS_{Treatment}}) = \frac{E(\mathrm{SS_{Treatment}})}{k-1}.$$

7.1-9 Prove the calculation formula for $\mathrm{SS_{Treatment}}$.

7.2   Other Inferences in One-Factor Experiments

Once we have concluded that the treatment means are not the same by rejecting the hypothesis of their equality, we must investigate how they differ. For instance, in Example 7.1-1, are the means different because the deflection of steel beams (group A) is larger than the deflection of beams made of alloys (B, C), which have similar deflection, or are there differences among all three means?

G. E. P. Box, W. G. Hunter, and J. S. Hunter in *Statistics for Experimenters* (New York: Wiley, 1978) describe a graphical procedure that is very useful in visually assessing the differences among k treatments. Their procedure involves plots of the treatment means together with that of a certain reference distribution. Let us assume that the sample sizes are the same, that is, $n_1 = n_2 = \cdots = n_k = n$. If the sample sizes are almost the same, we can set $n = \sum_{i=1}^{k} n_i/k$. Now if the k treatments had all the same mean μ, the sampling distribution of the treatment means $\bar{Y}_i$ would be normal with mean μ and variance σ^2/n. Replacing σ^2 by its estimate $\mathrm{MS_{Error}}$ from the ANOVA table, we find that $(\bar{Y}_i - \mu)/(\sqrt{\mathrm{MS_{Error}}/n})$ has a t-distribution with $N - k$ degrees of freedom. Thus we can approximate the distribution of treatment means by a scaled

t-distribution that is centered around μ. It is called "scaled" because we have to stretch the axes by the estimate of the standard deviation, $\sqrt{MS_{Error}/n}$. Box, Hunter, and Hunter refer to this distribution as the approximate *reference distribution* of the treatment averages $\bar{Y}_i$. Given the appropriate tables for the probability density function of a t-distribution, we could graph this density directly. However, in the absence of such tables (note that Table C.6 gives only selected percentage points, not the p.d.f.), we can proceed as follows.

Determine the upper $\alpha = 0.05$ percentage point of the t-distribution with $N - k$ degrees of freedom. Then the 5th and 95th percentiles of the reference distribution for $\bar{Y}_i$ are given by $\mu - t(0.05; N - k)\sqrt{MS_{Error}/n}$ and $\mu + t(0.05; N - k)\sqrt{MS_{Error}/n}$; for the moment, assume that μ is an arbitrary constant. In Example 7.1-1, $N - k = 17$, $t(0.05; 17) = 1.74$, $n = 20/3 = 6.67$, and $MS_{Error} = 6.0$; thus the percentiles are $\mu \pm (1.74)\sqrt{6.0/6.67}$ or $\mu \pm 1.65$, and the probability that the treatment average $\bar{Y}_i$ falls outside these limits should be about 10 percent. Of course, the density of the t-distribution reaches its maximum at μ, and the ordinate of the density at μ is approximately four to five times larger than the ordinate at the 5th and 95th percentile. For example, this factor is 4.8 for a t-distribution with 10 degrees of freedom, 4.3 for 20 degrees of freedom, 4.1 for 30 degrees of freedom, and 3.9 for the normal distribution. We can use this information to construct a reference distribution. In our example in Figure 7.2-1, we have *arbitrarily* centered the distribution at $\mu = 78$. If the ordinates at the 5th and 95th percentiles are one unit, the ordinate of the density at $\mu = 78$ is approximately 4.3, because $N - k = 17$ is reasonably close to 20. Since the shape of the p.d.f. of the t-distribution is similar to that of the normal distribution but with thicker tails, it is reasonable to draw an approximate bell-shaped curve through these three points to approximate that t-density.

Imagine sliding the reference distribution along the horizontal axis. Note that in our example there is no place to center the distribution so that the three treatment averages appear to be typical randomly selected realizations from this reference distribution. Figure 7.2-1 provides evidence that the three treatment means are not the same. This is the graphical equivalent of what was formally shown by the significant F-statistic. In addition, the reference

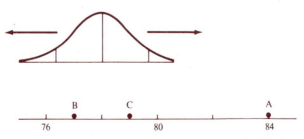

FIGURE 7.2-1 Three treatment averages and their reference distribution.

distribution shows that although μ_A (the mean deflection of steel beams) is probably larger than μ_B and μ_C, the data do not permit us to distinguish between deflection means, μ_B and μ_C, of the beams made of alloys.

7.2-1 Confidence Intervals for a Particular Difference

Let us assume that we want to obtain a confidence interval for the difference of the means of two particular *preselected* treatments, say treatments r and s. An estimate of $\mu_r - \mu_s$ is given by the difference of the respective sample means $\bar{Y}_r - \bar{Y}_s$. The variance of this difference of independent averages is given by

$$\text{var}(\bar{Y}_r - \bar{Y}_s) = \text{var}(\bar{Y}_r) + \text{var}(\bar{Y}_s) = \sigma^2\left(\frac{1}{n_r} + \frac{1}{n_s}\right),$$

which is estimated by

$$\text{MS}_{\text{Error}}\left(\frac{1}{n_r} + \frac{1}{n_s}\right).$$

Thus a $100(1 - \alpha)$ percent confidence interval for $\mu_r - \mu_s$ is given by

$$(\bar{Y}_r - \bar{Y}_s) \pm t(\alpha/2; v)\sqrt{\text{MS}_{\text{Error}}}\sqrt{\frac{1}{n_r} + \frac{1}{n_s}},$$

where $v = N - k$ are the degrees of freedom that are associated with MS_{Error}.

Example 7.2-1 Assume that prior to running the experiment, the engineer has decided to compare the deflection means of the two alloy beams (B, C). A 95 percent confidence interval for $\mu_C - \mu_B$ is given by

$$(79 - 77) \pm (2.11)\sqrt{6.0}\sqrt{\frac{1}{6} + \frac{1}{6}},$$

or $(-0.98 \leq \mu_C - \mu_B \leq 4.98)$. Since this interval includes zero, we cannot conclude from this limited amount of data that the deflection means of the two alloy beams are different. ■

7.2-2 Tukey's Multiple Comparison Procedure

The preceding interval controls the significance level of *one particular* preselected comparison. However, if there are k treatments, we can make many possible paired comparisons; as a matter of fact, there are $\binom{k}{2} = k(k - 1)/2$ of them. If α is the probability of error for one particular comparison, the probability of making at least one error in $k(k - 1)/2$ comparisons will be much larger than α. For example, assume that there are only two comparisons, each at the α level, and that the error in the first comparison is independent of the one in the second. Then the probability of making at least one error (which is the complement of making no error in both) is given by $1 - (1 - \alpha)^2 = \alpha(2 - \alpha)$, which, for small α, is almost twice as large as α. Therefore, if we want a $100(1 - \alpha)$ percent confidence statement for *all possible paired comparisons*, we must make the intervals much wider than the ones for individual differences of two means.

This is exactly what is done in Tukey's multiple comparison procedure. There the confidence intervals for $\mu_r - \mu_s$ are calculated from

$$(\bar{Y}_r - \bar{Y}_s) \pm \frac{q(\alpha; k, v)}{\sqrt{2}} \sqrt{MS_{Error}} \sqrt{\frac{1}{n_r} + \frac{1}{n_s}},$$

where $q(\alpha; k, v)$ is the $100(1 - \alpha)$ percentile of the *Studentized range* distribution for comparing k means with $v = N - k$ degrees of freedom for the mean square error. A table of upper percentage points of the Studentized range distribution is given in Table C.8. Since, for $k > 2$, $q(\alpha; k, v)/\sqrt{2} > t(\alpha/2; v)$, these intervals will always be wider than the confidence intervals that use the t-distribution. We should point out that, strictly speaking, this procedure is valid only for equal sample sizes. However, it is a good approximation if the n_i are not too different.

Example 7.2-2   In Example 7.1-1 we studied the differences among the deflection means of three types of beams. In this case there are a total of $(3)(2)/2 = 3$ pairwise comparisons, those associated with $\mu_A - \mu_B$, $\mu_A - \mu_C$, and $\mu_C - \mu_B$. Since $q(0.05; 3, 17) = 3.62$ and $[q(0.05; 3, 17)/\sqrt{2}]\sqrt{MS_{Error}} = 2.56\sqrt{6.0} = 6.27$, Tukey's multiple comparison intervals are

$$(84 - 77) \pm 6.27\sqrt{\frac{1}{8} + \frac{1}{6}} \quad \text{or} \quad 3.61 \le \mu_A - \mu_B \le 10.39,$$

$$(84 - 79) \pm 6.27\sqrt{\frac{1}{8} + \frac{1}{6}} \quad \text{or} \quad 1.61 \le \mu_A - \mu_C \le 8.39,$$

$$(79 - 77) \pm 6.27\sqrt{\frac{1}{6} + \frac{1}{6}} \quad \text{or} \quad -1.62 \le \mu_C - \mu_B \le 5.62.$$

From these multiple comparisons, we conclude that μ_A is probably larger than μ_B and μ_C, but that μ_B and μ_C are not much different. This is the same conclusion that we reached using the technique involving the reference distribution.

7.2-3   Model Checking

The single-factor ANOVA model assumes that the observations are independent and normally distributed with the same variance in each treatment group. The diagnostic checking procedures focus on the *residuals*, $e_{ij} = Y_{ij} - \bar{Y}_i$; these are differences between the observations and their respective group averages. We usually construct a histogram (or a dot diagram) of the residuals to see if the normal assumption is realistic; see Figure 7.2-2(a). One could also make a normal probability plot of the residuals to check whether the plotted observations fall more or less on a straight line; see Section 3.4. To check whether or not the variances in the treatment groups are about the same, we compare the dot diagrams of the residuals from each group in Figure 7.2-2(b). Also, we plot the residuals against their corresponding group averages $\bar{Y}_i$ in Figure 7.2-2(c). The variability should not depend on the level of $\bar{Y}_i$. If it does, this is often an indication that we should consider a transformation of the data. For example, if the variability grows with the level, a transformation such as $\log Y$ or $\sqrt{Y}$ might be appropriate. To check whether the observa-

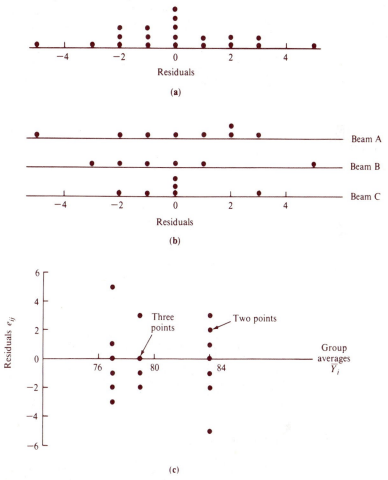

FIGURE 7.2-2   Various residual plots for the data in Example 7.1-1: (a) overall dot diagram of the residuals; (b) plot of residuals for each group separately; (c) plot of residuals against group averages.

tions are independent, we can plot the residuals against the time (run) order in which the experiment was performed. Patterns in the residuals, such as "runs" of positive or negative residuals or patterns with alternating signs, indicate that the errors from measurements taken closely together in time are not independent. Such patterns would occur if there is a carryover effect from one experiment to the next, deterioration in the measurement instrument, or operator fatigue. Such patterns suggest that time (run order) is an important factor and that it should be included as a factor (blocking variable) in our experiment. "Blocking" of experiments is considered in Section 7.3; there it is illustrated that such blocking arrangements will increase the precision of the comparison.

7.2-4   The Random-Effects Model

The one-factor analysis of variance model can also be written as

$$Y_{ij} = \mu + \tau_i + \varepsilon_{ij}, \qquad i = 1, 2, \ldots, k; \quad j = 1, 2, \ldots, n_i;$$

where $\mu = (1/N) \sum_{i=1}^{k} n_i \mu_i$ is the overall mean and where $\tau_i = \mu_i - \mu$, for $i = 1, \ldots, k$, are the treatment effects (see Exercise 7.1-7).

We can distinguish two different situations with respect to the treatment effects. In the first, the treatments are specifically chosen by the experimenter, (e.g., the three different types of beams in Example 7.1-1), and the tests of the hypotheses apply only to these specific factor levels. The conclusions that are reached cannot be extended to other treatments that were not explicitly considered. In this particular model, the treatment effects τ_i are unknown *constants*, and the model is called the *fixed-effects model*; it is the one that we have considered so far in this chapter. We have estimated the unknown fixed treatment means μ_i by $\bar{Y}_i$ and the treatment effects τ_i by $\bar{Y}_i - \bar{Y}$. Also, in the derivation of the result $E(MS_{Treatment}) = \sigma^2 + (\sum_{i=1}^{k} n_i \tau_i^2)/(k-1)$ in Exercise 7.1-8, it was assumed that the τ_i are fixed nonrandom constants.

In the second situation, the population treatment means μ_i, $i = 1, 2, \ldots, k$, can be thought of as a random sample of size k from a larger population of treatment means. As an example, consider the situation in which we investigate differences in yield that are due to various batches of raw material. In this situation we would like to extend the conclusions from our sample of treatments (batches) to all treatments in the population. Here if the k batches are selected at random from many possible batches, the treatment effects τ_i are random variables; thus this model is called the *random-effects model*.

In the random-effects model the observation

$$Y_{ij} = \mu + \tau_i + \varepsilon_{ij}$$

is a sum of two random variables, τ_i and ε_{ij}, and the unknown μ. Let us assume that τ_i and ε_{ij} are independently distributed random variables, with respective normal distributions, $N(0, \sigma_\tau^2)$ and $N(0, \sigma^2)$. This implies that

$\operatorname{var}(Y_{ij}) = \sigma_\tau^2 + \sigma^2$ is the sum of two variance components: One is due to the treatment and the other is due to the error.

In this situation we are not interested in testing the equality of the k randomly chosen treatment means. We are interested in the variability of the treatment effects in general; that is, we want to test $H_0: \sigma_\tau^2 = 0$ against $H_1: \sigma_\tau^2 > 0$. Despite the fact that the random-effects model differs from the fixed-effects model, the analysis of variance for the single-factor experiment is conducted in *identical fashion*. The F-test discussed earlier is also appropriate in this case.

The only difference in the two models appears in the expected mean square due to treatment. In the random-effects model

$$E(\text{MS}_{\text{Treatment}}) = \sigma^2 + \tilde{n}\sigma_\tau^2, \quad \text{where } \tilde{n} = \frac{1}{k-1}\left(N - \frac{\sum n_i^2}{\sum n_i}\right).$$

Here $\tilde{n} = n$ if each sample is the same size n. The entries in the ANOVA table can be used to estimate the variance components. Since $E(\text{MS}_{\text{Error}}) = \sigma^2$, it follows that estimates of the variance components are given by

$$\hat{\sigma}^2 = \text{MS}_{\text{Error}}$$

and

$$\hat{\sigma}_\tau^2 = \frac{1}{\tilde{n}} (\text{MS}_{\text{Treatment}} - \text{MS}_{\text{Error}}).$$

Occasionally, the latter expression may lead to a negative estimate. Since the variance σ_τ^2 is nonnegative, we say that a negative estimate, $\hat{\sigma}_\tau^2$, is evidence that the true variance, σ_τ^2, is indeed zero.

Example 7.2-3   A certain dairy has received several complaints from its customers that its milk tends to spoil prematurely. Milk spoilage is measured by the number of bacteria that are found in milk after it has been stored for 12 days. The dairy receives the raw milk for processing in large truck shipments from farmers in the surrounding area. Thus there is concern that the milk supply may have an important effect on the spoilage of the processed milk. In order to study a possible shipment (batch) effect, the company selects five shipments at random. After processing each batch, six cartons of milk are selected at random and are stored for 12 days. After that time, the bacteria counts (SPC, standard plate counts in units of 100) are made. From considerations that are explained in a later comment, a square-root transformation is made; the square roots of the bateria counts are given in Table 7.2-1.

This is clearly an example of a random-effects model, since the batches are taken from a larger population. The analysis, however, is identical to the one in the fixed-effects model, and the ANOVA table is given in Table 7.2-2. We have used a computer program to calculate the entries in the analysis-of-variance table. If such a program is not available, one can easily calculate

TABLE 7.2-1   Milk Shipment Bacteria Data

Batch	Observations (Square Roots)						Sample Mean
1	24	15	21	27	33	23	23.83
2	14	7	12	17	14	16	13.33
3	11	9	7	13	12	18	11.67
4	7	7	4	7	12	18	9.17
5	19	24	19	15	10	20	17.83

TABLE 7.2-2   ANOVA Table for Bacteria in Milk Shipments

Source	SS	df	MS	F
Treatment	803.0	4	200.8	9.01
Error	557.2	25	22.3	
Total	1360.2	29		

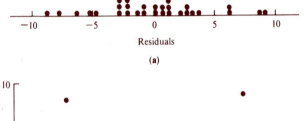

Residuals

(a)

Residuals e_{ij}

Group averages $\bar{Y}_i$

(b)

FIGURE 7.2-3   Various residual plots for the data in Example 7.2-3: (a) overall dot diagram of the residuals; (b) plot of residuals against group averages.

these numbers with a calculator. Since $n_i = n$, the calculation for the treatment sum of squares is simply

$$SS_{Treatment} = \frac{1}{n} \sum_{i=1}^{k} \left(\sum_{j=1}^{n} Y_{ij} \right)^2 - \frac{(\sum_{i=1}^{k} \sum_{j=1}^{n} Y_{ij})^2}{kn}.$$

The F-statistic, $F = 9.01$, is significant at the $\alpha = 0.01$ significance level since it exceeds $F(0.01; 4, 25) = 4.18$. Thus the company can conclude that there is considerable variation from shipment to shipment.

We can estimate the variance components, σ_{τ}^2 and σ^2, from the mean squares in the ANOVA table. The estimates are

$$\hat{\sigma}^2 = MS_{Error} = 22.3,$$

$$\hat{\sigma}_{\tau}^2 = \frac{1}{6}(200.8 - 22.3) = 29.75,$$

because each sample size is $n = 6$, and thus $\tilde{n} = n$.

The adequacy of the fitted model should always be checked before the conclusions from the estimated model are accepted. The residuals $e_{ij} = Y_{ij} - \bar{Y}_i$ are analyzed in Figure 7.2-3. It appears from these plots that the assumptions of the one-factor ANOVA model (normality and equal variances) are reasonably satisfied. ■

Remark   Note that we have analyzed transformed data: that is, $Y = \sqrt{\text{counts}}$. Bacteria counts often follow a Poisson distribution. This implies that groups with higher average counts also have higher variability, because the mean and the variance in the Poisson distribution are the same. This violates two of our assumptions: normality and constant variance. It can be shown that the square root of a Poisson random variable does stabilize the variance and also provides a variable that has an approximate normal distribution. ■

Exercises 7.2

7.2-1 In Exercises 7.1-3 to 7.1-6 we have asked you to construct the ANOVA tables for these one-factor experiments and to test whether the treatment means are different.

(a) Here we ask you to perform the appropriate diagnostic checks. In particular, you should construct overall dot diagrams of the residuals, compare dot diagrams of the residuals for the various treatment groups, and plot residuals against treatment averages.

(b) Also, we ask you to conduct the follow-up tests that are discussed in this section. In particular, plot the treatment averages and their reference distribution and calculate 95 percent confidence intervals that control for all possible paired comparisons.

Remark   There are $k(k-1)/2$ possible comparisons of k treatments. It is often convenient to order the treatment averages from smallest to largest and display the $k(k-1)/2$ treatment differences in the upper triangle of a $k \times k$ table. For example, pairwise differences of the $k = 4$ ordered averages $\bar{Y}_A$, $\bar{Y}_B$, $\bar{Y}_C$, and $\bar{Y}_D$ can be displayed as

$$\bar{Y}_B - \bar{Y}_A, \quad \bar{Y}_C - \bar{Y}_A, \quad \bar{Y}_D - \bar{Y}_A$$
$$\bar{Y}_C - \bar{Y}_B, \quad \bar{Y}_D - \bar{Y}_B$$
$$\bar{Y}_D - \bar{Y}_C.$$

Differences that are significantly different from zero [i.e., greater than $q(\alpha; k, v)\sqrt{MS_{Error}/n}$ if all sample sizes $n_i = n$ are the same] are usually circled. ■

7.2-2 We are interested in the effect of nozzle type on the rate of fluid flow. Three specific nozzle types are under study. Five runs through each of the three nozzle types led to the following results:

Nozzle Type	Rate of Flow (cubic centimeters)				
A	96.6	97.2	96.4	97.4	97.8
B	97.5	96.4	97.0	96.2	96.8
C	97.0	96.0	95.6	95.8	97.0

(a) Test whether the nozzle type has an effect on fluid flow. Use significance level $\alpha = 0.05$.
(b) Plot the treatment averages, together with their reference distribution.
(c) Perform and interpret the results of the appropriate diagnostic checks.

7.2-3 A company is concerned about the level of impurity in its manufactured product. One possible source of impurity is the raw material that is used in the production. To check this hypothesis the company selects six batches of raw material at random. Three products are then selected at random from those that were produced from each batch, and the impurities are counted.

Batch	Impurities		
1	15	20	17
2	12	16	15
3	20	18	14
4	9	10	13
5	12	14	8
6	21	16	19

(a) Is this a random-effects or a fixed-effects model?
(b) Test whether there are differences from batch to batch.
(c) Estimate the variance components.

7.2-4 A large bakery receives its flour in large batches of 50-pound bags. The company suspects that the batches furnished by the supplier differ significantly in weight. To check this suspicion, the company selects four batches at random. Five bags from each batch are weighed, and their weights are recorded as follows:

Batch	Weight $(y - 50)$				
1	0.09	−0.04	−0.08	−0.01	0.00
2	0.01	0.14	−0.04	0.02	−0.01
3	−0.22	−0.10	−0.13	−0.10	−0.11
4	−0.04	−0.02	−0.11	0.06	−0.10

Is the suspicion justified? Discuss.

7.2-5 Consider the aldrin concentrations (or their logarithms if you think that the data should be transformed) in Exercise 1.4-3. Calculate the ANOVA table and test whether the vertical distribution of aldrin in the river is homogeneous. What assumptions did you have to make here? For your analysis to be appropriate, how should the sampling procedure have been carried out? Would your analysis be appropriate if the experiment were conducted over a period of 10 days and the measurements in the 10 rows of the table in Exercise 1.4-3 came from samples that were taken on different days?

7.2-6 A company employs three workers who manufacture brake disks. Being randomly assigned to machines and material, they each make 10 disks. The absolute errors in the actual and specified diameter are recorded (see the summary data given below). Construct the ANOVA table and answer the following questions.
(a) Are there differences among the mean precisions of the three workers ($\alpha = 0.05$)?
(b) Construct a reference distribution for the three averages.
(c) What is the width of the 95 percent confidence interval obtained by Tukey's multiple comparison procedure?

Worker, i	n_i	$\bar{y}_i$	s_i^2
1	10	1.2	3.2
2	10	3.1	2.4
3	10	0.8	2.1

7.2-7   Your job in the quality assurance department at Northstar Steel is to analyze the metallurgic consistency of the production of 1/4-inch steel rods. An item of particular interest is the depletion of carbon, as it is related to the strength of these rods.

Every 30 minutes a rod is picked from the production line and the depletion of carbon is determined. The observations are displayed in a time-sequence plot, and at the end of each week the histogram of the $48 \times 7 = 336$ observations is displayed. The histogram tells us about the variability in our production. Specification limit(s) drawn on this histogram tell whether we are in compliance with customer specifications.

There are many factors that influence the depletion of carbon in the final product. Rods are extruded from billets, and billets are produced in batches (called *heats*). During each heat scrap metal is melted in huge buckets and then poured in forms to produce several billets. The billets from a single heat are sufficient for a 6-hour production of rods. Assume that the first 12 observations in our time-sequence plot come from heat 1, observations 13 to 24 from heat 2, and so on. How can you analyze the data (both graphically as well as analytically) to study whether the production from the same heat is more uniform than the one from different heats?

*7.3   Randomized Complete Block Designs

Suppose that we want to compare a number of treatments, say k of them, on certain experimental units: for example, k plant varieties on certain plots of land, k drugs on certain animals, or k test procedures on certain specimens. In designing efficient experiments, we attempt to control the variability that arises from extraneous sources, and some of this variability may come from differences among the experimental units. For example, not all plots of land, especially if far apart, may be of the same quality, or not all specimens, especially if they are from different batches, may be exactly the same. In a completely randomized experiment, we allocate the experimental units to the k treatments at random. Such an arrangement is successful in spreading fairly the differences of the experimental units among the k treatments. However, these differences do create a larger mean square error in the corresponding one-factor ANOVA table, and thus it is more difficult to detect differences among the treatments.

More precise comparisons can be made by grouping the experimental units into homogeneous blocks such that the units within a given block resemble each other more than they resemble the units in the other blocks. Then the experimental units within each block are assigned to the k treatments at random. For example, a block may consist of k adjacent plots of land, k animals from the same litter, or k specimens from the same batch. Since all k treatments are used within the same block, we can compare treatments on the same block and thus adjust for the variability between blocks.

If every one of the k treatments is represented in each block, we call the arrangement a *complete block design*. *Incomplete* block designs, on the other hand, arise when we are unable to include all k treatments in each block. Such a situation arises, for example, if we compare $k = 4$ different fabrics on a Martindale wear tester possessing the feature that only three different pieces of cloth can be compared in a single run. Here the block size (three) is smaller than the number of treatments (four). As another example, in a comparison of k test procedures, it may be impossible to run all k tests on the same day, which could be considered a block. The analysis of data from incomplete block designs is more difficult and is not considered in this book.

We call the arrangement a *randomized* complete block design because within each block we assign the k treatments to the experimental units at random. For example, within each block of k adjacent plots of land, we use a random mechanism (drawing numbers from a hat or using random numbers) to decide which plant variety is planted on which plot. Note that this is a *restricted* randomization since the blocks impose a constraint on how to allocate the experimental units.

Let us begin with an example taken from a study of compressive strength of concrete. The $k = 3$ treatments correspond to three different drying methods of molded concrete cylinders which are 100 mm in diameter and 200 mm long. Concrete is mixed in batches that are just large enough to produce three cylinders. Although great care is taken to achieve uniformity between batches, one can expect variability from batch to batch.

The experimental units in this example are the molded concrete cylinders. In a completely randomized experiment, with $n = b$ replications for each treatment, we would divide, at random, the $N = kn = kb$ cylinders into k groups and then assign the k treatments to these groups at random. However, a more precise comparison can be achieved by blocking the experiment and assigning, at random, the $k = 3$ cylinders from each batch to the three drying methods. This procedure was followed, and the results of a strength test on $b = 5$ batches are given in Table 7.3-1. For example, the number 49 in row 2 and column 3 represents the compressive strength of a cylinder from batch 3 that was dried according to method B.

In general, the data from a randomized complete block experiment can be represented as in Table 7.3-2. Here Y_{ij}, for $i = 1, 2, \ldots, k$ and $j = 1, 2, \ldots, b$, is

TABLE 7.3-1   Compressive Strength of Concrete (100 pounds per square inch)

Treatment	Batch					Treatment Mean
	1	2	3	4	5	
A	52	47	44	51	42	47.2
B	60	55	49	52	43	51.8
C	56	48	45	44	38	46.2
Batch mean	56	50	46	49	41	48.4

TABLE 7.3-2   Data from a Randomized Complete Block Experiment

Treatment	Block 1	Block 2	$\cdots$	Block j	$\cdots$	Block b	Treatment Mean
1	Y_{11}	Y_{12}	$\cdots$			Y_{1b}	$\bar{Y}_{1\cdot}$
2	Y_{21}	Y_{22}	$\cdots$			Y_{2b}	$\bar{Y}_{2\cdot}$
$\vdots$	$\vdots$	$\vdots$		$\vdots$		$\vdots$	$\vdots$
i	$\cdots$	$\cdots$	$\cdots$	Y_{ij}	$\cdots$	$\cdots$	$\bar{Y}_{i\cdot}$
$\vdots$	$\vdots$	$\vdots$		$\vdots$		$\vdots$	$\vdots$
k	Y_{k1}	Y_{k2}	$\cdots$			Y_{kb}	$\bar{Y}_{k\cdot}$
Block mean	$\bar{Y}_{\cdot 1}$	$\bar{Y}_{\cdot 2}$	$\cdots$	$\bar{Y}_{\cdot j}$	$\cdots$	$\bar{Y}_{\cdot b}$	$\bar{Y}_{\cdot\cdot}$

the observation on the ith treatment in the jth block. The treatment means are given by

$$\bar{Y}_{i\cdot} = \frac{1}{b} Y_{i\cdot} = \frac{1}{b} \sum_{j=1}^{b} Y_{ij},$$

the block means are

$$\bar{Y}_{\cdot j} = \frac{1}{k} Y_{\cdot j} = \frac{1}{k} \sum_{i=1}^{k} Y_{ij},$$

and the grand mean is

$$\bar{Y}_{\cdot\cdot} = \frac{1}{kb} Y_{\cdot\cdot} = \frac{1}{kb} \sum_{i=1}^{k} \sum_{j=1}^{b} Y_{ij}.$$

The dot in the notation for the sums ($Y_{i\cdot}$, $Y_{\cdot j}$, $Y_{\cdot\cdot}$) and the means ($\bar{Y}_{i\cdot}$, $\bar{Y}_{\cdot j}$, $\bar{Y}_{\cdot\cdot}$) indicates the index over which the sum or average is taken.

In the completely randomized one-factor experiment in Sections 7.1 and 7.2 we have written the model that generates the data as $Y_{ij} = \mu_i + \varepsilon_{ij} = \mu + \tau_i + \varepsilon_{ij}$, where $\tau_1, \tau_2, \ldots, \tau_k$, are the treatment effects. Each treatment changes the mean by a certain amount τ_i. In the randomized complete block design we have two factors that may affect the response: (1) the treatments and (2) the blocks. The model

$$Y_{ij} = \mu + \tau_i + \beta_j + \varepsilon_{ij}$$

incorporates both factors: μ is an overall mean; $\tau_1, \tau_2, \ldots, \tau_k$ are the treatment effects; $\beta_1, \beta_2, \ldots, \beta_b$ are the block effects, and the ε_{ij}'s are independent $N(0, \sigma^2)$ random variables. The treatment and block effects may be either fixed or random. If we treat them as fixed, this implies that they are nonrandom deviations from an overall mean that satisfy $\sum_{i=1}^{k} \tau_i = 0$ and $\sum_{j=1}^{b} \beta_j = 0$.

We could also take the treatment and block effects as random. In fact, in many cases in which we block with respect to batches, it would be more reasonable to consider the block effects as random. That is, the β_j are taken to be independent random variables from a $N(0, \sigma_\beta^2)$ distribution. It turns out that our analysis is unchanged if blocks or treatments are random; only the interpretation is different. If the blocks are random, we expect the inferences about the treatments to be the same throughout the population of blocks from which those used in the experiment were randomly selected.

It should also be emphasized that this model assumes that the treatment and block effects are *additive*. This means that if block j leads to an increase of $\beta_j = 5$ units in the response, and treatment i to an increase of $\tau_i = 2$ units, then the combined effect is $5 + 2 = 7$. Also, this model implies that the increase of $\beta_j = 5$ units in block j is the same for all treatments, and similarly the increase $\tau_i = 2$ for treatment i is the same for all blocks. Although this additive model is often adequate, there may be cases where it should not be used. The effect of treatment i may, in fact, depend on block j. The specific conditions in a specific block (batch) may make a certain treatment completely ineffective. Then we say that there are *interactions* between blocks and treatments. Later, in our discussion of model diagnostics, we will check whether an additive model structure is appropriate.

7.3-1　Estimation of Parameters and ANOVA

The estimate of the overall mean μ is given by the grand mean

$$\bar{Y}_{..} = \frac{1}{kb} \sum_{i=1}^{k} \sum_{j=1}^{b} Y_{ij}.$$

The estimate of the treatment effect τ_i is given by $\bar{Y}_{i.} - \bar{Y}_{..}$, the difference of the ith treatment mean from the grand mean. The estimate of the block effect β_j is $\bar{Y}_{.j} - \bar{Y}_{..}$, the difference of the jth block mean from the grand mean. Accordingly, an approximation of the error $\varepsilon_{ij} = Y_{ij} - (\mu + \tau_i + \beta_j)$ is given by the residual

$$e_{ij} = Y_{ij} - [\bar{Y}_{..} + (\bar{Y}_{i.} - \bar{Y}_{..}) + (\bar{Y}_{.j} - \bar{Y}_{..})] = Y_{ij} - \bar{Y}_{i.} - \bar{Y}_{.j} + \bar{Y}_{..}.$$

The residual represents the component of Y_{ij} that is left over after allowing for the overall mean and the treatment and block effects.

Associated with the model decomposition

$$Y_{ij} = \mu + \tau_i + \beta_j + \varepsilon_{ij}$$

we find a corresponding data decomposition,

$$Y_{ij} = \bar{Y}_{..} + (\bar{Y}_{i.} - \bar{Y}_{..}) + (\bar{Y}_{.j} - \bar{Y}_{..}) + (Y_{ij} - \bar{Y}_{i.} - \bar{Y}_{.j} + \bar{Y}_{..}).$$

A corresponding decomposition of the total sum of squares is

$$\text{SSTO} = \sum_{i=1}^{k} \sum_{j=1}^{b} (Y_{ij} - \bar{Y}..)^2$$

$$= \sum_{i=1}^{k} \sum_{j=1}^{b} [(\bar{Y}_{i\cdot} - \bar{Y}..) + (\bar{Y}_{\cdot j} - \bar{Y}..) + (Y_{ij} - \bar{Y}_{i\cdot} - \bar{Y}_{\cdot j} + \bar{Y}..)]^2$$

$$= b \sum_{i=1}^{k} (\bar{Y}_{i\cdot} - \bar{Y}..)^2 + k \sum_{j=1}^{b} (\bar{Y}_{\cdot j} - \bar{Y}..)^2 + \sum_{i=1}^{k} \sum_{j=1}^{b} (Y_{ij} - \bar{Y}_{i\cdot} - \bar{Y}_{\cdot j} + \bar{Y}..)^2$$

$$= \text{SS}_{\text{Treatment}} \qquad + \text{SS}_{\text{Block}} \qquad + \text{SS}_{\text{Error}} .$$

The cross-product terms resulting from the squaring of the trinomial,

$$2 \sum_i \sum_j (\bar{Y}_{i\cdot} - \bar{Y}..)(\bar{Y}_{\cdot j} - \bar{Y}..), \qquad 2 \sum_i \sum_j (\bar{Y}_{i\cdot} - \bar{Y}..)(Y_{ij} - \bar{Y}_{i\cdot} - \bar{Y}_{\cdot j} + \bar{Y}..),$$

and

$$2 \sum_i \sum_j (\bar{Y}_{\cdot j} - \bar{Y}..)(Y_{ij} - \bar{Y}_{i\cdot} - \bar{Y}_{\cdot j} + \bar{Y}..),$$

are all equal to zero (see Exercise 7.3-7).

The sum of squares due to treatment, $\text{SS}_{\text{Treatment}}$, measures the variation among the k treatment means. The sum of squares due to block, SS_{Block}, measures the variation among the b block means. The sum of squares due to error, SS_{Error}, measures the variability in the residuals.

Equivalent computational formulas for the total, the treatment, the block, and the error sum of squares are

$$\text{SSTO} = \sum_i \sum_j (Y_{ij} - \bar{Y}..)^2 = \sum_i \sum_j Y_{ij}^2 - \frac{(Y..)^2}{kb}, \qquad 10126.4$$

$$\text{SS}_{\text{Treatment}} = b \sum_{i=1}^{k} (\bar{Y}_{i\cdot} - \bar{Y}..)^2 = \frac{1}{b} \sum_{i=1}^{k} (Y_{i\cdot})^2 - \frac{(Y..)^2}{kb}, \qquad b^2$$

$$\text{SS}_{\text{Block}} = k \sum_{j=1}^{b} (\bar{Y}_{\cdot j} - \bar{Y}..)^2 = \frac{1}{k} \sum_{j=1}^{b} (Y_{\cdot j})^2 - \frac{(Y..)^2}{kb},$$

$$\text{SS}_{\text{Error}} = \text{SSTO} - \text{SS}_{\text{Treatment}} - \text{SS}_{\text{Block}},$$

respectively. One component can always be found from the other three.

Since the $N = kb$ components in SSTO satisfy one restriction, namely that $\sum_i \sum_j (Y_{ij} - \bar{Y}..) = 0$, the total sum of squares component has $kb - 1$ degrees of freedom. The k components in $\text{SS}_{\text{Treatment}}$ add to zero, that is, $\sum_{i=1}^{k} (\bar{Y}_{i\cdot} - \bar{Y}..) = 0$; thus $\text{SS}_{\text{Treatment}}$ has $k - 1$ degrees of freedom. Similarly, SS_{Block} has $b - 1$ degrees of freedom. SS_{Error} is the sum of squares of kb residuals. It is easy to show [see Exercise 7.3-7(a)] that

$$\sum_{i=1}^{k} e_{ij} = 0, \quad j = 1, 2, \ldots, b \qquad \text{and} \qquad \sum_{j=1}^{b} e_{ij} = 0, \quad i = 1, \ldots, k.$$

TABLE 7.3-3   ANOVA for Data from a Randomized Complete Block Design

Source	SS	df	MS	F
Treatment	$SS_{Treatment}$	$k-1$	$MS_{Treatment} = SS_{Treatment}/(k-1)$	$MS_{Treatment}/MS_{Error}$
Block	SS_{Block}	$b-1$	$MS_{Block} = SS_{Block}/(b-1)$	MS_{Block}/MS_{Error}
Error	SS_{Error}	$(k-1)(b-1)$	$MS_{Error} = SS_{Error}/(k-1)(b-1)$	
Total	SSTO	$kb-1$		

Thus we can regard the residuals as entries in a kb table, where each row and column adds to zero. With these restrictions we need only $(k-1)(b-1)$ entries to specify the table completely. Thus the error sum of squares has $(k-1)(b-1)$ degrees of freedom.

Corresponding to the sum-of-squares decomposition

$$SSTO = SS_{Treatment} + SS_{Block} + SS_{Error},$$

we observe the corresponding decomposition of the degrees of freedom

$$kb - 1 = (k-1) + (b-1) + (k-1)(b-1).$$

This information is written in form of the ANOVA table, Table 7.3-3. The MS column in this table lists the mean squares; these are the sums of squares divided by their corresponding degrees of freedom. The F column is explained in the following section.

7.3-2   Expected Mean Squares and Tests of Hypotheses

Before the observations are actually taken, $Y_{ij} = \mu + \tau_i + \beta_j + \varepsilon_{ij}$ and hence the mean squares are random variables. Therefore, it is appropriate to investigate the distribution and the expected values of these random variables.

The residuals $e_{ij} = Y_{ij} - \bar{Y}_{i\cdot} - \bar{Y}_{\cdot j} + \bar{Y}_{\cdot\cdot}$ correspond to the errors ε_{ij}. The mean square error is an unbiased estimator of σ^2; that is, $E(MS_{Error}) = \sigma^2$. Since the residuals are adjusted for possible treatment and/or block effects, this is true whether or not there are treatment or block effects present. One can also show, in the fixed-effects model, that

$$E(MS_{Treatment}) = \sigma^2 + b\frac{\sum_{i=1}^{k} \tau_i^2}{k-1}$$

and

$$E(MS_{Block}) = \sigma^2 + k\frac{\sum_{j=1}^{b} \beta_j^2}{b-1}.$$

Our main interest is in testing whether there are *treatment effects*. The objective is to test the null hypothesis $H_0: \tau_1 = \tau_2 = \cdots = \tau_k = 0$ against the alternative H_1: at least one τ_i, for $i = 1, \ldots, k$, is different from zero. Under H_0, both $MS_{Treatment}$ and MS_{Error} are unbiased estimates of σ^2, and their ratio should vary around 1. Moreover, we can show that under H_0, the sampling distribution of $F_{Treatment} = MS_{Treatment}/MS_{Error}$ is an F-distribution with $k - 1$ and $(k - 1)(b - 1)$ degrees of freedom. Under H_1, this F-statistic tends to be larger than what can be expected under H_0. If $F_{Treatment}$ is an observed value of this F-statistic, the

$$p \text{ value} = P[F(k - 1, (k - 1)(b - 1)) \geq F_{Treatment}]$$

expresses how likely it is that an observed F value of at least this size occurs by chance. If it is smaller than a chosen significance level α, we conclude that there are differences among treatments. Many computer packages calculate the probability value. If this value is not given, we choose a significance level α and use the upper percentage point $F(\alpha; k - 1, (k - 1)(b - 1))$ as the critical value. If $F_{Treatment}$ is greater than or equal to this value, we conclude, at significance level α, that the treatment means are different.

Usually, the treatment comparisons are of primary interest. Blocks are chiefly the means of reducing the experimental error, and often we are not really interested in testing for their effects. In some instances, however, it may be of interest to test for block effects because if there are no differences, blocking may not be necessary in future experiments. From the expected mean squares, we find that the hypothesis $H_0: \beta_1 = \beta_2 = \cdots = \beta_b = 0$ may be tested by comparing $F_{Block} = MS_{Block}/MS_{Error}$ to $F(\alpha; (b - 1), (k - 1)(b - 1))$. Note that the degrees of freedom in the appropriate F-distributions are easy to remember because they correspond to those in the numerator and denominator in these F-ratios.

Example 7.3-1   For the data in Table 7.3-1, we find that $\sum_i \sum_j y_{ij}^2 = 35{,}638$, $\sum_i \sum_j y_{ij} = 726$, and thus $SSTO = 35{,}638 - (726)^2/15 = 499.6$. Also, $y_1. = 236$, $y_2. = 259$, $y_3. = 231$, and

$$SS_{Treatment} = \frac{1}{5}(236^2 + 259^2 + 231^2) - \frac{(726)^2}{15} = 89.2.$$

In addition, $y._1 = 168$, $y._2 = 150$, $y._3 = 138$, $y._4 = 147$, $y._5 = 123$, and

$$SS_{Block} = \frac{1}{3}(168^2 + 150^2 + 138^2 + 147^2 + 123^2) - \frac{(726)^2}{15} = 363.6.$$

Of course, $SS_{Error} = 499.6 - 89.2 - 363.6 = 46.8$. This leads to the following ANOVA table:

Source	SS	df	MS	F
Treatment	89.2	2	44.6	7.62
Block	363.6	4	90.9	15.54
Error	46.8	8	5.85	
Total	499.6	14		

The fact that $F_{\text{Treatment}} = 7.62$ indicates that there are differences among the treatment means. The probability value $P[F(2, 8) \geq 7.62] \cong 0.02$ is quite small and the observed differences among the treatment averages cannot easily be explained as a chance result. ■

7.3-3   Increased Efficiency by Blocking

Of the sum of squares that is not accounted for by the treatments, $499.6 - 89.2 = 410.4$, the major part (363.6 or 89 percent) is due to the differences among the blocks. Thus, if we had run a completely randomized experiment, obtained the same observations, and analyzed the data according to a one-factor analysis of variance, then the batch variability would have increased the mean square error. That is, that design would not have been as sensitive as the randomized complete block design. In fact, the MS_{Error} from the one-factor ANOVA would have been $(363.6 + 46.8)/(4 + 8) = 34.2$, and the resulting F-statistic for testing treatment effects, $44.6/34.2 = 1.30$, would have been insignificant.

This example demonstrates the advantage of blocking if we suspect variability among the experimental units and are able to group the units into homogeneous blocks. On the other hand, if blocking is not needed and if we had run the experiment according to a completely randomized design with $n = b$ replicates, then the degrees of freedom for the error sum of squares would have been $k(b - 1)$. This is larger than $(k - 1)(b - 1)$ in the randomized complete block design. Blocking, when not needed, has cost us $b - 1$ degrees of freedom for error and has made the analysis less sensitive to detecting differences. Usually, however, the gains from blocking outweigh the small loss in degrees of freedom, and one should as a rule block whatever is reasonably possible.

7.3-4   Follow-Up Tests

A large value of $F_{\text{Treatment}}$ provides evidence that the treatment means are different. To study how they differ, it is useful to display the treatment means, which are averages of b observations, together with their reference distribution. This is done in Figure 7.3-1. The reference distribution for the treatment

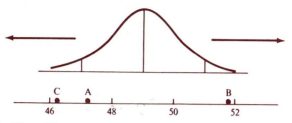

FIGURE 7.3-1   Plot of the treatment averages and their reference distribution.

means $\bar{Y}_{i\cdot}$ is given by a scaled t-distribution with $\nu = (k-1)(b-1) = 8$ degrees of freedom, scaled by the factor $\sqrt{MS_{Error}/b} = \sqrt{5.85/5} = 1.08$. In Figure 7.3-1 we have centered, arbitrarily, the reference distribution at 49. Since the 95th percentile of the $t(8)$ distribution is $t(0.05; 8) = 1.86$, 10 percent of the probability of the reference distribution is outside $49 \pm (1.86)(1.08)$, that is, 49 ± 2.01. We have marked a unit ordinate at these points. The ordinate at the mean 49 is approximately five times higher. The graph of a "t-like" distribution through these three points yields the reference distribution, given in Figure 7.3-1. Although making such a plot is certainly not an "exact" approach, it provides a good approximation. The reference distribution confirms the conclusion of the F-test. It is difficult to center the reference distribution to make the treatment means seem to be a typical sample from that distribution. It also illustrates that μ_A and μ_C are most likely the same, but that μ_B is different from both.

A more formal multiple comparison can be made with Tukey's paired-comparison procedure. The $100(1-\alpha)$ percent confidence intervals for differences in treatment means that take account of all possible pairwise comparisons are given by

$$(\bar{Y}_{r\cdot} - \bar{Y}_{s\cdot}) \pm \frac{q(\alpha; k, \nu)}{\sqrt{2}} \sqrt{MS_{Error}} \sqrt{\frac{2}{b}},$$

where $q(\alpha; k, \nu)$ is the upper 100α percentage point of the Studentized range distribution. In our case, $q(0.05; 3, 8) = 4.04$, and $(4.04/\sqrt{2})\sqrt{5.85}\sqrt{2/5} = 4.37$. Thus 95 percent confidence intervals for the treatment differences are

$$\mu_A - \mu_C: \quad 1.0 \pm 4.37$$

$$\mu_B - \mu_A: \quad 4.6 \pm 4.37$$

$$\mu_B - \mu_C: \quad 5.6 \pm 4.37$$

This confirms the conclusions that we have drawn from the reference distribution in Figure 7.3-1; the intervals for $\mu_B - \mu_A$ and $\mu_B - \mu_C$ do not include zero.

We could also construct a reference distribution for the block means, which is a scaled $t[(k-1)(b-1)]$ distribution with scale $\sqrt{MS_{Error}/k}$. However, inferences on block differences are usually not of major importance.

7.3-5   Diagnostic Checking

Before we accept the results of statistical tests, we should *always* convince ourselves that the assumptions on which those tests are based are actually satisfied. Violations of model assumptions will often invalidate the test results.

The diagnostic checks in the randomized complete block arrangement follow closely the ones for the completely randomized experiment. We check the

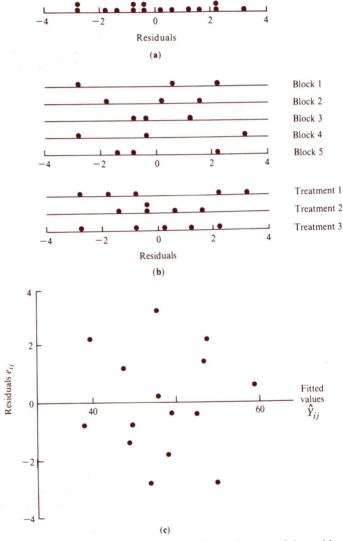

FIGURE 7.3-2   Various residual plots: (a) overall dot diagram of the residuals; (b) dot diagrams of the residuals by block and treatment; (c) plot of residuals against fitted values.

residuals $e_{ij} = Y_{ij} - \bar{Y}_{i\cdot} - \bar{Y}_{\cdot j} + \bar{Y}_{\cdot\cdot}$, which are approximations of the errors, to see if they are about normally distributed. We must also check whether the variability in the various treatment and block groups is roughly the same and whether a plot of residuals against fitted values $\hat{Y}_{ij} = \bar{Y}_{i\cdot} + \bar{Y}_{\cdot j} - \bar{Y}_{\cdot\cdot}$ shows any patterns. We call $\bar{Y}_{i\cdot} + \bar{Y}_{\cdot j} - \bar{Y}_{\cdot\cdot} = \bar{Y}_{\cdot\cdot} + (\bar{Y}_{i\cdot} - \bar{Y}_{\cdot\cdot}) + (\bar{Y}_{\cdot j} - \bar{Y}_{\cdot\cdot})$ the *fitted value* since it represents the estimate of the mean $\mu_{ij} = \mu + \tau_i + \beta_j$ in the ith treatment group and jth block. With $kb = 15$ observations, as in our example in Figure 7.3-2, it is often difficult to check these assumptions completely. For example, it may well be that the variability for the second treatment or the third block is somewhat smaller than for the other groups. However, we want to point out that the visual impression can change quickly by adding or removing a single point. At any rate, in small data sets, we can only hope to spot gross violations of the assumptions. In our example, none can be found.

The plot of residuals against fitted values is of particular interest here since a nonrandom pattern would suggest that the block and treatment effects are not additive. Recall that in our analysis we have assumed that the treatment and block effects in the model $Y_{ij} = \mu_{ij} + \varepsilon_{ij} = \mu + \tau_i + \beta_j + \varepsilon_{ij}$ are additive. However, "interactions" may be present and the magnitude of treatment effects may depend on the particular block; a detailed discussion of interactions is given in Section 8.1. In some cases the model may be nonadditive in the original observations, but additive for a certain transformation of the data. For example, the logarithmic transformation changes the multiplicative model $\mu_{ij} = \mu \tau_i \beta_j$ into an additive one, $\mu_{ij}^* = \mu^* + \tau_i^* + \beta_j^*$. A nonrandom pattern in the plot of e_{ij} against $\hat{Y}_{ij}$, like a curvilinear one, is an indication that the model is not additive and that a transformation should be considered.

Exercises 7.3

7.3-1 Four different fabrics are compared on a Martindale wear tester that can compare four materials in a single run (block). The weightloss (in milligrams) from five runs is measured and the following results are obtained:

	Run (Block)				
Fabric	1	2	3	4	5
A	36	17	30	30	25
B	38	18	39	40	25
C	36	26	41	38	28
D	30	17	34	33	21

(a) Our main interest is in comparing the four fabrics. Calculate the ANOVA table and test whether there are differences among treatment means. Conduct appropriate follow-up tests.
(b) Has the blocking arrangement been useful? Investigate whether there are differences among the block means.
(c) Check the adequacy of the model.
7.3-2 A certain type of film composition resistor used in electronic equipment is mounted on ceramic plates. An investigation was designed to determine the effects of four different geometric shapes on the current noise of these resistors. Four resistors could be mounted on each ceramic plate, and their loca-

tion was randomized. The results, measured in the logarithm of the noise measurement, for six ceramic plates are as follows:

	Plate (Block)					
Shape	1	2	3	4	5	6
A	1.11	1.70	1.60	1.20	1.85	1.50
B	0.95	1.42	1.28	1.05	1.45	1.10
C	1.00	1.45	1.25	1.15	1.55	1.15
D	0.82	1.30	1.10	0.90	1.40	1.10

(a) Estimate the overall mean, the treatment effects, and the block effects.

(b) Calculate the ANOVA table and investigate whether there are treatment differences. Plot the treatment means and construct a reference distribution. Calculate Tukey's 95 percent confidence intervals, which control for all possible pairwise comparisons.

(c) Check the model assumptions.

(d) Has blocking been helpful in making the treatment comparisons more precise?

7.2-3 The plant manager wants to investigate the productivity of three groups of workers: those with little, average, and considerable experience. Since the productivity depends to some degree on the day-to-day variability of the available raw materials, which affects all groups in a similar fashion, the manager suspects that the comparison should be blocked with respect to day. The results from five production days are as follows:

	Day (Block)				
Experience Level	1	2	3	4	5
A	53	58	49	52	60
B	55	57	53	57	64
C	60	62	55	64	69

(a) Are there differences in productivity among the three groups? Investigate how they differ.

(b) Has blocking made a difference? Test whether there are block effects.

(c) Check the model assumptions.

7.3-4 A psychologist studies the effect of background noise on reaction time. Each subject in this study is exposed to three levels of background noise: no noise, classical music, and rock music. At each level, the subject has to perform a variety of tasks and an overall estimate of its reaction time is determined. The particular order of the experiments is randomized for each subject. The results from seven randomly selected subjects are as follows:

	Subject (Block)						
Noise Level	1	2	3	4	5	6	7
A	10	7	14	10	12	15	8
B	10	8	13	8	11	12	9
C	14	10	17	12	14	18	6

(a) Are there differences among the three noise levels? Discuss.

(b) Are there differences among the subjects? Discuss.

(c) Is the additive model $Y_{ij} = \mu + \tau_i + \beta_j + \varepsilon_{ij}$ appropriate? Plot residuals against fitted values.

7.3-5 Consider the aldrin concentrations (or their logarithms if you think that the data should be transformed) in Exercise 1.4-3. Assume that the experiment was conducted over a period of 10 days and suppose that the measurements in each row of the table in Exercise 1.4-3 come from samples that were taken on the same day. Analyze the data and discuss whether the vertical distribution of aldrin in the river is homogeneous.

7.3-6 Grab samples were collected every 10 minutes for a period of 2 hours at six different sampling locations in the lateral transect of a large river. Separated by approximately 120 feet in the lateral direction, the sampling points were 2 miles downstream from a sewage treatment plant. Sodium was chosen as the water-quality variable to assess the spatial variability in the river's cross section. It is easily detected by spectrophotometry. The sampling points (the boats) were on a line that was perpendicular to the west bank; each person in the boat sampled approximately 1.5 feet from the water surface. The absorbances, which are linearly related to the sodium concentrations, are given in the accompanying table. Analyze the data and discuss whether the absorbances vary across the lateral transect of the river.

Time	Location 1	2	3	4	5	6
1	0.266	0.239	0.227	0.230	0.226	0.231
2	0.299	0.277	0.279	0.274	0.273	0.273
3	0.264	0.247	0.238	0.238	0.231	0.237
4	0.273	0.244	0.244	0.246	0.250	0.244
5	0.263	0.237	0.247	0.238	0.243	0.243
6	0.269	0.246	0.241	0.241	0.247	0.252
7	0.256	0.241	0.249	0.253	0.244	0.247
8	0.260	0.241	0.238	0.246	0.246	0.240
9	0.264	0.244	0.237	0.235	0.235	0.224
10	0.253	0.234	0.222	0.231	0.234	0.222
11	0.271	0.246	0.229	0.229	0.236	0.234
12	0.246	0.226	0.234	0.225	0.235	0.241
Distance from west bank (feet)	155	247	347	474	595	820

[T. G. Sanders, *Principles of Network Design for Water Quality Monitoring* (Fort Collins, Colo.: Colorado State University, 1980).]

7.3-7 The residuals are given by $e_{ij} = Y_{ij} - \bar{Y}_{i\cdot} - \bar{Y}_{\cdot j} + \bar{Y}_{\cdot\cdot}$. Show that

(a) $\sum_{j=1}^{b} e_{ij} = 0$ for $i = 1, \ldots, k$ and $\sum_{i=1}^{k} e_{ij} = 0$ for $j = 1, \ldots, b$.

(b) $\sum_i \sum_j (\bar{Y}_{i\cdot} - \bar{Y}_{\cdot\cdot})e_{ij} = \sum_i \sum_j (\bar{Y}_{\cdot j} - \bar{Y}_{\cdot\cdot})e_{ij} = 0$.

(c) $\sum_i \sum_j (\bar{Y}_{i\cdot} - \bar{Y}_{\cdot\cdot})(\bar{Y}_{\cdot j} - \bar{Y}_{\cdot\cdot}) = 0$.

7.3-8 This exercise requires more effort and should be assigned as a project. It makes use of the discussion in Chapters 6 and 7 and the material on data analysis in Chapter 1.

Select a convenient spot along a road and obtain data on traffic flow and traffic mix. For three days (Wednesday, Friday, and Sunday) and four periods (8:00–8:30, 13:00–13:30, 17:00–17:30, 21:00–21:30) obtain data on traffic counts and vehicle mix (trucks/cars; foreign/domestic). Analyze the resulting information.

Specify the relevant operational definitions (e.g., What is a truck? What do you do if you are uncertain whether a vehicle is domestic or foreign made?). Your analysis should discuss differences in traffic volume and vehicle mix for different days and different hours of the day. Display the information graphically. For example, you may want to plot traffic counts against time of day, separately for each day, and overlay the plots. Or, plot them against day, separately for each hour of day. Repeat plots for vehicle mix, displaying appropriate ratios.

Assume that you are interested in traffic volume (mix) for the following week. How confident are you in predicting traffic volume (traffic mix) for next Monday, Tuesday, and Wednesday? Are you more confident about your prediction for Wednesday? Why?

*7.4   Designs with Two Blocking Variables: Latin Squares

In Section 7.3 concerning randomized complete block designs, we discussed how to design a comparison of k treatments that adjusts for the variability introduced by a single blocking variable. Our approach was to assign at random each of the k treatments to each level of the blocking variable. Here we extend this principle to two blocking variables. We design the experiment such that each of the k treatments is assigned to each level of each of the two blocking variables in a very special way.

Let us explain this with a simple illustration. Let us say that we want to compare the yields of $k = 4$ different corn hybrids (A, B, C, and D) from an experiment that is carried out on a plot of land that consists of $4 \times 4 = 16$ subplots (see Table 7.4-1). Since the soil composition, and thus the "fertility," might vary from plot to plot, we can expect that the variability in fertility

TABLE 7.4-1   **Various Blocking Arrangements: Agricultural Experiment**

C	A	C	B
D	A	B	C
A	C	A	D
B	D	B	D

A	C	D	B
B	C	A	D
A	D	C	B
D	C	A	B

B	C	A	D
D	A	C	B
A	D	B	C
C	B	D	A

(a)
Completely
randomized

(b)
One blocking
variable (row)

(c)
Two blocking
variables;
Latin square

might introduce differences among the treatments. To spread this risk evenly among the treatments, one can assign each treatment to four of the 16 subplots at random; this corresponds to the completely randomized arrangement; see Table 7.4-1(a). However, the precision of the comparisons can probably be increased if we block the experiment. In particular, it is reasonable to assume that fertility might vary from row to row. Treating the rows as the levels of our first blocking variable, we can assign the four treatments to the four subplots in each row at random; this is the randomized complete block design in Table 7.4-1(b). However, it is just as reasonable to assume that fertility might vary from column to column. Thus we want an arrangement in which each column also contains all k treatments. Since there are now two blocking variables, rows and columns, we want a design in which each row and each column contains each of the k treatments exactly once. Such arrangements are called *Latin squares*. A Latin square for $k = 4$ is given in Table 7.4-1(c).

7.4-1   Construction and Randomization of Latin Squares

There exist many different Latin square arrangements for a given number of treatments k. For $k = 3$ there are 12 different tables, where each row and each column receives each treatment exactly once. In Table 7.4-2 we have listed three such tables. The first arrangement is called a *standard Latin square*. It is called "standard," since the treatments in the first row and the first column are

TABLE 7.4-2   **Three Possible Latin Squares for $k = 3$ Treatments**

A	B	C
B	C	A
C	A	B

C	B	A
A	C	B
B	A	C

A	C	B
C	B	A
B	A	C

arranged in standard (alphabetical) order. For $k = 4$ treatments there are 576 different Latin squares; for $k = 5$ treatments, there are 161,280. The number of different Latin squares increases rapidly with k.

Under randomization one should select one of these tables at random. As each table has the same chance of being chosen, the risk of uncontrolled factors is spread evenly among the k treatments. Clearly, it is often not feasible to list all possible Latin squares such that one can be selected at random. A different strategy has to be adopted.

It turns out that standard Latin squares can be utilized to achieve the desired randomization. From each standard Latin square we can obtain all other Latin squares by permuting rows as well as columns. In Table 7.4-3 we have listed the standard Latin squares for various values of k. For $k = 3$ there is only one standard Latin square; for $k = 4$ there are four. For $k = 5$ there are 56; however, we have shown only one. It is easy to remember the construction

TABLE 7.4-3   Selected Standard Latin Squares

$k = 3$

A	B	C
B	C	A
C	A	B

$k = 4$

A	B	C	D
B	A	D	C
C	D	B	A
D	C	A	B

A	B	C	D
B	C	D	A
C	D	A	B
D	A	B	C

A	B	C	D
B	D	A	C
C	A	D	B
D	C	B	A

A	B	C	D
B	A	D	C
C	D	A	B
D	C	B	A

$k = 5$

A	B	C	D	E
B	C	D	E	A
C	D	E	A	B
D	E	A	B	C
E	A	B	C	D

$k = 6$

A	B	C	D	E	F
B	C	D	E	F	A
C	D	E	F	A	B
D	E	F	A	B	C
E	F	A	B	C	D
F	A	B	C	D	E

of at least one standard Latin square. From the first row, given in standard order, we generate the entries in the other rows by rearranging the letters; the first letter of a line becomes the last letter in the subsequent one. Such an arrangement is also shown for $k = 6$; however, note that there are many other standard Latin squares which are not shown.

In the randomization for $k = 3$ we start with the single Latin square in Table 7.4-3 and rearrange (permute) the order of the rows and columns. For example, the second square in Table 7.4-2 is obtained after rearranging the rows of the standard Latin square in the order (312) (i.e., the third row becomes the first, the first becomes the second, and the second row becomes the third), and then rearranging the columns of the resulting table in order (132) (i.e., first column stays first, third column becomes second, and second column becomes third).

For $k = 4$ treatments there are four different standard Latin squares. Under our randomization procedure we first select a standard Latin square at random and then randomize the rows and columns. For example, the arrangement in Table 7.4-1(c) is obtained from the fourth standard Latin square in Table 7.4-3 after arranging the rows in order (1324) and the columns in order (2314).

For $k = 5$ treatments there are 56 standard Latin squares, and it is not practical to list and select from these 56 tables one at random. An alternative approach is to start with one particular standard Latin square, such as the one in Table 7.4-3, and then randomize the rows, the columns, and, *in addition*, the letters that characterize the treatments. The randomization of rows and columns was discussed before. The randomization of the treatments tries to make up for the fact that we did not start with a randomly selected standard Latin square. For example, the permutation (31524) means that the previous letter C replaces A, the previous letter A replaces B, and so on. Even though this particular randomization procedure is not based on all possible Latin squares, it is based on a very large subset that is sufficient for our purposes.

7.4-2   Analysis of Data from a Latin Square

In total there are k^2 observations, Y_{ij}, $i = 1, 2, \ldots, k$; $j = 1, 2, \ldots, k$. We can calculate the grand total G, the row totals R_i, the column totals C_j, and the treatment totals T_h, $h = 1, \ldots, k$. Furthermore, we can calculate the corresponding averages, say, $\bar{G}$, $\bar{R}_i$, $\bar{C}_j$, and $\bar{T}_h$. The analysis-of-variance table (Table 7.4-4) partitions the total variation

$$\text{SSTO} = \sum_i \sum_j (Y_{ij} - \bar{G})^2 = \sum_i \sum_j Y_{ij}^2 - \frac{G^2}{k^2}$$

into four components: sums of squares due to treatment, due to rows, due to columns, and due to error.

TABLE 7.4-4   ANOVA Table for the $k \times k$ Latin Square

Source	SS		df	MS
Treatment	$k \sum_{h=1}^{k} (\bar{T}_h - \bar{G})^2$	$= \frac{1}{k} \sum_{h=1}^{k} T_h^2 - \frac{1}{k^2} G^2$	$k-1$	$MS_{Treatment}$
Row	$k \sum_{i=1}^{k} (\bar{R}_i - \bar{G})^2$	$= \frac{1}{k} \sum_{i=1}^{k} R_i^2 - \frac{1}{k^2} G^2$	$k-1$	MS_R
Column	$k \sum_{j=1}^{k} (\bar{C}_j - \bar{G})^2$	$= \frac{1}{k} \sum_{j=1}^{k} C_j^2 - \frac{1}{k^2} G^2$	$k-1$	MS_C
Error	$SSTO - SS_{Treatment} - SS_R - SS_C$		$k^2 - 3k + 2$	MS_{Error}
Total	$\sum_{i=1}^{k} \sum_{j=1}^{k} Y_{ij}^2 - \frac{1}{k^2} G^2$		$k^2 - 1$	

The main interest is usually in testing whether there are significant treatment effects. If $MS_{Treatment}/MS_{Error}$ exceeds the critical value from an F-distribution with $k - 1$ and $k^2 - 1 - 3(k-1) = k^2 - 3k + 2$ degrees of freedom, there is significant evidence against the null hypothesis that there are no treatment differences.

Example 7.4-1   The yields (in bushels per 1/10 of an acre) of the $k = 4$ corn hybrids from our earlier example are given in Table 7.4-5. The row, column, and treatment totals are also given in this table. Calculate the entries of the ANOVA table as an exercise. You will find that the test statistic $MS_{Treatment}/MS_{Error} = (72.5/3)/(10.5/6) = 13.8$. Since this is larger than $F(0.01; 3, 6) = 9.78$, we can conclude that there are differences among the mean yields of the four corn hybrids.   ■

TABLE 7.4-5   Latin Square for $k = 4$ Corn Hybrids

	Columns				Row Total	Treatment Total
Rows	10(A)	14(B)	7(C)	8(D)	39	$T_A = 53$
	7(D)	18(A)	11(B)	8(C)	44	$T_B = 44$
	5(C)	10(D)	11(A)	9(B)	35	$T_C = 30$
	10(B)	10(C)	12(D)	14(A)	46	$T_D = 37$
Column Total	32	52	41	39	164	

Exercises 7.4

7.4-1 Carry out the computati[...]
the Latin square design in Examp[...]
7.4-2 Fisher discusses an expe[...]
compares the root weights of fi[...]
of marigolds. The experiment w[...]
plot of land that was divideɑ[...]
according to five rows and five [...]
ments (varieties A through E) we[...]
to a Latin square arrangement,[...]
results:

	Colum[...]
	376(D) 371(E) 355(C[...]
	316(B) 338(D) 336(E[...]
Rows	326(C) 326(A) 335(B[...]
	317(E) 343(B) 330(A[...]
	321(A) 332(C) 317(D[...]

(a) Construct the ANOVA tabl[...]
there are differences in mean roo[...]
five varieties.
(b) Discuss whether this pɑ[...]
arrangement has increased the pr[...]
parison. That is, suppose that [...]
numbers in a corresponding one[...]

TABLE 8.1-3   Two Examples of Cell Means

Illustration 1

	Factor B			$\bar{\mu}_{i\cdot}$
Factor A	1	2	3	
1	1	2	6	3
2	3	4	8	5
$\bar{\mu}_{\cdot j}$	2	3	7	4

$\alpha_1 = 3 - 4 = -1$ $\beta_1 = 2 - 4 = -2$
$\alpha_2 = 5 - 4 = 1$ $\beta_2 = 3 - 4 = -1$
$\quad$ $\beta_3 = 7 - 4 = 3$

$(\alpha\beta)_{11} = 1 - 3 - 2 + 4 = 0$
$(\alpha\beta)_{12} = 2 - 3 - 3 + 4 = 0$
$(\alpha\beta)_{13} = 6 - 3 - 7 + 4 = 0$

$(\alpha\beta)_{21} = 3 - 5 - 2 + 4 = 0$
$(\alpha\beta)_{22} = 4 - 5 - 3 + 4 = 0$
$(\alpha\beta)_{23} = 8 - 5 - 7 + 4 = 0$

Illustration 2

	Factor B			$\bar{\mu}_{i\cdot}$
Factor A	1	2	3	
1	1	2	6	3
2	5	8	2	5
$\bar{\mu}_{\cdot j}$	3	5	4	4

$\alpha_1 = 3 - 4 = -1$ $\beta_1 = 3 - 4 = -1$
$\alpha_2 = 5 - 4 = 1$ $\beta_2 = 5 - 4 = 1$
$\quad$ $\beta_3 = 4 - 4 = 0$

$(\alpha\beta)_{11} = 1 - 3 - 3 + 4 = -1$
$(\alpha\beta)_{12} = 2 - 3 - 5 + 4 = -2$
$(\alpha\beta)_{13} = 6 - 3 - 4 + 4 = 3$

$(\alpha\beta)_{21} = 5 - 5 - 3 + 4 = 1$
$(\alpha\beta)_{22} = 8 - 5 - 5 + 4 = 2$
$(\alpha\beta)_{23} = 2 - 5 - 4 + 4 = -3$

from level 1 to level 2 of factor A is the same at all levels of factor B, and the two corresponding graphs in Figure 8.1-1 are parallel. In illustration 2 this is not the case. For example, the effect is positive at level 1 of B, but is negative at level 3 of B. The two factors interact and thus the corresponding graphs in Figure 8.1-1 are not parallel.

Our discussion and the definition of row, column, and interaction effects have shown that we can always reparameterize the ab cell means as

$$\mu_{ij} = \bar{\mu}_{\cdot\cdot} + \alpha_i + \beta_j + (\alpha\beta)_{ij}.$$

Substituting this expression into the data-generating model

$$Y_{ijk} = \mu_{ij} + \varepsilon_{ijk}$$

leads to

$$Y_{ijk} = \bar{\mu}_{\cdot\cdot} + \quad \alpha_i \quad + \quad \beta_j \quad + \quad (\alpha\beta)_{ij} \quad + \varepsilon_{ijk}$$
$$= \bar{\mu}_{\cdot\cdot} + (\bar{\mu}_{i\cdot} - \bar{\mu}_{\cdot\cdot}) + (\bar{\mu}_{\cdot j} - \bar{\mu}_{\cdot\cdot}) + (\mu_{ij} - \bar{\mu}_{i\cdot} - \bar{\mu}_{\cdot j} + \bar{\mu}_{\cdot\cdot}) + \varepsilon_{ijk}.$$

The parameters μ_{ij}, and consequently the implied effects α_i, β_j, and $(\alpha\beta)_{ij}$, are unknown and must be estimated from sample data. From the observations in Table 8.1-1 we estimate the means, μ_{ij}, $\bar{\mu}_{i\cdot}$, $\bar{\mu}_{\cdot j}$, and $\bar{\mu}_{\cdot\cdot}$, by the respective sample averages,

$$\bar{Y}_{ij\cdot} = \frac{1}{n} Y_{ij\cdot} = \frac{1}{n} \sum_{k=1}^{n} Y_{ijk},$$

$$\bar{Y}_{i\cdot\cdot} = \frac{1}{bn} Y_{i\cdot\cdot} = \frac{1}{bn} \sum_{j=1}^{b} \sum_{k=1}^{n} Y_{ijk},$$

$$\bar{Y}_{\cdot j \cdot} = \frac{1}{an} Y_{\cdot j \cdot} = \frac{1}{an} \sum_{i=1}^{a} \sum_{k=1}^{n} Y_{ijk},$$

$$\bar{Y}_{\cdots} = \frac{1}{abn} Y_{\cdots} = \frac{1}{abn} \sum_{i=1}^{a} \sum_{j=1}^{b} \sum_{k=1}^{n} Y_{ijk}.$$

Thus the row effects α_i are estimated by $\bar{Y}_{i\cdot\cdot} - \bar{Y}_{\cdots}$, the column effects β_j by $\bar{Y}_{\cdot j \cdot} - \bar{Y}_{\cdots}$, and the interaction effects $(\alpha\beta)_{ij}$ by $\bar{Y}_{ij\cdot} - \bar{Y}_{i\cdot\cdot} - \bar{Y}_{\cdot j\cdot} + \bar{Y}_{\cdots}$. Approximations of the errors ε_{ijk} are given by the residuals $e_{ijk} = Y_{ijk} - \bar{Y}_{ij\cdot}$.

Corresponding to the data-generating model, we observe the data decomposition

$$Y_{ijk} = \bar{Y}_{\cdots} + (\bar{Y}_{i\cdot\cdot} - \bar{Y}_{\cdots}) + (\bar{Y}_{\cdot j\cdot} - \bar{Y}_{\cdots}) + (\bar{Y}_{ij\cdot} - \bar{Y}_{i\cdot\cdot} - \bar{Y}_{\cdot j\cdot} + \bar{Y}_{\cdots}) + (Y_{ijk} - \bar{Y}_{ij\cdot}).$$

The corresponding sum of squares decomposition is

$$\text{SSTO} = \text{SS}_A + \text{SS}_B + \text{SS}_{AB} + \text{SS}_{\text{Error}},$$

where

$$\text{SSTO} = \sum_i \sum_j \sum_k (Y_{ijk} - \bar{Y}_{\cdots})^2 = \sum_i \sum_j \sum_k Y_{ijk}^2 - \frac{(Y_{\cdots})^2}{abn},$$

$$\text{SS}_A = bn \sum_i (\bar{Y}_{i\cdot\cdot} - \bar{Y}_{\cdots})^2 = \frac{1}{bn} \sum_i (Y_{i\cdot\cdot})^2 - \frac{(Y_{\cdots})^2}{abn},$$

$$\text{SS}_B = an \sum_j (\bar{Y}_{\cdot j\cdot} - \bar{Y}_{\cdots})^2 = \frac{1}{an} \sum_j (Y_{\cdot j\cdot})^2 - \frac{(Y_{\cdots})^2}{abn},$$

$$\text{SS}_{AB} = n \sum_i \sum_j (\bar{Y}_{ij\cdot} - \bar{Y}_{i\cdot\cdot} - \bar{Y}_{\cdot j\cdot} + \bar{Y}_{\cdots})^2$$

$$= \frac{1}{n} \sum_i \sum_j (Y_{ij\cdot})^2 - (Y_{\cdots})^2/abn - \text{SS}_A - \text{SS}_B,$$

$$\text{SS}_{\text{Error}} = \sum_i \sum_j \sum_k (Y_{ijk} - \bar{Y}_{ij\cdot})^2 = \text{SSTO} - \text{SS}_A - \text{SS}_B - \text{SS}_{AB},$$

are the respective sums of squares associated with the total, factor A, factor B, interaction, and error. It is easy to show this decomposition. Note that $(Y_{ijk} - \bar{Y}_{\cdots})$ can be written as the sum of four terms. We square the expression of $(Y_{ijk} - \bar{Y}_{\cdots})$ and sum the squares over all replications k ($k = 1, \ldots, n$), levels of factor A ($i = 1, \ldots, a$), and levels of factor B ($j = 1, \ldots, b$). You will notice that all cross-product terms sum to zero. The sums of squares are displayed in the ANOVA table in Table 8.1-4.

A short note on the computation of these sums of squares is in order. Computer programs are usually available to obtain the entries in the ANOVA table and there is no need for hand calculations. However, knowledge of what these sums of squares measure also makes it straightforward to calculate them by hand if no computer is available. Also note that it is only necessary to calculate four sums of squares, as the fifth one can be obtained from the identity. It is probably easiest first to calculate SSTO, which is the sum of the

TABLE 8.1-4   **Analysis-of-Variance Table in the Two-Factor Factorial Experiment: Fixed Effects**

Source	SS	df	MS	F
A	SS_A	$a-1$	MS_A	$F_A = MS_A/MS_{Error}$
B	SS_B	$b-1$	MS_B	$F_B = MS_B/MS_{Error}$
AB	SS_{AB}	$(a-1)(b-1)$	MS_{AB}	$F_{AB} = MS_{AB}/MS_{Error}$
Error	SS_{Error}	$ab(n-1)$	MS_{Error}	
Total	SSTO	$abn-1$		

squared deviations from the overall mean. Next calculate SS_A. It is the sum of the squared distances from the row means to the overall mean, multiplied by nb, the number of observations that go into calculating each row mean. SS_B is calculated in a similar manner. The error sum of squares SS_{Error} is also easy to calculate, as we simply add up the ab sums of squares that are associated with the ab cells (of course, each of these sums is computed by summing the squared deviations from the respective cell mean $\bar{Y}_{ij\cdot}$). The interaction sum of squares can be obtained from the identity; $SS_{AB} = SSTO - SS_A - SS_B - SS_{Error}$. Of course, one can also calculate these sums from the computation equations above. These computations are a little more difficult, but in a sense, better, as they are not subject to so many rounding errors.

The third column in the ANOVA table lists the degrees of freedom for the various sums of squares. Because of the restrictions among the main and interaction effects, there are $(a-1)$ degrees of freedom for SS_A, $(b-1)$ for SS_B, and $(a-1)(b-1)$ for SS_{AB}. The degrees of freedom for SS_{Error} are $ab(n-1)$ since we combine ab error sums of squares, each with $(n-1)$ degrees of freedom. The sum of these degrees of freedom equals $abn-1$, which is the degrees of freedom for SSTO. The fourth column lists the mean squares and the fifth gives the respective F-statistics, which are explained later.

The expected values of these mean squares suggest how to conduct tests of certain null hypotheses: that is, about interactions in which $(\alpha\beta)_{ij} = 0$ for all $i = 1, \ldots, a$ and $j = 1, \ldots, b$; about main effects of factor A in which $\alpha_1 = \cdots = \alpha_a = 0$; and about main effects of factor B in which $\beta_1 = \cdots = \beta_b = 0$. It is quite useful to know whether interactions are present or not, as their absence implies that the effects are additive and that the effects of changes in factor A do not depend on the particular level of factor B. Furthermore, it is important to know about main effects as they tell us about the effects of factor A (or B) on the mean response.

In the derivation of the expected mean squares we must distinguish between *fixed* and *random* effects. In the *fixed-effects model* we assume that the α_i, β_j, and $(\alpha\beta)_{ij}$ are nonrandom unknown quantities, and that our comparisons are restricted to the specifically chosen factor levels. The only random components are the errors ε_{ijk}. After some algebra, which is similar to that in the one-factor comparison, it can be shown that

$$E(\text{MS}_A) = \sigma^2 + bn \frac{\sum_i \alpha_i^2}{a - 1},$$

$$E(\text{MS}_B) = \sigma^2 + an \frac{\sum_j \beta_j^2}{b - 1},$$

$$E(\text{MS}_{AB}) = \sigma^2 + n \frac{\sum_i \sum_j (\alpha\beta)_{ij}^2}{(a - 1)(b - 1)},$$

$$E(\text{MS}_{\text{Error}}) = \sigma^2.$$

Thus the F-ratios in Table 8.1-4 are the appropriate statistics for testing the significance of main and interaction effects. The statistic $F_{AB} = \text{MS}_{AB}/\text{MS}_{\text{Error}}$ tests the significance of the interactions; it is compared to the critical value $F[\alpha; (a - 1)(b - 1), ab(n - 1)]$ for a test with significance level α. The statistic $F_A = \text{MS}_A/\text{MS}_{\text{Error}}$ tests the significance of the factor A main effects by comparing it to $F[\alpha; a - 1, ab(n - 1)]$. Also, $F_B = \text{MS}_B/\text{MS}_{\text{Error}}$ provides a test of the significance of the factor B main effects by comparing it to $F[\alpha; b - 1, ab(n - 1)]$.

The significance of the main effects of a factor is determined by comparing the averages of the observations at the various levels of this factor. Since the averaging is over all levels of the other factor, it is meaningful to talk about and test for the significance of main effects only if there are fairly small and unimportant interactions. If there are large interaction effects, we should ignore the test for main effects and display the nature of the interactions by plotting the sample averages, as we did with the population means μ_{ij} in Figure 8.1-1. Frequently, transformations of the response, such as $\log Y$, $1/Y$, or $\sqrt{Y}$, take a model with interactions into one without interactions. A simple illustration, in which the logarithmic transformation leads to a simplification, is the multiplicative model, $\mu_{ij}^* = \mu^* \alpha_i^* \beta_j^*$, which becomes

$$\log \mu_{ij}^* = \log \mu^* + \log \alpha_i^* + \log \beta_j^* \qquad \text{or} \qquad \mu_{ij} = \mu + \alpha_i + \beta_j$$

in a notation that is obvious.

You should be aware that there can be situations in which we observe zero main effects (namely $\alpha_i = 0$ for all $i = 1, \ldots, a$), but where some interactions are nonzero. Such a situation does *not* imply that changes in factor A have no effect on the mean response. They do have an effect. However, because of the nonzero interactions, the effects of changes in A depend on the level of factor B. It would be a mistake to gloss over the important interactions and conclude that A is not important, just because their effects "average out" to zero, when averaging is done over all levels of B. To emphasize this point, take $a = 2$, $b = 3$, and $\mu_{11} = 1$, $\mu_{12} = -2$, $\mu_{13} = 1$, $\mu_{21} = -1$, $\mu_{22} = 2$, and $\mu_{23} = -1$. All main effects of A (as well as B) are zero. But it is obvious that changes in factor A affect the mean response. A change in A from level 1 to level 2 leads to a reduction of 2 units if B is at level 1, an increase of 4 units if B is at level 2, and a reduction of 2 units if B is at level 3.

If no interaction effects are present, we can also conduct *follow-up tests* on the row (factor A) and column (factor B) means. We can display the row averages $\bar{Y}_{i..}$, together with their reference distribution, which in this case is the scaled $t[v = ab(n-1)]$ distribution, with scale $\sqrt{MS_{Error}/bn}$. Similarly, we can display the column averages $\bar{Y}_{.j.}$, together with their reference distribution, which is the scaled $t[v = ab(n-1)]$ with scale $\sqrt{MS_{Error}/an}$.

Diagnostic checks should always be conducted before the conclusions from an analysis are adopted. As before, the primary tool is residual analysis, where the residuals $e_{ijk} = Y_{ijk} - \bar{Y}_{ij.}$ are the deviations from the cell averages. A dot diagram or a histogram of these residuals allows us to check roughly whether the error distribution is approximately normal. Dot diagrams of the residuals, separately for each of the ab cells but displayed on the same scale, provide information as to whether the variances in the ab cells are approximately the same. Also, a plot of the residuals e_{ijk} against the fitted values $\bar{Y}_{ij.}$ should show no apparent nonrandom patterns. A pattern where the variability is related to the level of the cell would violate the equal-variance assumption.

Example 8.1-1   The yield (in cups of popped corn from 1/4 cup of popcorn) is the variable of interest. We wish to test the effects of two factors. Factor A is the type of popcorn maker. We compare an "oil-based" popper (level 1) with a certain "air-based" popper (level 2). Factor B is popcorn brand; level 1 corresponds to a gourmet-type popcorn (its cost is $1.10 per pound), level 2 is a national brand (cost $0.50 per pound), and level 3 is a generic brand (cost $0.38 per pound). A 2×3 factorial experiment with $n = 3$ replications was performed, where the order of the 18 experiments was randomized to spread the variability that results from other uncontrolled factors evenly among all treatment groups. Table 8.1-5 lists the outcomes from these experiments. From the data we calculate the following sums of squares:

$$SSTO = 472 - \frac{(90)^2}{18} = 22,$$

$$SS_A = \left(\frac{1}{9}\right)[(40.5)^2 + (49.5)^2] - \frac{(90)^2}{18} = 4.5,$$

$$SS_B = \left(\frac{1}{6}\right)[(37.5)^2 + (28.5)^2 + (24)^2] - \frac{(90)^2}{18} = 15.75,$$

$$SS_{AB} = \left(\frac{1}{3}\right)[(17)^2 + (20.5)^2 + (13)^2 + (15.5)^2 + (10.5)^2 + (13.5)^2]$$

$$- \frac{(90)^2}{18} - 4.5 - 15.75 = 0.0833,$$

$$SS_{Error} = 22 - 4.5 - 15.75 - 0.0833 = 1.6667.$$

TABLE 8.1-5   Results for Popcorn Example

Popper	Gourmet	National Brand	Generic	Row Sum	Row Average
Oil	5.5, 5.5, 6	4.5, 4.5, 4	3.5, 4, 3	40.5	4.50
Air	6.5, 7, 7	5, 5.5, 5	4, 5, 4.5	49.5	5.50
Column Sum	37.5	28.5	24.0	$y_{...} = 90.0$	
Column Average	6.25	4.75	4.00	$\bar{y}_{...} = 5.00$	
				$\sum\sum\sum y_{ijk}^2 = 472$	

Alternatively, we could have calculated these sums of squares from their definitions. This provides the following ANOVA table:

Source	SS	df	MS	F
A (Popper)	4.5	1	4.5	32.4
B (Brand)	15.75	2	7.8750	56.7
AB	0.0833	2	0.0417	0.3
Error	1.6667	12	0.1389	
Total	22.0	17		

There is no indication of an interaction; $F_{AB} = 0.3$ is much smaller than the critical value $F(0.01; 2, 12) = 6.93$. Also, the plot of the cell averages in Figure 8.1-2(a) shows the absence of interaction; the two graphs are almost parallel. Thus it is appropriate to investigate the factor main effects. Both factors (popper and brand) are highly significant: 32.4, compared with $F(0.01; 1, 12) = 9.33$, and 56.7, compared with $F(0.01; 2, 12) = 6.93$. That is, there is very strong evidence that these differences cannot be explained as being chance results. The dot diagram of the residuals [Figure 8.1-2(b)] and the plot of the residuals against fitted values [Figure 8.1-2(c)] do not point to any major inadequacies of the fitted model. The variability of the residuals that correspond to low fitted values does appear to be a bit larger. However, due to the small sample size, it is difficult to tell whether this is a serious violation of the assumption of constant variance.

Our analysis shows that the gourmet brand leads to a much higher yield than the other two brands. However, if we take the differences in prices into account, the conclusion changes. If we use the cost of the generic popcorn as a base and recalling that it yields 4 cups on the average, the national brand yields $(4.75)(0.38)/(0.50) = 3.61$ cups for the same cost and the gourmet brand only $(6.25)(0.38)/(1.10) = 2.16$ cups. Thus, *judging on volume alone*, it does not pay to buy the gourmet brand. Also, the air-based popper is much better than

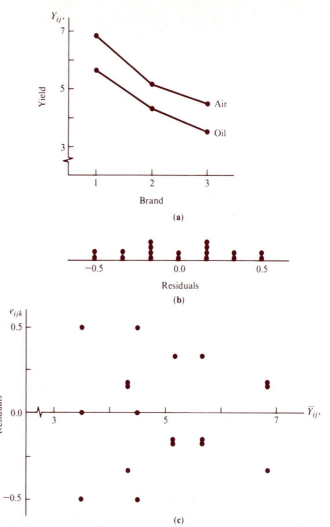

FIGURE 8.1-2 Popcorn example: (a) plot of cell means; (b) dot diagram of the residuals; (c) plot of residuals against fitted values.

the oil-based popper, using volume yield as a measure. Clearly, *taste* will play some role in the determination of the type of popcorn and popper a consumer will purchase.   ■

8.1-1   Graphics in the Analysis of Two-Factor Experiments

It is always an excellent strategy to display the response averages for the various levels of each factor. Furthermore, in order to recognize the joint effects of factors *A* and *B*, we recommend that for each level of one factor you plot and connect the cell means that correspond to the various levels of the other factor. You can overlay these graphs, as we have done in Figures 8.1-1 and 8.1-2. Roughly parallel curves suggest a model in which the effects of A and B are additive, that is, the interaction is zero.

If there are many observations, we can also calculate the quartiles, the interquartile range, and the standard deviation for each of the ab cells. Box-and-whisker diagrams can be prepared for each cell, and the ab diagrams can be put side by side. For example, we can display the b box-and-whisker diagrams for level 1 of factor A; next to it, on the same scale, the b diagrams that correspond to level 2 of A; and so on. Also, instead of displaying these a groups of diagrams (each of size b) side by side, we can try to overlay these box plots, as we have done with the cell averages in Figures 8.1-1 and 8.1-2. Looking across the interquartile ranges in these diagrams, we can assess whether the variability in these cells is roughly the same. It is important to check this, as the F-test in the analysis of variance assumes equal variances. If the variability is not constant, we should check whether it is related to the level of the observations. A plot of the ab interquartile ranges, or the standard deviations, against the cell averages is often very helpful in selecting an appropriate transformation. If the interquartile ranges (or standard deviations) grow proportional to the cell averages, the logarithm of the response is the appropriate transformation.

If we look across the box-and-whisker diagrams, we can also check whether the patterns among the first b diagrams [those for cells $(1, 1)$, $(1, 2)$, ..., $(1, b)$] are different from the patterns in the second group of b [those for cells $(2, 1)$, $(2, 2)$, ..., $(2, b)$], in the third group, and so on. If they are just shifted by constant amounts, we can adopt an additive model. In such a situation we can average over the other factor. For example, we can ignore factor B and construct for each level of factor A a box-and-whisker diagram from the bn observations; these diagrams can be compared side by side. A similar plot can be shown for the b levels of factor B.

Usually, there is no single best way of displaying a data set. It depends on the particular problem and, of course, the imagination of the investigator.

8.1-2   Special Case: $n = 1$

If there is only a single observation Y_{ij} in each cell, the model $\mu_{ij} = \bar{\mu}.. + \alpha_i + \beta_j + (\alpha\beta)_{ij}$ includes the same number of parameters as observations. Thus the error sum of squares is zero, and it is not possible to make inferences about the parameters. Accordingly, simplifying assumptions must be made about the model before we can make inferences. One such simplification assumes that the model is additive, $Y_{ij} = \bar{\mu}.. + \alpha_i + \beta_j + \varepsilon_{ij}$. This implies that the interaction sum of squares can be used as the error sum of squares. It follows that the analysis is the same as the one in the randomized complete block arrangement (Section 7.3), with the second factor replacing the blocking variable.

8.1-3   Random Effects

So far we have assumed that the factor levels of A and B are fixed. Now let us assume that the factor levels are chosen at random from larger populations; thus our inference is about all possible levels in these populations, not just the ones that we have selected. The coefficients, except $\bar{\mu}..$, in the model

$$Y_{ijk} = \bar{\mu}.. + \alpha_i + \beta_j + (\alpha\beta)_{ij} + \varepsilon_{ijk}$$

are now random variables: The α_i values are from $N(0, \sigma_\alpha^2)$, the β_j values from $N(0, \sigma_\beta^2)$, the $(\alpha\beta)_{ij}$ values from $N(0, \sigma_{\alpha\beta}^2)$, and the ε_{ijk} from $N(0, \sigma^2)$. In addition, we assume that these random variables are mutually independent.

The basic analysis-of-variance table in the random-effects model is the same as that for the fixed-effects model; the sums of squares, degrees of freedom, and mean squares are calculated the same way. However, the expected mean squares are now

$$E(\text{MS}_A) = \sigma^2 + n\sigma_{\alpha\beta}^2 + bn\sigma_\alpha^2,$$

$$E(\text{MS}_B) = \sigma^2 + n\sigma_{\alpha\beta}^2 + an\sigma_\beta^2,$$

$$E(\text{MS}_{AB}) = \sigma^2 + n\sigma_{\alpha\beta}^2,$$

$$E(\text{MS}_{\text{Error}}) = \sigma^2.$$

Thus, in the test of main effects, the correct denominator in the F ratios is the interaction mean square MS_{AB}, not MS_{Error} as it is in the fixed-effects model. For example, to test whether there is variability due to factor A ($H_0: \sigma_\alpha^2 = 0$), we compare $F = \text{MS}_A/\text{MS}_{AB}$ to the critical value $F[\alpha; (a-1), (a-1)(b-1)]$. The entries in the mean-square column of the ANOVA table can also be used to estimate the variance components. It is straightforward to show that the estimates are

$$\hat{\sigma}^2 = \text{MS}_{\text{Error}}, \qquad \hat{\sigma}_{\alpha\beta}^2 = \frac{\text{MS}_{AB} - \text{MS}_{\text{Error}}}{n},$$

$$\hat{\sigma}_\beta^2 = \frac{\text{MS}_B - \text{MS}_{AB}}{an} \qquad \hat{\sigma}_\alpha^2 = \frac{\text{MS}_A - \text{MS}_{AB}}{bn}.$$

Consider the example in Exercise 8.1-5. There a manufacturer of 13-inch brakewheels is concerned about the quality of its production; here the quality is measured by the differences of specified and actual diameters. Since operators and machines were thought to be important factors, the quality control engineer selected three operators and three machines at random and took samples of size $n = 5$ at each of the nine operator–machine combinations.

Exercises 8.1

8.1-1 Consider the following 2×4 table of cell means, μ_{ij}, $i = 1, 2; j = 1, 2, 3, 4$.

	Factor *B*			
Factor *A*	1	2	3	4
1	2	5	6	6
2	4	5	7	9

Calculate the row, column, and interaction effects.

8.1-2 For the popcorn example, plot the three brand averages and their reference distribution. Plot the two popper averages and their reference distribution.

8.1-3 A company wants to evaluate the effectiveness of three different training methods (factor *B*) designed to improve the job performance of its entering sales work force. New workers are classified on the basis of educational background (factor *A*): high school and college graduates. A random sample of 12 high school graduates is randomly divided into three groups of four. Each subgroup is then randomly assigned to one of the three job training programs. An analogous procedure is followed for a random sample of 12 college graduates. The sales (in $10,000) for the first quarter after their training are as follows:

	Training		
Education	1	2	3
High School	8, 4, 2, 3	10, 8, 6, 7	8, 6, 4, 7
College	14, 10, 6, 9	8, 9, 7, 10	15, 13, 9, 12

Use graphs to display the information. Calculate the ANOVA table and conduct the appropriate tests. Summarize your findings. Check the assumptions of your model.

8.1-4 An engineer in a textile mill studies the effect of temperature and time in a process involving dye on the brightness of a synthetic fabric. Several small randomly selected fabric specimens were dyed under each temperature and time combination. The brightness of the dyed fabric was measured on a 50-point scale.

	Temperature		
Time (cycles)	350°F	375°F	400°F
40	38, 32, 30	37, 35, 40	36, 39, 43
50	40, 45, 36	39, 42, 46	39, 48, 47

Display the information through well-chosen graphs. Estimate the row, column, and interaction effects. Construct the ANOVA table, and conduct tests for interaction and main effects, if appropriate. Check the adequacy of your model.

8.1-5 A company is concerned about the quality of its production of 13-inch brakewheels. The engineer who is in charge of quality control suspects that machines and operators may influence the quality of the final product. She conducts a small experiment to investigate the validity of her suspicion by selecting three machines and three operators at random. Each operator uses each machine. At each of the nine machine–operator combinations she takes a sample of $n = 5$ brakewheels and determines the difference in actual and specified diameter (in units of 1/100 inch). The results are as follows:

		Operator		
Machine		1	2	3
	1	2, 3, 2.5, 3.5, 3	3.5, 3, 4.5, 3, 3	2.5, 3, 2, 2.5, 1.5
	2	3, 3, 3.5, 3, 4	4, 5, 3, 2.5, 2.5	2, 2, 2.5, 3, 3
	3	3.5, 2.5, 3, 3, 4	5, 4, 2.5, 3.5, 4	2, 2.5, 3, 3, 2

(a) Are the operator and machine effects fixed or random effects? Discuss.

(b) Calculate the ANOVA table.

(c) Test whether there is interaction.

(d) Test for operator and machine main effects.

Remark The expected mean squares in the random-effects model in Section 8.1-3 show that the appropriate denominator in the test for main effects, say of factor A, is the interaction mean square MS_{AB}. Note, however, that it makes sense to interpret and to test for main effects only if the interactions are negligible. But if there are no interactions, the mean square MS_{AB} is also an estimate of σ^2. In this situation we can pool SS_{AB} and SS_{Error} to obtain a new and better estimate of σ^2,

$$MS_{Error(pooled)} = \frac{SS_{AB} + SS_{Error}}{(a-1)(b-1) + ab(n-1)}.$$

Since $\sigma^2_{\alpha\beta} = 0$ in $E(MS_A)$, we can use this estimate as the denominator in the test for the main effects of factor A, and compare $MS_A/MS_{Error(pooled)}$ with the percentage points of the

$$F[a-1, (a-1)(b-1) + ab(n-1)]$$

distribution. This test will be more reliable because pooling increases the degrees of freedom in the denominator.   ■

8.1-6 Show that

$$n \sum_i \sum_j (\bar{Y}_{ij\cdot} - \bar{Y}_{...})^2 = SS_A + SS_B + SS_{AB}.$$

This result says that the variability of the cell averages around the overall average can be written as the sum of the main effects and interaction sums of squares. Use this fact to show that

$$SS_{AB} = n \sum_i \sum_j (\bar{Y}_{ij\cdot} - \bar{Y}_{i\cdot\cdot} - \bar{Y}_{\cdot j\cdot} + \bar{Y}_{...})^2$$

$$= \frac{1}{n} \sum_i \sum_j (Y_{ij\cdot})^2 - \frac{(Y_{...})^2}{abn} - SS_A - SS_B.$$

8.1-7 The partially completed ANOVA table from a two-factor 3×4 factorial experiment with $n = 3$ observations in each cell is given below.

Source	SS	df	MS	F
A	10.12			
B	15.21			
AB	25.52			
Error				
Total	102.00	35		

(a) Complete the ANOVA table and test (at significance level $\alpha = 0.05$) whether an interaction of the two factors is present.

(b) What assumptions can be checked on the basis of the residuals and by what means?

8.1-8 Consider a factorial design in which a response is measured at four temperatures and three treatments, with four independent observations at each combination of temperature and treatment. A summary table of means is given below.

Table of Means (Four Observations per Cell)

Treatment	Temperature (°C)			
	0	5	10	15
A	6	8	12	17
B	10	14	18	23
C	12	8	7	6

Furthermore, we are told that $SS_{Error} = 550$. Construct the ANOVA table and carry out appropriate tests. Interpret your findings. Use graphical methods to support your conclusions.

8.1-9 Volunteers who had a smoking history classified as heavy, moderate, and nonsmoker were accepted until nine men were in each category. Three men in each category were randomly assigned to each of three stress tests: bicycle ergometer, treadmill, and step tests. Time until maximum oxygen uptake was recorded in minutes. The data follows.

Smoking History	Test		
	Bicycle	Treadmill	Step
Nonsmoker	12.8	16.2	22.6
	13.5	18.1	19.3
	11.2	17.8	18.9
Moderate	10.9	15.5	20.1
	11.1	13.8	21.0
	9.8	16.2	15.9
Heavy	8.7	14.7	16.2
	9.2	13.2	16.1
	7.5	8.1	17.8

(a) Analyze the results of this experiment. Obtain the ANOVA table and test for main effects and interactions.

(b) Construct reference distributions for the row (smoking history) means and the column (test) means.

*8.2 Nested Factors and Hierarchical Designs

Excessive variability among manufactured items should be a major concern for companies that are committed to high-quality production. To increase the quality of the production, we have to identify factors that affect the variable of interest and that contribute the most to its variability. The $\bar{x}$- and R-charts in Chapter 5 are very useful first steps in identifying these factors. An $\bar{x}$-chart, for example, may show segments of time where the plotted averages are particularly low (or high). If these periods coincide with different operators or shifts (day/night, weekday/weekend), or with changed input variables or changes in manufacturing conditions, we can tentatively identify these factors as contributors to the variation.

The analysis of nested or hierarchical designs gives us a more formal method of identifying and estimating the sources of the variability. Let us begin with an illustration. An engineer working for a company believes that the variability in a measured property of manufactured forgings is excessive. The raw material for the forgings are rods that the company purchases from a nearby foundry. The forgings are stamped from the rods, and measurements on the property of interest are made on each forging. The engineer wants to identify the sources for the excessive variability. The variability may be due to that among the purchased rods, variability among the stamped forgings, or variability due to measurement. It is important to know about these variance components. If the company finds that the variability is due mostly to rods, it would insist that the supplier of the rods strengthen its quality control program. If it is due to forgings, the company would look for improved stamping methods. If measurement variability is the major factor, it would carefully review its measurement procedures.

To estimate the variance components, the engineer conducts the following experiment. A total of a rods are selected at random. Then b forgings are taken at random from each of the selected rods. Finally, n independent measurements are made on each resulting forging. Figure 8.2-1 illustrates the design for $a = 5$ rods, $b = 3$ forgings, and $n = 2$ measurements. Such an arrangement is called a *nested* or *hierarchical design*.

It is important to recognize the difference between the arrangement in Figure 8.2-1 and the $a \times b$ factorial experiment. In the factorial, or *crossed*,

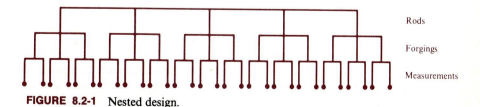

Rods

Forgings

Measurements

FIGURE 8.2-1 Nested design.

The following experiment was performed. (1) Five representative small parts were selected. (2) The first part was placed in the measurement fixture, all the while following the usual measurement system process description, and the measurement of interest was taken. Then four additional measurements were taken without disturbing the small part in any way. Note that from this series of five measurements we can estimate the "short-term" measurement variability, which is the variability due to the measurement *instrument*. (3) The first part is removed from the apparatus, and the next one is set up in the measurement fixture, and five measurements are taken in rapid succession without disturbing the small part in any way. (4) After each of the small parts have been measured (similarly) five times, the experimenter again sets up one of the five parts in the equipment and measures its size rapidly five more times. Similarly, measurements are obtained on the four other parts. (5) The process is repeated three more times, until five rounds of measurements have been obtained, each involving the same five small parts; in each round each part is measured five times in rapid succession. Note that the variability of the averages that are calculated from each of the five rapid succession quintuples measures the "long-term" measurement variability, the variability that is due to the measurement *process* (i.e., due to the setup procedure, adjustment of the measurement instrument, etc.).

This experiment leads to a total of 125 observations; the Y_{ijk} corresponds to the kth rapid measurement in setup j of part i. Explain how you would set up the ANOVA table and discuss what information you could extract from this experiment. [Coleman, D. E. "Measuring Measurements," *RCA Engineer*, 30(3): 16–23 (1985).]

Remark The tolerance limits for measurement errors listed by the manufacturer of a measurement instrument usually address only the short-term measurement variability. They do not incorporate the long-term variability, which is caused by factors that enter the measurement *process*. ■

8.2-7 A paper company is concerned about excessive variability in the rupture strength of its tissue. To study the sources of variability, the company selected five batches at random; from each batch, it took three samples and made four independent measurements on strength. Complete the ANOVA table, estimate the variance components, and interpret the results.

Source	SS	df	MS	F
Batch	119.6			
Sample (batch)				
Error	77.0			
Total	320.4			

8.3   General Factorial and 2^k Factorial Experiments

In Section 8.1 we studied the factorial experiment with two factors, A and B. Since each of the a levels of factor A is combined with each of the b levels of factor B, there is a total of ab level combinations of the two factors. The cell means, denoted by μ_{ij}, were modeled as $\mu_{ij} = \bar{\mu}.. + \alpha_i + \beta_j + (\alpha\beta)_{ij}$. Recall that the ith main effect of factor A, $\alpha_i = \bar{\mu}_{i.} - \bar{\mu}..$, is the difference between the average response at the ith level of factor A and the overall average. Similarly, the jth main effect of factor B equals $\beta_j = \bar{\mu}_{.j} - \bar{\mu}..$. The two-factor interaction,

$$(\alpha\beta)_{ij} = \mu_{ij} - (\bar{\mu}.. + \alpha_i + \beta_j) = \mu_{ij} - \bar{\mu}_{i.} - \bar{\mu}_{.j} + \bar{\mu}..,$$

is that part of μ_{ij} that cannot be explained by the main effects alone. A nonzero interaction implies that the effect of one factor depends on the level of the other.

Now if we consider three factors, say factors A, B, and C with a, b, and c levels, respectively, there is a total of abc level combinations of the three factors and thus abc cell means μ_{ijh}, $i = 1, \ldots, a$; $j = 1, \ldots, b$; $h = 1, \ldots, c$. Since there are three factors, we can define the main effects, the two-factor interactions (between A and B, A and C, and B and C), and now three-factor interactions. Main effects and two-factor interactions need little additional explanation, since they were defined earlier. The only difference from the two-factor experiment is that now we have to average over the levels of yet another factor. For example, the main effects of factor C are given by $\gamma_h = \bar{\mu}_{\cdot\cdot h} - \bar{\mu}_{\cdot\cdot\cdot}$, and the two-factor interactions between factors A and C are $(\alpha\gamma)_{ih} = \bar{\mu}_{i\cdot h} - \bar{\mu}_{i\cdot\cdot} - \bar{\mu}_{\cdot\cdot h} + \bar{\mu}_{\cdot\cdot\cdot}$. The three-factor interactions represent that part of μ_{ijh} that is not explained by a model that includes only main effects and two-factor interactions:

$$(\alpha\beta\gamma)_{ijh} = \mu_{ijh} - [\bar{\mu}_{\cdot\cdot\cdot} + \alpha_i + \beta_j + \gamma_h + (\alpha\beta)_{ij} + (\alpha\gamma)_{ih} + (\beta\gamma)_{jh}].$$

A nonzero three-factor interaction implies that the two-factor interactions depend on the levels of the third factor. The "dot notation" should be fairly obvious; a dot in place of an index means that we have averaged over this particular index.

For the three-factor factorial experiment with n replications in each cell, the ANOVA table is given in Table 8.3-1. Computer programs are usually available to calculate the entries in the ANOVA table and there is no reason to illustrate the computation of the various sums of squares.

If we assume that the three factors are fixed, the test statistics for main and interaction effects are the ratios of the corresponding mean squares and the mean square due to error. Since two-factor interactions and main effects are meaningful only if there are no three-factor interactions, we should first test

TABLE 8.3-1   ANOVA Table for the Factorial Experiment with Three Factors: Fixed Effects

Source	SS	df	MS	F
A	SS_A	$a - 1$	MS_A	MS_A/MS_{Error}
B	SS_B	$b - 1$	MS_B	MS_B/MS_{Error}
C	SS_C	$c - 1$	MS_C	MS_C/MS_{Error}
AB	SS_{AB}	$(a - 1)(b - 1)$	MS_{AB}	$MS_{AB}/MS_{\text{Error}}$
AC	SS_{AC}	$(a - 1)(c - 1)$	MS_{AC}	$MS_{AC}/MS_{\text{Error}}$
BC	SS_{BC}	$(b - 1)(c - 1)$	MS_{BC}	$MS_{BC}/MS_{\text{Error}}$
ABC	SS_{ABC}	$(a - 1)(b - 1)(c - 1)$	MS_{ABC}	$MS_{ABC}/MS_{\text{Error}}$
Error	SS_{Error}	$abc(n - 1)$	MS_{Error}	
Total	SSTO	$abcn - 1$		

for the presence of three-factor interaction. There we compare $\text{MS}_{ABC}/\text{MS}_{\text{Error}}$ with the critical value $F[\alpha; (a-1)(b-1)(c-1), abc(n-1)]$. Tests for two-factor interactions and main effects are constructed in a similar fashion.

Factorial experiments with three or more factors require many experimental runs, especially if each factor is studied at several levels and if the experiment is replicated at each combination $(n > 1)$. The number of runs can be reduced if we study the factors at only two levels. This leads us to factorial experiments with k factors at two levels each.

8.3-1 2^k Factorial Experiment

Here we assume that each of the k factors occurs at two levels: a "high" level, coded as $+1$ or just as $+$, and a "low" level, coded as -1 or as $-$. A complete factorial arrangement leads to a total of 2^k runs.

The 2^2 Factorial   Let us start with $k=2$ factors and the $2^2 = 4$ factor combinations (low, low), (high, low), (low, high), and (high, high). In coded units the four runs are $(-1, -1)$, $(1, -1)$, $(-1, 1)$, and $(1, 1)$. We have arranged these runs in Table 8.3-2 in what is called the *standard order*. There we start the levels of factor 1 with one minus and alternate the signs: $-, +, -, +$. The levels of factor 2 start with two minuses and the signs alternate in blocks of two: $-, -, +, +$. In Table 8.3-2 we display the levels of factor 1 in a column called x_1 and those of factor 2 in a column called x_2. The display of the factor levels in these two columns is called the *design matrix*. The standard order is a convenient systematic list of all possible factor-level combinations. The actual order in which the experiments are carried out, however, should always be randomized. A particular order may be: run 3, run 1, run 2, run 4.

There are four observations in this unreplicated 2^2 factorial; only a single observation is taken at each factor–level combination. Hence we can estimate at most four quantities: the overall mean, the two main effects, and the interaction between factors 1 and 2. The overall mean is estimated by

$$\text{average} = \frac{Y_1 + Y_2 + Y_3 + Y_4}{4}.$$

The main effect of factor 1, denoted by (1), is one-half of the difference between the averages of the responses at the high and low levels of factor 1,

$$(1) = \frac{1}{2}\left(\frac{Y_2 + Y_4}{2} - \frac{Y_1 + Y_3}{2}\right) = \frac{-Y_1 + Y_2 - Y_3 + Y_4}{4}.$$

Similarly, the main effect of factor 2 is estimated by

$$(2) = \frac{1}{2}\left(\frac{Y_3 + Y_4}{2} - \frac{Y_1 + Y_2}{2}\right) = \frac{-Y_1 - Y_2 + Y_3 + Y_4}{4}.$$

TABLE 8.3-2   The 2^2 Factorial Experiment

	Design				
Run	x_1	x_2	$x_1 x_2$	Observation	
1	$-$	$-$	$+$	Y_1	
2	$+$	$-$	$-$	Y_2	
3	$-$	$+$	$-$	Y_3	
4	$+$	$+$	$+$	Y_4	

The interaction between the two factors is estimated as one-half of the difference between the main effect of factor 1 at the high level of factor 2, $(Y_4 - Y_3)/2$, and that at the low level of factor 2, $(Y_2 - Y_1)/2$. That is, it is

$$(12) = \frac{1}{2}\left(\frac{Y_4 - Y_3}{2} - \frac{Y_2 - Y_1}{2}\right) = \frac{Y_1 - Y_2 - Y_3 + Y_4}{4}.$$

Note that this is the same as one-half of the difference between the main effects of factor 2 at the high and low levels of factor 1. If the main effects of one factor are the same at the high and low levels of the other, there is no interaction.

There is an easy way to remember the calculation of these effects. The sequences of $+$ and $-$ signs in columns x_1 and x_2 tell us how to combine the observations to get the main effects. The column $x_1 x_2$ of the products of x_1 and x_2 in Table 8.3-2 contains the appropriate coefficients for the interaction. All linear combinations are then divided by $2^2 = 4$.

Remarks   This definition of main and interaction effects is consistent with our definition in the general $a \times b$ factorial experiment in Section 8.1; see Exercise 8.3-2. Some other books define main effects as the difference between the averages at the high and low levels of a factor, not as one-half of this difference as we do here. If this alternative definition is adopted, we must divide the linear combinations by $2^{2-1} = 2$, the number of plus signs (or minus signs) in the coefficient columns. The effects are then twice as large as the ones that result from our definition. They measure the effect of moving from the low (-1) to the high ($+1$) level of a factor, which corresponds to a change of 2 units; the effects in our definition express the effect of a 1-unit change. ■

Example 8.3-1   The effects of temperature (factor 1) and reaction time (factor 2) on percent yield of a certain chemical reaction (response Y) are studied. There are two levels of temperature, 110°C (coded as $-$) and 130°C (coded as $+$), and two levels of reaction time, 50 minutes ($-$) and 70 minutes ($+$). The 2^2 factorial experiment was replicated ($n = 2$) and the order of the eight runs was randomized. The results are given in Table 8.3-3. The average yields from the two replications are used to estimate the effects. The individual observa-

TABLE 8.3-3   Example of a 2^2 Factorial Experiment

Run	Design x_1	Design x_2	$x_1 x_2$	Average Yield	Individual Observations
1	−	−	+	55.0	55.5, 54.5
2	+	−	−	60.6	60.2, 61.0
3	−	+	−	64.2	64.5, 63.9
4	+	+	+	68.2	67.7, 68.7

$$\text{Average} = (55.0 + 60.6 + 64.2 + 68.2)/4 = 62.0$$
$$(1) = (-55.0 + 60.6 - 64.2 + 68.2)/4 = 2.4$$
$$(2) = (-55.0 - 60.6 + 64.2 + 68.2)/4 = 4.2$$
$$(12) = (55.0 - 60.6 - 64.2 + 68.2)/4 = -0.4$$

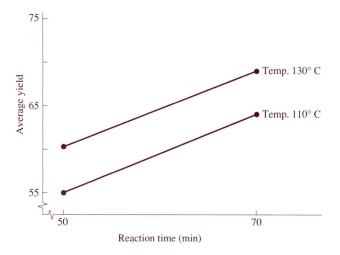

tions are used later to calculate standard errors of the estimated effects. Since we find that the interaction is quite small, we can proceed to interpret the main effects. The temperature main effect is 2.4. This means that on the average a temperature increase of 10°C leads to a 2.4 percent increase in yield. Stating this differently, we find that a temperature increase from the low level of 110°C to the high level of 130°C leads to a (2)(2.4) = 4.8 percent increase in yield. The time main effect is estimated as 4.2. This implies that a 10-minute increase in reaction time increases the yield by 4.2 percent. That is, changing reaction time from 50 minutes to 70 minutes increases the yield by (2)(4.2) = 8.4 percent on average. This information is shown graphically in the plots on the bottom of Table 8.3-3. As the interaction is negligible, the two lines on the graph are virtually parallel.

These results show that yield can be increased by increasing temperature and reaction time. Since the coded time (x_2) effect is 4.2/2.4 = 1.75 times greater than the coded temperature (x_1) effect, we should increase these factors along the line $x_2 = 1.75x_1$. This is called the path of *steepest ascent*. For example, the experiments with coded points $(x_1 = 0.5, x_2 = 0.875)$, $(x_1 = 1.0, x_2 = 1.75)$, $(x_1 = 1.5, x_2 = 2.625)$ would, based on the information from our initial 2^2 factorial experiment, move us quickly toward higher yields. These points are equivalent to (125°C, 68.75 minutes), (130°C, 77.5 minutes), and (135°C, 86.25 minutes), respectively. We would then conduct further experiments along this path of steepest ascent. The determination of optimal conditions is discussed in detail in Section 9.6. ■

The 2^3 Factorial   In the 2^3 factorial we have a total of eight runs. The levels of the three factors are listed in standard order in the columns x_1, x_2, and x_3 in Table 8.3-4. For example, the first run puts all three factors at their low levels; the second run sets factor 1 at the high level and factors 2 and 3 at low levels; and so on. From this list it is easy to become familiar with the standard order of the 8 runs in the 2^3 factorial experiment. Start the x_1 column with one minus and then alternate the signs until the 8th run is reached. Start the x_2 column with two minuses and alternate the signs in blocks of two. The x_3 column starts with four minuses, and we alternate the signs in blocks of four.

TABLE 8.3-4   **The 2^3 Factorial Experiment**

Run		Design						Observation
	x_1	x_2	x_3	x_1x_2	x_1x_3	x_2x_3	$x_1x_2x_3$	
1	−	−	−	+	+	+	−	Y_1
2	+	−	−	−	−	+	+	Y_2
3	−	+	−	−	+	−	+	Y_3
4	+	+	−	+	−	−	−	Y_4
5	−	−	+	+	−	−	+	Y_5
6	+	−	+	−	+	−	−	Y_6
7	−	+	+	−	−	+	−	Y_7
8	+	+	+	+	+	+	+	Y_8

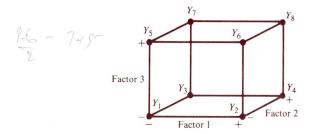

From the eight observations in the 2^3 factorial we can estimate a mean, three main effects, three two-factor interactions, and one three-factor interaction. The mean is estimated by

$$\text{average} = \frac{Y_1 + Y_2 + Y_3 + Y_4 + Y_5 + Y_6 + Y_7 + Y_8}{8}.$$

The main effect of factor i ($i = 1, 2, 3$) is one-half of the difference between the averages of the responses at the high and low levels of factor i. Thus from the cube in Table 8.3-4 we find that

$$(1) = \frac{1}{2}\left(\frac{Y_2 + Y_4 + Y_6 + Y_8}{4} - \frac{Y_1 + Y_3 + Y_5 + Y_7}{4}\right)$$

$$= \frac{-Y_1 + Y_2 - Y_3 + Y_4 - Y_5 + Y_6 - Y_7 + Y_8}{8},$$

$$(2) = \frac{1}{2}\left(\frac{Y_3 + Y_4 + Y_7 + Y_8}{4} - \frac{Y_1 + Y_2 + Y_5 + Y_6}{4}\right)$$

$$= \frac{-Y_1 - Y_2 + Y_3 + Y_4 - Y_5 - Y_6 + Y_7 + Y_8}{8},$$

$$(3) = \frac{1}{2}\left(\frac{Y_5 + Y_6 + Y_7 + Y_8}{4} - \frac{Y_1 + Y_2 + Y_3 + Y_4}{4}\right)$$

$$= \frac{-Y_1 - Y_2 - Y_3 - Y_4 + Y_5 + Y_6 + Y_7 + Y_8}{8}.$$

The interaction between factors i and $j \neq i$ is one-half of the difference between the main effect of factor i at the high level of factor j and that at the low level of factor j. Thus

$$(12) = \frac{1}{2}\left[\frac{1}{2}\left(\frac{Y_4 + Y_8}{2} - \frac{Y_3 + Y_7}{2}\right) - \frac{1}{2}\left(\frac{Y_2 + Y_6}{2} - \frac{Y_1 + Y_5}{2}\right)\right]$$

$$= \frac{Y_1 - Y_2 - Y_3 + Y_4 + Y_5 - Y_6 - Y_7 + Y_8}{8},$$

$$(13) = \frac{1}{2}\left[\frac{1}{2}\left(\frac{Y_6 + Y_8}{2} - \frac{Y_5 + Y_7}{2}\right) - \frac{1}{2}\left(\frac{Y_2 + Y_4}{2} - \frac{Y_1 + Y_3}{2}\right)\right]$$

$$= \frac{Y_1 - Y_2 + Y_3 - Y_4 - Y_5 + Y_6 - Y_7 + Y_8}{8},$$

$$(23) = \frac{1}{2}\left[\frac{1}{2}\left(\frac{Y_7 + Y_8}{2} - \frac{Y_5 + Y_6}{2}\right) - \frac{1}{2}\left(\frac{Y_3 + Y_4}{2} - \frac{Y_1 + Y_2}{2}\right)\right]$$

$$= \frac{Y_1 + Y_2 - Y_3 - Y_4 - Y_5 - Y_6 + Y_7 + Y_8}{8}.$$

The three-factor interaction is one-half of the difference between the two-factor interactions between factors 1 and 2 at the high and low levels of factor 3. Note that due to symmetry it is the same as one-half of the difference between the (13) interactions at high and low levels of factor 2 or between the (23) interactions at high and low levels of factor 1:

$$(123) = \frac{1}{2}\left[\frac{1}{2}\left(\frac{Y_8 - Y_7}{2} - \frac{Y_6 - Y_5}{2}\right) - \frac{1}{2}\left(\frac{Y_4 - Y_3}{2} - \frac{Y_2 - Y_1}{2}\right)\right]$$

$$= \frac{-Y_1 + Y_2 + Y_3 - Y_4 + Y_5 - Y_6 - Y_7 + Y_8}{8}.$$

Again, it is easy to remember the calculation of these effects from the + and − signs in Table 8.3-4. The signs in x_1, x_2, and x_3 tell us how to combine the observations for the main effects. The signs in the remaining product columns, x_1x_2, x_1x_3, x_2x_3, and $x_1x_2x_3$, which are also called the calculation columns, tell us how to calculate the interaction effects. These linear combinations are then divided by $2^k = 2^3 = 8$. Also, it is always useful to draw a cube, as we have done in Table 8.3-4, and display the responses at its vertices.

The 2^k Factorial   With k factors at two levels each, we have a total of 2^k runs. It is easy to write down these runs in standard order. Start column x_1 with one minus sign and alternate the signs until you reach row (run) 2^k. Start x_2 with two minus signs and alternate signs in blocks of 2 until row 2^k is reached. Start x_3 with $2^2 = 4$ minus signs and alternate in blocks of 4; start x_4 with $2^3 = 8$ minus signs and alternate signs in blocks of 8; and continue until you reach column x_k; it consists of 2^{k-1} minus signs, followed by 2^{k-1} plus signs.

Example 8.3-2   As an illustration of a 2^4 factorial we use the data from an experiment designed to evaluate the effect of laundering on certain fire-retardant treatments for fabrics. [M. G. Natrella, *Experimental Statistics, National Bureau of Standards Handbook 91* (Washington, D.C.: U.S. Government Printing Office, 1963).] Factor 1 is the type of fabric (sateen or monk's cloth), factor 2 corresponds to two different fire-retardant treatments, factor 3 describes the laundering condition (no laundering, after one laundering), and factor 4 corresponds to two different methods of conducting the flame test. The observations in Table 8.3-5 are inches burned, measured on a standard size sample fabric after a flame test.

The estimated effects are also listed in Table 8.3-5. Each is a linear combination of the observations, where the weights are the elements of the appropriate calculation column. For example, to get the (123) interaction, you initially multiply the x_1, x_2, and x_3 columns to obtain $x_1x_2x_3$; the signs in this column tell you how to combine the observations; finally, you divide this combination by $2^4 = 16$. The expression (1234) corresponds to the four-factor interaction. It is one-half of the difference between the three-factor interactions

TABLE 8.3-5   A 2^4 Factorial Experiment

x_1	x_2	x_3	x_4	y	Effect
$-$	$-$	$-$	$-$	42	Average $= 575/16 = 35.94$
$+$	$-$	$-$	$-$	31	$(1) = -129/16 = -8.06$
$-$	$+$	$-$	$-$	45	$(2) = 1.56$
$+$	$+$	$-$	$-$	29	$(3) = -0.56$
$-$	$-$	$+$	$-$	39	$(4) = -0.56$
$+$	$-$	$+$	$-$	28	$(12) = -2.19$
$-$	$+$	$+$	$-$	46	$(13) = -0.31$
$+$	$+$	$+$	$-$	32	$(14) = -1.56$
$-$	$-$	$-$	$+$	40	$(23) = 0.81$
$+$	$-$	$-$	$+$	30	$(24) = 0.06$
$-$	$+$	$-$	$+$	50	$(34) = -0.31$
$+$	$+$	$-$	$+$	25	$(123) = 0.31$
$-$	$-$	$+$	$+$	40	$(124) = -1.19$
$+$	$-$	$+$	$+$	25	$(134) = -0.56$
$-$	$+$	$+$	$+$	50	$(234) = -0.44$
$+$	$+$	$+$	$+$	23	$(1234) = 0.06$

For example, the $x_1 x_2 x_3$ column reads (written as a row)
$$- + + - + - - + - + + - + - - +\,.$$
Thus
$$(123) = \frac{\begin{array}{l} -42 + 31 + 45 - 29 + 39 - 28 - 46 + 32 \\ - 40 + 30 + 50 - 25 + 40 - 25 - 50 + 23 \end{array}}{16} = 0.31.$$

at the high and low levels of the fourth factor. If these three-factor interactions are the same, the four-factor interaction is zero. For the estimate of this four-factor interaction, we combine the observations according to the coefficients in the product column $x_1 x_2 x_3 x_4$ and divide by $2^4 = 16$.

After you have completed and checked these computations, you will agree that the calculation of the average and the 15 effects is quite cumbersome. In particular, you have had to form 16 sequences of $+$ and $-$ signs and then use them to form 16 linear combinations. Luckily, there is a shortcut method, the *Yates algorithm*. ■

Yates Algorithm   We start with the column of y's that correspond to the standard order of the factorial experiment. It is important to start in that particular order, as otherwise this method does not work. Then we form a new column, call it *col 1*, which we get by successive sums and differences of non-overlapping pairs of elements in the observation column. The sums are written down first: $y_2 + y_1$, $y_4 + y_3$, $y_6 + y_5$, ...; then the differences $y_2 - y_1$, $y_4 - y_3$, $y_6 - y_5$, ... Next, we form a second column, *col 2*, by repeating this summing and differencing operation on the pairs in *col 1*. That is, *col 2* is formed by first summing nonoverlapping pairs of *col 1* and then differencing

TABLE 8.3-6   Yates Algorithm for the Data in Example 8.3-2

x_1	x_2	x_3	x_4	y	col 1	col 2	col 3	col 4	Effect
$-$	$-$	$-$	$-$	42	73	147	292	575	Average $=$ 35.94
$+$	$-$	$-$	$-$	31	74	145	283	-129	(1) $= -8.06$
$-$	$+$	$-$	$-$	45	67	145	-52	25	(2) $=$ 1.56
$+$	$+$	$-$	$-$	29	78	138	-77	-35	(12) $= -2.19$
$-$	$-$	$+$	$-$	39	70	-27	12	-9	(3) $= -0.56$
$+$	$-$	$+$	$-$	28	75	-25	13	-5	(13) $= -0.31$
$-$	$+$	$+$	$-$	46	65	-35	-8	13	(23) $=$ 0.81
$+$	$+$	$+$	$-$	32	73	-42	-27	5	(123) $=$ 0.31
$-$	$-$	$-$	$+$	40	-11	1	-2	-9	(4) $= -0.56$
$+$	$-$	$-$	$+$	30	-16	11	-7	-25	(14) $= -1.56$
$-$	$+$	$-$	$+$	50	-11	5	2	1	(24) $=$ 0.06
$+$	$+$	$-$	$+$	25	-14	8	-7	-19	(124) $= -1.19$
$-$	$-$	$+$	$+$	40	-10	-5	10	-5	(34) $= -0.31$
$+$	$-$	$+$	$+$	25	-25	-3	3	-9	(134) $= -0.56$
$-$	$+$	$+$	$+$	50	-15	-15	2	-7	(234) $= -0.44$
$+$	$+$	$+$	$+$	23	-27	-12	3	1	(1234) $=$ 0.06

those same pairs. Then *col 3* is formed by applying the same operations on *col 2*, and so on. This gets repeated successively until we obtain *col k*. The elements of *col k* are then divided by 2^k. After that division, the resulting column lists the effects, in a very particular order: the first entry is the average; then (1), (2), and (12); next (3), (13), (23), (123); then (4), (14), (24), (124), (34), (134), (234), (1234); and so on.

Table 8.3-6 shows these calculations for the data in Example 8.3-2. For $k = 4$ we must carry out the summation/difference operation four times. The Yates algorithm represents a considerable savings over our earlier procedure that required the computation of 16 linear combinations.

8.3-2   Significance of Estimated Effects

We distinguish two situations. In the first we calculate the standard errors of the effects from several independent observations at each of the 2^k different factor-level combinations. That is, we have repeated the 2^k design at least once. In the second unreplicated situation, we use *normal probability plots* to assess the importance of the estimated effects.

Let us assume that there are n independent observations Y_{i1}, Y_{i2}, ..., Y_{in} with variance estimate $S_i^2 = [\sum_{j=1}^{n} (Y_{ij} - \bar{Y}_i)^2]/(n - 1)$ at each of the 2^k level combinations, $i = 1, 2, ..., 2^k$. The 2^k variance estimates can be pooled to obtain the overall variance estimate

$$S^2 = \frac{1}{2^k} \sum_{i=1}^{2^k} S_i^2 = \frac{1}{(n-1)2^k} \sum_{i=1}^{2^k} \sum_{j=1}^{n} (Y_{ij} - \bar{Y}_i)^2.$$

Since the estimate of the variance of an average $\bar{Y}_i$ at a particular level combination is S^2/n, and since the overall average and each estimated effect can be written as $(1/2^k) \sum_{i=1}^{2^k} c_i \bar{Y}_i$, where the coefficients c_i are either $+1$ or -1, we find that the estimate of the variance of an effect is

$$\text{var(effect)} = \text{var(average)} = \frac{1}{(2^k)^2} \sum_{i=1}^{2^k} \text{var}(\bar{Y}_i) = \frac{S^2}{n(2^k)}.$$

The estimates, together with the estimates of their standard deviations, which are also known as standard errors, indicate the statistical significance of the various effects.

Remark   Insignificance of an effect does not necessarily imply that this particular factor is unimportant. It just says that the response is unaffected if the factor is varied over a certain *range* (from -1 to $+1$ in coded units). For example, it could be that a factor is very important, but that a change over a certain small range has no effect on the response.   ■

Example 8.3-3   For the data in Table 8.3-3, and using the result in Exercise 8.3-1, we find that

$$s^2 = \frac{1}{4} \left[\frac{(55.5 - 54.5)^2}{2} + \frac{(60.2 - 61.0)^2}{2} + \frac{(64.5 - 63.9)^2}{2} + \frac{(67.7 - 68.7)^2}{2} \right]$$

$$= 0.375,$$

$$\text{var(effect)} = \text{var(average)} = \frac{1}{8}(0.375) = 0.0469,$$

and

$$[\text{var(effect)}]^{1/2} = [\text{var(average)}]^{1/2} = 0.22.$$

Thus the 2-sigma limits around the estimates are 60.0 ± 0.44 for the mean, 2.4 ± 0.44 for the main effect of factor 1, 4.2 ± 0.44 for the main effect of factor 2, and -0.40 ± 0.44 for the two-factor interaction. These intervals are approximate 95 percent confidence intervals. They indicate large main effects, but negligible interactions.   ■

In the second situation, we have only one observation at each factor-level combination. Thus we cannot estimate the standard error of the effects from replications. However, a *normal probability plot* (see the discussion in Section 3.4) of the estimates can shed some light on the importance of the various effects. If all effects are zero, then the observations are like a random sample drawn from a normal distribution with a fixed mean. It follows that the $2^k - 1$ main and interaction effects are normally distributed about zero. The ordered effects would therefore plot on normal probability paper about as a straight line. Those effects that do not fit reasonably well on a straight line are not easily explained as chance occurrences, and therefore are treated as "significant" effects.

Example 8.3-4 Let us consider the results from the 2^4 factorial in Example 8.3-2. The estimated effects, ordered from smallest to largest, are given in the second column of Table 8.3-7. The ranks are given in the third column; in case of ties, we assign the average rank. The ordered effects, effect$_{(i)}$, $i = 1, 2, \ldots,$ $m = 2^k - 1$, are the quantiles of order $P_i = (i - 0.5)/m$. The values of P_i are listed in the fourth column of the table.

Now, if all effects are zero and the estimated effects are just a sample from a normal distribution with mean zero, a scatter plot of P_i against effect$_{(i)}$ on ordinary graph paper should resemble the "S-shaped" c.d.f. of a normal distribution. Furthermore, since the mean of the normal distribution is zero, this curve should pass through the point $(0, 0.5)$. We could also plot the points (effect$_{(i)}$, P_i) on normal probability paper and should find that they fall more or less on a straight line that goes through the point $(0, 0.5)$.

Alternatively, with today's computers we can easily calculate z_i, the normal scores that correspond to the effects. The normal scores are the quantiles of order P_i from the standard normal distribution; that is, they satisfy $P_i = P(Z \le z_i) = \Phi(z_i)$. The normal scores are listed in the fifth column of Table 8.3-7. If all effects are zero, the points (effect$_{(i)}$, z_i), when plotted on ordinary graph paper, should lie on a straight line. Furthermore, since the mean of the distribution is zero, the line should go through the point $(0, 0)$. In the case of Example 8.3-2, this plot is given in Figure 8.3-1. Note that the point associated with effect (1) is far from a straight line going through the other points. Hence the main effect of factor 1, the type of fabric, appears to be nonzero. ■

Normal Scores of the $m = 2^4 - 1 = 15$
Estimated Effects: Example 8.3-2

Identity of Effect	Effect by Magnitude	Rank	$P_i = \dfrac{i - 0.5}{m}$	z_i
(1)	−8.06	1	0.033	−1.84
(12)	−2.19	2	0.100	−1.28
(14)	−1.56	3	0.167	−0.97
(124)	−1.19	4	0.233	−0.73
(3)	−0.56	6	0.367	−0.34
(4)	−0.56	6	0.367	−0.34
(134)	−0.56	6	0.367	−0.34
(234)	−0.44	8	0.500	0.00
(13)	−0.31	9.5	0.600	0.25
(34)	−0.31	9.5	0.600	0.25
(24)	0.06	11.5	0.733	0.62
(1234)	0.06	11.5	0.733	0.62
(123)	0.31	13	0.833	0.97
(23)	0.81	14	0.900	1.28
(2)	1.56	15	0.967	1.84

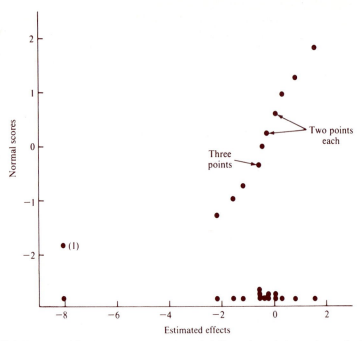

FIGURE 8.3.1   Dot diagram and normal probability plot of the estimated effects in Example 8.3-2.

Exercises 8.3

8.3-1 Show that the sample variance from a sample of $n = 2$ observations is one-half of the squared difference of the two observations. Thus, for $n = 2$, the variance estimate in the replicated 2^k factorial in Section 8.3-2 is

$$s^2 = \frac{1}{2^{k+1}} \sum_{i=1}^{2^k} (y_{i1} - y_{i2})^2.$$

8.3-2 The main and interaction effects in the general two-factor factorial experiment in Section 8.1 were defined as $\alpha_i = \bar{\mu}_{i\cdot} - \bar{\mu}_{\cdot\cdot}$, $\beta_j = \bar{\mu}_{\cdot j} - \bar{\mu}_{\cdot\cdot}$, and $(\alpha\beta)_{ij} = \mu_{ij} - \bar{\mu}_{i\cdot} - \bar{\mu}_{\cdot j} + \bar{\mu}_{\cdot\cdot}$, for $i = 1, \ldots, a$ and $j = 1, \ldots, b$. For $a = b = 2$, and, using an obvious notation for the four means μ_{--}, μ_{+-}, μ_{-+}, and μ_{++}, show that

(a) $\alpha_+ = -\alpha_- = (-\mu_{--} + \mu_{+-} - \mu_{-+} + \mu_{++})/4.$
(b) $\beta_+ = -\beta_- = (-\mu_{--} - \mu_{+-} + \mu_{-+} + \mu_{++})/4.$

(c) $(\alpha\beta)_{++} = -(\alpha\beta)_{-+} = -(\alpha\beta)_{+-} = (\alpha\beta)_{--}$
$= (\mu_{--} - \mu_{+-} - \mu_{-+} + \mu_{++})/4.$

8.3-3 Percent yields from a certain chemical reaction for changing temperature (factor 1), reaction time (factor 2), and concentration (factor 3) are as follows, where each $\bar{y}$ is computed from $n = 5$ replications:

x_1	x_2	x_3	$\bar{y}$
−	−	−	79.7
+	−	−	74.3
−	+	−	76.7
+	+	−	70.0
−	−	+	84.0
+	−	+	81.3
−	+	+	87.3
+	+	+	73.7

(a) Estimate the main effects, the three two-factor interactions, and the three-factor interaction.

(b) The variance estimate from $n = 5$ replications in each cell is $s^2 = 40$. Calculate standard errors for the estimated effects and interpret your findings.

8.3-4 Box, Hunter, and Hunter studied the effects of catalyst charge (10 pounds, 20 pounds), temperature (220°C, 240°C), pressure (50 psi, 80 psi) and concentration (10 percent, 12 percent) on percent conversion of a certain chemical (Y). The results of a 2^4 factorial experiment, in standard order, are given in the accompanying table. The actual order of the 16 experiments was randomized.

x_1	x_2	x_3	x_4	y	Order of Run
−	−	−	−	71	8
+	−	−	−	61	2
−	+	−	−	90	10
+	+	−	−	82	4
−	−	+	−	68	15
+	−	+	−	61	9
−	+	+	−	87	1
+	+	+	−	80	13
−	−	−	+	61	16
+	−	−	+	50	5
−	+	−	+	89	11
+	+	−	+	83	14
−	−	+	+	59	3
+	−	+	+	51	12
−	+	+	+	85	6
+	+	+	+	78	7

(a) Estimate the main effects and the two-, three-, and four-factor interactions. Use the Yates algorithm.

(b) Make a normal probability plot of the estimated effects and assess the significance of the various effects.

[G. E. P. Box, W. G. Hunter, and J. S. Hunter, *Statistics for Experimenters* (New York: Wiley, 1978), p. 325.]

8.3-5 Anderson and McLean discuss a 2^4 factorial experiment that arose in the finishing of metal strips in a metallurgical process. The measured response was a score for smoothness of the surface finish,

where a small reading was desirable and a large number indicated roughness. The factors (two levels each) that were included in this experiment were solution temperature (x_1), solution concentration (x_2), roll size (x_3) and roll tension (x_4).

x_1	x_2	x_3	x_4	y	x_1	x_2	x_3	x_4	y
−	−	−	−	17	−	−	−	+	11
+	−	−	−	14	+	−	−	+	18
−	+	−	−	8	−	+	−	+	8
+	+	−	−	16	+	+	−	+	21
−	−	+	−	11	−	−	+	+	14
+	−	+	−	15	+	−	+	+	21
−	+	+	−	9	−	+	+	+	12
+	+	+	−	4	+	+	+	+	13

(a) Estimate the main effects and all possible interactions. Use the Yates algorithm.

(b) Make a normal probability plot of the estimated effects and discuss the importance of the various effects.

[V. L. Anderson and R. A. McLean, *Design of Experiments: A Realistic Approach* (New York: Marcel Dekker, 1974), p. 232.]

8.3-6 Gunter, Tadder, and Hemak use factorial designs to improve the picture-tube phosphor screening process at RCA's picture-tube manufacturing facility. The phosphor screening process involves applying, exposing, and developing a photosensitive phosphor slurry to the inside of the picture-tube faceplate. This operation requires precise control of the slurry's chemical and physical properties. A slurry is a mixture of numerous chemicals. Included in the slurry are three surfactant additives, *A*, *B*, and *C*, that help make the slurry smoother and more able to wet the panel surface.

When Gunter, Tadder, and Hemak started their investigation, the process was already in a state of good statistical control, which means that the results were consistent over time. However, to reduce costs, it was essential to reduce the losses, which were measured by screen-room process rejects. Process personnel had a great deal of knowledge about the process and had found satisfactory levels for the three surfactant additives, but systematic statistical studies had not been made before, either in the laboratory or on-line in the plant.

They used an *evolutionary operation* (or EVOP for short) approach, in which small changes in the process levels are made without interfering significantly with the ongoing process. Small changes in these key variables are made according to a predetermined pattern (i.e., a design); and the resulting changes in the response are recorded, analyzed, and interpreted. [For a more detailed description of EVOP, refer to G. E. P. Box and N. R. Draper, *Evolutionary Operation* (New York: Wiley, 1969).]

Here the three surfactant additives were varied according to a 2^3 factorial experiment. The current settings of the three additives were varied slightly, and low ($-$) and high ($+$) levels were determined. In addition to these eight combinations of high and low settings, it was decided to run two experiments at the standard settings (each coded variable equals zero). The 10 runs required about 14 production days. The order of these runs was randomized, except that in each week a run with standard settings was conducted. The losses from the $2^3 = 8$ factorial runs were as follows:

| | Surfactant Additive | | | |
	A	B	C	Loss
	−	−	−	1.28
	+	−	−	1.93
	−	+	−	0.94
	+	+	−	1.31
	−	−	+	0.36
	+	−	+	1.11
	−	+	+	1.16
	+	+	+	1.58

(a) Calculate the main and interaction effects.

(b) The replications at the center point (i.e., experiments at the standard settings) led to losses of 0.83 and 1.40 units. Use these two values to calculate a very crude estimate of the variance of an individual observation, and estimate roughly the standard error of the estimated effects.

(c) Use the standard error in part (b) to interpret the

results of your experiment. How would you change the surfactant additives to reduce your losses? Why would it be reasonable to use the $(-, -, +)$ point of the 2^3 cube as the center point of a new EVOP cube and to start a new cycle around this point?
[B. H. Gunter, A. L. Tadder, and C. M. Hemak, "Improving the Picture Tube Phosphor Screening Process with EVOP," *RCA Engineer*, 30(3): 54–59 (1985).]

8.3-7 Ronald Snee (in a personal communication) describes the application of a factorial design in a product impurity study at du Pont. The experiment was carried out by an engineer who had taken a du Pont short course on the strategy of experimentation. The objective of his study was to find ways of reducing the level of impurity of a chemical product. Three factors were thought to be important: the *type* of polymer that was used (the engineer compared the standard polymer B, with a new but more expensive one, A), the polymer *concentration* (concentration was varied between the low level, 0.01 percent, and high level, 0.04 percent), and the amount of a certain *additive* (which was varied from a low level of 2 pounds to the high level of 12 pounds). The additive was known to have an effect at 2 pounds and it was of interest to determine whether higher levels would be of benefit. A factorial experiment with factors at these low and high levels was conducted and the percentage impurities from these runs are given in the accompanying table. Note there are replications at some (but not all) design points.

Polymer	Polymer Concentration (percent)	Additive (pounds)	Impurity (percent)
A	0.01	2	1.0
B	0.01	2	1.0, 1.2
A	0.04	2	0.2
B	0.04	2	0.5
A	0.01	12	0.9, 0.7
B	0.01	12	1.1
A	0.04	12	0.2, 0.3
B	0.04	12	0.5

(a) Give a graphic representation of the information

in the table. You may want to draw a cube and display the impurities at its vertices. Interpret the results.

(b) Estimate the main and interaction effects (use the averages from the replications in your calculations). Calculate an estimate of the process variance σ^2 and an estimate of the variance of the effects.

Hint   Use the three cases with replications to get an estimate of σ^2. Use this to calculate the variances of the responses (which are either individual observations or averages of replicates). For example, $\mathrm{var}(Y_1) = \sigma^2$, $\mathrm{var}(\bar{Y}_2) = \sigma^2/2$, since we took the average of 1.0 and 1.2 when we calculated the effects, and so on. Adding these variances and dividing by $(8)^2 = 64$ will give you the variance of an effect.

(c) You will find that a switch from the standard polymer B to the more expensive polymer A will decrease the impurities. Is this sufficient reason to switch to polymer A, or should additional analyses be conducted?

Hint   Recall cost-benefit analysis.

(d) Is it appropriate to conclude that the additive has "no effect" on impurity? What recommendations would you make concerning the level of the additive?   (usduty; (str (o), lot not (2))

(e) What level of polymer concentration would you recommend? What considerations would you evaluate to reach a decision?

8.3-8   An experiment is performed to compare the cleaning action of two detergents, detergent A and detergent B. Thirty-two swatches of cloth are soiled with grease; 16 are washed with detergent A and 16 with detergent B in an agitator machine and then measured for "whiteness." Criticize the following aspects of the experiment.

(a) The entire experiment is performed with soft water.

(b) To accelerate the testing procedure, the experimenter used very hot water and 10-minute washing times.

(c) All experiments with detergent A were done first.

(d) Briefly discuss how the experiment should be done. Assume that softness of the water, water temperature, and washing time might be important.

8.3-9   The yields (in percent) of a certain chemical reaction for changing levels of temperature (factor 1), reaction time (factor 2), and concentration (factor 3) are given below (each $\bar{y}$ is computed from $n = 3$ observations):

Temp. (°F)	Time (min)	Concentration (percent)	$\bar{y}$
250	50	3	71.8
200	50	5	81.5
250	60	5	71.2
250	50	5	78.8
200	50	3	77.2
200	60	3	74.2
200	60	5	84.8
250	60	3	67.5

Note that these runs are given in the actual randomized order, not in standard order.

(a) Estimate the main effects and the two- and three-factor interactions.

(b) The variance estimate from the three replications in each cell is $s^2 = 24$; find standard errors of the estimated effects, calculate approximate confidence intervals for the effects, and interpret your findings.

8.3-10   A chemical engineer is trying to improve the efficiency of a reaction that converts a raw material into a product. The response variable Y is called the *degree of conversion*. The engineer varies three factors: catalyst type (C), reactant concentration (R), and reaction temperature (T); two replications were made in each cell. The data in coded form (Y-59) are presented below.

	Catalyst, C			
	Type 1		Type 2	
	Reactant Concentration, R			
Temperature, T	0.1%	0.5%	0.1%	0.5%
120°	25	26	2	8
	16	33	1	15
160°	29	27	4	27
	23	31	0	35

(a) Estimate main and interaction effects, obtain their standard errors, and interpret your findings.

(b) Display the results graphically. For example, separately, for each level of catalyst, display the cell means of the other two factors (as in Table 8.3-3). Use this plot to describe the nature of the three-factor interaction.

(c) Which factor-level combination produces the greatest degree of conversion?

8.4 2^{k-p} Fractional Factorial Experiments

Investigators frequently have an extensive list of factors that may possibly have an effect on the response. However, it is often not feasible to conduct a full 2^k factorial experiment when the number of factors k is large since this would require experiments (runs) at all combinations of two levels of each of k factors. The number of runs increases rapidly with k; for example, a full factorial with seven factors requires $2^7 = 128$ runs. In this section we show that certain well-chosen parts of the 2^k factorial design allow us to estimate the main relationships without too much loss of information. If that part is only $1/2^p$ of the full 2^k factorial design, it is called a 2^{k-p} *fractional factorial design*. If $p = 1$, we talk about a half fraction as we perform one-half of the original; if $p = 2$, a quarter fraction; and so on.

8.4-1   Half Fractions of 2^k Factorial Experiments

A 2^{3-1} Fractional Factorial   Let us consider an illustration with $k = 3$ factors. Instead of studying the response at all eight factor-level combinations in the 2^3 factorial, we consider a half fraction ($p = 1$). The question now becomes: Which four runs from the cube in Figure 8.4-1 should be selected in

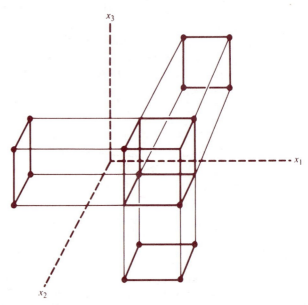

FIGURE 8.4-1   The 2^{3-1} fractional factorial design and its projection into three 2^2 factorials.

TABLE 8.4-1   The 2^{3-1} Fractional Factorial with $x_3 = x_1 x_2$

Run	Design x_1	x_2	x_3	Y
1	−	−	+	Y_1
2	+	−	−	Y_2
3	−	+	−	Y_3
4	+	+	+	Y_4

$$L_0 = (Y_1 + Y_2 + Y_3 + Y_4)/4 \rightarrow \mu + (123)$$
$$L_1 = (-Y_1 + Y_2 - Y_3 + Y_4)/4 \rightarrow (1) + (23)$$
$$L_2 = (-Y_1 - Y_2 + Y_3 + Y_4)/4 \rightarrow (2) + (13)$$
$$L_3 = (Y_1 - Y_2 - Y_3 + Y_4)/4 \rightarrow (3) + (12)$$

the 2^{3-1} fractional factorial design? One possible, and in fact, very good half fraction uses the factor-level combinations listed in Table 8.4-1. These points correspond to the circled corners of the cube in Figure 8.4-1.

Figure 8.4-1 illustrates that this particular fraction supplies a complete factorial in each of the three pairs of factors because any projection of the 2^{3-1} design into a two-dimensional plane produces a complete 2^2 factorial experiment. Such a design is therefore good in screening situations in which it can reasonably be assumed that out of three factors, no more than two are of importance.

Obviously, since there are only four runs, we cannot estimate three main effects, three two-factor interactions, and the three-factor interaction separately. In fact, we note from Table 8.4-1 that the levels of the third factor in x_3 are selected so that $x_3 = x_1 x_2$. Thus the linear combination that corresponds to the third column, denoted by $L_3 = (Y_1 - Y_2 - Y_3 + Y_4)/4$, *confounds* the main effect (3) and the two-factor interaction (12). Our notation in Table 8.4-1, $L_3 \rightarrow (3) + (12)$, expresses the fact that L_3 estimates the sum of (3) and (12).

The formal multiplication of one column by itself gives a column of + signs, which is denoted by I; that is, $I = x_1 x_1 = x_2 x_2 = x_3 x_3$ and $Ix_1 = x_1$, $Ix_2 = x_2$, and $Ix_3 = x_3$. Thus $x_3 = x_1 x_2$ is equivalent to $I = x_1 x_2 x_3$, as can be seen from the multiplication with x_3. Hence it is also true that $x_1 = x_1 x_1 x_2 x_3 = x_2 x_3$. Accordingly, we find that $L_1 = (-Y_1 + Y_2 - Y_3 + Y_4)/4$ confounds (1) and (23). In addition, the fact that $x_2 = x_2 x_1 x_2 x_3 = x_1 x_3$ means $L_2 = (-Y_1 - Y_2 + Y_3 + Y_4)/4$ confounds (2) and (13). Finally, since the $x_1 x_2 x_3$ product column is equal to a column of + signs, which we denote by I, the average $L_0 = (Y_1 + Y_2 + Y_3 + Y_4)/4$ confounds the overall mean level μ and the three-factor interaction (123).

The relationship that generates the levels of the third factor, $x_3 = x_1 x_2$, is equivalent to $x_3 x_3 = x_1 x_2 x_3$ and thus $I = x_1 x_2 x_3$. This relationship is called the *generator* of the 2^{3-1} fractional factorial. As seen earlier, the confounding patterns can be obtained from the equation $I = x_1 x_2 x_3$:

$$Ix_1 = x_1(x_1 x_2 x_3) \quad \text{or} \quad x_1 = x_2 x_3, \quad \text{since } x_1 x_1 = I,$$

$$Ix_2 = x_2(x_1 x_2 x_3) \quad \text{or} \quad x_2 = x_1 x_3, \quad \text{since } x_2 x_2 = I,$$

$$Ix_3 = x_3(x_1 x_2 x_3) \quad \text{or} \quad x_3 = x_1 x_2, \quad \text{since } x_3 x_3 = I.$$

The factor-level combinations and the confounding patterns in the 2^{3-1} fractional factorial are summarized in Table 8.4-1.

Since pairs of effects have been confounded, we cannot tell which member of a pair might cause a significant measurement. Thus we say that one member of such a pair is the *alias* of the other. In this illustration, we have alias pairs (1) and (23), (2) and (13), and (3) and (12).

A 2^{4-1} Fractional Factorial   In our next illustration, we study $k = 4$ factors in eight runs. This calls for a half fraction ($p = 1$) of the 2^4 factorial, or a 2^{4-1} fractional factorial. Since we have $2^3 = 8$ runs, we construct our fractional factorial by first writing down a complete factorial in any three factors and then associating one of the interaction terms with the levels of the fourth factor. We can use any of the two- or three-factor interactions. However, it is usually best to confound the levels of the fourth factor with the highest possible interaction. Thus we select the generator $x_4 = x_1 x_2 x_3$ or, equivalently, $I = x_1 x_2 x_3 x_4$ because $x_4 x_4 = I$.

Table 8.4-2 lists the factor-level combinations for the eight runs. Run 1 sets all four factors at their low levels. Run 2 sets factors 1 and 4 at their high levels and factors 2 and 3 at their low ones. Run 3 has factors 1 and 3 at their low levels and factors 2 and 4 at their high ones; and so on. Table 8.4-2 also shows the confounding patterns that result from this particular fraction. For example, since $x_1 = x_2 x_3 x_4$, the linear combination $L_1 = (-Y_1 + Y_2 - Y_3 + Y_4 - Y_5 + Y_6 - Y_7 + Y_8)/8$ estimates the sum of (1) and (234).

We say that this fractional factorial design is of *resolution* IV. The reason for this terminology is that main effects are confounded with three-factor interactions $(1 + 3 = 4)$ and two-factor interactions are confounded with two-factor interactions $(2 + 2 = 4)$, but main effects are not confounded with other main effects or with two-factor interactions. We denote it by 2^{4-1}_{IV} and call it a 2^{4-1} fractional factorial of resolution IV.

If one assumes that three- and four-factor interactions are negligible, which is a very reasonable assumption in most cases, then the linear combinations L_1, L_2, L_3 and L_7 in this fractional factorial arrangement provide unconfounded estimates of the main effects. The two-factor interactions, however, are confounded with other two-factor interactions.

Note that the 2^{4-1}, with $I = x_1 x_2 x_3 x_4$, is not the only possible fractional design of four factors in eight runs. For example, we could have selected the levels of the fourth factor, x_4, such that $x_4 = x_1 x_2$. However, this design confounds the main effect of factor 4 with the (12) interaction and thus is of

TABLE 8.4-2   **The 2_{IV}^{4-1} Fractional Factorial Design with $x_4 = x_1 x_2 x_3$**

Run	x_1	x_2	x_3	$x_1 x_2$	$x_1 x_3$	$x_2 x_3$	x_4 $x_1 x_2 x_3$	y
1	−	−	−	+	+	+	−	$y_1 = 21$
2	+	−	−	−	−	+	+	$y_2 = 23$
3	−	+	−	−	+	−	+	$y_3 = 27$
4	+	+	−	+	−	−	−	$y_4 = 24$
5	−	−	+	+	−	−	+	$y_5 = 23$
6	+	−	+	−	+	−	−	$y_6 = 26$
7	−	+	+	−	−	+	−	$y_7 = 33$
8	+	+	+	+	+	+	+	$y_8 = 37$

Design   Design

$$26.75 = L_0 = (y_1 + y_2 + y_3 + y_4 + y_5 + y_6 + y_7 + y_8)/8 \to \mu + (1234)$$
$$0.75 = L_1 = (-y_1 + y_2 - y_3 + y_4 - y_5 + y_6 - y_7 + y_8)/8 \to (1) + (234)$$
$$3.50 = L_2 \to (2) + (134)$$
$$3.00 = L_3 \to (3) + (124)$$
$$-0.50 = L_4 = (y_1 - y_2 - y_3 + y_4 + y_5 - y_6 - y_7 + y_8)/8 \to (12) + (34)$$
$$1.00 = L_5 \to (13) + (24)$$
$$1.75 = L_6 \to (23) + (14)$$
$$0.75 = L_7 = (-y_1 + y_2 + y_3 - y_4 + y_5 - y_6 - y_7 + y_8)/8 \to (4) + (123)$$

resolution III. It is not as desirable as the resolution IV design. We have already studied one resolution III design, the 2_{III}^{3-1} with generator $I = x_1 x_2 x_3$.

Example 8.4-1   This example of a 2_{IV}^{4-1}, with $I = x_1 x_2 x_3 x_4$, comes from a producer of cake mixes concerned about the texture of its cake frostings. Four different constituents that go into the manufacture of cake frosting were thought to have an effect on texture. A 2_{IV}^{4-1} fractional factorial was conducted; the texture readings and the estimated effects are given in Table 8.4-2. The results show that there are three large estimates, $L_2 = 3.50$, $L_3 = 3.00$, and $L_6 = 1.75$. The most reasonable interpretation of these results is that the main effects of factors 2 and 3, together with their interaction (23), are important. Another interpretation would be that main effects (2) and (3) and the (14) interaction are important. However, this is less plausible because models that include only interactions of factors, such as (14), and not their main effects, (1) and (4) here, are not as common.

We treat the estimates L_2, L_3, and L_6 as important effects, since they are large compared to the others. Ideally, however, we should assess their significance by comparing them with a standard error estimate from replications. If replications are not available, we should make a normal probability plot of the effects. (Refer to the discussion in Section 8.3.)

A 2^{5-1} Fractional Factorial　As another illustration, consider a 2^{5-1} fractional factorial to study five factors in $2^4 = 16$ runs. We can generate the design points by first writing down four columns associated with a full 2^4 factorial in four factors together with the 11 columns given by the various products $(x_1x_2, x_1x_3, \ldots, x_1x_2x_3, \ldots, x_1x_2x_3x_4)$. Finally, we associate the levels of the fifth factor with the four-factor interaction; that is, we choose the generator as $x_5 = x_1x_2x_3x_4$ or $I = x_1x_2x_3x_4x_5$ because $x_5x_5 = I$. In Exercise 8.4-2, you are asked to write down the level combinations of this design and determine the confounding patterns. For example, we find that L_1 estimates $(1) + (2345)$, since $x_1 = x_2x_3x_4x_5$; L_5, the combination that corresponds to the signs in x_1x_2, estimates $(12) + (345)$, because $x_1x_2 = x_3x_4x_5$. This fractional factorial design confounds main effects with four-factor interactions, and two-factor interactions with three-factor interactions. Thus it is said to be of resolution V, because $1 + 4 = 5$ and $2 + 3 = 5$. We denote it by 2_V^{5-1}. If we can assume that interactions of three or more factors are zero, a resolution V design leads to unconfounded estimates of all main effects and two-factor interactions.

8.4-2　Higher Fractions of 2^k Factorial Experiments

So far we have considered only half fractions of 2^k factorials, that is, 2^{k-1} fractional factorials. Now let us consider higher fractions. For example, let us consider a design to study seven factors in only $2^3 = 8$ runs. Since $2^7 = 128$, this is one 16th fraction, or a 2^{7-4} fractional factorial.

One can generate the eight design points by first writing down a full 2^3 factorial in three factors, and then associating the two- and three-factor interaction columns with the four additional factors. Thus there are four generators: $x_4 = x_1x_2$, $x_5 = x_1x_3$, $x_6 = x_2x_3$, and $x_7 = x_1x_2x_3$. Multiplying these by x_4, x_5, x_6, and x_7, respectively, and noting $x_4x_4 = x_5x_5 = x_6x_6 = x_7x_7 = I$, we obtain the *generating relation*

$$I = x_1x_2x_4 = x_1x_3x_5 = x_2x_3x_6 = x_1x_2x_3x_7.$$

The factor-level combinations for the 2^{7-4} fractional factorial are given in Table 8.4-3. The linear combinations $L_0, L_1, \ldots, L_7$ will confound main effects and interactions. How can one determine these relationships? A straightforward approach, which, however, is often laborious if there are several generators, is now being described. Note that the products of any number of the four expressions in the generating relationship will again lead to I. Considering all possible products of two, three, and four of these expressions, we find that

$$\begin{aligned}
I &= x_1x_2x_4 = x_1x_3x_5 = x_2x_3x_6 = x_1x_2x_3x_7 \\
&= x_2x_3x_4x_5 = x_1x_3x_4x_6 = x_3x_4x_7 = x_1x_2x_5x_6 \\
&= x_2x_5x_7 = x_1x_6x_7 = x_4x_5x_6 = x_1x_4x_5x_7 \\
&= x_2x_4x_6x_7 = x_3x_5x_6x_7 = x_1x_2x_3x_4x_5x_6x_7.
\end{aligned}$$

TABLE 8.4-3   The 2_{III}^{7-4} Fractional Factorial Design

Run	x_1	x_2	x_3	x_4 $x_1 x_2$	x_5 $x_1 x_3$	x_6 $x_2 x_3$	x_7 $x_1 x_2 x_3$	y
1	−	−	−	+	+	+	−	$y_1 = 68.4$
2	+	−	−	−	−	+	+	$y_2 = 77.7$
3	−	+	−	−	+	−	+	$y_3 = 66.4$
4	+	+	−	+	−	−	−	$y_4 = 81.0$
5	−	−	+	+	−	−	+	$y_5 = 78.6$
6	+	−	+	−	+	−	−	$y_6 = 41.2$
7	−	+	+	−	−	+	−	$y_7 = 68.7$
8	+	+	+	+	+	+	+	$y_8 = 38.7$

Design

$$65.1 = L_0 \rightarrow \mu$$
$$-5.4 = L_1 \rightarrow (1) + (24) + (35) + (67)$$
$$-1.4 = L_2 \rightarrow (2) + (14) + (36) + (57)$$
$$-8.3 = L_3 \rightarrow (3) + (15) + (26) + (47)$$
$$1.6 = L_4 \rightarrow (4) + (12) + (56) + (37)$$
$$-11.4 = L_5 \rightarrow (5) + (13) + (46) + (27)$$
$$-1.7 = L_6 \rightarrow (6) + (23) + (45) + (17)$$
$$0.3 = L_7 \rightarrow (7) + (34) + (25) + (16)$$

We call this the *defining relation*. Since there are four generators in the 2^{7-4}, there are $2^4 = 16$ expressions (including I) in the defining relation.

The precise confounding patterns can be obtained from the defining relation. For example, multiplying this relation by x_1, we find that the linear combination L_1 estimates

$$(1) + (24) + (35) + (1236) + (237) + (12345) + \cdots + (234567).$$

The resolution of this design is III, since it confounds main effects with two-factor interactions. The confounding relations in Table 8.4-3 are obtained after we assume that interactions of three or more factors can be disregarded (i.e., assuming these interactions are essentially zero).

Due to the very small fraction, (1/16 of a full 2^7 factorial), we confound main effects with two-factor interactions even after assuming that higher-order interactions are equal to zero. Thus, at first, there may be considerable ambiguity due to the confounding of particular estimates. However, fractional factorial experiments are of considerable value in situations where experiments are performed in sequence. Having performed one fraction, the results can be reviewed; and if there is ambiguity, a further group of experiments can be selected to resolve the uncertainty. The basic ideas behind this sequential approach to fractional factorial experimentation are outlined briefly in Exercises 8.4-6 and 8.4-7. For a more detailed discussion, the reader should consult books on the design of experiments, such as G. E. P. Box, W. G. Hunter, and J. S. Hunter, *Statistics for Experimenters*, (New York: Wiley, 1978).

Example 8.4-2 Box and Hunter [in "The 2^{k-p} Fractional Factorial Designs," *Technometrics*, 3: 311-351 (1961)] describe a specific application of a 2_{III}^{7-4} factorial design in which a company experienced considerable difficulties at the filtration stage in the startup of a new manufacturing unit. Various explanations for the much longer filtration times were discussed, and the following seven variables were proposed as being possibly responsible: water supply (town, local well), raw material (two suppliers), temperature at filtration (low, high), recycling (included, omitted), rate of addition of caustic soda (slow, fast), type of filter cloth (old, new), and hold-up time (two different storage times prior to filtration). The results in Table 8.4-3 show three large estimates, $L_1 = -5.4$, $L_3 = -8.3$, and $L_5 = -11.4$. The simplest interpretation would be that the main effects of factors 1, 3, and 5 are important. However, other interpretations are also possible. It could be that factors 3 and 5 and their interaction (35), or factors 1 and 5 and (15), or 1 and 3 and (13) are important. At this stage we do not know. However, following up the design with another fraction could resolve the ambiguities due to the confounding of the estimates. For example, Exercise 8.4-6 shows that a "foldover" of the original design would leave all main effects unconfounded. Changing the levels of a particular factor, say the fifth one, would leave the main effect of factor 5 and all two-factor interactions with factor 5 unconfounded (Exercise 8.4-7). ∎

The 2_{III}^{7-4} design just considered is also called a *saturated design* because every calculation column in the original 2^3 factorial generates the levels of an additional four factors. Another example of a saturated design is the 2_{III}^{15-11} design. It allows us to study 15 variables in 16 runs. Every interaction column from the original 2^4 factorial generates the levels of an additional factor ($x_5 = x_1 x_2$, $x_6 = x_1 x_3$, ..., $x_{11} = x_1 x_2 x_3$, ..., $x_{15} = x_1 x_2 x_3 x_4$). These designs are very useful in screening situations in which a large number of factors could possibly have an effect on the response.

Exercises 8.4

8.4-1 Consider the 2_{IV}^{4-1} fractional factorial design with generator $I = x_1 x_2 x_3 x_4$. Show that the confounding patterns in Table 8.4-2 are correct.

8.4-2 Consider the 2_V^{5-1} fractional factorial design with generator $I = x_1 x_2 x_3 x_4 x_5$. Specify the factor-level combinations for this design and obtain the confounding patterns.

Hint Start with the 2^4 factorial design and write down the two-, three-, and four-factor interaction columns. Associate the levels of the fifth factor with $x_1 x_2 x_3 x_4$, the four-factor interaction.

8.4-3 Consider the 2^{5-2} fractional factorial with generators $x_4 = x_1 x_2$ and $x_5 = x_1 x_2 x_3$. Specify the factor-level combinations for this design and determine the confounding patterns. What is the resolution of this design?

Hint   Start with a 2^3 factorial design and specify all interaction columns. Associate x_4 with $x_1 x_2$ and x_5 with $x_1 x_2 x_3$. Since there are two generators, there are $2^2 = 4$ terms in the defining relation, $I = x_1 x_2 x_4 = x_1 x_2 x_3 x_5 = x_3 x_4 x_5$.

8.4-4   Consider the 2^{6-2} fractional factorial with $x_5 = x_1 x_2 x_3$ and $x_6 = x_2 x_3 x_4$. Repeat Exercise 8.4-3 but start with a 2^4 factorial design.

8.4-5   Consider the 2_{III}^{7-4} design given in this section. Assuming that interactions among three or more factors are zero, show that we obtain the confounding patterns that are given in Table 8.4-3.

8.4-6   The 2_{III}^{7-4} design in Table 8.4-3 was one particular fraction of the 2^7 with generators $x_4 = x_1 x_2$, $x_5 = x_1 x_3$, $x_6 = x_2 x_3$, and $x_7 = x_1 x_2 x_3$. Consider another fraction, which you obtain by changing all the signs in the $x_1, x_2, x_3, x_4, x_5, x_6, x_7$ columns in Table 8.4-3. This is called the *foldover* of the original fraction.

(a) Convince yourself that these eight runs are the same as the ones that you get by writing down a 2^3 and selecting the levels of the other four factors as $x_4 = -x_1 x_2$, $x_5 = -x_1 x_3$, $x_6 = -x_2 x_3$, and $x_7 = x_1 x_2 x_3$.

(b) Using the generators in part (a), write down the defining relation for this fractional design.

(c) Assuming that interactions of three or more factors are zero, determine the confounding relationships for the estimates in this fractional design. Call the estimates $L_0', L_1', \ldots, L_7'$.

(d) Combine the linear combinations from the original (L_i) and the second (L_i') fraction, and form $(L_i + L_i')/2$ and $(L_i - L_i')/2$. Show that these linear combinations lead to unconfounded estimates of all seven main effects, while two-factor interactions are still confounded. For example, we find that $(L_1 + L_1')/2 \to (1)$ and $(L_1 - L_1')/2 \to (24) + (35) + (67)$.

8.4-7   Consider the same original 2_{III}^{7-4} design as in Exercise 8.4-6. But now consider another fraction, which we obtain by changing the signs of a single factor, say factor 5, in the original design.

(a) Convince yourself that these eight new runs are the same as the ones you obtain by writing down a 2^3 and selecting the levels of the other four factors as $x_4 = x_1 x_2$, $x_5 = -x_1 x_3$, $x_6 = x_2 x_3$, and $x_7 = x_1 x_2 x_3$.

(b) Using these generators, write down the defining relation for this fractional design.

(c) Assuming that interactions of three or more factors are zero, determine the confounding relationships for the estimates, say $L_0'', L_1'', \ldots, L_7''$.

(d) Combine these estimates with the ones from the original 2_{III}^{7-4} and form $(L_i + L_i'')/2$ and $(L_i - L_i'')/2$. Show that this will lead to unconfounded estimates of the main effect of factor 5 and of all two-factor interactions with factor 5.

8.4-8   Snee reports on a study that was designed to determine the factors that affect the color of a certain chemical product. A study of the process identified five factors that were thought to be important. It was decided to study these variables over the following ranges:

Process Variable	Low (−)	High (+)
x_1 = solvent/reactant	Low	High
x_2 = catalyst/reactant	0.025	0.035
x_3 = temperature (°C)	150	160
x_4 = reactant purity (percent)	92	96
x_5 = pH of reactant	8.0	8.7

The variables were studied using a 2^{5-1} fractional factorial design with generator $x_5 = x_1 x_2 x_3 x_4$ or, equivalently, $I = x_1 x_2 x_3 x_4 x_5$. Determine the confounding patterns that are implied by this particular fraction. The color of the product (in coded units) produced in each of the 16 runs (which were carried out in random order) is given in the accompanying table. Analyze the data. Plot the estimated effects on normal probability paper or, equivalently, use the computer to plot the normal scores of the effects against the effects. In your analysis you can assume that the interactions of order three or greater are zero.

Run	x_1	x_2	x_3	x_4	x_5	Color
1	−	−	−	−	+	−0.63
2	+	−	−	−	−	2.51
3	−	+	−	−	−	−2.68
4	+	+	−	−	+	−1.66
5	−	−	+	−	−	2.06
6	+	−	+	−	+	1.22
7	−	+	+	−	+	−2.09

Run	x_1	x_2	x_3	x_4	x_5	Color
8	+	+	+	−	−	1.93
9	−	−	−	+	−	6.79
10	+	−	−	+	+	6.47
11	−	+	−	+	+	3.45
12	+	+	−	+	−	5.68
13	−	−	+	+	+	5.22
14	+	−	+	+	−	9.38
15	−	+	+	+	−	4.30
16	+	+	+	+	+	4.05

[R. D. Snee, "Experimenting with a Large Number of Variables," in *Experiments in Industry: Design, Analysis and Interpretation of Results*, R. D. Snee, L. B. Hare, and J. R. Trout, eds. (Milwauke, Wis.: American Society for Quality Control, 1985).]

8.4-9   A study (also described by Snee in the book listed in Exercise 8.4-8) was initiated because of the perceived large variation in viscosity measurements obtained by an analytical laboratory. It was decided to conduct a "ruggedness test" of the measurement process to determine which variables, if any, were influencing the measurement process. The following seven variables were thought to be important:

Variable	Low (−)	High (+)
x_1 = sample preparation	M1	M2
x_2 = moisture measurement	Volume	Weight
x_3 = mixing speed (rpm)	800	1600
x_4 = mixing time (hours)	0.5	3
x_5 = healing time (hours)	1	2
x_6 = spindle	S1	S2
x_7 = protective lid	Absent	Present

The sample was prepared by one of two methods (M1, M2), using moisture measurements made on a volume or weight basis. The sample was then put into a machine, mixed at a given speed for a specified time period, and allowed to "heal" for 1 to 2 hours. There were two different spindles used in the mixer; the apparatus had a protective lid and it was decided to run tests with and without the lid. A 2^{7-3} fractional factorial design with generators $x_5 = x_2 x_3 x_4$, $x_6 = x_1 x_3 x_4$, and $x_7 = x_1 x_2 x_3$ was used. The viscosity measurements of the 16 runs, all made on samples from a common product source, are listed in the accompanying table. To guard against effects from other, unspecified sources, the experiments were conducted in random order. Determine the confounding patterns that are implied by this particular fraction. Construct a normal probability plot of the estimated effects. Interpret the results, assuming that interactions of order 3 or greater are zero.

Run	x_1	x_2	x_3	x_4	x_5	x_6	x_7	Viscosity
1	−	−	−	−	−	−	−	27.9
2	+	−	−	−	−	+	+	24.6
3	−	+	−	−	+	−	+	29.0
4	+	+	−	−	+	+	−	23.2
5	−	−	+	−	+	+	+	27.5
6	+	−	+	−	+	−	−	37.7
7	−	+	+	−	−	+	−	24.2
8	+	+	+	−	−	−	+	33.8
9	−	−	−	+	+	+	−	22.2
10	+	−	−	+	+	−	+	25.5
11	−	+	−	+	−	+	+	20.8
12	+	+	−	+	−	−	−	24.1
13	−	−	+	+	−	−	+	32.2
14	+	−	+	+	−	+	−	23.8
15	−	+	+	+	+	−	−	32.0
16	+	+	+	+	+	+	+	23.6

Hint   Use the Yates algorithm to estimate the effects; the estimates are arranged in a particular order (see Section 8.3). The defining relation of this fractional factorial tells you about the confounding patterns. For example, the (13) interaction (which is the sixth row of the Yates table) is confounded with (46) and (27).

8.4-10   This exercise requires considerable effort and should be assigned as a project. We want to investigate the effects of five factors on the growth of pinto beans. These factors are

Soaking fluid: water (−) or beer (+)

Salinity: no salt (−) or salt (+)

Acidity: no vinegar (−) or vinegar (+)

Soaking temperature: refrigerator temp (−) or room temp (+)

Soaking time: 2 hours (−) or 6 hours (+)

Use 3 tablespoons of soaking fluid to soak each bean. Use regular beer, as light beer may act like water. For salt, add 1/4 teaspoon to the soaking fluid. For vinegar, add 1 teaspoon to the soaking fluid.

Select one of the following exercises.

(a) Design, set up, and execute the experiment above as a 2^5 factorial experiment. Conduct three replications, which may be run concurrently. Analyze the effects of the factors, reporting your analysis with the appropriate summary statistics and plots.

(b) Perform a fractional factorial experiment in 16 runs. Write out the factor-level combinations, and set up and run the experiment. Comment on the confounding patterns. Conduct three replications, which may be run concurrently. Analyze the effects of the factors, reporting your analysis with the appropriate summary statistics and plots.

(c) Repeat experiment (b), but study the factors in eight runs.

The analysis of the next two projects should not be restricted to the topics studied in Chapter 8. The analysis should draw on all the materials considered thus far.

8.4-11 In Chapter 1 we discussed the 14 points by W. Edwards Deming. The fifth point, "never-ending improvement of the system of production and services," implies that any process, organizational or personal, is subject to improvement. Carry out a project that is aimed at the improvement of a *personal process*. Professor Harry Roberts uses such projects with great success in his courses at the University of Chicago. The following examples are based on his ideas.

(a) *Improvement of cardiovascular fitness.* Possible measurements include resting pulse, exercise pulse, and post-exercise pulse. Describe how you measure these variables. Give a detailed description of your measurement procedure. Design an exercise program aimed at improving fitness. For example, design a stair climbing exercise that is repeated several times during an exercise program. Set an exercise schedule and keep careful records of your data. Display your data over time and draw conclusions.

(b) *Improvement of sports skills.* For example, improve your free-throw shooting percentage by varying some of the key factors (relaxation before taking shot, shooting angle, use of backboard, etc.).

(c) Improvement of the efficiency of daily tasks, such as getting started in the morning, planning good work routines, or study habits.

8.4-12 As manager of a large collection agency you are looking for ways to increase the success of collecting overdue bills. The initial step in your collection process is to send a letter to the debtor. You are not certain whether a nice reminder or a threatening letter works best, nor do you know whether the letter should be sent by the collection agency or by a lawyer.

(a) Describe how you would set up a simple experiment to settle some of these open questions. You have available a large number of overdue accounts to select from, and for each account you know its size as well as the length of time it has been overdue. This is important information as the success of your strategy may depend on these characteristics. To simplify the situation you may assume that you have small and large, and recent and long-overdue accounts.

You have to give some thought on how to measure success. One possibility is to count the number of debts that are collected.

Can you determine the economic feasibility of your letter-writing strategy? Make the appropriate assumptions that allow you to carry out such an analysis. Assume that it costs a_1 to send a letter (and $a_2 > a_1$ to send it through the lawyer), and that you are paid c_1 for bringing in an overdue small account and c_2 for bringing in a large one. (Also the length of time that the account has been overdue may enter.)

(b) There are usually many delinquent clients who do not respond to a letter. Follow up on your non-respondents with a phone call that can be either threatening or nicely reminding. How would you design this follow-up experiment, and how would you analyze the resulting information? Does a threatening phone call work best in all situations? Is it always worthwhile to make a follow-up phone call? (Assume that it costs a_3 to make a call.) Can you identify situations where it would be beneficial to call?

Exercises 9.1

9.1-1 The attendance at a race track (x) and the amount that was bet (y) on $n = 10$ selected days is given in the following table:

Attendance, x (hundreds)	117	128	122	119
Amount Bet, y (millions of dollars)	2.07	2.80	3.14	2.26

	131	135	125	120	130	127
	3.40	3.89	2.93	2.66	3.33	3.54

(a) Make a scatter plot of y against x.
(b) Fit a simple linear regression model to the data and calculate the least-squares estimates, the fitted values, and the residuals. (It is useful to calculate these estimates once "by hand" to appreciate the computations that are involved. However, after having done this once, we recommend that a computer be used.)

9.1-2 An experiment was conducted to study the relationship between baking temperature x (in units of $10°$ Fahrenheit) and yield y (as percentage) of a popular cake mix.

Baking Temperature, x	10	10	11	11	12
Percent Yield, y	21.2	19.9	22.5	23.7	25.0

15	17	19	20	20	23	25	27	30
30.3	36.1	38.6	41.5	42.7	45.0	50.0	53.9	62.1

(a) Make a scatter plot of y against x.
(b) Estimate the parameters of the simple linear regression model by least squares and calculate the fitted values and the residuals.

9.1-3 The following data of Snedecor and Cochran show the initial weights and gains in weight (in grams) of 15 female rats on a high-protein diet that was administered from the 24th day to the 84th day of their age. The interest in these data is whether the weight gain depends on the initial weight.

Initial Weight, x	50	64	76	64	74	60	69	68
Weight Gain, y	128	159	158	119	133	112	96	126

	56	48	57	59	46	45	65
	132	118	107	106	82	103	104

(a) Make a scatter plot of y against x.
(b) Calculate the least-squares estimates of the parameters in the simple linear regression model. Calculate the fitted values and the residuals.
[G. W. Snedecor and W. G. Cochran, *Statistical Methods*, 6th ed. (Ames, Iowa: Iowa State University Press, 1967).]

9.1-4 Show that the fitted regression line $\hat{y} = \hat{\beta}_0 + \hat{\beta}_1 x$ goes through the point $(\bar{x}, \bar{y})$.
Hint Substitute $\bar{x}$ in $\hat{\beta}_0 + \hat{\beta}_1 x$ and show that the result equals $\bar{y}$.

9.1-5 Show that the least-squares estimate $\hat{\beta}_1$ can be written as

$$\hat{\beta}_1 = \frac{\sum (x_i - \bar{x}) y_i}{\sum (x_i - \bar{x})^2} = r(s_y/s_x),$$

where

$$r = \sum (x_i - \bar{x})(y_i - \bar{y})/[\sum (x_i - \bar{x})^2 \sum (y_i - \bar{y})^2]^{1/2}$$

is the sample correlation coefficient discussed in Section 1.5, and s_x and s_y are the respective sample standard deviations.

9.1-6 Consider the least-squares estimator of the intercept β_0, which is $\hat{\beta}_0 = \bar{Y} - \hat{\beta}_1 \bar{x}$.
(a) Show that $\hat{\beta}_0 = \sum k_i Y_i$, where $k_i = (1/n) - \bar{x} c_i$, $c_i = (x_i - \bar{x})/\sum (x_j - \bar{x})^2$. Thus $\hat{\beta}_0$, a linear function of $Y_1, Y_2, \ldots, Y_n$, has a normal distribution.
(b) Recalling that $\sum c_i = 0$, $\sum c_i x_i = 1$, and $\sum c_i^2 = 1/\sum (x_i - \bar{x})^2$, show that $E(\hat{\beta}_0) = \beta_0$ and also that $\text{var}(\hat{\beta}_0) = \sigma^2[(1/n) + \bar{x}^2/\sum (x_i - \bar{x})^2]$.

9.1-7 In the notation of this section show that

$E[(\hat{\beta}_0 - \beta_0)(\hat{\beta}_1 - \beta_1)] = \sigma^2 \sum k_i c_i$. Substituting $k_i = (1/n) - \bar{x}c_i$, prove that this equals

$$E[(\hat{\beta}_0 - \beta_0)(\hat{\beta}_1 - \beta_1)] = -\bar{x}\sigma^2 / \sum (x_i - \bar{x})^2$$

$$= -\bar{x}\,\text{var}(\hat{\beta}_1).$$

9.1-8 Consider the simple linear regression model through the origin, $Y_i = \beta x_i + \varepsilon_i$.

(a) Using principles from calculus, determine the least-squares estimate $\hat{\beta}$ that minimizes

$$\sum_{i=1}^{n} (y_i - \beta x_i)^2.$$

(b) Prior to sampling the Y_i are random variables. Show that the least-squares estimator $\hat{\beta}$ can be written as a linear function of $Y_1, Y_2, \ldots, Y_n$ and derive its mean and variance.

9.1-9 Assume that you are interested in estimating the effect of a variable x on a certain response variable. You have the opportunity to design the experiment (i.e., to choose the levels of the x variable) before you estimate the simple linear regression model $Y_i = \beta_0 + \beta_1 x_i + \varepsilon_i$. In designing your experiment you are restricted to the feasible range (c_1, c_2) of your x variable.

Assuming that your sample size is even, show that the best arrangement of the x levels is to allocate $n/2$ experiments to $x = c_1$ and $n/2$ experiments to $x = c_2$; this arrangement minimizes the variance of $\hat{\beta}_1$. Discuss why this arrangement is not very good if we want to check the adequacy of the linear model.

9.2   Inferences in the Regression Model

Regression analysis attempts to use the information from the explanatory variable to explain some of the variability in the response variable Y. Ignoring the information that is contained in $x_1, x_2, \ldots, x_n$, we can measure the variability among the responses $Y_1, Y_2, \ldots, Y_n$ by $\sum (Y_i - \bar{Y})^2$. This is called the *total sum of squares* and is written as

$$\text{SSTO} = \sum_{i=1}^{n} (Y_i - \bar{Y})^2 = \sum_{i=1}^{n} Y_i^2 - \frac{(\sum_{i=1}^{n} Y_i)^2}{n}.$$

Some of the variation in $Y_1, Y_2, \ldots, Y_n$ may be due to the different levels, $x_1, x_2, \ldots, x_n$, of the explanatory variable. For example, in the mileage data set of Section 9.1, we consider cars that range from 1900 to 4100 pounds in weight. Having cars with different weights in our sample is bound to lead to large variation among fuel consumption values, gpm. The regression model, however, expresses the relationship between the response and the explanatory variable, which partially "explains" the observation Y_i through the fitted value $\hat{Y}_i = \hat{\beta}_0 + \hat{\beta}_1 x_i$, $i = 1, 2, \ldots, n$. The variation of these fitted values about the mean $\bar{Y}$ measures the variability that is explained by the regression model. The sum of squares

$$\text{SSR} = \sum_{i=1}^{n} (\hat{Y}_i - \bar{Y})^2$$

is called the *sum of squares due to regression* or simply the *regression sum of squares*.

Usually, however, not all the variation is explained by the regression model; that is, part of the variation is left unexplained. The residuals, $e_i = Y_i - \hat{Y}_i$, $i = 1, 2, \ldots, n$, express that unexplained component. The unexplained variation is measured by

$$\text{SSE} = \sum_{i=1}^{n} e_i^2,$$

which is called the *sum of squares due to error*, or the *error sum of squares*.

We have introduced three sums of squares: the total sum of squares SSTO, the regression sum of squares SSR, and the error sum of squares SSE. In fact, one can show that

$$\text{SSTO} = \text{SSR} + \text{SSE}.$$

The proof of this decomposition of the total sum of squares is

$$\text{SSTO} = \sum_{i=1}^{n} (Y_i - \bar{Y})^2 = \sum_{i=1}^{n} [(Y_i - \hat{Y}_i) + (\hat{Y}_i - \bar{Y})]^2$$

$$= \sum_{i=1}^{n} (\hat{Y}_i - \bar{Y})^2 + \sum_{i=1}^{n} (Y_i - \hat{Y}_i)^2 + 2 \sum_{i=1}^{n} (\hat{Y}_i - \bar{Y})(Y_i - \hat{Y}_i)$$

$$= \text{SSR} + \text{SSE},$$

since

$$\sum_{i=1}^{n} (\hat{Y}_i - \bar{Y})(Y_i - \hat{Y}_i) = \sum_{i=1}^{n} e_i(\hat{Y}_i - \bar{Y}) = \sum_{i=1}^{n} e_i(\hat{\beta}_0 + \hat{\beta}_1 x_i) - \bar{Y} \sum_{i=1}^{n} e_i$$

$$= \hat{\beta}_0 \sum_{i=1}^{n} e_i + \hat{\beta}_1 \sum_{i=1}^{n} e_i x_i - \bar{Y} \sum_{i=1}^{n} e_i = 0$$

if we recall that $\sum e_i = \sum e_i x_i = 0$.

Let us illustrate these three sums of squares with the following two special cases: First, consider $\hat{\beta}_1 = 0$, which says that the explanatory variable has no linear association with the response. Then all fitted values are $\hat{Y}_i = \bar{Y}$, irrespective of the level x, and SSR = 0 and SSE = SSTO. This says that the regression model and the so-called explanatory variable x explain none of the variation in $Y_1, Y_2, \ldots, Y_n$. In the second situation assume that the fitted regression line passes through each observation; that is, $\hat{Y}_i = Y_i$. Then SSR = SSTO and SSE = 0. This says that the regression model with the variable x explains all the variability in $Y_1, Y_2, \ldots, Y_n$.

Remarks on Computation The calculation of all three sums of squares is very easy. Fitted values and residuals are needed in the calculation of SSR and SSE. Virtually every statistics computer software, as well as most sophisticated pocket calculators, calculate these sums of squares. Should hand calculation be necessary, one can use the following computation formula for SSR. Since $\bar{Y} = \hat{\beta}_0 + \hat{\beta}_1\bar{x}$ (see Exercise 9.1-4), we have

$$SSR = \sum_{i=1}^{n} (\hat{Y}_i - \bar{Y})^2 = \sum_{i=1}^{n} [\hat{\beta}_0 + \hat{\beta}_1 x_i - (\hat{\beta}_0 + \hat{\beta}_1 \bar{x})]^2$$

$$= \hat{\beta}_1^2 \sum_{i=1}^{n} (x_i - \bar{x})^2 = \frac{[\sum x_i Y_i - (\sum x_i)(\sum Y_i)/n]^2}{\sum x_i^2 - (\sum x_i)^2/n}.$$

This avoids some of the rounding that is necessary if fitted values are used. Of course, SSE can be obtained from SSE = SSTO − SSR. ■

9.2.1 Coefficient of Determination

The *coefficient of determination, R^2,* provides a summary statistic that measures how well the regression equation fits the data. It is given by

$$R^2 = \frac{SSR}{SSTO} = 1 - \frac{SSE}{SSTO},$$

since SSR = SSTO − SSE. This coefficient expresses the variability that is explained by the regression model as a fraction of the total sum of squares. Since $0 \leq SSR \leq SSTO$, it follows that

$$0 \leq R^2 \leq 1.$$

An $R^2 = 0$ means that SSR = 0 and SSE = SSTO. In such a case, the simple linear regression model explains none (i.e., zero percent) of the variation in the Y values. On the other hand, $R^2 = 1$ means that SSR = SSTO and SSE = 0. In this case all n observations lie on the fitted regression line and all (i.e., 100 percent) of the variation in $Y_1, Y_2, \ldots, Y_n$ is explained by the linear relationship with the explanatory variable.

The coefficient of determination in the simple linear regression model is related to the sample correlation coefficient that we have studied in Section 1.5. Substitution of SSR, as expressed in the previous computation formula, into $R^2 = SSR/SSTO$ leads to

$$R^2 = \frac{[\sum x_i Y_i - (\sum x_i)(\sum Y_i)/n]^2}{[\sum x_i^2 - (\sum x_i)^2/n][\sum Y_i^2 - (\sum Y_i)^2/n]}.$$

This shows that R^2 is the square of the sample correlation coefficient.

Example 9.2-1   For the mileage data in Table 9.1-1 we find that

$$SSTO = 207.31 - \frac{(43.9)^2}{10} = 14.589,$$

$$SSR = \frac{[135.80 - (29.0)(43.9)/10]^2}{89.28 - (29.0)^2/10} = 13.915,$$

and

$$SSE = 14.589 - 13.915 = 0.674.$$

Alternatively, we could have also calculated SSE by summing the squares of the residuals given in Table 9.1-2. It follows that $R^2 = 13.915/14.589 = 0.954$. This means that the explanatory variable, weight, explains 95.4 percent of the variability in the y values. Or, to say this differently, the simple linear regression model reduces the variability in the y values by 95.4 percent. ■

9.2-2 Analysis-of-Variance Table and the F-Test

The decomposition of the total sum of squares is usually summarized in an analysis-of-variance (ANOVA) table, similar to the ones we discussed in Chapters 7 and 8 for data from designed experiments. The first column in Table 9.2-1 shows the sources of variation. The second column gives the corresponding sums of squares; the total sum of squares is partitioned into a sum of squares due to regression (SSR) and a sum of squares due to error (SSE).

The third column contains the degrees of freedom for the various sums of squares that are given above. The degrees of freedom can be thought of as the number of independent components that are necessary to calculate a sum of squares. For example, the degrees of freedom for SSTO $= \sum (Y_i - \bar{Y})^2$ are $n - 1$. There are n deviations $Y_i - \bar{Y}$ in this sum of squares; however, since $\sum (Y_i - \bar{Y}) = 0$, one needs only $n - 1$ deviations to calculate SSTO, as the remaining one can always be calculated from the others. The degrees of freedom for the error sum of squares is $n - 2$, which is n minus the number of estimated coefficients in the regression function. There are n residuals in SSE $= \sum e_i^2$. However, there are two restrictions among the residuals ($\sum e_i = \sum e_i x_i = 0$). Thus, for given x values, we need only $n - 2$ residuals to calculate this sum of squares. Since there is only one explanatory variable, there is only one degree of freedom for the regression sum of squares. The equation SSR $= \hat{\beta}_1^2 \sum (x_i - \bar{x})^2$ shows that, apart from the given x values, we need only one quantity, the estimate $\hat{\beta}_1$, to calculate this sum of squares.

The fourth column in the ANOVA table is called the mean-square column; it contains the ratios of the various sums of squares and their degrees of freedom. MSR $=$ SSR/1 is the *mean square due to regression*, and MSE $=$ SSE/$(n - 2)$ is the *mean square due to error* or the *mean-square error*.

TABLE 9.2-1   ANOVA Table for the Simple Linear Regression Model

Source	SS	df	MS	F
Regression	SSR	1	MSR = SSR/1	MSR/MSE
Error	SSE	$n - 2$	MSE = SSE/$(n - 2)$	
Total	SSTO	$n - 1$		

The F-ratio, $F = \text{MSR/MSE}$, in the fifth column provides a statistic for testing whether or not $\beta_1 = 0$. In order to understand this test, we must investigate the sampling distribution of this F-ratio. Let us first discuss its sampling distribution when $\beta_1 = 0$. In this case the explanatory variable x has no effect on the response and $Y_i = \beta_0 + \varepsilon_i$, $i = 1, \ldots, n$, are independent random variables from a normal distribution with mean β_0 and variance σ^2. We know from earlier chapters that in this situation SSTO/σ^2 follows a chi-square distribution with $n - 1$ degrees of freedom. Next, let us consider the regression sum of squares and determine the distribution of SSR/σ^2. Using the expression for SSR at the end of Section 9.2-1, we can write

$$\frac{\text{SSR}}{\sigma^2} = \frac{\hat{\beta}_1^2 \sum_{i=1}^{n} (x_i - \bar{x})^2}{\sigma^2} = \left[\frac{\hat{\beta}_1 - 0}{\sigma / \sqrt{\sum (x_i - \bar{x})^2}} \right]^2.$$

Since $\sigma^2 / \sum (x_i - \bar{x})^2$ is the variance of $\hat{\beta}_1$ we find that for $\beta_1 = 0$, SSR/σ^2 is the square of a $N(0, 1)$ random variable, and hence $\chi^2(1)$.

So far we have shown that the first two expressions in the identity

$$\frac{\text{SSTO}}{\sigma^2} = \frac{\text{SSR}}{\sigma^2} + \frac{\text{SSE}}{\sigma^2}$$

follow chi-square distributions with $n - 1$ and 1 degrees of freedom, respectively. What can we say about the distribution of the last term, SSE/σ^2? Applying a well-known decomposition theorem from mathematical statistics [see R. V. Hogg and A. T. Craig, *Introduction to Mathematical Statistics*, 4th ed. (New York: Macmillan, 1978)], we can also show that SSE/σ^2 follows a chi-square distribution, with $n - 2$ degrees of freedom, and that SSR and SSE are independent. Note that the degrees of freedom on the right side of the identity above add up to the degrees of freedom on the left side: $n - 1 = 1 + (n - 2)$.

The chi-square distributions for SSR/σ^2 and SSE/σ^2 imply that both $\text{MSR} = \text{SSR}/1$ and $\text{MSE} = \text{SSE}/(n - 2)$ provide unbiased estimates of σ^2 if $\beta_1 = 0$. This follows from the fact that the mean of a chi-square random variable is equal to its degrees of freedom (see Section 3.3). The independence of SSR and SSE also implies that

$$F = \frac{(\text{SSR}/\sigma^2)/1}{(\text{SSE}/\sigma^2)/(n - 2)} = \frac{\text{SSR}/1}{\text{SSE}/(n - 2)} = \frac{\text{MSR}}{\text{MSE}}$$

follows an F-distribution with 1 and $n - 2$ degrees of freedom.

Next, let us consider the situation when $\beta_1 \neq 0$. One can show that, also in this case, the standardized error sum of squares, SSE/σ^2, follows a $\chi^2(n - 2)$ distribution. Thus, in either case ($\beta_1 = 0$ or $\beta_1 \neq 0$), $\text{MSE} = \text{SSE}/(n - 2)$ is an unbiased estimator of σ^2. This is not surprising as the residuals approximate the unknown error components. However, if $\beta_1 \neq 0$, MSR is no longer an unbiased estimator of σ^2. In fact, we show in Exercise 9.2-2 that $E(\text{MSR}) = \sigma^2 + \beta_1^2 \sum (x_i - \bar{x})^2$ is always larger than σ^2. Therefore, the F-ratio, $F = \text{MSR}/\text{MSE}$, will tend to be larger when $\beta_1 \neq 0$ than when $\beta_1 = 0$.

Large F-ratios indicate that β_1 is different from zero. This implies the following decision rule for testing the null hypothesis $H_0: \beta_1 = 0$ against the alternative $H_1: \beta_1 \neq 0$. Calculate the F-ratio from the data. If it exceeds the upper 100α percentage point of the $F(1, n-2)$ distribution, namely, if $F \geq F(\alpha; 1, n-2)$, we reject $H_0: \beta_1 = 0$ in favor of $H_1: \beta_1 \neq 0$ at significance level α. On the other hand, if $F < F(\alpha; 1, n-2)$, we do not reject H_0; that is, we conclude that with these data there is insufficient evidence to say that β_1 is different from zero.

Example 9.2-2 The ANOVA table for the mileage data in Table 9.1-1 follows.

Source	SS	df	MS	F
Regression	13.195	1	13.915	165.2
Error	0.674	8	0.084	
Total	14.589	9		

The mean square error $\text{MSE} = 0.084$ is the estimate of σ^2. The F-ratio is much larger than the critical value $F(0.01; 1, 8) = 6.03$; thus we conclude that $\beta_1 \neq 0$. ■

9.2-3 Confidence Intervals and Tests of Hypotheses for Regression Coefficients

In Section 9.1 we obtained the variance of the least-squares estimate $\hat{\beta}_1$, namely, $\text{var}(\hat{\beta}_1) = \sigma^2/\sum (x_i - \bar{x})^2$. There we also showed that the standardized variable

$$Z = \frac{\hat{\beta}_1 - \beta_1}{\sqrt{\text{var}(\hat{\beta}_1)}} = \frac{\hat{\beta}_1 - \beta_1}{\sqrt{\sigma^2/\sum (x_i - \bar{x})^2}}$$

follows a $N(0, 1)$ distribution and used this result to obtain confidence intervals for β_1. This, however, required that σ^2 is known.

In practice, σ^2 is unknown and must be estimated from the data. Replacing σ^2 in $\text{var}(\hat{\beta}_1)$ by the mean square error $\text{MSE} = \text{SSE}/(n-2)$ and taking the square root, we obtain an estimate of the standard deviation of $\hat{\beta}_1$,

$$s(\hat{\beta}_1) = \sqrt{\frac{\text{MSE}}{\sum (x_i - \bar{x})^2}};$$

we also call this the standard error of the estimate $\hat{\beta}_1$. Replacing the standard deviation $\sqrt{\mathrm{var}(\hat{\beta}_1)}$ in the denominator of Z by its estimate changes the sampling distribution slightly. We can show that

$$\frac{\hat{\beta}_1 - \beta_1}{s(\hat{\beta}_1)} = \frac{\hat{\beta}_1 - \beta_1}{\sqrt{\mathrm{MSE}/\sum (x_i - \bar{x})^2}}$$

follows a t-distribution with $n - 2$ degrees of freedom. The degrees of freedom are easy to remember, as they correspond to the degrees of freedom of the error sum of squares in the ANOVA table.

In the proof of this result we use the fact that SSE/σ^2 is $\chi^2(n - 2)$ and independent of $\hat{\beta}_1$. Dividing the standard normal variable Z given above by $\sqrt{(\mathrm{SSE}/\sigma^2)/(n - 2)}$, the square root of a $\chi^2(n - 2)$ variable divided by its degrees of freedom, leads to $(\hat{\beta}_1 - \beta_1)/\sqrt{\mathrm{MSE}/\sum (x_i - \bar{x})^2}$ that has a $t(n - 2)$ distribution.

We can use this sampling distribution result to construct confidence intervals for β_1 as well as test hypotheses about β_1 following the general discussion in Chapters 4 and 6. A $100(1 - \alpha)$ percent confidence interval for β_1 is given by

$$\hat{\beta}_1 \pm t(\alpha/2; n - 2)s(\hat{\beta}_1).$$

This interval covers the true but unknown β_1 in $100(1 - \alpha)$ percent of the cases.

To test the null hypothesis $H_0: \beta_1 = \beta_{10}$ against the alternative $H_1: \beta_1 \neq \beta_{10}$, where β_{10} is some given value, we compare the test statistic $(\hat{\beta}_1 - \beta_{10})/s(\hat{\beta}_1)$ to critical values from the $t(n - 2)$ distribution. At significance level α, we accept H_1 if

$$\frac{|\hat{\beta}_1 - \beta_{10}|}{s(\hat{\beta}_1)} \geq t(\alpha/2; n - 2).$$

Otherwise, there is insufficient evidence to reject H_0.

Frequently, we are interested in testing $H_0: \beta_1 = 0$ against $H_1: \beta_1 \neq 0$. If H_0 is not rejected, we conclude that the explanatory variable x is not important in explaining the variability in the response variable Y. On the other hand, concluding H_1 implies that x does have a significant linear association with Y. In this particular case $(\beta_{10} = 0)$ the test statistic becomes $t_{\hat{\beta}_1} = \hat{\beta}_1/s(\hat{\beta}_1)$; it is called the *t-statistic*, or *t-ratio*. At significance level α, we accept H_1 if

$$|t_{\hat{\beta}_1}| \geq t(\alpha/2; n - 2).$$

Otherwise, there is not enough evidence to reject $H_0: \beta_1 = 0$. Applied statisticians call the estimate $\hat{\beta}_1$ statistically *significant* if H_1 $(\beta_1 \neq 0)$ is accepted. They call $\hat{\beta}_1$ *insignificant* if H_0 $(\beta_1 = 0)$ is accepted.

The test involving the t-statistic is equivalent to the F-test, which was discussed previously. Since

$$(t_{\hat{\beta}_1})^2 = \frac{\hat{\beta}_1^2}{s^2(\hat{\beta}_1)} = \frac{\hat{\beta}_1^2 \sum (x_i - \bar{x})^2}{\mathrm{MSE}} = \frac{\mathrm{MSR}}{\mathrm{MSE}} = F,$$

the inequalities

$$|t_{\hat{\beta}_1}| \geq t(\alpha/2; n-2) \quad\text{and}\quad F \geq F(\alpha; 1, n-2)$$

provide exactly the same test of $H_0: \beta_1 = 0$ against $H_1: \beta_1 \neq 0$. This follows from the fact that the percentiles of the $t(r)$ and $F(1, r)$ distributions are related by

$$[t(\alpha/2; r)]^2 = F(\alpha; 1, r);$$

see Exercise 9.2-4.

Alternatively, we can conduct the test of H_0 using the p value. The p value is the probability, under H_0, of obtaining a value of the test statistic at least as "extreme" as the one actually observed. We know that under H_0 the t-statistic, $t_{\hat{\beta}_1}$, follows a t-distribution with $n-2$ degrees of freedom. Thus, in the case of the two-sided test,

$$p \text{ value} = 2P[t(n-2) \geq |t_{\hat{\beta}_1}|],$$

where $t_{\hat{\beta}_1}$ is the observed value of the test statistic. Of course, the p value can be looked up in extensive t-tables, but it is usually part of the computer output. If this p value is less than or equal to the chosen significance level α, we reject H_0 and accept H_1. That is, the probability, under H_0, of getting a sample value $\hat{\beta}_1$ of that size or larger is just too small for us to believe in H_0: $\beta_1 = 0$. On the other hand, if the p value is greater than α, we do not reject H_0; that is, the sample result $\hat{\beta}_1$ is not extreme enough to doubt our null hypothesis H_0.

Example 9.2-3   For the mileage data set, the estimate of β_1 is $\hat{\beta}_1 = 1.639$. Since $\text{MSE} = 0.084$ and $\sum (x_i - \bar{x})^2 = 5.18$, we find that the estimated variance of $\hat{\beta}_1$ is $s^2(\hat{\beta}_1) = 0.084/5.18 = 0.0162$; the standard error of $\hat{\beta}_1$ is $s(\hat{\beta}_1) = 0.127$. A 95 percent confidence interval for β_1 is given by $1.639 \pm (2.306)(0.127)$, since $t(0.025; 8) = 2.306$. This equals 1.639 ± 0.293 or, equivalently, $1.35 \leq \beta_1 \leq 1.93$. The confidence interval provides strong evidence that $\beta_1 > 0$, and that heavier cars do indeed require more fuel to operate (higher gpm values). More formally, one could test $H_0: \beta_1 = 0$ against the one-sided alternative hypothesis $H_1: \beta_1 > 0$. Note that this requires a one-sided test; in this case the critical value is given by $t(\alpha; n-2)$, with $\alpha = 0.05$ and $n = 10$. The t-statistic is given by $t_{\hat{\beta}_1} = 1.639/0.127 = 12.91$. It is much larger than the critical value $t(0.05; 8) = 1.86$, and thus there is very strong evidence that $\beta_1 > 0$. ■

In Section 9.1-3 we also obtained the variance of $\hat{\beta}_0$, the least-squares estimate of the intercept of the regression line. Replacing σ^2 in this expression by MSE and taking the square root gives us the standard error of $\hat{\beta}_0$,

$$s(\hat{\beta}_0) = \sqrt{\text{MSE}\left[\frac{1}{n} + \frac{\bar{x}^2}{\sum (x_i - \bar{x})^2}\right]}.$$

Since $(\hat{\beta}_0 - \beta_0)/s(\hat{\beta}_0)$ is $t(n-2)$, we find a $100(1-\alpha)$ percent confidence interval for β_0, namely

$$\hat{\beta}_0 \pm t(\alpha/2; n-2)s(\hat{\beta}_0).$$

Exercises 9.2

9.2-1 In the linear regression situation, $Y_i = \beta_0 + \beta_1 x_i + \varepsilon_i$, with the usual assumptions (normality, independence, and common variance), we compute from $n = 16$ points,

$$\hat{\beta}_1 = 0.35, \quad \text{MSE} = 2.3, \quad \sum (x_i - \bar{x})^2 = 100.0.$$

Test at the $\alpha = 0.05$ significance level $H_0: \beta_1 = 0.20$ against $H_1: \beta_1 > 0.20$. Obtain a 90 percent confidence interval for β_1.

9.2-2 Consider Exercises 9.1-1 to 9.1-3. For each of the three exercises obtain the ANOVA table, calculate and interpret R^2, and test whether or not the slope β_1 is different from zero. In addition, obtain and interpret 95 percent confidence intervals for the slope β_1 and the intercept β_0.

9.2-3 In the notation of this section, show, for a general β_1, that

$$E(\text{MSR}) = E[\hat{\beta}_1^2 \sum (x_i - \bar{x})^2] = \sigma^2 + \beta_1^2 \sum (x_i - \bar{x})^2.$$

Thus, if $\beta_1 = 0$, $F = \text{MSR/MSE}$ should be near 1 since $E(\text{MSR}) = E(\text{MSE}) = \sigma^2$. If $\beta_1 \neq 0$, F tends to be larger.

Hint Recall that $E(\hat{\beta}_1^2) = \text{var}(\hat{\beta}_1) + [E(\hat{\beta}_1)]^2$.

9.2-4 In general, $t(r) = Z/\sqrt{\chi^2(r)/r}$, where Z is a standard normal variable and independent of $\chi^2(r)$.

(a) Argue that $[t(r)]^2 = (Z^2/1)/[\chi^2(r)/r]$ is $F(1, r)$.

Hint What is the distribution of Z^2? See Exercise 4.4-5.

(b) Take $r = 10$ and $\alpha = 0.05$, and note that $t^2(0.025; 10) = F(0.05; 1, 10)$ by observing these respective values in the t- and F-tables.

9.2-5 *Estimation of the mean response.* Let $\hat{\beta}_0$, $\hat{\beta}_1$, and MSE be the unbiased estimators of β_0, β_1, and σ^2 as given in this section. Let us consider the estimation of the *mean response*, $E(Y_k) = \beta_0 + \beta_1 x_k$, at a certain level $x = x_k$. The obvious estimator is $\tilde{Y}_k = \hat{\beta}_0 + \hat{\beta}_1 x_k$. This is an unbiased estimator of $E(Y_k)$, since $E(\tilde{Y}_k) = \beta_0 + \beta_1 x_k$.

(a) Show that, using the results of Section 9.1 and Exercises 9.1-6 and 9.1-7,

$$\text{var}(\tilde{Y}_k) = \text{var}(\hat{\beta}_0) + x_k^2 \, \text{var}(\hat{\beta}_1)$$
$$+ 2x_k E[(\hat{\beta}_0 - \beta_0)(\hat{\beta}_1 - \beta_1)]$$
$$= \sigma^2 \left[\frac{1}{n} + \frac{(x_k - \bar{x})^2}{\sum (x_i - \bar{x})^2} \right],$$

where the sums in $\bar{x} = \sum x_i/n$ and $\sum (x_i - \bar{x})^2$ do not include the new level x_k. Observe that this variance is smallest if $x_k = \bar{x}$, the center of the experimental region. Can you think of an intuitive explanation of this fact?

(b) Argue that

$$\frac{[\tilde{Y}_k - (\beta_0 + \beta_1 x_k)]/\sqrt{\text{var}(\tilde{Y}_k)}}{\sqrt{\dfrac{\text{SSE}}{\sigma^2} \Big/ (n-2)}}$$

$$= \frac{\tilde{Y}_k - (\beta_0 + \beta_1 x_k)}{\sqrt{\text{MSE}\left[\dfrac{1}{n} + \dfrac{(x_k - \bar{x})^2}{\sum (x_i - \bar{x})^2} \right]}}$$

has a $t(n-2)$ distribution.

(c) Hence

$$\hat{\beta}_0 + \hat{\beta}_1 x_k \pm t(\alpha/2; n-2) \sqrt{\text{MSE}\left[\frac{1}{n} + \frac{(x_k - \bar{x})^2}{\sum (x_i - \bar{x})^2} \right]}$$

provides a $100(1-\alpha)$ percent confidence interval for the mean response $E(Y_k) = \beta_0 + \beta_1 x_k$.

(d) Use the mileage data set and show that for an automobile weighing $x_k = 2500$ pounds a 95 percent confidence interval for $E(Y_k)$ is given by $3.73 \pm (2.306)(0.105)$ or, equivalently, $3.49 \leq E(Y_k) = \beta_0 + \beta_1 x_k \leq 3.97$.

9.2-6 Consider the *prediction* of a new observation $Y_k = \beta_0 + \beta_1 x_k + \varepsilon_k$ at the level $x = x_k$. Note that this is different from Exercise 9.2-5, where we estimate the mean response.

Use $\tilde{Y}_k = \hat{\beta}_0 + \hat{\beta}_1 x_k$ as the prediction and define the prediction error as $W = Y_k - \tilde{Y}_k$. Using the result in Exercise 9.2-5, show that

$$\text{var}(W) = \sigma^2 + \text{var}(\tilde{Y}_k) = \sigma^2 \left[1 + \frac{1}{n} + \frac{(x_k - \bar{x})^2}{\sum (x_i - \bar{x})^2} \right]$$

(b) Argue that

$$\frac{W/\sqrt{\text{var}(W)}}{\sqrt{\dfrac{\text{SSE}}{\sigma^2} \Big/ (n-2)}} = \frac{Y_k - (\hat{\beta}_0 + \hat{\beta}_1 x_k)}{\sqrt{\text{MSE}\left[1 + \dfrac{1}{n} + \dfrac{(x_k - \bar{x})^2}{\sum (x_i - \bar{x})^2} \right]}}$$

has a $t(n-2)$ distribution.

(c) Hence

$$\hat{\beta}_0 + \hat{\beta}_1 x_k$$

$$\pm t(\alpha/2; n-2) \sqrt{\text{MSE}\left[1 + \frac{1}{n} + \frac{(x_k - \bar{x})^2}{\sum (x_i - \bar{x})^2} \right]}$$

provides a $100(1 - \alpha)$ percent *prediction interval* for Y_k. This interval is always wider than the confidence interval for the mean response. Give an intuitive explanation.

(d) Use the mileage data set and show that for an automobile weighing $x_k = 2500$ pounds a 95 percent prediction interval for Y_k is $3.73 \pm (2.306)(0.308)$ or, equivalently, $3.02 \leq Y_k \leq 4.44$.

9.2-7   Consider the data in Exercise 9.1-3. Use the result in Exercise 9.2-5(c) to construct a 95 percent confidence interval for the mean weight gain of rats with an initial weight of 60 grams. Repeat your calculations for rats with an initial weight of 100 grams. Would you put much trust in this second interval? Discuss.

9.2-8   Consider the data in Exercise 9.1-1. Use the result in Exercise 9.2-6(c) to construct a 90 percent prediction interval for amount bet when the attendance at the track is 12,000.

9.3   The Adequacy of the Fitted Model

9.3-1   Residual Checks

A simple linear regression model should only be fit to data that exhibit at least a rough linear relationship. A linear fit is not appropriate for data that follow a quadratic (or a more complicated) pattern. Such a pattern would not be consistent with the assumptions associated with a simple linear regression model. Moreover, this regression model should only be fit to data for which the variability in the Y values is approximately constant for all values of x. For example, it is not appropriate with data in which the variability in Y increases with increasing or decreasing levels of x or Y. This would violate the constant-variance assumption.

A standard regression analysis is also not appropriate if the error terms ε_i are correlated, as this violates the independence assumption. Correlation among the errors may occur if the observations (x_i, Y_i), $i = 1, 2, \ldots, n$, are collected sequentially in time and the index i stands for time or run order. One such example would be observations on the yield Y and a certain input variable x from consecutive batches in a chemical production process. In such a situation it is very likely that there is a "carryover" effect from batch to batch. This carryover could introduce correlation among the errors.

It is very important to always check whether the assumptions of the regression model are satisfied. Computers and hand-held calculators now make it so easy to estimate regression functions that a number of different models are frequently fit to the data. Thus it becomes especially important that the users of regression methods check to see if these models are really appropriate.

Our main tools in model checking are various residual plots. In particular, for $i = 1, 2, \ldots, n$:

1. A plot of the residuals e_i against the fitted values $\hat{y}_i$.

2. A plot of the residuals e_i against x_i.

3. Plots of the residuals e_i against other explanatory variables that were not included in the original model (e.g., time or run order if the data are collected sequentially).

4. A plot of the residuals e_i against the lagged residuals e_{i-1} if we collected the data sequentially in time.

If the regression assumptions are satisfied, we should see no patterns in these scatter plots. The residuals should give the impression of varying independently within a 2σ horizontal band around zero. That is, since the residuals are estimates of independent $N(0, \sigma^2)$ errors, most of the residuals (roughly 95 percent) should fall within $\pm 2\sqrt{\text{MSE}}$ of zero. Or, equivalently, we could calculate standardized residuals $e_i/\sqrt{\text{MSE}}$; 95 percent of these should fall within ± 2 of zero.

To illustrate the residual checks, we consider two cases in which some of the assumptions are violated. In case 1 the regression function is specified incorrectly: the data follow a curvilinear (quadratic) relationship, but a simple linear regression model is fitted [see Figure 9.3-1(a)]. In case 2 the equal-variance assumption is violated because the variability grows with the level of Y [see Figure 9.3-1(b)]. In each case we have calculated the fitted values and the residuals from the simple linear regression model. The respective plots of e_i against $\hat{y}_i$ are given in Figure 9.3-1(c) and (d); and those of e_i against x_i are given in Figure 9.3-1(e) and (f), respectively. In both cases we can recognize patterns in the residual plots. For example, in the first one (c), the residuals are negative for low and high fitted values, and positive for the intermediate range. In the second case (d), the variability in the residuals grows with the fitted values. These residuals certainly do not give the impression of varying independently within a horizontal band around zero. The graphs in (e) and (f), in which we plot the residuals against the x values, convey similar information.

Just the recognition that there is a problem with the regression model is not enough. Actions must be taken to fix the inadequacies in the model. In the case of fitting the incorrect model form, one has to revise the regression function. For our first example, we would fit the quadratic model $Y_i = \beta_0 + \beta_1 x_i + \beta_2 x_i^2 + \varepsilon_i$ (see Section 9.4). In the case of variances that are not constant, we should look for a transformation of the response variable Y that stabilizes the variance and then relate the transformed observations to the explanatory variable. We know that the logarithmic transformation (log Y) is appropriate if

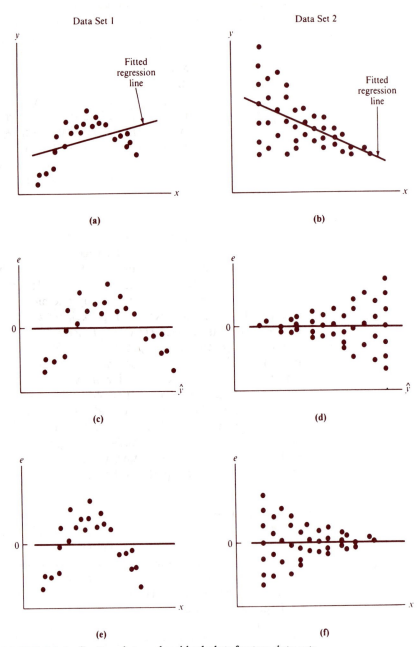

FIGURE 9.3-1   Scatter plots and residual plots for two data sets.

the *standard deviation* of Y increases proportional to the level of Y. If the *variance* of Y increases proportional to the level of Y, then we should try the square root transformation ($\sqrt{Y}$). In practice, we try various transformations, such as $1/Y$, $\log Y$, $\sqrt{Y}$, or other powers of Y. Plots of these transformed observations against their x values indicate which particular transformation stabilizes the variance the best.

Transformations of the response variable Y, as well as those of the explanatory variable x, may also help us simplify the regression function. The fact that the variables are measured in a particular metric is usually not a good enough reason to analyze them in the same metric. For example, fuel efficiency is usually given in miles per gallon (mpg). However, we have illustrated that gpm = 100/mpg (gallons per 100 miles) is a more sensible metric when analyzing the relationship between fuel efficiency and weight.

Example 9.3-1   In Exercise 9.3-6 we give the weights and fuel efficiencies [Y = mpg (miles per gallon)] of $n = 38$ cars. A scatter plot of mpg against weight is given in Figure 9.3-2(a), together with the linear fit. The residual plots (against fitted values and weights, respectively) are given in Figure 9.3-2(b) and (c). There are patterns in these plots indicating that the simple linear regression model is not an appropriate model. For example, most of the residuals for cars with low and high weights are positive, while the ones for cars with weights in the intermediate range are negative.

One way to correct this problem is to fit a more general model, say one that allows for a quadratic component, namely, $Y = \beta_0 + \beta_1 x + \beta_2 x^2 + \varepsilon$. Another possibility is to look for transformations that simplify the model structure. In fact, we have given some explanation of why the transformation gpm = 100/mpg should be appropriate. A scatter plot of gpm against weight is given in Figure 9.3-3(a) together with the linear fit. The residual plots (against fitted values and weights, respectively) are given in Figure 9.3-3(b) and (c). We notice that this model fits better; in particular, the residuals in Figure 9.3-3 show fewer nonrandom patterns than the ones in Figure 9.3-2. ■

Plots of residuals against other possible explanatory variables (other than the one already in the model) may also be useful. Patterns in these plots may tell us that the unexplained component in the regression model can be "explained" by these other variables. For example, in this mileage data set, one could plot the residuals against the number of cylinders, engine displacement, or horsepower. Associations in these plots indicate that these variables are important and that they should be included in the model.

We also assume that the errors in the regression model are independent. If an experiment is conducted sequentially in time, it may happen that the error at time i depends on the error at time $i - 1$. Consider, for example, a chemical batch process with a certain amount of carryover from batch to batch. This carryover could be negative if a lower-than-average yield from batch $i - 1$

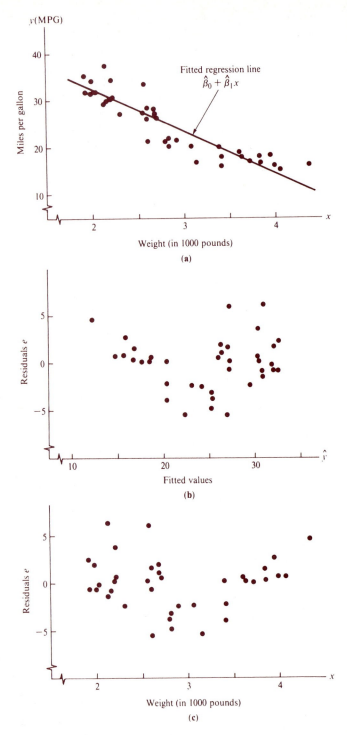

FIGURE 9.3-2 Plots for Example 9.3-1: (a) mpg against weight; (b) residuals against fitted values; (c) residuals against weight. Fitted values and residuals are from the model mpg $= \beta_0 + \beta_1$(weight) $+ \varepsilon$.

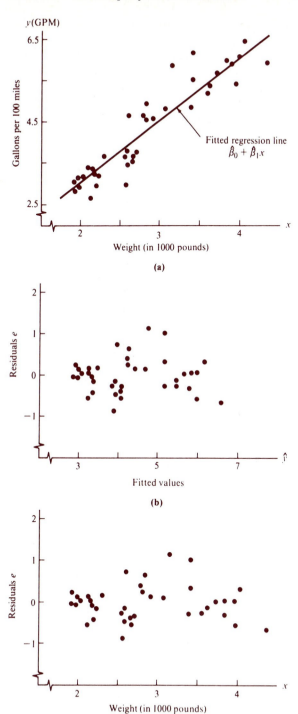

(a)

(b)

(c)

FIGURE 9.3-3 Plots for Example 9.3-1: (a) gpm = 100/mpg against weight; (b) residuals against fitted values; (c) residuals against weight. Fitted values and residuals are from the model gpm = $\beta_0 + \beta_1$(weight) + ε.

usually means a higher-than-average yield from the next batch. Of course, the carryover could also be positive. Since the residuals e_i are estimates of the errors ε_i, a plot of e_i against e_{i-1} in these cases of influential carryover would show a negative (or positive) association. An example of a plot of (e_{i-1}, e_i), $i = 2, 3, \ldots, n$, which points to a violation of the independence assumption is given in Figure 9.3-4.

We could carry this analysis one step further and calculate the correlation coefficient between the residuals and the lagged residuals. Substituting $x_i = e_{i-1}$ and $y_i = e_i$ into the equation for the correlation coefficient given in Section 1.5, we can calculate the correlation from the $n - 1$ pairs (e_1, e_2), $(e_2, e_3), \ldots, (e_{n-1}, e_n)$. Of course, the n residuals sum to zero; thus it is *approximately* true that

$$\bar{x} = \frac{\sum_{i=2}^n e_{i-1}}{n-1} \approx 0, \qquad \bar{y} = \frac{\sum_{i=2}^n e_i}{n-1} \approx 0$$

and if n is reasonably large,

$$\sum_{i=2}^n e_{i-1}^2 \approx \sum_{i=2}^n e_i^2 \approx \sum_{i=1}^n e_i^2.$$

With these approximations, the correlation coefficient is about equal to

$$r_1 = \frac{\sum_{i=2}^n e_{i-1}e_i}{\sum_{i=1}^n e_i^2}.$$

This is called the *lag 1 autocorrelation* of the residuals. It is of lag 1 because it calculates the approximate correlation coefficient between adjacent residuals. It is called an *auto*correlation, since there is only one series involved; that is, it

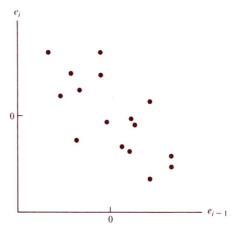

FIGURE 9.3-4   Plot of the residuals e_i against the lagged residuals e_{i-1}.

is a correlation of a series with itself. Note that we can extend this concept to *lag k autocorrelations*:

$$r_k = \frac{\sum_{i=k+1}^{n} e_{i-k} e_i}{\sum_{i=1}^{n} e_i^2}, \qquad k = 1, 2, 3, \ldots .$$

If the lag 1 autocorrelation is close to zero, we can conclude that adjacent residuals (and therefore errors) are uncorrelated. If its absolute value, $|r_1|$, is large (say, larger than $2/\sqrt{n}$), then the independence of the errors would be seriously questioned. Here we are using the fact that if there is no correlation among the errors, then the sampling distribution of r_1 is approximately $N(0, 1/n)$.

Alternatively, the *Durbin–Watson statistic* could be calculated:

$$DW = 2(1 - r_1).$$

Since r_1 is a correlation coefficient and thus between -1 and $+1$, the Durbin–Watson statistic is between 0 and 4. If DW is close to 2, so that r_1 is close to zero, we can safely assume that there is no lag 1 autocorrelation among the errors. If DW is much different from 2 (toward either zero or 4), we would have to question the independence.

What should we do if we notice correlation among the errors? Clearly, the techniques we have discussed are not applicable. The answer to this question is beyond the scope of this introductory book. The interested reader is referred to books on *time-series analysis*.

Remark   The plots of e_i against e_{i-1}, the lag 1 autocorrelation r_1, and the Durbin–Watson test statistic DW are meaningful only if the index i refers to time or run order. They are not appropriate, for example, in the mileage example, where i is just an arbitrary index; that is, we could have arranged the order of the cars in many different ways.   ■

9.3-2   Output from Computer Programs

Virtually every statistics computer software package includes programs for regression analysis; SAS, SPSS, BMDP, and MINITAB are just a few examples of well-known comprehensive packages. There are also numerous statistics packages for microcomputers that include regression routines. The output from these packages is very similar. It usually includes a listing of the least-squares estimates, their standard errors, t-ratios, the analysis-of-variance table, R^2, the fitted values, the residuals, and the Durbin–Watson test statistic. These programs also allow the user to store the residuals and fitted values in order to perform various diagnostic residual checks.

Example 9.3-2   The data in Table 9.3-1 give the monthly steam consumption Y (in pounds of steam used) and the average monthly atmospheric temperature x (in degrees Fahrenheit) for 25 consecutive months. These are taken

TABLE 9.3-1   Steam Usage and Average Temperature for 25 Consecutive Months.

Month	Steam Usage (pounds)	Average Temperature (°F)
1	10.98	35.3
2	11.13	29.7
3	12.51	30.8
4	8.40	58.8
5	9.27	61.4
6	8.73	71.3
7	6.36	74.4
8	8.50	76.7
9	7.82	70.7
10	9.14	57.5
11	8.24	46.4
12	12.19	28.9
13	11.88	28.1
14	9.57	39.1
15	10.94	46.8
16	9.58	48.5
17	10.09	59.3
18	8.11	70.0
19	6.83	70.0
20	8.88	74.5
21	7.68	72.1
22	8.47	58.1
23	8.86	44.6
24	10.36	33.4
25	11.08	28.6

from a steam plant of a large industrial company and are part of a larger data set that includes many other variables, such as the number of operating days per month and the total production. For a detailed analysis, see Draper and Smith, *Applied Regression Analysis*, 2nd ed. (New York: Wiley, 1981). The objective of this analysis is to find a model that explains the variation in steam consumption. An obvious starting point is to relate steam consumption, Y, to the average atmospheric temperature, x. The scatter plot in Figure 9.3-5 shows an approximate linear relationship, which suggests the simple linear regression model

$$Y_i = \beta_0 + \beta_1 x_i + \varepsilon_i, \quad i = 1, 2, \ldots, 25.$$

The output (somewhat edited) from a computer run is given in Table 9.3-2.

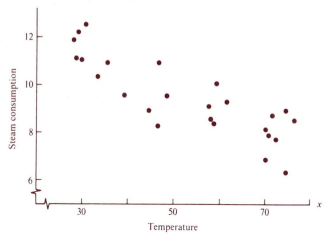

FIGURE 9.3-5 Scatter plot of monthly steam consumption against average monthly temperature.

The parameter of primary interest β_1 is estimated as $\hat{\beta}_1 = -0.0798$; its standard error is $s(\hat{\beta}_1) = 0.0105$ and the corresponding t-ratio is $t_{\hat{\beta}_1} = \hat{\beta}_1/s(\hat{\beta}_1) = -7.59$. Since this is much larger in absolute value than the critical value $t(0.025; 23) = 2.069$, we find that there is strong evidence that $\beta_1 \neq 0$. The estimate of β_1 implies that we can expect, on average, a 0.0798-pound reduction in steam use for each $1°$ increase in temperature. The R^2 from the

TABLE 9.3-2 **Edited Computer Output from the Simple Linear Regression of Steam Usage on Average Temperature**

The fitted regression equation is
$\hat{y} = 13.62 - 0.0798x$

Coefficient	Estimate	Standard Error	t-Ratio
β_0	13.62	0.58	23.43
β_1	-0.0798	0.0105	-7.59

$\sqrt{\text{MSE}} = 0.890$; $R^2 = 0.714$.

ANOVA table:

Source	SS	df	MS	F
Regression	45.592	1	45.592	57.5
Error	18.223	23	0.792	
Total	63.816	24		

Durbin–Watson statistic $= 2.70$.

simple linear regression model is $R^2 = 0.714$. This implies that temperature explains 71.4 percent of the variation in steam use.

The fitted values, $\hat{y}_i$, and residuals, e_i, are listed in Table 9.3-3. The respective residual plots of e_i against $\hat{y}_i$ and e_i against x_i in Figure 9.3-6(a) and (b) show no apparent patterns. The residuals fall within two horizontal bands around zero. Moreover, the variance of the errors seems to be unaffected by the level of the response variable or the explanatory variable. Thus the simple linear regression model seems quite adequate.

Since the data were collected sequentially, it is of interest to check whether adjacent residuals are correlated. The plot of e_i against e_{i-1} in Figure 9.3-6(c) indicates some, but rather minor, negative correlation. The lag one autocorrelation is

$$r_1 = \frac{(0.17)(-0.12) + (-0.12)(1.35) + \cdots + (-0.60)(-0.26)}{(0.17)^2 + (-0.12)^2 + \cdots + (-0.26)^2} = -0.35,$$

and the Durbin–Watson statistic is DW $= 2(1 - r_1) = 2.70$. We could use the

TABLE 9.3-3   Observations, Fitted Values, and Residuals for the Steam Usage Data

i	x_i	y_i	$\hat{y}_i$	$e_i = y_i - \hat{y}_i$
1	35.3	10.98	10.81	0.17
2	29.7	11.13	11.25	−0.12
3	30.8	12.51	11.16	1.35
4	58.8	8.40	8.93	−0.53
5	61.4	9.27	8.72	0.55
6	71.3	8.73	7.93	0.80
7	74.4	6.36	7.68	−1.32
8	76.7	8.50	7.50	1.00
9	70.7	7.82	7.98	−0.16
10	57.5	9.14	9.03	0.11
11	46.4	8.24	9.92	−1.68
12	28.9	12.19	11.32	0.87
13	28.1	11.88	11.38	0.50
14	39.1	9.57	10.50	−0.93
15	46.8	10.94	9.89	1.05
16	48.5	9.58	9.75	−0.17
17	59.3	10.09	8.89	1.20
18	70.0	8.11	8.04	0.07
19	70.0	6.83	8.04	−1.21
20	74.5	8.88	7.68	1.20
21	72.1	7.68	7.87	−0.19
22	58.1	8.47	8.98	−0.51
23	44.6	8.86	10.06	−1.20
24	33.4	10.36	10.96	−0.60
25	28.6	11.08	11.34	−0.26

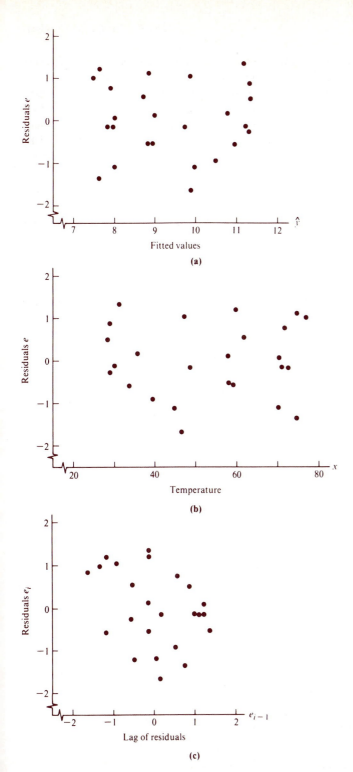

FIGURE 9.3-6 Various residual plots for the steam data: (a) residuals e against fitted values $\hat{y}$; (b) residuals e against temperature x; (c) residuals e_i against lagged residuals e_{i-1}.

critical values in tables that are provided by Durbin and Watson; in fact, we would find that the correlation is significant at the $\alpha = 0.05$ level. A simpler, but only approximate test is to check whether $|r_1| = |-0.35|$ exceeds 2 times the standard error of r_1, which is approximately equal to $1/\sqrt{n} = 1/\sqrt{25} = 0.20$. Here $|r_1|$ is slightly smaller than 0.40. This is a borderline case of a possible moderate correlation among the residuals.   ■

9.3-3   The Importance of Scatter Plots in Regression

Scatter plots of the regression variables are absolutely necessary in any regression analysis. Figure 9.3-7 illustrates this very clearly. There we show plots of four equal-sized data sets that all yield the same regression summaries (i.e., same estimates, same standard errors, same ANOVA table, same R^2). But in only one of them, namely in part (a), is it really appropriate to fit a linear model. The pattern in part (b) is quadratic, and it would be a mistake to

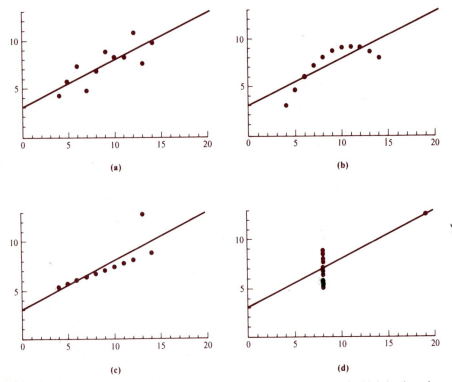

FIGURE 9.3-7   Anscombe's plots of four equal-sized data sets, all of which lead to the same regression summaries. The line refers to the least-squares fit. [Reproduced with permission from F. J. Anscombe, "Graphs in Statistical Analysis," *The American Statistician*, 27: 17–21 (1973).]

approximate it with a linear function, at least over the range from $x = 5$ to $x = 15$. The figures in parts (c) and (d) show the effect of a single observation on the regression estimates. Ten observations in part (c) lie on a straight line, but one response, the one at $x = 13$, does not follow their pattern. This one observation, called an *outlier* in the response variable y, changes the slope of the regression line. The plot in part (d) is also interesting because it illustrates the influence of a single observation whose x value is far from all others in the experiment, that is, outside the usual experimental region. Since least squares minimizes the sum of the squared distances from the observations to the regression line, we find that the fitted line in part (d) is not very far from the response that corresponds to this outlying x value. Different responses at this particular x level would lead to very different fitted regression lines.

If data are just fed into a regression computer program and if the data, or the residuals from the regression fit, are not plotted, certain features of a data set would not be recognized. Scatter plots are important, as they alert the investigator to special features, such as outlying observations. These plots should then be followed by an investigation of the particular circumstances that were present at the time the observations were taken. Frequently, special experimental conditions or errors in measuring or recording the data are the causes of outliers. Since we do not want one observation to have a very large influence on the fitted regression line, we usually drop such observations from the data set. But we also want to emphasize that very often much useful information can be uncovered by studying how these points were actually obtained.

Exercises 9.3

9.3-1   Previously, you were asked to fit simple linear regression models to the data in Exercises 9.1-1 to 9.1-3. Check the appropriateness of the simple linear regression model for each of these data sets by constructing appropriate residual plots.

9.3-2   Consider the following four fictitious data sets, each consisting of eleven (x, y) pairs. For the first three data sets the x values are the same, and they are listed only once.

Show that for each of the four data sets the simple linear regression fit leads to the same output (i.e., same estimates and standard errors, same ANOVA table, same R^2).

Carry out appropriate diagnostics and convince yourself that the simple linear regression model is only appropriate for one data set.

x	y	y	y	x	y
10	8.04	9.14	7.46	8	6.58
8	6.95	8.14	6.77	8	5.76
13	7.58	8.74	12.74	8	7.71
9	8.81	8.77	7.11	8	8.84
11	8.33	9.26	7.81	8	8.47
14	9.96	8.10	8.84	8	7.04
6	7.24	6.13	6.08	8	5.25
4	4.26	3.10	5.39	19	12.50
12	10.84	9.13	8.15	8	5.56
7	4.82	7.26	6.42	8	7.91
5	5.68	4.74	5.73	8	6.89

[F. J. Anscombe, "Graphs in Statistical Analysis," *The American Statistician*, 27: 17–21 (1973).]

9.3-3 In a regression problem with $n = 10$ pairs of (x_i, y_i) we find $\sum x_i = 15$, $\sum y_i = 20$, $\sum x_i y_i = 33$, $\sum x_i^2 = 31.5$, $\sum y_i^2 = 49$.
(a) Find the least-squares estimates of the regression coefficients in the simple linear regression model.
(b) Why is it important to look at a scatter plot of y against x?

9.3-4 Show that in the simple linear regression model the relationship between the F-statistic and R^2 is given by $F = (n - 2)R^2/(1 - R^2)$.

9.3-5 Box, Hunter, and Hunter have analyzed the dispersion of an aerosol spray as a function of its age. The dispersion Y is measured as the reciprocal of the number of particles in a unit volume. Age x is measured in minutes. The experiments were performed in random order, but they are listed here in increasing order of x.

Age, x	8	22	35	40	57
Dispersion, y	6.16	9.88	14.35	24.06	30.34

73	78	87	98
32.17	42.18	43.23	48.76

(a) Make a scatter plot of the observations.
(b) Calculate the least-squares estimates, the ANOVA table, and R^2.
(c) Construct a test of $\beta_1 = 0$ against $\beta_1 > 0$.
(d) Test whether $\beta_0 = 0$. Can you simplify the model? Are dispersion and age proportional?
(e) Estimate the mean response at age $x_k = 110$. Construct a 95 percent confidence interval. Discuss the possible dangers of such an extrapolation.
Hint See Exercise 9.2-5.
[G. E. P. Box, W. G. Hunter, and J. S. Hunter, *Statistics for Experimenters* (New York: Wiley, 1978).]

9.3-6 Consider the regression model that relates gas mileage and weight of automobiles. Thirty-eight cars from the model year 1978–1979 were selected and their weights (in units of 1000 pounds) and fuel efficiencies mpg (miles per gallon) were measured. The results are listed in the accompanying table. These data are analyzed in Example 9.3-1. Here we ask you to repeat the analysis with the locally available computer software.

Weight	mpg	Weight	mpg
4.360	16.9	3.830	18.2
4.054	15.5	2.585	26.5
3.605	19.2	2.910	21.9
3.940	18.5	1.975	34.1
2.155	30.0	1.915	35.1
2.560	27.5	2.670	27.4
2.300	27.2	1.990	31.5
2.230	30.9	2.135	29.5
2.830	20.3	2.670	28.4
3.140	17.0	2.595	28.8
2.795	21.6	2.700	26.8
3.410	16.2	2.556	33.5
3.380	20.6	2.200	34.2
3.070	20.8	2.020	31.8
3.620	18.6	2.130	37.3
3.410	18.1	2.190	30.5
3.840	17.0	2.815	22.0
3.725	17.6	2.600	21.5
3.955	16.5	1.925	31.9

(a) Make a scatter plot of mpg against weight and discuss whether the simple linear regression model mpg $= \beta_0 + \beta_1(\text{weight}) + \varepsilon$ is appropriate.
(b) Plot gpm $= 100/\text{mpg}$ (gallons per 100 miles traveled) against weight. Discuss whether the simple linear regression model gpm $= \beta_0 + \beta_1(\text{weight}) + \varepsilon$ is appropriate.
(c) Consider the regression model in part (b). Compute the least-squares estimates, their standard errors, and the t-ratios. Interpret your findings.
(d) Discuss whether the model fitted in part (c) leads to an adequate representation. Plot the residuals against fitted values and against weight. Can you see patterns in these plots? If so, suggest modifications.
(e) Estimate the mean fuel consumption (gpm) of cars with a weight of 3500 pounds. Construct a 90 percent confidence interval for the mean response.
[H. V. Henderson and P. F. Velleman, "Building Multiple Regression Models Interactively," *Biometrics*, 37: 391–411 (1981).]

9.3-7 By using the notation associated with the simple linear regression model, the *adjusted* R^2 is defined as

$$R_a^2 = 1 - \frac{\text{SSE}/(n-2)}{\text{SSTO}/(n-1)} = \frac{\text{SSTO}/(n-1) - \text{MSE}}{\text{SSTO}/(n-1)}.$$

The term "adjusted" refers to the fact that the sums

of squares are adjusted by their respective degrees of freedom. Then since $[\text{SSE}/(n-2)]/[\text{SSTO}/(n-1)]$ represents the fraction of variance remaining after fitting the regression line, R_a^2 represents the fractional reduction from $\text{SSTO}/(n-1)$ to $\text{MSE} = \text{SSE}/(n-2)$, that is, the reduction in variance that can be attributed to the regression. The fractional reduction in standard deviation is

$$\frac{\sqrt{\text{SSTO}/(n-1)} - \sqrt{\text{MSE}}}{\sqrt{\text{SSTO}/(n-1)}} = 1 - \sqrt{1 - R_a^2}.$$

(a) Show that $1 \geq R^2 \geq R_a^2 \geq 1 - \sqrt{1 - R_a^2}$.

(b) For the mileage data in Table 9.1-1, compute and interpret R_a^2 and $1 - \sqrt{1 - R_a^2}$.

9.3-8 The University of Iowa student enrollment for the fall and spring semesters combined (given in units of 1000 students) from 1963–1964 (time $x = 1$) to 1979–1980 ($x = 17$) is given in the accompanying table.

(a) Plot enrollment against time. Fit the regression model $Y_i = \beta_0 + \beta_1 x_i + \varepsilon_i$. Calculate the least-squares estimates, fitted values, residuals, and the entries in the ANOVA table.

Time, x	Enrollment, y	Time, x	Enrollment, y
1	25.3	10	39.1
2	28.3	11	39.8
3	32.2	12	41.6
4	34.6	13	43.6
5	36.4	14	43.5
6	37.9	15	44.2
7	39.2	16	44.6
8	40.1	17	45.6
9	39.6		

(b) Check the appropriateness of the regression model by constructing residual plots. Calculate the lag 1 autocorrelation of the residuals and the Durbin–Watson statistic. Interpret your findings.

Note It can be shown that the standard error $s(\hat{\beta}_1) = \sqrt{\text{MSE}/\sum (x_i - \bar{x})^2}$ underestimates the true standard error of $\hat{\beta}_1$ if there is positive autocorrelation among the residuals. Thus it is inappropriate in these cases to use the t-ratio $\hat{\beta}_1/s(\hat{\beta}_1)$ for testing $H_0: \beta_1 = 0$.

9.4   The Multiple Linear Regression Model

In Section 9.3 we studied the *simple linear regression model* $Y_i = \beta_0 + \beta_1 x_i + \varepsilon_i$. There was only *one* explanatory variable; moreover, the model was particularly simple, as it involved a linear relationship.

Models that are linear in the explanatory variable x are often good approximations of complicated nonlinear functional relationships, especially if the range of the x values is not too large. Over a small enough region, many complicated nonlinear functions can be approximated by a linear one; for example, consider Taylor's series expansion through only the linear term(s). However, there are cases where nonlinear relationships are needed; for example, we could fit the *quadratic* $Y_i = \beta_0 + \beta_1 x_i + \beta_2 x_i^2 + \varepsilon_i$, or, more generally, the *polynomial* $Y_i = \beta_0 + \beta_1 x_i + \cdots + \beta_k x_i^k + \varepsilon_i$. These relationships are nonlinear in the explanatory variable. However, they are still linear in the regression coefficients $\beta_0, \beta_1, \ldots, \beta_k$, and for this reason they are called *linear regression models*.

Polynomials are not the only nonlinear relationships that we can consider. Models of the form $Y_i = (\beta_0 + \beta_1 x_i)e^{\beta_2 x_i} + \varepsilon_i$, or $Y_i = \beta_0 x_i/(1 + \beta_1 x_i) + \varepsilon_i$, are also nonlinear in x. In addition, they are nonlinear in the regression coefficients, and for this reason they are called *nonlinear regression models*.

All the models that we described so far include just *one* explanatory variable. Frequently, more than one variable has an influence on the response. For example, gas mileage depends not only on weight, but may also depend on the engine design and the wind resistance of the car. Also, the yield of a chemical process may not only be influenced by the concentration, but in addition by the temperature and by the type of catalyst that is used in the reaction.

To study such situations, let us initially consider models with two explanatory variables, x_1 and x_2. We use the following notation: Y_i is the response that corresponds to the level x_{i1} of the first variable x_1 and level x_{i2} of the second variable x_2, $i = 1, 2, \ldots, n$. The linear model

$$Y_i = \beta_0 + \beta_1 x_{i1} + \beta_2 x_{i2} + \varepsilon_i, \qquad i = 1, 2, \ldots, n,$$

where $\varepsilon_1, \varepsilon_2, \ldots, \varepsilon_n$ are independent $N(0, \sigma^2)$ random variables, is probably the simplest regression model with two explanatory variables. The expected value $E(Y) = \beta_0 + \beta_1 x_1 + \beta_2 x_2$ defines a plane in three-dimensional space. The coefficient β_j measures the effect on the response of a unit change in variable $x_j, j = 1, 2$.

A slightly more complicated model is given by

$$Y_i = \beta_0 + \beta_1 x_{i1} + \beta_{11} x_{i1}^2 + \beta_2 x_{i2} + \beta_{22} x_{i2}^2 + \varepsilon_i.$$

The effect of the variable x_j $(j = 1, 2)$ is now quadratic. The model

$$Y_i = \beta_0 + \beta_1 x_{i1} + \beta_{11} x_{i1}^2 + \beta_2 x_{i2} + \beta_{22} x_{i2}^2 + \beta_{12} x_{i1} x_{i2} + \varepsilon_i$$

is even more general and somewhat different from the previous ones. Due to the term $\beta_{12} x_{i1} x_{i2}$, the effect of a unit change in variable x_1 depends on the value of the second explanatory variable x_2 (it did not in the previous models). We say that the variables interact, and the term $\beta_{12} x_{i1} x_{i2}$ is called an *interaction* component.

Here we have given three different models with two explanatory variables. The first is linear in the two x variables; the other two are quadratic in x_1 and x_2; in the last one, the variables x_1 and x_2 interact. Note that all these models are linear in the regression coefficients and thus are linear regression models.

Now let us define the *multiple linear regression model* with p explanatory variables (or regressors) $x_1, x_2, \ldots, x_p$ as

$$Y_i = \beta_0 + \beta_1 x_{i1} + \beta_2 x_{i2} + \cdots + \beta_p x_{ip} + \varepsilon_i, \qquad i = 1, 2, \ldots, n,$$

where $\varepsilon_1, \varepsilon_2, \ldots, \varepsilon_n$ are independent $N(0, \sigma^2)$ random variables. The random variable Y_i is the ith response that corresponds to the levels $x_{i1}, x_{i2}, \ldots, x_{ip}$ of the p regressors $x_1, x_2, \ldots, x_p$, $i = 1, 2, \ldots, n$. The p regressors can be p different variables, or functions (such as products) of a smaller set of variables. For example, in the model

$$Y_i = \beta_0 + \beta_1 x_{i1} + \beta_{11} x_{i1}^2 + \beta_2 x_{i2} + \beta_{22} x_{i2}^2 + \beta_{12} x_{i1} x_{i2} + \varepsilon_i$$

there are only two variables, x_1 and x_2, but there are $p = 5$ variables (regressors) in the regression model: x_1, x_1^2, x_2, x_2^2, and $x_1 x_2$. To use the general linear multiple regression model in this case, we redefine these $p = 5$ regressors to be x_1, x_2, x_3, x_4, and x_5, respectively.

9.4-1   Estimation of the Regression Coefficients

The regression coefficients $\beta_0, \beta_1, \ldots, \beta_p$, as well as the variance of the errors, $\mathrm{var}(\varepsilon_i) = \sigma^2$, are usually unknown and have to be estimated from observations $(y_i, x_{i1}, \ldots, x_{ip})$, $i = 1, 2, \ldots, n$. As in the simple linear regression model, we can use the *least-squares criterion* to determine the estimates of the regression coefficients. There we choose the estimates of $\beta_0, \beta_1, \ldots, \beta_p$ such that the sum of the squared deviations between the observations and the regression surface, namely

$$S(\beta_0, \beta_1, \ldots, \beta_p) = \sum_{i=1}^{n} [y_i - (\beta_0 + \beta_1 x_{i1} + \cdots + \beta_p x_{ip})]^2,$$

is minimized. If we equate the partial derivatives $\partial S(\beta_0, \beta_1, \ldots, \beta_p)/\partial \beta_j, j = 0, 1, \ldots, p$, to zero, we obtain the $p + 1$ equations,

$$\sum_{i=1}^{n} [y_i - (\beta_0 + \beta_1 x_{i1} + \cdots + \beta_p x_{ip})](-1) = 0,$$

$$\sum_{i=1}^{n} [y_i - (\beta_0 + \beta_1 x_{i1} + \cdots + \beta_p x_{ip})](-x_{ij}) = 0, \qquad j = 1, 2, \ldots, p.$$

The solutions of these equations are the least-squares estimates, $\hat{\beta}_0, \hat{\beta}_1, \ldots, \hat{\beta}_p$, since it can be shown that the second partial derivatives evaluated at $\hat{\beta}_0, \hat{\beta}_1, \ldots, \hat{\beta}_p$ satisfy the conditions for a relative minimum of $S(\beta_0, \beta_1, \ldots, \beta_p)$. Rearranging some of the terms in these equations and substituting $\hat{\beta}_j$ for β_j leads to the following $(p + 1)$ equations in the $(p + 1)$ estimates $\hat{\beta}_0, \hat{\beta}_1, \ldots, \hat{\beta}_p$:

$$n\hat{\beta}_0 + (\sum x_{i1})\hat{\beta}_1 + (\sum x_{i2})\hat{\beta}_2 + \cdots + (\sum x_{ip})\hat{\beta}_p = \sum y_i,$$

$$(\sum x_{i1})\hat{\beta}_0 + (\sum x_{i1}^2)\hat{\beta}_1 + (\sum x_{i1}x_{i2})\hat{\beta}_2 + \cdots + (\sum x_{i1}x_{ip})\hat{\beta}_p = \sum x_{i1}y_i,$$

$$\vdots \qquad\qquad\qquad\qquad\qquad \vdots$$

$$(\sum x_{ip})\hat{\beta}_0 + (\sum x_{i1}x_{ip})\hat{\beta}_1 + (\sum x_{i2}x_{ip})\hat{\beta}_2 + \cdots + (\sum x_{ip}^2)\hat{\beta}_p = \sum x_{ip}y_i.$$

These are called the *normal equations*. It is quite easy to solve the normal equations and determine the least-squares estimates. In fact, we can write each estimate as a linear combination of the responses, $y_1, \ldots, y_n$; the coefficients in these linear combinations depend only on the x_{ij} values ($i = 1, \ldots, n$ and $j = 1, \ldots, p$). Since computer programs for least-squares estimation are generally available, we do not discuss the numerical solution, nor do we introduce the solution in matrix notation. We expect that you use the locally available computer software.

A Further Remark on Estimation   There is yet another, somewhat simpler method for calculating the least-squares estimates. This is achieved by writing the regression model as

$$Y_i = \beta_0^* + \beta_1(x_{i1} - \bar{x}_1) + \cdots + \beta_p(x_{ip} - \bar{x}_p) + \varepsilon_i,$$

where $\beta_0^* = \beta_0 + \beta_1\bar{x}_1 + \cdots + \beta_p\bar{x}_p$ is a new intercept and $\bar{x}_j = (1/n)\sum_{i=1}^n x_{ij}$ is the average level of variable $x_j, j = 1, \ldots, p$. Replacing the x_{ij} in the first normal equation by $x_{ij} - \bar{x}_j$ leads to the least-squares estimate $\hat{\beta}_0^* = \bar{y} = (1/n)\sum_{i=1}^n y_i$. This shows that the multiple linear regression model can be written in a "mean-corrected" form:

$$(Y_i - \bar{Y}) = \beta_1(x_{i1} - \bar{x}_1) + \cdots + \beta_p(x_{ip} - \bar{x}_p) + \varepsilon_i, \qquad i = 1, 2, \ldots, n.$$

Thus the number of normal equations is reduced from $p + 1$ to p, and $\hat{\beta}_0$ can be calculated from $\hat{\beta}_0 = \bar{y} - \hat{\beta}_1\bar{x}_1 - \cdots - \hat{\beta}_p\bar{x}_p$.

We can use this representation to obtain explicit expressions for the least-squares estimates in the linear regression model with $p = 2$ explanatory variables. The substitution of $y_i - \bar{y}$ for y_i and $x_{ij} - \bar{x}_j$ for x_{ij} in the $p = 2$ remaining normal equations leads to

$$s_{11}\hat{\beta}_1 + s_{12}\hat{\beta}_2 = s_{1y},$$

$$s_{12}\hat{\beta}_1 + s_{22}\hat{\beta}_2 = s_{2y},$$

where $s_{11} = \sum(x_{i1} - \bar{x}_1)^2$, $s_{22} = \sum(x_{i2} - \bar{x}_2)^2$, $s_{12} = \sum(x_{i1} - \bar{x}_1)(x_{i2} - \bar{x}_2)$, $s_{1y} = \sum(x_{i1} - \bar{x}_1)(y_i - \bar{y})$, and $s_{2y} = \sum(x_{i2} - \bar{x}_2)(y_i - \bar{y})$. The solution of these two equations is given by

$$\hat{\beta}_1 = \frac{s_{22}s_{1y} - s_{12}s_{2y}}{s_{11}s_{22} - s_{12}^2}$$

$$\hat{\beta}_2 = \frac{-s_{12}s_{1y} + s_{11}s_{2y}}{s_{11}s_{22} - s_{12}^2}$$

The estimate of the intercept can be calculated from $\hat{\beta}_0 = \bar{y} - \hat{\beta}_1\bar{x}_1 - \hat{\beta}_2\bar{x}_2$. ∎

9.4-2   Residuals, Fitted Values, and the Sum-of-Squares Decomposition

With the least-squares estimates $\hat{\beta}_0, \hat{\beta}_1, \ldots, \hat{\beta}_p$ we can calculate the *fitted values*

$$\hat{y}_i = \hat{\beta}_0 + \hat{\beta}_1 x_{i1} + \cdots + \hat{\beta}_p x_{ip}, \qquad i = 1, 2, \ldots, n,$$

and the residuals

$$e_i = y_i - \hat{y}_i = y_i - (\hat{\beta}_0 + \hat{\beta}_1 x_{i1} + \cdots + \hat{\beta}_p x_{ip}), \qquad i = 1, 2, \ldots, n.$$

Since there are $p + 1$ regression coefficients, we find that there are $p + 1$ restrictions among the n residuals. These are, as can be seen by evaluating the

$p + 1$ first partial derivatives of $S(\beta_0, \beta_1, \ldots, \beta_p)$ at the least-squares estimates, given by $\sum_{i=1}^{n} e_i = 0$ and $\sum_{i=1}^{n} e_i x_{ij} = 0$ for $j = 1, \ldots, p$.

The components in the regression sum-of-squares decomposition, SSTO = SSR + SSE, can be calculated from SSTO $= \sum (y_i - \bar{y})^2 = \sum y_i^2 - (\sum y_i)^2/n$, SSR $= \sum (\hat{y}_i - \bar{y})^2$ and SSE $= \sum (y_i - \hat{y}_i)^2 = \sum e_i^2 = $ SSTO $-$ SSR. As in the simple linear regression model, we display the sums of squares in an ANOVA table, Table 9.4-1. The error sum of squares, SSE, now has $n - p - 1$ degrees of freedom, since there are $p + 1$ restrictions among the n residuals. A more formal explanation is that under the assumption that the errors $\varepsilon_1, \varepsilon_2, \ldots, \varepsilon_n$ are independent $N(0, \sigma^2)$ variables, the sampling distribution of SSE$/\sigma^2 = \sum (Y_i - \hat{Y}_i)^2/\sigma^2$ is a chi-square distribution with $n - (p + 1)$ degrees of freedom. The regression sum of squares, SSR, has p degrees of freedom because there are p explanatory variables in the model. The mean square due to error, MSE $=$ SSE$/(n - p - 1)$, and the mean square due to regression, MSR $=$ SSR$/p$, are given in the fourth column of the ANOVA table. The mean-square error, MSE $=$ SSE$/(n - p - 1)$, is an unbiased estimate of σ^2.

From the ANOVA table we can calculate the coefficient of determination,

$$R^2 = \frac{\text{SSR}}{\text{SSTO}} = 1 - \frac{\text{SSE}}{\text{SSTO}}, \qquad 0 \le R^2 \le 1.$$

It expresses the regression sum of squares as a fraction of the total sum of squares. A high R^2 value indicates that the regression model with the p explanatory variables explains a large proportion of the variability among the observations $y_1, y_2, \ldots, y_n$. However, this value by itself does not tell us which of the p variables are the most important ones.

A closely related measure of fit of an estimated regression model compares the variance estimates with and without the explanatory variables. That is, the sample variance of the observations $y_1, y_2, \ldots, y_n$, which is SSTO$/(n - 1)$, can be compared to the variance estimate in the regression model, MSE $=$ SSE$/(n - p - 1)$. The proportionate reduction in variance due to regression is the adjusted R^2, namely,

$$R_a^2 = 1 - \frac{\text{SSE}/(n - p - 1)}{\text{SSTO}/(n - 1)}.$$

It can be shown that $R_a^2 \le R^2$.

TABLE 9.4-1   ANOVA for the Multiple Linear Regression Model

Source	SS	df	MS	F
Regression	SSR	p	MSR $=$ SSR$/p$	MSR/MSE
Error	SSE	$n - p - 1$	MSE $=$ SSE$/(n - p - 1)$	
Total	SSTO	$n - 1$		

9.4-3   Inference in the Multiple Linear Regression Model

The regression model includes a random component ε, and thus the response variable Y is also a random variable. The least-squares estimates, the sums of squares in the ANOVA table, and R^2 are all functions of $Y_1, \ldots, Y_n$. Thus, prior to sampling, they are random variables and each has a sampling distribution. To make statistical inferences, we must know these sampling distributions, at least when we make the usual normal assumptions.

Frequently, the first question that one wants answered is whether or not the regressors $x_1, \ldots, x_p$ explain some of the variation in the response variable Y. Thus we are interested in testing $H_0 : \beta_1 = \beta_2 = \cdots = \beta_p = 0$ against the alternative H_1 that not all $\beta_j = 0$. Under the null hypothesis, the regression model reduces to the simple model $Y_i = \beta_0 + \varepsilon_i$, that is, the model in which the normal variables $Y_1, Y_2, \ldots, Y_n$ are independent and identically distributed, since none of the x variables are involved. Under the alternative, there is *at least one* x variable that explains some of the variation in the Y. The appropriate test statistic is the F-ratio from the ANOVA table, $F = \text{MSR/MSE}$.

If $\varepsilon_1, \varepsilon_2, \ldots, \varepsilon_n$ are independent normal random variables with mean zero and common variance σ^2, the distribution of SSE/σ^2 is chi-square with $n - p - 1$ degrees of freedom and thus $E(\text{MSE}) = \sigma^2$. Now, if H_0 is true, it is also true that SSR/σ^2 is $\chi^2(p)$ and $E(\text{MSR}) = \sigma^2$. Since it can be shown that SSE and SSR are independent, $F = \text{MSR/MSE}$ follows an F-distribution with p and $n - p - 1$ degrees of freedom. If, however, H_1 is true, then $E(\text{MSR}) > \sigma^2$ and the F-ratio will tend to be much larger than what can be expected under H_0. This leads to the following decision rule: Calculate $F = \text{MSR/MSE}$ from the ANOVA table and if $F \geq F(\alpha; p, n - p - 1)$, accept H_1 at significance level α; otherwise, do not reject H_0. Alternatively, many computer programs calculate the p value $= P[F(p, n - p - 1) \geq F]$, where F is the calculated F. If this p value is small (less than the significance level α), it is very unlikely that we have found such a large F-ratio by chance alone. We accept H_1 and conclude that the regressor variables explain some of the variation in the response variable Y. Also note that the F-ratio and R^2 are related through the very simple equation

$$F = \frac{R^2}{1 - R^2} \left(\frac{n - p - 1}{p} \right).$$

A high R^2 implies a large value for the F-ratio.

The conclusion that there is a significant regression relationship is only the first step in our analysis. Next we want to assess the significance of each individual regression coefficient $\hat{\beta}_j$. Prior to sampling, $\hat{\beta}_j$ is a random variable and has a sampling distribution. Since it is a linear combination of the normal random variables $Y_1, Y_2, \ldots, Y_n$, say, $\hat{\beta}_j = \sum_{i=1}^{n} c_{ij} Y_i, j = 0, 1, \ldots, p$, it is normally distributed. The c_{ij}'s depend only on the nonrandom levels of the x variables, and it is possible to write down explicit expressions for these coefficients. However, this is not done here because computer programs are available for their calculation. As in the simple linear regression model, we can show that $\hat{\beta}_j$ is an unbiased estimator of β_j, that is, $E(\hat{\beta}_j) = \beta_j$. Moreover, we can find the variance, $\text{var}(\hat{\beta}_j) = \sigma^2 \sum_{i=1}^{n} c_{ij}^2$, of these sampling distributions, $j = 0, 1, \ldots, p$. Thus the standardized random variable $(\hat{\beta}_j - \beta_j)/\sqrt{\text{var}(\hat{\beta}_j)}$ follows a $N(0, 1)$ distribution. Replacing the unknown variance σ^2 by its estimate MSE leads to the estimated variance of $\hat{\beta}_j$, namely $s^2(\hat{\beta}_j) = \text{MSE} \sum_{i=1}^{n} c_{ij}^2$. The square roots of these quantities, the standard errors $s(\hat{\beta}_j)$, are displayed in the regression output. With this standard error, the sampling distribution of $(\hat{\beta}_j - \beta_j)/s(\hat{\beta}_j)$ is $t(n - p - 1)$, where the degrees of freedom, $n - p - 1$, in the t-distribution come from the degrees of freedom of the error sum of squares in the ANOVA table.

With this sampling distribution, we can calculate $100(1 - \alpha)$ percent confidence intervals for β_j, namely, $\hat{\beta}_j \pm t(\alpha/2; n - p - 1)s(\hat{\beta}_j)$. Also, to test the significance of an individual regression coefficient, we test $H_0: \beta_j = 0$ against $H_1: \beta_j \neq 0$. The appropriate test statistic is the t-ratio, $t_{\hat{\beta}_j} = \hat{\beta}_j/s(\hat{\beta}_j)$, and if $|t_{\hat{\beta}_j}| \geq t(\alpha/2; n - p - 1)$, we conclude H_1 at significance level α; otherwise, we do not reject $\beta_j = 0$. Alternatively, one can compare the p value $= 2P[t(n - p - 1) \geq |t_{\hat{\beta}_j}|]$, where $t_{\hat{\beta}_j}$ is the computed value of the t-statistic, with the significance level α. If the p value is less than or equal to α, we conclude that the regressor variable x_j has a significant impact on the response. These t-tests are also called *partial t-tests*, since they assess the partial (or additional) significance of the variable x_j, over and above the impact of all other variables in the model. There is more on this in the next section.

Exercises 9.4

9.4-1   The model $Y_i = \beta_0 + \beta_1 x_{i1} + \beta_2 x_{i2} + \varepsilon_i$ is fit to $n = 8$ observations. The calculation results in

$$\sum y_i = 8, \qquad \sum x_{i1} = \sum x_{i2} = \sum x_{i1} x_{i2} = 0,$$

$$\sum x_{i1}^2 = 20, \qquad \sum x_{i2}^2 = 40, \qquad \sum x_{i1} y_i = 10,$$

$$\sum x_{i2} y_i = 30.$$

Using the normal equations, calculate the least-squares estimates of β_0, β_1, and β_2.

9.4-2   Consider data on per capita beer consumption (y), per capita real income (x_1), and relative price of beer (x_2). The linear regression model $Y_i = \beta_0 + \beta_1 x_{i1} + \beta_2 x_{i2} + \varepsilon_i$ is estimated from $n = 17$ observations.

(a) Using a regression program, we find that the estimates and their standard errors (given in parentheses) are $\hat{\beta}_0 = 1.37$ (0.35), $\hat{\beta}_1 = 1.14$ (0.16), and $\hat{\beta}_2 = -0.83$ (0.20). Calculate 95 percent confidence intervals for β_1 and β_2. Conduct partial t-tests at the $\alpha = 0.05$ significance level. Interpret your results.

(b) The partially completed ANOVA table follows:

Source	SS	df	MS	F
Regression				
Error	34			
Total	100			

Complete the table, calculate R^2, and use the F-statistic to test $H_0: \beta_1 = \beta_2 = 0$ at the $\alpha = 0.05$ level.

9.4-3 A linear regression model $Y_i = \beta_0 + \beta_1 x_{i1} + \beta_2 x_{i2} + \varepsilon_i$ was fit to $n = 20$ data points. It was found that SSTO = 200 and SSR = 66.

(a) Construct the ANOVA table.

(b) Calculate and interpret R^2.

(c) Test $H_0: \beta_1 = \beta_2 = 0$ at the $\alpha = 0.05$ significance level.

(d) The individual t-statistics were $t_{\hat{\beta}_0} = 4.30$, $t_{\hat{\beta}_1} = -3.60$, and $t_{\hat{\beta}_2} = 0.80$. Make appropriate tests about the parameters and interpret the results. Does it seem that the regression model can be simplified?

9.5 More on Multiple Regression

9.5-1 Multicollinearity Among the Explanatory Variables

In this section we discuss how multicollinearity affects the regression analysis. Multicollinearity refers to a condition in the explanatory variables. It occurs when explanatory variables convey very similar information, and when there is "near" linear dependence among the variables $x_1, x_2, \ldots, x_p$.

To discuss multicollinearity among the explanatory variables, let us consider the multiple regression model with $p = 2$ regressors. In the *mean-corrected* form, the basic model can be written as

$$Y_i - \bar{Y} = \beta_1(x_{i1} - \bar{x}_1) + \beta_2(x_{i2} - \bar{x}_2) + \varepsilon_i.$$

If the explanatory variables x_1 and x_2 convey the same, or very similar information, we say that there is multicollinearity. If they express the same information through an approximate linear relationship between x_1 and x_2, then the absolute value of the correlation coefficient

$$r_{12} = \frac{\sum (x_{i1} - \bar{x}_1)(x_{i2} - \bar{x}_2)}{[\sum (x_{i1} - \bar{x}_1)^2 \sum (x_{i2} - \bar{x}_2)^2]^{1/2}}$$

is close to 1. On the other hand, if x_1 and x_2 provide different and independent information, r_{12} is close to zero.

As a simple and trivial example, consider the mileage data with gpm as the dependent variable Y, with weight in kilograms as x_1 and weight in pounds as x_2. Obviously, x_1 and x_2 express the same information because x_1 and x_2 are proportional; thus $r_{12} = 1$. In many practical and nontrivial applications, r_{12} will not be 1 exactly, but may be very large. For example, heavy cars tend to have larger engines and hence the correlation between weight and engine displacement of cars may be quite high.

If the correlation coefficient between x_1 and x_2 is $r_{12} = 0$, we also say that x_1 and x_2 are *orthogonal*. An example of such a situation arises in the context of factorial experiments (see Section 8.3). In a 2^2 factorial experiment the investigator conducts the experiment at two levels for each of the two variables: the low level is coded as -1 and the high level is given by $+1$. There are $n = 4$ observations if there are no replications, and the data are given by $(y_1, -1, -1)$, $(y_2, 1, -1)$, $(y_3, -1, 1)$, and $(y_4, 1, 1)$. It is easy to check that the correlation coefficient between x_1 and x_2 is $r_{12} = 0$.

If $r_{12} = 0$, the normal equations in Section 9.4 simplify as they reduce to

$$[\sum (x_{i1} - \bar{x}_1)^2]\hat{\beta}_1 = \sum (x_{i1} - \bar{x}_1)(y_i - \bar{y}),$$
$$[\sum (x_{i2} - \bar{x}_2)^2]\hat{\beta}_2 = \sum (x_{i2} - \bar{x}_2)(y_i - \bar{y}).$$

The estimates of the regression coefficients are

$$\hat{\beta}_1 = \frac{\sum (x_{i1} - \bar{x}_1)(y_i - \bar{y})}{\sum (x_{i1} - \bar{x}_1)^2} = \frac{s_{1y}}{s_{11}},$$

$$\hat{\beta}_2 = \frac{\sum (x_{i2} - \bar{x}_2)(y_i - \bar{y})}{\sum (x_{i2} - \bar{x}_2)^2} = \frac{s_{2y}}{s_{22}}.$$

These estimates are the same as the ones that we get by estimating β_1 and β_2 in the two individual models, $(Y_i - \bar{Y}) = \beta_1(x_{i1} - \bar{x}_1) + \varepsilon_i$ and $(Y_i - \bar{Y}) = \beta_2(x_{i2} - \bar{x}_2) + \varepsilon_i$. In other words, since $r_{12} = 0$, the addition of the second variable x_2 to our model and estimating β_1 and β_2 jointly does not change our estimate of β_1.

Of course, this is not true if $r_{12} \neq 0$ because from the normal equations in Section 9.4 we have that

$$\hat{\beta}_1 = \frac{s_{22}}{s_{11}s_{22} - s_{12}^2} s_{1y} - \frac{s_{12}}{s_{11}s_{22} - s_{12}^2} s_{2y}.$$

Since $r_{12} = s_{12}/\sqrt{s_{11}s_{22}}$, we can rewrite this estimate as

$$\hat{\beta}_1 = \left(\frac{1}{1 - r_{12}^2}\right) \frac{s_{1y}}{s_{11}} - \left(\frac{r_{12}}{1 - r_{12}^2}\right) \frac{s_{2y}}{\sqrt{s_{11}s_{22}}}.$$

From this equation it becomes clear that, in general, when $r_{12} \neq 0$, the estimate of β_1 will change if we include another variable x_2 in the model. This is the reason why we emphasized the *partial* nature of individual regression coefficients and of the corresponding t-tests. We always have to consider the contribution of an explanatory variable in relation to all other variables in the regression model.

This should be kept in mind when we interpret the multiple regression output. For example, if individual t-tests show that both $\hat{\beta}_1$ and $\hat{\beta}_2$ are insignificant, this does *not* imply that both x_1 and x_2 are unimportant and can be omitted from the model. Since $t_{\hat{\beta}_2}$ is a partial test statistic, it tests only the additional importance of the variable x_2 over and above the contribution of x_1. It is like adding an extra explanatory variable to the model and then asking for its contribution beyond all other variables in the model. Similarly, $t_{\hat{\beta}_1}$ tests the significance of the regression contribution of x_1 over and above that explained by x_2. If x_1 and x_2 are highly correlated, it could be that both individual t-statistics are insignificant, even though the response Y is related to each of them. In such a case the F-statistic, which tests H_0: $\beta_1 = \beta_2 = 0$ against the alternative that at least one of the coefficients is nonzero, would be significant. In summary, this discussion implies that we must proceed cautiously when simplifying regression models. We should not omit all insignificant coefficients at once, but should proceed sequentially, omitting one insignificant variable at a time and reestimating the remaining parameters each time.

Example 9.5-1 An engineer in the paint division of a chemical company studies the effects of latex solid contents (x_1) and drying temperature (x_2) on the stiffness of the paint. The engineer varies latex contents between 40 and 50 percent, and drying temperature between 75 and 95°F. In order to study possible interaction effects between latex solid contents and drying temperature, she varies these two variables simultaneously. The experiment is run at the following four conditions of latex solid contents and drying temperature: (40 percent, 75°F), (50 percent, 75°F), (40 percent, 95°F), (50 percent, 95°F). This is a two-level factorial experiment since each of the two levels of one variable (factor) is combined with each of the two levels of the other. Following our notation in Sections 8.3 and 8.4, we code the two levels as ± 1. We let $x_1 = -1$ if latex contents is 40 percent, and $x_1 = +1$ if it is 50 percent; thus a unit change in x_1 corresponds to a 5 percent change in latex solid contents. Similarly, $x_2 = -1$ if temperature is at 75°F, and $x_2 = +1$ if temperature is at 95°F; a unit change in x_2 corresponds to a 10°F change in temperature. Also suppose that at each level combination, the engineer conducts two separate and independent experiments. That is, a total of eight experiments are run. To guarantee the validity of the resulting inference, the engineer randomizes the order of these eight experiments and obtains the data given in Table 9.5-1.

We want to estimate the regression model

$$Y_i = \beta_0 + \beta_1 x_{i1} + \beta_2 x_{i2} + \beta_3 x_{i3} + \varepsilon_i, \qquad i = 1, 2, \ldots, 8,$$

where $x_{i3} = x_{i1} x_{i2}$. We observe that $\bar{x}_1 = \bar{x}_2 = \bar{x}_3 = 0$; thus we know from the first normal equation in Section 9.4 that $\hat{\beta}_0 = \bar{y} = 135$. Furthermore, we note

TABLE 9.5-1 **Data from a Replicated 2^2 Factorial Design**

x_1	x_2	$x_3 = x_1 x_2$	y
-1	-1	1	120
-1	-1	1	125
1	-1	-1	140
1	-1	-1	145
-1	1	-1	125
-1	1	-1	135
1	1	1	140
1	1	1	150

TABLE 9.5-2   ANOVA Table for Example
9.5-1

Source	SS	df	MS	F
Regression	675	3	225	7.20
Error	125	4	31.25	
Total	800	7		

that the correlation coefficients between the three explanatory variables are
$r_{12} = r_{13} = r_{23} = 0$; so the three x variables are orthogonal. The estimates,
with standard errors in parentheses, are given by $\hat{\beta}_0 = 135$ (1.98), $\hat{\beta}_1 = 8.75$
(1.98), $\hat{\beta}_2 = 2.5$ (1.98), and $\hat{\beta}_3 = -1.25$ (1.98). The fact that these standard
errors are the same arises because of the very special nature of the x values in
this example. The ANOVA table is given in Table 9.5-2. The coefficient of
determination is $R^2 = 675/800 = 0.84$. The overall regression model is significant because $F = 225/31.25 = 7.20$ is larger than the critical value $F(0.05; 3,
4) = 6.59$.

The model can be simplified because the coefficient that corresponds to the
interaction $x_3 = x_1 x_2$ is insignificant. Its t-ratio, $t_{\hat{\beta}_3} = -1.25/1.98 = -0.63$, is
much smaller in absolute value than the critical value $t(0.025; 4) = 2.776$. This
leads us to the *main-effects* model, $Y_i = \beta_0 + \beta_1 x_{i1} + \beta_2 x_{i2} + \varepsilon_i$. Such a model
is much easier to interpret since the effect of a unit change in one variable does
not depend on the level of the other. In general, we should estimate β_1 and β_2
again, since omitting a variable from the model will lead to different estimates
of the remaining coefficients. In our special case, however, the three sets of x
variables are orthogonal; thus the estimates remain unchanged.

Finally, we summarize in Table 9.5-3 the results of the estimation of three
regression models, where we have eliminated the explanatory variables in a
logical order in moving from one model to the next. For this orthogonal
example, we note that (1) the regression coefficient estimates do not change as
we omit the other explanatory variables from the model. The standard errors

TABLE 9.5-3   Regression Estimates and Standard Errors (in
Parentheses) for Example 9.5-1

Regression on:	β_0	β_1	β_2	β_3	MSE
$x_1, x_2, x_3 = x_1 x_2$	135.00	8.75	2.50	-1.25	31.25
	(1.98)	(1.98)	(1.98)	(1.98)	
x_1, x_2	135.00	8.75	2.50		27.50
	(1.85)	(1.85)	(1.85)		
x_1	135.00	8.75			31.25
	(1.98)	(1.98)			

change somewhat because the estimates of σ^2 are different. (2) The second variable x_2 (temperature) is insignificant; the t-ratio from the model with x_1 and x_2, $t_{\beta_2} = 2.5/1.85 = 1.35$, is smaller than the critical value $t(0.025; 8 - 3 = 5) = 2.571$. (3) In summary, it appears that over the ranges considered x_1 is the only important variable because $t_{\beta_1} = 8.75/1.98 = 4.43$ is larger than $t(0.025; 8 - 2 = 6) = 2.447$. A 5 percent change in latex solid contents leads to an 8.75 unit change (increase) in the stiffness rating. Of course, this statement applies only for changes in the 40 to 50 percent range of latex contents. Since we have no data outside this region, it would be dangerous to extrapolate too far.

You may wonder whether it is also possible to include quadratic terms x_1^2 and x_2^2 in this regression model. With our data it is not possible to estimate quadratic effects, since we have only two levels and there is no way to determine a quadratic curve from just two points. If we want to fit a quadratic model, we need observations at more than two levels. For example, including a center point where $x_1 = x_2 = 0$, or considering a factorial experiment with three levels for each variable, resulting in the nine (x_1, x_2) design points, $(-1, -1), (0, -1), (1, -1), (-1, 0), (0, 0), (1, 0), (-1, 1), (0, 1)$, and $(1, 1)$, would provide the necessary information to fit a quadratic model. ■

Example 9.5-2 Consider the mileage data shown in Section 9.1. There we found a strong positive linear association between gpm (y) and weight (x_1). Now we add a second variable, horsepower (x_2), and consider the multiple regression model: $Y_i = \beta_0 + \beta_1 x_{i1} + \beta_2 x_{i2} + \varepsilon_i$. Since more powerful cars require more fuel, we expect a positive association between gpm and horsepower and thus a positive estimate for β_2. The weights and horsepowers of the 10 cars in our sample are given in Table 9.5-4.

The plot of horsepower against weight in Figure 9.5-1, with a correlation

TABLE 9.5-4   Gpm, Weight, and Horsepower of 10 Selected Cars

Gpm, y	Weight (1000 pounds), x_1	Horsepower, x_2
5.5	3.4	120
5.9	3.8	130
6.5	4.1	142
3.3	2.2	68
3.6	2.6	95
4.6	2.9	109
2.9	2.0	65
3.6	2.7	80
3.1	1.9	71
4.9	3.4	105

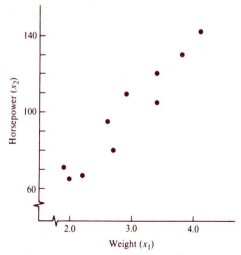

FIGURE 9.5-1   Scatterplot of horsepower against weight.

coefficient of $r_{12} = 0.98$, indicates a strong linear relationship between these two explanatory variables. The explanatory variables for this particular data set constitute a very "poor design" for estimating their effects because one is essentially a linear function of the other. In order to study the partial effects of weight and horsepower on fuel consumption, we would need the gpm of heavy cars with low horsepower and the gpm of light cars with high horsepower. However, such cars are not part of our sample and may, in fact, not even exist. To illustrate why it is difficult to partition the effects in such a situation, let us assume that the linear relationship between x_2 and x_1 is exact; that is, say that $x_2 = \alpha_0 + \alpha_1 x_1$. For our data $\alpha_1 \approx 35$. If we substitute this for x_2 into $Y = \beta_0 + \beta_1 x_1 + \beta_2 x_2 + \varepsilon$, we obtain $Y = \beta_0 + \beta_1 x_1 + \beta_2(\alpha_0 + \alpha_1 x_1) + \varepsilon = \beta_0^* + \beta_1^* x_1 + \varepsilon$. Now $\beta_1^* = \beta_1 + \alpha_1 \beta_2$ may be estimated with good precision. For example, in Section 9.1 we found a highly significant regression coefficient for the variable weight, x_1; its value was $\hat{\beta}_1^* = 1.64$. But there are many solutions to $1.64 = \beta_1 + 35\beta_2$; in fact, there are an infinite number of possibilities. One of them is $\beta_1 = 1.64$ and $\beta_2 = 0.0$; another is $\beta_1 = 0.0$ and $\beta_2 = 0.047$; a third is $\beta_1 = 0.82$ and $\beta_2 = 0.024$; and so on. If the linear relationship between x_2 and x_1 is not exact but only approximate, there is still considerable uncertainty regarding how to estimate the coefficients β_1 and β_2. This uncertainty is reflected in the large standard errors of these estimates. In a multicollinear situation they tend to be much larger than the standard errors in the simplified models in which we have omitted one of the collinear explanatory variables. This is exactly what we observe in this example. The estimation results for the three models $Y_i = \beta_0 + \beta_1 x_{i1} + \beta_2 x_{i2} + \varepsilon_i$, $Y_i = \beta_0 + \beta_1 x_{i1} + \varepsilon_i$, and $Y_i = \beta_0 + \beta_2 x_{i2} + \varepsilon_i$ in Table 9.5-5 show that the standard errors of the estimates of β_1 and β_2 are much larger in the full model than in either of the simplified models.

TABLE 9.5-5   Regression Estimates and Standard Errors (in Parentheses) for Example 9.5-2

Regression on:	β_0	β_1	β_2	R^2
x_1, x_2	−0.33	0.82	0.024	0.974
	(0.30)	(0.36)	(0.010)	
x_1 (weight)	−0.36	1.64		0.954
	(0.38)	(0.13)		
x_2 (horsepower)	−0.12		0.046	0.955
	(0.36)		(0.003)	

This table leads to the following observations. (1) The estimate of β_1 has changed from 1.64 in the regression on weight only to 0.82 in the more general model that includes both weight and horsepower as explanatory variables. The same observation can be made for the coefficient of horsepower; it changes from 0.046 to 0.024 when weight is introduced as an additional explanatory variable. (2) Weight still has a significant partial effect (at significance level $\alpha = 0.10$) after horsepower has been included in the model. However, its significance is greatly reduced: from $1.64/0.13 = 12.85$ in the regression on weight only to $0.82/0.36 = 2.26$ in the regression on both weight and horsepower. The same observation applies to the coefficient of horsepower. (3) The coefficient of determination R^2 changes very little. Also, the fitted values that are implied by these three models are very similar. This means that all three models lead to similar fitted surfaces. However, this is true only as long as one is interested in the mean responses to values from the experimental region, which is this narrow band of values in the scatterplot of x_2 against x_1 in Figure 9.5-1. The extrapolations for x_1 and x_2 values that lie outside this region will be quite different for the three fitted models. Since there are no data points to check the adequacy of the models outside this experimental region, it is difficult to determine which of the three models is more appropriate. ■

9.5-2   Another Example of Multiple Regression

Data concerning pavement durability is given in Table 9.5-6. There we list measurements of the change in rut depth (y) of 31 experimental asphalt pavements that were prepared under different conditions specified by the values of five explanatory variables: viscosity of asphalt (x_1), percentage of asphalt in surface course (x_2), percentage of asphalt in base course (x_3), percentage of fines in surface course (x_4), and percentage of voids in surface course (x_5). The sixth variable, x_6, is an *indicator variable* that separates the results for 16 pavements tested in one set of runs from those 15 tested in the second run. Note that asphalt viscosity is considerably higher in the second set of runs. The data are taken from a study by J. W. Gorman and R. J. Toman, "Selection of Variables for Fitting Equations to Data" [*Technometrics*, 8:

27–51 (1966)], who also give a detailed description of the experiment. An analysis of these data is also given in a book by C. Daniel and F. S. Wood, *Fitting Equations to Data*, 2nd ed. (New York: Wiley, 1980).

An objective of this experiment is to determine the important variables that affect the change in rut depth. Viscosity of the asphalt is certainly one of them

TABLE 9.5-6   Pavement Durability Data[a]

y	x_1	x_2	x_3	x_4	x_5	x_6
6.75	2.80	4.68	4.87	8.4	4.916	−1
13.00	1.40	5.19	4.50	6.5	4.563	−1
14.75	1.40	4.82	4.73	7.9	5.321	−1
12.60	3.30	4.85	4.76	8.3	4.865	−1
8.25	1.70	4.86	4.95	8.4	3.776	−1
10.67	2.90	5.16	4.45	7.4	4.397	−1
7.28	3.70	4.82	5.05	6.8	4.867	−1
12.67	1.70	4.86	4.70	8.6	4.828	−1
12.58	0.92	4.78	4.84	6.7	4.865	−1
20.60	0.68	5.16	4.76	7.7	4.034	−1
3.58	6.00	4.57	4.82	7.4	5.450	−1
7.00	4.30	4.61	4.65	6.7	4.853	−1
26.20	0.60	5.07	5.10	7.5	4.257	−1
11.67	1.80	4.66	5.09	8.2	5.144	−1
7.67	6.00	5.42	4.41	5.8	3.718	−1
12.25	4.40	5.01	4.74	7.1	4.715	−1
0.76	88.00	4.97	4.66	6.5	4.625	1
1.35	62.00	5.01	4.72	8.0	4.977	1
1.44	50.00	4.96	4.90	6.8	4.322	1
1.60	58.00	5.20	4.70	8.2	5.087	1
1.10	90.00	4.80	4.60	6.6	5.971	1
0.85	66.00	4.98	4.69	6.4	4.647	1
1.20	140.00	5.35	4.76	7.3	5.115	1
0.56	240.00	5.04	4.80	7.8	5.939	1
0.72	420.00	4.80	4.80	7.4	5.916	1
0.47	500.00	4.83	4.60	6.7	5.471	1
0.33	180.00	4.66	4.72	7.2	4.602	1
0.26	270.00	4.67	4.50	6.3	5.043	1
0.76	170.00	4.72	4.70	6.8	5.075	1
0.80	98.00	5.00	5.07	7.2	4.334	1
2.00	35.00	4.70	4.80	7.7	5.705	1

Source: J. W. Gorman and R. J. Toman, "Selection of Variables for Fitting Equations to Data," *Technometrics*, 8: 27–51 (1966).

[a] y, Change in rut depth in inches per million wheel passes; x_1, viscosity of asphalt; x_2, percentage of asphalt in surface course; x_3, percentage of asphalt in base course; x_4, percentage of fines in surface course; x_5, percentage of voids in surface course; x_6, indicator variable to separate two sets of runs.

as we can see from the plot in Figure 9.5-2(a). The relationship between Y (change of rut depth) and x_1 (asphalt viscosity) is highly nonlinear. In many cases, transformations of the response variable as well as of the explanatory variables may lead to simplifications of the relationship. Logarithmic transformations are usually the first ones tried, especially when variables are bounded

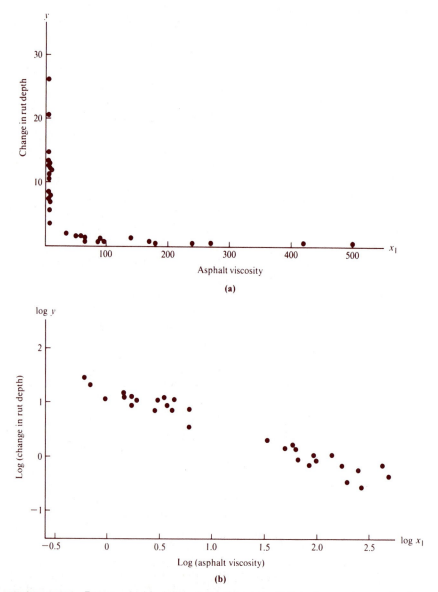

FIGURE 9.5-2   Pavement durability data: (a) plot of the change in rut depth, y, against viscosity of asphalt, x_1; (b) plot of log y against log x_1.

from below, as is the case in the change of rut depth. The plot of log y against log x_1 is given in Figure 9.5-2(b), and it shows that these logarithmic (base 10) transformations lead to a relationship that is approximately linear. Thus we start with a model of the form $\log Y_i = \beta_0 + \beta_1 \log x_{i1} + \varepsilon_i$.

We mentioned that the experiment was run in two batches. Thus one may be interested in learning whether there is an effect due to the two different sets of runs. This can be achieved by including the indicator variable, x_6, in the model, and considering $\log Y_i = \beta_0 + \beta_1 \log x_{i1} + \beta_6 x_{i6} + \varepsilon_i$. An indicator variable is a variable that expresses the absence or presence of a condition. It is either zero or 1 or, as in our example, -1 or $+1$. A nonzero value of β_6 would change the intercept in the linear regression model to $\beta_0 - \beta_6$ for the first group and $\beta_0 + \beta_6$ for the second. Thus β_6 measures the additional effect that is due to the different sets of runs, after having adjusted for the different levels of asphalt viscosity. Note that the term $\beta_6 x_6$ affects only the intercept of the relationship between log y and log x_1; the slope (which measures the effect of log x_1) stays the same. In other words, we assume that the effects of log x_1 and x_6 are additive.

Also, the remaining variables $x_2, \ldots, x_5$ may have a significant impact on the response variable log Y. To study their effects, we consider the model

$$\log Y_i = \beta_0 + \beta_1 \log x_{i1} + \beta_2 x_{i2} + \beta_3 x_{i3} + \beta_4 x_{i4} + \beta_5 x_{i5} + \beta_6 x_{i6} + \varepsilon_i.$$

The reader may ask the question why we have included these variables in their original metric and not considered a transformation (possibly logarithmic). For one, individual scatter plots of log y against x_2 through x_5 show more or less linear relationships. Furthermore, the range of these variables is rather small. Since over a limited range most nonlinear functions can be approximated by linear ones, it does not matter too much whether we use x_j or log x_j.

The regression output for this general model with the six explanatory variables is given in Table 9.5-7. This regression explains 97.2 percent of the variation in log Y. This regression is highly significant because $F = 140.1 > F(0.01; 6, 24) = 3.67$. That is, the null hypothesis $H_0: \beta_1 = \beta_2 = \cdots = \beta_6 = 0$ is rejected in favor of H_1: not all $\beta_j = 0$, $j = 1, \ldots, 6$. Looking at the partial (individual) t-tests, and comparing the t-ratios with $t(0.025; 24) = 2.064$, we find that the important variables that affect the change in rut depth (as measured by its logarithm) are asphalt viscosity as measured by log x_1, percent of asphalt in surface course (x_2), and percent of voids in surface course (x_5). In addition, it appears that the runs in the second set lead to smaller changes in rut depth than the runs in the first set. Thus there are some differences in the rutting rates from the two sets of runs that are not accounted for by the change in asphalt viscosity, the percent of asphalt, or the percent of voids in the surface course. This change may be due to a difference between the batches of asphalt, but could also be due to changes of tires on test machines, slightly different uncontrolled test conditions, and so on. We really do not know.

To check the adequacy of the fitted models, we perform various residual

TABLE 9.5-7   **Regression Output for the Example**

	Estimate	Standard Error	t-Ratio
Constant	-2.645	1.091	-2.43
$\log x_1$	-0.513	0.073	-7.03
x_2	0.498	0.115	4.32
x_3	0.101	0.142	0.71
x_4	0.019	0.034	0.55
x_5	0.138	0.048	2.87
x_6	-0.134	0.064	-2.10

ANOVA table:

Source	SS	df	MS	F
Regression	10.752	6	1.792	140.1
Error	0.307	24	0.0128	
Total	11.059	30		

$R^2 = 10.752/11.059 = 0.972$.

plots that we have discussed in Section 9.3. One of them, a plot of residuals against fitted values, is given in Figure 9.5-3. It shows no apparent patterns. In addition, we also find that the plots of residuals against the explanatory variables show no model inadequacies. Thus it appears that the model in Table 9.5-7 gives an appropriate representation of the data.

Two of the coefficients in this model were found insignificant. One can simplify the model by omitting insignificant variables. However, we cautioned earlier that the variables should be omitted one by one, estimating the coefficients of the new model at each stage. In Table 9.5-7, the coefficient with the smallest t-ratio, in absolute value, is x_4 (percentage of fines in surface course). Since it is insignificant, we drop it from the model and use

$$\log Y_i = \beta_0 + \beta_1 \log x_{i1} + \beta_2 x_{i2} + \beta_3 x_{i3} + \beta_5 x_{i5} + \beta_6 x_{i6} + \varepsilon_i.$$

The estimation results for this model are summarized in the first three columns of Table 9.5-8. We note that x_3 is insignificant (t-ratio $= 0.99$). This leads to a further simplification of the model,

$$\log Y_i = \beta_0 + \beta_1 \log x_{i1} + \beta_2 x_{i2} + \beta_5 x_{i5} + \beta_6 x_{i6} + \varepsilon_i.$$

The estimates, standard errors, and t-ratios for this model are given in the last three columns of Table 9.5-8. The smallest t-ratio is the one associated with the indicator variable x_6. It is still significant at the $\alpha = 0.10$ level because $t(0.05; 31 - 5 = 26) = 1.706$. Thus we should not simplify this model further and should consider it as our best description of the relationship. In summary,

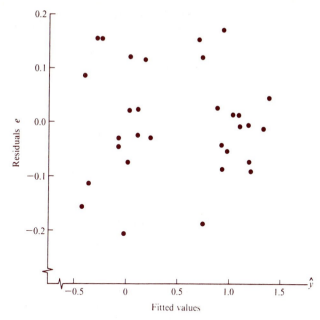

FIGURE 9.5-3   Pavement durability data. Plot of residuals against fitted values.

we find that asphalt viscosity, percent of asphalt in surface course, and percent of voids in the surface course have an effect on the change in rut depth. In addition, we note some differences in the rutting rates from the two sets of runs.

The selection procedure that we have described here is called *backward elimination*. One starts with the largest possible model and omits insignificant variables, one at a time. Many other "search" procedures to choose the best-fitting model have been developed. For example, we could start with the simplest model with just one explanatory variable and then add variables if they are found significant. Such an approach is known as *forward selection*.

TABLE 9.5-8   **Results of Estimation for the Example**

	Estimate	Standard Error	t-Ratio	Estimate	Standard Error	t-Ratio
Constant	-2.692	1.072	-2.51	-1.853	0.658	-2.81
$\log x_1$	-0.522	0.070	-7.42	-0.547	0.065	-8.36
x_2	0.502	0.114	4.43	0.465	0.107	4.35
x_3	0.129	0.130	0.99			
x_4						
x_5	0.146	0.045	3.24	0.144	0.045	3.20
x_6	-0.131	0.063	-2.09	-0.111	0.059	-1.87
		$R^2 = 0.972$			$R^2 = 0.971$	

Another approach that is usually preferable to the backward elimination and forward selection procedures examines the results of all possible regressions. The number of all possible regressions is large in most cases; for p regressor variables there are $2^p - 1$ possible regression models: p models with one variable, $p(p - 1)/2$ models with two variables, ..., and one model with all variables included. Today's computers, however, can perform these estimations very rapidly. Various criteria for comparing the fitted models are suggested in the literature. For example, one can select the model that leads to the smallest mean-square error. The resulting "optimal" model, as well as every other model that achieves a mean-square error which is close to the minimum and which includes not more variables than the optimal model, should be considered for a more detailed study. Texts on regression analysis, such as Draper and Smith, *Applied Regression Analysis* (New York: Wiley, 1981) and Neter, Wasserman, and Kutner, *Applied Linear Regression Models* (Homewood, Ill.: Irwin, 1983) give a detailed description of these procedures.

Our model for the change in rut depth is linear in the transformed variables. We could ask whether it is necessary to include interaction terms. In particular, one may be interested in interactions with the indicator variable x_6. An interaction with an indicator variable amounts to a slope change in the regression model. Consider, for example, adding the term $\beta_{16}(\log x_1)x_6$ to our model to obtain

$$\log Y = \beta_0 + \beta_1(\log x_1) + \beta_2 x_2 + \beta_5 x_5 + \beta_6 x_6 + \beta_{16}(\log x_1)x_6 + \varepsilon.$$

The coefficient β_6 amounts to a change in the intercept; β_{16} measures the change in the regression coefficient of $\log x_1$. If $x_6 = -1$, as in the first set of runs, the regression coefficient for $\log x_1$ is $\beta_1 - \beta_{16}$; if $x_6 = 1$, it is $\beta_1 + \beta_{16}$. The model with the added interaction component was also estimated. However, we found that the estimate of β_{16} is insignificant.

Exercises 9.5

9.5-1 Ten randomly selected rats were fed various doses of a dietary supplement (x, in grams), and the growth rates (y, in coded units) are given in the accompanying table.

(a) A simple linear regression was fitted to the data (i.e., $Y = \beta_0 + \beta_1 x + \varepsilon$). Calculate the ANOVA table and test whether $\beta_1 = 0$. Check the adequacy of the fitted model.

(b) The experimenter also considered a second-order model $Y = \beta_0 + \beta_1 x + \beta_2 x^2 + \varepsilon$. Use the available computer software, calculate the least-squares estimates, and test $\beta_2 = 0$ at the $\alpha = 0.05$ significance level.

Observation Number	Amount of Supplement, x	Growth Rate, y
1	10	73
2	10	78
3	15	85
4	20	90
5	20	91
6	25	87
7	25	86
8	25	91
9	30	75
10	35	65

(c) How can a residual analysis of the model in part (a) indicate whether the simple linear regression model is adequate?

9.5-2 The cloud point of a liquid is a measure of the degree of crystallization in a stock that can be measured by the refractive index. It has been suggested that the percentage of I-8 in the base stock is an excellent predictor of cloud point. The data in the accompanying table were collected on stocks with known percentages of I-8.

Percent I-8, x	Cloud Point, y	Percent I-8, x	Cloud Point, y
0	22.1	0	21.9
1	24.5	2	26.1
2	26.0	4	28.5
3	26.8	6	30.3
4	28.2	8	31.5
5	28.9	10	33.1
6	30.0	0	22.8
7	30.4	3	27.3
8	31.4	6	29.8
		9	31.8

(a) Make a scatter plot of the data.
(b) Consider the linear model $Y = \beta_0 + \beta_1 x + \varepsilon$. Calculate the least-squares estimates, the ANOVA table, and R^2. Conduct appropriate diagnostic checks and assess the adequacy of this first-order model.
(c) Consider the second-order model $Y = \beta_0 + \beta_1 x + \beta_2 x^2 + \varepsilon$. Repeat the analysis in part (b). Which model would you prefer?
[N. R. Draper and H. Smith, *Applied Regression Analysis*, 2nd ed. (New York: Wiley, 1981), p. 283.]
9.5-3 An experimenter performs a 2^2 factorial experiment to study the effects of temperature and concentration on the yield of a chemical reaction. The experimenter conducted two runs at each of the four possible combinations of temperature and concentration; this provided a total of eight runs. The levels for temperature were 120 and 140°F, and the levels for concentration were 15 and 25 percent. These are denoted by ±1. The order of the eight experiments was randomized.

Temperature, x_1	Concentration, x_2	Yield, y
−1	−1	58
−1	−1	63
+1	−1	75
+1	−1	85
−1	+1	65
−1	+1	59
+1	+1	88
+1	+1	94

Consider the regression model $Y = \beta_0 + \beta_1 x_1 + \beta_2 x_2 + \beta_3 x_1 x_2 + \varepsilon$.
(a) Calculate the least-squares estimates, the ANOVA table, and R^2.
(b) Test for overall significance of the regression; that is, test $H_0: \beta_1 = \beta_2 = \beta_3 = 0$ against H_1: at least one regression coefficient different from zero. Consider partial t-tests, and interpret your findings.
9.5-4 A certain response Y is measured at 2-minute intervals. It is well established that the response variable increases linearly with time, x_1. At time zero, a "treatment" is applied, and it is hypothesized that this causes the response curve to shift by a constant but positive amount. Use an indicator variable, x_2, and formulate an appropriate regression model. Estimate the parameters from the following data.

x_1	x_2	y
−5	−1	5
−3	−1	7
−1	−1	10
1	1	14
3	1	17
5	1	18

Using $\alpha = 0.10$, is there significant evidence that such a shift has occurred?
9.5-5 Snedecor and Cochran have described an investigation of the source from which corn plants in various Iowa soils obtain their phosphorus. The concentrations (in parts per million) of inorganic (x_1) and organic (x_2) phosphorus in the soils were determined chemically. The phosphorus content (y, in ppm) of corn plants grown in these soils was also

measured. The results appear in the accompanying table.

Soil Sample	x_1	x_2	y
1	0.4	53	64
2	0.4	23	60
3	3.1	19	71
4	0.6	34	61
5	4.7	24	54
6	1.7	65	77
7	9.4	44	81
8	10.1	31	93
9	11.6	29	93
10	12.6	58	51
11	10.9	37	76
12	23.1	46	96
13	23.1	50	77
14	21.6	44	93
15	23.1	56	95
16	1.9	36	54
17	26.8	58	168
18	29.9	51	99

(a) Estimate the multiple regression model $Y_i = \beta_0 + \beta_1 x_{i1} + \beta_2 x_{i2} + \varepsilon_i$.

(b) Check the adequacy of the fitted model. Conduct residual plots. In particular, check whether there are outliers among the data.

Note An outlier is a point that does not follow the general patterns that are exhibited by the other observations in the data set. A residual that is more than $3\sqrt{\text{MSE}}$ from zero is usually a good indication that the corresponding observation is different from the rest. If an outlier is indicated, the experimenter should scrutinize this point and check whether the observation is due to a recording error or to some other special circumstance that is not captured in the data (variables) recorded. In the absence of such specific information, the outlying data point may be omitted and the model reestimated.

(c) Calculate the ANOVA table, R^2, and test the overall significance of the regression model. Use $\alpha = 0.05$.

(d) Calculate the standard errors of the estimates and the t-ratios. Test the significance of the individual regression coefficients. Use $\alpha = 0.05$. Can you simplify the model? If so, estimate the new model and interpret your findings.

[G. W. Snedecor and W. G. Cochran, *Statistical Methods*, 6th ed. (Ames, Iowa: Iowa State University Press, 1967).]

9.5-6 Business schools are interested in predicting the GPA (y) of their MBA students as a function of the GMAT test score (x_1) and their undergraduate grade-point average (x_2). The data for a sample of 12 students are as follows:

x_1	x_2	y
560	3.32	3.20
540	3.23	3.44
520	2.97	3.70
580	2.79	3.10
520	3.35	3.00
620	2.90	4.00
660	3.52	3.38
630	3.54	3.83
550	2.64	2.67
550	3.06	2.75
600	2.41	2.33
537	3.44	3.75

(a) Estimate the regression model $Y = \beta_0 + \beta_1 x_1 + \beta_2 x_2 + \varepsilon$, test the significance of the regression estimates, and draw conclusions.

(b) Speculate on why GMAT test scores and undergraduate grade-point averages may not appear to be such important predictor variables.

Hint Consider the limited range of the explanatory variables, the fact that the experiment is not designed, the fact that other important predictor variables may be missing, and so on.

9.5-7 T. Kyotani et al. have studied the variation in the traction coefficients of 25 lubricating oils. Traction measurements were obtained on a special two-disk machine. After applying oil to the cleaned faces of the two disks, the disks are pressed into contact by a spring. A certain load is applied and the rotating speed of one disk is increased from 44 centimeters per second (cm/s) to 52 cm/s, while the speed of the other disk is kept constant at 45 cm/s. The variation in the traction coefficients with sliding speed is measured, and the maximum is recorded as in the accompanying table. Loads of 100 kg and 150 kg are used in the experiment.

Fluid	Maximum Traction Coefficient $f_{max} \times 10^3$		Flow Activation Volume, FAV (cm^3/mol)
	Load (100 kg)	Load (150 kg)	
1	66	74	51.8
2	65	68	50.7
3	65	70	51.0
4	59	60	40.1
5	54	56	40.4
6	58	58	39.5
7	63	63	39.5
8	57	57	39.7
9	83	77	76.1
10	74	75	61.5
11	91	93	67.8
12	92	93	92.2
13	90	88	80.5
14	88	87	87.8
15	88	89	88.7
16	91	93	91.5
17	87	88	94.4
18	69	75	57.2
19	67	68	53.0
20	69	72	53.9
21	66	66	57.6
22	76	75	58.7
23	76	74	73.5
24	76	78	61.2
25	85	83	71.9

It is thought that the traction coefficients increase with the rigidity of the molecular structure of these different lubricating fluids. The flow activation volume (FAV) is taken as a measure of rigidity. It measures the average size of holes into which the flow segments are required to move. Since flexible molecules can separate into small flow segments with ease, most of these molecules have small values of FAV. Conversely, rigid molecules have large values of FAV.

(a) Consider the traction coefficients at a load of 100 kg. Plot traction coefficients against flow activation volume. Develop a regression model that explains the variability in the traction coefficients.

(b) Repeat this exercise for traction coefficients at a load of 150 kg.

(c) Use the graphs and discuss whether the two fitted regression lines (surfaces) are the same.

[T. Kyotani, H. Yoshitake, T. Ito, and Y. Tamai, "Correlation Between Flow Properties and Traction of Lubricating Oils," *Transactions of the American Society of Lubricating Engineers*, 29: 102–106 (1986).]

9.5-8 The mean rate of oxygenation from the atmospheric reaeration process for a stream depends on the mean velocity of stream flow and the average depth of the stream bed. The data from 12 experiments are as follows:

Mean Velocity, x_1 (ft/sec)	Mean Depth, x_2 (ft)	Mean Oxygenation Rate, y (ppm per day)
3.69	5.09	1.44
3.07	3.27	2.27
2.10	4.42	0.98
2.68	6.14	0.50
2.78	5.66	0.74
2.64	7.17	1.13
2.92	11.41	0.28
2.47	2.12	3.36
3.44	2.93	2.79
4.65	4.54	1.57
2.94	9.50	0.46
2.51	6.29	0.39

Consider the following two models:

$$(1) \quad E(Y) = \beta_0 + \beta_1 x_1 + \beta_2 x_2.$$
$$(2) \quad E(Y) = \beta_0 x_1^{\beta_1} x_2^{\beta_2}.$$

Determine the least-squares estimates of the coefficients and discuss the adequacy of these two models. Which model would you prefer?

Hint   Consider a logarithmic transformation for the model in (2).

9.5-9 Indicator variables are variables that express the absence and presence of a certain condition. They take on the values 0 and 1 (or -1 and $+1$ as in the example in Section 9.5-2). Assume that the response variable Y is linearly related to an explanatory variable x. At a certain known threshold, say x_*, the slope coefficient changes as shown in the following graph. Explain how you would set up the regression model to test the significance of the slope change.

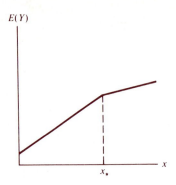

$E(Y)$

x_* x

9.5-10   William J. Hill and Robert A. Wiles ["Plant Experimentation (PLEX)," *Journal of Quality Technology*, 7: 115–122 (1975)] describe an experiment on a large continuous chemical operation consisting of several separate reaction steps. The variable of interest in their investigation is percent yield. The factors believed to affect yield are the concentration of reactant A in solvent S (x_1), the ratio of reactant B to reactant A (x_2), and the temperature in the reactor (x_3). The coded variables are given in the following table. (Note that the paper does not provide us with original units.) The 15 runs in this experiment were performed in random order over a period of 10 days, with 8 hours at each operating condition.

x_1	x_2	x_3	Percent yield	
-1	-1	-1	75.4	
1	-1	-1	73.9	
-1	1	-1	76.8	
1	1	-1	72.8	
-1	-1	1	75.3	75.3
1	-1	1	71.4	
-1	1	1	76.5	77.2
1	1	1	72.3	
0	0	0	74.4	74.5
-2	0	0	79.0	78.4
2	0	0	69.2	

Note that there are replicates at some of the operating conditions. In reading your data into a

computer program you may have to enter them as $(-2, 0, 0, 79.0)$, $(-2, 0, 0, 78.4)$, and so on.

Develop a model that relates yield to these explanatory variables. Consider quadratic terms if necessary. Carefully check the adequacy of your fitted model(s) and discuss their implications. For example, what does it mean if the regression coefficients associated with a variable are found insignificant?

9.5-11   S. Weisberg [*Applied Linear Regression*, 2nd ed. (New York: Wiley, 1985)] describes the results of an experiment that evaluates the performance of a cutting-tool material in cutting steel on a lathe. The aim of the experiment is to understand how tool life (measured in minutes) varies with cutting speed (in feet per minute) and feed rate (in thousandths of an inch per revolution). The following table lists the results of the experiment.

S	F	Life							
-1	-1	54.5	66.0						
1	-1	11.8	14.0						
-1	1	5.2	3.0						
1	1	0.8	0.5						
0	$-\sqrt{2}$	86.5							
0	$\sqrt{2}$	0.4							
$-\sqrt{2}$	0	20.1							
$\sqrt{2}$	0	2.9							
0	0	3.8	2.2	3.2	4.0	2.8	3.2	4.0	3.5

The levels of the two factors are coded and centered to give $S = (\text{speed} - 900)/300$ and $F = (\text{feed rate} - 13)/6$. The order of the runs was randomized.

Analyze the information. Use graphical procedures as well as analytic methods. You may want to consider transformations of the response variable.

Are there certain observations that you would question? If there are, repeat your analysis without these observations. (Of course, the analyst should always discuss any unusual observations with the scientist who carried out the experiment. Sometimes unusual observations arise because something went wrong in the experiment. But often these unusual observations help us make our models more realistic, as they point to factors that we had ignored previously.)

9.6   Response Surface Methods

Often, experimenters wish to find the conditions under which a certain process attains the optimal results. That is, they want to determine the levels of the design (explanatory) variables at which the response reaches its optimum. This optimum could be either a maximum or a minimum of a function of the design variables. For example, consider a chemical process whose yield is a function of temperature and pressure; it is of interest to determine the levels of temperature and pressure that lead to the largest possible yield. Or consider a biologist who wants to maximize the growth of an organism as a function of the percentage of glucose, the concentration of yeast extract, and the time allowed for organism growth. Or a production engineer may be trying to maximize the seal strength of a certain plastic wrap by varying the sealing temperature and the percentage of a polyethelene additive. Methods for determining the optimum conditions and for exploring the response surface in the neighborhood of these "best" conditions are discussed in books on *response surface methods*. Here we give only a brief introduction to this topic.

We start our discussion by emphasizing that the "change one variable at a time" approach, which is still widely used in industry, is a very inefficient and usually unsuccessful method for determining the optimum conditions. A much better strategy results by changing the variables simultaneously in a systematic way.

Experimentation is often started in a region that may be far from optimal. However, strategies for reaching the optimum region through successive iterative experimentation have been developed. A good approach consists of first performing a factorial experiment in the initial region, approximating the unknown response surface by a linear function of the design variables and determining the path of steepest ascent. Once the neighborhood of the optimum is reached, we can design a more elaborate experiment and estimate second-order models that include quadratic and interaction components. We discuss briefly two such designs: the 3^k factorial and the central composite design. We also illustrate how the optimum conditions, as well as the nature of the response surface in their vicinity, can be determined from the estimated second-order model.

9.6-1   The "Change One Variable at a Time" Approach

Let us describe this approach and its associated difficulties with a simple example. Let us assume that a chemist wants to maximize the yield of a chemical reaction by varying the reaction time (T) and the reaction pressure (P). Suppose that the contours of the true response function, which is unknown to the chemist, is as given in Figure 9.6-1. The curves on such a contour plot connect points that lead to the same yield.

In the "change one variable at a time" approach the experimenter fixes a certain level for one of the factors. Assume that he starts with a reaction temperature of 220°C. He then conducts experiments for different levels of pressure: say, at 80, 90, 100, 110, and 120 psi. Results are obtained at those five experimental points, and they are plotted in Figure 9.6-2a. With temperature fixed at 220°C, he finds that the maximum yield is obtained at a pressure of about 100 psi. In the next step, pressure is fixed at this "best" value and temperature is varied. With pressure fixed at 100 psi, results are obtained at temperatures of 180, 200, 240, and 260°C, as plotted in Figure 9.6-2b. The experimenter finds that for this "best" value of pressure (best to be understood in the sense that this particular pressure has led to the highest response when temperature is fixed at 220°C), the best value of temperature is not far from the temperature 220°C (possibly a little higher) that was used in the first set of runs. Thus it might seem justified to conclude that the *overall* maximum is achieved with a temperature of 220°C (or somewhat higher) and a pressure of 100 psi.

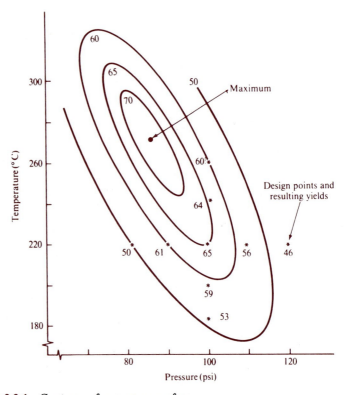

FIGURE 9.6-1   Contours of a response surface.

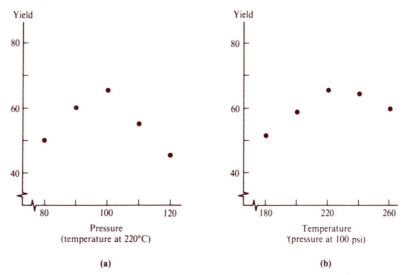

FIGURE 9.6-2 "Change one variable at a time" approach: (a) plot of yield against pressure, at fixed temperature of 220°C; (b) plot of yield against temperature, at fixed pressure of 100 psi.

However, this reasoning is incorrect, as it is shown by the contour plot in Figure 9.6-1. The maximum yield is obtained when temperature is about 270°C and pressure is at 85 psi. Why has this approach failed? The graphs in Figure 9.6-2(a) and (b) show that if either temperature or pressure, *individually*, is changed from the operating condition (220°C, 100 psi), the yield will decrease. But Figure 9.6-1 also shows that yield will increase if we change temperature and pressure *together* and move toward the upper left-hand corner in Figure 9.6-1. The "change one variable at a time" approach has failed here, since it assumes that the effects of changes in one factor are independent of the effects of changes in the other. This is, however, usually not true. An alternative and more successful approach is to change the variables *together*.

9.6-2   Method of Steepest Ascent

Experimentation is often started in a region that may be far from optimal. However, a sequence of well-designed experiments should lead us toward the optimum. We may start with a 2^k factorial, possibly with several center points added. Experience from previous experiments may help us in selecting the initial levels of the factors. Once those are chosen, we can express the design points in coded form by $(x_1 = \pm 1, x_2 = \pm 1, ..., x_k = \pm 1)$ and $(x_1 = 0, x_2 = 0, ..., x_k = 0)$ for the center point. Initially, the response surface is approximated by a first-order (or linear) model, and the results from this initial experiment are used to estimate the coefficients in $Y = \beta_0 + \beta_1 x_1 + \cdots + \beta_k x_k + \varepsilon$ by least squares. Even though the linear model may not be an adequate description of the relationship, it usually provides a good starting point for our analysis.

The objective is now to find the path of *steepest ascent* that leads us to the optimum as quickly as possible. We want to locate the point, among all points that are a fixed distance, say R units, from the center $(0, 0, \ldots, 0)$, that gives the largest response. In mathematical terms, this involves the maximization of $\hat{\beta}_0 + \hat{\beta}_1 x_1 + \cdots + \hat{\beta}_k x_k$, subject to the constraint $\sum_{i=1}^{k} x_i^2 = R^2$, where $\hat{\beta}_0, \hat{\beta}_1, \ldots, \hat{\beta}_k$ are the estimates of $\beta_0, \beta_1, \ldots, \beta_k$. It can be shown (see Exercise 9.6-8) that the maximum is achieved at the point with coordinates

$$x_i = \frac{R\hat{\beta}_i}{(\sum_{j=1}^{k} \hat{\beta}_j^2)^{1/2}}, \qquad i = 1, \ldots, k.$$

Thus the path of steepest ascent from the center $(0, 0, \ldots, 0)$ is in the direction of the point

$$(x_1, \ldots, x_k) = \left(\frac{R\hat{\beta}_1}{(\sum \hat{\beta}_j^2)^{1/2}}, \ldots, \frac{R\hat{\beta}_k}{(\sum \hat{\beta}_j^2)^{1/2}} \right).$$

Since the coded design points of the original 2^k factorial are one unit from the origin, and since we should not trust extrapolations that go much beyond the experimental region, it is reasonable to generate points on this path by taking $R = 1, 2, 3, \ldots$, and by conducting new experiments at these levels. Assume, for illustration, that this is done and that we find that the responses along this path reach their maximum for a certain R. Then the corresponding design point is taken as the center point for a new and usually more elaborate experiment.

A Remark on Center Points in 2^k Factorial Experiments   Observations at the center point in a 2^k factorial experiment have no effect on the slope estimates $\hat{\beta}_1, \ldots, \hat{\beta}_k$ in the linear model $Y = \beta_0 + \beta_1 x_1 + \cdots + \beta_k x_k + \varepsilon$, and they do not affect the path of steepest ascent. This is easy to see from the normal equations in Section 9.4-1; observations at the center point with $x_{ij} = 0$ do not contribute to the sums in the normal equations.

Why then would we want to run experiments at the center point in a 2^k factorial? There are several reasons for doing so. One is that replications at the center point give us an estimate of the variability in the observations, and this information can be used to obtain standard errors for the estimates. A second reason is that observations at the center point can tell us about the curvature of the surface. If there is no curvature and if the linear model is appropriate over the region of our initial experiment, the average of the n_1 observations at the center point, say $\bar{Y}_1$, and the average of the 2^k observations in the factorial, say $\bar{Y}_2$, are both estimates of β_0, and they should be roughly equal. A nonzero difference of these two averages indicates that there is curvature. The sample variance s^2, calculated from the n_1 observations at the center point, can be used to obtain a standard error for this difference. Since var$(\bar{Y}_1) \approx s^2/n_1$ and var$(\bar{Y}_2) \approx s^2/2^k$, we find that var$(\bar{Y}_1 - \bar{Y}_2) \approx s^2[(1/n_1)$ $+ (1/2^k)]$. The standardized difference $(\bar{Y}_1 - \bar{Y}_2)/\sqrt{\mathrm{var}(\bar{Y}_1 - \bar{Y}_2)}$ can be used to assess its statistical significance.

Why is it so important to know that over a certain region there is curvature in the surface? The reason is that we base our path of steepest ascent on a linear approximation of the surface. If there is sizable curvature, our path may be poor and we may find that on this path responses will soon start to decrease. In such a situation it is important to perform another simple experiment and recalculate the direction of the path of steepest ascent.

There is another lesson to be learned from this discussion: Experimentation must be iterative. It is important to incorporate any prior knowledge into designing the experiment at the next stage. It is usually inefficient to perform one big experiment that uses up most of the allocated resources, because such a strategy does not allow for subsequent learning. This is the reason why many experimenters recommend to spend only 25 or 30 percent of one's budget on the initial stage of an experiment. ■

9.6-3 Designs for Fitting Second-Order Models: The 3^k Factorial and the Central Composite Design

First-order models do not lead to surfaces that describe maxima or minima. For that one needs at least a second-order model. The 2^k factorial cannot be used to estimate the coefficients in a second-order model

$$Y = \beta_0 + \sum_{i=1}^{k} \beta_i x_i + \sum_{i=1}^{k} \beta_{ii} x_i^2 + \sum \sum_{i<j} \beta_{ij} x_i x_j + \varepsilon$$

because we need at least three different levels for each factor to estimate a second-order function. One can use a 3^k factorial experiment, where each factor is observed at three levels: a low (-1), an intermediate (0), and a high $(+1)$ level. For $k = 2$ factors this involves the nine design points that are given in Table 9.6-1.

TABLE 9.6-1   **The 3^2 Factorial**

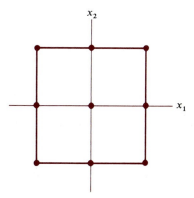

x_1	x_2
-1	-1
0	-1
$+1$	-1
-1	0
0	0
$+1$	0
-1	$+1$
0	$+1$
$+1$	$+1$

TABLE 9.6-2   **Central Composite Design for $k = 2$ Factors**

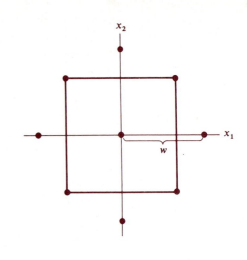

x_1	x_2	
-1	-1	
$+1$	-1	2^2
-1	$+1$	
$+1$	$+1$	
$-w$	0	
w	0	axial or
0	$-w$	"star" points
0	w	
0	0	
$\vdots$	$\vdots$	center points
0	0	

One problem with 3^k factorials is that the number of runs increases very rapidly with k. Thus other arrangements, such as the *central composite design* (*ccd*), have been developed. There we start with the ordinary 2^k factorial and add $2k$ axial or "star" points $(\pm w, 0, \ldots, 0)$, $(0, \pm w, 0, \ldots, 0)$, $\ldots$, $(0, \ldots, 0, \pm w)$. In addition, several observations are taken at the center point

TABLE 9.6-3   **Central Composite Design for $k = 3$ Factors**

x_1	x_2	x_3	
-1	-1	-1	
$+1$	-1	-1	
-1	$+1$	-1	
$+1$	$+1$	-1	
-1	-1	$+1$	2^3
$+1$	-1	$+1$	
-1	$+1$	$+1$	
$+1$	$+1$	$+1$	
$-w$	0	0	
w	0	0	
0	$-w$	0	axial or
0	w	0	"star" points
0	0	$-w$	
0	0	w	
0	0	0	
$\vdots$	$\vdots$	$\vdots$	center points
0	0	0	

$(0, 0, \ldots, 0)$, say n_1 of them. This leads to a total of $n = 2^k + 2k + n_1$ runs, a number that is usually much smaller than 3^k. Furthermore, if $w \neq 1$, each variable is actually measured at five different levels, namely, $-w$, -1, 0, 1, and w; this allows us to get a better estimate of the curvature.

The central composite design for $k = 2$ factors is given in Table 9.6-2. The value of w is selected by the experimenter. Various criteria can be used in making this choice. For example, we can choose $w = \sqrt{2}$. Then the design is *rotatable* because, geometrically, all design points lie on a circle of radius $\sqrt{2}$.

The central composite design for $k = 3$ factors is given in Table 9.6-3. Frequently, with $k = 3$, w is chosen as $w = 2^{3/4} = 1.682$. Note that with one center point ($n_1 = 1$) this design consists of only 15 runs, while the 3^3 factorial requires 27. For more than three variables, the advantage, in terms of the number of runs, of the central composite design over the factorial arrangement with three levels increases even more.

9.6-4   Interpretation of the Second-Order Model

A second-order model with $k = 2$ variables is given by

$$E(Y) = \beta_0 + \beta_1 x_1 + \beta_2 x_2 + \beta_{11} x_1^2 + \beta_{22} x_2^2 + \beta_{12} x_1 x_2;$$

depending on the values of its coefficients, it can describe several different response surfaces. The three most common ones are those with a maximum, a minimum, or a saddle point. Contour plots of these three types of surfaces are given in Figure 9.6-3. Exercise 9.6-1 gives several examples of second-order models that lead to such surfaces.

For most readers, surfaces with a maximum (or a minimum) need very little explanation: Leaving the critical point (the point of the optimum) in any direction results in a decrease (or increase) of the response. However, in the case of

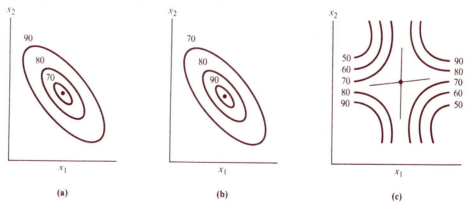

FIGURE 9.6-3   Contour plots for three second-order models: (a) minimum; (b) maximum; (c) saddle point.

a saddle point, the experimenter may get an increase or a decrease in the response when moving away from that critical point, depending on which direction is taken. The surface looks like a saddle; thus its name.

To determine the critical point, which is sometimes also called the stationary point, we set the two first partial derivatives equal to zero:

$$\frac{\partial E(Y)}{\partial x_1} = \beta_1 + 2\beta_{11}x_1 + \beta_{12}x_2 = 0,$$

$$\frac{\partial E(Y)}{\partial x_2} = \beta_2 + 2\beta_{22}x_2 + \beta_{12}x_1 = 0.$$

This leads to the stationary point

$$x_{1,0} = \frac{\beta_{12}\beta_2 - 2\beta_{22}\beta_1}{4\beta_{11}\beta_{22} - \beta_{12}^2},$$

$$x_{2,0} = \frac{\beta_{12}\beta_1 - 2\beta_{11}\beta_2}{4\beta_{11}\beta_{22} - \beta_{12}^2}.$$

Note that if the denominator in these expressions is zero, the solution corresponds to what is called a *ridge* (see Exercise 9.6-2).

To determine the nature of the surface at the stationary point, one has to investigate the second derivatives:

$$\frac{\partial^2 E(Y)}{\partial x_1^2} = 2\beta_{11}, \qquad \frac{\partial^2 E(Y)}{\partial x_1 \, \partial x_2} = \beta_{12}, \qquad \frac{\partial^2 E(Y)}{\partial x_2^2} = 2\beta_{22}.$$

If the two solutions of the quadratic equation $(2\beta_{11} - \lambda)(2\beta_{22} - \lambda) - \beta_{12}^2 = 0$, say λ_1 and λ_2, are both negative, the function has a maximum at the stationary point $(x_{1,0}, x_{2,0})$. If they are both positive, it is a minimum; however, if they are of different sign, it is a saddle point.

Now there are various analytic methods that can be used to investigate the nature of the response surface. For example, in the case of a saddle point, these methods indicate the direction in which we must move in order to increase the response. In the case of a maximum, they show in which direction the decrease in the response is slowest. This information is important, since it tells the experimenter about the direction in which the response is least sensitive to changes in the input factors. We do not discuss these methods here because they are beyond the scope of an introductory book. Also, with only $k = 2$ factors, we can always plot the contours of the estimated second-order surface and make these assessments from the graph. Computer programs for contour plotting are a part of most statistical packages.

9.6-5   An Illustration

An experimenter attempts to gain insight into the influence of the sealing temperature (T) and the percentage of a polyethelene additive (P) on the seal strength (Y, measured in grams per centimeter) of a certain plastic wrap.

Assume that *unknown to our experimenter* the response function is given by

$$E(Y) = -20 + (0.85)T + (1.5)P - (0.0025)T^2 - (0.375)P^2 + (0.025)TP.$$

The contours of this response surface are given in Figure 9.6-4. Its maximum is at temperature $T = 216°C$ and percentage of polyethelene additive $P = 9.2$ percent. Of course, due to the uncontrolled variability in raw materials, lab conditions, measurement errors, and so on, the actual results of the experiment will vary around these expected values.

Our experimenter starts his investigation at a temperature of 140°C and additive of 4 percent. This combination was suggested by a colleague who had experimented with a similar additive. He performs a factorial experiment around this center point. In his experiment a unit change in temperature corresponds to 20°C; and a unit change in P corresponds to 2 percentage points.

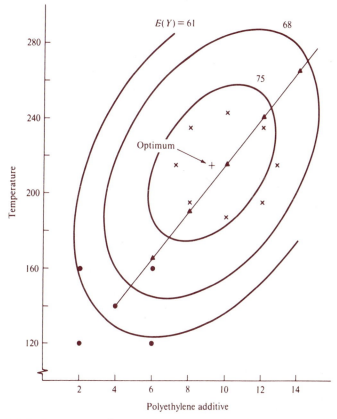

FIGURE 9.6-4 Response surface and design points for the example in Section 9.6-5. The symbol ● corresponds to the design points of the initial 2^2 factorial design with one center point; ▲ corresponds to the design points on the path of steepest ascent; × corresponds to the design points of the central composite design.

TABLE 9.6-4 Results from the 2² Factorial with Two Center Points

T	P	Coded T	P	y
120	2	−1	−1	52
160	2	+1	−1	62
120	6	−1	+1	60
160	6	+1	+1	70
140	4	0	0	63
140	4	0	0	65

The coded levels are obtained as

$$x_1 = \frac{T - 140}{20} \quad \text{and} \quad x_2 = \frac{P - 4}{2}.$$

The results of the 2² factorial with two center points are given in Table 9.6-4. The observations were generated by adding small random errors to the mean response $E(Y)$. From these results the experimenter fits the linear model and obtains the least-squares equation $\hat{y} = 62 + 5x_1 + 4x_2$. The results in Section 9.6-2 are used and the path of steepest ascent is obtained. It is described by the points on $(5R/\sqrt{41}, 4R/\sqrt{41})$ or, equivalently, $(1.25R_1, R_1)$.

Experiments on this path are conducted when $R_1 = 1, 2, \ldots, 5$, and the results are given in Table 9.6-5. The responses on this path of steepest ascent seem to reach their maximum at about $(x_1 = 3.75$ and $x_2 = 3)$ or, in terms of uncoded variables, at $T = 215°C$ and $P = 10$ percent. This point is then taken as the center point of a central composite design. Choosing the rotatable design with $w = \sqrt{2}$, our experimenter conducts the nine runs in Table 9.6-6: The first four points are those of a 2² factorial design, the next four are axial

TABLE 9.6-5 Results of Experiments on Path of Steepest Ascent

T	P	Coded T	P	y
165	6	1.25	1	72
190	8	2.50	2	77
215	10	3.75	3	79
240	12	5.00	4	76
265	14	6.25	5	70

TABLE 9.6-6 **Results from the Central Composite Design**

T	P	Coded T	Coded P	y	
195	8	2.75	2	78	
235	8	4.75	2	76	2^2
195	12	2.75	4	72	
235	12	4.75	4	75	
187	10	2.34	3	74	
243	10	5.16	3	76	
215	7.2	3.75	1.59	77	axial points
215	12.8	3.75	4.41	72	
215	10	3.75	3	80	center point

points, and the last is a center point. Note that we kept the initial coding $x_1 = (T - 140)/20$ and $x_2 = (P - 4)/2$; the coded levels in the central composite design are expressed in relation to the original center point at $T = 140°C$ and $P = 4$ percent. A second-order model is fitted to the data in Table 9.6-6. The estimated second-order equation is

$$\hat{y} = 40.44 + 14.57x_1 + 9.33x_2 - 2.38x_1^2 - 2.63x_2^2 + 1.25x_1x_2.$$

The stationary solution is given by

$$x_{1,0} = \frac{(1.25)(9.33) - 2(-2.63)(14.57)}{4(-2.38)(-2.63) - (1.25)^2} = 3.76,$$

$$x_{2,0} = \frac{(1.25)(14.57) - 2(-2.38)(9.33)}{4(-2.38)(-2.63) - (1.25)^2} = 2.67.$$

This corresponds to a temperature of $T = 215°C$ and $P = 9.3$ percent additive. Since the solutions of

$$[2(-2.38) - \lambda][2(-2.63) - \lambda] - (1.25)^2 = 0$$

are both negative, the stationary point is indeed a maximum. It is very close to the maximum of $E(Y)$, which was at $T = 216$ and $P = 9.2$, but of course this is unknown to the experimenter. Thus despite the fact that the experiment started in a region that is not optimal, a sequence of iterative experiments has led to the optimum fairly quickly. Of course, the variability of the error component around the expected response surface will influence the variability in the direction of the path of steepest ascent. This, in turn, may affect how quickly the optimum is reached.

In our example the variability is rather small. We can see this from the replications at the design point $T = 140°$, $P = 4$ percent (leading to responses

63 and 65) and at the design point $T = 215°$, $P = 10$ percent (leading to responses 79 and 80). The variance of an observation is estimated by $s^2 = [(63 - 64)^2 + (65 - 64)^2 + (79 - 79.5)^2 + (80 - 79.5)^2]/2 = 1.25$. The standard deviation $s = 1.12$ is rather small, considering that the observations from the initial 2^2 factorial experiment range from 52 to 70, and those from the central composite design from 72 to 80. Thus it is not surprising that we reach the optimum rather quickly.

Exercises 9.6

9.6-1 Consider the following second-order models.

(a) $E(Y) = 3 + 2x_1 + 4x_2 - 0.6x_1^2 - 0.9x_2^2 - 0.4x_1x_2$.

(b) $E(Y) = 13 - 2x_1 - 4x_2 + 0.6x_1^2 + 0.9x_2^2 + 0.4x_1x_2$.

(c) $E(Y) = 13 + 2x_1 + 4x_2 + 0.2x_1^2 - 0.7x_2^2 - 1.2x_1x_2$.

(d) $E(Y) = 6 + 3x_1 + 5x_2 - 4x_1^2 - 3x_2^2 - 2x_1x_2$.
Determine the stationary solution and discuss the nature of the response surface. Sketch its contours.

9.6-2 Consider the second-order model

$$E(Y) = 10 + 2x_1 + 4x_2 - x_1^2 - 4x_2^2 - 4x_1x_2.$$

In this case, $4\beta_{11}\beta_{22} - \beta_{12}^2 = 0$. Sketch the contours of this response surface. Show that its maximum is described by the points that satisfy the equation $x_1 + 2x_2 = 1$. We call such a surface a *stationary ridge*.

9.6-3 The percentage concentration of a certain input material and the temperature at which the reaction takes place are thought to be important factors in determining the yield of a chemical batch process. A 2^2 factorial experiment (replicated once) led to the following results:

Concentration (percent)	Temperature (°C)	Yield (in grams)
12	100	70, 73
14	100	78, 80
12	110	84, 86
14	110	85, 88

Determine the path of steepest ascent. Where should the next observations be taken?

9.6-4 A 3^2 factorial experiment is conducted to determine the effect of temperature (x_1) and reaction time (x_2) on the yield $(y$, in grams) of a chemical reaction. The coded factors are given by

$$x_1 = \frac{\text{temperature} - 145°C}{5}$$

and

$$x_2 = \frac{\text{time} - 90 \text{ minutes}}{10}.$$

The results are as follows:

x_1	x_2	y
-1	-1	31.1
0	-1	33.7
$+1$	-1	30.7
-1	0	31.1
0	0	34.1
$+1$	0	32.2
-1	$+1$	28.4
0	$+1$	33.4
$+1$	$+1$	31.9

Estimate a second-order response surface, determine its stationary solution (expressed in coded as well as original units), and discuss its nature.

9.6-5 A central composite design with $k = 2$, $w = \sqrt{2}$, and four center points is used in an experiment on the precipitation of stoichiometric dihydrate of calcium hydrogen orthophosphate. The response is percentage yield. The two factors are the mole ratio of NH_3 to $CaCl_2$ in the calcium chloride solution, and the starting pH of the $NH_4H_2PO_4$ solution used. The coded factors are

$$x_1 = \frac{(NH_3/CaCl_2) - 0.85}{0.09},$$

$$x_2 = \frac{pH - 3.5}{0.9}.$$

The data are given in the following table.

x_1	x_2	y
-1	-1	54.1
1	-1	66.0
-1	1	74.5
1	1	80.6
$-\sqrt{2}$	0	68.1
$\sqrt{2}$	0	89.2
0	$-\sqrt{2}$	40.8
0	$\sqrt{2}$	78.0
0	0	72.3
0	0	75.9
0	0	74.6
0	0	75.5

Estimate a second-order response surface and determine its stationary solution. Discuss the nature of the estimated response surface.

9.6-6 Assume that the expected response surface is given by

$$E(Y) = 50 + 2.6x_1 + 1.4x_2 - 0.25x_1^2$$
$$- 0.20x_2^2 - 0.05x_1x_2;$$

but, of course, the experimenter does not know this response surface.

(a) The experimenter starts her investigation with a 2^2 factorial, with one center point; that is, she takes observations at $(-1, -1)$, $(1, -1)$, $(-1, 1)$, $(1, 1)$, and $(0, 0)$. Generate random responses at these design points as follows. Perform a sequence of coin tosses. If the result is "heads," add 1 to $E(Y)$; otherwise, subtract 1.

(b) These results are given to our experimenter. Calculate the path of steepest ascent. The experimenter performs additional runs along this path. Use the procedure in part (a) to calculate the responses for these design points.

(c) After the experimenter has located the maximum on this path, she performs a central composite design with $w = \sqrt{2}$. Generate the responses at these design points and estimate a second-order model. Determine the stationary solution, describe the nature of the response surface, and discuss whether the true maximum has been reached.

9.6-7 Myers conducted an experiment to explore the synthesis of mercaptobenzothiazole (MBT) as a function of reaction time and temperature. A rotatable central composite design with coded factors

$$x_1 = \frac{time \ (hours) - 12}{5.6}$$

and

$$x_2 = \frac{temperature \ (°C) - 250}{20}$$

was conducted, and the following results were observed:

x_1	x_2	y
-1	-1	81.3
$+1$	-1	85.3
-1	$+1$	83.1
$+1$	$+1$	72.7
$-\sqrt{2}$	0	82.9
$\sqrt{2}$	0	81.7
0	$-\sqrt{2}$	84.7
0	$\sqrt{2}$	57.9
0	0	82.9
0	0	81.2
0	0	82.4

Estimate the second-order model, determine the stationary point, and discuss the nature of the response surface (in coded as well as original units).

Hint To facilitate the interpretation, draw the contours for $\hat{y} = 75$, 80, and 85. You should obtain a saddle point.

[R. H. Myers, *Response Surface Methodology* (Boston: Allyn and Bacon, 1971).]

9.6-8 Determine the values of x_i, $i = 1, \ldots, k$, that maximize $\beta_0 + \beta_1 x_1 + \cdots + \beta_k x_k$, subject to the constraint $\sum_{i=1}^{k} x_i^2 = R^2$.

Hint　Use a Lagrange multiplier and maximize

$$Q(x_1, \ldots, x_k) = \hat{\beta}_0 + \hat{\beta}_1 x_1 + \cdots + \hat{\beta}_k x_k$$
$$- \lambda\left(\sum_{i=1}^{k} x_i^2 - R^2\right).$$

9.6-9　Du Pont has developed an Automatic Clinical Assay System that allows the clinician in a hospital to determine the concentrations of substances in a patient's blood and urine. Measurements of many chemical substances can be made with the du Pont Discrete Clinical Analyzer and custom-made analytical test packs. The analyzer assays a sample of the blood serum for a certain substance by transferring a fixed volume of the specimen into a method-specific test pack and adding a controlled amount of a certain buffer solution. The pack contains, in several different compartments, all the reagents that are necessary to complete the assay. Reagents are added to the test sample in a predetermined manner. Initiation of a chemical reaction is followed by timed measurements of the absorbance of light, of known wavelength, by the pack. From these absorbance measurements the concentration of the chemical substance in the sample can be calculated from a calibration curve.

The pack configuration affects the assay sensitivity, which is defined as the unit absorbance change per unit concentration of the chemical substance that is in the sample. The configuration is, among many other factors, a function of the reagents and their concentrations, and of the buffer and its pH. Response surface methodology is used to develop the relationships between sensitivity and these factors and to select the conditions that optimize the sensitivity.

Humphries, Melnychuk, Donegan, and Snee discuss the use of the Discrete Clinical Analyzer in determining the concentration of plasma ammonia. In this case the chemical reaction is initiated by the enzyme glutamate dehydrogenase (GLDH). Response surface methods were used to determine the optimum values for the GLDH concentration (x_1), and the pH (x_2) and molarity (x_3) of the buffer, which in this case was a certain sulfonic acid, to be used in the pack.

A central composite design with $w = 1$ was used to study the effects of these $k = 3$ factors on assay sensitivity. Note that for $w = 1$, the "star points" in

the central composite design correspond to the centers of the six sides of the cube. Hence this design is frequently called a *face-centered-cube design*. The concentration of GLDH was varied from 90 (low), 125 (medium), to 160 units (high); pH was varied from 7.25 (low), 7.45 (medium), to 7.65 (high); and the molarity (mol/liter) of the buffer was varied from 0.04 (low), 0.05 (medium), to 0.06 (high). Three assays were run for each experimental test combination, and the results are shown in the accompanying table (note that several responses are missing).

GLDH Concentration, x_1	pH, x_2	Molarity, x_3	Sensitivity, y
−	−	−	148, 143, 147
+	−	−	175, 188
−	+	−	175, 178, 180
+	+	−	167, 166, 173
−	−	+	141, 139
+	−	+	178, 175
−	+	+	187, 170, 181
+	+	+	164, 177, 170
−	0	0	180, 184, 176
+	0	0	178, 179, 175
0	−	0	173, 160
0	+	0	185, 171, 180
0	0	−	187, 182, 175
0	0	+	181, 182, 180
0	0	0	193, 181, 188

Note　$x_1 = \dfrac{\text{concentration} - 125}{35}$, $\quad x_2 = \dfrac{\text{pH} - 7.45}{0.20}$,

$\quad x_3 = \dfrac{\text{molarity} - 0.05}{0.01}$.

(a) Estimate the quadratic model

$$Y = \beta_0 + \beta_1 x_1 + \beta_2 x_2 + \beta_3 x_3 + \beta_{11} x_1^2 + \beta_{22} x_2^2$$
$$+ \beta_{33} x_3^2 + \beta_{12} x_1 x_2 + \beta_{13} x_1 x_3 + \beta_{23} x_2 x_3 + \varepsilon.$$

(b) You should find that in this model the t-ratios for the coefficients $\beta_3, \beta_{33}, \beta_{13}$, and β_{23} are insignificant. This suggests that molarity (x_3) has no effect on the response over the range 0.04 to 0.06 mol/liter.

(c) Omit molarity from the model and estimate

$$Y = \beta_0 + \beta_1 x_1 + \beta_2 x_2 + \beta_{11} x_1^2$$
$$+ \beta_{22} x_2^2 + \beta_{12} x_1 x_2 + \varepsilon.$$

Determine the stationary point of the response surface that is implied by this model in coded as well as original units. Determine its nature (maximum, minimum, or saddle point). Plot the contours of the response function over the region $7.25 < \text{pH} < 7.65$ and $100 < \text{concentration (GLDH)} < 180$.

(d) What levels of GLDH, molarity, and pH would you recommend to maximize sensitivity?

(e) Your recommendations from part (d) are used to manufacture packs. In practice it is sufficient to be within 3 percent of the highest attainable sensitivity. Will the resulting packs be insensitive to (i.e., robust to) variations in the actual levels of GLDH, pH, and molarity? Recall that because of manufacturing process variation, the levels of the pack ingredients will not be *identical* to the target values. What process variations can be tolerated without affecting the performance of the pack, that is, the sensitivity of the analysis?

[B. A. Humphries, M. Melnychuk, E. J. Donegan, and R. D. Snee, "Automated Enzymatic Assay for Plasma Ammonia," *Clinical Chemistry*, 25: 26–30 (1979).]

9.6-10 Consider the 2^k factorial experiment. Discuss the importance of adding center points. In particular, explain how the n_1 observations at the center point can be used to (1) estimate the standard errors of main effects and interactions, and (2) assess whether quadratic components, such as x_1^2, x_2^2, and so on, are needed in the model.

Two Experimental Design Case Studies

BERTON H. GUNTER, Statistical Consultant

Introduction

One of the virtues of the statistical design of experiments (DOX) is that it encourages consideration of issues and attention to detail that may otherwise be ignored. Particularly in industrial work, a good design can mean the difference between the success or failure of an experimental program. By success we mean that definitive conclusions can be drawn, not that a particular idea is demonstrated. By framing the *process* of experimentation with an elegant structure, DOX gives an experimenter new and powerful tools with which to probe nature. The effectiveness of these tools in catalyzing scientific understanding cannot be matched by conventional approaches. It is the purpose of these case studies to demonstrate these ideas with two real industrial applications.

The student encountering DOX for the first time may get the impression that the ideas are complex, mathematical, and far too difficult to apply routinely in practice. It may also appear that the analysis of a designed experiment involves forbidding algebraic computation, and that design is a black art. Nothing could be further from the truth. The analysis of a well-designed experiment often requires nothing more than a few plots or an appropriate tabular display of the data. The number of designs typically encountered in practice are relatively few and easily mastered. The Pareto principle applies: A small fraction of the tools handle a large fraction of the problems that occur.

The two case studies presented here illustrate these points. In both cases it was the discipline and the systematic methodology demanded by DOX rather than any elaborate statistical sophistication that led to success. In both examples, nearly trivial analyses were sufficient to tell the tale, and in both cases, straightforward two-level factorial designs of the type discussed in Sections 8.3 and 8.4 were used.

It should be emphasized that DOX amounts to much more than choosing a particular design and/or applying special analytical techniques. In particular, DOX affects the selection of variables to be included in an experiment, an area generally thought to lie exclusively within the realm of the subject matter expert. Because the effects of many factors and their interactions can be studied economically with relatively simple and parsimonious designs, the experimenter with knowledge of DOX has more flexibility in deciding what variables to study and how to study them. In complex industrial situations, it is not unusual to encounter situations in which dozens of variables may be important. The ability to screen large subsets of these variables efficiently through the use of, for example, fractional factorials, can be crucial to achieving success within the limitations of practical economic constraints.

The principles of randomization, blocking, and replication are integral components of the DOX approach. Randomization is an experimental strategy that protects against the intrusion of Murphy's law by minimizing the chance that variables not in the experiment may confuse the results. Blocking allows an experimenter to study subtle effects even in the presence of large systematic variation. Replication gives a clear picture of the experimental error so that the experimenter can decide whether an estimated effect amounts to more than just random noise. Application of these principles is essential in engineering work within industry.

Most important, DOX encourages good experimental practice. By promoting systematic thinking about the experimental process, it can help the experimenter avoid errors that could distort results or lead to erroneous conclusions.

The following two case studies discuss various design issues and illustrate the benefits of carefully designed experiments. Minor details have been altered, and the data have been coded to avoid compromising proprietary issues. In all essentials, however, the discussions give an accurate picture of what actually took place.

Case Study 1: Problems in the Production of High-Reliability Electrical Components

The manufacturer of a line of high-reliability electrical components, primarily resistors for military applications, experienced a drastic increase in the failure rate of the components during environmental testing. The testing consisted of subjecting sampled resistors to extreme temperature and humidity conditions in one of two environmental test chambers. Although there were some differences in the failure incidences between the two chambers (lots that consistently failed in one chamber would pass the test in the other), the situation deteriorated over the course of several production runs so that failure became consistent no matter which chamber was used. As a result, contractual requirements forced the company to stop shipping current production. The plant was in danger of losing the business, as the depletion of its inventory forced its customer to look to other suppliers.

This situation precipitated drastic reaction on the part of management. Great effort was expended trying to find the source of the problem. Unfortunately, the production process was extremely complex, involving everything from the "sputtering" of exotic thin-film chemistries onto ceramic substrates, to the deposition of protective plastic coatings over the finished components. Although it was this last step that was mainly suspected as the source of the problem (the coating was not doing its job), it was difficult to rule out other factors. The investigations therefore ranged from checking the incoming materials, to overhauling the elaborate equipment, to checking for contamination in the plumbing and cleaning systems. Not surprisingly, many things were found that required adjustment or replacement. Each time a change was made, a small test batch of product was manufactured and tested environmentally to see if the problem had been fixed. Because the testing facilities were limited and the test itself took 2 to 3 days, it always took several days until the data became available. Unfortunately, nothing seemed to work. The plant was out of production for 6 months when management decided to call in a staff statistician to see if a more systematic approach using DOX could help.

The statistician started the investigation by identifying critical variables. To do this, process experts were brought together to determine what variables should be considered as possible causes of the problem. The result of these discussions was a list of more than three dozen variables which were thought to be plausible suspects. Opinions differed radically as to which were the most likely; generally, each expert thought it was the variables that did not fall within his or her area of responsibility.

Logistical considerations made it impossible to study all these factors in a single experiment. Consequently, the experimental team decided to adopt a sequential approach. Variables that affected individual process steps were grouped together. For example, one set of variables was concerned with the incoming ceramic substrates, another with the deposition of the thin films, another with the machinery used to set the nominal resistances, and yet another with the protective coating. It was decided to work on each of the process steps separately. The procedure was to sample from and randomize across the steps that were not directly involved, but to change the variables at each studied step according to an appropriate statistical design. Although this "divide-and-conquer" strategy had the risk of overlooking some of the interprocess interactions, it was thought to be a realistic approach given the practical constraints involved.

Initial efforts concentrated on the protective plastic coating. Five variables were thought to be of primary importance:

1. Supplier of a basic component of the plastic (there were two).
2. Viscosity of the coating at the time of application.
3. Temperature of the first bake (dry) cycle.
4. Temperature of the second bake (cure) cycle.
5. Speed of the conveyor (i.e., time in the cycle).

A half fraction of a 2^5 factorial (i.e., a 2^{5-1} fractional factorial) was chosen as the design. This called for runs at 16 different experimental settings. Each test chamber could hold about 100 resistors, so 10 resistors in a row were produced for each run and then split randomly into two groups of five for testing. This resulted in a full set of 16 groups of five in each test chamber. The number of failures among each run of 10 resistors was recorded. This test procedure assured that possible chamber differences would not bias the effects of the five factors being studied.

One other feature comprised the experimental design, although it was by no means statistical. At the planning stage of this experiment, the statistician raised the issue of whether there might be differences between experimental runs and runs under normal production conditions. This issue is always important, since the experiment should simulate what actually occurs in production. The process experts felt that the major difference was that normal production was a high-volume, continuous operation, while the experiment would consist of a succession of small batches. One concern that was raised in this discussion was that the process might not have a chance to achieve thermal equilibrium during the experimental runs, whereas in production thermal equilibrium was naturally achieved as a result of steady-state conditions. This point had not been raised before; it was identified only as a consequence of the extensive probing that is required for DOX.

To address this concern, it was decided to "buffer" each group of 10 experimental resistors with a bunch of "dummy" resistors immediately preceding and following the experimental batch (see Figure A.1). These dummies, which were just ordinary resistors that received no special treatment, would act as a heat sink to allow the experimental runs to better simulate normal production. They would not require any of the special tracking and identification procedures of the experimental batch and would simply be discarded as scrap.

This, then, was the essence of the experimental strategy. Considerable planning, personnel, and logistical support was necessary to assure that the strategy was properly executed. The fact that a solution to the problem had to be found before the plant could go back into operation provided the necessary incentive for this effort. The experiment was carried out as planned and the results came in. What was causing the problem?

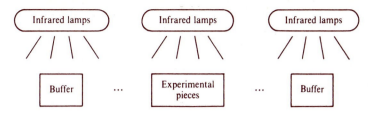

FIGURE A.1 Process flow for experimental runs.

In a word, *nothing!* Because of the careful experimental design (randomization of the run order and attention to the measurement protocol), it could be confidently stated that it was highly improbable that any of the variables studied or their interactions had an effect. Even more surprising, there were practically no test failures. All experimental conditions produced good results. Because this was such a striking departure from the previous 6 months' history, the whole experiment was repeated. Again, the results came out essentially the same. A further experiment was designed in which additional factors in another step of the process were tested. Again, the results came out the same way; nothing made much difference, and everything seemed to be fine. This all took about 6 weeks, and after puzzling over it and wondering what it meant, management decided that the problem must have gone away and resumed production. To their delight, the environmental test failures had indeed disappeared.

So what *had* happened? What variables were responsible? Unfortunately, no one knows for sure. The disaster that had struck 6 months before had been real—there was no doubt about that. But the experiment demonstrated that none of the variables suspected by the experts had anything to do with it. The general consensus was that whatever had been wrong (some oil contamination in high-pressure air lines and possible problems with the cleaning procedures were deemed most likely) had been fixed. However, the sloppiness of the earlier experimental procedures—in particular, failing to make sure that thermal equilibrium was achieved—had caused enough new problems so that no one could see that the earlier problems had gone away. Only when the attention to detail required by DOX removed this sloppiness was the true state of affairs revealed. Subsequent theoretical analysis confirmed that thermal extremes similar to that seen in the earlier experimentation could cause slight bubbling of the plastic coating. This, in turn, could have resulted in porosity that would lead to failure in the small batch testing.

The moral of this tale is simple: Statistical DOX encourages good experimental practice. The benefits of such practice are always substantial.

Case Study 2: Improving a Photolithographic Process

Photolithography, using chemicals to etch patterns on a substrate by sensitizing the substrate through a photographic exposure process, is widely used in industry. Printed-circuit boards, integrated microcircuits, TV screens, and magazines are just a few of many products that are produced photolithographically. The particular process considered here is not important. Suffice it to say that it involved the production of a regular grid of lines spaced 6 to 8 mils apart (a mil is 0.001 inch) over an approximately rectangular surface about the size of a TV screen.

One of the key chemicals of this photolithographic process is polyvinyl alcohol (PVA). Because it is both cheap and rather harmless, PVA is a widely used and well-studied industrial chemical. Unfortunately, however, the nature of the chemical makes it highly variable, even in its "pure" form. Even low-level contamination can radically alter its properties. Since different manufacturers of PVA use slightly different production methods, the resulting PVAs, although chemically identical, can behave differently in end users' processes. This was the situation in the photolithographic process that is described in this case study.

Our manufacturer wanted to switch PVA suppliers. Supplier A's PVA tended to be lumpy. This lumpiness caused defects (small holes or streaks) in the grid pattern deposited. Supplier B's PVA was free of this granularity, but unfortunately required an unacceptably long exposure time in the pattern exposure "camera" that printed the pattern on the sensitive PVA-based emulsion. As a result, it was not possible to use B's PVA in production.

Three other components of the emulsion were used to control exposure sensitivity. They were components T, D, and F, comprising nominally 5, 12, and 1.5 percent by volume of the total emulsion. The engineer in charge of this process felt that by adjusting the amount of these three components he could lower the required exposure time so that supplier B's PVA could be used in production. To achieve this reduction, he started to experiment with the amounts of each of these three components. For example, he would add a little more of T and then see if he could adjust the exposure time so that his grid patterns were of the right dimension. If that did not work, he would increase or decrease D or F and again try to adjust exposure time to get the right pattern dimensions. This approach was used partly because it avoided the production of bad panels, and partly because it was standard experimental practice to vary only one chemical at a time. This went on for some time, but without any luck. Finally, the experimenter consulted a statistician and asked him to help with a designed experiment.

Experimental Design

The approach that was used in the designed experiment was different. Instead of trying to make changes in one variable at a time and then adjusting camera exposure time to get acceptable results, it was decided to vary T, D, and F systematically according to a simple statistical design, leave the exposure time constant, and measure the resulting grid. This information would be used to construct a statistical model that related the component proportions to grid widths. This would then determine how to alter the proportions of the chemicals to get proper grid dimensions at the nominal exposure time.

A 2^3 factorial experiment with a replicated center point was chosen as the design. The center point was set at the nominal production conditions, while the corner points of the cube were set at the levels that are shown in Table A.1. The settings are percent volume of the total emulsion. The astute reader may realize that because the settings are calibrated in percent volume of the total emulsion, a way must be found to adjust other components of the batch to assure that their sum adds to 100 percent. For example, at the $(-, -, -)$ setting, the three chemicals occupy only 11 percent of the total volume, while at the $(+, +, +)$ setting they occupy 26 percent. In this case, the adjustment was not a problem. Distilled water and PVA were inert components that could be adjusted without affecting the overall properties of the emulsion.

Each run involved the production of five consecutive grids, one right after the other, at the required factor settings. As each piece came off the line, it was

TABLE A.1 Factor Levels and Coded Experimental Runs

Component	Coding of Variables		
	$-$ (low)	0 (nominal)	$+$ (high)
T	3%	5%	7%
D	8%	12%	16%
F	0%	1.5%	3%

Run	T	D	F
1	$-$	$-$	$-$
2	$+$	$-$	$-$
3	$-$	$+$	$-$
4	$+$	$+$	$-$
5	$-$	$-$	$+$
6	$+$	$-$	$+$
7	$-$	$+$	$+$
8	$+$	$+$	$+$
9	0	0	0
10	0	0	0

TABLE A.2   **Line Widths (in mils) at Various Locations of the Rectangular Array**

Note: Corner Identification Is by Clock Position

10:00	2:00
Center	
8:00	4:00

Run	Center	Corner				Corner Average
		2:00	4:00	8:00	10:00	
1	6.8	3.9	4.0	3.9	4.2	4.000
	6.5	4.4	3.6	4.2	4.3	4.125
	6.7	4.1	3.9	4.2	4.1	4.075
	6.3	4.5	3.7	3.7	4.2	4.025
	6.8	4.7	4.1	4.1	4.4	4.325
2	6.7	4.9	4.4	4.8	4.8	4.725
	6.9	5.2	4.5	4.9	5.0	4.900
	7.3	5.0	4.2	4.7	4.6	4.625
	7.2	5.1	4.7	4.5	4.7	4.750
	6.9	5.0	4.2	4.6	4.9	4.675
3	9.7	7.3	7.1	7.0	7.4	7.200
	9.9	7.2	7.1	7.3	7.2	7.200
	9.3	7.2	7.2	7.2	7.2	7.200
	9.6	7.0	7.2	7.2	7.0	7.100
	9.9	7.0	7.2	7.0	7.4	7.150
4	9.5	7.7	7.2	7.3	7.5	7.425
	9.1	7.8	7.2	7.4	7.5	7.475
	9.5	7.5	7.2	7.4	7.5	7.400
	9.2	7.8	7.3	7.4	7.1	7.400
	9.6	7.4	6.7	6.9	7.1	7.025
5	6.9	5.1	4.7	4.9	5.3	5.000
	7.2	5.4	4.9	4.7	4.6	4.900
	7.2	5.3	4.7	4.9	5.5	5.100
	7.5	5.5	5.1	5.2	5.2	5.250
	7.4	5.2	5.2	4.6	5.1	5.025
6	8.0	6.2	5.8	6.0	6.0	6.000
	7.4	5.9	5.2	5.6	5.5	5.550
	7.4	6.0	5.1	5.5	5.3	5.475
	7.2	5.4	5.2	5.5	5.3	5.350
	7.8	5.8	5.4	5.2	5.6	5.500
7	10.3	7.9	7.9	7.6	7.7	7.775
	10.2	8.0	7.5	7.7	7.3	7.625
	9.8	7.6	7.5	7.5	7.5	7.525

| Run | Center | Corner | | | | Corner Average |
		2:00	4:00	8:00	10:00	
	9.7	7.8	7.4	7.6	7.8	7.650
	10.1	7.8	7.5	7.7	7.7	7.675
8	10.1	8.1	8.0	8.0	8.0	8.025
	10.0	8.1	8.0	8.0	8.1	8.050
	9.7	7.7	7.5	7.7	7.9	7.700
	9.3	7.6	7.5	7.6	7.8	7.625
	10.1	8.2	8.1	8.3	8.1	8.175
9	8.4	6.5	6.6	6.5	6.6	6.550
	8.3	6.4	6.4	6.3	6.7	6.450
	8.2	6.6	6.1	6.7	6.6	6.500
	8.7	6.7	6.4	6.6	6.7	6.600
	8.4	6.3	6.5	6.5	6.3	6.400
10	8.6	7.1	7.2	6.9	7.1	7.075
	8.0	7.1	6.2	6.2	6.4	6.475
	8.3	6.6	6.5	6.3	6.5	6.475
	8.8	7.1	6.7	6.7	6.7	6.800
	8.3	6.9	6.6	6.6	6.9	6.750

measured in five places: at the center and the four corners. This was done because the center was supposed to be at a nominal which was about 2 mils higher than the nominals at the four corner points, and it was important to be correct in all areas. The actual run order of the 10 runs was randomized, except that the (0, 0, 0) runs were taken as the first and last runs. This was done both to "calibrate" the process and to get a rough idea of possible run-to-run variability. It took about 2 to 3 hours to perform the experiment. However, the planning and the setup of the various solutions took considerably longer.

A total of 50 pieces was produced and measured. The results of the experiment (in standard order, which is not the order in which the experiment was carried out) are given in Table A.2. Note that the measurements do not come from a completely randomized design. In a completely randomized design, the 50 pieces would have received the various test conditions in a completely random order, not in 10 groups of size 5. This fact becomes important when the magnitudes of the factor effects are assessed.

Data Analysis

In this experiment, each item was measured at five different places: at the center and the four corner points. A cursory inspection of the data shows that the measurements at the center are always about 2 mils higher than those at the corners. This was expected as the system was designed for a larger center-line width. The graph in Figure A.2, where the corner averages are plotted against the measurements at the center, illustrates the relationship. The least-squares line

$$\text{corner average} = -2.10 + (1.00)\ \text{center}$$

confirms that the relationship is nearly linear with a slope of about 1. However, the plot of the residuals from this fit against the center measurements (i.e., the explanatory variable in the regression) in Figure A.3 reveals some lack of fit. The curvature of the residual plot suggests that the center/ corner offset is not quite constant. The offset is closer to 1.8 for medium-sized center values (here the residuals are positive, as the fitted values are too low), and about 2.4 when the center values tend to either end of their range. In Figure A.3 residuals that come from the "control" runs, where all factors are at their nominal levels, are circled. This suggests that control runs and experimental runs are somewhat different. As we shall see shortly, in this particular experiment there is a plausible explanation for these offset differences.

From a practical standpoint, the curvature is quite small in comparison to the range of the center values. But to be on the safe side, a prudent analysis should look at the corners and centers separately. Although the two results should be similar, it may, nevertheless, be informative to study their differences. For this reason two separate analyses are carried out: one for the center values and one for the corner averages.

The five runs in each of the 10 blocks are used to calculate the averages in Table A.3. The first eight averages correspond to the runs in the 2^3 factorial;

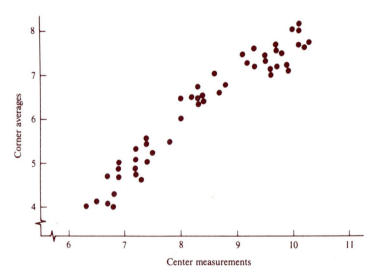

FIGURE A.2   Scatterplot of corner averages against center measurements.

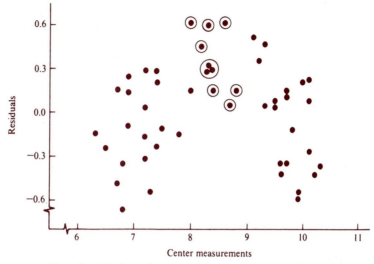

FIGURE A.3 Plot of residuals against center measurements. Residuals that come from the control runs are circled.

the last two correspond to the control runs where the process was run under nominal conditions.

Before these averages are analyzed any further, one should check to see whether outliers are present. A small percentage of outliers can lead some statistical procedures to conclusions quite different from those that would be drawn if the outliers were not present. This does not mean that the outliers should be excluded automatically. Indeed, outliers often provide the most interesting information to the experimenter. But they should be identified and their effect on the conclusions should be determined. For this data set, the 50

TABLE A.3 **Center and Corner Averages of the 10 Runs**

T	D	F	Center	Corners
−	−	−	6.62	4.11
+	−	−	7.00	4.74
−	+	−	9.68	7.17
+	+	−	9.38	7.35
−	−	+	7.24	5.06
+	−	+	7.56	5.58
−	+	+	10.02	7.65
+	+	+	9.84	7.92
0	0	0	8.40	6.50
0	0	0	8.40	6.72

center measurements should be plotted against the run (group) number to check for consistency of the measurements in each group. Similarly, the 50 corner averages should be plotted against the run number. If you try this as an exercise, you will find that there are one or two corner averages that look slightly different than the other averages in their respective groups. For example, the last average in group 4 and the first average in group 6 look suspicious. You could omit these points, revise the entries in Table A.3, and analyze the revised averages. However, for these data, the conclusions are largely unaffected.

The Yates algorithm, which is described in Section 8.3, is used to calculate the effects based on the averages of the $2^3 = 8$ factor-level combinations. The first column of data in Table A.4 lists these averages in standard order. The next three columns are obtained by successively applying an algorithm where the entries in each column are obtained by taking sums and differences of nonoverlapping pairs of entries from the previous column. For example, in column (a), the first four entries are the sums:

$$13.62 = 6.62 + 7.00; \quad 19.06 = 9.68 + 9.38; \quad \text{etc.}$$

The last four entries are the differences:

$$0.38 = 7.00 - 6.62; \quad -0.30 = 9.38 - 9.68; \quad \text{etc.}$$

TABLE A.4   Calculation of Effects Using the Yates Algorithm

Run	Average	(a)	(b)	(c)	Effect	Identity of Effect
			Center			
1	6.62	13.62	32.68	67.34	8.42	Mean
2	7.00	19.06	34.66	0.22	0.03	(T)
3	9.68	14.80	0.08	10.50	1.31	(D) ← significant
4	9.38	19.86	0.14	-1.18	-0.15	(TD)
5	7.24	0.38	5.44	1.98	0.25	(F) ← ?
6	7.56	-0.30	5.06	0.06	0.01	(TF)
7	10.02	0.32	-0.68	-0.38	-0.05	(DF)
8	9.84	-0.18	-0.50	0.18	0.02	(TDF)
			Corner			
1	4.11	8.85	23.37	49.58	6.20	Mean
2	4.74	14.52	26.21	1.60	0.20	(T)
3	7.17	10.64	0.81	10.60	1.33	(D) ← significant
4	7.35	15.57	0.79	-0.70	-0.09	(TD)
5	5.06	0.63	5.67	2.84	0.36	(F) ← ?
6	5.58	0.18	4.93	-0.02	-0.00	(TF)
7	7.65	0.52	-0.45	-0.74	-0.09	(DF)
8	7.92	0.27	-0.25	0.20	0.03	(TDF)

The "effect" column is obtained by dividing column (c) by 8 and lists the estimates of the effects in the order given in the last column. Alternatively, these estimates could have been obtained by regressing the averages on the columns of 1's and −1's of the design variables and their cross-products (see Sections 9.4 and 9.5).

Interpretation of the Results

Which of the effects look real, that is, different from noise? Recall that the effects were calculated from the run (group, block) *averages*. The failure to randomize the order of the testing completely means that we cannot obtain an error estimate by the usual procedure of pooling the within-run variances. The resulting estimate of the standard deviation of the estimated effects would tend to underestimate the true effect variability. It fails to account for the fact that the variability of the 50 test units run in a completely random order would probably be greater than that seen when the units are run in 10 groups of five identical treatments, as actually occurred.

Without a direct line of reasoning to assess random variability, an indirect approach must be used. All of the effects are calculated as sums and differences of eight data values. If a variable or interaction had no effect, the estimate of that effect obtained by the calculation represents nothing more than random error. Moreover, the central limit theorem assures that the distribution of this random error should be approximately normal. As a result, the estimates of main effects or interactions with negligible influence should fall approximately on a straight line through the origin on a normal probability plot (Sections 3.4 and 8.3). Those estimates falling far from such a line are likely to represent effects that are real (i.e., significantly different from random error).

The normal probability plot for the seven effects at the grid center is given in Figure A.4(a). Upon fitting a by-eye straight line through the origin to the points, it is apparent that the main effect of factor D looks real. With the possible exception of the main effect of F, all other estimates look like noise. The analysis for the corner averages is also given in Table A.4 and the normal probability plot is given in Figure A.4(b). Again, D appears to be a significant factor, while F may have an additional, but much smaller, effect.

The normal probability plots indicate that factor D has a large and probably real effect on both corner and center line-widths. With the possible exception of the main effect of F, all other effects appear negligible. Following the principle of parsimony (the simplest explanation that does well), D, and possibly F, were candidates for a final model. Because the engineers involved had reason to believe that F was marginally important, it was included. This yielded the two fitted models,

$$\text{center} = 8.42 + (1.31)D + (0.25)F$$

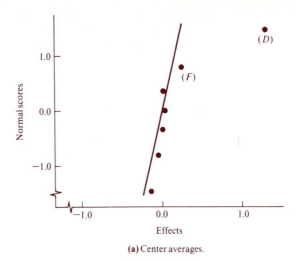

(a) Center averages.

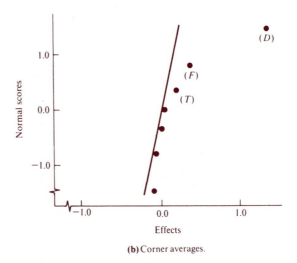

(b) Corner averages.

FIGURE A.4   Normal probability plots of the estimated effects for center and corner averages. The line through the origin is fitted "by eye." Points that are far from this line correspond to significant effects.

and

$$corner = 6.20 + (1.33)D + (0.36)F,$$

where D and F are still given in their coded values of -1, 0, and $+1$.

The fitted values and residuals from these models are given in Table A.5. The error (residual) sum of squares for corner averages is considerably larger than that for the center averages. This suggests that behavior at the corners is more variable than at the center. Moreover, the model underpredicts the

TABLE A.5   Averages, Fitted Values, and Residuals from the Model That Includes the Main Effects of *D* and *F*

	Center			Corner		
Run	Average	Fitted Value	Residual	Average	Fitted Value	Residual
1	6.62	6.86	−0.24	4.11	4.51	−0.40
2	7.00	6.86	0.14	4.74	4.51	0.23
3	9.68	9.48	0.20	7.17	7.17	0.00
4	9.38	9.48	−0.10	7.35	7.17	0.18
5	7.24	7.36	−0.12	5.06	5.23	−0.17
6	7.56	7.36	0.20	5.58	5.23	0.35
7	10.02	9.98	0.04	7.65	7.89	−0.24
8	9.84	9.98	−0.14	7.92	7.89	0.03
9	8.40	8.42	−0.02	6.50	6.20	0.30
10	8.40	8.42	−0.02	6.72	6.20	0.52
		SSE = 0.20			SSE = 0.82	

corner averages of the control runs. This reflects the fact that the center/corner offset averaged 2.22 mils for the eight factorial test runs, but only 1.79 mils for the two control runs.

It turns out that there is a straightforward explanation for these phenomena. The greater variability seen at the grid corners was completely expected and typical. The nature of the exposure process was well known to be the source. The smaller center/corner offset of the control runs was also not surprising, although the explanation was more subtle. Each of the eight experimental runs required manually dispensing an experimental mixture as each piece came around in a carrier to the dispensing station on the manufacturing line. The two control runs required no such hand dispensing because for these runs the automated procedures could be used. Unfortunately, it was not possible to achieve as complete a dispersion of the emulsion with a manual dispense as could be achieved by the automated procedures. As a result, the corners tended not to be adequately covered for the factorial runs, which caused their center/corner offsets to be different than those of the control runs.

On the basis of these results, several changes were made. First, it became clear that the *D* component alone could be used to control grid width at the nominal exposure time. This information resulted in the appropriate setting for *D* to enable supplier *B*'s PVA to be used in production. In addition, an even more important and unexpected benefit resulted. The fact that changes in the *F* component over the range 0 to 3 percent had at most a marginal effect was a surprise. *F* had originally been added as a "promoter" because engineers felt that it was needed to enhance the effect of the *D* component. However, since the experiment showed that *F* was unnecessary, it could be eliminated. Because it was both expensive and involved costly waste treatment procedures to discharge, this development resulted in a large cost reduction, far beyond that which had originally been expected.

Such bonuses are often the result of good experimental design. Well-designed experiments can yield dividends that "one variable at a time" approaches cannot deliver. Moreover, these benefits require little, if any, additional experimental cost or effort. The experiment and analysis described here took only a few days to plan and organize and only a day or so to perform and analyze. The payback from these efforts was immediate and significant.

APPENDIX

B

Bibliography

Anderson, V. L., and R. A. McLean. *Design of Experiments: A Realistic Approach.* New York: Marcel Dekker, Inc., 1974.

Box, G. E. P., and N. R. Draper. *Evolutionary Operation.* New York: John Wiley & Sons, Inc., 1969.

Box, G. E. P., W. G. Hunter, and J. S. Hunter. *Statistics for Experimenters.* New York: John Wiley & Sons, Inc., 1978.

Daniel, C., and F. S. Wood. *Fitting Equations to Data*, 2nd ed. New York: John Wiley & Sons, Inc., 1980.

Deming, W. E. *Out of the Crisis.* Cambridge, Mass.: MIT Center for Advanced Engineering Study, 1986.

Deming, W. E. *Quality, Productivity, and Competitive Position.* Cambridge, Mass.: MIT Center for Advanced Engineering Study, 1982.

Draper, N. R., and H. Smith. *Applied Regression Analysis*, 2nd ed. New York: John Wiley & Sons, Inc., 1981.

Eisenhart, C., M. W. Hastay, and W. A. Wallis. *Selected Techniques of Statistical Analysis.* New York: McGraw-Hill Book Company, 1947.

Fisher, R. A. *Statistical Methods for Research Workers.* Edinburgh: Oliver & Boyd, 1925.

Grant, E. L. *Statistical Quality Control*, 2nd ed. New York: McGraw-Hill Book Company, 1952.

Hogg, R. V., and A. T. Craig. *Introduction to Mathematical Statistics*, 4th ed. New York: Macmillan Publishing Company, 1978.

Hogg, R. V., and E. A. Tanis. *Probability and Statistical Inference*, 3rd ed. New York: Macmillan Publishing Company, 1988.

Ishikawa, K. *Guide to Quality Control.* Tokyo: Asian Productivity Organization, 1982.

Montgomery, D. C. *Design and Analysis of Experiments*, 2nd ed. New York: John Wiley & Sons, Inc., 1984.

Myers, R. H. *Response Surface Methodology.* Boston: Allyn and Bacon, Inc., 1971.

Natrella, M. G. *Experimental Statistics, National Bureau of Standards Handbook 91.* Washington, D.C.: U.S. Government Printing Office, 1963.

Nelson, W. *Applied Life Data Analysis.* New York: John Wiley & Sons, Inc., 1982.

Neter, J., W. Wasserman, and M. H. Kutner. *Applied Linear Regression Models.* Homewood, Ill.: Richard D. Irwin, Inc., 1983.

Snedecor, G. W., and W. G. Cochran. *Statistical Methods*, 6th ed. Ames, Iowa: Iowa State University Press, 1967.

Snee, R. D., L. B. Hare, and J. R. Trout. *Experiments in Industry. Design, Analysis and Interpretation of Results.* Milwaukee: American Society for Quality Control, 1985.

Tukey, J. W. *Exploratory Data Analysis.* Reading,

Mass.: Addison-Wesley Publishing Company, Inc., 1977.

Velleman, P. F., and D. C. Hoaglin. *Applications, Basics, and Computing of Exploratory Data Analysis.* Boston: Duxbury Press, 1981.

Weisberg, S. *Applied Linear Regression*, 2nd ed. New York: John Wiley & Sons, Inc., 1985.

Wetherill, G. B. *Elementary Statistical Methods*, 3rd ed. London: Methuen & Company Ltd., 1982.

Woodward, R. H., and P. L. Goldsmith. *Cumulative Sum Techniques.* Edinburgh: Oliver & Boyd, 1964.

Statistical Tables

TABLE C.1 **Factors for Determining the 3σ Control Limits in $\bar{x}$-Charts and R-Charts**

Number of Observations in Sample, n	Factors for $\bar{x}$-Charts		Factors for R-Chart	
	Using $\bar{s}$ A_3	Using $\bar{R}$ A_2	D_3	D_4
2	2.66	1.88	0	3.27
3	1.95	1.02	0	2.57
4	1.63	0.73	0	2.28
5	1.43	0.58	0	2.11
6	1.29	0.48	0	2.00
7	1.18	0.42	0.08	1.92
8	1.10	0.37	0.14	1.86
9	1.03	0.34	0.18	1.82
10	0.98	0.31	0.22	1.78
11	0.93	0.29	0.26	1.74
12	0.89	0.27	0.28	1.72
13	0.85	0.25	0.31	1.69
14	0.82	0.24	0.33	1.67
15	0.79	0.22	0.35	1.65
16	0.76	0.21	0.36	1.64
17	0.74	0.20	0.38	1.62
18	0.72	0.19	0.39	1.61
19	0.70	0.19	0.40	1.60
20	0.68	0.18	0.41	1.59

Source: Reproduced and adapted with permission from E. L. Grant, *Statistical Quality Control*, 2nd ed. (New York: McGraw-Hill, 1952), pp. 513 and 514.

TABLE C.2   Binomial Distribution Function

$$P(X \le x; p) = \sum_{k=0}^{x} \frac{n!}{k!(n-k)!} p^k (1-p)^{n-k}$$

$$P(X \le x; p) = P(X \ge n - x; 1 - p) = 1 - P(X \le n - x - 1; 1 - p)$$

n	x	p									
		0.05	0.10	0.15	0.20	0.25	0.30	0.35	0.40	0.45	0.50
2	0	0.9025	0.8100	0.7225	0.6400	0.5625	0.4900	0.4225	0.3600	0.3025	0.2500
	1	0.9975	0.9900	0.9775	0.9600	0.9375	0.9100	0.8775	0.8400	0.7975	0.7500
	2	1.0000	1.0000	1.0000	1.0000	1.0000	1.0000	1.0000	1.0000	1.0000	1.0000
3	0	0.8574	0.7290	0.6141	0.5120	0.4219	0.3430	0.2746	0.2160	0.1664	0.1250
	1	0.9928	0.9720	0.9392	0.8960	0.8438	0.7840	0.7182	0.6480	0.5748	0.5000
	2	0.9999	0.9990	0.9966	0.9920	0.9844	0.9730	0.9571	0.9360	0.9089	0.8750
	3	1.0000	1.0000	1.0000	1.0000	1.0000	1.0000	1.0000	1.0000	1.0000	1.0000
4	0	0.8145	0.6561	0.5220	0.4096	0.3164	0.2401	0.1785	0.1296	0.0915	0.0625
	1	0.9860	0.9477	0.8905	0.8192	0.7383	0.6517	0.5630	0.4752	0.3910	0.3125
	2	0.9995	0.9963	0.9880	0.9728	0.9492	0.9163	0.8735	0.8208	0.7585	0.6875
	3	1.0000	0.9999	0.9995	0.9984	0.9961	0.9919	0.9850	0.9744	0.9590	0.9375
	4	1.0000	1.0000	1.0000	1.0000	1.0000	1.0000	1.0000	1.0000	1.0000	1.0000
5	0	0.7738	0.5905	0.4437	0.3277	0.2373	0.1681	0.1160	0.0778	0.0503	0.0312
	1	0.9774	0.9185	0.8352	0.7373	0.6328	0.5282	0.4284	0.3370	0.2562	0.1875
	2	0.9988	0.9914	0.9734	0.9421	0.8965	0.8369	0.7648	0.6826	0.5931	0.5000
	3	1.0000	0.9995	0.9978	0.9933	0.9844	0.9692	0.9460	0.9130	0.8688	0.8125
	4	1.0000	1.0000	0.9999	0.9997	0.9990	0.9976	0.9947	0.9898	0.9815	0.9688
	5	1.0000	1.0000	1.0000	1.0000	1.0000	1.0000	1.0000	1.0000	1.0000	1.0000
6	0	0.7351	0.5314	0.3771	0.2621	0.1780	0.1176	0.0754	0.0467	0.0277	0.0156
	1	0.9672	0.8857	0.7765	0.6553	0.5339	0.4202	0.3191	0.2333	0.1636	0.1094
	2	0.9978	0.9842	0.9527	0.9011	0.8306	0.7443	0.6471	0.5443	0.4415	0.3438
	3	0.9999	0.9987	0.9941	0.9830	0.9624	0.9295	0.8826	0.8208	0.7447	0.6562
	4	1.0000	0.9999	0.9996	0.9984	0.9954	0.9891	0.9777	0.9590	0.9308	0.8906
	5	1.0000	1.0000	1.0000	0.9999	0.9998	0.9993	0.9982	0.9959	0.9917	0.9844
	6	1.0000	1.0000	1.0000	1.0000	1.0000	1.0000	1.0000	1.0000	1.0000	1.0000
7	0	0.6983	0.4783	0.3206	0.2097	0.1335	0.0824	0.0490	0.0280	0.0152	0.0078
	1	0.9556	0.8503	0.7166	0.5767	0.4449	0.3294	0.2338	0.1586	0.1024	0.0625
	2	0.9962	0.9743	0.9262	0.8520	0.7564	0.6471	0.5323	0.4199	0.3164	0.2266
	3	0.9998	0.9973	0.9879	0.9667	0.9294	0.8740	0.8002	0.7102	0.6083	0.5000
	4	1.0000	0.9998	0.9988	0.9953	0.9871	0.9712	0.9444	0.9037	0.8471	0.7734
	5	1.0000	1.0000	0.9999	0.9996	0.9987	0.9962	0.9910	0.9812	0.9643	0.9375
	6	1.0000	1.0000	1.0000	1.0000	0.9999	0.9998	0.9994	0.9984	0.9963	0.9922
	7	1.0000	1.0000	1.0000	1.0000	1.0000	1.0000	1.0000	1.0000	1.0000	1.0000

TABLE C.2   Binomial Distribution Function (*continued*)

n	x	0.05	0.10	0.15	0.20	0.25	0.30	0.35	0.40	0.45	0.50
						p					
8	0	0.6634	0.4305	0.2725	0.1678	0.1001	0.0576	0.0319	0.0168	0.0084	0.0039
	1	0.9428	0.8131	0.6572	0.5033	0.3671	0.2553	0.1691	0.1064	0.0632	0.0352
	2	0.9942	0.9619	0.8948	0.7969	0.6785	0.5518	0.4278	0.3154	0.2201	0.1445
	3	0.9996	0.9950	0.9786	0.9437	0.8862	0.8059	0.7064	0.5941	0.4770	0.3633
	4	1.0000	0.9996	0.9971	0.9896	0.9727	0.9420	0.8939	0.8263	0.7396	0.6367
	5	1.0000	1.0000	0.9998	0.9988	0.9958	0.9887	0.9747	0.9502	0.9115	0.8555
	6	1.0000	1.0000	1.0000	0.9999	0.9996	0.9987	0.9964	0.9915	0.9819	0.9648
	7	1.0000	1.0000	1.0000	1.0000	1.0000	0.9999	0.9998	0.9993	0.9983	0.9961
	8	1.0000	1.0000	1.0000	1.0000	1.0000	1.0000	1.0000	1.0000	1.0000	1.0000
9	0	0.6302	0.3874	0.2316	0.1342	0.0751	0.0404	0.0207	0.0101	0.0046	0.0020
	1	0.9288	0.7748	0.5995	0.4362	0.3003	0.1960	0.1211	0.0705	0.0385	0.0195
	2	0.9916	0.9470	0.8591	0.7382	0.6007	0.4628	0.3373	0.2318	0.1495	0.0898
	3	0.9994	0.9917	0.9661	0.9144	0.8343	0.7297	0.6089	0.4826	0.3614	0.2539
	4	1.0000	0.9991	0.9944	0.9804	0.9511	0.9012	0.8283	0.7334	0.6214	0.5000
	5	1.0000	0.9999	0.9994	0.9969	0.9900	0.9747	0.9464	0.9006	0.8342	0.7461
	6	1.0000	1.0000	1.0000	0.9997	0.9987	0.9957	0.9888	0.9750	0.9502	0.9102
	7	1.0000	1.0000	1.0000	1.0000	0.9999	0.9996	0.9986	0.9962	0.9909	0.9805
	8	1.0000	1.0000	1.0000	1.0000	1.0000	1.0000	0.9999	0.9997	0.9992	0.9980
	9	1.0000	1.0000	1.0000	1.0000	1.0000	1.0000	1.0000	1.0000	1.0000	1.0000
10	0	0.5987	0.3487	0.1969	0.1074	0.0563	0.0282	0.0135	0.0060	0.0025	0.0010
	1	0.9139	0.7361	0.5443	0.3758	0.2440	0.1493	0.0860	0.0464	0.0233	0.0107
	2	0.9885	0.9298	0.8202	0.6778	0.5256	0.3828	0.2616	0.1673	0.0996	0.0547
	3	0.9990	0.9872	0.9500	0.8791	0.7759	0.6496	0.5138	0.3823	0.2660	0.1719
	4	0.9999	0.9984	0.9901	0.9672	0.9219	0.8497	0.7515	0.6331	0.5044	0.3770
	5	1.0000	0.9999	0.9986	0.9936	0.9803	0.9527	0.9051	0.8338	0.7384	0.6230
	6	1.0000	1.0000	0.9999	0.9991	0.9965	0.9894	0.9740	0.9452	0.8980	0.8281
	7	1.0000	1.0000	1.0000	0.9999	0.9996	0.9984	0.9952	0.9877	0.9726	0.9453
	8	1.0000	1.0000	1.0000	1.0000	1.0000	0.9999	0.9995	0.9983	0.9955	0.9893
	9	1.0000	1.0000	1.0000	1.0000	1.0000	1.0000	1.0000	0.9999	0.9997	0.9990
	10	1.0000	1.0000	1.0000	1.0000	1.0000	1.0000	1.0000	1.0000	1.0000	1.0000
11	0	0.5688	0.3138	0.1673	0.0859	0.0422	0.0198	0.0088	0.0036	0.0014	0.0005
	1	0.8981	0.6974	0.4922	0.3221	0.1971	0.1130	0.0606	0.0302	0.0139	0.0059
	2	0.9848	0.9104	0.7788	0.6174	0.4552	0.3127	0.2001	0.1189	0.0652	0.0327
	3	0.9984	0.9815	0.9306	0.8389	0.7133	0.5696	0.4256	0.2963	0.1911	0.1133
	4	0.9999	0.9972	0.9841	0.9496	0.8854	0.7897	0.6683	0.5328	0.3971	0.2744
	5	1.0000	0.9997	0.9973	0.9883	0.9657	0.9218	0.8513	0.7535	0.6331	0.5000
	6	1.0000	1.0000	0.9997	0.9980	0.9924	0.9784	0.9499	0.9006	0.8262	0.7256
	7	1.0000	1.0000	1.0000	0.9998	0.9988	0.9957	0.9878	0.9707	0.9390	0.8867
	8	1.0000	1.0000	1.0000	1.0000	0.9999	0.9994	0.9980	0.9941	0.9852	0.9673
	9	1.0000	1.0000	1.0000	1.0000	1.0000	1.0000	0.9998	0.9993	0.9978	0.9941
	10	1.0000	1.0000	1.0000	1.0000	1.0000	1.0000	1.0000	1.0000	0.9998	0.9995
	11	1.0000	1.0000	1.0000	1.0000	1.0000	1.0000	1.0000	1.0000	1.0000	1.0000

TABLE C.2   Binomial Distribution Function (*continued*)

n	x	0.05	0.10	0.15	0.20	0.25	0.30	0.35	0.40	0.45	0.50
						p					
12	0	0.5404	0.2824	0.1422	0.0687	0.0317	0.0138	0.0057	0.0022	0.0008	0.0002
	1	0.8816	0.6590	0.4435	0.2749	0.1584	0.0850	0.0424	0.0196	0.0083	0.0032
	2	0.9804	0.8891	0.7358	0.5583	0.3907	0.2528	0.1513	0.0834	0.0421	0.0193
	3	0.9978	0.9744	0.9078	0.7946	0.6488	0.4925	0.3467	0.2253	0.1345	0.0730
	4	0.9998	0.9957	0.9761	0.9274	0.8424	0.7237	0.5833	0.4382	0.3044	0.1938
	5	1.0000	0.9995	0.9954	0.9806	0.9456	0.8822	0.7873	0.6652	0.5269	0.3872
	6	1.0000	0.9999	0.9993	0.9961	0.9857	0.9614	0.9154	0.8418	0.7393	0.6128
	7	1.0000	1.0000	0.9999	0.9994	0.9972	0.9905	0.9745	0.9427	0.8883	0.8062
	8	1.0000	1.0000	1.0000	0.9999	0.9996	0.9983	0.9944	0.9847	0.9644	0.9270
	9	1.0000	1.0000	1.0000	1.0000	1.0000	0.9998	0.9992	0.9972	0.9921	0.9807
	10	1.0000	1.0000	1.0000	1.0000	1.0000	1.0000	0.9999	0.9997	0.9989	0.9968
	11	1.0000	1.0000	1.0000	1.0000	1.0000	1.0000	1.0000	1.0000	0.9999	0.9998
	12	1.0000	1.0000	1.0000	1.0000	1.0000	1.0000	1.0000	1.0000	1.0000	1.0000
13	0	0.5133	0.2542	0.1209	0.0550	0.0238	0.0097	0.0037	0.0013	0.0004	0.0001
	1	0.8646	0.6213	0.3983	0.2336	0.1267	0.0637	0.0296	0.0126	0.0049	0.0017
	2	0.9755	0.8661	0.6920	0.5017	0.3326	0.2025	0.1132	0.0579	0.0269	0.0112
	3	0.9969	0.9658	0.8820	0.7473	0.5843	0.4206	0.2783	0.1686	0.0929	0.0461
	4	0.9997	0.9935	0.9658	0.9009	0.7940	0.6543	0.5005	0.3530	0.2279	0.1334
	5	1.0000	0.9991	0.9924	0.9700	0.9198	0.8346	0.7159	0.5744	0.4268	0.2905
	6	1.0000	0.9999	0.9987	0.9930	0.9757	0.9376	0.8705	0.7712	0.6437	0.5000
	7	1.0000	1.0000	0.9998	0.9988	0.9944	0.9818	0.9538	0.9023	0.8212	0.7095
	8	1.0000	1.0000	1.0000	0.9998	0.9990	0.9960	0.9874	0.9679	0.9302	0.8666
	9	1.0000	1.0000	1.0000	1.0000	0.9999	0.9993	0.9975	0.9922	0.9797	0.9539
	10	1.0000	1.0000	1.0000	1.0000	1.0000	0.9999	0.9997	0.9987	0.9959	0.9888
	11	1.0000	1.0000	1.0000	1.0000	1.0000	1.0000	1.0000	0.9999	0.9995	0.9983
	12	1.0000	1.0000	1.0000	1.0000	1.0000	1.0000	1.0000	1.0000	1.0000	0.9999
	13	1.0000	1.0000	1.0000	1.0000	1.0000	1.0000	1.0000	1.0000	1.0000	1.0000
14	0	0.4877	0.2288	0.1028	0.0440	0.0178	0.0068	0.0024	0.0008	0.0002	0.0001
	1	0.8470	0.5846	0.3567	0.1979	0.1010	0.0475	0.0205	0.0081	0.0029	0.0009
	2	0.9699	0.8416	0.6479	0.4481	0.2811	0.1608	0.0839	0.0398	0.0170	0.0065
	3	0.9958	0.9559	0.8535	0.6982	0.5213	0.3552	0.2205	0.1243	0.0632	0.0287
	4	0.9996	0.9908	0.9533	0.8702	0.7415	0.5842	0.4227	0.2793	0.1672	0.0898
	5	1.0000	0.9985	0.9885	0.9561	0.8883	0.7805	0.6405	0.4859	0.3373	0.2120
	6	1.0000	0.9998	0.9978	0.9884	0.9617	0.9067	0.8164	0.6925	0.5461	0.3953
	7	1.0000	1.0000	0.9997	0.9976	0.9897	0.9685	0.9247	0.8499	0.7414	0.6047
	8	1.0000	1.0000	1.0000	0.9996	0.9978	0.9917	0.9757	0.9417	0.8811	0.7880
	9	1.0000	1.0000	1.0000	1.0000	0.9997	0.9983	0.9940	0.9825	0.9574	0.9102
	10	1.0000	1.0000	1.0000	1.0000	1.0000	0.9998	0.9989	0.9961	0.9886	0.9713
	11	1.0000	1.0000	1.0000	1.0000	1.0000	1.0000	0.9999	0.9994	0.9978	0.9935
	12	1.0000	1.0000	1.0000	1.0000	1.0000	1.0000	1.0000	0.9999	0.9997	0.9991
	13	1.0000	1.0000	1.0000	1.0000	1.0000	1.0000	1.0000	1.0000	1.0000	0.9999
	14	1.0000	1.0000	1.0000	1.0000	1.0000	1.0000	1.0000	1.0000	1.0000	1.0000

TABLE C.2   Binomial Distribution Function (*continued*)

						p					
n	*x*	0.05	0.10	0.15	0.20	0.25	0.30	0.35	0.40	0.45	0.50
15	0	0.4633	0.2059	0.0874	0.0352	0.0134	0.0047	0.0016	0.0005	0.0001	0.0000
	1	0.8290	0.5490	0.3186	0.1671	0.0802	0.0353	0.0142	0.0052	0.0017	0.0005
	2	0.9638	0.8159	0.6042	0.3980	0.2361	0.1268	0.0617	0.0271	0.0107	0.0037
	3	0.9945	0.9444	0.8227	0.6482	0.4613	0.2969	0.1727	0.0905	0.0424	0.0176
	4	0.9994	0.9873	0.9383	0.8358	0.6865	0.5155	0.3519	0.2173	0.1204	0.0592
	5	0.9999	0.9978	0.9832	0.9389	0.8516	0.7216	0.5643	0.4032	0.2608	0.1509
	6	1.0000	0.9997	0.9964	0.9819	0.9434	0.8689	0.7548	0.6098	0.4522	0.3036
	7	1.0000	1.0000	0.9994	0.9958	0.9827	0.9500	0.8868	0.7869	0.6535	0.5000
	8	1.0000	1.0000	0.9999	0.9992	0.9958	0.9848	0.9578	0.9050	0.8182	0.6964
	9	1.0000	1.0000	1.0000	0.9999	0.9992	0.9963	0.9876	0.9662	0.9231	0.8491
	10	1.0000	1.0000	1.0000	1.0000	0.9999	0.9993	0.9972	0.9907	0.9745	0.9408
	11	1.0000	1.0000	1.0000	1.0000	1.0000	0.9999	0.9995	0.9981	0.9937	0.9824
	12	1.0000	1.0000	1.0000	1.0000	1.0000	1.0000	0.9999	0.9997	0.9989	0.9963
	13	1.0000	1.0000	1.0000	1.0000	1.0000	1.0000	1.0000	1.0000	0.9999	0.9995
	14	1.0000	1.0000	1.0000	1.0000	1.0000	1.0000	1.0000	1.0000	1.0000	1.0000
	15	1.0000	1.0000	1.0000	1.0000	1.0000	1.0000	1.0000	1.0000	1.0000	1.0000
16	0	0.4401	0.1853	0.0743	0.0281	0.0100	0.0033	0.0010	0.0003	0.0001	0.0000
	1	0.8108	0.5147	0.2839	0.1407	0.0635	0.0261	0.0098	0.0033	0.0010	0.0003
	2	0.9571	0.7892	0.5614	0.3518	0.1971	0.0994	0.0451	0.0183	0.0066	0.0021
	3	0.9930	0.9316	0.7899	0.5981	0.4050	0.2459	0.1339	0.0651	0.0281	0.0106
	4	0.9991	0.9830	0.9209	0.7982	0.6302	0.4499	0.2892	0.1666	0.0853	0.0384
	5	0.9999	0.9967	0.9765	0.9183	0.8103	0.6598	0.4900	0.3288	0.1976	0.1051
	6	1.0000	0.9995	0.9944	0.9733	0.9204	0.8247	0.6881	0.5272	0.3660	0.2272
	7	1.0000	0.9999	0.9989	0.9930	0.9729	0.9256	0.8406	0.7161	0.5629	0.4018
	8	1.0000	1.0000	0.9998	0.9985	0.9925	0.9743	0.9329	0.8577	0.7441	0.5982
	9	1.0000	1.0000	1.0000	0.9998	0.9984	0.9929	0.9771	0.9417	0.8759	0.7728
	10	1.0000	1.0000	1.0000	1.0000	0.9997	0.9984	0.9938	0.9809	0.9514	0.8949
	11	1.0000	1.0000	1.0000	1.0000	1.0000	0.9997	0.9987	0.9951	0.9851	0.9616
	12	1.0000	1.0000	1.0000	1.0000	1.0000	1.0000	0.9998	0.9991	0.9965	0.9894
	13	1.0000	1.0000	1.0000	1.0000	1.0000	1.0000	1.0000	0.9999	0.9994	0.9979
	14	1.0000	1.0000	1.0000	1.0000	1.0000	1.0000	1.0000	1.0000	1.0000	0.9997
	15	1.0000	1.0000	1.0000	1.0000	1.0000	1.0000	1.0000	1.0000	1.0000	1.0000
	16	1.0000	1.0000	1.0000	1.0000	1.0000	1.0000	1.0000	1.0000	1.0000	1.0000
17	0	0.4181	0.1668	0.0631	0.0225	0.0075	0.0023	0.0007	0.0002	0.0000	0.0000
	1	0.7922	0.4818	0.2525	0.1182	0.0501	0.0193	0.0067	0.0021	0.0006	0.0001
	2	0.9497	0.7618	0.5198	0.3096	0.1637	0.0774	0.0327	0.0123	0.0041	0.0012
	3	0.9912	0.9174	0.7556	0.5489	0.3530	0.2019	0.1028	0.0464	0.0184	0.0063
	4	0.9988	0.9779	0.9013	0.7582	0.5739	0.3887	0.2348	0.1260	0.0596	0.0245
	5	0.9999	0.9953	0.9681	0.8943	0.7653	0.5968	0.4197	0.2639	0.1471	0.0717
	6	1.0000	0.9992	0.9917	0.9623	0.8929	0.7752	0.6188	0.4478	0.2902	0.1662
	7	1.0000	0.9999	0.9983	0.9891	0.9598	0.8954	0.7872	0.6405	0.4743	0.3145
	8	1.0000	1.0000	0.9997	0.9974	0.9876	0.9597	0.9006	0.8011	0.6626	0.5000
	9	1.0000	1.0000	1.0000	0.9995	0.9969	0.9873	0.9617	0.9081	0.8166	0.6855

TABLE C.2   Binomial Distribution Function (*continued*)

n	x	0.05	0.10	0.15	0.20	0.25	0.30	0.35	0.40	0.45	0.50
							p				
	10	1.0000	1.0000	1.0000	0.9999	0.9994	0.9968	0.9880	0.9652	0.9174	0.8338
	11	1.0000	1.0000	1.0000	1.0000	0.9999	0.9993	0.9970	0.9894	0.9699	0.9283
	12	1.0000	1.0000	1.0000	1.0000	1.0000	0.9999	0.9994	0.9975	0.9914	0.9755
	13	1.0000	1.0000	1.0000	1.0000	1.0000	1.0000	0.9999	0.9995	0.9981	0.9936
	14	1.0000	1.0000	1.0000	1.0000	1.0000	1.0000	1.0000	0.9999	0.9997	0.9988
	15	1.0000	1.0000	1.0000	1.0000	1.0000	1.0000	1.0000	1.0000	1.0000	0.9999
	16	1.0000	1.0000	1.0000	1.0000	1.0000	1.0000	1.0000	1.0000	1.0000	1.0000
18	0	0.3972	0.1501	0.0536	0.0180	0.0056	0.0016	0.0004	0.0001	0.0000	0.0000
	1	0.7735	0.4503	0.2241	0.0991	0.0395	0.0142	0.0046	0.0013	0.0003	0.0001
	2	0.9419	0.7338	0.4797	0.2713	0.1353	0.0600	0.0236	0.0082	0.0025	0.0007
	3	0.9891	0.9018	0.7202	0.5010	0.3057	0.1646	0.0783	0.0328	0.0120	0.0038
	4	0.9985	0.9718	0.8794	0.7164	0.5187	0.3327	0.1886	0.0942	0.0411	0.0154
	5	0.9998	0.9936	0.9581	0.8671	0.7175	0.5344	0.3550	0.2088	0.1077	0.0481
	6	1.0000	0.9988	0.9882	0.9487	0.8610	0.7217	0.5491	0.3743	0.2258	0.1189
	7	1.0000	0.9998	0.9973	0.9837	0.9431	0.8593	0.7283	0.5634	0.3915	0.2403
	8	1.0000	1.0000	0.9995	0.9957	0.9807	0.9404	0.8609	0.7368	0.5778	0.4073
	9	1.0000	1.0000	0.9999	0.9991	0.9946	0.9790	0.9403	0.8653	0.7473	0.5927
	10	1.0000	1.0000	1.0000	0.9998	0.9988	0.9939	0.9788	0.9424	0.8720	0.7597
	11	1.0000	1.0000	1.0000	1.0000	0.9998	0.9986	0.9938	0.9797	0.9463	0.8811
	12	1.0000	1.0000	1.0000	1.0000	1.0000	0.9997	0.9986	0.9942	0.9817	0.9519
	13	1.0000	1.0000	1.0000	1.0000	1.0000	1.0000	0.9997	0.9987	0.9951	0.9846
	14	1.0000	1.0000	1.0000	1.0000	1.0000	1.0000	1.0000	0.9998	0.9990	0.9962
	15	1.0000	1.0000	1.0000	1.0000	1.0000	1.0000	1.0000	1.0000	0.9999	0.9993
	16	1.0000	1.0000	1.0000	1.0000	1.0000	1.0000	1.0000	1.0000	1.0000	0.9999
19	0	0.3774	0.1351	0.0456	0.0144	0.0042	0.0011	0.0003	0.0001	0.0000	0.0000
	1	0.7547	0.4203	0.1985	0.0829	0.0310	0.0104	0.0031	0.0008	0.0002	0.0000
	2	0.9335	0.7054	0.4413	0.2369	0.1113	0.0462	0.0170	0.0055	0.0015	0.0004
	3	0.9868	0.8850	0.6841	0.4551	0.2630	0.1332	0.0591	0.0230	0.0077	0.0022
	4	0.9980	0.9648	0.8556	0.6733	0.4654	0.2822	0.1500	0.0696	0.0280	0.0096
	5	0.9998	0.9914	0.9463	0.8369	0.6678	0.4739	0.2968	0.1629	0.0777	0.0318
	6	1.0000	0.9983	0.9837	0.9324	0.8251	0.6655	0.4812	0.3081	0.1727	0.0835
	7	1.0000	0.9997	0.9959	0.9767	0.9225	0.8180	0.6656	0.4878	0.3169	0.1796
	8	1.0000	1.0000	0.9992	0.9933	0.9713	0.9161	0.8145	0.6675	0.4940	0.3238
	9	1.0000	1.0000	0.9999	0.9984	0.9911	0.9674	0.9125	0.8139	0.6710	0.5000
	10	1.0000	1.0000	1.0000	0.9997	0.9977	0.9895	0.9653	0.9115	0.8159	0.6762
	11	1.0000	1.0000	1.0000	1.0000	0.9995	0.9972	0.9886	0.9648	0.9129	0.8204
	12	1.0000	1.0000	1.0000	1.0000	0.9999	0.9994	0.9969	0.9884	0.9658	0.9165
	13	1.0000	1.0000	1.0000	1.0000	1.0000	0.9999	0.9993	0.9969	0.9891	0.9682
	14	1.0000	1.0000	1.0000	1.0000	1.0000	1.0000	0.9999	0.9994	0.9972	0.9904
	15	1.0000	1.0000	1.0000	1.0000	1.0000	1.0000	1.0000	0.9999	0.9995	0.9978
	16	1.0000	1.0000	1.0000	1.0000	1.0000	1.0000	1.0000	1.0000	0.9999	0.9996
	17	1.0000	1.0000	1.0000	1.0000	1.0000	1.0000	1.0000	1.0000	1.0000	1.0000

TABLE C.2   Binomial Distribution Function (*continued*)

n	x	0.05	0.10	0.15	0.20	0.25	0.30	0.35	0.40	0.45	0.50
20	0	0.3585	0.1216	0.0388	0.0115	0.0032	0.0008	0.0002	0.0000	0.0000	0.0000
	1	0.7358	0.3917	0.1756	0.0692	0.0243	0.0076	0.0021	0.0005	0.0001	0.0000
	2	0.9245	0.6769	0.4049	0.2061	0.0913	0.0355	0.0121	0.0036	0.0009	0.0002
	3	0.9841	0.8670	0.6477	0.4114	0.2252	0.1071	0.0444	0.0160	0.0049	0.0013
	4	0.9974	0.9568	0.8298	0.6296	0.4148	0.2375	0.1182	0.0510	0.0189	0.0059
	5	0.9997	0.9887	0.9327	0.8042	0.6172	0.4164	0.2454	0.1256	0.0553	0.0207
	6	1.0000	0.9976	0.9781	0.9133	0.7858	0.6080	0.4166	0.2500	0.1299	0.0577
	7	1.0000	0.9996	0.9941	0.9679	0.8982	0.7723	0.6010	0.4159	0.2520	0.1316
	8	1.0000	0.9999	0.9987	0.9900	0.9591	0.8867	0.7624	0.5956	0.4143	0.2517
	9	1.0000	1.0000	0.9998	0.9974	0.9861	0.9520	0.8782	0.7553	0.5914	0.4119
	10	1.0000	1.0000	1.0000	0.9994	0.9961	0.9829	0.9468	0.8725	0.7507	0.5881
	11	1.0000	1.0000	1.0000	0.9999	0.9991	0.9949	0.9804	0.9435	0.8692	0.7483
	12	1.0000	1.0000	1.0000	1.0000	0.9998	0.9987	0.9940	0.9790	0.9420	0.8684
	13	1.0000	1.0000	1.0000	1.0000	1.0000	0.9997	0.9985	0.9935	0.9786	0.9423
	14	1.0000	1.0000	1.0000	1.0000	1.0000	1.0000	0.9997	0.9984	0.9936	0.9793
	15	1.0000	1.0000	1.0000	1.0000	1.0000	1.0000	1.0000	0.9997	0.9985	0.9941
	16	1.0000	1.0000	1.0000	1.0000	1.0000	1.0000	1.0000	1.0000	0.9997	0.9987
	17	1.0000	1.0000	1.0000	1.0000	1.0000	1.0000	1.0000	1.0000	1.0000	0.9998
	18	1.0000	1.0000	1.0000	1.0000	1.0000	1.0000	1.0000	1.0000	1.0000	1.0000

TABLE C.3   Poisson Distribution Function

$$P(X \le x) = \sum_{k=0}^{x} \frac{\lambda^k e^{-\lambda}}{k!}$$

	$\lambda = E(X)$									
x	0.1	0.2	0.3	0.4	0.5	0.6	0.7	0.8	0.9	1.0
0	0.905	0.819	0.741	0.670	0.607	0.549	0.497	0.449	0.407	0.368
1	0.995	0.982	0.963	0.938	0.910	0.878	0.844	0.809	0.772	0.736
2	1.000	0.999	0.996	0.992	0.986	0.977	0.966	0.953	0.937	0.920
3	1.000	1.000	1.000	0.999	0.998	0.997	0.994	0.991	0.987	0.981
4	1.000	1.000	1.000	1.000	1.000	1.000	0.999	0.999	0.998	0.996
5	1.000	1.000	1.000	1.000	1.000	1.000	1.000	1.000	1.000	0.999
6	1.000	1.000	1.000	1.000	1.000	1.000	1.000	1.000	1.000	1.000

x	1.1	1.2	1.3	1.4	1.5	1.6	1.7	1.8	1.9	2.0
0	0.333	0.301	0.273	0.247	0.223	0.202	0.183	0.165	0.150	0.135
1	0.699	0.663	0.627	0.592	0.558	0.525	0.493	0.463	0.434	0.406
2	0.900	0.879	0.857	0.833	0.809	0.783	0.757	0.731	0.704	0.677
3	0.974	0.966	0.957	0.946	0.934	0.921	0.907	0.891	0.875	0.857
4	0.995	0.992	0.989	0.986	0.981	0.976	0.970	0.964	0.956	0.947
5	0.999	0.998	0.998	0.997	0.996	0.994	0.992	0.990	0.987	0.983
6	1.000	1.000	1.000	0.999	0.999	0.999	0.998	0.997	0.997	0.995
7	1.000	1.000	1.000	1.000	1.000	1.000	1.000	0.999	0.999	0.999
8	1.000	1.000	1.000	1.000	1.000	1.000	1.000	1.000	1.000	1.000

x	2.2	2.4	2.6	2.8	3.0	3.2	3.4	3.6	3.8	4.0
0	0.111	0.091	0.074	0.061	0.050	0.041	0.033	0.027	0.022	0.018
1	0.355	0.308	0.267	0.231	0.199	0.171	0.147	0.126	0.107	0.092
2	0.623	0.570	0.518	0.469	0.423	0.380	0.340	0.303	0.269	0.238
3	0.819	0.779	0.736	0.692	0.647	0.603	0.558	0.515	0.473	0.433
4	0.928	0.904	0.877	0.848	0.815	0.781	0.744	0.706	0.668	0.629
5	0.975	0.964	0.951	0.935	0.916	0.895	0.871	0.844	0.816	0.785
6	0.993	0.988	0.983	0.976	0.966	0.955	0.942	0.927	0.909	0.889
7	0.998	0.997	0.995	0.992	0.988	0.983	0.977	0.969	0.960	0.949
8	1.000	0.999	0.999	0.998	0.996	0.994	0.992	0.988	0.984	0.979
9	1.000	1.000	1.000	0.999	0.999	0.998	0.997	0.996	0.994	0.992
10	1.000	1.000	1.000	1.000	1.000	1.000	0.999	0.999	0.998	0.997
11	1.000	1.000	1.000	1.000	1.000	1.000	1.000	1.000	0.999	0.999
12	1.000	1.000	1.000	1.000	1.000	1.000	1.000	1.000	1.000	1.000

TABLE C.3   Poisson Distribution Function (*continued*)

| | | | | | $\lambda = E(X)$ | | | | | |
x	4.2	4.4	4.6	4.8	5.0	5.2	5.4	5.6	5.8	6.0
0	0.015	0.012	0.010	0.008	0.007	0.006	0.005	0.004	0.003	0.002
1	0.078	0.066	0.056	0.048	0.040	0.034	0.029	0.024	0.021	0.017
2	0.210	0.185	0.163	0.143	0.125	0.109	0.095	0.082	0.072	0.062
3	0.395	0.359	0.326	0.294	0.265	0.238	0.213	0.191	0.170	0.151
4	0.590	0.551	0.513	0.476	0.440	0.406	0.373	0.342	0.313	0.285
5	0.753	0.720	0.686	0.651	0.616	0.581	0.546	0.512	0.478	0.446
6	0.867	0.844	0.818	0.791	0.762	0.732	0.702	0.670	0.638	0.606
7	0.936	0.921	0.905	0.887	0.867	0.845	0.822	0.797	0.771	0.744
8	0.972	0.964	0.955	0.944	0.932	0.918	0.903	0.886	0.867	0.847
9	0.989	0.985	0.980	0.975	0.968	0.960	0.951	0.941	0.929	0.916
10	0.996	0.994	0.992	0.990	0.986	0.982	0.977	0.972	0.965	0.957
11	0.999	0.998	0.997	0.996	0.995	0.993	0.990	0.988	0.984	0.980
12	1.000	0.999	0.999	0.999	0.998	0.997	0.996	0.995	0.993	0.991
13	1.000	1.000	1.000	1.000	0.999	0.999	0.999	0.998	0.997	0.996
14	1.000	1.000	1.000	1.000	1.000	1.000	0.999	0.999	0.999	0.999
15	1.000	1.000	1.000	1.000	1.000	1.000	1.000	1.000	1.000	0.999
16	1.000	1.000	1.000	1.000	1.000	1.000	1.000	1.000	1.000	1.000

x	6.5	7.0	7.5	8.0	8.5	9.0	9.5	10.0	11.0	12.0
0	0.002	0.001	0.001	0.000	0.000	0.000	0.000	0.000	0.000	0.000
1	0.011	0.007	0.005	0.003	0.002	0.001	0.001	0.000	0.000	0.000
2	0.043	0.030	0.020	0.014	0.009	0.006	0.004	0.003	0.001	0.001
3	0.112	0.082	0.059	0.042	0.030	0.021	0.015	0.010	0.005	0.002
4	0.224	0.173	0.132	0.100	0.074	0.055	0.040	0.029	0.015	0.008
5	0.369	0.301	0.241	0.191	0.150	0.116	0.089	0.067	0.038	0.020
6	0.527	0.450	0.378	0.313	0.256	0.207	0.165	0.130	0.079	0.046
7	0.673	0.599	0.525	0.453	0.386	0.324	0.269	0.220	0.143	0.090
8	0.792	0.729	0.662	0.593	0.523	0.456	0.392	0.333	0.232	0.155
9	0.877	0.830	0.776	0.717	0.653	0.587	0.522	0.458	0.341	0.242
10	0.933	0.901	0.862	0.816	0.763	0.706	0.645	0.583	0.460	0.347
11	0.966	0.947	0.921	0.888	0.849	0.803	0.752	0.697	0.579	0.462
12	0.984	0.973	0.957	0.936	0.909	0.876	0.836	0.792	0.689	0.576
13	0.993	0.987	0.978	0.966	0.949	0.926	0.898	0.864	0.781	0.682
14	0.997	0.994	0.990	0.983	0.973	0.959	0.940	0.917	0.854	0.772
15	0.999	0.998	0.995	0.992	0.986	0.978	0.967	0.951	0.907	0.844
16	1.000	0.999	0.998	0.996	0.993	0.989	0.982	0.973	0.944	0.899
17	1.000	1.000	0.999	0.998	0.997	0.995	0.991	0.986	0.968	0.937
18	1.000	1.000	1.000	0.999	0.999	0.998	0.996	0.993	0.982	0.963
19	1.000	1.000	1.000	1.000	0.999	0.999	0.998	0.997	0.991	0.979
20	1.000	1.000	1.000	1.000	1.000	1.000	0.999	0.998	0.995	0.988
21	1.000	1.000	1.000	1.000	1.000	1.000	1.000	0.999	0.998	0.994
22	1.000	1.000	1.000	1.000	1.000	1.000	1.000	1.000	0.999	0.997
23	1.000	1.000	1.000	1.000	1.000	1.000	1.000	1.000	1.000	0.999

TABLE C.4   **Standard Normal Distribution Function**

$$P(Z \le z) = \Phi(z) = \int_{-\infty}^{z} \frac{1}{\sqrt{2\pi}} e^{-w^2/2}\, dw$$

$$\Phi(-z) = 1 - \Phi(z)$$

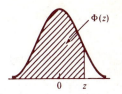

z	0.00	0.01	0.02	0.03	0.04	0.05	0.06	0.07	0.08	0.09
0.0	0.5000	0.5040	0.5080	0.5120	0.5160	0.5199	0.5239	0.5279	0.5319	0.5359
0.1	0.5398	0.5438	0.5478	0.5517	0.5557	0.5596	0.5636	0.5675	0.5714	0.5753
0.2	0.5793	0.5832	0.5871	0.5910	0.5948	0.5987	0.6026	0.6064	0.6103	0.6141
0.3	0.6179	0.6217	0.6255	0.6293	0.6331	0.6368	0.6406	0.6443	0.6480	0.6517
0.4	0.6554	0.6591	0.6628	0.6664	0.6700	0.6736	0.6772	0.6808	0.6844	0.6879
0.5	0.6915	0.6950	0.6985	0.7019	0.7054	0.7088	0.7123	0.7157	0.7190	0.7224
0.6	0.7257	0.7291	0.7324	0.7357	0.7389	0.7422	0.7454	0.7486	0.7517	0.7549
0.7	0.7580	0.7611	0.7642	0.7673	0.7703	0.7734	0.7764	0.7794	0.7823	0.7852
0.8	0.7881	0.7910	0.7939	0.7967	0.7995	0.8023	0.8051	0.8078	0.8106	0.8133
0.9	0.8159	0.8186	0.8212	0.8238	0.8264	0.8289	0.8315	0.8340	0.8365	0.8389
1.0	0.8413	0.8438	0.8461	0.8485	0.8508	0.8531	0.8554	0.8577	0.8599	0.8621
1.1	0.8643	0.8665	0.8686	0.8708	0.8729	0.8749	0.8770	0.8790	0.8810	0.8830
1.2	0.8849	0.8869	0.8888	0.8907	0.8925	0.8944	0.8962	0.8980	0.8997	0.9015
1.3	0.9032	0.9049	0.9066	0.9082	0.9099	0.9115	0.9131	0.9147	0.9162	0.9177
1.4	0.9192	0.9207	0.9222	0.9236	0.9251	0.9265	0.9279	0.9292	0.9306	0.9319
1.5	0.9332	0.9345	0.9357	0.9370	0.9382	0.9394	0.9406	0.9418	0.9429	0.9441
1.6	0.9452	0.9463	0.9474	0.9484	0.9495	0.9505	0.9515	0.9525	0.9535	0.9545
1.7	0.9554	0.9564	0.9573	0.9582	0.9591	0.9599	0.9608	0.9616	0.9625	0.9633
1.8	0.9641	0.9649	0.9656	0.9664	0.9671	0.9678	0.9686	0.9693	0.9699	0.9706
1.9	0.9713	0.9719	0.9726	0.9732	0.9738	0.9744	0.9750	0.9756	0.9761	0.9767
2.0	0.9772	0.9778	0.9783	0.9788	0.9793	0.9798	0.9803	0.9808	0.9812	0.9817
2.1	0.9821	0.9826	0.9830	0.9834	0.9838	0.9842	0.9846	0.9850	0.9854	0.9857
2.2	0.9861	0.9864	0.9868	0.9871	0.9875	0.9878	0.9881	0.9884	0.9887	0.9890
2.3	0.9893	0.9896	0.9898	0.9901	0.9904	0.9906	0.9909	0.9911	0.9913	0.9916
2.4	0.9918	0.9920	0.9922	0.9925	0.9927	0.9929	0.9931	0.9932	0.9934	0.9936
2.5	0.9938	0.9940	0.9941	0.9943	0.9945	0.9946	0.9948	0.9949	0.9951	0.9952
2.6	0.9953	0.9955	0.9956	0.9957	0.9959	0.9960	0.9961	0.9962	0.9963	0.9964
2.7	0.9965	0.9966	0.9967	0.9968	0.9969	0.9970	0.9971	0.9972	0.9973	0.9974
2.8	0.9974	0.9975	0.9976	0.9977	0.9977	0.9978	0.9979	0.9979	0.9980	0.9981
2.9	0.9981	0.9982	0.9982	0.9983	0.9984	0.9984	0.9985	0.9985	0.9986	0.9986
3.0	0.9987	0.9987	0.9987	0.9988	0.9988	0.9989	0.9989	0.9989	0.9990	0.9990

Selected Upper Percentage Points

Tail probability, α	0.100	0.050	0.025	0.010	0.005
Upper percentage point, $z(\alpha)$	1.282	1.645	1.960	2.326	2.576

Source: Reproduced in abridged form from Table 1 of E. S. Pearson and H. O. Hartley, *Biometrika Tables for Statisticians*, Vol. 1 (Cambridge: Cambridge University Press, 1954).

**TABLE C.5   Upper Percentage Points of
the Chi-Square Distribution:
Values of $\chi^2(\alpha; r)$**

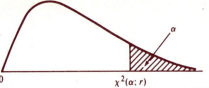

r	$\alpha = 0.995$	$\alpha = 0.99$	$\alpha = 0.975$	$\alpha = 0.95$	$\alpha = 0.05$	$\alpha = 0.025$	$\alpha = 0.01$	$\alpha = 0.005$	r
1	0.0^4393	0.0^3157	0.0^3982	0.00393	3.841	5.024	6.635	7.879	1
2	0.0100	0.0201	0.0506	0.103	5.991	7.378	9.210	10.597	2
3	0.0717	0.115	0.216	0.352	7.815	9.348	11.345	12.838	3
4	0.207	0.297	0.484	0.711	9.488	11.143	13.277	14.860	4
5	0.412	0.554	0.831	1.145	11.070	12.832	15.086	16.750	5
6	0.676	0.872	1.237	1.635	12.592	14.449	16.812	18.548	6
7	0.989	1.239	1.690	2.167	14.067	16.013	18.475	20.278	7
8	1.344	1.646	2.180	2.733	15.507	17.535	20.090	21.955	8
9	1.735	2.088	2.700	3.325	16.919	19.023	21.666	23.589	9
10	2.156	2.558	3.247	3.940	18.307	20.483	23.209	25.188	10
11	2.603	3.053	3.816	4.575	19.675	21.920	24.725	26.757	11
12	3.074	3.571	4.404	5.226	21.026	23.337	26.217	28.300	12
13	3.565	4.107	5.009	5.892	22.362	24.736	27.688	29.819	13
14	4.075	4.660	5.629	6.571	23.685	26.119	29.141	31.319	14
15	4.601	5.229	6.262	7.261	24.996	27.488	30.578	32.801	15
16	5.142	5.812	6.908	7.962	26.296	28.845	32.000	34.267	16
17	5.697	6.408	7.564	8.672	27.587	30.191	33.409	35.718	17
18	6.265	7.015	8.231	9.390	28.869	31.526	34.805	37.156	18
19	6.844	7.633	8.907	10.117	30.144	32.852	36.191	38.582	19
20	7.434	8.260	9.591	10.851	31.410	34.170	37.566	39.997	20
21	8.034	8.897	10.283	11.591	32.671	35.479	38.932	41.401	21
22	8.643	9.542	10.982	12.338	33.924	36.781	40.289	42.796	22
23	9.260	10.196	11.688	13.091	35.172	38.076	41.638	44.181	23
24	9.886	10.856	12.401	13.848	36.415	39.364	42.980	45.558	24
25	10.520	11.524	13.120	14.611	37.652	40.646	44.314	46.928	25
26	11.160	12.198	13.844	15.379	38.885	41.923	45.642	48.290	26
27	11.808	12.879	14.573	16.151	40.113	43.194	46.963	49.645	27
28	12.461	13.565	15.308	16.928	41.337	44.461	48.278	50.993	28
29	13.121	14.256	16.047	17.708	42.557	45.722	49.588	52.336	29
30	13.787	14.953	16.791	18.493	43.773	46.979	50.892	53.672	30

Source: Reproduced with permission from Table 8 of E. S. Pearson and H. O. Hartley, *Biometrika Tables for Statisticians,*
Vol. 1 (Cambridge: Cambridge University Press, 1954).

TABLE C.6 Upper Percentage Points of the Student's t-Distribution: Values of $t(\alpha; r)$

r	$\alpha = 0.10$	$\alpha = 0.05$	$\alpha = 0.025$	$\alpha = 0.01$	$\alpha = 0.005$
1	3.078	6.314	12.706	31.821	63.657
2	1.886	2.920	4.303	6.965	9.925
3	1.638	2.353	3.182	4.541	5.841
4	1.533	2.132	2.776	3.747	4.604
5	1.476	2.015	2.571	3.365	4.032
6	1.440	1.943	2.447	3.143	3.707
7	1.415	1.895	2.365	2.998	3.499
8	1.397	1.860	2.306	2.896	3.355
9	1.383	1.833	2.262	2.821	3.250
10	1.372	1.812	2.228	2.764	3.169
11	1.363	1.796	2.201	2.718	3.106
12	1.356	1.782	2.179	2.681	3.055
13	1.350	1.771	2.160	2.650	3.012
14	1.345	1.761	2.145	2.624	2.977
15	1.341	1.753	2.131	2.602	2.947
16	1.337	1.746	2.120	2.583	2.921
17	1.333	1.740	2.110	2.567	2.898
18	1.330	1.734	2.101	2.552	2.878
19	1.328	1.729	2.093	2.539	2.861
20	1.325	1.725	2.086	2.528	2.845
21	1.323	1.721	2.080	2.518	2.831
22	1.321	1.717	2.074	2.508	2.819
23	1.319	1.714	2.069	2.500	2.807
24	1.318	1.711	2.064	2.492	2.797
25	1.316	1.708	2.060	2.485	2.787
26	1.315	1.706	2.056	2.479	2.779
27	1.314	1.703	2.052	2.473	2.771
28	1.313	1.701	2.048	2.467	2.763
29	1.311	1.699	2.045	2.462	2.756
30	1.310	1.697	2.042	2.457	2.750
40	1.303	1.684	2.021	2.423	2.704
60	1.296	1.671	2.000	2.390	2.660
120	1.289	1.658	1.980	2.358	2.617
∞	1.282	1.645	1.960	2.326	2.576

Source: Reproduced with permission from Table 12 of E. S. Pearson and H. O. Hartley, *Biometrika Tables for Statisticians*, Vol. 1 (Cambridge: Cambridge University Press, 1954).

TABLE C.7 Upper Percentage Points of the F-Distribution:
Values of $F(0.05; r_1, r_2)$

$\alpha = 0.05$

$F(0.05; r_1, r_2)$

r_2 = Degrees of freedom for denominator	r_1 = Degrees of freedom for numerator																		
	1	2	3	4	5	6	7	8	9	10	12	15	20	24	30	40	60	120	∞
1	161.4	199.5	215.7	224.6	230.2	234.0	236.8	238.9	240.5	241.9	243.9	245.9	248.0	249.1	250.1	251.1	252.2	253.3	254.3
2	18.51	19.00	19.16	19.25	19.30	19.33	19.35	19.37	19.38	19.40	19.41	19.43	19.45	19.45	19.46	19.47	19.48	19.49	19.50
3	10.13	9.55	9.28	9.12	9.01	8.94	8.89	8.85	8.81	8.79	8.74	8.70	8.66	8.64	8.62	8.59	8.57	8.55	8.53
4	7.71	6.94	6.59	6.39	6.26	6.16	6.09	6.04	6.00	5.96	5.91	5.86	5.80	5.77	5.75	5.72	5.69	5.66	5.63
5	6.61	5.79	5.41	5.19	5.05	4.95	4.88	4.82	4.77	4.74	4.68	4.62	4.56	4.53	4.50	4.46	4.43	4.40	4.36
6	5.99	5.14	4.76	4.53	4.39	4.28	4.21	4.15	4.10	4.06	4.00	3.94	3.87	3.84	3.81	3.77	3.74	3.70	3.67
7	5.59	4.74	4.35	4.12	3.97	3.87	3.79	3.73	3.68	3.64	3.57	3.51	3.44	3.41	3.38	3.34	3.30	3.27	3.23
8	5.32	4.46	4.07	3.84	3.69	3.58	3.50	3.44	3.39	3.35	3.28	3.22	3.15	3.12	3.08	3.04	3.01	2.97	2.93
9	5.12	4.26	3.86	3.63	3.48	3.37	3.29	3.23	3.18	3.14	3.07	3.01	2.94	2.90	2.86	2.83	2.79	2.75	2.71
10	4.96	4.10	3.71	3.48	3.33	3.22	3.14	3.07	3.02	2.98	2.91	2.85	2.77	2.74	2.70	2.66	2.62	2.58	2.54
11	4.84	3.98	3.59	3.36	3.20	3.09	3.01	2.95	2.90	2.85	2.79	2.72	2.65	2.61	2.57	2.53	2.49	2.45	2.40
12	4.75	3.89	3.49	3.26	3.11	3.00	2.91	2.85	2.80	2.75	2.69	2.62	2.54	2.51	2.47	2.43	2.38	2.34	2.30
13	4.67	3.81	3.41	3.18	3.03	2.92	2.83	2.77	2.71	2.67	2.60	2.53	2.46	2.42	2.38	2.34	2.30	2.25	2.21
14	4.60	3.74	3.34	3.11	2.96	2.85	2.76	2.70	2.65	2.60	2.53	2.46	2.39	2.35	2.31	2.27	2.22	2.18	2.13
15	4.54	3.68	3.29	3.06	2.90	2.79	2.71	2.64	2.59	2.54	2.48	2.40	2.33	2.29	2.25	2.20	2.16	2.11	2.07
16	4.49	3.63	3.24	3.01	2.85	2.74	2.66	2.59	2.54	2.49	2.42	2.35	2.28	2.24	2.19	2.15	2.11	2.06	2.01
17	4.45	3.59	3.20	2.96	2.81	2.70	2.61	2.55	2.49	2.45	2.38	2.31	2.23	2.19	2.15	2.10	2.06	2.01	1.96
18	4.41	3.55	3.16	2.93	2.77	2.66	2.58	2.51	2.46	2.41	2.34	2.27	2.19	2.15	2.11	2.06	2.02	1.97	1.92
19	4.38	3.52	3.13	2.90	2.74	2.63	2.54	2.48	2.42	2.38	2.31	2.23	2.16	2.11	2.07	2.03	1.98	1.93	1.88
20	4.35	3.49	3.10	2.87	2.71	2.60	2.51	2.45	2.39	2.35	2.28	2.20	2.12	2.08	2.04	1.99	1.95	1.90	1.84
21	4.32	3.47	3.07	2.84	2.68	2.57	2.49	2.42	2.37	2.32	2.25	2.18	2.10	2.05	2.01	1.96	1.92	1.87	1.81
22	4.30	3.44	3.05	2.82	2.66	2.55	2.46	2.40	2.34	2.30	2.23	2.15	2.07	2.03	1.98	1.94	1.89	1.84	1.78
23	4.28	3.42	3.03	2.80	2.64	2.53	2.44	2.37	2.32	2.27	2.20	2.13	2.05	2.01	1.96	1.91	1.86	1.81	1.76
24	4.26	3.40	3.01	2.78	2.62	2.51	2.42	2.36	2.30	2.25	2.18	2.11	2.03	1.98	1.94	1.89	1.84	1.79	1.73
25	4.24	3.39	2.99	2.76	2.60	2.49	2.40	2.34	2.28	2.24	2.16	2.09	2.01	1.96	1.92	1.87	1.82	1.77	1.71
26	4.23	3.37	2.98	2.74	2.59	2.47	2.39	2.32	2.27	2.22	2.15	2.07	1.99	1.95	1.90	1.85	1.80	1.75	1.69
27	4.21	3.35	2.96	2.73	2.57	2.46	2.37	2.31	2.25	2.20	2.13	2.06	1.97	1.93	1.88	1.84	1.79	1.73	1.67
28	4.20	3.34	2.95	2.71	2.56	2.45	2.36	2.29	2.24	2.19	2.12	2.04	1.96	1.91	1.87	1.82	1.77	1.71	1.65
29	4.18	3.33	2.93	2.70	2.55	2.43	2.35	2.28	2.22	2.18	2.10	2.03	1.94	1.90	1.85	1.81	1.75	1.70	1.64
30	4.17	3.32	2.92	2.69	2.53	2.42	2.33	2.27	2.21	2.16	2.09	2.01	1.93	1.89	1.84	1.79	1.74	1.68	1.62
40	4.08	3.23	2.84	2.61	2.45	2.34	2.25	2.18	2.12	2.08	2.00	1.92	1.84	1.79	1.74	1.69	1.64	1.58	1.51
60	4.00	3.15	2.76	2.53	2.37	2.25	2.17	2.10	2.04	1.99	1.92	1.84	1.75	1.70	1.65	1.59	1.53	1.47	1.39
120	3.92	3.07	2.68	2.45	2.29	2.17	2.09	2.02	1.96	1.91	1.83	1.75	1.66	1.61	1.55	1.50	1.43	1.35	1.25
∞	3.84	3.00	2.60	2.37	2.21	2.10	2.01	1.94	1.88	1.83	1.75	1.67	1.57	1.52	1.46	1.39	1.32	1.22	1.00

Source: Reproduced with permission from Table 18 of E. S. Pearson and H. O. Hartley, *Biometrika Tables for Statisticians*, Vol. 1 (Cambridge: Cambridge University Press, 1954).

TABLE C.7 Upper Percentage Points of the F-Distribution (continued): Values of $F(0.01; r_1, r_2)$

$\alpha = 0.01$

$F(0.01; r_1, r_2)$

r_1 = Degrees of freedom for numerator

r_2 = Degrees of freedom for denominator	1	2	3	4	5	6	7	8	9	10	12	15	20	24	30	40	60	120	∞
1	4052	4999.5	5403	5625	5764	5859	5928	5982	6022	6056	6106	6157	6209	6235	6261	6287	6313	6339	6366
2	98.50	99.00	99.17	99.25	99.30	99.33	99.36	99.37	99.39	99.40	99.42	99.43	99.45	99.46	99.47	99.47	99.48	99.49	99.50
3	34.12	30.82	29.46	28.71	28.24	27.91	27.67	27.49	27.35	27.23	27.05	26.87	26.69	26.60	26.50	26.41	26.32	26.22	26.13
4	21.20	18.00	16.69	15.98	15.52	15.21	14.98	14.80	14.66	14.55	14.37	14.20	14.02	13.93	13.84	13.75	13.65	13.56	13.46
5	16.26	13.27	12.06	11.39	10.97	10.67	10.46	10.29	10.16	10.05	9.89	9.72	9.55	9.47	9.38	9.29	9.20	9.11	9.02
6	13.75	10.92	9.78	9.15	8.75	8.47	8.26	8.10	7.98	7.87	7.72	7.56	7.40	7.31	7.23	7.14	7.06	6.97	6.88
7	12.25	9.55	8.45	7.85	7.46	7.19	6.99	6.84	6.72	6.62	6.47	6.31	6.16	6.07	5.99	5.91	5.82	5.74	5.65
8	11.26	8.65	7.59	7.01	6.63	6.37	6.18	6.03	5.91	5.81	5.67	5.52	5.36	5.28	5.20	5.12	5.03	4.95	4.86
9	10.56	8.02	6.99	6.42	6.06	5.80	5.61	5.47	5.35	5.26	5.11	4.96	4.81	4.73	4.65	4.57	4.48	4.40	4.31
10	10.04	7.56	6.55	5.99	5.64	5.39	5.20	5.06	4.94	4.85	4.71	4.56	4.41	4.33	4.25	4.17	4.08	4.00	3.91
11	9.65	7.21	6.22	5.67	5.32	5.07	4.89	4.74	4.63	4.54	4.40	4.25	4.10	4.02	3.94	3.86	3.78	3.69	3.60
12	9.33	6.93	5.95	5.41	5.06	4.82	4.64	4.50	4.39	4.30	4.16	4.01	3.86	3.78	3.70	3.62	3.54	3.45	3.36
13	9.07	6.70	5.74	5.21	4.86	4.62	4.44	4.30	4.19	4.10	3.96	3.82	3.66	3.59	3.51	3.43	3.34	3.25	3.17
14	8.86	6.51	5.56	5.04	4.69	4.46	4.28	4.14	4.03	3.94	3.80	3.66	3.51	3.43	3.35	3.27	3.18	3.09	3.00
15	8.68	6.36	5.42	4.89	4.56	4.32	4.14	4.00	3.89	3.80	3.67	3.52	3.37	3.29	3.21	3.13	3.05	2.96	2.87
16	8.53	6.23	5.29	4.77	4.44	4.20	4.03	3.89	3.78	3.69	3.55	3.41	3.26	3.18	3.10	3.02	2.93	2.84	2.75
17	8.40	6.11	5.18	4.67	4.34	4.10	3.93	3.79	3.68	3.59	3.46	3.31	3.16	3.08	3.00	2.92	2.83	2.75	2.65
18	8.29	6.01	5.09	4.58	4.25	4.01	3.84	3.71	3.60	3.51	3.37	3.23	3.08	3.00	2.92	2.84	2.75	2.66	2.57
19	8.18	5.93	5.01	4.50	4.17	3.94	3.77	3.63	3.52	3.43	3.30	3.15	3.00	2.92	2.84	2.76	2.67	2.58	2.49
20	8.10	5.85	4.94	4.43	4.10	3.87	3.70	3.56	3.46	3.37	3.23	3.09	2.94	2.86	2.78	2.69	2.61	2.52	2.42
21	8.02	5.78	4.87	4.37	4.04	3.81	3.64	3.51	3.40	3.31	3.17	3.03	2.88	2.80	2.72	2.64	2.55	2.46	2.36
22	7.95	5.72	4.82	4.31	3.99	3.76	3.59	3.45	3.35	3.26	3.12	2.98	2.83	2.75	2.67	2.58	2.50	2.40	2.31
23	7.88	5.66	4.76	4.26	3.94	3.71	3.54	3.41	3.30	3.21	3.07	2.93	2.78	2.70	2.62	2.54	2.45	2.35	2.26
24	7.82	5.61	4.72	4.22	3.90	3.67	3.50	3.36	3.26	3.17	3.03	2.89	2.74	2.66	2.58	2.49	2.40	2.31	2.21
25	7.77	5.57	4.68	4.18	3.85	3.63	3.46	3.32	3.22	3.13	2.99	2.85	2.70	2.62	2.54	2.45	2.36	2.27	2.17
26	7.72	5.53	4.64	4.14	3.82	3.59	3.42	3.29	3.18	3.09	2.96	2.81	2.66	2.58	2.50	2.42	2.33	2.23	2.13
27	7.68	5.49	4.60	4.11	3.78	3.56	3.39	3.26	3.15	3.06	2.93	2.78	2.63	2.55	2.47	2.38	2.29	2.20	2.10
28	7.64	5.45	4.57	4.07	3.75	3.53	3.36	3.23	3.12	3.03	2.90	2.75	2.60	2.52	2.44	2.35	2.26	2.17	2.06
29	7.60	5.42	4.54	4.04	3.73	3.50	3.33	3.20	3.09	3.00	2.87	2.73	2.57	2.49	2.41	2.33	2.23	2.14	2.03
30	7.56	5.39	4.51	4.02	3.70	3.47	3.30	3.17	3.07	2.98	2.84	2.70	2.55	2.47	2.39	2.30	2.21	2.11	2.01
40	7.31	5.18	4.31	3.83	3.51	3.29	3.12	2.99	2.89	2.80	2.66	2.52	2.37	2.29	2.20	2.11	2.02	1.92	1.80
60	7.08	4.98	4.13	3.65	3.34	3.12	2.95	2.82	2.72	2.63	2.50	2.35	2.20	2.12	2.03	1.94	1.84	1.73	1.60
120	6.85	4.79	3.95	3.48	3.17	2.96	2.79	2.66	2.56	2.47	2.34	2.19	2.03	1.95	1.86	1.76	1.66	1.53	1.38
∞	6.63	4.61	3.78	3.32	3.02	2.80	2.64	2.51	2.41	2.32	2.18	2.04	1.88	1.79	1.70	1.59	1.47	1.32	1.00

TABLE C.8   **Upper Percentage Points of the Studentized Range Distribution: Values of $q(0.05; k, v)$**

Degrees of Freedom v	Number of Treatments k								
	2	3	4	5	6	7	8	9	10
1	18.0	27.0	32.8	37.2	40.5	43.1	45.4	47.3	49.1
2	6.09	8.33	9.80	10.89	11.73	12.43	13.03	13.54	13.99
3	4.50	5.91	6.83	7.51	8.04	8.47	8.85	9.18	9.46
4	3.93	5.04	5.76	6.29	6.71	7.06	7.35	7.60	7.83
5	3.64	4.60	5.22	5.67	6.03	6.33	6.58	6.80	6.99
6	3.46	4.34	4.90	5.31	5.63	5.89	6.12	6.32	6.49
7	3.34	4.16	4.68	5.06	5.35	5.59	5.80	5.99	6.15
8	3.26	4.04	4.53	4.89	5.17	5.40	5.60	5.77	5.92
9	3.20	3.95	4.42	4.76	5.02	5.24	5.43	5.60	5.74
10	3.15	3.88	4.33	4.66	4.91	5.12	5.30	5.46	5.60
11	3.11	3.82	4.26	4.58	4.82	5.03	5.20	5.35	5.49
12	3.08	3.77	4.20	4.51	4.75	4.95	5.12	5.27	5.40
13	3.06	3.73	4.15	4.46	4.69	4.88	5.05	5.19	5.32
14	3.03	3.70	4.11	4.41	4.64	4.83	4.99	5.13	5.25
15	3.01	3.67	4.08	4.37	4.59	4.78	4.94	5.08	5.20
16	3.00	3.65	4.05	4.34	4.56	4.74	4.90	5.03	5.15
17	2.98	3.62	4.02	4.31	4.52	4.70	4.86	4.99	5.11
18	2.97	3.61	4.00	4.28	4.49	4.67	4.83	4.96	5.07
19	2.96	3.59	3.98	4.26	4.47	4.64	4.79	4.92	5.04
20	2.95	3.58	3.96	4.24	4.45	4.62	4.77	4.90	5.01
24	2.92	3.53	3.90	4.17	4.37	4.54	4.68	4.81	4.92
30	2.89	3.48	3.84	4.11	4.30	4.46	4.60	4.72	4.83
40	2.86	3.44	3.79	4.04	4.23	4.39	4.52	4.63	4.74
60	2.83	3.40	3.74	3.98	4.16	4.31	4.44	4.55	4.65
120	2.80	3.36	3.69	3.92	4.10	4.24	4.36	4.47	4.56
∞	2.77	3.32	3.63	3.86	4.03	4.17	4.29	4.39	4.47

Source: Reproduced with permission from Table 29 of E. S. Pearson and H. O. Hartley, *Biometrika Tables for Statisticians*, Vol. 1 (Cambridge: Cambridge University Press, 1954).

TABLE C.9   Factors k for Tolerance Limits

| n | $1 - \alpha = 0.95$ | | | $1 - \alpha = 0.99$ | | |
	$p = 0.90$	$p = 0.95$	$p = 0.99$	$p = 0.90$	$p = 0.95$	$p = 0.99$
2	32.019	37.674	48.430	160.193	188.491	242.300
3	8.380	9.916	12.861	18.930	22.401	29.055
4	5.369	6.370	8.299	9.398	11.150	14.527
5	4.275	5.079	6.634	6.612	7.855	10.260
6	3.712	4.414	5.775	5.337	6.345	8.301
7	3.369	4.007	5.248	4.613	5.488	7.187
8	3.136	3.732	4.891	4.147	4.936	6.468
9	2.967	3.532	4.631	3.822	4.550	5.966
10	2.839	3.379	4.433	3.582	4.265	5.594
11	2.737	3.259	4.277	3.397	4.045	5.308
12	2.655	3.162	4.150	3.250	3.870	5.079
13	2.587	3.081	4.044	3.130	3.727	4.893
14	2.529	3.012	3.955	3.029	3.608	4.737
15	2.480	2.954	3.878	2.945	3.507	4.605
16	2.437	2.903	3.812	2.872	3.421	4.492
17	2.400	2.858	3.754	2.808	3.345	4.393
18	2.366	2.819	3.702	2.753	3.279	4.307
19	2.337	2.784	3.656	2.703	3.221	4.230
20	2.310	2.752	3.615	2.659	3.168	4.161
25	2.208	2.631	3.457	2.494	2.972	3.904
30	2.140	2.549	3.350	2.385	2.841	3.733
35	2.090	2.490	3.272	2.306	2.748	3.611
40	2.052	2.445	3.213	2.247	2.677	3.518
45	2.021	2.408	3.165	2.200	2.621	3.444
50	1.996	2.379	3.126	2.162	2.576	3.385
55	1.976	2.354	3.094	2.130	2.538	3.335
60	1.958	2.333	3.066	2.103	2.506	3.293
65	1.943	2.315	3.042	2.080	2.478	3.257
70	1.929	2.299	3.021	2.060	2.454	3.225
75	1.917	2.285	3.002	2.042	2.433	3.197
80	1.907	2.272	2.986	2.026	2.414	3.173
85	1.897	2.261	2.971	2.012	2.397	3.150
90	1.889	2.251	2.958	1.999	2.382	3.130
95	1.881	2.241	2.945	1.987	2.368	3.112
100	1.874	2.233	2.934	1.977	2.355	3.096
150	1.825	2.175	2.859	1.905	2.270	2.983
200	1.798	2.143	2.816	1.865	2.222	2.921
250	1.780	2.121	2.788	1.839	2.191	2.880
300	1.767	2.106	2.767	1.820	2.169	2.850
400	1.749	2.084	2.739	1.794	2.138	2.809
500	1.737	2.070	2.721	1.777	2.117	2.783
600	1.729	2.060	2.707	1.764	2.102	2.763
700	1.722	2.052	2.697	1.755	2.091	2.748
800	1.717	2.046	2.688	1.747	2.082	2.736
900	1.712	2.040	2.682	1.741	2.075	2.726
1000	1.709	2.036	2.676	1.736	2.068	2.718
∞	1.645	1.960	2.576	1.645	1.960	2.576

Source: Reprinted with permission from C. Eisenhart, M. W. Hastay, and W. A. Wallis, *Selected Techniques of Statistical Analysis* (New York: McGraw-Hill, 1947), p. 102.

TABLE C.10   2000 Random Digits

98086	24826	45240	28404	44999	08896	39094	73407	35441	31880
33185	16232	41941	50949	89435	48581	88695	41994	37548	73043
80951	00406	96382	70774	20151	23387	25016	25298	94624	61171
79752	49140	71961	28296	69861	02591	74852	20539	00387	59579
18633	32537	98145	06571	31010	24674	05455	61427	77938	91936
74029	43902	77557	32270	97790	17119	52527	58021	80814	51748
54178	45611	80993	37143	05335	12969	56127	19255	36040	90324
11664	49883	52079	84827	59381	71539	09973	33440	88461	23356
48324	77928	31249	64710	02295	36870	32307	57546	15020	09994
69074	94138	87637	91976	35584	04401	10518	21615	01848	76938
09188	20097	32825	39527	04220	86304	83389	87374	64278	58044
90045	85497	51981	50654	94938	81997	91870	76150	68476	64659
73189	50207	47677	26269	62290	64464	27124	67018	41361	82760
75768	76490	20971	87749	90429	12272	95375	05871	93823	43178
54016	44056	66281	31003	00682	27398	20714	53295	07706	17813
08358	69910	78542	42785	13661	58873	04618	97553	31223	08420
28306	03264	81333	10591	40510	07893	32604	60475	94119	01840
53840	86233	81594	13628	51215	90290	28466	68795	77762	20791
91757	53741	61613	62269	50263	90212	55781	76514	83483	47055
89415	92694	00397	58391	12607	17646	48949	72306	94541	37408
77513	03820	86864	29901	68414	82774	51908	13980	72893	55507
19502	37174	69979	20288	55210	29773	74287	75251	65344	67415
21818	59313	93278	81757	05686	73156	07082	85046	31853	38452
51474	66499	68107	23621	94049	91345	42836	09191	08007	45449
99559	68331	62535	24170	69777	12830	74819	78142	43860	72834
33713	48007	93584	72869	51926	64721	58303	29822	93174	93972
85274	86893	11303	22970	28834	34137	73515	90400	71148	43643
84133	89640	44035	52166	73852	70091	61222	60561	62327	18423
56732	16234	17395	96131	10123	91622	85496	57560	81604	18880
65138	56806	87648	85261	34313	65861	45875	21069	85644	47277
38001	02176	81719	11711	71602	92937	74219	64049	65584	49698
37402	96397	01304	77586	56271	10086	47324	62605	40030	37438
97125	40348	87083	31417	21815	39250	75237	62047	15501	29578
21826	41134	47143	34072	64638	85902	49139	06441	03856	54552
73135	42742	95719	09035	85794	74296	08789	88156	64691	19202
07638	77929	03061	18072	96207	44156	23821	99538	04713	66994
60528	83441	07954	19814	59175	20695	05533	52139	61212	06455
83596	35655	06958	92983	05128	09719	77433	53783	92301	50498
10850	62746	99599	10507	13499	06319	53075	71839	06410	19362
39820	98952	43622	63147	64421	80814	43800	09351	31024	73167

Source: Reprinted with permission from pages 1–2 of *A Million Random Digits with 100,000 Normal Deviates,* by The Rand Corporation. New York: The Free Press, 1955. Used by permission.

Answers
TO SELECTED EXERCISES

Chapter 1

1.2-1 **(b)** $\bar{x} = 15.375$ (psi), $s^2 = 3.4107$ (psi^2),
$s = 1.85$ (psi).
(c) $Q_1 = (14 + 15)/2 = 14.5$,
$Q_2 = (15 + 16)/2 = 15.5$,
$Q_3 = (16 + 17)/2 = 16.5$, $Q_3 - Q_1 = 2$.

1.2-2 **(b)** $\bar{x} = 320.1$, $s^2 = 45.6326$, $s = 6.76$,
$Q_1 = 316$, $Q_2 = 320$, $Q_3 = 325$.

1.2-3 **(b)** $\bar{x} = 7.29$, $s^2 = 4.1025$, $s = 2.03$,
$Q_1 = 6.05$, $Q_2 = 6.95$, $Q_3 = 8.45$,
$Q_3 - Q_1 = 2.40$.

1.2-6 Calculate averages and differences of the replications. The 10 averages describe the variability due to the actual size differences; the 10 differences describe the measurement variability.

1.2-9 **(a)** $Q_1 = 61.12$, $Q_2 = 87.94$, $Q_3 = 117.89$,
$Q_3 - Q_1 = 56.77$.
(b) $\bar{x} = 94.25$ (grams), $s^2 = 2193.79$,
$s = 46.84$ (grams).

1.3-3 **(a)** $\bar{x} = 189.0$; **(b)** logarithmic transformation.

1.3-4 $\bar{x} = 74.4$, $s = 2.11$, $Q_1 = 73.1$,
$Q_2 = 74.55$, $Q_3 = 75.6$.

1.4-1 **(a)** $\bar{x} = 9.42$, $s = 2.08$, $x_{min} = 2.9$,
$Q_1 = 8.65$, $Q_2 = 9.40$, $Q_3 = 10.25$,
$x_{max} = 16.7$; lead concentrations have increased; variability in the two groups is about the same.

1.4-3 **(a)**

	x_{min}	Q_1	Q_2	Q_3	x_{max}
Surface	3.08	3.67	4.33	4.40	5.17
Middepth	3.17	4.26	5.04	6.17	6.57
Bottom	3.76	4.90	5.53	7.30	8.79

Variability increases with level. Logarithmic transformation should be tried.

1.5-2 $\hat{\beta} = \sum x_i y_i / \sum x_i^2 = 1.25$.

1.5-4 $\hat{\alpha} = 3.2761$, $\hat{\beta} = 0.3098$.

1.5-6 **(c)** CO concentrations are related to traffic density. Wind plays the role of transport (under calm conditions or when $WS_p < 0$ only part of the emissions are transported to the measurement site) and diffusion (strong winds diffuse part of the emissions before they reach the measurement site).

Ledolter and Tiao consider models of the form

$$CO = \alpha + \beta_1(TD)\exp[-\beta_2(WS_p - \beta_3)^2],$$

where α is a parameter measuring background, β_1 is a parameter proportional to emissions, and β_2 and β_3 are parameters that model the effect of WS_p.

1.5-8 $r = 0.63$.

Chapter 2

2.1-1 0.06, 0.08, 0.12, 0.02.

2.1-3 $\{1, 2, 3, 4, 5, 6\}$, 1/6, 1/2.

2.1-6 0.095.

2.2-3 0.000865.

2.2-5 2^7, 1/128, 7/128.

2.2-7 0.4095.

2.2-8 (a) No;   (b) 1/2, 2/5, 1/5, 7/10;
(c) Yes.

2.2-9 (a) 0.06;   (b) 0.94;   (c) 2/7;
(d) 1/93.

2.2-14 (a) 64/105;   (b) 7/32.

2.3-1 (a) 0.3;   (b) 0.9;   (c) 3;   (d) 1.

2.3-2 (a) 1/325;   (b) 1/36;   (c) 2.

2.3-3 (b) $1 - (5/6)^x$; $x = 1, 2, 3, \ldots$;
(c) 0.2996;   (d) 6.

2.3-5 1.3, 0.81, 0.9.

2.3-6 34/15.

2.4-1 (a) 0.8171;   (b) 2.

2.4-3 $n = 22$.

2.4-4 (a) 0.1143;   (b) \$810, \$270.

2.4-10 (a) 0.50.

2.4-11 (b) 0.813.

2.5-1 (a) 0.018;   (b) 0.196;   (c) 0.215.

2.5-3 0.014.

2.5-4 (a) 0.143;   (b) 0.865;   (c) \$2000.

2.5-5 \$30,000.

Chapter 3

3.1-4 (a) 0.604;   (b) 0.216;   (c) 0.343.

3.1-5 (a) 2/3, 1/18;   (b) 1/2, 1/20.

3.1-6 (a) 0.841, 0.707, 0.931, 0.974;
(b) 0.693, 0.288, 1.386, 2.303.

3.1-7 (a) $(x - a)/(b - a)$, $a \le x < b$;
(b) $(a + b)/2$; $(b - a)^2/12$.

3.2-1 (a) 0.6612;   (b) 0.2850;   (c) 0.2455.

3.2-3 (a) 7.30;   (b) 4.28;   (c) 8.29;
(d) 3.92.

3.2-6 (a) 0.1057;   (b) 0.0062;   (c) 0.2113;
(d) 0.0784;   (e) 0.2946.

3.2-7 100.82.

3.3-2 (a) 0.368.

3.3-4 (a) Gamma with $\alpha = 2$ and $\beta = 4/3$;
(b) 0.690.

3.3-5 0.908, 0.017.

Chapter 4

4.1-1 $-6, 86$.

4.1-3 1/2, 1/200.

4.1-5 (a) 15.87%;   (b) 0.0228.

4.1-7 (b) 0, 1;   (c) $(2/3 + u/3\sqrt{2})^2$,
$-2\sqrt{2} \le u < \sqrt{2}$.

4.1-8 $y^2/2, 0 < y \le 1$; $1 - (2 - y)^2/2, 1 < y \le 2$.

4.2-1 0.77.

4.2-5 (a) 0.7701;   (b) 0.7455;   (c) No.

4.2-6 (a) 0.5963;   (b) 0.5934.

4.3-1 (47.83, 50.57).

4.3-3 43.

4.3-5 $(-168.9, -105.1)$.

4.4-1 (a) (2.32, 2.48),   (b) (2.31, 2.49);
(c) (1.86, 2.94).

4.4-2 (a) 12, 24;
(b) 21.026, 3.571, 28.300, 4.404.

4.4-3 (a) 0, 11/9;   (b) 1.796;   (c) 2.201.

4.4-7 $(-5.6, 11.0)$.

4.5-3 (0.09, 0.23).

4.5-5 (358.4, 1037.3).

4.5-6 (a) 289;   (b) 385.

4.6-2 $(1 + x/\beta)e^{-x/\beta}$, $x/(\beta^2 + x)$.

4.6-3 (a) $\lambda = 0.021$;   (b) 47.6;
(c) $e^{-1} = 0.368$.

4.6-6 $z_p = [-\ln(1 - p^{1/k})]/\lambda$.

Chapter 5

5.1-2 $\bar{x} = 5.16$. $\bar{R} = 1.18$; control limits for $\bar{x}$-chart:
4.48, 5.84; control limits for R-chart: 0, 2.49;
process is under control.

5.1-3 Control limits for p-chart: 0, 0.0305; process
has gone out of control.

5.1-4 LCL $= 0$; UCL $= 0.072 < 0.08$.

5.1-5 UCL $= 4.486$, 0.053, 0.58.

5.1-7 UCL $= 7.40$, yes.

5.2-3 $h = 2.66$, RQL ≈ 11; $d_r < 2.66$ for $r = 1, 2,$
$\ldots, 30$; cans have not been overfilled.

5.2-4 $d_{12}^* = -2.90 < -2.66$; filling weight has
become too low.

5.2-5 $h = 5.55$, RQL ≈ 6; $d_{19} = 7.2 > 5.55$; deflection has become too large.

5.2-6 $n = 3$; if $d_r^* < -11.72$, conclude that breaking strength is unacceptable.

5.3-2   **(b)** 0.143;   **(c)** 0.010;
(d) AOQL ≈ 0.02.

5.3-4   **(a)** 0.122, 0.199;   **(b)** AOQL ≈ 0.0028.

5.3-5 $n = 100$, Ac $= 4$ gives $\alpha = 0.053$, $\beta = 0.100$.

5.3-6   0.9123.

Chapter 6

6.1-2   0.9452, 0.7257, 0.3446, 0.0808, 0.0548.

6.1-3   0.0256, reject.

6.1-5 $z = -1.35$, p value $= 0.0885$, do not reject H_0.

6.1-7   24, 33.66.

6.1-8   589, 0.227.

6.2-1 $|-2.15| > 1.96$, reject H_0.

6.2-4 $4.03 > 1.725$, reject H_0.

6.2-6 $-2.27 < -1.645$, reject H_0.

6.2-9   **(a)** $24.12/7.82 = 3.08 > 2.48$; reject H_0.

6.3-1 $6.1 < 11.070$, do not reject H_0.

6.3-2 $36.37 > 5.991$, reject H_0.

6.3-3 $9.00 < 12.592$, accept independence.

6.3-5 $1.7 < 7.815$, do not reject H_0.

Chapter 7

7.1-2

Source	SS	df	MS	F
Treatment	31.112	2	15.56	22.3
Error	29.260	42	0.70	
Total	60.372	44		

$F_{\text{Treatment}} = 22.3 > F(0.05; 2, 42) = 3.22$; mean lengths are different.

7.1-3   **(a)**

Source	SS	df	MS	F
Treatment	475.76	4	118.94	14.76
Error	161.20	20	8.06	
Total	636.96	24		

$F_{\text{Treatment}} = 14.76 > F(0.05; 4, 20) = 2.87$, differences among the mean breaking strengths.

7.1-4   **(a)**

Source	SS	df	MS	F
Treatment	193,011	2	96,506	12.5
Error	85,160	11	7,742	
Total	278,171	13		

Since $F = 12.5 > F(0.05; 2, 11) = 3.98$, we can conclude that there are differences among mean weight gains.

7.1-5

Source	SS	df	MS	F
Treatment	1.5474	2	0.774	1.08
Error	17.2022	24	0.717	
Total	18.7496	26		

$F_{\text{Treatment}} = 1.08 < F(0.05; 2, 24) = 3.40$; no significant differences.

7.2-2   **(a)**

Source	SS	df	MS	F
Treatment	1.6333	2	0.817	2.34
Error	4.1840	12	0.349	
Total	5.8173	14		

$F = 2.34 < F(0.05; 2, 12) = 3.89$; insufficient evidence to conclude that nozzle type affects the flow.
(b) Scaled t-distribution with 12 degrees of freedom and scale factor $(MS_{\text{Error}}/5)^{1/2} = 0.26$.

7.2-3   **(a)** Random-effects model.
(b)

Source	SS	df	MS	F
Batch	170.94	5	34.19	5.13
Error	80.00	12	6.67	
Total	250.94	17		

Since $F = 5.13 > F(0.05; 5, 12) = 3.11$, we find significant batch variability.
(c) $\hat{\sigma}^2 = 6.67$, $\hat{\sigma}_\tau^2 = 9.17$.

7.3-1   **(a)**

Source	SS	df	MS	F
Treatment	165.8	3	55.3	7.5
Block	905.3	4	226.3	30.6
Error	88.7	12	7.4	
Total	1159.8	19		

$F_{\text{Treatment}} = 7.5 > F(0.05; \ 3, \ 12) = 3.49$; differences among the fabrics. Use a scaled t-distribution with 12 degrees of freedom and scale factor $(7.4/5)^{1/2} = 1.22$ to compare the treatment averages.

(b) $F_{\text{Block}} = 30.6 > F(0.05; \ 4, \ 12) = 3.26$; the blocking arrangement is very useful. If blocks are ignored, the estimate of the error variance is

$$\frac{(905.3 + 88.7)}{4 + 12} = 62.1;$$

then the resulting F-statistic for treatment differences in the completely randomized arrangement,

$$\frac{55.3}{62.1} = 0.89 < F(0.05; 3, 16) = 3.24,$$

is insignificant. Blocking has increased the precision of our comparison.

7.3-3 (a)

Source	SS	df	MS	F
Treatment (experience)	147.73	2	73.87	24.3
Block (day)	231.73	4	57.93	19.1
Error	24.27	8	3.03	
Total	403.73	14		

$F_{\text{Treatment}} = 24.3 > F(0.05; \ 2, \ 8) = 4.46$; we find that there are differences in productivity among the three groups.

The group averages (already ordered in magnitude) are $\bar{y}_A = 54.4$, $\bar{y}_B = 57.2$, $\bar{y}_c = 62.0$. Significant entries in the table of pairwise comparisons

$$\bar{y}_B - \bar{y}_A = 2.8 \qquad \bar{y}_C - \bar{y}_A = \boxed{7.6}$$
$$\bar{y}_C - \bar{y}_B = \boxed{4.8}$$

are circled; $q(0.05; 3, 8) \sqrt{MS_{\text{Error}}/b} = 3.15$ is used to determine significance.

Plot the treatment averages and compare them with the scaled $t(v = 8)$ distribution with scale factor $\sqrt{3.03/5} = 0.78$. Group C is very different from A and B.

(b) $F_{\text{Block}} = 19.1 > F(0.05; 4, 8) = 3.84$.

7.4-2 (a)

Source	SS	df	MS	F
Treatment	330.24	4	82.56	0.56
Row	4240.24	4	1060.06	7.25
Column	701.84	4	175.46	1.20
Error	1754.32	12	146.19	
Total	7026.64	24		

Since $F_{\text{Treatment}} = 0.56 < F(0.05; 4, 12) = 3.26$, the differences among mean root weights are not significant.

(b) Blocking has increased the precision of our comparison. If the same data were obtained from a completely randomized one-factor experiment, we would have found $SS_{\text{Error}} = 4240.24 + 701.84 + 1754.32 = 6696.4$, with $4 + 4 + 12 = 20$ degrees of freedom. The resulting estimate of error variance, $6696.4/20 = 334.8$, is 2.5 times larger than $MS_{\text{Error}} = 146.19$.

Chapter 8

8.1-3

Source	SS	df	MS	F
A(background)	100.04	1	100.04	19.02
B(training)	20.25	2	10.12	1.92
AB	33.58	2	16.79	3.19
Error	94.75	18	5.26	
Total	248.62	23		

Fixed effects.
Interaction is insignificant, since

$$F_{AB} = 3.19 < F(0.05; 2, 18) = 3.55.$$

Main effect B is insignificant, since

$$F_B = 1.92 < F(0.05; 2, 18).$$

Main effect A is significant, since

$$F_A = 19.02 > F(0.05; 1, 18) = 4.41.$$

Residual plots show no major model inadequacies.

8.1-4

Source	SS	df	MS	F
A(time)	150.2	1	150.2	9.69
B(temperature)	80.8	2	40.4	2.61
AB	3.4	2	1.7	0.11
Error	186.0	12	15.5	
Total	420.4	17		

Interaction is clearly insignificant, since $F_{AB} < 1$.
Temperature main effect is insignificant, since

$$F_B = 2.61 < F(0.05; 2, 12) = 3.89;$$

temperature changes in the range 350 to 400°
do not affect the brightness.
Time is an important factor;

$$F_A = 9.69 > F(0.05; 1, 12) = 4.75$$

is significant.
Residual plots show no major model inadequacies.

8.1-5 (a) The machine and operator effects are *random*.
(b)

Source	SS	df	MS
A(machine)	0.878	2	0.439
B(operator)	9.211	2	4.606
AB	0.489	4	0.122
Error	16.400	36	0.456
Total	26.978	44	

(c) $F_{AB} = MS_{AB}/MS_{Error} = 0.27 < F(0.05; 4, 36) = 2.61$; interaction is insignificant.
(d) $MS_A/MS_{AB} = 3.6 < F(0.05; 2, 4) = 6.94$; the machine effect is insignificant. $MS_B/MS_{AB} = 37.7 > F(0.05; 2, 4)$; operator effect is highly significant.
Conclusions do not change if $MS_{Error(pooled)} = 0.4222$ is used.

8.2-1 (a)

Source	SS	df	MS	F
A . . . batch	1210.93	14	86.495	1.49
B(A). . . sample (batch)	869.75	15	57.983	63.23
Error	27.50	30	0.917	
Total	2108.18	59		

$MS_{B(A)}/MS_{Error} = 63.23 > F(0.05; 15, 30) = 2.01$; sample variability is significant.
$MS_A/MS_{B(A)} = 1.49 < F(0.05; 14, 15) = 2.43$; batch variability is insignificant.
(b) Measurement: $\hat{\sigma}^2 = 0.92$
Sample: $\hat{\sigma}_\beta^2 = 28.53$
Batch: $\hat{\sigma}_\alpha^2 = 7.13$
Sampling procedure should be improved.

8.2-3

Source	SS	df	MS	F
A . . . batch	109.6	5	21.92	1.06
B(A) . . . sample (batch)	124.2	6	20.70	4.64
Error	107.0	24	4.46	
Total	340.8	35		

$MS_{B(A)}/MS_{Error} = 4.64 > F(0.05; 6, 24) = 2.51$; sample variability is significant.
$MS_A/MS_{B(A)} = 1.06 < F(0.05; 5, 6) = 4.39$; batch variability is insignificant.
$\hat{\sigma}^2 = 4.46$; $\hat{\sigma}_\beta^2 = 5.41$; $\hat{\sigma}_\alpha^2 = 0.20$.

8.3-3 (a) Average = 78.375 (12) = −1.525
(1) = −3.55 (13) = −0.525
(2) = −1.45 (23) = 0.375
(3) = 3.20 (123) = −1.20.
(b) Main effects of factors 1 and 3 are significant.

8.3-4 (a) Average = 72.25 (4) = −2.75
(1) = −4.00 (14) = 0.00
(2) = 12.00 (24) = 2.25
(12) = 0.50 (124) = 0.25
(3) = −1.13 (34) = −0.13
(13) = 0.38 (134) = −0.13
(23) = −0.63 (234) = −0.38
(123) = −0.38 (1234) = −0.13.
(b) Normal probability plot of the 15 effects shows that (1), (2), (4), and (24) are large.

8.3-6 (a) Average = 1.209 (AB) = −0.076
(A) = 0.274 (AC) = 0.019
(B) = 0.039 (BC) = 0.279
(C) = −0.156 (ABC) = −0.006.
(b) $s^2 = (0.83 - 1.40)^2/2 = 0.1625$ is a very crude variance estimate from the two replications at the center point; var (effect) = $s^2/8 = 0.0203$; standard error (effect) = 0.14.

(c) (A) and (BC) are large (two standard errors from zero).

Factor A does not interact with the other factors. Its main effect is positive; we should set additive A at its low level in order to reduce losses.

The results at the low level of A show that we should set B at the low level, and C at the high one.

8.4-3 Start with a 2^3 factorial, specify the four interaction columns, and associate x_4 with x_1x_2 and x_5 with $x_1x_2x_3$:

Run	x_1	x_2	x_3	x_4 x_1x_2	x_1x_3	x_2x_3	x_5 $x_1x_2x_3$
1	−	−	−	+	+	+	−
2	+	−	−	−	−	+	+
3	−	+	−	−	+	−	+
4	+	+	−	+	−	−	−
5	−	−	+	+	−	−	+
6	+	−	+	−	+	−	−
7	−	+	+	−	−	+	−
8	+	+	+	+	+	+	+

Design variables

Defining relation:

$$I = x_1x_2x_4 = x_1x_2x_3x_5 = x_3x_4x_5.$$

Resolution III.

The eight linear combinations estimate:

$$L_0 \to \mu + (124) + (1235) + (345)$$
$$L_1 \to (1) + (24) + (235) + (1345)$$
$$L_2 \to (2) + (14) + (135) + (2345)$$
$$L_3 \to (3) + (1234) + (125) + (45)$$
$$L_4 \to (12) + (4) + (35) + (12345)$$
$$L_5 \to (13) + (234) + (25) + (145)$$
$$L_6 \to (23) + (134) + (15) + (245)$$
$$L_7 \to (123) + (34) + (5) + (1245).$$

8.4-6 **(c)** The linear combinations from the fold-over estimate:

$$L_0' \to \mu$$
$$L_1' \to (1) - (24) - (35) - (67)$$
$$L_2' \to (2) - (14) - (36) - (57)$$
$$L_3' \to (3) - (15) - (26) - (47)$$
$$L_4' \to (4) - (12) - (37) - (56)$$
$$L_5' \to (5) - (13) - (27) - (46)$$
$$L_6' \to (6) - (23) - (17) - (45)$$
$$L_7' \to (7) - (34) - (25) - (16).$$

8.4-8 Using the Yates algorithm, we obtain the following estimates:

$$2.8750 \to \mu$$
$$0.8225 \to (1)$$
$$-1.2525 \to (2)$$
$$0.0550 \to (12)$$
$$0.3838 \to (3)$$
$$0.0638 \to (13)$$
$$0.0413 \to (23)$$
$$0.0013 \to (123) + (45) = (45)$$
$$2.7925 \to (4)$$
$$-0.0950 \to (14)$$
$$-0.0450 \to (24)$$
$$-0.2875 \to (124) + (35) = (35)$$
$$-0.3138 \to (34)$$
$$0.1863 \to (134) + (25) = (25)$$
$$-0.3063 \to (234) + (15) = (15)$$
$$-0.8713 \to (1234) + (5) = (5).$$

The defining relation $I = x_1x_2x_3x_4x_5$ is used to determine the confounding patterns. For example, the linear combination that corresponds to the $x_1x_2x_3$ column estimates $(123) + (45) = (45)$, since we assume that interactions of three or more factors are zero. A normal probability plot shows that the main effects of factors 1, 2, 4, and 5 are large.

Chapter 9

9.1-1 **(b)** $\hat{\beta}_0 = -7.877, \hat{\beta}_1 = 0.08676$;
$\hat{y}_1 = -7.877 + (0.08676)(117) = 2.27$,
$e_1 = 2.07 - 2.27 = -0.20$;
$\hat{y}_2 = -7.877 + (0.08676)(128) = 3.23$,
$e_2 = 2.80 - 3.23 = -0.43$;
etc.

9.1-2 **(b)** $\hat{\beta}_0 = 0.989, \hat{\beta}_1 = 1.99463$;
$\hat{y}_1 = 0.989 + (1.99463)(10) = 20.94$,
$e_1 = 21.2 - 20.94 = 0.26$;
$\hat{y}_3 = 0.989 + (1.99463)(11) = 22.93$,
$e_3 = 22.5 - 22.93 = -0.43$;
etc.

9.1-3 **(b)** $\hat{\beta}_0 = 54.95, \hat{\beta}_1 = 1.0641$;
$\hat{y}_1 = 54.95 + (1.0641)(50) = 108.16$,
$e_1 = 128 - 108.16 = 19.84$;
$\hat{y}_2 = 54.95 + (1.0641)(64) = 123.05$,
$e_2 = 159 - 123.05 = 35.95$;
etc.

9.1-8 (a) $\hat{\beta} = \sum x_i y_i / \sum x_i^2$;

(b) $\text{var}(\hat{\beta}) = \sigma^2 / \sum x_i^2$.

9.2-1 $\hat{\beta}_1 = 0.35$, $s(\hat{\beta}_1) = (2.3/100)^{1/2} = 0.152$.
Test statistic $= (0.35 - 0.20)/0.152 = 0.99 <$
$t(0.05; 16 - 2 = 14) = 1.761$; insufficient evidence to reject H_0: $\beta_1 = 0.20$; we accept H_0;
$(0.08 \leq \beta_1 \leq 0.62)$.

9.2-2 For Exercise 9.1-1:

Source	SS	df	MS	F
Regression	2.306	1	2.306	28.9
Error	0.639	8	0.080	
Total	2.945	9		

$R^2 = 2.306/2.945 = 0.783$.
$\hat{\beta}_1 = 0.087$, $s(\hat{\beta}_1) = 0.016$, $t_{\hat{\beta}_1} = \hat{\beta}_1 / s(\hat{\beta}_1) = 5.37$; since $|t_{\hat{\beta}_1}| = 5.37$ is larger than $t(0.025; 8) = 2.306$, we reject H_0: $\beta_1 = 0$ in favor of $H_1: \beta_1 \neq 0$; $(0.050 \leq \beta_1 \leq 0.124)$.
$\hat{\beta}_0 = -7.877$, $s(\hat{\beta}_0) = 2.027$, $t_{\hat{\beta}_0} = \hat{\beta}_0 / s(\hat{\beta}_0) = -3.89$; since $|t_{\hat{\beta}_0}| = 3.89$ is larger than $t(0.025; 8) = 2.306$, we reject H_0: $\beta_0 = 0$ in favor of $H_1: \beta_0 \neq 0$.

For Exercise 9.1-2:

Source	SS	df	MS	F
Regression	2306.4	1	2306.4	1949
Error	14.2	12	1.18	
Total	2320.6	13		

$R^2 = 2306.4/2320.6 = 0.994$.
$t_{\hat{\beta}_1} = \hat{\beta}_1 / s(\hat{\beta}_1) = 1.9946/0.0452 = 44.1 >$
$t(0.025; 12) = 2.179$; reject H_0: $\beta_1 = 0$ in favor of $H_1: \beta_1 \neq 0$ at significance level $\alpha = 0.05$. The p value is extremely small; very strong evidence that $\beta_1 \neq 0$. $t_{\hat{\beta}_0} = \hat{\beta}_0 / s(\hat{\beta}_0) = 0.989/0.859 = 1.15 < t(0.025; 12) = 2.179$; conclude that $\beta_0 = 0$.

For Exercise 9.1-3:

Source	SS	df	MS	F
Regression	1522.9	1	1522.9	4.09
Error	4834.9	13	371.9	
Total	6357.7	14		

$R^2 = 0.24$.
$\hat{\beta}_1 = 1.0641$; $s(\hat{\beta}_1) = 0.526$; $\hat{\beta}_1 / s(\hat{\beta}_1) = 2.02$ is larger than $t(0.05; 13) = 1.771$; reject H_0: $\beta_1 = 0$ in favor of $H_1: \beta_1 \neq 0$ at significance level $\alpha = 0.10$.

9.2-7 $x_k = 60$: $(108.04 \leq E(Y_k) \leq 129.56)$;
$x_k = 100$: $(114.72 \leq E(Y_k) \leq 208.00)$.

9.3-5 (b) $\hat{\beta}_0 = 0.839$, $\hat{\beta}_1 = 0.489$.

Source	SS	df	MS	F
Regression	1830.7	1	1830.7	202
Error	63.3	7	9.04	
Total	1893.9	8		

$R^2 = 0.967$.

(c) Here $t_{\hat{\beta}_1} = \hat{\beta}_1 / s(\hat{\beta}_1) = 0.489/0.034 = 14.2$ is much larger than the critical value $t(0.025; 7) = 2.365$; strong evidence that $\beta_1 > 0$.

(d) $t_{\hat{\beta}_0} = \hat{\beta}_0 / s(\hat{\beta}_0) = 0.839/2.15 = 0.39$ is smaller than the critical value 2.365; conclude that $\beta_0 = 0$. Dispersion and age are proportional.

(e) $(49.59 \leq E(Y_k) \leq 59.67)$; extrapolation is dangerous because $x_k = 110$ is outside the experimental region.

9.3-8 (a) $\hat{\beta}_0 = 29.01$, $\hat{\beta}_1 = 1.06$.

Source	SS	df	MS	F
Regression	459.74	1	459.74	106
Error	65.17	15	4.34	
Total	524.92	16		

$R^2 = 0.876$.

(b) Residual plots show curvilinear patterns. Lag 1 autocorrelation $r_1 = 0.62$ is larger than $2/\sqrt{17} = 0.49$. The DW test is very small; positive autocorrelation among the residuals.

9.4-1 $\hat{\beta}_0 = 1$, $\hat{\beta}_1 = 0.5$, $\hat{\beta}_2 = 0.75$.

9.4-2 (a) $1.14 \pm (2.145)(0.16)$
or $(0.80 \leq \beta_1 \leq 1.48)$;
$-0.83 \pm (2.145)(0.20)$
or $(-1.26 \leq \beta_2 \leq -0.40)$.

(b) $R^2 = 66/100 = 0.66$;
$F = 13.59 > F(0.05; 2, 14) = 3.74$; reject
$H_0: \beta_1 = \beta_2 = 0$ in favor of H_1 that at least one of the coefficients is different from zero.

9.4-3 (a)

Source	SS	df	MS	F
Regression	66	2	33	4.19
Error	134	17	7.88	
Total	200	19		

(b) $R^2 = 0.33$.
(c) $F = 4.19 > F(0.05; 2, 17) = 3.59$; we reject $H_0: \beta_1 = \beta_2 = 0$.
(d) $t(0.025; 17) = 2.11$. Estimate $\hat{\beta}_2$ is not significantly different from zero. We can simplify the regression model to $Y_i = \beta_0 + \beta_1 x_{i1} + \varepsilon_i$.

9.5-1 (a) $\hat{\beta}_0 = 86.436$, $\hat{\beta}_1 = -0.202$.

Source	SS	df	MS	F
Regression	24.5	1	24.5	0.29
Error	686.4	8	85.8	
Total	710.9	9		

$t_{\hat{\beta}_1} = \hat{\beta}_1/s(\hat{\beta}_1) = -0.202/0.377 = -0.53$.
Since $|t_{\hat{\beta}_1}| < t(0.025; 8) = 2.306$, we accept H_0. Residual plots reveal serious model inadequacies; quadratic term x^2 missing in the model.
(b) $\hat{\beta}_0 = 35.66$, $\hat{\beta}_1 = 5.26$, $\hat{\beta}_2 = -0.128$;
$s(\hat{\beta}_0) = 5.62$, $s(\hat{\beta}_1) = 0.56$, $s(\hat{\beta}_2) = 0.013$
$|t_{\hat{\beta}_2}| = 9.97 > t(0.025; 7) = 2.365; \beta_2 \neq 0$.
9.5-2 (b) $\hat{y} = 23.35 + 1.045x$; $R^2 = 0.955$. Residuals point to problems with this model; quadratic component x^2 is missing.
(c) $\hat{y} = 22.56 + 1.668x - 0.068x^2$;
$R^2 = 0.988$; $\hat{\beta}_2/s(\hat{\beta}_2) = -6.59$ is significant; residuals look much better.
9.5-3 (a) $\hat{y} = 73.4 + 12.1x_1 + 3.12x_2 + 2.37x_1x_2$.

Source	SS	df	MS	F
Regression	1299.37	3	433.12	17.6
Error	98.50	4	24.62	
Total	1397.87	7		

$R^2 = 0.93$.

(b) $F = 17.6 > F(0.01; 3, 4) = 16.69$; reject $H_0: \beta_1 = \beta_2 = \beta_3 = 0$ at significance level $\alpha = 0.01$. The t-ratios for $\hat{\beta}_1$, $\hat{\beta}_2$, and $\hat{\beta}_3$ are given by 6.91, 1.78, and 1.35, respectively. Comparing these ratios with $t(0.025; 4) = 2.776$, we find that $\beta_1 \neq 0$. Only the main effect of temperature is significant.

9.5-5 (a) $\hat{y} = 56.25 + 1.79x_1 + 0.087x_2$.
(b) 17th soil sample is an outlier.
(c) After omitting this observation, we find that $\hat{y} = 66.47 + 1.29x_1 - 0.11x_2$; $R^2 = 0.525$.
(d) The simplified model is given by $\hat{y} = 62.57 + 1.23x_1$; $R^2 = 0.519$.

9.5-6 (a) $\hat{y} = 0.022 + 0.00131x_1 + 0.804x_2$;
$R^2 = 0.347$. $F = MSR/MSE = 2.39 < F(0.05; 2, 9) = 4.26$; very little reason to reject $H_0: \beta_1 = \beta_2 = 0$. For this particular data set the GMAT scores have little explanatory power. The largest t-ratio fails to exceed $t(0.025; 9) = 2.262$.

9.6-1 (a) $x_{1,0} = 1, x_{2,0} = 2$; maximum.
(b) $x_{1,0} = 1, x_{2,0} = 2$; minimum.
(c) $x_{1,0} = 1, x_{2,0} = 2$; saddle point.
(d) $x_{1,0} = 0.18, x_{2,0} = 0.77$; maximum.

9.6-2 $E(Y) = 11 - (x_1 + 2x_2 - 1)^2$.

9.6-3 Fitting the first-order model to the coded variables

$$x_1 = C - 13 \quad \text{and} \quad x_2 = \frac{T - 105}{5},$$

we obtain

$$\hat{y} = 80.5 + (2.25)x_1 + (5.25)x_2.$$

The design points on the path of steepest ascent are given by $(x_1 = 0.39, x_2 = 0.92)$ or $(C = 13.39, T = 109.6)$, $(x_1 = 0.78, x_2 = 1.84)$ or $(C = 13.78, T = 114.2)$, $(x_1 = 1.17, x_2 = 2.76)$, or $(C = 14.17, T = 118.8)$, and so on.

9.6-4 $\hat{y} = 34.36 + 0.7x_1 - 0.3x_2 - 2.83x_1^2 - 0.93x_2^2 + 0.98x_1x_2$.
Stationary point $(x_{1,0} = 0.1054, x_{2,0} = -0.1058)$ or (temperature $= 145.53$, time $= 88.94$) corresponds to a maximum.

9.6-7 $\hat{y} = 82.17 - 1.01x_1 - 6.09x_2 + 1.02x_1^2$
$- 4.48x_2^2 - 3.60x_1x_2$.
Stationary point $(x_{1,0} = -0.4121,\ x_{2,0} = -0.5141)$ or (time = 9.69, temperature = 239.72) corresponds to a saddle point.

9.6-9 **(a)** $\hat{y} = 183.94 + 4.89x_1 + 6.48x_2 - 0.71x_3$
$- 4.42x_1^2 - 10.41x_2^2 - 1.92x_3^2$
$- 10.94x_1x_2 + 0.04x_1x_3 + 1.68x_2x_3$.
(c) $\hat{y} = 183.31 + 4.80x_1 + 6.39x_2$
$- 4.78x_1^2 - 10.95x_2^2 - 10.84x_1x_2$.

Stationary point $(x_{1,0} = 0.3903,\ x_{2,0} = 0.0986)$ or (GLDH = 138.7, pH = 7.47) corresponds to a maximum.
(e) Sketch the contours for $\hat{y} = (0.97)(184.56) = 179.02$; insensitive.

9.6-10 The sample variance s^2 from the n_1 responses at the center point provides an estimate of σ^2.

var(effect) $= s^2/2^k$.
var(difference of the two averages)
$= (s^2/2^k) + (s^2/n_1)$.

Index

Design of experiments

Design	Model
Completely randomized one-factor experiment: Assign experimental units to the k treatment groups at random	$Y_{ij} = \mu + \tau_i + \varepsilon_{ij}$ $j = 1, 2, \ldots, n_i; \ i = 1, 2, \ldots, k;$ $\sum n_i = N$ ε_{ij} independent $N(0, \sigma^2)$
Randomized complete block experiment: Group kb units into b homogeneous blocks of size k. Assign the units in each block to the k treatments at random	$Y_{ij} = \mu + \tau_i + \beta_j + \varepsilon_{ij}$ ε_{ij} independent $N(0, \sigma^2)$
Two-factor factorial experiment: Assign n units to each of ab combinations of factors A and B at random	$Y_{ijk} = \mu + \alpha_i + \beta_j + (\alpha\beta)_{ij} + \varepsilon_{ijk}$ ε_{ijk} independent $N(0, \sigma^2)$
Nested factors: The b levels of factor B are nested within a levels of factor A. The a batches and b samples from each batch are chosen at random; n measurements are taken from each group	$Y_{ijk} = \mu + \alpha_i + \beta_{j(i)} + \varepsilon_{k(i, j)}$ α_i independent $N(0, \sigma_\alpha^2)$ $\beta_{j(i)}$ independent $N(0, \sigma_\beta^2)$ $\varepsilon_{k(i, j)}$ independent $N(0, \sigma^2)$

2^k factorial and 2^{k-p} fractional factorial experiments: k factors, each at a low ($-$) and high ($+$) level. For example, 2^3 and 2^{4-1}. In the latter, use 2^3 and take the fourth factor by $x_4 = x_1 x_2 x_3$. Various products, like $x_2 x_3$, give the signs that apply to the corresponding responses in determining effects, like (23).

Run	x_1	x_2	x_3	Response
1	$-$	$-$	$-$	Y_1
2	$+$	$-$	$-$	Y_2
3	$-$	$+$	$-$	Y_3
4	$+$	$+$	$-$	Y_4
5	$-$	$-$	$+$	Y_5
6	$+$	$-$	$+$	Y_6
7	$-$	$+$	$+$	Y_7
8	$+$	$+$	$+$	Y_8